Homosexuality/Heterosexuality

THE KINSEY INSTITUTE SERIES

June Machover Reinisch, *General Editor*

Masculinity/Femininity
Basic Perspectives
Edited by June Machover Reinisch, Leonard Rosenblum,
and Stephanie A. Sanders

Homosexuality/Heterosexuality
Concepts of Sexual Orientation
Edited by David P. McWhirter, Stephanie A. Sanders,
and June Machover Reinisch

Homosexuality/Heterosexuality

Concepts of Sexual Orientation

Edited by

David P. McWhirter, M.D.

Stephanie A. Sanders, Ph.D.

June Machover Reinisch, Ph.D.

New York   Oxford
Oxford University Press
1990

Oxford University Press

Oxford   New York   Toronto
Delhi   Bombay   Calcutta   Madras   Karachi
Petaling Jaya   Singapore   Hong Kong   Tokyo
Nairobi   Dar es Salaam   Cape Town
Melbourne   Auckland

and associated companies in
Berlin   Ibadan

Library of Congress Cataloging-in-Publication Data
Homosexuality/heterosexuality : concepts of sexual orientation
edited by David P. McWhirter, Stephanie A. Sanders,
June Machover Reinisch.
p.   cm.—(Kinsey Institute series ; v. 2)
Based on papers of an institute conference held in May 1986.
Includes bibliographies and index.
ISBN 0-19-505205-6
1. Homosexuality—Congresses.   I. McWhirter, David P., 1932–
II. Sanders, Stephanie A.   III. Reinisch, June Machover.   IV. Series.
[DNLM: 1. Homosexuality—psychology—congresses.   WM 610 H768 1986]
HQ76.25.H6765   1990   306.7'66—dc19   DNLM/DLC
for Library of Congress   89-3114

9 8 7 6 5 4 3 2 1

Printed in the United States of America on acid-free paper

Dedication

To John Money, scientist, scholar, clinician, teacher,
and father of human psychoendocrinology,
whose dedication to his research and practice
has brought the world to a fuller and more humane understanding
of human sexuality.

Preface

Homosexuality/Heterosexuality: Concepts of Sexual Orientation is the second volume in *The Kinsey Institute Series*. In each volume, researchers from a wide range of academic disciplines draw on their own data and on the viewpoints of their own areas of expertise to address the central issues in a specific arena of discourse. The chapters of each volume are written after the contributors participate in a *Kinsey Symposium* on the topic. As a result, they reflect the diverse perspectives that emerge during sustained discussions among colleagues from many different fields. The editors of each volume provide an introduction based on the full range of discussions at the Symposium and the contents of the final contributions. This overview highlights the central themes and research findings of the volume as well as major issues for future consideration.

We would like to acknowledge the support of Indiana University. The Kinsey Institute is also grateful to the Institute for Sexual Behavior, Inc., including Drs. Klein, McWhirter, and Mattison, for their generous contribution which permitted the videotaping of the symposium. Special thanks go to Ruth Beasley, Kathryn Fisher, Sandra Ham, J. Susan Straub, Mary Ziemba-Davis, and the other members of The Kinsey Institute staff for their assistance in planning and conducting the Second Kinsey Symposium and in helping to prepare this book. We also thank Terry Sare who helped typed the manuscript and its revisions, and Joan Bossert, Stan George, and Louise Chang at Oxford University Press. We are deeply indebted to Elizabeth Roberge for her exemplary efforts in compiling this volume.

Bloomington, Indiana　　　　　　　　　　　　　　　　D.P.M.
January 1990　　　　　　　　　　　　　　　　　　　　S.A.S.
　　　　　　　　　　　　　　　　　　　　　　　　　　J.M.R.

Contents

Contributors

JOHN BANCROFT, M.D.
Clinical Consultant
M.R.C. Reproductive Biology Unit
Edinburgh, Scotland

PHILIP BLUMSTEIN, PH.D.
Professor, Department of Sociology
University of Washington
Seattle, Washington

JOHN E. BOSWELL, PH.D.
Professor, Department of History
Yale University
New Haven, Connecticut

VERN L. BULLOUGH, PH.D., R.N.
SUNY Distinguished Professor
Departments of History, Sociology,
   and Nursing
State University of New York at Buffalo
Buffalo, New York

VIVIENNE C. CASS, PH.D.
Clinical Psychologist
Department of Social Inquiry
Psychological Section
Murdoch University
Murdoch, Western Australia

SUSAN D. COCHRAN, PH.D.
Associate Professor, Department of
   Psychology
California State University, Northridge
Northridge, California

ELI COLEMAN, PH.D.
Associate Professor
Program in Human Sexuality
University of Minnesota Medical
   School
Minneapolis, Minnesota

JOHN P. DE CECCO, PH.D.
Professor of Psychology and Human
   Sexuality Studies
Director, Human Sexuality Studies
   Program
Director, Center for Research and
   Education in Sexuality (CERS)
San Francisco State University
Editor, *Journal of Homosexuality*
San Francisco, California

JOHN H. GAGNON, PH.D.
Professor, Department of Sociology
  and Psychology
State University of New York at Stony
  Brook
Stony Brook, New York

DAVID C. GEARY, PH.D.
Department of Psychology
University of Missouri
Columbia, Missouri

LOUIS GOOREN, M.D., PH.D.
Department of Internal Medicine
Free University Hospital
Amsterdam, The Netherlands

GILBERT HERDT, PH.D.
Associate Professor and Chairman of
  the Committee on Human
  Development
Department of Psychology and Com-
  mittee on Human Develpment
The University of Chicago
Chicago, Illinois

RICHARD A. ISAY, M.D.
Clinical Professor of Psychiatry
Cornell Medical College
Faculty, Columbia Center for Psycho-
  analytic Training and Research
New York, New York

FRANK JOHNSON, PH.D.
Department of Biology
University of Southern California
Los Angeles, California

FRITZ KLEIN, M.D.
Clinical Institutes
San Diego, California

NORETTA KOERTGE, PH.D.
Professor, Departments of History
  and Philosophy of Science
Indiana University
Bloomington, Indiana

DAVID P. MCWHIRTER, M.D.
Associate Clinical Professor of
  Psychiatry
Medical Director
San Diego County Psychiatric
  Hospital
San Diego, California

JOHN MONEY, PH.D.
Professor of Medical Psychology and
  Pediatrics, Emeritus
The Johns Hopkins University and
  Hospital
Balitmore, Maryland

RONALD D. NADLER, PH.D.
Research Professor
Yerkes Regional Primate Research
  Center
Emory University
Atlanta, Georgia

MARGARET NICHOLS, PH.D.
Executive Director, Institute for Per-
  sonal Growth
New Brunswick, New Jersey
Project Director, Northern Brooklyn
  AIDS Partner Study
Brooklyn. New York

LETITIA ANNE PEPLAU, PH.D.
Professor, Department of Psychology
Acting Director, Center for Study of
  Women
University of California, Los Angeles
Los Angeles, California

RICHARD PILLARD, M.D.
Associate Professor of Psychiatry
Director, Family Studies Laboratory
Director, Research Training Program
Department of Biobehavioral Sciences
Division of Psychiatry
Boston University School of Medicine
Boston, Massachusetts

JUNE MACHOVER REINISCH,
   PH.D.
Director, The Kinsey Institute for Re-
   search in Sex, Gender, and
   Reproduction
Professor of Psychology and
   Psychiatry
Indiana University
Bloomington, Indiana

LEONARD A. ROSENBLUM, PH.D.
Professor, Department of Psychiatry
The State University of New York
Health Science Center at Brooklyn
Brooklyn, New York

STEPHANIE A. SANDERS, PH.D.
Assistant Director
The Kinsey Institute for Research in
   Sex, Gender, and Reproduction
Indiana University
Bloomington, Indiana

PEPPER SCHWARTZ, PH.D.
Associate Professor,
Department of Sociology
University of Washington
Seattle, Washington

BRUCE VOELLER, PH.D.
President
The Mariposa Education and Re-
   search Foundation
Topanga, California

JAMES D. WEINRICH PH.D.
Assistant Research Psychobiologist
Department of Psychiatry
University of California, San Diego
San Diego, California

RICHARD E. WHALEN, PH.D.
Department of Psychology
University of California
Riverside, California

Prologue

David P. McWhirter

August 1956 was a landmark month for sexology. On August 24, Alfred Kinsey died. Six days later a young research associate in psychology from University of California at Los Angeles, Dr. Evelyn Hooker, presented her subsequently published paper "The Adjustment of the Male Overt Homosexual" (Hooker, 1957) at the Annual Meeting of the American Psychological Association in Chicago.* The reverberations of Kinsey's premature death that eclipsed his pioneering work and the publication of Hooker's paper continue to this day.

Prior to Hooker's research there had been, with the exception of Alfred Kinsey's and Havelock Ellis's work, little of significance in the scientific literature other than the pathological model for understanding sexual orientation. Hooker's work, which documented normal psychological adjustment patterns in nonclinical samples of male homosexuals, was overlooked for many years, especially by the psychoanalysts who continued to insist on a psychopathological explanation for homosexuality.

In September 1967, a Task Force on Homosexuality was appointed by Stanley F. Yolles, M.D., Director of the National Institute of Mental Health. Based on her previous work, Dr. Evelyn Hooker was appointed chairperson of that task force. Its final report was issued on October 10, 1969, just six months after the Stonewall riots in New York City, which heralded the beginning of the Gay Liberation Movement. Many of the Task Force's

---

*E. A. Hooker, The adjustment of the male overt homosexual. *Journal of Projective Techniques, 21,* 17–31, 1957.

recommendations, especially those relating to social policy, were applauded by the then organizing gay community, while others relating to prevention and treatment were less welcomed. The recommendations regarding further research continue to be carried out—indeed many of the contributors to this volume have followed the research recommendations of the National Institute of Mental Health Task Force on Homosexuality.

Attitudes about homosexuality have undergone many changes in the past few decades. The American Psychiatric Association decision in 1973 to eliminate homosexuality per se as a disease listed in the *Diagnostics and Statistics Manual* was an important contribution to these changes. Effects on the public attitude of the Acquired Immune Deficiency Syndrome (AIDS) epidemic, still at its most virulent, have yet to be fully realized. It will take years of retrospective study to place AIDS into historical perspective.

AIDS has been responsible for putting the existence of homosexuality on the front page of newspapers and on prime-time television throughout America since 1982. Many scientists and clinicians who have become involved in the fight against this major public health crisis have been confronted with the need to better understand human sexuality, particularly issues of sexual orientation. Therefore, the discussion of theoretical issues in this volume, which carefully examines the empirical data and scientific thinking on sexual orientation from Kinsey's time to the present, has direct practical application at this point in history.

During the past 50 years researchers have continued to use the time-honored, seven-point "Kinsey Scale" to characterize sexual orientation. Using questions about the current usefulness of the Kinsey Scale, a group of well-known researchers were brought together at The Kinsey Institute in May 1986 to discuss sexual orientation and then to write the chapters in this book. The volume represents a confluence of thinking with a multidisciplinary approach.

The introduction of the concept of "discontinuities" in the development of sexual orientation may seem to cast suspicion on the Kinsey Scale as universally applicable. Some would have us believe the scale was devised to apply to white, middle-class American males, hardly explaining the diversity found in other cultures and other times. New approaches to expanding the scale have broad clinical implications but become methodological problems in research application because of the potential number of variables.

Fifty years ago, Alfred Kinsey devised a simple seven-point scale based on his interpretation of the answers supplied by his subjects. In many ways that scale radicalized how human sexual behavior was categorized. Criticized as it may be, we have yet to find a broadly accepted replacement. Discussions about sexual orientation will continue for decades to come. This volume represents the state of the art at the end of the 1980s.

Homosexuality/Heterosexuality:
An Overview

*Stephanie A. Sanders, June Machover Reinisch, and
David P. McWhirter*

The world is not to be divided into sheep and goats. Not all things are black nor all things white. It is a fundamental of taxonomy that nature rarely deals with discrete categories. Only the human mind invents categories and tries to force facts into separated pigeon-holes. The living world is a continuum in each and every one of its aspects. The sooner we learn this concerning human sexual behavior the sooner we shall reach a sound understanding of the realities of sex.

Sexual Behavior in the Human Male, Kinsey, Pomeroy, & Martin, 1948

It is a characteristic of the human mind that it tries to dichotomize in its classification of phenomena. Things are either so, or they are not so. Sexual behavior is either normal or abnormal, socially acceptable or unacceptable, heterosexual or homosexual; and many persons do not want to believe that there are gradations in these matters from one to the other extreme.

Sexual Behavior in the Human Female, Kinsey, Pomeroy, Martin, & Gebhard, 1953

Homosexuality/Heterosexuality: Concepts of Sexual Orientation provides a current multidisciplinary overview of (1) what has been learned from various research perspectives about the nature of sexual orientation and what factors shape or alter orientation, and (2) how different assumptions about the nature of sexual orientation may influence research findings. This era of AIDS (Acquired Immune Deficiency Syndrome) has, in one manner or another, affected all people's lives, and current scholarly thought on topics of sexual behavior have become crucial not only to students and scholars of behavioral and psychological development, but it also has become central to the development of sound research designs and education programs designed to slow this growing public health crisis.

Perhaps the most important message of this volume, particularly with respect to the AIDS crisis, is the recurrent theme that dichotomous categories, such as heterosexual and homosexual, fail to reflect adequately the complex realities of sexual orientation, and human sexuality in general. This insight eloquently expressed years ago by Alfred C. Kinsey and his colleagues, and all too often ignored in subsequent years, is once again voiced throughout this volume from historic, religious, psychobiological, evolutionary, cultural, sociological, developmental, relational, conceptual, and theoretical perspectives. The danger of such categorical thinking can be exemplified as follows. It is a common assumption that the labels heterosexual, homosexual, and bisexual reasonably reflect actual sexual behavior patterns, but such an assumption leads to gross underestimates of the prevalence of behavioral bisexuality, an essential component for accurately describing human sexual behavior and indeed for deriving epidemiological predictions about the spread of Human Immunodeficiency Virus (HIV) (Reinisch, Sanders, & Ziemba-Davis, 1988, Reinisch, Ziemba-Davis & Sanders, in press). Thus, the theoretical and empirical concepts related to sexual orientation discussed in this volume are directly relevant to any scientist, scholar, or clinician concerned with human sexuality, regardless of his or her particular academic discipline.

Conceptualizations of sexual orientation appear to be evolving in a fashion somewhat parallel to our changing views of masculinity and femininity. Therefore, a brief review of the development of scientific thought on these gender-role concepts is instructive with respect to our understanding of heterosexuality and homosexuality. However, sexual orientation (heterosexual/bisexual/homosexual), the expression of gender role (masculine/feminine), and gender identity (an individual's identification as either male or female) are conceptually distinct phenomena, although in reality some overlap may occur among them. (For a detailed consideration of the interrelationships among these concepts, see Chapter 4 by Money, Chapter 22 by Koertge, and Chapter 5 by Whalen, Geary, and Johnson.

In the past, masculinity and femininity were viewed as discrete, dichotomous categories equated with maleness and femaleness, respectively. An individual whose behavior was not concordant with the expectations for his or her sex was considered to be abnormal. The early quantification techniques used for psychological assessment placed masculinity and femininity at opposite ends of a single unidimensional continuum. Such a bipolar model implies that the more masculine an individual is the less feminine he or she is, and vice versa.

Current psychological models of psychological masculinity and femininity often measure these qualities in terms of instrumental, agentic (task-oriented, self-promoting), and expressive, communal (emotional, other-oriented) traits, respectively. These dimensions are not bipolar opposites, but instead are independent (orthogonal) or semi-independent (oblique) continua and, therefore, are not inversely related in a mathematical sense (see Bem, 1974; Reinisch, 1976; Reinisch & Sanders, 1987, in press;

Spence, Helmreich, & Stapp, 1974; Whalen, 1974). That is, for example, high "femininity" (expressivity) is not necessarily associated with low "masculinity" (instrumentality). An individual can be (1) high on both "masculinity" and "femininity" (androgynous), (2) high on "masculinity" and low on "femininity" (masculine), (3) high on "femininity" and low on "masculinity" (feminine), or (4) low on both scales (undifferentiated).

In addition to the advances made with respect to our understanding that both masculinity and femininity can coexist within an individual of either sex, scientists and scholars have also attempted to identify the various components of and appropriate units of measurement for masculinity and femininity. There are multiple dimensions along which each of these concepts might be measured—for example, there are physical, behavioral, cognitive, personality, and social dimensions each with component subfactors. (In fact, some researchers now avoid the use of the terms "masculinity" and "femininity," which are overly inclusive and misleading, in favor of using specific terms such as "instrumentality" and "expressivity," which more accurately label the dimensions that are measured.) Furthermore, while some individuals exhibit a consistent pattern of "masculinization" or "feminization" across these multiple factors, others do not. Some scientists have addressed the cultural and contextual dependence of the very definitions of masculinity and femininity and issues of sex-role conformity. Others have explored the relative contributions of biological and sociocultural factors in the development and expression of masculine and feminine traits, unfortunately often entering into a nature versus nurture debate. [See Reinisch, Rosenblum, & Sanders, 1987 (Volume 1 in The Kinsey Institute Series) for a multidisciplinary consideration of the concepts of masculinity and femininity.]

Many of the same theoretical and empirical issues arise with respect to sexual orientation. Prior to the pioneering work of Dr. Alfred C. Kinsey, "homosexual" and "heterosexual" were viewed as dichotomous categories; that is, a person was considered to be either a heterosexual or a homosexual. Some allowed for a third category of bisexual, but others believed that a bisexual was a homosexual in disguise (trying to pass as heterosexual) or a heterosexual who was experimenting (see part A in the figure on page xxii). Such a categorical model is also apparent in the traditional psychoanalytic view of sexual orientation in which there is an assumption that some "true" underlying heterosexuality or homosexuality exists (that might best be identified through analysis of erotic fantasies), but that a person might repress such thoughts and exhibit behavior inconsistent with this true identity. (See Isay, Chapter 17, for a more detailed consideration of the psychoanalytic perspective.) The categorical view of sexual orientation is still held by many and certainly reflects how people are labeled in many societies.

One of the major contributions of Kinsey's research was his challenge of such dichotomous categorization. In their empirical documentation of

Models Of Sexual Orientation

A. Dichotomous—Psychoanalytic

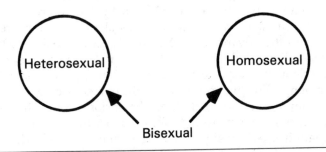

B. Unidimensional—Bipolar (Kinsey, 1948, 1953)

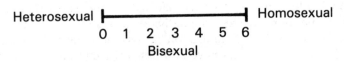

C. Two-dimensional—Orthogonal (Storms, 1978, 1980)

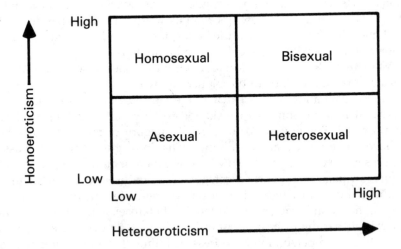

human sexual behavior patterns, he and his colleagues found that homosexual experience was not uncommon and that engaging in homosexual acts did not necessarily make a person a "homosexual." Independent of sexual self-labeling (i.e., what a person calls himself or herself), behavioral bisexuality among men and women was not uncommon even forty to fifty years ago. For example, in 1948 Kinsey and his colleagues reported that 50% of single, married, and previously married white men between the ages of 16 and 55 had responded erotically to other men, and 37% had engaged in sexual activity with a male to the point of orgasm since puberty (Kinsey et al., 1948). Similarly, 28% of single, married, and previously married white women between the ages of 12 and 45 reported that they had responded erotically to women, and 13% had engaged in sexual activity with a female to the point of orgasm (Kinsey et al., 1953). Kinsey and his colleagues also reported that, across a lifetime, a person's sexual behavior pattern could change, sometimes dramatically. There appeared to be a continuum of sexuality (Kinsey used a 0–6 scale) from exclusively heterosexual to exclusively homosexual (see part B of the figure on page xxii). The Kinsey scale and modifications thereof have been widely applied in sex research during the past 40 years.

The Kinsey scale has met with the same types of criticism as the unidimensional bipolar model of masculinity/femininity. It implies an inverse or reciprocal relationship—that is, the more homosexual an individual is, the less heterosexual he or she must be. Parallel to the development of orthogonal models of "masculinity" (instrumentality) and "femininity" (expressivity) (Bem, 1974; Spence & Helmreich, 1978), Storms (1978, 1980) proposed that homoeroticism and heteroeroticism are independent, orthogonal continua (see part C of the figure on page xxii). In this model, a bisexual is high on both homoeroticism and heteroeroticism, a heterosexual is high on heteroeroticism and low on homoeroticism, a homosexual is high on homoeroticism and low on heteroeroticism, and a person low on both dimensions would be asexual. To date, Storm's orthogonal model of sexual orientation has not been as widely utilized in sex research as have various modifications of the Kinsey scale.

As was the case with the gender-role concepts of masculinity and femininity, issues of (1) multidimensionality, (2) appropriate units of measurement, and (3) concordance or discordance across various dimensions of heterosexuality and homosexuality have been raised. In fact, most researchers who have modified the Kinsey scale have done so by using bipolar ratings of heterosexuality/homosexuality on multiple dimensions that are components of sexual orientation based on the belief that a single scale was inadequate to evaluate sexual orientation. Specifically, sexual behavior, sexual fantasy, who the person falls in love with, which sex is more "attractive," and so on, can be independently assessed. Each of these may be further subdivided. When asking about sexual behavior, for example, all of the following dimensions might be addressed: (1) the number of partners of each sex, (2) the frequency of sexual activity with each sex, or (3) the frequency of orgasm with each sex. As with the construct of masculinity/femininity, some individuals may exhibit similar levels of heterosexuality/homosexuality across relevant dimensions, while others do not. Discussions related to the appropriate dimensions through which to measure sexual orientation are found throughout this volume (particularly in Chapter 15 by Coleman, Chapter 16 by Klein, Chapter 21 by De Cecco, and Chapter 22 by Koertge).

Developmental changes and apparent discontinuities in sexual behavior patterns and homosexual identity across the lifespan raise important theoretical issues regarding the nature of sexual orientation and pose interesting challenges for the empiricist attempting to assess orientation (see Herdt, Chapter 13; Cass, Chapter 14; Nichols, Chapter 20). The fact that sexual behavior patterns and sexual self-labeling can change dramatically and sometimes several times (e.g., from heterosexual to homosexual and back to heterosexual) within an individual over time challenges the view that sexual orientation is fixed or determined early in life and remains constant.

Concordance or discordance across the multiple dimensions of sexual orientation or over time warrants further investigation. For example, based on traditional psychoanalytic views, a clinician might view an inconsistency between the frequency of homosexual erotic fantasies and actual homosexual behavior as reflecting repression of one's "true" sexual desires. However, Nichols (Chapter 20) has reported that, especially among women, fantasy content and behavior may be highly discordant and not reflect psychological maladjustment. A woman may consider herself to be heterosexual and have only male partners during one period of her life in which her fantasies may be predominately homosexual. She may then fall in love with a woman and live a lesbian lifestyle, during which her fantasies may be predominantly heterosexual. Certainly such case histories challenge the repression hypothesis and suggest that sexual orientation may change during the life span. Transitions in sexual orientation, however, do not necessarily imply that there can be conscious control over or choice of sexual orientation.

Cass (Chapter 14) has discussed the development of sexual identity, which involves the labeling of oneself as homosexual or heterosexual or bisexual. Since numerous factors affect an individual's acceptance and interpretation of his or her sexual orientation and the contexts, if any, in which he or she is identified as homosexual or bisexual, the use of such labels, although they may be important to one's identity, are not necessarily good predictors of sexual behavior patterns. For example, in a recent Kinsey Institute study of 262 self-identified lesbian women, 75% had had sex with men since age 18 and 43% of those who had always identified themselves as lesbian had done so (Reinisch, Sanders, & Ziemba-Davis, 1988, in press).

Analogous with the construct of masculinity/femininity, the very definitions of, attitudes toward, and expression of homosexuality and heterosexuality are dependent on cultural and contextual factors (see Bullough, Chapter 1; Boswell, Chapter 2; Voeller, Chapter 3; Gagnon, Chapter 12; and Herdt, Chapter 13). As Dr. Boswell points out, homosexuality may either be "marked" (i.e., something that is labeled as different) or "unmarked" in a given cultural, historical, and religious context.

Also parallel to the construct of masculinity/femininity, there is a great deal of interest in identifying the "causes" of sexual orientation, and these dialogs often are framed as a nature versus nurture debate regarding the relative contributions of biological and socioenvironmental factors instead of applying the more productive interactionist perspective (see Money, Chapter 4; Whalen, Geary, and Johnson, Chapter 5; Gooren, Chapter 6; Pillard, Chapter 7; Bancroft, Chapter 8; Weinreich, Chapter 9). For example, animals have been studied in an attempt to understand biological and evolutionary components of sexual orientation, and the limitations of animal models are also discussed (see Whalen, Geary, and Johnson, Chapter 5; Weinreich, Chapter 9; Nadler, Chapter 10; Rosenblum, Chapter 11). As the chapters in this volume reveal, there does not appear to be a single cause or a simple developmental path that determines sexual orientation, be it homosexual or heterosexual. Both biological and socioenvironmental factors have been identified that may affect the development of sexual orientation, and different factors may play varying roles in different individuals. The development of better scientific understanding of the origins of sexual orientation will be greatly facilitated by recognition and consideration of the following: (1) the existence of substantial diversity among individuals who identify themselves as homosexual similar to that among "heterosexuals," (2) the possibility that there may be many homosexualities, and (3) the likelihood that there may be multiple pathways to a common sexual orientation—homosexual, bisexual, or heterosexual (Bell & Weinberg, 1978).

By simultaneously examining the variables of sex (male or female), gender role (masculinity and femininity), and sexual orientation as they affect sexual and relational patterns, a number of contributors provide an invaluable clarification of the meaning of each of these concepts (Blumstein & Schwartz, Chapter 18; Peplau & Cochran, Chapter 19; Nichols, Chapter 20). For example, Drs. Blumstein and Schwartz have noted that, in general, lesbian couples exhibit a lower frequency of sexual activity and gay male couples exhibit a higher frequency of sexual activity than do heterosexual couples. They discuss these differences in sexual frequency within the context of the sex of the partners within each couple type; that is, in our society males generally initiate sexual activity more often than do females. Thus, the higher sexual frequency in gay male couples and the lower sexual frequency in lesbian couples may best be interpreted as relating to the sex of the partners, and perhaps to sex-role expectations, rather than to their sexual orientation.

Finally, as we noted in our earlier volume *Masculinity/Femininity: Basic Perspectives* (Reinisch et al., 1987), an overview of the chapters in this volume reminds us of the story of the three baseball umpires that bears repeating, perhaps because this parable speaks to the very nature of scientific inquiry itself. The first umpire says, "I call 'em the way I *see* 'em!" The second umpire responds, "Not me, I call 'em the way they *are!*" The third, presumably an older and wiser umpire, counters these confident views with "They aren't anything until I *call* them!" As with all aspects of science, our understanding of the nature and origins of sexual orientation develops as a function of the questions we ask, the methods by which we seek the answers, and how we interpret the data—all further limited by the cultural context in which we work and the lens through which we view the world. Because our "calls" form the substance of scientific knowledge, it is imperative that we compare various perspectives on a topic, as is accomplished in this volume, in an attempt to examine the lenses through which we look and the biases they introduce.

In summary, sexual orientation cannot be understood in terms of simple dichotomies or unidimensional models. Sexual orientation is multidimensional in its essence, and its development is affected by many factors. Although nominal categories of heterosexual, homosexual, and bisexual exist, the application of such labels reflects a complex set of social, political, and developmental factors and does not always accurately reflect actual sexual behavior patterns or erotic desire. These as well as other theoretical and empirical issues addressed in this volume have diverse, direct, practical implications for all scientists, scholars, and clinicians whose work involves the issues of sexual orientation and sexual behavior patterns. For example, the distinction between homosexual/heterosexual behavior and homosexual/heterosexual identity highlights that, when we need to know about what people are doing (as in attempts to predict the spread of HIV, or sexually transmitted diseases in general), we must concentrate on the behaviors expressed and not on categories of self-identification or labels, or we will be confused and misguided in the practical decisions we make.

Acknowledgments

We would like to thank C. A. Hill and M. Ziemba-Davis for their thoughtful editorial commentary.

References

Bell, A. P. & Weinberg, M. S. (1978). *Homosexualities: A Study of Diversity Among Men and Women*. New York: Simon and Schuster.

Bem, S. L. (1974). The measurement of psychological androgyny. *Journal of Consulting and Clinical Psychology, 42*, 155–162.

Kinsey, A. C., Pomeroy, W. B., & Martin, C. E. (1948). *Sexual Behavior in the Human Male*. Philadelphia: W. B. Saunders Company.

Kinsey, A. C., Pomeroy, W. B., Martin, C. E., & Gebhard, P. H. (1953). *Sexual Behavior in the Human Female*. Philadelphia: W. B. Saunders Company.

Reinisch, J. M. (1976). Effects of prenatal hormone exposure on physical and psychological development in humans and animals: With a note on the state of the field. In E. J. Sacher (Ed.), *Hormones, Behavior, and Psychopathology* (p. 69–94). New York: Raven Press.

Reinisch, J. M., Rosenblum, L. A., & Sanders, S. A. (1987). *Masculinity/Femininity: Basic Perspectives. The Kinsey Institute Series, Volume 1*. New York: Oxford University Press.

Reinisch, J. M., Rosenblum, L. A., & Sanders, S. A. (1987). Masculinity/Femininity: An Introduction. In J. M. Reinisch, L. A. Rosenblum, & S. A. Sanders (Eds.), *Masculinity/Femininity: Basic Perspectives. The Kinsey Institute Series, Volume 1*. New York: Oxford University Press.

Reinisch, J. M., Sanders, S. A. (1987). Behavioral influences of prenatal hormones. In C. B. Nemeroff and P. T. Loosen (Eds.), *Handbook of Clinical Psychoneuroendocrinology*, New York: The Guilford Press.

Reinisch, J. M., & Sanders S. A. (in press). Prenatal hormonal contributions to sex differences in human cognitive and personality development. In H. Moltz, I. L. Ward, & A. A. Gerall (Eds.), *Handbook of Behavioral Neurobiology (Vol. 10), Sexual Differentiation: A Lifespan Approach*. New York: Plenum Publishing Corporation.

Reinisch, J. M., Sanders, S. A., & Ziemba-Dais, M. M. (1988). The study of sexual behavior in relation to the transmission of Human Immunodeficiency Virus: Caveats and Recommendations, *American Psychologist, 43*((11): 921–927.

Reinisch, J. M., Sanders, S. A., & Ziemba-Davis, M. (in press). Self-labeled sexual orientation, sexual behavior, and knowledge about AIDS: Implications for biomedical research and education programs. In S. J. Blumenthal, A. Eichler, and G. Weissman (Eds.), Proceedings of NIMH/NIDA Workshop, *Women and Aids: Promoting Healthy Behaviors*.

Reinisch, J. M., Ziemba-Davis, M., & Sanders, S. A. (In press). Sexual behavior and AIDS: Lessons from art and sex research. In B. Voeller, J. M. Reinisch, & M. Gottlieb (Eds.) *AIDS and Sex: An Integrated Biomedical and Biobehavioral Approach*. New York: Oxford University Press.

Spence, J. T., & Helmreich, R. L. (1978). *Masculinity and Femininity: Their Psychological Dimensions, Correlates, and Antecedents*. Austin: University of Texas Press.

Spence, J. T., Helmrich, R. L., & Stapp, J. (1974). The PAQ: A Measure of sex-role stereotypes and M-F. *JSAS Catalogue of Selected Documents in Psychology, 4*, 127.

Storms, M. D. (1981) A theory of erotic orientation development. *Psychological Review, 88*(4): 340–353.

Storms, M. D. (1980). Theories of sexual orientation. *Journal of Personality and Social Psychology, 38*(5): 783–792.

Voeller, B., Reinisch, J. M., & Gottlieb, M. (in press). *AIDS and Sex: An Integrated Biomedical and Biobehavioral Approach. The Kinsey Institute Series, Volume 4*. New York: Oxford University Press.

Whalen, R. E. (1974). Sexual differentiation: Models, methods and mechanisms. In R. C. Friedman, R. M. Richart, & R. L. Vande Wiele (Eds.), *Sex Differences in Behavior*, (pp. 467–481). New York: Wiley.

I
HISTORICAL
AND RELIGIOUS
PERSPECTIVES

1

The Kinsey Scale
in Historical Perspective

Vern Bullough

Kinsey, as we all know, put sexual behavior on a continuum from 0 to 6, with exclusively heterosexual behavior on one end (0) and exclusively homosexual or lesbian behavior on the other (6). The effect of this was to emphasize the variety of sexual activity and to demonstrate that homosexuality and lesbianism were more or less a natural aspect of human behavior. On the basis of this classification, Kinsey reported that 37% of the male population had some homosexual experience to the point of orgasm between adolescence and old age, 13% had more homosexual than heterosexual experience, and 4% were exclusively homosexual. Similar, though lower figures were given for women and lesbianism (Kinsey, Pomeroy & Martin, 1948; Kinsey, Pomeroy, Martin, & Gebhard, 1953).

Note that I speak of Kinsey as doing this, even though the research was a collaborative effort, because the scale was not developed after the research was done but either before the research was undertaken or by the time the first 60 interviews were completed (Pomeroy, 1986). Although the Kinsey scale, as I have claimed elsewhere, is not the only way to describe sexual behavior (Bullough, 1979), nor in light of what we now know is it probably the best way, from a historical viewpoint it was extremely valuable.

Background

Homosexual activity is universal throughout history. I do not know of any historical area or period or any culture in which there is not some record of homosexual activity, although different societies and cultures have looked upon these activities with a wide range of attitudes (Bullough, 1976).

Regardless of the kind of source material one uses, religious, medical, legal, or poetry, drama, fiction, or history, there is a vast amount of information about sexual activities in general and homosexual activity in particular. For example, from the surviving Egyptian legends about the gods Seth and Horus, we learn about early attitudes toward homosexuality (Bullough, 1973). It is from the Gilgamesh story of creation and the flood that we find the earliest attitudes about homosexuality of the Mesopotamian peoples of the Tigris Euphrates (Bullough, 1971).The same comments can be made for the religious traditions of India and China (Bullough, 1976).

When we leave the mythological survivals of the ancient gods and goddesses and come to those historical religions that still survive, we have even richer sources. Though Christianity, Judaism, and Islam are religions of the book, with a canon of sacred scriptures, including the Bible and the Koran, the richest source of sex information in these religions can be found in the traditional amplification of the scriptures. In Judaism it is the Talmud, in Islam it is the various legal commentators upon the Koran, and in Christianity it is a rich variety of sources ranging from theological treatises to canon law to confessional literature to saints' lives (Bullough, 1976).

Sexuality in fact was a major focus of early Christian literature. Almost every early Christian Father dealt with sexuality, some in great detail with widespread discussions about same-sex activity. In the case of St. Augustine (n.d.) we even have a sexual confession involving the issue of celibacy versus any sexual activity at all. Although homosexual activity was condemned, so were most other forms of sexual activity with the exception of sex undertaken for the purpose of procreation. Even then it had to be in the proper position and with the proper parts of the anatomy, that is, penis and vagina, with the female on her back. At the same time the Christian church developed institutions that would encourage same-sex activity, such as all-male monasteries and all-female convents. Evidence that the church was concerned about this derives from the documentation of efforts of numerous monastic officials from St. Benedict on to lessen the temptation of same-sex activity (Delatte, 1950).

The problem, with such data, however, is the ambiguity about what constitutes homosexuality. This problem also appears in the legal data, where again there is a plethora of references in legal codes, legal commentaries, and lawsuits dealing with same-sex activities. In the West, canon (or church) law is particularly valuable in this respect because the legal commentators were dealing with prohibited activity and were attempting to describe the degree of sin or punishment involved (Bullough & Brundage, 1982). To do this they often made up imaginary cases or pulled real cases from the literature. James Brundage, the scholar who has most thoroughly investigated sex and the canon law, found that about 10% of canon law texts in the medieval-early modern period dealt with sexual topics, as did approximately 6% of the civil law texts. He also found that fornication was the subject discussed most frequently, whereas sodomy (read this to include homosexuality) was not discussed very often (Brundage, 1982).

The mention of the term *sodomy* emphasizes the confusion about same-sex activity. For example, English legal commentators, the source of much of American law, usually did not attempt to distinguish between various forms of forbidden intercourse. Sir Edward Coke, one of the major commentators, wrote the following:

> Buggery is a detestable, and abominable sin, amongst Christians not to be named, committed by carnal knowledge against the ordinance of the Creator, and order of nature, by mankind, or with brute beast, or by womankind with brute beast. (Coke, 1628/1797, pp. 58–59)

Obviously there is a lumping of what we now call bestiality with some aspects of same-sex activity, but the exclusion of sexual activity between two women leads one to wonder if same-sex activity was thought to occur only if there was penetration or emission of semen. Coke also made no distinction about the number of times a person engaged in such activities; by definition the person who did so even once was a sodomist.

This confusion of legal authorities appears in the first reported trial for a homosexual offense after the sixteenth- century revision of the English common law took place in 1631. In this case the Earl of Castlehaven, who was both married and a father, was charged with committing sodomy with one of his male servants as well as raping his own wife. Castlehaven was convicted and executed. A commentator on the case has argued that he was convicted more for violating the social norms of mixing the classes than for his sexual activity (Bingham, 1971).

Within what is now the United States, the earliest conviction for a homosexual offense occurred in 1624, when Richard Cornish was executed for allegedly forcing a young man to have sexual relations with him (McIlwaine, 1924). In New England the first conviction took place in 1637, when two males were found "guilty of lude behavior and unclean carriage one with another, by often spending their seed one upon another" (*Records*, 1855). At least in this last case the term *often* was used, and we can surmise it was not an isolated incident.

This same ambiguity existed in other kinds of sources. Plato, for example, made a case for homosexuality in the *Symposium*, although it was not for exclusive homosexuality but for a bisexuality with homoerotic contacts taking place primarily between older adult men and adolescent boys

(Plato, 1953). Aristotle (1927) recognized the existence of people who would rate a 6 on the Kinsey scale, but only rarely do we have enough information to classify people. Even so, several people have compiled lists of possible individuals (Bullough, 1979; Rowse, 1977).

Even if someone clearly seems to be entirely oriented toward the same sex, we still have the problem of distinguishing between behavior and attitudes because attitudes do not always equate with behavior. Even if they did, there still is a problem of language. An example culled from the writings of St. Bernard will illustrate this point. Bernard was the person most responsible for the rise and influence of the Cistercians, an order formed eight years before he was born. Sometime after Bernard joined the order, he was chosen to head a branch house at Clairvaux and proceeded to attract so many new monks that 65 new houses were founded. The motivating force behind St. Bernard seems to have been love, the weak frail love of men for each other and for God, and the masterful overpowering love of God for all. A good illustration of this is the letter he wrote to a certain Robert, a cousin of his, who apparently had fled the monastery to which his parents had dedicated him in child-hood. Bernard was overcome with grief at the loss of this young man. This letter stands first in the collection of his correspondence. It is clear that St. Bernard believed that his love for the young man would bring him back and to this end he dictated this letter(still preserved on the parchment on which it was written):

> I am not writing in order to contend, but to end contention. To flee persecution is no fault in him who flees, but in him who pursues: I do not deny it. I pass over what has happened; I do not ask why or how it happened. I do not discuss faults, I do not dispute as to the circumstances, I have no memory for injuries. I speak only what is in my heart. Wretched me, that I lack thee, that I do not see thee, that I am living without thee, for whom to die would be to live; without whom to live is to die. I ask not why thou hast gone away; I complain only that thou dost not return. Come, and there shall be peace; return, and all shall be made good. (Taylor, 1949)

He goes on like this for several pages. Is St. Bernard a homosexual? Or is this a form of expression much like we find existed among women in nineteenth-century America (Smith-Rosenberg, 1975)?

In the nineteenth century, terms of endearment and affection were commonplace among women. Susan B. Anthony's letters to her young proteges, most notably Anna Dickinson, for example, included such en-dearing terms as "Dicky darling Anna" and "Dear Chick-a-dee," and she was constantly wanting to give Anna "one awful long squeeze." She encouraged Anna not to marry a "man" and requested that she visit her in

New York, where although the quarters were plain, there was a double bed "big enough and good enough to take you in." When Anna was planning to visit her, Anthony wrote that she could hardly wait for her, "for the scolding and pinched ears and everything I know awaits me. . . . What world of experience since I last snuggled the wee child in my long arms." Anna was not the only one to whom Anthony wrote such letters. As she wrote in 1895 to Anna, "I have had several lovely Anna girls— 'nieces'—they call themselves now-a-day—since my first Anna—but none of them—has or ever can fill the niche in my heart that you did" (Sinclair, 1965).

There are numerous other such surviving letters between women of the time. Antoinette Brown, for example, fell in love with Lucy Stone, and she begged Lucy, her "dearest little cowboy," to come and visit her. "I love you Lucy any way, and if you would only come and take a nap with me here on my bed my head would get rested a great deal faster for it is aching now" (Sinclair, 1965).

What is one to make of such references, whether they are found in the High Middle Ages or in nineteenth-century America? If we do read homoerotic feelings into them, as I do, can we classify these people as homosexuals, or are such references just a form of endearing expression, as some would argue?

This leads one to ask whether one homosexual experience or homo-erotic experience can make someone a homosexual. Obviously, the law did not distinguish in the past, but it was a problem that bothered Kinsey and other researchers in the past. Although we have often classified peo-ple in the past as homosexual, there was really no standard of agreement about what it was to be homosexual. One of the more fascinating cases in American history is that of Walt Whitman, who illustrates some of the problems in defining who was homosexual. Among the poems in *Leaves of Grass*, first published in 1860, is a group of 45 poems known as the "Cala-mus" group, usually interpreted as focusing on the spiritual love of man for man. The calamus is a plant, sometimes known as the sweet flag, whose fascicles, clinging together for support, supposedly represented the "adhesive love" of friendship. Many readers of the poems saw some-thing more than spiritual love. John Addington Symonds, a nineteenth-century closet homosexual and collaborator with Havelock Ellis on his study of homosexuality, believed that Whitman clearly was homosexual.

> [The] language of "Calamus."..has a passionate glow, a warmth of emotional tone, beyond anything to which the modern world is used in the celebration of the love of friends. It recalls to our mind the early Greek enthusiasm. . . . Nor does the poet himself appear to be unconscious that there are dangers and difficulties involved in the highly pitched emotions he is praising. (Symonds, 1891)

To remove all doubts, Symonds, the author of a biography of Whitman, wrote to him. Whitman delayed several years in answering the question, but Symonds persisted and Whitman finally replied:

> [That] the Calamus part has ever allowed the possibility of such construction as mentioned is terrible. I am fain to hope the pages themselves are not to be even mentioned for such gratuitous and quite at the same time undreamed and unwished possibility of morbid inferences—which are disavowed by me and seem damnable. (Symonds, 1891)

This reply, however, is quite simply untruthful. We know from other sources that Whitman was homosexual, very active in the nineteenth-century equivalent of the twentieth-century gay life. We even know the names of some of the men he propositioned in New York bars and streets during certain periods in his life (Cowley, 1946; Smith, 1949).

In that period and time, however, Whitman was unwilling to be identified, even to a person as empathic and understanding as John Addington Symonds. Perhaps this was simply the better part of discretion as evidenced by the furor that arose in more recent times over the Delaware River Port Authority's decision in July 1955 to name the then new bridge connecting South Philadelphia and Camden, New Jersey (where Whitman died), after the poet. The Reverend Edward B. Lucitt of the Camden diocese sent a letter on behalf of Roman Catholics in Camden and surrounding counties protesting the name of Walt Whitman Bridge because Whitman's life and works were "personally objectionable" as evidenced by the fact that a recent biographer had called him "homoerotic." This letter was followed by a series of letters from 58 Catholic schools in the Camden diocese asking to find a less objectionable man from New Jersey for whom the bridge could be named. The chairman of the Delaware River Port Authority issued a bulletin stating that the authority had asked three historical societies (never named) and could find no evidence that Whitman was homosexual. G. W. Allen, the author who had called Whitman homoerotic, also issued a bulletin, saying, "I used the term '*homoerotic*' rather than '*homosexual*' because the latter suggests sex perversion. There is absolutely no evidence that Whitman engaged in any perverted practice" (Smith, 1949).

Research into Homosexuality

If we have difficulty in defining people of the past as homosexual, one of the major problems is what constituted homosexuality then. Attempts to find labels for people who engage in same-sex activity and to define what it means did not originate with Kinsey. One of the most complete descriptions in the medical literature is that made by Soranus, a Greek physician of the second century A.D., whose work on acute and chronic diseases has been preserved in a Latin translation by Caelius Aurelianus. Soranus (or Aurelianus) included a brief chapter on effeminate men, whom he called *subactors* or *pathics*.

> Now this condition is different from a bodily disease; it is rather an affliction of a diseased mind. Indeed, often out of passion and in rare cases out of respect for certain persons to whom they are beholden, these pathics suddenly change their character and for a while try to give proof of their virility. But since they are not aware of their limitations, they are again the victims of excesses, subjecting their virility to too great a strain and consequently involving themselves in worse vices . . . Indeed, the victims of this malady may be compared to the women who are called *tribades* because they pursue both kinds of love. These women are more eager to lie with women than with men; in fact, they pursue women with almost masculine jealousy. (Aurelianus, 1950)

Although there are many flaws in Soranus's description, its value is that generally it is nonjudgmental. Those parts that are judgmental are now believed to have been inserted at a later date by Christian scribes.

It was not until the nineteenth century that researchers (many of them homosexuals themselves) tried to find more accurate ways of describing same-sex behavior and activities. Undoubtedly, they were driven to this by confusion over the terms as well as the judgmental connotation of many of the terms. One of the pioneers in calling for new terms was Johann Ludwig Casper, author of the standard nineteenth-century work on forensic medicine. Casper originally used the term *paederastia* as a catchall classification but quickly realized it was a poor term because at least some of the same-sex activity was between adults. Casper also included references to lesbianism and sodomy, although the latter was defined almost solely in terms of animal contacts (Casper, 1864). Later editions, edited by Carl Liman, also called for greater precision in terminology, particularly the need to recognize and distinguish between congenital or innate homosexuals (perhaps a 6 on the Kinsey scale) and those who turned to homosexuality later because, in his terms, of a "satiety with other, more normal pleasures" (Casper & Liman, 1889).

One of the first to try to develop a new nomenclature and description was Swiss milliner Heinrich Hössli (1836), who used the term *Mannerliebe* (man-love). This had the advantage of being a neutral term, but it was somewhat ambivalent in meaning. Karl Heinrich Ulrichs, also known as Numa Numantius, used the term *mannmännliche Liebe* (love between men), perhaps based upon Hössli's term, but hunted for precise definitions. Ulrichs, a homosexual himself, wanted to demonstrate that "abnormal" instincts were inborn and therefore natural, and he was especially concerned with finding nonderogatory terms to describe individuals born with same-sex inclinations. He originally coined the term *Uranian*, derived from an illusion to Uranus in Plato's *Symposium*, and later Germanized this into *urning* for the male, *uringin* for the female, and referred to the condition itself as *urningtum* (Ulrichs, 1864, 1865).

Ulrichs distinguished a threefold division in sexuality, male, female, and urning or uringin; the last were individuals who had the physical features of one sex but whose sexual instinct failed to correspond to their sexual organs, resulting in an inversion of sexual desires. Ulrichs also held that the line of physical differentiation between males and females had been overemphasized; as proof he pointed out that normal males have rudimentary breasts and normal females, a rudimentary penis. Many people, he wrote, fail to develop along expected lines in their physiology, and it was easily understandable to him why a body might have one physiological sex and the soul another (1869a, 1869b). Essentially, however, Ulrichs was concerned with 6s on the Kinsey scale.

Independently of Ulrichs, Karl Maria Kertbeny (born Karl Maria Benkert) coined the term *homosexual* (1869a, 1869b). This word was picked up by Gustav Jager (1884) and by Richard von Krafft-Ebing (1894), who popularized it in the various translations of his work. For a time, other terms competed with the term *homosexual*. Carl Westphal, a professor of psychiatry at Berlin, published a case history of a young woman who from her earliest years liked to dress as a boy, cared for boy's games, and found herself only attracted to women (a 6 on the Kinsey scale?). Westphal (1869) believed that the phenomenon he observed was congenital and entitled it the *konträre sexualempfindug*, which was usually translated into English as "inverted sexual instinct," although that is not the literal translation.

John Addington Symonds used the term *inversion* (1891),and Havelock Ellis, who was his coauthor on the original German edition of Ellis's study *Sexual Inversion* (1936), used both the terms *inversion* and *homosexuality*. Ellis distinguished sexual inversion from homosexuality, with homosexuality including all sexual attractions between people of the same sex, even when seemingly due to the accidental absence of the natural objects of sexual attraction. Sexual inversion was a constitutional abnormality and would probably be equivalent to a Kinsey 6 (Ellis, 1936, p. 1). Though Ellis dealt with a real problem, his terms were not adopted. Instead, with the use of the term *homosexuality* by Magnus Hirschfeld (1914), the term *homosexual* more or less carried the day. There remained ambiguities, however, about what the term meant, and a series of investigators labored with the problem of distinguishing who could be called a 6 on the Kinsey scale from others who engaged in homosexual activity. Various terms were proposed to distinguish the levels of homosexuality, or homosexualities, to use a more recent concept. *Sexual inversion* was one term used, as well as *bisexual, psychosexual hermaphrodite*, and manyother terms. The problem was made more difficult by the conceptions of latent homosexuality advanced by Sigmund Freud (Freud, 1910, 1922, 1924–1950, 1938).

There were numerous investigators (Bullough, 1976), but the underlying problem of what constituted homosexuality was a question that had not been resolved when Kinsey appeared on the scene. He hit upon an answer very early in his research, namely, the bipolar seven-point scale (Pomeroy, 1986). It is the kind of scale a biologist might construct, and since five-, six-, and seven-point scales seem to be the most popular, Kinsey probably did not search for much further refinement, believing as most scale constructors of the time did that further refinement would simply make it more difficult to score.

For whatever reason, it was a stroke of political genius. Note the term *political*. Although I think the Kinsey scale can be improved upon, and it does not measure all the things I want to measure, it does two things of great importance. It offers comfort to both homosexuals and heterosexuals. Kinsey, in effect, demonstrated that some homosexual activity was widespread in the American population, almost a normative aspect of growing up. By so doing he gave assurance to many worried heterosexuals that they were not homosexuals and could relax in their "normality." Homosexuals, on the other hand, found that they were more numerous than the general public (and perhaps they themselves) realized and that others had at least experimented with homosexuality. The result was an outburst of books assuring homosexuals of their own normality, with titles implying everything from the fact that one person in twenty was gay to one person in ten to even lower ratios.

Kinsey's findings and the publicity about them has been particularly valuable in assuring many a parent and many a client that one experience does not a homosexual make. On the other hand, his findings that a significant percentage of his sample were exclusively homosexual or almost exclusively homosexual allowed American society to come to terms with the facts of life and to recognize the widespread existence of homosexuality. These are extremely important contributions, and I do not think the modern gay movement would have come into being without them (Bullough, 1984).

I am, however, at this point in my research, convinced that the Kinsey scale has outlived its political usefulness and we need a more effective scholarly measuring tool. In fact, the Kinsey scale offers the same kind of difficulty that the traditional masculine-feminine scale did until it was realized that women could have masculine traits and still be feminine and vice versa. This led to the development of the Bem scale (Bem, 1974) and others. A more complex scale could have numerous research advantages by not only allowing us to research over again what we have done before but also allowing us to ask different kinds of questions and to forge different kinds of answers. We know a large number of factors are associated with sexual identity, and as a historian I know that researchers such as Kinsey themselves have an effect upon not only what society believes but how it behaves. Something made possible by the Kinsey scale and its rise is the individual's self-identification as a homosexual. In social movements (and the gay movement is a social one) involving stigmatized groups (and certainly homosexuals were stigmatized in the past and some of this stigmatism still remains), individuals have found a need to define themselves in terms that distinguish them from others. In a sense this is what some of the early research into homosexuality mentioned in this chapter also tried to do.

What probably needs to be emphasized in any scale is not the polarization of sex into homosexuality and heterosexuality but how much alike even in sexual behavior people are. Evelyn Hooker (1957) emphasized the similarities of the psychosocial aspects of homosexuals with her heterosexual sample, but we need to do similar things in terms of sexual activity itself. We have taken some steps in this direction by emphasizing homosexualities instead of homosexuality, but if this is the case there are also heterosexualities and bisexualities as well. I do not think a bipolar scale can do this, and I personally believe that the more we know about sexual behavior the less valuable a bipolar scale becomes.

In sum, Kinsey answered a problem for his generation. Like the work of others before him in science, however, his work now becomes a stepping-stone from which we need to advance in new directions.

References

Aristotle (1927). *Problemata, 4, 26* (879–880A) (E. S. Forster, Trans.). In W. D. Ross (Ed.), *The works of Aristotle* (Vol. 7). Oxford, England: Clarendon Press.

Augustine, St. *Confessions.* Various editions.

Aurelianus, C. (1950). *On acute diseases and on chronicdiseases* (0. W. Tempkins, Trans.). Chicago: University of Chicago Press, Book 4, sec. 9, lines 131–137.

Bem, S. L. (1974). The measurement of psychological androgyny. *Journal of Consulting and Clinical Psychology, 42,* 155–162.

Bingham, C. (1971). Seventeenth-century attitudes toward deviant sex. *Journal of Interdisciplinary History, 1,* 447–467.

Brundage, J. (1982). Sex and canon law. In V. L. Bullough & J. Brundage, *Sexual practices and the medieval church,* (pp. 88–101). Buffalo, NY: Prometheus.

Bullough, V. L. (1971). Attitudes toward deviant sex in ancient Mesopotamia. *Journal of Sex Research, 7,* 184–203.

Bullough, V. L. (1973). Homosexuality as submissive behavior: An example from Egyptian mythology. *Journal of Sex Research, 9,* 283–88.

Bullough, V. L. (1976). *Sexual variance in society and history.* Chicago: University of Chicago Press.

Bullough, V. L. (1979). *Homosexuality: A history.* New York: New American Library.

Bullough, V. L. (1984). Weighing the shift from sexual identity to sexual relationship. *Journal of Homosexuality, 10,* 3–6.

Bullough, V. L. & Brundage, J. (1982). *Sexual practices and the medieval church.* Buffalo, NY: Prometheus.

Casper, J. L. (1864). *A handbook of the practice of forensic medicine* (pp. 330–346). (G. W.

Balfour, Trans., third German ed., Vols. 1–4). London: New Syndeham Society.

Casper, J. L., & Liman, C. (1889). *Handbuch der Gerichtlichen Medicine*, [Handbook of Judicial Medicine] Berlin: Hirschwald.

Coke, E. (1797). *Institutes of the laws of England* (Part III). London: E. and R. Brooke. (Original work published 1628).

Cowley, M. (1946). Walt Whitman, "The Miracle," Walt Whitman, "The Secret." *New Republic*.

Delatte, D. P. (1950). *The rule of St. Benedict*, Cap. 22. (D. M. McCann, Trans.). Reprinted: Latrobe, PA. The Arch Abbey Press.

Ellis, H. (1936). *Sexual inversion*: Part 4, Vol. 1. *Psychology of sex*. New York: Random House. This volume was originally conceived as a collaboration between Ellis and Symonds. The first volume was published in Germany because of problems with English censorship, but before the work appeared in 1896, Symonds had died. When an English version was published in 1897, Symond's family sought to remove his name from it. Failing to do so, they bought up most of the English edition and destroyed it, after which they secured an agreement that Ellis would publish it under his own name.

Freud, S. (1910). *Three contributions to sexual theory*. New York: Journal of Nervous and Mental Diseases Publishing Co.

Freud, S. (1922). *Leonardo da Vinci*, (A. A. Brill, Trans.). London: Kegan, Paul, Trench, Trubner and Co.

Freud, S. (1924–1950). *Collected papers*. London: Imago Publishers.

Freud, S. (1938). *Basic writings*. New York: Basic Books.

Hirschfeld, M. (1920). *Die Homosexualität des Mannes und des Weibes* (2nd ed.). [The Homosexuality of the Man and of the Woman] Berlin: Louis Marcus.

Hooker, E. (1957). The adjustment of the male overt homosexual. *Journal of Projective Techniques*, 21, 18–31.

Hössli, H. (1836). *Eros Die Mannerliebe der Griechen ihre Beziehung zur Geshichte Erziehung, Literatur und Gesetzgebung aller Zeiten* (Vol. 1). [Eros the male love of the Greeks, their relationship to the history, education, literature and love of all times]. St. Gallen, Switzerland: E. P. Scheitlin.

Jager, G. (1884). *Entdeckung der Seele*. [Discovery of the soul]. Leipzig, Germany: E. Gunther.

Kertbenny, K. M. (1869a). *Das Gemeinschadliche des Section 143 des Preusichen Strafgesetzbuches vom 14 April 1851 und daher seine notwendige Tilgung als Section 152 im Entwurfe eines Strafgesetzbuches für den Norrdeutschen Bund.* [The public nuisance section (Section 143) of the Prussian Penal Code from 14 April, 1851 and its necessary sucession as Section 152 in the draft of a Penal code for the Confederation of North German states]. Leipzig: Serbe.

Kertbenny, K. M. (1869b). *Section 142 des preuszichen Strafgesetzbuches vom 14 April 1851 und seine Aufrechterhaltung als section 152 im Entwurfe eines Strafgesetzbuches fur den norddeutschen Bund.* [Section142 of the Prussian Penal code of April 14, 1851 and its continuation as Section 152 in the draft of a penal codefor the Confederation of North German states]. Leipzig: Serbe. Reprinted in 1905 by Magnus Hirschfeld in *Jahrbuch für sexuelle Zwischenstufen*, 6, 3–66.

Kinsey, A. C., Pomeroy, W. B. & Martin, C. E. (1948). *Sexual behavior in the human male*. Philadelphia: W. B. Saunders.

Kinsey, A. C., Pomeroy, W. B., Martin, C. E., & Gebhard, P. H. (1953). *Sexual behavior in the human female*. Philadelphia: W.B. Saunders.

Krafft-Ebing, R. von (1894). *Psychopathia Sexualis* (C. H. Chaddock, Trans.). Philadelphia: F. A. Davis.

McIlwaine, H. R. (Ed.). (1924). *Minutes of the council and general court of colonial Virginia, 1622–1632, 1670–76.* Richmond, Va: Virginia State Library.

Plato (1953). *Symposium* (W. R. M. Lamb, Ed. and Trans.). London: William Heinemann.

Pomeroy, Wardell (1986). [Interview with Vern Bullough].

Records of the Colony of New Plymouth in New England. (1855). Boston: William White.

Rowse, A. L. (1977). *Homosexuals in history.* New York: MacMillan.

Sinclair, A. (1965). *The better half: The emancipation of the American woman.* New York: Harper & Row.

Smith, A. E. (1959, Winter). The curious controversy over Whitman's sexuality. *One Institute Quarterly, 4,* p. 6.

Smith-Rosenberg, C. (1975). The female world of love and ritual: Relations between women in nineteenth-century America, *Signs, 1,* 1–30.

Symonds, J. A. (1891). *A problem in modern ethics.* London: privately printed. This was published anonymously, with no author given.

Taylor, H. 0. (1949). *The medieval mind* (Vols. 1 and 2). Cambridge, MA: Harvard University Press.

Ulrichs, K. H. (1864). *"Vindex." Social-Juristische Studien über mannmännliche Geschlectsliebe.* [Socio-legal studies on male-male sexual love]. Leipzig: Matthes.

Ulrichs, K. H. (1865). *"Formatrix." Anthropologische Studien über urnische Liebe.* [Anthropological studies in homosexual love]. Leipzig: Matthes.

Ulrichs, K. H. (1869a). *"Argonauticus." Eastrow und die Urninge des pietisitischen, ultra montanen und freidenkenden Lagers.* [Eastrow and the male homosexual from the religious ultra montanen and the free thinking factions]. Leipzig: Serbe.

Ulrichs, K. H. (1869b). *"Incubus." Urningsliebe und Blutgier. Eine Erorterung über krankhafte Gemuthsaf fectionen und Zurecht-nungsfahigkeit, veranlässt durch den Berliner Criminalfall v. Zastrow.* [Male homosexual love and blood thirstiness. A discussion of the pathological mental disorder and responsibility on the occasion of the Berlin criminal case of Zastrow].Leipzig: Serbe.

Westphal, C. (1869). Die Konträre Sexualempfindung. [The inverted sexual instinct]. *Archiven für Psychiatrie & Nervenkrankheiten 2,* 73–108.

2

Sexual and Ethical Categories in Premodern Europe

John Boswell

A central problem in assessing the utility of the Kinsey scale for understanding sexuality in premodern Europe is that the scale is designed to answer a question earlier societies would not themselves have raised. Social and ideological constructions[1] of sexuality inevitably vary according to time and place. Equally inevitably, they shape contemporary thought about as well as perceptions of sexuality. Public discourse about sexuality in ancient and medieval Europe was markedly different from its modern descendants and rarely directed attention to the issues subsumed under or implied by the rubrics "orientation," "preference," or "identity" addressed by the Kinsey scale.[2]

In the Mediterranean city-states of the ancient world (ca. 400 B.C.-400 A.D.), both public and private "norms" for human conduct were largely social and behavioral (as opposed, e.g., to intentional, psychological, or spiritual) and based on codes of public conduct and behavior anyone could follow, regardless of (what modern writers would call) "sexual orientation."[3] Ideals of human action focused on the fulfillment of social roles and expectations: being a good citizen by serving in the army or civil service or donating resources or labor to the state; being a responsible family member by treating one's spouse properly and caring well for children; being a dutiful child by obeying one's father and mother, bringing honor to the family through achievement, caring for aged parents; being a faithful friend in joy and sorrow, good fortune and bad. "Sexual identity" had little to do with any of these—including the roles of spouse and parent, since marriage and parenthood were not thought to depend on erotic attachment.

Opportunities for sexual expression also tended to obviate questions of orientation. Marriage was a duty for all Roman citizens, in the eyes of the family and the state, but was not generally supposed to fulfill erotic needs.[4] Every male was expected to marry, as were most females, regardless of whether or not conjugal relations afforded an opportunity for erotic satisfaction. In the case of males, extramarital sexuality was normal and accepted; in the case of married females, it was not, but for the latter, erotic fulfillment was not a public issue—fair treatment, affection, and respect were the expected rewards of being a good wife and mother. (Sexual fulfillment for women was appropriate only for courtesans, who could, if they wished, have recourse to either males or females, as could unmarried men. Nevertheless, there are hints, especially in sensational contexts, that married women also had recourse to slaves or masturbation for sexual needs, and there were of course instances of adultery involving married women. It seems unlikely on the face of it that public lack of interest in the sexual fulfillment of married women reflects a corresponding lack of interest on their part.)

Ethical ideals (as opposed to ordinary behavior)[5] were slightly more complicated and can be distinguished according to three general approaches, depending on whether they emphasized (1) the responsibilities, (2) the dangers, or (3) the religious significance of human sexuality.

The moral views on human sexuality of the "average Greco-Roman" were rarely articulated and are difficult to reconstruct with precision. They seem to have presupposed that sexuality is good or neutral so long as it is responsible, that is, does not interfere with duties to the state or family and does not involve the abuse of freeborn children or married women. This loose code is implicit in much of Greek and Roman literature, art, mythology, and law, and it is against it that a second, more ascetic, approach urged that sexuality is an inherently dangerous force and should be avoided as much as possible. Some adherents of this view would call their followers to celibacy, some would limit sexual expression to marriage, others to procreative acts within marriage. Although the last two prescriptions would apply to homosexual and heterosexual acts differentially (since the former would be categorically precluded, while the latter would only be circumscribed), they were not aimed at homosexuality or predicated on any invidious distinction between homosexual and heterosexual. Their objective was primarily to curtail promiscuous or pleasure-centered heterosexual activity. They excluded homosexual acts incidentally or along with activities—such as masturbation—that were not special to any group.

A few specific religions attached theological or ceremonial significance to particular aspects of sexuality. Traditional Romans idealized the sacrifice of sexual pleasure made by vestal virgins, while others embraced mystery cults that incorporated sexual acts in religious observance. Jews had very detailed rules about licit sexuality. Such practices and proscriptions had little impact on popular views; both Jews and vestal virgins were considered distinctive precisely because the standards they followed were exceptional. Apart from Judaism, no religion of the ancient world categorically prohibited homosexual relations, although some preached celibacy.[6]

There was thus relatively little reason for Romans to confront or pose questions of sexual orientation. Opportunities for erotic expression were organized around issues of class and age or marital status rather than gender; personal worth was measured in terms of public contributions and family responsibility, neither essentially related to personal erotic interest; private sexual behavior was not an arena of judgment or concern; and even ethical systems did not make the gender of sexual-object choice a criterion of moral action.

This does not mean that everyone was at liberty to perform any sort of sexual act with anyone of either gender. One's own gender, age, class, and social standing set limitations on the range of acceptable forms of sexual expression for each individual. With a few exceptions, the higher one's social status, the more restrictions would apply to sexual acts and the fewer to sexual partners. A wealthy and powerful adult male citizen, for example, at the top of the status hierarchy, could penetrate any other person without loss of social status (although a dispute might arise if the other party were the wife or child of another citizen). "What does it matter," Antony wrote to Augustus, "where or in whom you stick it?"[7] But for the same male to be penetrated—by anyone—would incur disrespect if it were known and might even subject him to loss of civil privilege. By contrast, although a slave (or even a freedman) would lose no status for performing any particular sexual act, including being penetrated, he might suffer greatly (a slave could forfeit his life) if he had intercourse with anyone other than a partner allowed him by his owner or an adult male citizen.[8]

The restrictions on the sexual behavior of adult male citizens were not the result of prejudice against homosexuality. The same man could penetrate as many other men as he wished without incurring any stigma. The code of propriety was related to gender. Penetration and power were associated with the prerogatives of the ruling male elite; surrendering to penetration was a symbolic abrogation of power and authority—but in a way that posed a polarity of domination-subjection rather than of homosexual-heterosexual.[9] It was generally acceptable for a member of a less powerful group to submit to penetration by a member of a more powerful one. This was not thought to characterize any defect of personality or indicate any special psychological constitution or status.

The urgent personal question in Augustan Rome was not the gender with whom one did it but what one did. Martial titillated his audience by speculating on the possibility of "passive"[10] sexual behavior on the part of well-known Roman citizens, and a number of prominent Athenians and Romans were the butt of humor because they had performed an activity inappropriate to their status.[11] Conversely, Juvenal composed a long satire on the several inversions of the prevailing ethic involved in a male prostitute's taking the active role with male citizen clients.[12] The issue in all such cases was behavior, not gender preference. No citizen was ridiculed for having recourse to passive partners of either sex; nor were prostitutes or slaves—male or female—pilloried for receptivity.

Beginning around 400 A.D., Christianity began to introduce a new sexual code, focused on religious concepts of "holiness" and "purity." The origins and sources of its norms—the New Testament, Alexandrian Judaism, popular taboos, neo-Platonic philosophy, Roman legal principles— are imperfectly understood and too complex to enter into here. For the most part, its regulations, like their Greco-Roman predecessors, were conceptually unrelated to sexual "identity" or "orientation." But because Christianity, unlike ancient ethical systems, used obedience to sexual ethics as a primary symbol and test of human conduct, its code was both more detailed and more prominent, and in practice it laid the groundwork for distinctions based on "orientation."

Two general approaches to Christian sexuality can be discerned in the early church, distinct in their relation to "orientation." The earliest, evident in the New Testament, is similar to the "sex is dangerous" approach of pagan ethics: eroticism is a troublesome aspect of a fallen world; Christians should attempt to control it through responsible use. This approach would not, in itself, create distinctions based on gender-object choice because it focuses on the permanence and fidelity of erotic relationships, qualities that could be and were present in both heterosexual and homosexual relationships in the ancient world. Long-lasting homosexual unions and even official marriages were known in Greece and Rome, and Christian ceremonies of union for males closely resembling, if not actually constituting, marriage were also common in parts of the Christian world throughout the early Middle Ages. They invoked well-known pairs of saints as models for permanent, erotic same-sex relationships.[13] Even in areas where such relationships were not recognized, there was, through the end of the twelfth century, a strong tradition in Christian thought that regarded homosexuality and heterosexuality as two sides of the same coin. Either could be put to good or bad use, depending on the extent to which it was directed toward godly or ungodly ends. Any faithful and selfless passion subordinated to God's love, according to tradition, might be holy and sanctifying, just as any selfish lust was sinful.[14]

An opposing school of thought held that to be sinless a sexual act must be procreative. Even nonprocreative sexual activity between husband and wife was sinful, because procreative purpose was the sole justification for any sexual act. This idea was almost certainly borrowed from strands of late antique pagan ethics and was at first limited to ascetic Christian writers deeply imbued with Hellenistic philosophy, especially in Alexandria. But it gradually spread throughout the Christian world and became the favored position of ascetics in the West since it both limited sexuality to the smallest possible arena and appealed to an easily articulated and understood principle. Ultimately, it became the standard of Catholic orthodoxy, although hardly inevitably: not for a millennium after it first appeared did it sweep all other approaches before it.

By the end of the Middle Ages, although in parts of the Catholic world the "separate but equal" tradition survived,[15] the majority of Catholic churchmen and states had accepted the principle of procreative justification, and as a result, nonprocreative sexual behavior was considered a serious sin everywhere in Western Europe. Most civil law codes included penalties for "unnatural acts," which were, theologically, the discharge of semen in any nonprocreative context: non-procreative heterosexual activity (i.e., oral or anal), masturbation, homosexual acts, bestiality.[16] At least from the time of Augustine influential theologians had argued that nonprocreative acts within marriage were even more sinful than those outside, but public legal systems found them difficult to detect and punish, and civil codes and popular attitudes often reduced the distinction to extramarital versus marital sexuality or heterosexual versus homosexual acts.

This created a kind of dichotomy related to sexual-object choice. Although much heterosexual activity—even in marriage—and masturbation suffered the same moral sanctions as homosexual acts, only the last two were categorically prohibited, whereas forms of the first could be entirely moral.[17] It is essential to note, nonetheless, that whereas this late medieval system placed homosexual activity generically in an inferior category, it did not create a concept of sexual dimorphism in which a homosexual "orientation" or erotic preference was stigmatized as characterizing a special category of person. Those who engaged in forbidden sexual activity, homosexual or heterosexual, were sinners, but everyone in Catholic Europe was a sinner. All humans in all times (except Adam and Eve before the fall and the Virgin Mary after) were sinners. The rationale that made homosexual acts morally reprehensible also condemned contraception, masturbation, sexual expression between husband and wife undertaken for reasons of affection or pleasure, divorce, lending at interest, and a host of other common, everyday activities familiar to (if not practiced by) most Europeans. "Sinner" was a universal, not a special, category, and if the particular vice that included someone in this category was unusual, the category itself was thoroughly familiar to his neighbors.

Moreover, being "sinful" was a temporary state, no matter how often or for how long one found oneself in it. Anyone could cease being "sinful" at any moment, through repentance and contrition, ideally but not necessarily solemnized in the sacrament of penance. In this regard the public discourse of Catholic Europe regarding sexual ethics was much like the public ethos of ancient city-states, despite the change from secular to religious justification. Both were predicated on norms of external, modifiable behavior rather than on internal disposition or inclination; and the ethical codes of both either treated homosexuality and heterosexuality as morally indistinguishable or focused on elements of sexual behavior that usually affected all varieties of sexual expression.

The splintering of the Christian tradition during the Reformation rendered it increasingly difficult in early modern Europe to sustain public codes of conduct based on a particular set of transcendental values, and religious concepts of holy versus sinful behavior gradually ceased to be the defining terms of public discourse about sexual conduct, even in officially Catholic countries. By the early twentieth century, scientific—especially medical—values had replaced the consensus once based on theological principles. As the public's attention focused less and less on the salvation of the soul and more and more on the body and its well-being, the paramount standard in both public and private codes came to be the norm of health, physical and psychological. The desirability of persons, actions, and things is generally assessed in modern industrial nations against the ultimate value "health:" what is physically or mentally "normal" is what would be found in a "healthy" person. That this is tautological is not particularly unusual or striking. What is more interesting is that "normality" and "health" are personal characteristics rather than modes of behavior, and one generally has less control over them than over actions or conduct.

The medieval notion of the unholiness of homosexual acts was transformed by this change into the abnormality of the homosexual "condition." The "condition" has been variously conceptualized as a genetic "trait," a psychological "state," an "inclination," or a "preference." Although these vary in their implications of permanence and mutability, all suggest an essential, internal characteristic of a person rather than an external, voluntary activity.

The importance of the difference between the modern view and preceding systems of conceptualizing sexuality can scarcely be exaggerated. Contemporary constructions have drastically altered social views of sexual behavior and its significance by focusing on sexual-object choice and correlating it with an inherent, defining personal characteristic. The majority supposes itself to have the trait, condition, or preference of heterosexuality, which is "healthy" and "normal," and believes that a minority of persons have the "opposite" trait, condition or preference, which is "unhealthy" and "not normal." The difference is rendered more profound and alienating by the fact that the "normal" or "healthy" state is generally considered, like *all* forms of sexuality in the past, to be primarily behavioral. Because "heterosexual" is conceived to be the norm, it is unmarked and unnoticed. "Heterosexual person" is unnecessary; *person* implies heterosexual without indication to the contrary. And yet the normal person is not "heterosexual" in any defining sense; he or she engages in heterosexual activity from time to time, but hardly any information about his or her character, behavior, life-style or interest can be inferred from this fact.

"Homosexual," on the other hand, is understood as a primary and permanent category, a constant and defining characteristic that implies a great deal beyond occasional sexual behavior about the person to whom the term is applied. Not only, it is imagined, does his or her sexuality define all other aspects of personality and life-style—which are implicitly subordinate to sex in the case of homosexuals but not heterosexuals—but the connotations of the term *homosexual* and its place in the modern construction of sexuality suggest that homosexuals are much more sexual than heterosexuals. The majority chooses sexual "orientation" or object-choice-based-identity as the key polarity in sexual discourse, marks certain people on the basis of this, and then imagines that its categorization corresponds to the *actual* importance in their lives of the characteristic so marked.

The conceptual distance between "homosexual" and "heterosexual" is vastly greater in modern understandings of sexuality than its nearest correlates in ancient or medieval systems. Though in the ancient world important distinctions between active and passive were related to gender and object choice, they also crossed gender-object lines, and their most prominent variables were age, social standing, and marital status, which affected the whole population. In the Middle Ages performance of homosexual acts—even preferring them to other forms of sexual unholiness— placed a woman or man in a universal, temporary category ("sinner") which also affected the rest of the populace. If a man committed sins of sodomy to which his neighbor felt no temptation, the neighbor still had his own temptations and vices, and whatever sins he did commit placed him in the same sinful moral category. The great divide was between sinless Mary and all other sinful human beings. Moreover, anyone could escape unholiness at will. No sinner was different in kind from the rest of the human race.

Most Americans and modern Europeans, however, do not imagine that they occupy or even share characteristics of the same category as "abnormal persons." They assume, by and large, that they represent the "norm" of health, at least psychologically, and that those who are "abnormal"— such as "homosexuals"—are essentially and categorically different from them. This provokes not only disapproval but fear and loathing of the "abnormal" and "unhealthy," in no small measure because there is widespread uncertainty and apprehension about how one gets into the undesirable categories and worry that "normal, healthy" people might themselves fall out of their category into one of the "unhealthy" ones, perhaps by "catching" whatever its defining defect is. And unlike the category "sinner," most of the modern categories offer no easy escape. Although one gets over minor physical illnesses and recovers "health," major bodily diseases (for instance, cancer) and most psychic problems render one irrevocably "abnormal." Simply having been to a psychiatrist is a permanent stigma for much of the population.

For these reasons "homosexual/heterosexual" is the major dialectical foundation of all modern discourse about sexuality—scientific, social, and ethical—and it seems urgent, intuitive, and profoundly important to most Americans. This greatly complicates analysis of either the discourse about or the reality of sexuality in premodern Europe, because these primary modern rubrics were of little import or interest to ancient and medieval writers, and the categories the latter employed (active/passive, sinful/holy) often filter or obscure information necessary to answer questions basic to modern interest about sexual taxonomy based on "orientation."

The Kinsey scale posits homosexuality and heterosexuality as end points, apparently recognizing dimorphic taxonomy based on orientation, and one might suppose that it also would pose difficulties of application to premodern data.[18] But in fact its combination of flexibility and specificity allow it to be deployed as a kind of bridge between modern and ancient constructions of sexuality in assessing the individual experiences often obscured by the overlay of other sexual constructs. Its apparent relation to prevailing modern conceptualizations of "orientation" is misleading: utilizing exclusive homosexuality and heterosexuality as the theoretical termini of a graded scale actually presupposes a broad range of empirical possibilities, undermining the implicit assumption of one normal and one abnormal "orientation." This is a considerable advance in sophistication. Rather than constituting the two possible categories of "sexuality," "homosexuality" and "heterosexuality" simply demarcate boundaries, and a middle ground subtler than "bisexuality" emerges, in which many or even most humans simply fall nearer to or further from each pole. Application of the scale to the data extractable from premodern sources is of course delicate. Since they were predicted on different constructs, they filter and baffle much information, and at best their indications are inexact. It is worth bearing in mind, however, that the scale is approximate, subjective, and variable even in the case of living subjects.

It would be a misprision to take the fact that ancient and medieval sexual constructions focused on other issues as demonstration of lack of awareness of sexual "orientation." Lack of interest in, nonrecognition of, and the actual absence of something are three separate phenomena. An idea can be widely present, even pervasive, and go unnoticed. Many aspects of social and cultural life, in fact, are unremarked in historical documents precisely because they are so common. Much less is known about eating habits in ancient societies than about philosophy, and yet eating was by any reasonable standard a vastly more common and arguably much more important aspect of life.

Perceptions of both the ordinary and the uncommon depend to a considerable extent on the agendas and views of those who shape social structures and discourse about them. Most Western societies (including our own), for example, have words to describe adults whose erotic interest is directed toward children. We do not have words to describe the obverse:

children who are erotically interested in adults. Whether or not such children exist, the absence of the term is almost certainly not related to empirical observation. It is a consequence of the fact that the discourse that generates the terminology is produced by and concerned with the sexual interests of adults and therefore coins terms to describe the variety of partners of interst to them. The same applies to gender. Many ancient treatises on sexual attraction address the issue of whether males or females are more desirable sexually—but only as partners for men. This is not because females did not have the same choice in partners but because the discourse and its concerns were generated by and for adult males, who had little or no interest in female erotic preferences.

Despite differing public constructions of sexuality and preoccupation with other issues, most ancient and medieval writers other than theologians did in fact evince awareness of a basic dimorphism in sexual attraction, and often commented on it explicitly; even theologians did so when writing about something other than theology. In the famous explanation of the etiology of romantic attachment in Plato's *Symposium*, Aristophanes plainly postulated a sexual taxonomy in which all humans are either inherently and permanently homosexual, heterosexual, or bisexual. He, indeed, seemed to have in mind Kinsey 0s, 3s, and 6s (although the mythic character of his speech may have induced him to use extremes as symbols of a phenomenon he knew to be empirically more fluid and complex).[19] What is clear is that he did not imagine a populace undifferentiated in experience or desire, responding circumstantially to individuals of either gender, but persons with lifelong preferences arising from innate character (or a mythic prehistory). In a work intended for a wider audience, *Daphnis and Chloe*, the novelist Longus describeda character with homosexual interest as possessing this desire "by nature" ("*fusei*" 4.11). In his twelfth-century discussion of sexuality, Allan of Lille said that "of those men who employ the grammar of Venus there are some who embrace the masculine, others who embrace the feminine, and some who embrace both."[20] Arnald of Vernhola, brought before the inquisition in France in the fourteenth century for homosexual acts and invited to repent of them, argued that his "nature" inclined him to sodomy.[21] He had, however, also had sex with women, and his "nature" appears to have been about a Kinsey 4. Avicenna's canon addressed the problem of "bisexuality" in men who seem to fall in the Kinsey 3–4 range and offered a remedy for this "constitutional problem."[22] Albertus Magnus considered homosexuality to be a contagious disease especially common among the wealthy, and Thomas Aquinas believed, like Aristotle, that some men were congenitally homosexual.[23] Whether any of them had in mind 5s or 6s is not perfectly clear, but it is apparent that they were describing people beyond 3, and that they imagined this was a personal characteristic rather than simply a question of opportunistic behavior.

Kinsey 5s and 6s are common in ancient and medieval writing. "My heart feels no love for women, but burns with an unquenchable flame for males."[24] Ganymede is generally an exclusively homosexual figure from Athens through the Renaissance, both desired by and desirous of other males, in contrast to figures like Adonis who might provoke desire in either gender.[25] The word (catamitus) in Latin for an exclusively passive male—necessarily a Kinsey 6[26]—is derived from his name. Although in several medieval poems his interest in men is related to the "sin of sodomy"—which is a behavioral construct—and efforts are made to interest him in women, these are generally futile, and at the outset of the most popular treatment of this subject he announces that he "will never marry" and despises the sexual attractions of females.[27] A thirteenth-century satire of a bishop accused the prelate not only of interest in males—which would not in itself constitute a Kinsey ranking—but of having no desire for females, which does seem to place him near the 6 end of the scale.[28] "Because I have never liked women or cunts," a sixteenth-century Frenchman asked, "does that mean I should not like passive men? Everyone has his preferences . . . In nature everyone has an orientation."[29] His contemporary, the Duc de Vendôme, was noted among his contemporaries for attraction to men *as opposed to women*.[30] Both men seem to have been 5 or 6 on the Kinsey scale.

In a few cases ancient writers depicted women who were exclusively attracted to other women, but because the vast majority of premodern writings about sexuality were male compositions addressed to other men and dealing with male erotic interests, lesbianism was very rarely a lively concern. Both Martial and Lucian described women who seemed to be by choice involved only in sexual activity with other women,[31] and the twelfth-century bishop Etienne de Fougères divided the women of his world into three categories: virtuous, adulterous, and lesbian.[32]

Ironically, what is now considered the "norm" of human sexuality is the hardest preference to locate in records of the past. Heterosexuality has very rarely elicited notice in the Western tradition, either because it is "normal" and "unmarked," as in the modern West, or because, as in the ancient world, orientation itself was generally not addressed. A few classical writers did consider it odd enough to mention. Clodius Albinus was noted for his aversion to homosexual activity.[33] Martial warned a friend interested in the wife of another man that if the adultery were discovered the friend need not imagine he could mollify the husband with sexual favors: "Do you trust in your buns? The husband is not interested in men"[34]—an apparent reference to a Kinsey 0, discernible even through layers of linguistic filter.

By contrast, there are many ostensible Kinsey 3s, so many that some historians have inferred that the whole populace of the ancient world fell into this category or that "orientation" was a concept irrelevant to antiquity.

"Zeus came as an eagle to godlike Ganymede, as a swan came he to the fair-haired mother of Helen. So there is no comparison between the two things: one person likes one, another likes the other; I like both."[35] It is easy to miss the fact that the writer was specifically identifying his bisexual interest as a point of note and contrasting it to homosexual or hetersexual preferences, clearly viewed as in some sense characteristic of the persons in question.[36]

Much medieval poetry celebrated or satirized bisexual inclinations, and it is a topos of parody that someone spared neither sex in his lechery. "Men and women please the pope; boys and girls please the pope; old men and old women please the pope; shame on him who refuses."[37] While such literary effusions may be evidence of Kinsey 3s, they presumably derive some of their effectiveness from the fact that such ambivalence of erotic interest is thought noteworthy rather than typical.

The sister-in-law of Louis XIV described the sexual preferences of men at the French court in terms almost exactly like modern sexual taxonomies: some prefer women, some like both men and women, some prefer men, some prefer children, and some have little interest in sex at all.[38]

The intermediate ranges around the middle are harder to quantify, both now and in the records of the past. Ovid said that homosexual relations appealed to him "less,"[39] implying a rating of 1 or 2? In the *Ephesiaca*, a romantic novel of late antiquity, sexual categories are not discussed but play a major role in the action. Habrocomes is involved throughout only with women, and when, after his long separation from his true love, Anthia, she desires to know if he has been faithful to her, she inquires only as to whether he has slept with other women, although she knows that men have been interested in him. He appears to be a Kinsey 0 or 1. Another character, Hippothoos, had been married to an older woman and attracted to Anthia but is apparently a 4 or a 5. The two great loves of his life are males (Hyperanthes and Habrocomes); he left all to follow each of these, and at the end of the story he erects a statue to the former and establishes his residence near that of the latter. No woman plays an important erotic role in his life, and his marriage was presumably a question of duty, as discussed above. The author tidied up all the couples at the end by reuniting Anthia and Habrocomes and introducing a new male lover (Clisthenes) for Hippothoos.

In the twelfth-century *Roman d'Énéas*, Aeneas, famous for his erotic relation to Dido, is said nonetheless to *prefer* males: "This wretch is of the sort who have hardly any interest in women. He prefers the opposite trade: he will not eat hens, but he loves very much the flesh of a cock . . . He does not know how to play with women, and would not parley at the wicket-gate; but he loves very much the breech of a young man."[40]

In addition to comments about preference or orientation, discussions of particular sexual practices sometimes disclose evidence relatable to the Kinsey scale. As noted, the issue of males being penetrated was problematic in some social contexts, and discussions of men who prefer to be penetrated provide indirect evidence of high Kinsey ratings since their sexual activity necessarily involved other males. Although slaves and boys may have accepted rather than sought a passive role, there is no reason to assume that some of them did not enjoy it.[41] Adult males who preferred to be penetrated were common enough not only to have special names (not derogatory for anyone other than an adult male citizen) but also to provoke scientific speculation on the origin of their unusual "orientation."[42] Satirists depicted passive adult citizens as hiring bisexual males to satisfy their needs and impregnate their wives—clearly indicating Kinsey 6s.[43]

Both Greek and Latin, moreover, contain verbs that primarily or exclusively denote a male's penetrating another male, as opposed to a female, suggesting that in addition to the most prominent distinctions between active and passive, there were common and familiar distinctions about preferred object choice.[44]

Cognizance of the social construction of sexual behavior in given times and places is fundamental to understanding both the reality and the perception of sexuality. These have varied so widely in the Western tradition that the most basic taxonomic distinctions of one age may seem almost entirely irrelevant to those of another. Primary ancient and medieval sexual constructs were unrelated to the modern differentiation between homosexual and heterosexual "orientation," "identity," or "preference." This does not, however, mean that there was no awareness of specifically homosexual or heterosexual "orientation" in earlier societies. Much evidence indicates that these were common and familiar concepts, which received little attention in the records of these cultures not because few people recognized them but because they had little social or ethical impact. Thomas Aquinas, for example, cautioned against eliminating prostitution on the grounds that if it were suppressed the world would be filled with "sodomy."[45] One could infer from this either that St. Thomas had no concept of sexual orientation at all or that he believed all those who frequented prostitutes to be Kinsey 3s. Denied access to the latter, they will naturally satisfy themselves with homosexual intercourse. But in fact it can be shown that Aquinas did not believe this, since elsewhere he discussed sexual "orientation" as innate and seemed to predicate his analysis on Kinsey 6s. His point about prostitutes is actually a moral one, derived from the prevailing ethical construct of sexuality in his day. The broadest and most urgent dichotomy among sexual acts was the division between "moral" and "immoral," which depended on whether they were undertaken to produce legitimate offspring or not. Since both prostitution and homosexual acts fall in the "immoral" category, it is logical to suppose that if one is removed, the other will take its place. Constructions and context shape the articulation of sexuality, but they do not efface recognition of erotic preference as a potential category.

The Kinsey scale is thus applicable, with caution, to premodern data despite the fact that the latter often evince little concern with the dichotomy on which the scale is based. Kinsey was far-sighted in two directions. He moved modern discourse away from a polarity based on one implicitly "normal" orientation and one "abnormal" one to a more empirical and less judgmental taxonomy, recognizing gradient varieties of human sexuality; and in doing so he created a scale that can be used to bridge the gap between sexual constructions of the past and those of the present.[46]

Notes

1. As opposed to many other writers on this subject, I use the term "construction," like "construct," as a noun derived from "to construe"—interpret, explain—rather than from "to construct" (build, create). Either sense suggests that sexuality as a social phenomenon owes much to human understanding and thought, but the latter derivation implies that humans create sexuality itself, which seems to me an exaggeration. As I try to make clear, I understand the data to show that humans establish patterns of behavior on the basis of *their interpretation of* the role of sexuality in their society. As a cultural phenomenon, sexuality is thus an interaction of organic and social-intellectual forces.

2. The terminology of sexual preference, identity, and orientation is not uniform, and there are no standard definitions or distinctions to cite. "Preference" and "orientation" can clearly mean different things, as other chapters in this volume will demonstrate, and either can be the basis of an "identity," but all three are often used interchangeably, even in scientific literature. It is not my intention to address questions of etiology or psychological autonomy here; I use these terms individually or in conjunction to designate that interaction of experience and fantasy that Kinsey et al. used in assigning persons a position on the Kinsey scale, and I explain in this chapter what I understand to be the social and scientific significance of this assignment.

3. No study of sexuality in the ancient world addresses these issues in this context or can be recommended without reservation. Michael Faucault offers a superficial but challenging overview of Greek and Roman sexual constructs in his *Histoire de la Sexualité*, especially volumes 2, *L'Usage des plaisirs* (Paris, 1984), and 3, *Le Souci de soi* (Paris, 1984). For bibliography of other approaches (to 1979), see Chapters 1 and 3 of Boswell, *Christianity, Social Tolerance and Homosexuality: Gay People in Western Europe from the Beginning of the Christian Era to the Fourteenth Century* (Chicago, 1980, [hereafter CSTH]). It omitted Paul Veyne's "La famille et l'amour sous le Haut-Empire romain," *Annales E.S.C.* 33 (1978) 3–23 and J. P. Sullivan's excellent "Martial's Sexual Attitudes," *Philologus. Zeitschrift für klassische Philologie* 123 (1979) 288–302. K. J. Dover's *Greek Homosexuality* (Cambridge, MA, 1978) appeared as CSTH was going to press. It is now the indispensable starting point for discussion of homosexuality in Attic literature, although I remain unconvinced by some of its assumptions and conclusions. For subsequent treatments of Greek homosexuality, see, for example, F. Buffière *Éros adolescent. La pédérastie dans la Grèce antique* (Paris, 1980); Jan Bremmer, "An Enigmatic Indo-European rite: Paederasty," *Arethusa* 13.2 (1980), 279–298; Gerda Kempter, *Ganymed: Studien zur Typologie, Ikonographie und Ikonologie* (Cologne, 1980), Harald Patzer, *Die Griechische Knabenliebe* (Wiesbaden, 1982), and D.S. Barrett, "The Friendship of Achilles and Patroclus," *Classical Bulletin* 57 (1981) 87–93, which includes a thorough review of the literature on homosexuality in Homer. Much less has appeared on Rome.

Neither Paul Veyne,"L'Homosexualité a Rome," *L'Histoire* 30:76–78 (1981) nor J. N. Adam, *The Latin Sexual Vocabulary* (Baltimore) takes cognizance of the chapter on Roman homosexuality in CSTH; Ramsay MacMullen, "Roman Attitudes to Greek Love," *Historia* 31, 4 (1982) 484–502, is sharply critical of it, while Saara Lilja, *Homosexuality in Republican and Augustan Rome* (Helsinki, 1982), is in general agreement. Robin Scroggs, *The New Testament and Homosexuality* (Philadelphia, 1983), although addressed to religious issues, provides a useful overview of sexual practices in the Mediterranean during the first centuries of the Christian Era. I disagree with some of his conclusions. I also find myself in substantial disagreement with the interpretations of Greek homosexuality in Bernard Sergent, *L'Homosexualité dans la mythologie grecque* (Paris, 1984) [English trans. *Homosexuality in Greek Myth,* by Arthur Goldhammer: Boston, 1986], and with the extremely erudite articles of David Halperin, "Plato and Erotic Reciprocity," *Classical Antiquity* 5.1 (April, 1986) 58–80, and "One Hundred Years of Homosexuality," *Diacritics* (Summer 1986) 34–35. For a more recent statement of my own views, see Boswell, "Revolutions, Universals and Sexual Categories," in *Salmagundi 58–59: Homosexuality: Sacrilege, Vision, Politics* (Fall 1982-Winter 1983) 89–113 [hereafter RUSC].

4. This is not to say that there were not persons who insisted that marriage *should* limit one's erotic focus, but they were manifestly arguing against a neutral assumption about this on the part of the general populace.

5. That is, standards proposed as to how people *should* behave as opposed to an empirical description of how they did behave. In some societies, for example, among Orthodox Jews, rules for proper conduct (such as laws of *kashrut*) may shape daily life, but among Greeks and Romans the ideals of patrician philosophers probably had little impact on the lives even of other members of their own class until Christian emperors began legislating morality in the fourth century.

6. It is easy to miss this point in a subplot of Apuleius's *Metamorphoses* and to project modern constructs onto ancient ones. A group of priests who have sex with a young man are accused of "execrable filthiness" (*execrandas foeditates*), but homosexuality is not at issue. The fact that they are sexually passive is even a minor aspect; the chief ground of criticism is that they have taken a public vow of celibacy (*insuper ridicule sacerdotum purissimam laudantes castimoniam*), which they are hypocritically violating. Lucius himself shrinks from becoming a priest at the end of the novel because he cannot face the requirement of celibacy.

7. "An refert, ubi et in qua arrigas?" Suetonius, *Augustus* 69. *Qua* may be feminine because Antony is thinking primarily of females, but it could also mean parts of the body, male or female. Cf. Martial 11.20.

8. Several aspects of this code are evident in the incident adduced by Seneca the Elder in a legal "controversy." A slave is prosecuted for adultery with his mistress, but the wife claims that the husband has so charged him only after she objected to the fact that he wanted the slave in their bed for his own purposes (*Controversiae* 2.1.34–35).

9. "For a man to be penetrated by a richer and older man is good: for it is customary to receive from such men. To be penetrated by a younger and poorer is bad: for it is the custom to give to such persons. It is also bad if the penetrator is older and poorer." Artemidorus Daldianus [2d century, A.D.], *Onirocriticon libri quinque*, ed. R. Park (Leipzig, 1963) 1.78, pp. 88–89.

10. As is standard usage, I employ "passive" to mean receptive, orally or anally. I do not mean to imply anything about personality or degree of involvement in the activity. "Active" is its corollary and describes only a physical role.

11. See discussion in Boswell, CSTH, pp. 74–76; Sullivan, as cited above, n.1.

12. Satire 9.

13. For the ancient world, see Boswell, CSTH, pp. 20–21, 26-27, 69, 82–84, 123,

225–26. No previous author, to my knowledge, has written about the Christian ceremony of union for males performed in Eastern churches from the fifth century into the twentieth century and in the West at least into the sixteenth century, when Montaigne mentioned it at Rome (*Journal de Voyage en Italie par la Suisse et l"Allemagne en 1580 et 1581*, ed. Charles Dedeyan [Paris, 1946], p. 231). Manuscripts of the ceremony survive in many parts of the Christian world, from the Middle East to France. I am preparing a critical edition and study of the ceremony and its significance.

14. See, for example, discussion in CSTH, Chapters 8 and 9.

15. Madame, the Princess Palatine and sister-in-law of Louis XIV, for example, recorded that many of her contemporaries criticized in private the "biblical prejudice" against homosexuality, noting that heterosexuality was necessary in earlier times to populate the planet but is no longer required, and she added that it is regarded as a sign of good breeding ("une gentillesse") to observe that since Sodom and Gomorrha the Lord has not punished anyone for such misdeeds (letter of 13 Dec., 1701).

16. The *locus classicus* for this is Thomas Aquinas, *Summa theologiae* 2a. 2ae. 154.11–12, but Thomas stands in the middle of a long, relatively consistent tradition. In addition to Boswell, CSTH, 202–204, 323–325, and *passim*, see John Noonan, *Contraception: A History of Its Treatment by the Catholic Theologians and Canonists* (Cambridge, MA, 1965), and studies of the penitential tradition (e.g., Pierre J. Payer, *Sex and the Penitentials* [Toronto, 1984]).

17. This fact sometimes justified considering homosexual sodomy as worse than other forms, although this position was not consistent and was easily conflated with the personal prejudice of heterosexual writers against homosexual acts as revolting. See n. 45.

18. I have in fact implied as much previously: CSTH, pp. 41–42.

19. Among many complex aspects of this speech as an indication of contemporary sexual constructs, two are especially notable. (1) Although it is the sole Attic reference to lesbianism as a concept, male homosexuality is of much greater concern as an erotic disposition in the ensuing discussion than either female homosexuality or heterosexuality. (2) This, in my view, accounts for the additional subtlety of age distinctions in male-male relations, suggesting a general pattern of older *erastes* and younger *eromenonos*. Age differential was unquestionably a part of the construct of sexuality among elements of the population in Athens, but it can easily be given more weight than it deserves. "Romantic love" of any sort was thought to be provoked by and directed toward the young, as is clearly demonstrated in Agathon's speech a little farther on, where he uses the greater beauty of young males and females *interchangeably* to prove that Love is a young god. In fact, most Athenian males married women considerably younger than themselves, but since marriage was not imagined to follow upon romantic attachment, this discrepancy does not appear in dialogues on *eros*.

20. Thomas Wright, (Ed.), *The Anglo-Latin Satirical Poets and Epigrammatists* (London, 1972) 2:463. The late antique and medieval debates on the most desirable gender erotically pose interesting problems in this regard since they sometimes seem to be discussions of which gender one should *choose* to love and at other times about whether it is better to be *inclined* to one gender or another. See discussion in CSTH, 124–127, 255–265.

21. His confession is translated in CSTH, pp. 401–402; for discussion see ibid., pp. 285–285, and E. Le Roy Ladurie, *Montaillou, village occitan de 1294 à 1324* (Poitiers, 1975), pp. 209–215.

22. *Liber Canonis* (Venice 1507, rpt. Hildesheim, 1964) fol. 358.

23. CSTH, pp. 316–329.

24. *The Greek Anthology* (Cambridge, MA, 1963) 12.17 (my translation).

25. See Boswell, CSTH, Chapter 9, "The Triumph of Ganymede," and James Saslow, *Ganymede in the Renaissance. Homosexuality in Art and Society* (New Haven, 1986).

26. Because he could only be "passive" with other men. On the other hand, a male with a very low Kinsey rating (e.g., 1 or 2) might also be exclusively passive in his relations with males. The correlation between preference for a given role and for a particular gender appears not to be predictable or regular.

27. But in the medieval poem "Ganymede and Helen" he abandons an exclusively homosexual orientation to marry Helen at the behest of the gods. See discussion in CSTH, pp. 254–60.

28. Translated ibid., p. 217.

29. "Moi qui n'ai jamais aimé la garce ni le con, faut-il pour cela que je n'aime point les bardaches? Chacun a son appetit . . . Dans la nature chacun a son inclination" "L'Ombre de Deschauffours," cited in Claude Courouve, *Vocabulaire de l'Homosexualité masculine* (Paris, 1985), p. 64.

30. "Ce jeune monsieur n'aimait pas les femmes . . . ; cf. "le gout de Monsieur n'était pas celui des femmes . . ." Courouve, pp. 47–49; cf. Marc Daniel, *Hommes du grand siècle* (Paris, n.d.), pp. 59–60.

31. Martial (7.67) and Lucian (*Dialogues of the Courtesans*, 5.3); see also CSTH, pp. 82–84. Such women are posited in Aristophanes' myth, cited earlier.

32. *Le Livre des manières*, ed. Anthony Lodge (Geneva, 1979), especially pp. 97–98. (I am grateful to Jeri Guthrie for bringing this to my attention.) Etienne's contemporary, the "monk of Eynsham" in England, had a vision in which he saw a crowd of women guilty of lesbianism in purgatory, but it is less clear in this case that he conceives of them as a distinct "type." "Vision of the Monk of Eynsham," in *Eynsham Cartulary*, ed. H.E. Salter 2 (Oxford, 1908) pp. 257–371. See also Judith Brown, *Immodest Acts: The Life of a Lesbian Nun in Renaissance Italy* (Oxford, 1985).

33. ". . . Aversa Veneris semper ignarus et talium persecutor" Capitolinus 11.7. The elliptical "talium" says much about the prevalence of concepts of "orientation."

34. *Epigrams* 2.47: "confidis natibus? non est pedico maritus;/ quae faciat duo sunt; irrumat aut futuit." "Irrumo" and "futuo" are verbs for "to get a blow job" and "to fuck a woman." For "pedicare" see below. Apuleius specifically describes a case of a husband taking sexual revenge on his wife's lover (*Metamorphoses*, 9.27–28). It is conceivable that Martial's threat is subtler: he might be warning the potential adulterer that he will have to fellate the husband to placate him rather than rely on his buns, but this seems highly unlikely to me. Penetrating a male anally was (and is) such a common metaphor for dominating or humiliating him that it would be counterintuitive to suggest *irrumo* as a pejorative alternative. When Catullus threatens to humiliate someone sexually, he mentions both as equally insulting ("Pedicabo ego vos et irrumabo . . ." 16. This poem is a subtle evocation of prejudices relating to male sexual roles with other males and their social implications.)

35. *The Greek Anthology*, 1.65 (trans. W. R. Paton). Cf. 5.19, which seems to suggest a change from homosexual to heterosexual orientation.

36. This is also true of Plutarch's discussion in his "Dialogue on Love" (*Moralia* 767), discussed in RUSC, p. 98.

37. Hilary the Englishman (first half of the twelfth century), "De papa scolastico," in *Hilarii versus et ludi*, ed. J. J. Champollion-Figeac (Paris, 1838), no. 14, pp. 41–42.

38. Passim in her correspondence (*Briefe 1676–1706* [Stuttgart, 1867], discussed in Daniel, passim), but see especially the letter of Dec. 1705, cited in Courouve, p. 54.

39. *Ars amatoria* 2.684: "hoc est quod pueri tangar amore minus."

40. *Eneas. A Twelfth-Century French Romance*, trans. John Yunck (New York, 1974), p. 226.

41. Petronius makes a great joke out of a man's wooing a boy with gifts to persuade him to allow this favor, which the boy then enjoys so much that he keeps the man awake all night asking for more: *Satyricon* 85–87.

42. For example, in the *Problems* attributed to Aristotle, 4.26 (880A). Cf. *Nicomachaen Ethics* 7.5.3ss, quoted by Aquinas in *Summa theologiae* 1a. 2ae.31.7.

43. For example, Juvenal, *Satire* 9; Martial, *Epigrams* 12.91. On loss of civil privileges, Paulus *Sententiae* 2.27.12; *Digest* 3.1.1.6. Both are discussed in CSTH, p. 122.

44. In Greek, *pugizein* means "fuck a male" and *binein* "fuck a female;" in Latin, the same distinction is reflected in *pedico* and *futuo*. Although *pugizein* can refer to anal intercourse with a female, this usage is extremely rare, and *pedico* is never used for females. A graffito such as "volo piidicarii," therefore (from Pompeii: CSTH, p. 57), although properly translated as "I want to fuck someone," is clear evidence of preference for male sexual partners. Arabic also has a verb (*lata*) that usually refers to a male's penetrating another male.

45. "Tolle meretrices de mundo et replebis ipsum sodomia" *De regimine principum* 4.14; this is perhaps inspired by Augustine's warning "Aufer meretrices, turbaveris omnia libidinibus." Although *sodomia* could refer to heterosexual intercourse, it is not a convincing interpretation of the word here. Indeed, one reason Aquinas would posit *sodomia* as a greater evil than prostitution is that the latter could conceivably involve procreative acts and be less sinful than the former. Another possibility is that popular prejudice against homosexuality, on the rise in the thirteenth century, often made it seem worse than the theological case against it would justify.

46. A further advantage of the Kinsey scale is its flexible relation to the social and personal extensions or associations of erotic preference. In many cultures, especially those with sanctions against homosexual behavior, secondary psychological or physical characteristics are thought to be concomitants of sexual preferences or "identities," especially in the case of males. Homosexual men (or passive males) are expected to be effeminate, or more creative, and so on. Here the scale lends itself to particularly subtle distinctions. In Roman society, for example, one might expect that whereas Kinsey 3s would not be thought effeminate simply because they had sex with males in addition to females, Kinsey 6s would be associated with effeminacy. In fact, a Kinsey 6 who was consistently active rather than passive—that is, a man who had sex mostly with other males but was not known to take the passive role (the Roman emperor Hadrian is an example)— would not have been thought effeminate. Only a preference for the "female role" inspired associations of femininity in men, and only adoption of an "active" role in women inspired connotations of inappropriate masculinity—not ranking according to the Kinsey scale. This is quite different from American society, where "exclusive homosexuality," that is, being a Kinsey 6, is usually associated with effeminacy in males, as opposed to bisexuality (Kinsey 3), which has few if any specific behavioral connotations. Apprehension of such differences is useful in distinguishing between issues of gender role and sexual-object choice, related but crucially distinct concepts.

3

Some Uses and Abuses of the Kinsey Scale

Bruce Voeller

Despite the brilliant and pioneering scientific contributions of Alfred Kinsey and his colleagues to an understanding of human sexuality, until recently, surprisingly little of their myth-exploding discoveries has infused the general public's thinking, or even that of scholars or the shapers of public policy. This is certainly true of the Kinsey group's discovery of the sheer extent of female sexuality and of homosexual fantasy and experience in both females and males. It is also true of the discovery that homosexuality is to be found throughout the length and breadth of America—in farm folk as well as city folk, among ministers and athletes, Caucasians and people of color, marrieds and singles. And it is true of the finding that homosexuality is not an "all or none" trait; rather, nearly half of all Americans have experienced varying degrees of homosexual erotic feelings, and many have acted on those feelings, some extensively. While the underlying basis for the country's blindness to the Kinsey group's discoveries relates to our culture's profound sex phobia, *politics* was a major force in undermining the Kinsey group's credibility and thence the magnitude of their contributions. As a nation, we have paid an incalculable price for our ignorance, AIDS being but the most recent example.

A witch-hunt began, following the 1953 publication of the second volume of the Kinsey group's studies. The tale of Senate investigations (which made sensational headlines of the scandalous idea that mothers, sisters, and daughters might be sexual) and the resultant termination of the Kinsey Institute's Rockefeller-linked financial support have been well documented by Pomeroy (1972). With the erosion of public trust, then funding, the group's capacity to enlighten the public and replace street information with fact was deeply undermined.

How ironic, I suspect, Kinsey would find the fact that eventually another form of *politics* would inject a new, sharpened awareness of female sexuality and of homosexuality into the minds of the public, namely, the Women's Movement and the Gay Movement.

With some important exceptions, the peri-Stonewall (1960s and 1970s) Gay Movement was peopled with young women and men who had modest educational backgrounds yet dared to be openly gay. And they were commonly mistrustful and unwelcoming to most of the more advantaged, closeted homosexuals in Citicorp, St. Patrick's Cathedral, the U.S. Congress, the Green Bay Packers, and the New York Psychoanalytic Association. These blue-denim elitists concentrated their talents, with dazzling impact, upon media-capturing street protests and colorful, effective "zaps" against homophobic officials and institutions (Voeller, 1980). For the most part, the nascent Gay Movement had neither time nor inclination to recruit reluctant professionals or to explore the link between their new movement and the corpus of sex research, ethology, genetics, ethnology, sociology, medicine, and psychiatry.

I saw an opportunity to make a contribution to this new movement by bringing some of these scholarly fields to it. As a married father and an associate professor at Rockefeller University, my long-unrequited homosexual impulse had comprised reading and rereading the two great "Kinsey" volumes (Kinsey, Pomeroy, & Martin, 1948; Kinsey, Pomeroy, Martin, & Gebhard, 1953), as well as Ford and Beach (1951). I had been dumbfounded to learn that 37% of males had had a postpubertal homosexual experience, as had 20% of women. I played with the Kinsey scale data on my calculator and was struck by the fact that for those who had *predominantly* homosexual experience (4s, 5s and 6s on the Kinsey scale), the percentages were about 7 percent for women and 13 percent for men (depending on just which data you used). As there are about equal numbers of each gender, an *average of 10% of the population could be designated as Gay*, that is, to the homosexual side of the midpoint 3 on the scale, a percentage Gebhard (1977), at the Kinsey Institute, recalculated and confirmed.

I also knew that the Kinsey group found surprisingly small fluctuations in the extent of same-gender experience when comparing a wide range of sociological slices of the population. Thus, as a scientist, I could see how handy it was to use the 10% figure. By merely moving a decimal point one digit to the left, any number for a particular population became the figure for the number of gay people in *that population*, whether in America (over 20 million gay Americans), in the Republican party, or in a lecture hall, so long as the size (*n*) of the population was not too statistically small. And 10% seemed a *fair* figure to use inasmuch as it did not include bisexual people who had less homosexual than heterosexual experience (1s and 2s

INDIANA UNIVERSITY

INSTITUTE FOR SEX RESEARCH, INC.

MORRISON HALL 416
BLOOMINGTON, INDIANA 47401
TEL. (812) 337-7686

Founded by Alfred C. Kinsey
Paul H. Gebhard, Director

TO: National Gay Task Force

FROM: Paul H. Gebhard

SUBJECT: Memorandum on the Incidence of
Homosexuals in the United States

DATE: March 18, 1977

It is quite evident that when one speaks of homosexuality one is talking about something which involves millions, not thousands, of U.S. citizens, and that homosexuality is a phenomenon which, with only slight variations, appears to cross all geographic, ethnic and socioeconomic barriers in this country.

There have been no studies to indicate how many U.S. citizens are self-described as homosexual. Existing statistical material has measured sexual activity or response rather than willingness to engage in loving relationships with members of the same sex. Most of the research is more than 15 years old, and various methodological and sampling defects plague all sex research. Nonetheless we believe that the interview data collected by Dr. Kinsey and the Institute staff between 1938 and 1963 leads inescapably to the above conclusion.

The Institute studies published in 1948 and 1953 indicated that 37% of the male and 20% of the female population had some form of overt homosexual experience after puberty and that only 63% of males and 80% of females were exclusively heterosexual up to the time they were interviewed. Although these figures have remained remarkably constant in subsequent research and reworking of the data, I wish to point out that our samples had an undue proportion of people of college age. If the average age of our samples were in the forties, the figures for homosexual experience might well be higher by several percentage points. I also believe that if the same resarch were conducted today, the percentages would be significantly higher by virtue of the increased sexual experimentation connected with the so-called "sexual revolution."

In the 1948 and 1953 studies, it was stated that 13% of the male and 7% of the female population had more homosexual experience or psychological response for at least three years between the ages of 16 and 55, for a combined percentage of 10% for the total population. These figures have been criticized for including psychological response along with overt experience. However, I have been recently reworking the 1938 to 1963 data to include only "experience" (defined as deliberate physical contact intended by at least one of the participants to produce sexual arousal).

Tabulations based on these criteria indicate that 13.95% of males and 4.25% of females, or a combined average of 9.13% of the total population had either extensive (21 or more partners or 52 or more experiences) or more than incidental (5–20 partners or 21–50 experiences) homosexual experience. I wish to point out that although the Institute did interview members of homosexual groups and organizations as part of its research, all such persons were excluded from the above tabulation.

I believe that however this data is interpreted, one can only conclude that a significant percentage of the American population is predominately homosexual in its sexual and affectional orientation.

Sincerely,

Paul Gebhard

Paul H. Gebhard
Director

Figure 3.1. Kinsey Institute estimate of homosexuality-bisexuality.

on the scale) or even equal amounts of each (3s)—all people who could have been arrested as "homosexuals" under the ubiquitous sodomy laws that existed then.

As I became openly active in the Gay Movement, I pressed for recognition of what the Kinsey scale meant: gays were a huge potential voting block ("The voting booth is the world's safest closet!"); we were, I argued, in every extended family in America ("We *are* your children!"). I asked:

How could 37% of American men be "unfit" for service in the U.S. armed forces? How could 37% of males be potential felons under sodomy laws throughout the United States? Were these men who escaped arrest only through the luck of not being discovered? How could 10% of American men be emotionally unbalanced, much less 37%, as had to be if the American Psychiatric Association were correct in its designation of homosexuality as a sickness? As I became a national Gay leader, I insisted to other Gay leaders that we needed to bring the messages of these questions home to the media, to judges and legislators, to ministers and rabbis, to psychiatrists—and most of all to our own potential constituents, gays who had been taught great self-hatred and that they were virtually alone in the world. Most of us hadn't had a clue we were surrounded by fellow gays.

While the initial peri-Stonewall Gay Movement was focused in a few "gay" cites such as New York, San Francisco, Washington, and Los Angeles—giving credence to the prevailing view of Americans that homosexuals were only in *other* people's towns—I campaigned with Gay groups and in the media across the country for the Kinsey-based finding that "We are everywhere." This slogan became a National Gay Task Force *leitmotiv*. And the issues derived from the implications in the Kinsey data became key parts of national political, educational, and legislative programs during my years at New York's Gay Activist Alliance and the National Gay Task Force.

At the same time, groups of gay students began to reveal themselves at universities nationwide, from the Dakotas, Maine, Idaho, and Louisiana. Our ubiquity grew more and more visible, and it belied the notion that we were all in Greenwich Village or San Francisco. It put tangible flesh on the bones of the Kinsey group's data—flesh that could not be ignored by the media's conspiracy of silence or the public's unseeing eyes.

Inasmuch as we were intrinsically almost as invisible to each other as we were to the public, we, too, needed to see the Kinsey group's data made flesh. Little by little this occurred, with the development of gay churches, athletic and recreational leagues, professional and political associations—and finally the great tragedy of AIDS, which has exposed so many of us, from Rock Hudson to Roy Cohn.

I realized I was involved in a new movement bent on uniting an invisible constituency, yet one intent on establishing itself as real. It had to create a self-image, much as women and blacks had been doing, but without a visible counterpart to gender or skin color. Inevitably, we would have to go through a period of exacerbating the traditional public myth of "them *or* us," of homosexual *or* heterosexual; we would simultaneously benefit from the Kinsey scale's evidence of our universal presence while ignoring it by insisting everyone was gay *or* heterosexual. We would correct a bit of the world's sexual myopia by expanding people from 0s versus 6s, to 0s versus 4s, 5s, and 6s. Even "they" could see that some of us were fathers and mothers, and thus not pure gay.

However, without the notion of "gay," we could not gain the support of our own people or create a gay civil rights agenda based on accessing the legitimacy of the existing civil rights movement of other minorities and women. Thus, sadly, we too became exclusive in terms of sexual orientation rather than inclusive; those of us who realized what we were creating justified it as a political necessity.

As Klein and others accurately make clear in this volume, many women and men in the Kinsey scale range of 1 through 5 ended up being told by the new gay movement, almost as forcibly as by the traditional culture, that they must make up their minds whether they were gay or nongay. People who ranged from 1 through 5 on the scale were perceived at best as transitional to gay, at worst as too cowardly to come all the way out of the closet. Unfortunately, a large number of us have subscribed to our own rhetoric. But our movement will only be successful when the distinction no longer has significance to anyone and persons can exist at any or a variety of Kinsey scale values without being shunned, shamed, or punished.

The Kinsey data were also one of a number of bases for some crippling internal battles within the gay movement. For example, most gay groups were overwhelmingly comprised of males. In some of these organizations women charged the males with sexist domination. The women claimed there were as many lesbian women as gay men. Thus, for women to have their fair share of decision-making power (the only way, they argued, to encourage other lesbians to join groups), women should have 50% of board seats and elective positions. To nearly everyone's dismay, some men shot back, "one man one vote." Others, who felt *some* accommodation was called for, argued for a Kinsey-based "power" ratio linked to the data that 7% of women are lesbians, 13% of men are gay.

While some discussion was beneficial in teaching the Gay movement the reality of sexism, parts of the movement became paralyzed by this debate. At the National Gay Task Force, fully aware of the issues and the risk of paralysis, we simply mandated gender equality in hiring, in numbers of women and men on the board, and in having co-executive directors, allowing us to get on with the work of the movement as we saw it.

In any case, after years of our educating those who inform the public and make its laws, the concept that 10% of the population is gay has become a generally accepted "fact." While some reminding always seems necessary, the 10% figure is regularly utilized by scholars, by the press, and in government statistics. As with so many pieces of knowledge (and myth), repeated telling made it so—incredible as the notion was to the world when the Kinsey group first put forth its data or decades later when the Gay Movement pressed that data into public consciousness.

Currently, the Kinsey scale still raises interesting issues linked with the Gay Movement, as in AIDS research, for example, where information about gays has only partially penetrated the thinking of researchers in an AIDS crisis that is primarily sexual and heavily affects gay males.

On an ongoing basis I have participated in the national discussion of protecting blood and blood products from contamination by the AIDS virus (HIV) ever since the first federal government meeting on that issue. Recently, a key federal panel spent quite some time attempting to explain why comparatively few of the nation's 12,000 hemophiliacs have contracted AIDS, despite the fact that the great majority of hemophiliacs are infected with the AIDS virus (through contamination of the mass-produced clotting agent factor VIII, which they must constantly inject). A part of the issue under discussion turned on the notion that hemophiliacs may have a viral inactivator or that in the procedure by which factor VIII is prepared the virus is converted to a less virulent form. Either notion might have implications for AIDS prevention. If these or similar explanations are valid, the panel wondered, why are there *any* cases of AIDS among hemophiliacs? Hoping my endless harping about Kinsey at these meetings would now occur to them, I waited out 15 minutes of discussion before pointing out that 13% of hemophiliac men are likely to be predominantly gay and thus have a *sexual* route for infection by the virus, in addition to the route through factor VIII—with all the consequences a study of this likelihood might have for distinguishing between a hemophiliac inactivator and HIV attenuation during factor VIII preparation. Members of the panel failed to note on their own that hemophiliac men might be gay, with consequences to interpreting AIDS data. Indeed, one nationally prominent blood expert was highly offended by my assertion that some hemophiliacs are homosexual.

Again in the AIDS area, it is fascinating that so relatively few AIDS cases occur among persons of Chinese, Korean, or Japanese heritage, even in heavily gay and heavily Asian-American AIDS-decimated cities such as San Francisco. Does this suggest a race-linked resistance, possibly an isolatable substance that enhances HIV immunity? Or is there a cultural difference in the incidence of homosexuality? In the amount of receptive anal intercourse (the sex act carrying highest relative risk for HIV infection)? In low levels of sexual contact between infected whites and blacks with Asians? Some fresh use of the Kinsey scale might help answer these interesting questions and provide new direction for AIDS prevention.

In addition, several bodies of data suggest that *hetero*sexual anal intercourse is very much more common than is recognized by most physicians or researchers. Bolling (1977) reported that about 8% of women engaged in it regularly for pleasure with their male partners and 25% had tried it. C. A. Tripp and Wardell Pomeroy (in personal communication) have each indicated that on the basis of their long research careers they believe these figures to be low estimates. Thus, a figure of 10% might be a fair, conservative estimate (Voeller, 1983).

Ten percent of this country's female population comes to over 11 million people, the adult portion of whom appear to be engaging in the single most risky of all sex acts in terms of contracting AIDS, *receptive* anal intercourse. Thirteen percent of American males, or almost 15 million people are homosexual and in the largest AIDS risk group. But only a *portion* of them are engaging in anal intercourse. And only a fraction of that portion are *receptive* partners in anal intercourse. Thus, roughly as many American women as homosexual men are anal receptive sex partners, possibly more.

While the number of sexual partners for the women in question is probably lower than in gay male circles, one may ask whether heterosexual anal intercourse can become a "hot spot" in the AIDS epidemic, both here in the United States and elsewhere (for example, in Brazil, where it is reportedly a common practice and where AIDS is firmly established).

In any case, these selected examples give a hint of the range of uses, and abuses, to which the Kinsey data and the Kinsey scale have been put in the educational and political growth of the Gay Movement, as well as a hint of some of the areas in which they might be instructive in the future.

Of the many people in the heterosexual community who deserve honor and recognition for their contribution to the Gay Movement, Kinsey and his colleagues and Dr. Evelyn Hooker have earned a singular place.

References

Bolling, D. R. (1977). Prevalence, goals and complications of heterosexual anal intercourse in a gynecologic population. *Journal of Reproductive Medicine, 19,* 120–124.

Ford, C. S. & Beach, F. (1951). *Patterns of sexual behavior.* New York: Harper & Row.

Kinsey, A. C., Pomeroy, W. B., & Martin, C. E. (1948). *Sexual behavior in the human male.* Philadelphia: W. B. Saunders.

Kinsey, A. C., Pomeroy, W. B., Martin, C. E., & Gebhard, P. H. (1953). *Sexual behavior in the human female.* Philadelphia: W. B. Saunders.

Pomeroy, W. B., (1972). *Dr. Kinsey and the Institute for Sex Research.* New York: Harper & Row.

Voeller, B. (1980). Society and the gay movement. In J. Marmor (Ed.), *Homosexual behavior: A modern reappraisal.* (pp. 232–252). New York: Basic Books.

Voeller, B. (1983). Heterosexual/anal intercourse. New York: The Mariposa Foundation.

II
PSYCHOBIOLOGICAL PERSPECTIVE

4

Agenda and Credenda
of the Kinsey Scale

John Money

Historical and Cultural Relativity

The phenomenon that is today named homosexuality did not have that name until it was coined by K. M. Benkert, writing under the pseudonym of Kertbeny, in 1869 (Bullough, 1976). Although he applied the term *homosexuality* to both males and females, he defined it on the criterion of erectile failure:

> In addition to the normal sexual urge in men and women, Nature in her sovereign mood has endowed at birth certain male and female individuals with the homosexual urge, thus placing them in a sexual bondage which renders them physically and psychically incapable—even with the best intention—of normal erection. This urge creates in advance a direct horror of the Opposite sex, and the victim of this passion finds it impossible to suppress the feeling which individuals of his own sex exercise upon him. (p. 637).

Instead of the criterion of genital sexuality, as in homo*sexual*, Benkert could have used the criterion of falling in love, as in homo*philic*, or the criterion of being attracted to those of the same sex, as in homo*genic*. Both terms were proposed by others, but *homosexual* won the day, probably because it was taken up in the early years of the twentieth century by Havelock Ellis (1942) and Magnus Hirschfeld (1948). Neither of these two writers recognized that the ethnocentricity of Benkert's definition of homosexuality as a sickness, though freeing it from being a sin or a crime, confines it too narrowly to pathological deviancy. It leaves no place for homosexuality as a status that is culturally ordained to be normal and healthy, as it is in societies that have, since time immemorial, institutionalized bisexuality. In bisexuality, homosexuality and heterosexuality may coexist concurrently, or they may be sequential, with a homosexual phase of development antecedent to heterosexuality and marriage. Concurrent bisexuality was exemplified in classical Athenian culture (Bullough, 1976). Sequential bisexuality is exemplified in various tribal Melanesian and related cultures.

There is a vast area of the world, stretching from the northwestern tip of Sumatra through Papua New Guinea to the outlying islands of Melanesia in the Pacific, in which the social institutionalization of homosexuality is shared by various ethnic and tribal people (Herdt, 1984; Money & Ehrhardt, 1972). More precisely, it is sequential bisexuality that is institutionalized in these societies. Their cultural tradition dictates that males between the ages of 9 and 19 reside no longer with their families but in the single longhouse in the village center where males congregate. Until the age of 19, the prescribed age of marriage, they all participate in homosexual activities. After marriage, homosexual activity either ceases or is sporadic.

The Sambia people (Herdt, 1981) of the eastern highlands of New Guinea are among those whose traditional folk wisdom provides a rationale for the policy of prepubertal homosexuality. According to this wisdom, a prepubertal boy must leave the society of his mother and sisters and enter the secret society of men in order to achieve the fierce manhood of a headhunter. Whereas in infancy he must have been fed women's milk in order to grow, in the secret society of men he must be fed men's milk, that is, the semen of mature youths and unmarried men, in order to become pubertal and become mature himself. It is the duty of the young bachelors to feed him their semen. They are obliged to practice institutionalized pedophilia. For them to give their semen to another who could already ejaculate his own is forbidden, for it robs a prepubertal boy of the substance he requires to become an adult. When a bachelor reaches the marrying age, his family negotiates the procurement of a wife and arranges the marriage. He then embarks on the heterosexual phase of his career. He could not, however, have become a complete man on the basis of heterosexual experience alone. Full manhood necessitates a prior phase of exclusively homosexual experience. Thus, homosexuality is universalized and is a defining characteristic of head-hunting, macho manhood.

In Sambia culture, omission of rather than participation in the homosexual developmental phase would be classified as sporadic in occurrence, if it occurred at all, and would stigmatize a man as deviant. In our own culture, by contrast, it is homosexual participation that is classified as sporadic and stigmatized as a deviancy in need of explanation. For us, heterosexuality, like health, is taken as a verity that needs no explanation other than being attributed to the immutability of the natural order of things. Since heterosexuality needs no explanation, then in bisexuality the homosexual component alone needs explanation. Consequently, there has been no satisfactory place for bisexuality in theoretical sexology. The universalization of sequential bisexuality, as in the Sambia tradition, is unexplainable in homosexual theory that is based exclusively on the concept of homosexuality as sporadic in occurrence and pathologically deviant (Stoller & Herdt, 1985).

Institutionalized homosexuality, in serial sequence with institutionalized heterosexuality and marriage, as among the Sambia and other tribal peoples, must be taken into account in any theory that proposes to explain homosexuality. The theory will be deficient unless it also takes heterosexuality into account. Culturally institutionalized bisexuality signifies either that bisexuality is a universal potential to which any member of the human species could be acculturated or that bisexuality is a unique potential of those cultures whose members have become selectively inbred for it. There are no data that give conclusive and absolute support to either alternative. However, genetically pure inbred strains are an ideal of animal husbandry, not of human social and sexual interaction. Therefore, it is likely that acculturation to bisexuality is less a concomitant of inbreeding than it is of the bisexual plasticity of all members of the human species. It is possible that bisexual plasticity may vary over the life span. Later in life it may give way to exclusive monosexuality—or it may not.

Preference versus Status or Orientation

In the human species, a person does not prefer to be homosexual instead of heterosexual or to be bisexual instead of monosexual. Sexual preference is a moral and political term. Conceptually, it implies voluntary choice, that is, that one chooses, or prefers, to be homosexual instead of heterosexual or bisexual, and vice versa. Politically, sexual preference is a dangerous term for it implies that if homosexuals choose their preference, then they can be legally forced, under threat of punishment, to choose to be heterosexual.

The concept of voluntary choice is as much in error here as in its application to handedness or to native language. You do not choose your native language as a preference, even though you are born without it. You assimilate it into a brain prenatally made ready to receive a native language from those who constitute your primate troop and who speak that language to you and listen to you when you speak it. Once assimilated through the ears into the brain, a native language becomes securely locked in—as securely as if it had been phylogenetically preordained to be locked in prenatally by a process of genetic determinism or by the determinism of fetal hormonal or other brain chemistries. So also with sexual status or orientation, which, whatever its genesis, also may become assimilated and locked into the brain as monosexually homosexual or heterosexual or as bisexually a mixture of both.

A sexual status (or orientation) is not the same as a sexual act. It is possible to participate in or be subjected to a homosexual act or acts without, thereby, becoming predestined to have a homosexual status, and vice versa with heterosexuality. The Skyscraper Test exemplifies the difference between act and status. One of the versions of this test applies to a person with a homosexual status who is atop the Empire State Building or other high building and is pushed to the edge of the parapet by a gun-toting, crazed sex terrorist with a heterosexual status. Suppose the homosexual is a man and the terrorist a woman who demands that he perform oral sex with her or go over the edge. To save his life, he might do it. If so, he would have performed a heterosexual act, but he would not have changed to have a heterosexual status. The same would apply if the tourist were a straight man and the terrorist a gay man. The tourist might perform a homosexual act, but would retain his heterosexual status, and so on.

By dramatizing the difference between act and status, the Skyscraper Test points to the criterion of falling in love as the definitive criterion of homosexual, heterosexual, and bisexual status. A person with a homosexual status is one who has the potential to fall in love only with someone who has the same genital and bodily morphology as the self. For a heterosexual, the morphology must be that of a person of the other sex. For the bisexual, it may be either.

It is not necessary for the masculine or feminine bodily morphology of the partner to be concordant with the chromosomal sex, the gonadal sex, or the sex of the internal reproductive anatomy. For example, a male-to-female, sex-reassigned transsexual with the body morphology transformed to be female in appearance is responded to as a women—and vice versa in female-to-male transsexualism.

Discordance between the body morphology and other variables of sex occurs also in some cases of intersexuality. For example, it is possible to be born with a penis and empty scrotum and to grow up with a fully virilized body and mentality, both discordant with the genetic sex (46 XX), the gonadal sex (two normal ovaries), and the internal sexual structures (uterus and oviducts). Conversely, it is possible to be born with a female vulva and to grow up with a fully feminized body and mentality both discordant with the genetic sex (46 XY), the gonadal sex (two testes), and the internal sexual structures (vestigiated feminine Mullerian-duct structures and differentiated masculine Wolffian-duct structures). Clinical photographic examples of these and many other syndromes are reproduced in Money (1968, 1974).

The 46 XX intersexed man who falls in love with and has a sex life with a 46 XX normal woman is regarded by everyone as heterosexual and so is his partner. The criterion of their heterosexuality is the sexual morphology of their bodies and masculinity or femininity of their mentality and behavior, not the sex of their chromosomes, gonads, or internal organs. The same principle applies conversely in the case of the feminized 46 XY intersexed woman whose sex life is with a normal 46 XY man.

Evolutionary Bisexuality

Any theory of the genesis of either exclusive homosexuality or exclusive heterosexuality must address primarily the genesis of bisexuality. Monosexuality, whether homosexual or heterosexual, is secondary and a derivative of the primary bisexual or ambisexual potential. Ambisexuality has its origins in evolutionary biology and in the embryology of sexual differentiation.

Ambisexuality has many manifestations in evolutionary biology. Oysters, garden worms, and snails, for example, are ambisexual. They are also classified as bisexual and as hermaphroditic. Many species of fish are capable of changing their sex from female to male, or male to female, in some species more than once (Chan, 1977). The change is so complete that the fish spends part of its life breeding as a male with testicles that make sperms and part as a female with ovaries that make eggs—an exceptionally thorough degree of sequential bisexuality.

A species of whiptail lizard from the Southwest, *Cnemedophorus uniparens*, offers a unique contribution to bisexual theory (Crews, 1982, 1987). This species has neither males nor females but is monecious and parthenogenic. Nonetheless, as judged by comparison with closely related two-sexed whiptail species, each individual lizard is able at different times to behave in mating as if a male, and as if a female. The one in whom a clutch of eggs is ripening, ready to be laid in the sand for sun hatching, is mounted by a mate whose ovaries are in a dormant, nonovulatory phase. This enactment is believed to affect the hormonal function of the pituitary of the ovulating lizard and to facilitate reproduction. At a later date, their roles reverse.

In this parthenogenic reptilian species, the brain is bisexual or ambisexual, even though the pelvic reproductive anatomy is not. According to MacLean's evolutionary theory of the triune brain, the mammalian brain is made up of an evolutionarily ancient reptilian brain overlaid by a paleocortex that is shared by all mammals and in turn is overlaid by the neocortex, which is most highly evolved in the human species (MacLean, 1972). Thus, the behavioral bisexuality of parthenogenic whiptail lizards may provide a key to understanding the bisexual potential of mammalian species.

It has long been known that the mammalian embryo, in the early stages of its development, is sexually bipotential. The undifferentiated gonads differentiate into either testes or ovaries. Thereafter, the Eve principle triumphs over the Adam principle: sexual differentiation proceeds to be that of a female unless masculinizing hormones are added, normally by being secreted by the fetal testis. One of the two masculinizing hormones from the fetal testes is actually a defeminizing hormone, MIH (Mullerian inhibiting hormone). It has a brief life span during which it vestigiates the two Mullerian ducts and prevents them from developing into a uterus and fallopian tubes (oviducts). The other hormone, testosterone, (or one of its metabolites), masculinizes. It presides over the two Wolffian ducts and directs their development into the male internal accessory organs, including the prostate gland and seminal vesicles.

Differentiation of the internal genitalia is ambitypic. That is to say, the male and female anlagen are both present to begin with, after which one set vestigiates while the other set proliferates. By contrast, differentiation of the external genitalia is unitypic. That is to say, there is a single set of anlagen that has two possible destinies, namely, to become either male or female. Thus, the clitoris and the penis are homologues of each other, as are the clitoral hood and the penile foreskin. The tissues that become the labia minora in the female wrap around the penis in the male and fuse along the midline of the underside to form the tubular urethra. The swellings that otherwise form the divided labia majora of the female fuse in the midline to form the scrotum of the male.

The Adam principle as applied to hormonal induction of sexual dimorphism of the genitalia applies also to dimorphism of the brain and its governance of the genitalia and their functioning. According to present evidence, hormone-induced brain dimorphism takes place later than that of the genitalia and, dependent on species, may extend into the first few days or weeks of postnatal life. The primary masculinizing hormone is testosterone, though it is not necessarily used in all parts of the brain as such. Within brain cells themselves, as within cells of the pelvic genitalia, it may be reduced to dihydrotestosterone. Paradoxically, it may also exert its masculinizing action only if first aromatized into estradiol, one of the sex steroids that received its name when it was considered to be exclusively an estrogenic, feminizing hormone. In both sexes, estradiol is metabolized from testosterone, which in turn is metabolized from progesterone, of which the antecedent is the steroidal substance cholesterol, from which all the steroidal hormones are derived.

On the basis of animal experimental studies of the effects of prenatal brain hormonalization on subsequent sexually dimorphic behavior, it is now generally acknowleged that the converse of brain masculinization is not feminization but demasculinization. The converse of feminization is defeminization. It is possible for masculinization to take place without defeminization and for feminization to take place without demasculinization (Baum, 1979; Baum, Gallagher, Martin, & Damassa, 1982; Beach, 1975; Ward, 1972, 1984; Ward & Weisz, 1980; Whalen & Edwards, 1967). That means that the differentiation of sexual dimorphism in the brain is not unitypic, like that of the external genitalia, but ambitypic, like that of the internal genitalia. Ambitypic differentiation allows for the possible coexistence of both masculine and feminine nuclei and pathways, as well as the behavior they govern, in some if not all parts of the brain. The two need not have equality. One may be more dormant than the other. To illustrate, when cows in a herd are in season, the central nervous system functions in such a way as to permit cow to mount cow, whereas when a bull is present, the cow is receptive and the bull does the mounting. Mounting is traditionally defined as masculine behavior, but it would be more accurately defined as ambisexual since it is shared by both sexes. On the criterion of mounting, cows are bisexual insofar as they mount and are mounted. Bulls are less so insofar as they are seldom mounted.

The first evidence of the hormonal induction of sexual dimorphism in the brain was inferred from its effects on behavior. The first experiment was done by Eugen Steinach (1940) early in the twentieth century. He demonstrated that the mating behavior of female guinea pigs would be masculinized if they had been neonatally castrated and then given an implant of testicular tissue. The theoretical implications of Steinach's finding were too advanced for their time. They lay dormant until William C. Young confirmed the experiment in the 1950s (Young, Goy, & Phoenix, 1964). Since then there has developed a whole new science of hormone-brain-behavior dimorphism.

By the 1970s it had become evident that hormone-mediated dimorphism of the brain was no longer an inference based on sexually dimorphic behavior but an actuality that could be neuroanatomically demonstrated directly in brain tissue. In 1969, Doerner and Staudt reported that the nuclear volume of nerve cells in the preoptic area and ventromedial nucleus in the rat hypothalamus was larger in females than males and that androgen administered in late prenatal and early neonatal life would reduce the volume of these cells in females and castrated males. In 1971, Raisman and Field reported their discovery of sexual dimorphism in the dendritic synapses of the preoptic area of the rat brain. Thus began a new era of research into the prenatal hormonal determinants of sex differences in the neuroanatomy of those regions of the brain that mediate mating behavior (see reviews by Arnold & Gorski, 1984; De Voogd, 1986; De Vries, De Brun, Uylings, & Corner, 1984).

Confirmatory findings followed in quick succession. In rats, Gorski and his research colleagues found and named the sexually dimorphic nucleus of the preoptic area (SDN-POA) (Gorski, Gordon, Shryne, & Southam, 1978). The corresponding sexually dimorphic tissues in the human brain Gorski refers to as the interstitial nuclei of the anterior hypothalamus. The SDN-POA of male rats is bigger than that of females and becomes so under the influence of steroid hormone from the testes (testosterone or its metabolite, estradiol), during the critical period of the first few days after birth (Doehler et al., 1982). Also in rats, Breedlove and Arnold (1980) discovered sexual dimorphism in the number of motor neurons innervating the perineal muscles in rats; and that it is during the critical period of the first few days that the larger number of these motor neurons in males is produced by the presence of steroid hormone from the testes (Breedlove, 1986).

In songbirds, as well as in rats, the presence of testicular hormone during a brief critical period proved to be the determinant in the male brain of the neuroanatomy that governs song (Nottebohm & Arnold, 1976). In the zebra finch, testicular hormone exerts its masculinizing effect once and forever during the early critical period. There is no backtracking. The song pattern of the first spring singing season persists unchanged in subsequent years. In the canary, by contrast, the entire process is reactivated each spring, which allows the male to change his song and learn a new one each year instead of having only the one that he learned in the first year of life. An adult female, provided she is treated with steroid hormone, is able to learn a song for the first time as an adult. Learning the song first as a newly hatched nestling is not imperative. Male songbirds copy the song they hear in the nest even though they do not sing it until weeks later.

The findings with respect to canary song demonstrate a type of sexual dimorphism in which the ambisexual window is not forever closed after the neonatal critical period but is reopened annually. Thus, a canary of either sex may sing one year but not the next, depending on the degree of steroidal hormonalization of the sexually dimorphic brain in the springtime of each year. As as result, as songsters, canaries have the possibility of being serially rather than concurrently bisexual.

Concurrent bisexuality would require two coexistent, dimorphic neuroanatomical systems, one subserving masculine and one feminine dimorphism of behavior, for example, mounting and lordosing, respectively. In rat experiments, Nordeen and Yahr (1982) found such a duality in the form of hemispheric asymmetry in the neighborhood of the sexually dimorphic nucleus of the preoptic area of the hypothalamus. They implanted pellets of the steroid hormone estradiol separately into the left and right sides of the hypothalamus of newborn female rat pups. The subsequent effect of the hormone on the left side was to defeminize, that is, to suppress lordosis, and the right side to masculinize, that is, to facilitate mounting behavior, after the rats become mature.

The lateral distribution in the brain of masculine to the right and feminine to the left means that the two sides may develop to be either concordant (one masculinized and the other defeminized or one feminized and the other demasculinized) or discordant (one masculinized and the other feminized or one demasculinized and the other defeminized). Disparities may come into being on the basis of the amount of hormone needed by and available to each side, the timing of its availability to each side, the synchrony or dissynchrony of the hormonal programming on each side, and the pulsatility or continuity of the hormonal supply on each side. Thus, there are alternative ways in which one side could be rendered masculine and the other feminine to a sufficient degree to constitute bisexuality. Likewise, there are alternative ways in which the brain may be masculinized when the genitals are feminized, or vice versa, so as to constitute homosexuality.

These alternative ways of predisposing the brain to be either bisexual or homosexual can, of course, be manipulated experimentally. They may also occur adventitiously as an unrecognized side effect of hormone imbalance secondary to nutritional, medicinal, or endocrine changes, including stress-derived changes, in the pregnant mother's bloodstream. Sleeping pills containing barbiturate, for example, may have a demasculinizing effect on the brain of the human fetus because the drug has been shown to have such an effect on male rat pups (reviewed in Reinisch & Sanders, 1982). Also in rats, maternal stress that alters maternal adrenocortical hormones may exert a prenatal demasculinizing effect on male pups, subsequently evident in their bisexual and homosexual mating behavior (Ward, 1984).

The dramatic power of the steroid hormones in prenatal life to foreordain the sexual orientation and mating behavior of adult life has been illustrated in several laboratory species in experiments in which fetal females are hormonally masculinized or males demasculinized. The hormonal intervention may be timed so as to change the sex first of the external genitalia and then of the brain or to spare the external genitalia and change the brain only.

There is a remarkable film (Clarke, 1977; Short & Clarke, n.d.) that shows how the brains and behavior of ewe lambs, independently of their bodies, can be masculinized in utero by implanting the pregnant mother with testosterone at the critical period of gestation, Day 50 and thereafter. The lamb grows up to be a lesbian ewe. Its brain is so effectively masculinized that its mating behavior (and also its urinating behavior), including mating rivalry and the proceptive courtship ritual, is exactly like that of a ram even though, at the same time, its own ovaries are secreting estrogen, not androgen. Moreover, the normal rams and ewes of the flock respond to the lesbian ewe's masculinized mating behavior as if it were that of a normal ram.

Sheep, cattle, swine (reviewed by D'Occhio & Ford, 1988), and other four-legged species are, more or less, hormonal robots insofar as a masculine or a feminine mating pattern can be foreordained on the basis of regulating the prenatal hormonalization of the brain. Even among sheep, however, the final outcome will be influenced by whether the lamb grew up in a normal flock of ewes and rams or in a sex-segregated herd. Primates are even more influenced by the social conditions of growing up and are less subject to hormonal robotization (Goldfoot, 1977; Goldfoot & Neff, 1987; Goldfoot & Wallen, 1978; Goldfoot, Wallen, Neff, McBriar, &

Goy, 1984; Phoenix & Chambers, 1982; Phoenix, Jensen, & Chambers, 1983).

Defining Criteria of Masculine and Feminine

A diecious species is one in which the male and female reproductive organs are housed in two separate and distinct individual beings. A monecious species is one that has the male and female organs housed in one individual being. Parthenogenic creatures, such as the whiptail lizards already mentioned, are a special instance of a monecious species, for their brains have two separate and distinct patterns of breeding behavior, though every member of the species has the same genital morphology and produces eggs exclusively. These eggs do not need to capture and join with a sperm in order to be fertile and produce young ones. Reproductively, the species is monomorphic. There are no sperm-bearing males. Without the dimorphism of male and female, there are therefore no females in the species. Nonetheless, so powerful is the dimorphism of language, that it is all but inevitable that when this same lizard, during an anovulatory phase, mounts another ovulatory lizard, the mounting behavior will be called masculine. The criterion of masculine in this instance is that it simulates the behavior of males in those whiptail species that are diecious and have sperm-bearing males as well as egg-bearing females.

In this example, one confronts the issue of the ultimate criterion of what is masculine, what is feminine, and what is bisexual. The workaday criterion is that if, in a diecious species, males do it, it is masculine, whereas if females do it, it is feminine. If both do it, it is sex-shared or bisexual. This criterion would be acceptable if it were applied with strict mathematical obedience to the statistical norm of what is manifested by males only, by females only, or by both. The statistical norm, however, insidiously yields to the ideological norm, which is not the norm of what males and females actually do but what they ought to do. Ideologically, what is masculine is what males ought to do, and what is feminine is what females ought to do, according to criteria that are assumed to be eternal verities but are actually culture-bound dogmas of history and the cultural heritage. Ideologically, there is practically no place for what is sex shared or ambisexual. The very term *ambisexual* is seldom used, being replaced by the word *bisexual*. Bisexual does not imply that something is shared in common by both males and females but, with pejorative overtones, that something appropriate to one sex is incongruously manifested by a deviant member of the other sex. We are heirs to a long history of a cultural fixation on sex divergency rather than sex sharing.

This fixation has insidiously infected sexual science so as to ensure that its focus is on explaining sex difference, not sex similarity. The naming of the sex hormones when they were isolated in the 1920s and subsequently synthesized is an example. Androgen (Gk. *andros*, "man") became the name for a male hormone, especially testosterone, secreted by testes. The female hormones were named estrogen (Gk. *oistrous*, "gadfly;" L. *oestrus*, "the period of sexual heat") and progesterone (L. *pro* + *gestatio*, "gestation," + *sterol*, as in cholesterol, + *one*). The progesterone level is higher during pregnancy than in the nonpregnant state. Simply by being characterized as masculinizing and feminizing, the gonadal hormones have insidiously supported the idea of sex difference, whereas in fact all three hormones are sex shared. Their ratio differs in males and females but not their occurrence. Moreover, as previously noted, the body synthesizes all three from cholesterol, the progression in both sexes being from progesterone to testosterone to estradiol.

One way out of the dilemma of relativity is to tolerate it. Thus, in genetics, one tolerates the stipulation that the genetic male is chromosomally XY and the female, XX, despite the undisputed evidence that some males are XX, XXY, and XYY, not to mention a multiplicity of chromosomal mosaics; and females are likewise XY, XO, XXX, and mosaic. In traditional biology, one tolerates the stipulation that males bear sperm and females bear eggs, despite their relativity in hermaphroditic species in which the same individual bears both eggs and sperms. In comparative sexology, one tolerates the stipulation that having a penis is the criterion of being male and having a vulva is the criterion of being female, despite the relativity of intersexes or hermaphrodites. The XY/XX, the sperm/egg and the penis/vulva criteria of, respectively, male/female impose a too rigid antithesis on the coding of what is male and what female in mating behavior by excluding the relativity of behavior that may be to some degree sex shared.

In human sexology, one tolerates the penis/vulva criterion as a good enough approximation for stipulating that masculine is what males do and feminine is what females do. As an approximation, however, it is far from perfect because of the high degree of cultural relativity in the social stipulation of gender coding. The hazard of cultural relativity is that it is conducive to cultural chauvinism. The danger of cultural chauvinism for a science of sexology is that the stipulations of one culture (usually one's own, of course) will be universalized, and the cultural lessons of human gender diversity will be lost.

Sex and Gender

Although the terms *sex* and *gender* are carelessly used synonymously, they are not synonymous. They are also not antonyms, though they are frequently used almost as if they were. In one such usage, sex is defined as what you are born with, as male or female, and gender is what you acquire as a social role, from a social script. This usage lends support to a second one in which gender is sex without the dirty part that belongs to the genitalia and reproduction. This is the Barbie-doll usage, in which human beings are cast in the role of Barbie and Ken dolls molded with nothing between their legs, though blatantly sexy in shape and clothing.

It is the Barbie-doll definition of gender that made possible the political term, *gender gap*, for which *sex gap* would be an unacceptable synonym because of its double meaning. In the politics of the women's movement, the separation of gender from sex was a godsend because it allowed sex differences in procreation to be set aside in the fight for gender equality in earning power and legal status.

Used strictly correctly, the word *gender* is conceptually more inclusive than the word *sex*. It is an umbrella under which are sheltered all the different components of sex difference, including the sex-genital, sex-erotic, and sex-procreative components. The need to find an umbrella term became for me an imperative in the early 1950s when I was writing about the manliness or womanliness of people with a history of having been born with indeterminate genital sex. They were hermaphrodites, and their genital sex was ambiguous. In some instances, they would grow up to live as women but would not have a woman's sex organs. In other instances, they would live as men without a man's sex organs. In the case of a man, by way of illustration, it made no sense to say that such a person had a male sex role when, in fact, he had no male external genitalia, could not urinate as a male, and would never be able to copulate as a male. No matter how manly he might otherwise be, his genital sex role was not that of a man. There was no word with which to name manliness despite the deficit of the very organs that are the criterion of being a man. That is why I turned to philology and linguistics and borrowed the term *gender* (Money, 1955). Then it became possible to say that the person had the gender role and also the gender identity of a man, but a deficient or partially deficient male sex role in his usage of the birth-defective sex organs. The new term made it also possible to formulate such statements as: a male gender role despite a female (46 XX) genetic sex. Without the term *gender*, one would get bogged down in statements such as this: a male sex role, except that his sex role with the sex organs was not male and his genetic sex was female.

In popular and in scientific usage, gender role and gender identity have become separated, whereas they are really two sides of the same coin. Other people infer your private and personal gender identity from the public evidence of your gender role. You alone have intimate access to your gender identity. The acronym G-I/R (gender-identity/role) unifies identity and role into a singular noun.

There is no finite limit to the number of adjectives that may be used to qualify a G-I/R. One classification is into homosexual, bisexual, or heterosexual G-I/R. A homosexual G-I/R itself ranges widely from that of a full-time drag queen or gynemimetic (one who mimes women) to that of a stereotypically macho football hero or marine-corps sergeant who has a masculine G-I/R except for the sex of the partner to whom he becomes erotically attracted and male bonded in a love affair. Some people would say that the macho homosexual has a masculine G-I/R except for a homosexual partner preference or object choice. The correct statement should be: masculine G-I/R except for the erotosexual and falling in love component.

Gender Coding

Reductionistic thinking as applied to gender coding is based on the split between sex and gender, according to which sex belongs to biology and which gender to social science. For reductionists, biological means genetic, neuroanatomic, endocrinologic, or in some other way physiologic. Reductionist theory fails to recognize that there is a biology of learning and remembering, the effects of which may become permanently cemented into the brain. Reductionism adopts the common, though erroneous, assumption that what the brain assimilates it may always discard—that learning may always be undone by unlearning, or that memory may always be undone by forgetting.

Reductionist theory is popular on both sides of the fence that falsely claims to separate biology from social learning. It allows its proponents on either side to earn a living by ignoring each other's specialty knowledge, training, and certification. The bureaucracy of scholars is not well suited to interdisciplinary knowledge or to the concept of multivariate, sequential determinants that cross the boundaries of scientific specialties. Gender coding is both multivariate and sequential, and it is neither exclusively biological nor exclusively social, but a product of both.

In the years of childhood, the gender-coded development of boys and girls invariably mirrors the masculine and feminine stereotypes of their social heritage. In the human species, there is no way in which to ascertain what culture-free masculinity and femininity would be like, for they are always packaged in culture, just as linguisitic ability is always packaged in a native language. Primordial masculinity and femininity are unascertainable in their entirety. It is possible, however, to gender code and classify male-female differences into those that are sex irreducible, sex derivative, sex adjunctive, and sex adventitious. These four classes are hierarchical in their relationship, with sex-irreducible coding at the top.

Sex-irreducible differences are specific to reproduction: men impregnate, and women menstruate, gestate, and lactate. Ovulation is omitted insofar as gestation does not take place without it. Lactation might be omitted insofar as modern nutritional technology has made it possible, though not desirable, for maternal neonatal breast-feeding to be replaced by a formula-milk substitute.

Immutability of the procreative sex difference will undoubtedly remain as if absolute for most men and women forever. However, in the light of contemporary experimental obstetrics, being pregnant is no longer an absolutely immutable sex difference. Twenty years ago, Cecil Jacobsen, geneticist, and the late Ray Hertz, endocrine oncologist, using the technique of embryo transplantation, got male baboons abdominally pregnant. In one case, 6 1/2 months later, they delivered a live baby by Caesarean section, two weeks premature. The experiment was designed to find out if pregnant women whose ovaries had to be removed because of ovarian cancer would be able to keep the pregnancy. Male baboons were used because males have no ovaries, and they demonstrated that a pregnancy can exist without ovarian hormones from the mother. "There is no question in my mind," Dr. Jacobsen recently stated, "that the hormones and stimuli required for normal fetal development are innate within the early embryo. Most developmental biologists are now coming round to that view. But back in the 1960's it was heresy" (Barsky, 1986).

Gender Crosscodification

It is necessary to have a conceptual term other than *paraphilia, perversion,* or *deviancy* for the name of whatever it is that makes homosexual different from heterosexual. In earlier writings, I used the term *gender transposition* to signify that, instead of complete concordance of all the components of either masculine or feminine, one or more is transposed so as to be, respectively, feminine or masculine. Gender transposition applies not only to homosexuality but to a range of phenomena that differ on the basis of the number of components involved and the persistence of their transposition (Table 4.1). In transexualism, for example, all the components of extrinsic gender coding are transposed (or crosscoded) relative to the criterion of the external genitalia; and the transposition is long-lasting—usually permanent.

Table 4.1
Gender Cross-Coding (Transposition)

	Continuous or Chronic	*Episodic or Alternating*
Total	Transexualism	Transvestophilia (fetishistic transvestism)
Partial unlimited	Gynemimesis Andromimesis	Transvestism (nonfetishistic transvestism)
Partial limited	Male Homophilia Female Homophilia	Homo/heterophilia (bisexualism)

The term *gender transposition* carries no connotations as to causality, immutability, or penetrance, all three of which require to be specified on the basis of empirical data. However, the term has proved to be a stumbling block for those who have a strong antipathy to homosexual science insofar as they believe that to classify homosexuality as a transposition is to stigmatize it as being abnormal. Their alternative is to classify homosexuality as a moral choice or preference for a same-sex partner, which in the vocabulary of psychoanalysis, is a same-sex object choice.

Many social science writers and sex therapists differentiate object choice, gender identity, and gender role. This enables them to say, for example, that a man is masculine in his gender identity and gender role but homosexual in orientation and object choice. The alternative is to say he has a masculine G-I/R (gender-identity/role) except for the sexuoerotic imagery and ideation of his love life and sex life in dreams and fantasies and in their translation into actual practices. This alternative formulation circumvents the scientific fallacy inherent in the term *object choice*, namely, that heterosexuality and homosexuality have their origin in voluntary choice and are therefore already fully explained by fiat, without the superfluous addition of more research—which is the fallacy of scientific nihilism.

Terminologically, gender transposition and gender crosscoding are synonymous. However, crosscoding carries more the connotation of extrinsic and arbitrary social coding than the connotation of genetic coding, hormonal coding, or coding of any other less arbitrary intrinsic origin. Thus, it is possible that the term *gender crosscoding* will prove less of a stumbling block than will *gender transposition*. Gender crosscoding should not be construed as being exclusively socially programmed, however. It may be prenatally programmed as well, for example, by hormonal crosscoding, at least in part if not in toto.

One way of classifying gender crosscoding is the simple seven-point (0 to 6) scale devised by Kinsey and now commonly referred to as the Kinsey scale. It is a scale constructed on the assumption that exclusive heterosexuality (rated 0) and exclusive homosexuality (rated 6) are polar extremes on the same continuum. It is a ratio scale insofar as bisexual is rated as the ratio of heterosexual to homosexual, with the 50:50 ratio given a rating of 3. As in all ratios, the absolute scores of prevalence or intensity are forfeited. For example, a person who has had bisexual experience with more than 5,000 different partners by age 50, with never fewer than two partners daily and with frequent participation in bisexual group-sex parties may get the same bisexual rating as another person who has had only two partners, one male and one female, and with a participation frequency no higher than twice a week.

Kinsey ratings are allocated on the basis of self-reported data on erotosexual imagery and ideation in fantasies and dreams as well as on actual erotosexual experiences. The Kinsey scale's criterion of homosexuality or heterosexuality is participation in a sexual act, actually and/or in imagery, without taking into account whether or not it is compatible with falling in love, homosexually, heterosexually, or both.

Because the Kinsey scale is a unidimensional ratio scale, a Kinsey rating does not take into account qualitative differences among the different categories, types, and syndromes of gender crosscoding. For example, a Kinsey rating does not disclose whether the person rated 6 is an exclusively homosexual drill sergeant, a full-time gynemimetic impersonator in the entertainment industry, a gay transvestophile, or a preoperative male-to-female transexual whose sexual partners are exclusively male.

It is possible, of course, to allocate a Kinsey rating to people who represent the qualitatively different manifestations of gender crosscoding. To do so, however, they must first be ascertained and classified as belonging to one subgroup or another. Table 4.1 presents such a classification.

To be empirically useful and scientific, a classification must be based on criteria that are exhaustive and mutually exclusive. That is, they must be able to accommodate all known cases or examples (and ideally all those remaining to be ascertained), and without overlap or ambiguity. Table 4.1 satisfies these conditions by classifying gender crosscoding according to the dual criteria of time (duration or persistence) and degree (penetrance or pervasiveness).

To avoid the pitfall of prematurely allocating causality, the classification of Table 4.1 expressly avoids any reference to psychogenic versus organogenic origin or etiology. Etiology in sexology can be established only by painstaking, laborious, empirical research, not by doctrinal revelation and not on the basis of diagnosis by exclusion, the trash-can method by which psychogenesis is all too often attributed. It is better to admit ignorance than to be pilloried for the folly of pretentious error. It is difficult to relinquish dogma. All present-day explanations of gender crosscoding are either social (nurture) or biological (nature) dogmas unless they are presented with the proviso that they are incompletely substantiated.

There is no evidence that gender crosscoding is either all nature or all nurture in its origins. The forces of nature meet the forces of nurture in the course of development from embryonic life onward. When they meet at a so-called critical or sensitive period of some aspect of development, together they program what the outcome of that development will be. In fetal life, for example, thalidomide in the intrauterine environment falsely nurtures what nature is growing from buds to limbs, with the result that the limbs become permanently deformed. A corresponding example in postnatal life is Konrad Lorenz's now famous demonstration of how newly hatched ducklings became imprinted (nature) not to a mother duck but to him (nurture) provided he squatted and waddled during the critical posthatching period. Subsequently, they followed him, and forever failed to follow a duck, as mother.

The old paradigm was nature/nurture. The new paradigm is nature/ critical period/nurture. The programming that takes place when nature and nurture interact at a critical period, whether in prenatal or postnatal life, may be irreversible and immutable.

Immutability is a key concept here. It is particularly relevant to gender crosscoding in the ideology of law, legislation, religion, and society, where the issue is not, as it is frequently assumed to be, innate versus acquired, that is, nature versus nurture, but immutability versus mutability.

As in the case of left-handedness, the immutability of any manifestation of gender crosscoding, for example, homophilic homosexuality, is not synonymous with whether its origin is ostensibly biological or not. In an earlier era, left-handedness was a deviation to be cured at school by tying the left hand behind the back and other punishments. The outcome was not right-handedness but poor writing, dyslexia, and delinquency in response to academic abuse. For society, it has been more expeditious not to punish but to tolerate left-handedness and to manufacture tools and artifacts to accommodate people with this status.

The lesson of left-handedness can be applied to gender crosscoding. It is more expedient and much less expensive for society to tolerate what it cannot change rather than to engage in trying to force a cure on what is already immutable. The false hope of curing left-handedness was based on the appearance of success in cases in which there was some degree of ambidexterity on which to capitalize. The counterpart in gender crosscoding is bisexuality that is wrongly classified as homosexuality. Most if not all the claimed cures of homosexuality prove, on more detailed investigation, to have been cases in which there was some degree of bisexuality on which to capitalize. It is in just such a case that the individual may experience a sense of the self divided and in conflict, for the resolution of which he or she seeks treatment to be monosexually one or the other, but not bisexually both together.

The homosexual person, like the bisexual or heterosexual, may be either normophilic or paraphilic. Paraphilia is independent of homosexuality or heterosexuality. If a paraphilia afflicts a heterosexual person, it is the paraphilia that needs treatment, not the heterosexuality. Likewise, it is the paraphilia and not the homosexuality that needs treatment when a homosexual person is paraphilically afflicted.

The canons of health and well-being do not discriminate between Kinsey 0 and Kinsey 6. They are disciplines of equal opportunity. They apply to us all.

Acknowledgment

This chapter was supported by USPHS Grant HD00325 and Grant 830-86900, William T. Grant Foundation.

References

Arnold, A. P., & Gorski, R. A. (1984). Gonadal steroid induction of structural sex differences in the central nervous system. *Annual Review of Neuroscience, 7*, 413–442.

Barsky, L. (1986). Holy hormones . . . male pregnancy? *Chatelaine, 59*(8):62–63, 123–124.

Baum, M. J. (1979). Differentiation of coital behavior in mammals: A comparative analysis. *Neuroscience and Biobehavioral Reviews, 3*, 265–284.

Baum, M. J., Gallagher, C. A., Martin, J. T., & Damassa, D. A. (1982). Effects of testosterone, dihydrotestosterone, or estradiol administered neonatally on sexual behavior of female ferrets. *Endocrinology, 111*, 773–780.

Beach, F. A. (1975). Hormonal modification of sexually dimorphic behavior. *Psychoneuroendocrinology, 1*, 3–23.

Breedlove, S. M. (1986). Cellular analyses of hormone influence on motoneuronal development and function. *Journal of Neurobiology, 17*, 157–176.

Breedlove, S. M., & Arnold, A. F. (1980). Hormone accumulation in a sexually dimorphic motor nucleus of the rat spinal cord. *Science, 210*, 564–566.

Bullough, V. L. (1976). *Sexual variance in society and history*. New York: John Wiley & Sons.

Chan, S. T. H. (1977). Spontaneous sex reversal in fishes. In J. Money & H. Musaph (Eds.), *Handbook of Sexology*. New York: Excerpta Medica.

Clarke, I. J. (1977). The sexual behavior of prenatally androgenized ewes observed in the field. *Journal of Reproduction and Fertility, 49*, 311–315.

Crews, D. (1982). On the origin of sexual behavior. *Psychoneuroendocrinology, 7*, 259–270.

Crews, D. (1987). Functional associations in behavioral endocrinology. In J. M. Reinisch, L. A. Rosenblum, & S. A. Sanders, (Eds.), *Masculinity/femininity: BasicPerspectives*. New York: Oxford University Press.

DeVoogd, T. J. (1986). Steroid interactions with structure and function of avian song control regions. *Journal of Neurobiology, 17*, 177–201.

De Vries, G. J., De Brun, J. F. C., Uylings, H. B. M., & Corner, M. A. (Eds.). (1984). *Sex differences in the brain: Relation between structure and function*. New York: Elsevier.

D'Occhio, M. J., & Ford, J. J. (1988). Contribution of studies in cattle, sheep, and swine to our understanding of the role of gonadal hormones in processes of sexual differentiation and adult sexual behavior. In J. M. A. Sitsen (Ed.), *Handbook of Sexology* (Vol. 7). New York: Elsevier.

Doerner, G., & Staudt, J. (1969). Perinatal structural sex differentiation of the hypothalamus in rats. *Neuroendocrinology, 5*, 103–106.

Doehler, K. D., Coquelin, A., Davis, F., Hines, M., Shryne, J. E., & Gorski, R. A. (1982). Differentiation of the sexually dimorphic nucleus in the preoptic area of the rat brain is determined by the perinatal hormone environment. *Neuroscience Letters, 33*, 295–299.

Ellis, H. (1942). *Studies in the psychology of sex* (Vols. 1 and 2). New York: Random House.

Goldfoot, D. A. (1977). Sociosexual behaviors of nonhuman primates during development and maturity: Social and hormonal relationships. In A. M. Schrier (Ed.), *Behavioral primatology, Advances in research and theory* (Vol. 1). Hillsdale, NJ: Lawrence Erlbaum.

Goldfoot, D. A., & Neff, D. A. (1987). On measuring behavioral sex differences in social contexts. In J. M. Reinisch, L. A. Rosenblum, & S. A. Sanders

(Eds.), *Masculinity/femininity: Basic perspectives*. New York: Oxford University Press.

Goldfoot, D. A., & Wallen, K. (1978). Development of gender role behaviors in heterosexual and isosexual groups of infant rhesus monkeys. In D. J. Chivers, & J. Herbert (Eds.), *Recent advances in primatology: Vol. 1. Behaviour*. London: Academic Press.

Goldfoot, D. A., Wallen, K., Neff, D. A., McBrair, M. C., & Goy, R. W. (1984). Social influences upon the display of sexually dimorphic behavior in rhesus monkeys: Isosexual rearing. *Archives of Sexual Behavior*, *13*, 395–412.

Gorski, R. A., Gordon, J. H., Shryne, J. E., & Southam, A. M. (1978). Evidence for a morphological sex difference within the medial preoptic area of the rat brain. *Brain Research*, *148*, 333–346.

Herdt, G. H. (1981). *Guardians of the flutes: Idioms of masculinity*. New York: McGraw-Hill.

Herdt, G. H. (Ed.). (1984). *Ritualized homosexuality in Melanesia*. Berkeley: University of California Press.

Hirschfeld, M. (1948). *Sexual anomalies: The origins, nature and treatment of sexual disorders*. New York: Emerson Books.

Jackson, P., Barrowclough, I. W., France, J. T., & Phillips, L. I. (1980). A successful pregnancy following total hysterectomy. *British Journal of Obstetrics and Gynaecology*, *87*, 353–355.

MacLean, P. D. (1972). *A triune concept of the brain and behavior*. The Hincks Memorial Lectures (T. Boag, Ed.). Toronto: Toronto University Press.

Money, J. (1955). Hermaphroditism, gender, and precocity in hyperadrenocorticism: Psychologic findings. *Bulletin of the Johns Hopkins Hospital*, *96*, 253–264.

Money, J. (1968). *Sex errors of the body: Dilemmas, education, counseling*. Baltimore: Johns Hopkins University Press.

Money, J. (1974). Prenatal hormones and postnatal socialization in gender identity differentiation. *Nebraska Symposium on Motivation*, *21*, 221–295.

Money, J. (1987). Propaedeutics of diecious G-I/R: Theoretical foundations for understanding dimorphic gender-identity/role. In J. M. Reinisch, L. A. Rosenblum, & S. A. Sanders (Eds.), *Masculinity/femininity: Basic perspectives*. New York: Oxford University Press.

Money, J., & Ehrhardt, A. A. (1972). *Man and woman, boy and girl: The differentiation and dimorphism of gender identity from conception to maturity*. Baltimore, MD: Johns Hopkins University Press.

Nordeen, E. J., & Yahr, P. (1982). Hemispheric asymmetries in the behavioral and hormonal effects of sexually differentiating mammalian brain. *Science*, *218*, 391–393.

Nottebohm, F., & Arnold, A. P. (1976). Sexual dimorphism in vocal control areas of the song-bird brain. *Science*, *194*, 211–213.

Phoenix, C. H., & Chambers, K. C. (1982). Sexual behaviour in adult gonadectomized female pseudohermaphrodite, female, and male rhesus macaques (*Macaca mulatta*) treated with estradiol benzoate and testosterone proprionate. *Journal of Comprehensive Physiology*, *96*, 823–833.

Phoenix, C. H., Jensen, J. N., & Chambers, K.C. (1983). Female sexual behavior displayed by androgenized female rhesus monkeys. *Hormones and Behavior*, *17*, 146–151.

Raisman, C., & Field, P. M. (1971). Sexual dimorphism in the preoptic area of the rat. *Science*, *173*, 731–733.

Reinisch, J. M., & Sanders, S. A. (1982). Early barbiturate exposure: The brain, sexually dimorphic behavior, and learning. *Neuroscience and Biobehavioral Reviews*, *6*, 311–319.

Short, R. V., & Clarke, I. J. (n.d.) *Masculinization of the female sheep*. Distributed by MRC Reproductive Biology Unit, 2 Forrest Road, Edinburgh, EHI 20W, U.K.

Steinach, E. (1940). *Sex and life. Forty years of biological and medical experiments*. New York: Viking.

Stoller, R. J., & Herdt, G. H. (1985). Theories of origins of male homosexuality. *Archives of General Psychiatry, 42*, 399–404.

Ward, I. L. (1972). Prenatal stress feminizes and demasculinizes the behavior of males. *Science, 175*, 82–84.

Ward, I. L. (1984). The prenatal stress syndrome: Current status. *Psychoneuroendocrinology, 9*, 3–11.

Ward, I. L., & Weisz, J. (1980). Maternal stress alters plasma testosterone in fetal males. *Science, 207*, 328–329.

Whalen, R. E., & Edwards, D. A. (1967). Hormonal determinants of the development of masculine and feminine behavior in male and female rats. *Anatomical Record, 157*, 173–180.

Young, W. C., Goy, R. W., & Phoenix, C. H. (1964). Hormones and sexual behavior. *Science, 143*, 212–218.

5

Models of Sexuality

Richard E. Whalen, David C. Geary, and Frank Johnson

Kinsey, Pomeroy, and Martin (1948) argued that lay concepts of heterosexuality/homosexuality, such as the belief that male homosexuals are more feminine than are male heterosexuals, were scientifically unsatisfactory. The scientific study of sexual orientation required first the reliable assessment of heterosexual and homosexual behavior. Rather than dichotomizing sexual orientation as either heterosexual or homosexual, Kinsey et al. (1948) argued that sexual orientation was better understood in terms of a unidimensional continuum in which an individual was rated in terms of a ratio of heterosexual to homosexual behavior. Moreover, they argued that homosexuality should be understood in relation to "the rest of the sexual pattern in each individual's history" (p. 838).

Unfortunately, the Kinsey scale obscures the nature of the individual's "sexual pattern." Two individuals with identical Kinsey ratings can be quite different in other aspects of their sexuality, for example, frequency of sexual behavior. Furthermore, these two individuals may differ in the quality and quantity of their heterosexual and/or homosexual contacts. Thus, the unidimensional Kinsey scale forces individuals with identical ratings to be treated as equivalent in all other aspects of their sexuality. Individual differences in other aspects of sexuality (e.g., masculinity/femininity) are left to clinical judgments and are not objectively measured.

We are going to argue that sexual orientation should be assessed within the framework of a multidimensional model of sexuality. The multidimensional model includes heterosexuality and homosexuality as orthogonal dimensions, and these dimensions are considered to be independent of the development of other aspects of sexuality, such as masculinity. A scale developed from a multidimensional model of sexuality would provide information on the "sexual pattern" of the individual, as suggested by Kinsey et al. (1948), and as such would provide more complete information on the sexuality of homosexuals and heterosexuals than is currently provided by the Kinsey scale. Factors that need to be considered in the development of a multidimensional scale of sexuality include, in addition to sexual preference, masculinity/femininity, sexual arousal, stability of sexual relationships, and so on. Further, factors influencing the development of any of these dimensions, such as early hormonal environment, also need to be considered if a theoretically sound and complete scale of sexuality is to be developed. Accordingly, we will review, briefly, hormonal and psychosexual aspects of sexuality and then propose a framework from which the development of a multidimensional scale of human sexuality could begin.

A logical starting point for the discussion of sexuality is the consideration of the influence of hormones on various aspects of sexuality. Indeed, our initial intention was to discuss the relationship between animal studies of the sexual differentiation process and human heterosexuality/ homosexuality. This intention derived from Whalen's (1974) postulation that sexual differentiation is best characterized by a model in which masculinization-demasculinization is orthogonal to, or independent of, feminization-defeminization. The Whalen model was based on the many studies published since the now classic paper by Phoenix, Goy, Gerall, and Young (1959) which demonstrated that testosterone treatment of pregnant guinea pigs decreased the sensitivity of female offspring to the estrogen/progesterone induction of sexual receptivity and increased the sensitivity of these female offspring to testosterone with respect to the induction of male-typical sexual behavior.

The Phoenix et al. (1959) finding led to the notion that testosterone treatment during a limited, sensitive period of development "masculinized" the brain. Given our historical penchant for equating "more masculine" with "less feminine" and "more feminine" with "less masculine," it was natural to characterize the change in sensitivity to testosterone and to estrogen with a unidimensional model; that is, increases in male-typical behavior lead to decreases in female-typical behavior.

Alternatively, Whalen (1964) described a similar sexual differentiation process in rats as one of "defeminization" rather than one of "masculinization." The data that led to this conceptualization came from a study by Whalen and Edwards (1967), in which male or female rats were castrated or sham castrated within 12 hours of birth. Some of these animals were also given a single injection of either testosterone or estradiol at the time of neonatal castration. When adult, these animals were treated with testosterone and tested with receptive females for the display of male-typical behavior (mounting) and were given estrogen and progesterone and then tested with sexually vigorous males for the display of female-typical sexual behavior (lordosis).

None of the neonatal treatments influenced the response to testosterone. Both male and female rats showed male-typical mounting responses when given testosterone, although genetic males mounted, on the average, more frequently than did genetic females (Whalen & Edwards, 1967). Lordotic behavior was displayed with the estrogen and progesterone treatment of females castrated in adulthood, females castrated at birth, and *males castrated at birth*.

Animals stimulated by hormone during the early postnatal period either endogenously (males castrated in adulthood) or exogenously (males or females castrated at birth and given either testosterone or estradiol) failed to show lordotic behavior when given estrogen and progesterone in adulthood. Thus, our early hormone treatments failed to enhance testosterone-induced male-typical behavior, but hormone treatments did reduce the sensitivity of both males and females to estrogen/progesterone-induced lordotic behavior. We suggested that the primary effect of early hormonal stimulation was to reduce sensitivity to ovarian hormones. We called this process *defeminization*.

Subsequent research by Beach and his colleagues (Beach, Kuehn, Spraque, & Anisko, 1972) with dogs and by ourselves with hamsters (DeBold & Whalen, 1975), and other investigators working with a variety of species, indicated that experimental manipulations could selectively decrease sensitivity to estrogen or increase sensitivity to testosterone. Thus, male-nonmale and female-nonfemale were considered orthogonal facets of sexual differentiation. The foregoing is a theoretical concept about the nature of sexual differentiation; it is not a statement about the sexual differentiation process of any particular species because species differ in the details of the differentiation process. Regardless, the evidence now indicates that in at least some strains of rats "masculinization" occurs predominantly before birth whereas "defeminization" occurs after birth. With normal pregnancies in which about half of the fetuses are female, male fetuses partially "masculinize" the female fetuses. Clemens (1974) reported that females from all female litters failed to show male-typical mounting when given testosterone in adulthood, whereas 88% of females from litters containing five males did mount other females when given testosterone. Since five males per litter is not uncommon, this accounts for the Whalen and Edwards (1967) finding that, on average, adult female rats show mounting behavior when given testosterone; that is, they appear to be masculinized prenatally.

Thus, because Phoenix et al. (1959) studied a species, the guinea pig, in which both masculinization and defeminization occur prenatally, they were led to the concept that masculinization is perfectly and negatively correlated with defeminization. Whalen and Edwards (1967), working with rats, were led to the concept that masculinization and defeminization are independent aspects of sexual differentiation.

We believe that the orthogonal model of differentiation has proven to be more powerful in terms of explaining the effects of hormonal stimulation during development on adult sexual behavior than has the unidimensional model proposed by Phoenix et al. (1959). Thus, it is reasonable to consider whether an analogous orthogonal model of human heterosexuality/homosexuality would also be more powerful than the undimensional model underlying the Kinsey scale.

At first glance, the Kinsey scale would appear to represent a unidimensional model of sexual differentiation, one that is conceptually parallel to the Phoenix et al. (1959) model for animals. However, we will argue that the unidimensional model of animal sexual differentiation is not an appropriate analogue for the Kinsey scale. *Most* studies of animal sexual differentiation focus on the potential of normal and perinatally hormonally manipulated animals to display homotypical and heterotypical sexual responses when treated with hormones in adulthood. We have asked, for example, whether male rats castrated in adulthood will show the female-typical lordosis response when given estrogen and progesterone in adulthood. It turns out that the answer to that question is "it depends." It depends upon whether the rats are American or Scandinavian. American male rats of the Sprague-Dawley strain rarely display lordosis, regardless of the amount of estrogen and progesterone given. In Sweden, intact male rats and castrated male rats given estrogen and progesterone frequently show lordosis (Sodersten, Enroth, Mode, & Gustafsson, 1985). In both countries, male rats castrated at birth do develop the potential to respond to ovarian hormones. As behavioral biologists both the Swedes and ourselves are interested in the genetic and hormonal control of this behavior, and we are curious as to how our rat strains differ. Neither of us, however, considers the Swedish rats to be homosexual because they show female-typical responses and American rats to be heterosexual because they do not.

In a similar vein, we do not conclude that neonatally androgenized female hamsters, which do show male-typical mounting responses when given testosterone in adulthood, are homosexual, even though our treatment clearly "masculinized" their behavior.

We have been studying the role of hormonal stimulation during development upon the sexual differentiation process, the process by which males become different from females with respect to sexual behavior. Others have studied the role hormones play in the differentiation of the internal reproductive organs, and still others have studied the actions of hormones on the differentiation of the genitalia. None of us would conclude that we are studying the dimension of heterosexuality/homosexuality.

Thus, sexual differentiation may be influenced in a variety of species through the experimental manipulation of hormone levels. Specifically, with the manipulation of hormone levels, an animal's behavior may be, for example, "masculinized" *or* "defeminized." However, we would not argue that these changes in the frequency of male-typical or female-typical sexual behaviors are analogous to human heterosexuality/ homosexuality. In fact, we would contend that the sexual differentiation process in animals and the development of human sexual preference are quite different.

It appears to us that there is a fundamental problem with our lexicon. We too often do not distinguish between male/female, masculine/feminine, and heterosexual/homosexual. Much too often we equate male homosexual with female and female homosexual with male. A case in point is the proliferation of studies since the 1971 study of Kolodny, Masters, Hendryx, and Toro on testosterone levels in male homosexuals (see Meyer-Bahlburg, 1984, for a review). Implicit to these studies is that either the male homosexual *should* have lower than normal levels of testosterone or a finding of lower levels of testosterone is causally related to sexual preference. However, as early as 1948, Kinsey argued that while testosterone may control the intensity of the sexual drive, testosterone does not control the focus of the sexual drive. Thus, as in 1966 (Whalen), we wish to clearly distinguish between sexual drive or motivation and object choice or sexual preference. In 1966 Whalen suggested that "Homosexual and heterosexual behaviors, in the present theory, are considered different habit states which may be activated by identical motivational states" (p. 161). Subsequent findings do not force a reconsideration of that postulation. The hormone-free heterosexual does not become femalelike, although he may become asexual. The testosterone-rich homosexual does not come to prefer females as erotic objects. Thus, hormone levels, which may relate to sexual urge and the intensity of sexual activity, are not logically or empirically relevant to the issue of heterosexuality/homosexuality.

Our second point concerning the sexual differentiation process and sexual preference deals with morphological sex differences. It has become clear that during development the testes secrete testosterone. Testosterone regulates the development of the internal reproductive structures, whereas its metabolite, dihydrotestosterone, controls the virilization of the external genitalia. In the absence of androgens (females) and in males who are unable to respond to their own androgens because of a genetic anomaly, female-typical genitalia develop (Wilson, 1982). We know of no evidence showing that human homosexuals routinely have atypical genital development indicative of unusual hormonal secretion patterns during fetal development.

With regard to the influence of early sex hormone exposure on sexuality, we come to the following conclusions. First, contrary to the argument presented by Dörner (1978), empirical evidence does not support the conclusion that male homosexuality is the result of a "feminized" brain or that female homosexuality is the result of a "masculinized" brain. Hormonal levels may influence the strength of arousal to specific sexual stimuli, but they do not influence sexual preference.

This leads into our third point, which concerns the concept of masculinity and femininity. Although, as pointed out by Spence (1984), our concepts of masculinity and femininity are rather ill-defined, and therefore difficult to measure in humans, we nonetheless feel the concept useful in characterizing individuals. In studies of animal behavior, we have tended to associate the relative frequencies of female-typical *behaviors* with femininity and male-typical *behaviors* with masculinity. The dimension is much more complex in humans because, in this species, our everyday assessment of masculinity and femininity includes not only observable sexual behaviors, but also sexual and nonsexual behaviors, beliefs, and attitudes. For instance, in the real world, both male and female rats always engage in vigorous outdoor activities. In our culture, we tend to characterize any person frequently engaging in vigorous outdoor activities as being masculine.

We feel that the inclusion of an assessment of masculinity and femininity is appropriate in any characterization of an individual's sexuality. However, we feel that a traditional M-F scale that equates "more masculine" with "less feminine" would be inadequate. On the basis of our animal model postulating orthogonal dimensions of masculinity and femininity, we would prefer independent assessments of masculinity and femininity, following the lead of Bem (1974) and Spence, Helmriech, and Stapp (1974). However, we have a fundamental objection to the underlying rationale associated with the development of popular sex-role inventories, such as the Bem Sex-Role Inventory (BSRI; Bem, 1974). Bem stated that a sex-typed individual is "someone who has internalized society's standards of desirable behavior for men and women" (p. 155). Accordingly, items comprising the BSRI were selected "on the basis of sex-typed social desirability" (p.155). Masculinity and femininity on the BSRI, or similar measures, are judged in terms of an individual's self-rating of how congruent or incongruent his or her behavior is in relation to "society's standards."

Definitions of masculinity and femininity based on the BSRI are rather different from definitions of masculinity and femininity based on the animal studies described earlier. Masculinity and femininity as depicted by the BSRI stem from perceived standards and completely ignore the influences from which definitions of masculinity and femininity were developed in the animal literature, that is, sex hormones. Any scale of human masculinity and femininity would need to give careful consideration to the factors affecting sex-typed behavior in animals. More specifically, there is evidence to suggest that early hormone exposure does influence the frequency of many sex-typed behaviors in humans. For example, girls with a history of prenatal exposure to excess androgens (e.g., congenital adrenal hyperplasia) frequently show levels of energy expenditure (e.g., aggressive outdoor play) more typical of males than of females.

Girls prenatally exposed to the synthetic estrogen diethylstilbestrol (DES), apparently show fewer female-typical behaviors (e.g., maternal doll play) but do not show a concurrent increase in male-typical behavior. Thus, sex hormones may influence the frequency of some masculine or feminine behaviors in humans, but there is little evidence to suggest that there is a correlated influence on sexual preference.

We are not arguing that a self-rating scale such as the BSRI or the Personal Attributes Questionnaire (PAQ; Spence et al., 1974) is not without merit. However, we would recommend the empirical development of a scale that included both self-rating (e.g., preference for one activity over another) *and* behavioral factors. Behavioral factors on such a scale might include those used by Money and Ehrhardt (1972): evidence of tomboyism, expenditure of energy in recreation and aggression, preferred clothing and adornment, anticipation and imagery of maternalism, marriage and romance. Many of these behaviors reliably distinguish individuals with progestin-induced hermaphroditism, the adrenogenital syndrome, and Turner's syndrome from matched controls, as well as girls exposed in utero to DES from matched controls (Ehrhardt, 1984).

Next we turn to the Kinsey scale. As noted earlier, we feel that this scale provides an inadequate characterization of sexuality, homo- or hetero-. We feel that it might be possible to develop an assessment device that yields, like the MMPI, a *profile* of sexuality that an investigator can then examine. While making no pretense in psychometrics, we suggest that the following dimensions might provide a reasonable starting point.

Dimension 1. Hetero- sexual and social activities, frequency and nature (intercourse, oral-genital activities, etc.).

Dimension 2. Homo- sexual and social activities, frequency and nature.

Dimension 3. Heterosexual fantasies, frequency and nature.

Dimension 4. Homosexual fantasies, frequency and nature.

Dimension 5. Masculinity; as noted above, such a scale should include an assessment of self-perception, as well as an assessment of behaviors known to be influenced by the early hormonal environment.

Dimension 6. Femininity; as noted above, such a scale should include as assessment of self-perception, as well as an assessment of behaviors known to be influenced by the early hormonal environment.

Dimension 7. Assessment of the masculinity/femininity of the preferred partner.

Dimension 8. An evaluation of sexual arousability (Whalen, 1966). How erotically arousable is an individual to preferred and nonpreferred sexual stimuli?

Dimension 9. Stability of sexual relationships.

An instrument that included independent scales for the assessment of various aspects of sexuality, such as the one just proposed, would provide the examiner with important information on the individual differences in sexuality of both the heterosexual and the homosexual, information on individual differences that is not provided by the Kinsey scale. To illustrate, consider the almost "feminine" asexual who has only occasional homosexual fantasies compared to another individual who is highly "masculine," highly arousable but who maintains a stable relationship with a same-sex partner. These two individuals are rather different, both psychologically and sexually, but both individuals would receive a Kinsey score of 6.

In other words, a complete understanding of homosexuality and heterosexuality and the development of sexual preference requires first the accurate assessment of *all* aspects of an individual's sexuality, not simply a ratio of heterosexual to homosexual experiences. We are suggesting that any scientific *analysis* must be preceded by an adequate *description*. The Kinsey scale does not provide that description either for homosexuality or for heterosexuality.

The fascinating analysis for the development of sexual preference by Bell, Weinberg, and Hammersmith (1981) provides an illustration. Their analysis was based upon previous theories of the development of homosexuality, but they assumed neutrality with respect to those theories and simply examined whether homosexuals and heterosexuals reported certain theorized relationships (e.g., strong mother and weak father). These researchers presented their findings in terms of percentages of homosexuals and heterosexuals who, for example, thought that they were their mother's favorite child or who thought that they were more similar to their mother than to their father, and so on. A path analysis was used to determine whether certain sequences of events (or perceptions) reliably predicted the development of homosexuality. The analysis failed to show one or a few dominant paths to homosexuality. This leads us to the conclusion that either there are many pathways to homosexuality or that there are many homosexualities. One cannot determine the correct conclusion from the available data, but we believe that Kinsey 0s and Kinsey 6s are in fact heterogeneous populations, and we propose that a more thorough description of these populations as outlined above, may one day reveal subtle sexual and psychological differences for both heterosexuals and homosexuals, each of which may have a unique developmental history.

In conclusion, animal studies of the sexual differentiation process have not provided useful insight into the biological basis of human sexual preference. They may, however, have led us to reconsider the notion that human sexuality is truly multidimensional and that many of these dimensions may in fact be orthogonal.

References

Beach, F. A., Kuehn, R. E., Sprague, R. H., & Anisko, J. J. (1972). Coital behavior in dogs. XI Effects of androgenic stimulation during development on masculine mating responses in females. *Hormones and Behavior, 3*, 143–168.

Bell, A. P., Weinberg, M. S., & Hammersmith, S. K. (1981). *Sexual preference: Its development in men and women.* Bloomington: Indiana University Press.

Bem, S. L. (1974). The measurement of psychological androgyny. *Journal of Consulting and Clinical Psychology, 42*, 155–162.

Clemens, L. G. (1974). Neurohormonal control of male sexual behavior. In W. Montagna and W. A. Sadler (Eds.), *Reproductive behavior* (pp. 23–53). New York: Plenum.

DeBold, J. F., & Whalen, R. E. (1975). Differential sensitivity of mounting and lordosis control systems to early androgen treatment in male and female hamsters. *Hormones and Behavior, 6*, 197–209.

Dorner, G. (1978). Hormones and sexual differentiation of the brain. In R. Porter & J. Whelen (Eds.), *Sex, hormones and behavior* (pp. 81–101). Ciba Foundation Symposium 62 (new series). Amsterdam: Exerpta Medica.

Ehrhardt, A. A. (1984). Gender Differences: A biosocial perspective. In T. B. Sonderegger (Ed.), *Nebraska Symposium on Motivation* (Vol. 32, pp. 37–57). Lincoln: University of Nebraska Press.

Kinsey, A. C., Pomeroy, W. B., & Martin, C. E. (1948). *Sexual behavior in the human male.* Philadelphia: W. B. Saunders.

Kolodny, R. C., Masters, W. H., Hendryx, J., & Toro, G. (1971). Plasma testosterone and semen analysis in male homosexuals. *New England Journal of Medicine, 285*, 1170–1174.

Meyer-Bahlburg, H. (1984). Psychoendocrine research on sexual orientation. Current status and future options. In G. J. DeVries, J. P. C. De Bruin, H. M. B. Uylings, & M. A. Corner (Eds.), *Progress in brain research*, (Vol. 61, pp. 375–398). Amsterdam: Elsevier.

Money, J., & Ehrhardt, A. A. (1972). *Man and woman, boy and girl.* New York: New American Library.

Phoenix, C. H., Goy, R. W., Gerall, A. A., & Young, W. C. (1959). Organizing action of prenatally administered testosterone propionate on the tissues mediating mating behavior in the female guinea pig. *Endocrinology, 65*, 369–382.

Sodersten, P., Enroth, P., Mode, A., & Gustafsson, J.-A. (1985). Mechanisms of androgen-activated sexual behavior in rats. In R. Gilles and J. Balthazart (Eds.), *Neurobiology: Current comparative approaches* (pp. 48–59). Berlin: Springer-Verlag.

Spence, J. T. (1984). Gender identity and its implications for the concepts of masculinity and femininity. In T. B. Sonderegger (Ed.), *Nebraska Symposium on Motivation* (Vol. 32, pp. 59–95). Lincoln: University of Nebraska Press.

Spence, J. T., Helmriech, R., & Stapp, J. (1974). The personal attributes questionnaire: a measure of sex-role stereotypes and masculinity-femininity. *JSAS Catalog of Selected Documents in Psychology, 4*, 43–44, MS 617.

Whalen, R. E. (1964). Physiology of reproductive behavior. *McGraw-Hill Yearbook of Science and Technology* (pp. 359–361). New York: McGraw-Hill.

Whalen, R. E. (1966). Sexual Motivation. *Psychological Review, 73*, 151–163.

Whalen, R. E. (1974). Sexual differentiation: Models, methods and mechanisms. In R. C. Friedman, R. M. Richart, & R. L. Vande Wiele (Eds.), *Sex differences in behavior* (pp. 467–481). New York: John Wiley & Sons.

Whalen, R. E., & Edwards, D. A. (1967). Hormonal determinants of the development of masculine and feminine behavior in male and female rats. *Anatomical Record, 157,* 173–180.

Wilson, J. D. (1982). Gonadal hormones and sexual behavior. In G. M. Besser & L. Martini (Eds.), *Clinical neuroendocrinology* (pp. 1–29). New York: Academic Press.

6

Biomedical Theories of Sexual Orientation: A Critical Examination

Louis Gooren

Biomedical Approach to Sexuality and, in Particular, Homosexuality

Biomedical sciences usually relate, if they do not equate, sexuality to reproductive behavior or reproductive biology. Therefore, subjects such as fertility, infertility, gestation, and parturition have been intensively studied while eroticism, pair-bonding and sexual lust, even in their biological aspects, have been grossly ignored and neglected in medicine (Money, 1981). The medical profession offers generous care for reproductive problems, but erotic or sexual aspects of reproduction are not well treated in medicine and therefore remain a patient's private problem left to his or her own capacity of solving it. Biomedicine is further characterized by a strong element of teleology, the belief that nature or natural processes are shaped by a purpose and directed toward an end by a driving force. Following this doctrine, eroticism and sexuality are the driving forces that subserve procreation and preservation of the species.

Procreation evidently requires the fusion of an egg and a sperm cell, the sexual union of a female and a male. Expressions of sexuality that preclude procreation by their very nature (such as homosexuality) have been regarded as unnatural. Another approach to the naturalness of homosexuality in humans has been the study of its prevalence in the animal world.

In an attempt to conceptualize homosexuality, biomedicine has departed from the procreational, the heterosexual paradigm. Nature dictates sexual desires and lust between man and woman. So, if a man experiences sexual desires toward another man, this man must have some female characteristics to explain why he has these "female" desires. By the same token a lesbian woman must have some "male characteristics."

In the middle of the last century, science discovered the principles governing sexual differentiation of men and women. The mechanisms directing the undifferentiated embryo along female or male lines were elucidated, and this knowledge enabled the understanding of phenomena such as hermaphroditism and pseudohermaphroditism. Since homosexuals do not show obvious differences from heterosexuals in gonadal and genital anatomy, it was reasoned that homosexuals have a degree of pseudohermaphroditism in the biological substrate of their sexual desiring, the central nervous system.

To understand pathophysiology, medicine widely employs animal experimentation. Much of the progress that medicine has made can be attributed to the testing and probing of medical hypotheses in laboratory animals; therefore, animal data are valued as representative for the human. There have been attempts to design animal models of homosexuality or at least of homosexual behavior through hormonal manipulations of the central nervous system resulting in a degree of pseudohermaphroditism. As Beach (1979) points out, the word *homosexual* has been used in animal research in two different circumstances: (1) as a description of individuals that exhibit coital responses typical of their genetic sex, but do so in response to a like-sexed partner, and (2) as a description of animals that exhibit coital patterns typical of the opposite sex. These animal observations have been regarded as valid models of human homosexuality. But as the eminent animal psychoendocrine sexologist Beach (1979) notes, (a) observations of sexual behavior in a certain animal model apply only to that model and to that species of animal, (b) great similarities in appearance of behavior observed among different species are not necessarily evidencing the same phenomena, and (c) for humans there are no exclusively masculine or feminine motor patterns of copulation. Therefore, extrapolation of animal data to the human with regard to the sex differentiation of copulatory motor patterns is not relevant. It is further of note that human homosexual behavior generally occurs between two subjects with a homosexual orientation. The simple fact that this interaction then takes place between two (approximately) identical "pseudohermaphrodites" has been overlooked in the animal experimental design of homosexuality, where often one hormonally manipulated animal and one nonmanipulated animal of the same sex are studied for their sexual interaction.

It is further questionable whether homosexuals will experience their sexual behavior as a derivative of behavior of the opposite gender unless there is a degree of gender dysphoria in addition to a homosexual orientation, which is sometimes the case.

Homosexuality from the Perspective of Sexual Differentiation

Since biomedicine views procreation as the goal of erotosexual activity, heterosexuality apparently needs no biological explanation and biomedical scientists have expressed little amazement about the occurrence of heterosexuality in nature. It is homosexuality frustrating the procreational objective that needs explanation. The origins of homosexuality are conceptualized as a disturbance of proper sexual differentiation of the male *versus* the female. To follow the reasoning applied to this subject by biomedical scientists, it is necessary to review biological sexual differentiation.

The process of sexual dimorphism begins with the sex differences of the chromosomes established at conception. The chromosomal pattern of the male comprises an X chromosome from the mother and a Y chromosome from the father, and for the female, an X chromosome from each parent. As for the human, there is currently no evidence that the extra X or Y chromosome present in all cells of the body has a direct effect on a person's erotosexual status simply by reason of its presence. It has rather an indirect and derivative influence by its determination of the nature of the embryonic gonadal anlage: a testis in the case of an Y chromosome, an ovary in the case of two X chromosomes. While the testis develops and becomes hormonally active approximately 8 weeks following conception, the ovary is quiescent until 16 weeks following conception. The testis starts secreting high levels of testosterone between 8 and 22 weeks following conception (Wilson, Griffin, George & Leshin, 1981), and this generates high levels of testosterone in the bloodstream of the male fetus. This constitutes an essential difference between the male and the female fetus. With androgens in the proper amount secreted, the fetus further differentiates as a male. In all its simplicity this rule applies across the species and irrespective of chromosomal and gonadal sex. It applies in mammals also irrespective of the source of androgens and the organ system involved. The constraints of this operative mechanism are the amount of hormone and the timing, there being a critical developmental period for the induction of a specific androgenic effect. The presence (in males) or absence (in females) of testosterone leads to the differentiation of the internal genitalia from two sets of mesonephric ducts present in both sexes. There is one exception to the rule of androgens determining the fate of sexual differentiation; that exception is the suppression of the development of the uterus in the male fetus by a nonsteroid testicular product (Mullerian inhibiting factor). The external genitalia are also formed from identical anlagen in males and females mediated by action of a testosterone, though testosterone has to be converted to a different molecular form, 5-alpha-dihydrotestosterone for this particular biological effect.

Up to this stage of development, it has been sufficiently established that the foregoing principles underlie human sexual differentiation. There is sufficient evidence from pathophysiology available in the human to support these theories. Less certain is the sexual differentiation of the brain in the human. In lower animals evidence has accumulated that the same organizing principle accounts for the sexual differentiation of the brain in that the same area of brain tissue is hormonally masculinized by the presence of testosterone or becomes feminized by the absence of such hormonal stimulation. There is evidence that at least in some species testosterone has to be taken up by the brain and converted by the enzyme aromatase to estradiol and possibly for other functions to 5-alpha-dihydrotestosterone by 5-alpha-reductase. (For reviews, see Baum, 1979; Döhler et al., 1984; Gorski, 1984; McEwen, 1983). Döhler et al., (1984) have provided evidence that the level of estrogens in rats causes the brain to differentiate into neural substrates and circuitries that will be able to respond in a female or male fashion in adulthood (see also Chapter 5 in this volume). Working with other species, Gorski found that in the same animal some functions both structurally and functionally undergo sexual differentiation by estrogens in one locus and by androgens in another. McEwen (1981) in particular has refined the concepts of brain androgenization. It was first assumed that as in the case with the female and male genitalia, an absolute and mutually exclusive dichotomy would exist in the brain following sex-steroid exposure. To be masculinized was assumed to be synonymous with being unfeminized, and to be feminized was synonymous with being unmasculinized. However, there is now experimental evidence to support the preservation of two schemas, each one having its own set of neural pathways. Development of one set does not reciprocally deactivate the other. Activation and deactivation are two distinct though possibly interrelated processes (see also Chapter 4 and Chapter 5 in this volume). In the view of McEwen (1983) defeminization encompasses the suppression of traits such as feminine sexual behavior and of the ability to ovulate, and it involves the aromatization pathway of testosterone. Defeminization is very likely nonexisting in the ferret, the monkey, and the human. Masculinization (the enhancement of traits such as male sexual and aggressive behavior) varies widely among species in its hormone metabolic pathway. In the rat, the masculizing pathway involves a combination of aromatization and reduction of testosterone to estradiol and 5-alpha-dihydrotestosterone, respectively. In guinea pigs and monkeys, 5-alpha-dihydrotestosterone is the masculinizing agent. For the human, little is known about defeminization and masculinization processes in the brain. A sex-dimorphic nucleus has been found in the brain the significance of which is as yet undetermined. Preliminary evidence suggests that in the human, masculinization rather than defeminization is the predominant mode of sexual differentiation, comparable to that in the rhesus monkey. Since human experimentation is not available for obvious reasons, we have to rely on the experiments of nature (androgen-insensivity syndrome or congenital adrenal hyperplasia) or the experiments of medicine (hormone exposure during pregnancy) to gain insight into brain differentiation processes.

Homosexuality and Prenatal Endocrine Influences

Investigations of the sexual orientation of subjects prenatally exposed to a hormonal environment atypical for their sex (androgen deficiency in men and androgen or estrogenexcess in women) are of great interest to the study of therelationship between hormones and homosexuality. This subject has been reviewed by Meyer-Bahlburg (1984). Available data will only be summarized here. Sources of information are the evidence from (1) prenatal endocrine disorders and (2) offspring of hormone-treated pregnancies.

1. a. Prenatally hypoandrogenized genetic males are represented by the syndrome of complete or partial androgen insensitivity (AIS). These genetic males produce high levels of circulating androgens, which are partially aromatized to estrogens. These subjects suffer from a lack of functional androgen receptors and therefore are born with female external genitalia. They are often not diagnosed until they are teenagers and fail to have menarche. They are sensitive to the effects of estrogens as evidenced by breast development at puberty. They are generally reared as girls, and develop a female gender indentity and a sexual orientation toward men (Money, Schwartz, & Lewis, 1984).
   b. Congenital adrenal hyperplasia (CAH) is an endocrine model of prenatal hyperandrogenization. In patients with this condition, an enzyme defect shifts the bulk of steroid hormone production by the adrenal from cortisol to androgens. The earlier data appeared to indicate an overriding influence of the sex of assignment and rearing of girls afflicted with this disease. A majority of the female subjects provided with proper corrective hormonal treatment were found to be heterosexual (Money & Schwartz, 1977). Later follow-up studies, however, found an unusual amount of bisexuality in imagery and/or sexual experience (Money et al., 1984), although a majority of affected subjects were heterosexual. When interpreting these findings, one must consider that these subjects present with a lifelong medical condition of corticosterone substitution with potential influence on their psychosexual development. Their medical condition has a profound effect on the parental attitude toward them. Money and Lewis (1982) have found that in male subjects afflicted

with this syndrome the incidence of homosexuality is less than in a control population of men. Almost all have a very early puberty.

2. Estrogens and progestogens were administered to pregnant women in the years between 1940 and 1970, and data on the sexual orientation of the offspring might provide information on the hormonal influence on the development of sexual orientation. Progesterone-related progestogens have, depending on their chemical formulae, an androgenic or an antiandrogenic biological effect. The overall impression is that no solid data show that exposure to progesterone affects future sexual orientation in an appreciable way (Kester, Green, Finch, & Williams, 1980; Money & Mathews, 1982). When evaluating the data on prenatal estrogen exposure, one must remember that part of the sexual brain differentiation in animals is brought about by the aromatization products of androgens that are estrogens. Therefore, prenatal exposure to estrogens is relevant to this problem. Diethylstilbestrol (DES), a very potent estrogen, has not shown a significant effect on heterosexual development of males exposed to this estrogen (Beral & Colwell, 1981; Kester et al., 1980; Yalom, Green, & Fisk, 1973). When evaluating these male subjects, one must consider the possibility that administration of estrogen has potentially interfered with their testicular steroidogenesis, and that these males have therefore potentially been exposed to less androgens than normal. Although early studies of DES-exposed females suggested that there was no significant effect on heterosexual development (Beral & Colwell, 1981; Hines, 1982), a more recent study by Ehrhardt, Meyer-Bahlburg, Feldman, & Ince (1984) reported that 25% of the sample of DES-exposed females showed increased levels of bisexuality and homosexuality and about 75% were exclusively or nearly exclusively heterosexual in their sexual behavior and imagery.

In summary, the evidence from prenatal endocrine disorders and from the offspring of hormone-treated pregnancies suggests that hormones may contribute to, but do not actually determine, the course of sexual orientation in individuals with an abnormal sex-steroid history during prenatal life. Even more confusion is generated when one attempts to find a unifying principle with regard to the nature of the prenatal hormonal exposure on future sexual orientation.

For the sake of comparison of men and women, a male heterosexual and a female homosexual will be labeled as gynephile (women-loving) and a male homosexual and a female heterosexual as androphile (men-loving) (see Table 6.1).

If we arbitrarily attribute + + for the degree of androgen exposure and

Table 6.1
Percentage Distribution of Androphiles and Gynephiles among Genetic Males and Females Exposed to Varying Levels of Androgens and Estrogens

| | Exposure to | | % | % |
	Androgens	Estrogens	Androphiles	Gynephiles
GENETIC MALES				
Normal	+ +	+	5	95
Congenital adrenal hyperplasia (CAH)	+ + +	+	—	>95
Androgenic insensitivity (AIS)	− −	+	100	—
Diethylstilbestrol (DES)	+	+ +	5	95
GENETIC FEMALES				
Normal	−	−	95	5
Congenital adrenal hyperplasia (CAH)	+ +	+	—	>5
Diethylstilbestrol (DES)	−	+ +	—	>5

+ for estrogen exposure for men without a history of an abnormal prenatal endocrine condition, men suffering from CAH have been relatively overexposed to androgens, and DES-exposed men have been relatively underexposed to androgens and overexposed to estrogens prenatally. Women suffering from CAH have been overexposed to both androgens and estrogens that result from androgen aromatization, and DES-exposed women have had an overexposure to estrogens. Upon inspection of the table, genetically male subjects afflicted with AIS present the clearest example. They have been prenatally exposed only to estrogens, and almost 100% of them develop androphile orientation. Not consistent with this finding is the normal distribution of androphilia in DES-exposed men and the above-normal gynephilia in DES-exposed women. If one finds a higher incidence of gynephilia in females with CAH as well as in females with a history of DES exposure, it is uncertain which hormonal factor (androgens or estrogens) has been contributing to the increased gynephilia in these groups. If it were estrogens, the exclusive androphilia of genetic males with AIS does not fit with that assumption. Potentially, an overexposure to androgens prenatally could induce a high degree of gynephilia in both men and women suffering from CAH. The preceding comparisons obviously do not allow the determination of a unifying concept of the prenatal influence of sex steroids on future sexual orientation.

From the psychosexual point of view, one can argue whether the androphilia of homosexual men equals the androphilia of heterosexual women and further whether the gynephilia of heterosexual men equals the gynephilia of lesbians. Remarkably enough, biomedical research seems predominantly interested in the genital sex of the partner rather than in motivational aspects of the selection of that partner. Obviously, the latter aspects lend themselves less to verification methods of experimentation in the biomedical sciences.

Peripheral Sex Steroid Levels and Homosexuality

The discovery of the principles governing the sexual differentiation of mammals and the role of testicular hormones therein and also the advent of techniques of hormone measurements have led to a surge in hormone investigations in homosexuals. These investigations have the following questions in mind. Do homosexual men have lower levels of testosterone ("male" hormone) and/or higher levels of estrogens ("female" hormone)? Do lesbians have higher testosterone levels and possibly lower estrogen levels? The pivotal role of testosterone and its metabolites in the sexual differentiation of the male has led to such considerations, which when critically examined, are not very rational from an endocrinological viewpoint.

Testosterone plays a primary role in the development of morphological sex differences in the fetus. The process of sexual differentation begins with the sex differences of the chromosomes at conception as already outlined. This genetic information induces sexual differentiation of the gonads. All further steps in sexual differentiation are hormonally determined. The fetal testes produce high levels of testosterone whereas the ovaries remain quiescent. The presence in males or the absence in females of testosterone leads to differentiation of the internal and external genitalia. Evidence is accumulating that in diverse species the brain also undergoes sexual differentiation. This differentiation follows a pattern similar to that of the external genitalia in that male differentiation is induced by the presence of testosterone and female differentiation develops only in the absence of such androgen stimulation. The impressive paradigm of this sexual differentiation is the fact that testicular products (predominantly testosterone) determine the fate of sexual differentiation of the fetus. Insufficient production or biological action of androgens leads to pseudohermaphroditism of the genitalia and of the brain as demonstrated in animal experiments. On the other hand, undue exposure of the female fetus to androgens leads to masculinization of the genitalia and the central nervous system.

Initially only folk wisdom but in recent years corroborated by scientific data, androgens appear to activate erotosexual behavior in males in adulthood (Davidson, Kwan, & Greenleaf, 1982). On the other hand, the role of sex hormones in the activation of sexual behavior in the human female remains unclear, though activation of female sex behavior by estrogens and progestogens is evident in lower mammals (Sanders & Bancroft, 1982). This dichotomy has, in addition to the preceding arguments, led to the belief that androgens are "male" hormones and that estrogens and progestagens are "female" hormones.

In line with the knowledge that androgens play a key role in the somatic sexual differentiation and in the activation of male erotosexual behavior, it was tacitly and implicitly assumed that phenomena in the human such as sexual orientation and gender identity/role were the product of "male " hormones in the male and of "female" hormones in the female, only appropriately developing in the male following an adequate androgen stimulus and only properly developing in the female if she were not exposed to androgens. Solid endocrine data were and are lacking to substantiate these notions. The semantics of male and female hormones and the frailties of referring to testosterone as a male hormone and to estrogen and progesterone as female hormones have been reviewed by Whalen (1984).

Since 1971, many studies testing the assumption that male homosexuals are underandrogenized and female homosexuals are overandrogenized have been published. For an excellent detailed review of these endocrine studies, including a critical approach to the methodology, the reader is referred to four papers of H. Meyer-Bahlburg (1977, 1979, 1982, 1984). His conclusion is that these studies make it highly unlikely that abnormalities in the peripheral sex steroid levels or hormone production after puberty can be held responsible for the development of a homosexual orientation, although Meyer-Bahlburg does not exclude the possibility that hormones are a contributing factor to the development of sexual orientation. The latter awaits further elucidation.

Upon review of the research efforts to relate sexual orientation to peripheral blood sex hormone levels, a number of obviously relevant topics come to the mind of the critical endocrinologist.

1. What happens to the sexual orientation of a male who loses his testicular function (following a surgical trauma, severe hematoma or extirpation because of a malignancy) and who consequently experiences a dramatic fall of testosterone levels? What happens to the sexual orientation of prostatic cancer patients treated with estrogens? What is the fate of sexual orientation of women harboring an androgen-producing adrenal and ovarium tumor or women who are treated with androgens because of breast cancer? Although I am unaware of any systematic research, it has never been reported that sexual orientation ever underwent a shift induced by the change of levels of androgens and estrogens.

2. What is the sexual orientation of men suffering from congenital syndromes associated with testicular insufficiency as in Kallmann's syndrome or Klinefelter's syndrome? The latter has an incidence of 1:500 in men. This 46 XXY chromosomopathy is associated with low testosterone levels in adulthood. It has not been found that men suffering from this syndrome are more frequently homosexual than controls (Vogt, 1984).

3. Attempts to change sexual orientation with high doses of synthetic androgens have invariably failed (Gartrell, 1982).

4. Men suffering from mild subclinical forms of androgen insensitivity have high peripheral testosterone levels because their hypothalamopituitary unit is less sensitive to the negative feedback action of androgens; therefore, a great amount of LH is secreted, resulting in high peripheral testosterone levels. These men present themselves with high testosterone levels while the bioactivity of testosterone is low in them because of their defect.
5. With the advent of the hormone receptor physiology, the relevance of peripheral hormone levels has become limited. Peripheral hormone levels indicate the strength of the hormonal signal, but the extent to which the hormonal message is expressed biologically in the organism is further determined by hormone receptor and postreceptor events. This biological action eludes peripheral hormone determinations, which evidences the relativity of levels of sex hormones to biological phenomena.

Collectively, the preceding points make it highly unlikely that study of peripheral hormone values may provide any clue to sexual orientation. Not only have the best-designed studies failed to find differences in hormone levels between homosexuals and heterosexuals, but the foregoing considerations derived from the scientific principles of endocrinology do not make that plausible.

Neuroendocrinology and Homosexuality

Dörner (1980) and Gladue, Green, and Hellman (1984) argue that the response of LH to estrogen administration discriminates men and women. Women react with an increase in LH levels to an estrogen stimulus (estrogen positive feedback effect), while men respond with a decrease in LH levels (estrogen negative feedback effect). The researchers hypothesize that the sex difference inthis neuroendocrine response reflects the sexual differentiation that takes place in the brain during the prenatal period. They have found that homosexual men display an LH response to estrogen administration intermediate between that of heterosexual men (with an estrogen negative feedback effect) and that of heterosexual women (with an estrogen positive feedback effect). From their data, they conclude that the brain organization controlling LH secretion in homosexual men is somewhat differentfrom that in heterosexual men, resembling to some extent that of women. There is, however, a technical endocrinological objection to be made against the view that men an women differ in theirneuroendocrine response of LH to estrogen administration. This notion of difference is typically derived from research data of nonprimate species.

In rats and other comparable species, this sex difference has been repeatedly demonstrated and is now an established factor of the neuroendocrinology of those species (McEwen, 1981). The situation in monkeys and humans is undoubtedly different. As early as 1973, Karsch, Dierschke, and Knobil demonstrated that in the macaque estradiol stimulated similar increments in serum LH levels in both males and females provided the animals were gonadectomized at the time estrogen was given. No such estrogen-induced surge of LH was seen in male macaques with intact gonads. The researchers then concluded that there is an apparent difference in the regulation of gonadotropin secretion in rodents and in primates. One series of investigations (Barbarino et al., 1982, 1983) demonstrated convincingly that daily estradiol injections in castrated men caused a significant depression in serum LH followed by a significant surge in LH secretion 120 hours after the onset of the estrogen treatment. Goh, Ratnam, and London (1984) showed that long-term estrogen treatment (more than 4 months) can induce feminization of the gonadotropin response to estrogen in nonorchidectomized transsexuals. Since long-term estrogen treatment of male subjects drastically reduces testosterone secretion, it would seem that testosterone is the inhibiting factor in men for the evocation of an estrogen positive feedback effect. Westphal, Stadelman, Horton, and Resko (1984), however, demonstrated that in monkeys, it is not testosterone but another (as yet unidentified) testicular product that inhibits the estrogen positive feedback in eugonadal primate males. This observation in monkeys was subsequently shown to apply to humans (Goh, Wong, & Ratnam, 1985). The lack of sexual differentiation in the physiological mechanisms that regulate the cyclic gonadotropin secretion in primates was more recently demonstrated in a fascinating way by Norman and Spies. Male macaque monkeys could be brought to secrete a cyclic gonadotropin upon an ovarian transplant after orchidectomy.

In one recent report (Gooren, 1986a), we demonstrated that transsexuals display an estrogen feedback response appropriate to their genetic sex before gonadectomy and cross-gender hormone treatment, whereas an opposite estrogen feedback response can be evoked after gonadectomy while receiving cross-gender treatment. From our study it appears that (1) in the same subject both types of estrogen feedback effect can be consecutively evoked, and (2) the type of response depends on the gonadal and/ or hormonal status of the subject involved. Apparently, it is not the brain-pituitary unit that determines the type of estrogen feedback response since this unit itself did not change in our subjects undergoing gender reassignment. However, there was a profound change in circulating sex steroids. It has been found that genetically male subjects suffering from the androgen insensivity syndrome display an estrogen negative feedback effect that has been assumed to indicate a male brain organization (Aono, Miyake, Kinugasa, Kurachi, & Matsumoto, 1978; Van Look et al., 1977). Upon review of the relevant literature, it appeared that these observations had been made in the subjects before orchidectomy. Other reports (including our own) on these subjects indicate that after orchidectomy an estrogen positive feedback response is found (Corsello et al., 1984; Zarate, Canales, Soria, & Caballo, 1974). These data argue, in support of the evidence of Westphal et al., that also in humans a testicular factor other than androgens (androgen- insensitive subjects are unresponsive to androgens by the nature of their defect) inhibits an estrogen positive feedback effect in intact males. On the basis of the preceding information, it seems safe to state that in humans the brain-pituitary unit responsible for the secretion of LH does not undergo a sexual differentiation and consequently it is highly unlikely that differences in gonadotropin secretion found between (groups of) subjects can be interpreted as reflecting differences in hormonal imprinting and organization of the prenatal brain.

Which factors, then, could potentially explain the differences in the response of LH to estrogen administration between homosexuals and heterosexuals reported by Dörner (1980) and Gladue, Green, & Hellman (1984), if the neuroendocrine organization of LH secretion does not?

In a study carefully replicating the investigations of Dörner and Gladue et al., (Gooren, 1986b), we were unable to demonstrate a statistically significant difference in LH response between homosexual and heterosexual men. In 5 of 15 heterosexual and 11 of 23 homosexual men, LH levels rose at day 4 following estrogen administration above pretreatment values at days -l and 0 (a female like response). In the remaining 10 heterosexual and 12 homosexual men LH levels on Day 4 after estrogen administration were lower than pretreatment values (a male like response). In an attempt to analyze the differences in responses within each category, we found that those men in whom testosterone levels had fallen farthest upon estrogen administration, LH levels had risen most. It therefore seemed that the suppression of testosterone levels induced by estrogen administration determined the type of LH response to estrogens. That a testicular factor is implicated was evidenced by the observation that those subjects who had shown the greatest fall of testosterone levels upon estrogen administration had a much lower response of testosterone to human chorionic gonadotropin (HCG) administration. HCG is an LH-like hormone and a very potent stimulus of testosterone secretion. Summarizing our findings, we established that a female like response of LH to estrogens could be found in heterosexual and homosexual men alike and further that the appearance of this type of response correlates with testicular factors such as the fall of testosterone following estrogen administration and the response of testosterone to HCG stimulation.

The data of Gladue et al. (1984) are presented as percentages of baseline values of hormones, which unfortunately masks interindividual variation in values and overlaps between homosexual and heterosexual men. A review of these data indicates that the homosexual men as a group displayed a greater fall of testosterone levels upon estrogen administration than the heterosexual men as a group and that the homosexual men had a greater rise of LH levels than the heterosexuals. These combined findings can then be interpreted as a simple feedback relationship within a hypothalamus-pituitary-endocrine organ axis (such as testis, thyroid, adrenal). A fall in hormone production in the target endocrine organ induces a rise in secretion of the pituitary stimulatory hormone. That this explanation is more likely to apply to the results of Dörner and Gladue et al., appeared further from our replication study of homosexual and heterosexual men. A true estrogen positive feedback response of LH in women is invariably associated with a greater response of LH to stimulation with the hypothalamic releasing hormone LHRH after estrogen exposure *versus* preadministration values (Young & Jaffe, 1976). When we applied this test to the homosexual men in our study, in all of them (including those who had shown a female like response of LH to estrogens), the LH response to LHRH stimulation had decreased following estrogen exposure. This disqualifies the observed LH rise after estrogen exposure in some men as a true estrogen positive feedback response and puts it in the category of a simple LH feedback reaction to the lowering of testosterone levels following estrogen administration.

A further part of our study also argues against a difference in brain mechanisms controlling LH secretion between heterosexuals and homosexuals. No difference could be established in the LH response to estrogens between six heterosexual and six homosexual women (Gooren, 1986b). The LH response to LHRH studied in these two categories indicated that the response was greater after estrogen exposure in a quantitatively identical fashion between the two groups. In other words, in both groups of women a nondiscriminating true estrogen positive feedback response had been elicited and the homosexual women in no way resembled the men tested in precisely the same way. As stated earlier, in our study homosexual men were not different from heterosexual men in their LH response to estrogens. The hormonal data collected by Dörner and Gladue et al. allowed, however, a distinction between homosexual and heterosexual men as groups.

If one rejects the explanation that this distinction is due to a different hormonal imprinting of the neuroendocrine system, what other factors can one consider? Our own experiments provided strong evidence that the type of response of LH to estrogens in men is determined by testicular factors. Could there be a difference in testicular functioning between heterosexual and homosexual men to explain the differences encountered by Dörner and Gladue et al.? Gladue (1985) admitted this possibility in a reply to a technical comment on his work by Baum et al. (1985), offering this alternative explanation of the Gladue et al. (1984) results and interpretation.

Which testicular factors could one think of? Our own preliminary results indicate that age is a factor to be considered. In a study comparing men over 65 years of age to men between 20 and 25 years of age, it was found that testosterone levels fell farther and LH levels rose more upon estrogen administration in the older men than in the young men, a finding supported by other literature data (Harman & Tsitouras, 1980).

It is further known that viral infections may affect testicular hormone production. The best-known example is the mumps virus, but other classes of viruses also affect testicular functioning (Frantz & Wilson, 1985). Use of recreational drugs (such as cannabis and alcohol), body weight (obesity and underweight), and vigorous exercise are known to affect the hypothalamo-pituitary-testicular endocrine axis (Griffin & Wilson, 1985). Also, psychological stress may alter the ratio of androgens to estrogen (Gooren & Daantje, 1986). All these factors have to be taken into account when comparing testicular functioning of two populations. In our study (Gooren, 1986b), we failed to find differences between homosexual and heterosexual men in the testosterone response to estrogens. All these men were hospital workers and their friends. Other methods of recruiting of test subjects may take in greater differences between homosexual and heterosexual subjects.

In summary, the evidence that regulation of gonadotropin secretion in primates is *not* sex-differentiated is solid. There is a clear difference in this respect with rodents (rat). Therefore, it seems untenable to regard the LH response to estrogen as an indication of prenatal brain imprinting. Authors who extrapolate data collected in the rat to primates ignore literature data available since 1973 and thereafter.

Conclusion

Biomedicine, departing from the reproductive, that is, the heterosexual, paradigm of human sexuality, has conceptualized homosexuality as a disturbance of sexual differentiation of the male *versus* the female. It attributes female biological markers to homosexual men and male biological markers to homosexual women.

Upon evaluation of neuroendocrine functions and peripheral sex steroid levels, one finds no convincing differences between homosexuals and heterosexuals.

Studies assessing the effects of prenatal hormonal influences on later sexual orientation have in a number of cases established positive correlations between prenatal sex-steroid exposure and homosexuality. Examination of the nature of the hormone does not disclose a unifying hypothesis with regard to prenatal hormonal influences on later sexual orientation. Therefore, other nonhormonal factors must be considered as well.

Correlation does not necessarily imply causality. Offspring from an endocrine-abnormal pregnancy may suffer from lifelong medical conditions with potential consequences for self-image and child-parent interaction. These and other factors may not be disregarded when the research data are interpreted.

Up to the present day, solid evidence of biological correlates of homosexuality is lacking. As in other fields of science only solid data can provide solid evidence. Statements such as an endocrine influence on sexual orientation cannot be excluded are too general to be credited.

References

Aono, T., Miyake, A., Kinugasa, T., Kurachi, K., & Matsumoto, K. (1978). Absence of positive feedback effect of estrogen on LH release in patients with testicular feminization syndrome. *Acta Endocrinologica, 87,* 259–267.

Barbarino, A., de Marinis, L., & Macini, A. (1983). Estradiol modulation of basal and gonadotropin-releasing hormone- induced gonadotropin release in intack and castrated men. *Neuroendocrinology, 36,* 105–111.

Barbarino, A., de Marinis, L., Mancini, A., Giustacchini, J., & Alcini, A. E. (1982). Biphasic effect of estradiol on LH reponse to gonadotropin-releasing hormone in castrated men. *Metabolism, 31,* 755–758.

Baum, M. J. (1979). Differentiation of coital behavior in mammals: A comparative analysis. *Neuroscience Biobehavioral Reviews, 39,* 265–284.

Baum, M. J., Caroll, R. S., Erskine, M. S. & Tobet, S. A. (1985). Neuroendocrine response to estrogen and sexual orientation. *Science, 230,* 960–961.

Beach, F. A. (1979). Animal models for human sexuality. In R. Porter & J. Whelen (Eds.), *Sex, hormones and behavior* (pp. 113–143). Ciba Foundation Symposium 62 (new series). Amsterdam: Excerpta Medica.

Beral, V., & Colwell, L. (1981). Randomized trial of high doses of stilboestrol and norethisterone therapy in pregnancy: Longterm follow-up of the children. *Journal of Epidemiology and Community Health, 35,* 155–160.

Corsello, S. M., De Rosa, G., Liberale, I., Merini, L., Moneta, E., & Pasargiklian, E. (1984). Effects of estrogens on LH release in testicular feminization syndrome before and after gonadectomy. *Obstetrics and Gynecology, 63,* 312–317.

Davidson, J. M., Kwan, M., & Greenleaf, W. J. (1982). Hormonal replacement and sexuality in men. *Clinics in Endocrinology and Metabolism, ll,* 599–625.

Döhler, K. D., Hancke, J. L., Srivastava, S. S., Hofmann, C., Shryne, J. E., & Gorski, R. A. (1984). Participation of estrogens in female sexual differentiation of the brain: Neuroanatomical, neuroendocrine, and behavioral evidence. In G. J. de Vries, J. P. C. de Bruin, H. B. M. Uylings, & M. A. Corner (Eds.), *Progress in brain research* (Vol. 61, pp. 99-l17). Amsterdam: Elsevier.

Dörner, G. (1980). Sexual differentiation of the brain. *Vitamins and Hormones, 38,* 325–381.

Ehrhardt, A. A., Meyer-Bahlburg, H. F. L., Feldman, J. F. & Ince, S. E. (1984). Sexdimorphic behavior in childhood subsequent to prenatal exposure to exogenous progestogens and estrogens. *Archives of Sexual Behavior, 13,* 457–479.

Frantz, A. G. & Wilson, J. D. (1985). Endocrine disorders of the breast. In J. D. Wilson & D. W. Foster (Eds.), *Textbook of endocrinology* (p. 413). Philadelphia: W. B. Saunders.

Gartrell, N. K. (1982). Hormones and homosexuality. In W. Paul, J. D. Weinrich, J. C. Gonsiorek, & M. E. Hotvedt (Eds.), *Homosexuality: Social, psychological and biological issues.* Beverly Hills: Sage.

Gladue, B. A. (1985). Reply to Baum et al. *Science, 230,* 961.

Gladue, B. A., Green, R., & Hellman, R. E. (1984). Neuroendocrine response to estrogen and sexual orientation. *Science, 225,* 1496–1498.

Goh, H. H., Ratnam, S. S., & London, D. R. (1984). The feminization of gonadotropin response in intact male transsexuals. *Clinical Endocrinology, 20,* 591–596.

Goh, H. H., Wong, P. C. & Ratnam, S. S.(1985). Effects of sex steroids on the positive estrogen feedback mechanism in intact women and castrated men. *Journal of Clinical Endocrinology and Metabolism, 61,* 1158–1164.

Gooren, L. (1986a). The neuroendocrine response of luteinizing hormone to estrogen administration in heterosexual, homosexual, and transsexual subjects. *Journal of Clinical Endocrinology and Metabolism, 63,* 583–588.

Gooren, L. (1986b). The neuroendocrine response of luteinizing hormone to estrogen administration in the human is not sex specific but dependent on the hormonal environment. *Journal of Clinical Endocrinology and Metabolism, 63,* 589–593.

Gooren, L. J. G., & Daantje, C. R. E. (1986). Psychological stress as a cause of intermittent gynecomastia. *Hormone and Metabolism Research, 18,* 424.

Gorski, R. A. (1984). Critical role for the medial preoptic area in the sexual differentiation of the brain. In G. J. de Vries, J. P. C. de Bruin, H. B. M. Uylings, & M. A. Corner (Eds.), *Progress in brain research* (Vol. 61, pp. 129–146). Amsterdam: Elsevier.

Griffin, J. E. & Wilson, J. D. (1985). Disorders of the testes and male reproductive tract. In J. D. Wilson & D. W. Forster (Eds.), *Textbook of endocrinology* (pp. 259–311). Philadelphia: W. B. Saunders.

Harman, S. M., & Tsitouras, P. D. (1980). Reproductive hormones in aging men: I. Measurements of sex-steroids, basal luteinizing hormone and Leydig cell response to human chorionic gonadotropin. *Journal of Clinical Endocrinology and Metabolism, 51,* 35–40.

Hines, M. (1982). Prenatal gonadal hormones and sex differences in human behavior. *Psychological Bulletin, 92,* 56–80.

Hirschfeld, M. (1906). Von Wesen der Liebe. Zugleich ein Beitrag zur Losung der Fragen der Bisexualitat. [The essence of love. At the same time a contribution to the solution of the question of bisexuality]. *Jahrbuch der Sexuellen Zwischenstufen, 8,* 1-284.

Karsch, F. J., Dierschke, D. J., & Knobil, E. (1973). Sexual differentiation of pituitary function: Apparent difference between primates and rodents. *Science, 179,* 484–486.

Kester, P., Green, R., Finch, S. J., & Williams, K. (1980). Prenatal "female hormone" administration and psychosexual development in human males. *Psychoneuroendocrinology, 5,* 269–285.

McEwen, B. S. (1981). Neural gonadal steroid interactions. *Science, 211,* 1303–1310.

McEwen, B. S. (1983). Gonadal steroid influences on brain development and sexual differentiation. In R. O. Group (Ed.), *Reproductive physiology IV: International review of physiology* (Vol. 27). Baltimore, MD: University Park Press.

Meyer-Bahlburg, H. F. L. (1977). Sex hormones and male homosexuality in comparative perspective. *Archives of Sexual Behavior, 6,* 297–325.

Meyer-Bahlburg, H. F. L. (1979). Sex hormones and female homosexuality: A critical examination. *Archives of Sexual Behavior, 8,* 101-119.

Meyer-Bahlburg, H. F. L. (1982). Hormones and psychosexual differentiation: Implications for the management of intersexuality, homosexuality and transsexuality. *Clinics in Endocrinology and Metabolism, 11,* 681–701.

Meyer-Bahlburg, H. F. L. (1984). Psychoendocrine research on sexual orientation: Current status and future options. In G. J. de Vries, J. P. C. de Bruin, H. B. M. Uylings & M.A. Corner (Eds.), *Progress in brain research* (Vol. 61, pp. 375–398. Amsterdam: Elsevier.

Money, J. (1981). The development of sexuality and eroticism in humankind. *Quarterly Review of Biology, 56,* 379–404.

Money, J., & Lewis, V. (1982). Homosexual/heterosexual status in boys at puberty: Idiopathic adolescent gynecomastia and congenital virilizing adrenocorticism compared. *Psychoneuroendocrinology, 7*, 339–346.

Money, J., & Mathews, D. (1982). Prenatal exposure to virilizing progestins: An adult follow-up study of twelve women. *Archives of Sexual Behavior, 11*, 73–83.

Money, J., & Schwartz, M. (1977). Dating, romantic and non romantic friendships, and sexuality in 17 early-treated adrenogenital females, aged 16–25. In P. A. Lee, L. P. Plotnick, A. A. Kowarski, & C. J. Migeon (Eds.), *Congenital adrenal hyperplasia* (pp. 419–431). Baltimore, MD: University Park Press.

Money, J., Schwartz, M., & Lewis, V. G. (1984). Adult erotosexual status and fetal hormonal masculinization and demasculinization: 46 XX congenital virilizing adrenal hyperplasia and 46 XY androgen insensitivity syndrome compared. *Psychoneuroendocrinology, 9*, 405–410.

Norman, R. L. & Spies, H. G. (1986). Cyclic ovarian function in a male macaque: Additional evidence for a lack of sexual differentiation in the physiological mechanisms that regulate the cyclic release of gonadotropins in males. *Endocrinology, 118*, 2608–2610.

Sanders, D., & Bancroft, J. (1982). Hormones and the sexuality of women: The menstrual cycle. *Clinics in Endocrinology and Metabolism, ll*, 639–661.

Van Look, P. F. A., Hunter, W. M., Corker, Ch. S., & Baird, D. T. (1977). Failure of positive feedback in normal men and subjects with testicular feminization. *Clinical Endocrinology, 7*, 353–366.

Vogt, H. J. (1984). Sexual behavior in Klinefelter's syndrome. In H. J. Bandeman & R. Breit (Eds.), *Klinefelter's syndrome*. Berlin: Springer-Verlag.

Whalen, R. E. (1984). Multiple actions of steroids and their antagonists. *Archives of Sexual Behavior, 13*: 497–502.

Westphal, P. K., Stadelman, H. L., Horton, L. E., & Resko, J. A. (1984). Experimental induction of estradiol positive feedback in intact male monkeys: Absence of inhibition by physiologic concentrations of testosterone. *Biology of Reproduction, 31*, 856–862.

Wilson, J. D., Griffin, J. E., George, F. W., & Leshin, M. (1981). The role of gonadal steroids in sexual differentiation. *Recent Progress in Hormone Research, 37*, 1–38.

Yalom, I. D., Green, R., & Fisk, N. (1973). Prenatal exposure to female hormones. *Archives of General Psychiatry, 28*, 554–561.

Young, J. R., & Jaffe, R. B. (1976). Strength duration characteristics of estrogen effect on gonadotropin response to gonadotropin-releasing hormone in women II: Effects of varying concentrations of estradiol. *Journal of Clinical Endocrinology and Metabolism, 42*, 432–437.

Zarate, A., Canales, E. S., Soria, J., & Caballo, O. (1974). Studies on the LH- and FSH-releasing mechanism in the testicular feminization syndrome. *American Journal of Obstetrics and Gynecology, 119*, 971–977.

7

The Kinsey Scale:
Is It Familial?

Richard C. Pillard

One of the purposes of this volume is to examine the present usefulness for clinicians and researchers of the Kinsey scale, a unidimensional, bipolar conceptualization of sexual orientation. This chapter will summarize some data from a family study in which the Kinsey scale was one of the criteria for subject selection. The chapter begins with some general comments on family study methodology and then presents summary results from an ongoing family study of sexual orientation. It concludes with a brief comment on the Kinsey scale as a research tool.

I will start with a brief anecdote about sexual orientation. Recently, I heard from a young American woman, a Chinese major at college, who had spent a year in China perfecting her language skills. She lived in a remote province, where she was befriended by a young Chinese woman who was learning English. These women spent many hours together comparing their two cultures. At one point, my American informant spoke about homosexuality and the lesbian and gay liberation movement. The Chinese woman was astounded. She had never heard of this—it did not exist in China, she was certain—there was no word for it in Chinese—and in any case, what could two women do together? The American woman took it as a challenge to rationalize this peculiarity of our culture, and after a while the Chinese woman found it less astonishing. By degrees, the two developed an intimacy that eventually became an intense physical and sexual intimacy.

At the end of the year of study, the American woman returned to her life as a student, including the relationship with her boyfriend, whom she fully intended to marry. The affair with her friend was one of the serial sexual liaisons expected of adolescents in our culture and even, by being bisexual, invested with a certain cachet. But matters were very different for the Chinese woman. She was emotionally devastated to have lost one to whom she had made a profound and, as she expected, permanent emotional commitment. She broke off an engagement with the fiance to whom her family had pledged her from infancy. My American informant wondered, with a mixture of concern and puzzlement, why an agreeable relationship had become for her friend the cause of such confusion and unhappiness.

The point of this anecdote is to illustrate the complex determination of sexual behaviors. I think it is likely that one's ultimate placement on the Kinsey scale is influenced by biological factors as yet unknown, but it is also influenced by what the culture makes available (as other chapters in this volume address) and to a certain extent by "error variance," or what we more simply refer to as fate.

Family studies have traditionally been undertaken by medical geneticists who have been concerned with the mode of transmission and with the pathophysiology of certain forms of illness. More recently, behavioral scientists have used the family study and family history methods to investigate personality traits, cognitive abilities, special talents, and the like. The study to be presented asked about the relationship of sexual orientation both to cognitive abilities and to certain forms of mental disorder. This fact prompts a disclaimer: The debate on homosexuality as a normal personality variant has been joined by many writers including myself (Bayer, 1981; Pillard, 1982). I will simply reiterate that nothing in the methodology of this study or in its results implies that a homosexual orientation is itself a mental disorder or anything other than a "normal" behavior.

Family studies, as they have been used in psychiatric research, are of two sorts: *family interview studies*, in which various members of a kindred are personally interviewed (or their hospital records examined) in order to determine who does and who does not possess a given trait, and *family history studies*, in which one or more members of the family serve as informants and provide data about the others. The pros and cons of the two methods are fairly obvious. Interview studies are more accurate, but the investigator has to recruit and obtain information from dozens or hundreds of people, with the attendant problem of what to do about those who cannot be found or who refuse to participate. The history method is easier to do, but it underestimates, to an unknown and frequently considerable degree, the occurrence of the trait of interest. One of the purposes of an interview study is to obtain an estimate of this "false negative" rate so that an appropriate correction factor or "threshold" can be built into the design and measurement instruments of history studies.

Another important strategy choice should be mentioned. Family studies might be aimed, as ours was, at getting data on particular family units, first-degree relatives usually, or siblings and half-siblings. Or they might try to develop large pedigrees, which can easily include hundreds of individuals of various degrees of relationship. A study plan might focus on twins, half-sibs, adopted-away offspring, or others, depending upon the investigator's objective.

The final outcome of a family study is most obviously to collect information bearing on a genetic contribution to the trait in question. A genetic influence may be detected in several ways: one is to examine the pedigree to see whether the trait is distributed according to the laws of Mendelian genetics. A trait controlled by a single gene of large or small effect (dominant or recessive) is usually indicated in this way. However, many traits are subject to a more complicated set of influences. A characteristic may be modified by several genes (polygenes) or by the presence of nonallelic genes elsewhere on the genome (epistatic interaction), or by environmental influences. A trait of uniform appearance may have diverse origins; for example, a clinical depression may result from tragic life events in one person, from the ingestion of certain drugs in another, from a neurochemical irregularity in a third, or from some combination of these.

It must also be said that in human beings, with one or two exceptions, no behavioral trait has been unquestionably established as the subject of genetic influence. The exceptions include some forms of alcoholism and bipolar mood disorder; but this entire topic is the subject of active debate and one's view of the topic of genetic influences on behavior continues to require an open mind.

A second, and I think more interesting, use of family study methodology is to identify the natural range of variation of a trait. By observing the forms or varieties of a trait *within* a family and by comparing this to the forms of the trait *between* families, one can hope to get a useful sense of typology, to "carve nature at the joints." (Examples of this approach in action come from studies by Winokur, Cloninger, Cadoret, Goodwin, and their colleagues and are nicely summarized in a review by Weissman et al., 1986.)

Notice that no commitment needs to be made about the *causes* of the condition under study. Heredity, environment, or some combination might be involved in the etiology of any of the traits under investigation. The power of the investigative method is that it identifies features that hang together empirically to form syndromes of behavior. In addition, as Weissman et al. (1986) point out, studies of young children of adult probands can give information about early signs of a trait and on risk or protective factors that mediate the development of the trait.

A number of interesting questions arise relevant to the subject of this volume. Do individuals who are at one position on the Kinsey scale, say, Kinsey 6s, have relatives who are also Kinsey 6s, or might the relatives show various degrees of bisexuality? Do male and female homosexuality

run together in a kindred, or do they tend to segregate in separate families? Are there traits besides sexual orientation itself that correlate with a
given orientation? Within the limits of the data we have collected, I will
try to make some comment on each of these questions.

The design of this study was logically simple (though logistically complex). We recruited a number of male and female probands by means of
newspaper and radio advertisements. The criteria for participation were
that subjects had to be currently unmarried (to avoid marital status as a
confounding variable), age 25 to 35 for men and 25 to 4O for women; they
had to be in reasonably good health, to speak English as a native language, and to have at least one sibling age 2O or over available for study.
Subjects responding to the advertisements and meeting these criteria
were brought to the Family Studies Laboratory for a day of interview and
psychological testing.

The data set included (a) demographic variables, (b) scores on cognitive
abilities taken from subtests of the WAIS, (c) "masculinity/femininity"
scores from the Fy scale of the California Psychological Inventory and
from the Bem Sex-Role Inventory, (d) ratings of "closeness/distance" to
first-degree family members taken from the Family Member Rating Scale,
developed by us, (e) estimates of lifetime episodes of mental disorder
from the Schedule of Affective Disorders and Schizophrenia, Lifetime
Version, a standardized structured interview schedule, (f) a brief health
questionnaire, and finally, (g) a sexual history that included information
on gender-typical behavior in childhood and sexual dysfunctions as well
as sexual orientation items from which a Kinsey rating could be made.

Information was gathered from each proband about the mental health
and sexual orientation of each sibling and parent. Then, the sibs themselves were recruited for study, either in person, by mailed questionnaire,
by telephone interview, or some combination of these. Thus, the study
included both the history and interview methodologies.

The reader is referred to publications from this study for details of
methodology and results (Pillard, Poumadere, & Carretta, 1982; Pillard &
Weinrich, 1986). I will summarize here those of our findings that are most
pertinent to the symposium topic.

Kinsey scale ratings were based on the sexual history interview. For
each subject, raters made ratings of both sexual behavior and erotic fantasy content: lifetime sexual behavior, sexual behavior for the past year,
lifetime sexual fantasy, and sexual fantasy for the past year—four ratings
in all. The great majority of male subjects showed a close correspondence
between their behavior and their sexual fantasies. Only two had substantial homosexual fantasies but little homosexual behavior.

Further, as Figure 7.1 shows, there were few men with a substantially
bisexual orientation (Kinsey 2–4) particularly if one considers sexual behavior during the preceding 12 months. This point deserves emphasis;
virtually all the men we interviewed seemed to have made the decision to

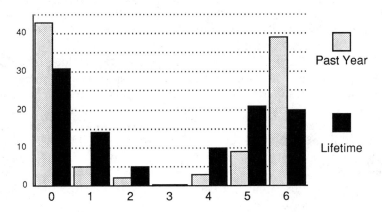

Figure 7.1. Past year and lifetime Kinsey ratings, male subjects.

label themselves as either heterosexual or homosexual (remember that these men were at least 25 years old). Of the few with substantial bisexual behavior, most said they knew, even during adolescence, that they were "really" one orientation or the other and they engaged in sexual behavior with people of the nonpreferred gender because of social expectation, or for some other reason, but not because of variability or doubt about partner preference.

Parenthetically, one of our graduate students became interested in the relative absence of bisexuals in the sample and attempted specifically to recruit an independent bisexual male sample. This proved difficult to do. Most of the self-identified bisexual men he found were in their late adolescence, that is, younger than the family study sample, or had a single woman sexual partner but serial male partners with predominately homoerotic fantasies or identified themselves as "in transition" from heterosexuality to homosexuality. Also of interest is the fact that many of these subjects who were self-identified as bisexuals were rated by us as Kinsey 5s and even Kinsey 6s. Clearly, factors other than a position on the Kinsey scale attend self-labeling as "bisexual."

Our raters found it more difficult to establish Kinsey ratings on the female subjects. Many of these women, though they were mature adults, were continuing to experience changes in their sexual lives. This made them reluctant to label themselves as homosexual or heterosexual—a situation that did not have a counterpart in the histories of the men (a fact noted by others in this volume). The women's sexual feelings seemed to depend more upon the partner they were with; in general, they seemed to have the ability for a "situational response," which the men lacked. Figure 7.2 shows the lowest and highest possible Kinsey ratings for these women in order to give an idea of the possible variability in the Kinsey ratings.

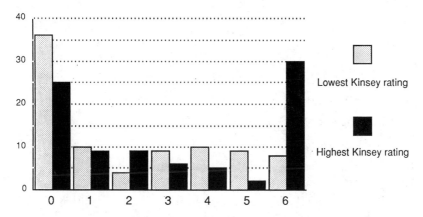

Figure 7.2. Highest and lowest Kinsey ratings, female subjects.

Again, there is a tendency for ratings of sexual orientation to cluster at the ends of the Kinsey scale, but this tendency was much weaker among the women than it was among the men.

The data in Figure 7.3 address the familiality of sexual orientation in sisters of the male probands. The 101 male probands were dichotomized into two groups: predominately homosexual (Kinsey 4–6) and predominately heterosexual (Kinsey 0–2). Sexual orientation of the sisters was similarly distributed across the two groups. Specifically, there was one Kinsey 5–6 sister of the mostly heterosexual men and two Kinsey 5–6 sisters for the homosexual men—obviously not a significant difference.

Figure 7.4 tabulates brothers of the male probands. Here, a difference is obvious. Thirteen brothers of the homosexual probands were also substantially homosexual, and two were bisexual. Heterosexual probands had only two homosexual brothers. This difference is statistically significant. We also asked about (but did not interview) second- and third-degree relatives. The male homosexual probands identified more uncles, nephews, and male cousins (by a ratio of about 6 to 1) than did the male heterosexual probands.

Male index subjects	Kinsey rating of sister		
	0-1	2-4	5-6
Kinsey 0-2	61	5	1
Kinsey 4-6	44	2	2

Figure 7.3. Familiality: sisters of male index subjects.

Male index subjects	Kinsey rating of brother		
	0-1	2-4	5-6
Kinsey 0-2	53	0	2
Kinsey 4-6	53	2	13

Figure 7.4. Familiality: brothers of male index subjects.

Figure 7.5 tabulates predominantly homosexual, bisexual, and hetero-sexual sisters of predominantly homosexual, bisexual, and heterosexual female probands. Here, as with the men, there was a clustering of homo-sexual and bisexual sisters—less obvious than for the males, but the differ-ence is still statistically significant. Figure 7.6 displays the orientation of the brothers of the female probands. There were, surprisingly, a few more gay male brothers of lesbian probands, a difference of borderline signifi-cance. As further data on this sample are being collected, we must await a final analysis.

Taken together, these findings suggest that a homosexual orientation does run in families within male and female lineages, perhaps as two independent familial traits. An interesting exception is the extended pedi-gree shown in Figure 7.7 of one family (not participants in the studies just described) with seven sibs, six of whom we were able to interview. Of the three males, all were homosexual or bisexual, and of the four females, three were homosexual or bisexual. One of the women in the sibship wrote a sociologic study of her family for a college project identifying sexual orientation and other characteristics. In this family, only one other member, a female maternal cousin, was identified as homosexual.

It is worth pointing out that this one family provides independent and powerful statistical evidence for the fact of familial homosexuality. The precise probability of finding a sibship with this many lesbian and gay

Female index subjects	Kinsey rating of sister		
	0-1	2-4	5-6
Kinsey 0-1	47	5	1
Kinsey 2-4	7	5	1
Kinsey 5-6	38	5	4

Figure 7.5. Familiality: sisters of female index subjects.

Female index subjects	Kinsey rating of brother		
	0-1	2-4	5-6
Kinsey 0-1	**44**	0	0
Kinsey 2-4	9	0	2
Kinsey 5-6	31	1	3

Figure 7.6. Familiality: brothers of male index subjects.

members depends upon the population frequency that one is willing to assume for these traits, but a conservative estimate would be that such a family aggregation would occur by chance less than one time in 25 million. Clearly, factors other than chance are operating here.

The next question prompted by these data is whether there are related traits that seem to be familial. With respect to sexual behavior itself, do gays in the same family prefer the same kind of sexual activity or the same type of partner? The summary answer appears to be that there is no within-family similarity on these behaviors as far as we could tell, but it would require larger samples than we have to investigate this question with sufficient statistical power.

We also investigated correlates of sex-role and gender-typical behavior using the Bem Sex-Role Inventory, the Strong-Campbell Vocational Interest Index, and the Fy scale from the California Psychological Inventory. Figure 7.8 shows Fy scale scores for the male sample. Higher (more homosexual) ratings on the Kinsey scale predict more feminine scores on the Fy scale. A comparison of heterosexual/homosexual brother pairs (data not shown) also shows that the gay brother is far more likely to have the higher (more "feminine") Fy score.

The Fy scale scores for women showed a different picture. Women with higher Kinsey scores did have slightly lower (more "masculine") scores, but the trend was not nearly as significant as for the men. This is consistent with data showing that in childhood, the lesbian-to-be is gender atypical much less often than the gay man-to-be (Zucker, 1983).

Discussions of gender atypicality seem to be unpopular in the gay community. It is as though we feel that there is something not quite correct in being "feminine." However, this finding turns up in virtually every one of the many studies I could find on this issue. Many, to be sure, are methodologically inadequate, but we ought to recognize that there is a powerful link between sexual orientation and gender role behavior, particularly in childhood, whatever that may mean for the ultimate understanding of these phenomena. Weinrich and I suggest that the situation is in fact more complicated than simply that gay men are more "feminine" and lesbian

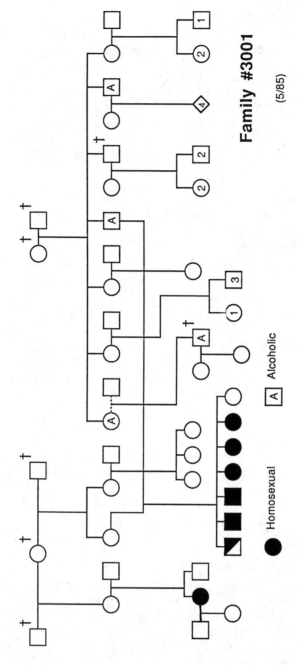

Family #3001

(5/85)

Homosexual   Alcoholic

Figure 7.7. Extended pedigree of family 3001.

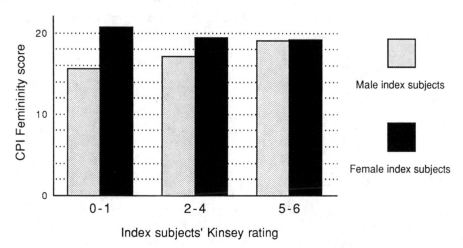

Figure 7.8. CPI Fy scores of male and female index subjects.

women, more "masculine." In brief, we suggest that gender behavior is the resultant of two dimensions, "masculinization" and "defeminization" and that gay men are masculinized but not defeminized (Pillard & Weinrich, 1987).

Many reports in the older literature suggest that gay men experience their fathers as cold, more psychologically remote, less "fatherly" than do heterosexual men. We investigated this issue by constructing a Likert-type scale asking subjects to rate themselves on how close or how distant they felt toward each first-degree family member during the developmental years, roughly through high school. Figure 7.9 shows that the pre-

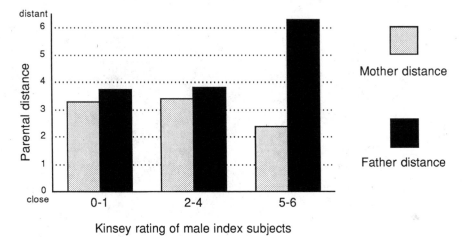

Figure 7.9. Father and mother "close/distant" ratings of male index subjects.

dominantly gay men and their gay brothers did report themselves as considerably more distant from their father than did the heterosexual men. And the gay men reported slightly but significantly greater closeness to their mother.

The significance of "father distance" has been repeatedly documented and discussed (Bell, Weinberg, & Hammersmith, 1981). This, however, is the only data set from which within-family comparisons can be made.

Figure 7.10 shows father-distance ratings treated in a different way. Three columns represent families in which there are no gay men, one gay man, and two or more gay men. We are trying to arrange the families according to a roughly made estimate of the pervasiveness of the homosexual trait. The ratings in the figure are made by the *heterosexual* brothers, and as the figure shows, heterosexual brothers rate themselves as relatively more distant from their father if they come from a family in which there are gay brothers. In addition, however, when pair comparisons are made, the gay brother rates himself as the more distant in 21 of 26 instances.

The next piece of evidence may illuminate the father-distant finding. We obtained Family History Research Diagnostic Criteria diagnoses of mental disorder on each first-degree family member from the standardized interview schedule of Endicott, Andreasen, and Spitzer, (1978). (I should underscore that the fathers and mothers were not themselves interviewed. A diagnostic assessment was made from information provided by their children according to Endicott et al.'s family history criteria.) For the fathers, as shown in Figure 7.11, one diagnosis stands out: alcoholism. More than twice as many fathers of homosexual subjects received an alcoholism diagnosis as did fathers of exclusively heterosexual sons. And this is a specific finding; other mental disorders were not reported in excess in the fathers of gay men.

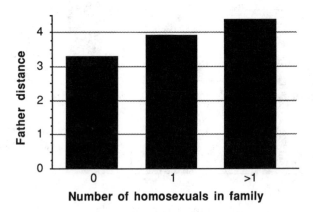

Figure 7.10. Father distance ratings for heterosexual men in families with none, one, and two gay brothers.

Fathers' Diagnoses by Son's Sexual Orientation

		Heterosexual	Homosexual
Depression:	unipolar	5	4
	bipolar	0	0
Hypomania		0	1
Alcoholism		4	13
	...with drug use	1	0
Drug use disorder		0	1
Other mental disorder		6	6
No mental disorder		32	24
(not counted)		2	1

Figure 7.11. Research diagnostic criteria diagnoses in fathers of male subjects.

This suggests a possible reason why heterosexual sons in families with a gay sib reported a more distant father: there seem to be more alcoholic fathers in these families and it is easy to imagine that alcoholic fathers are more "distant" from all of their sons. But this explanation is incomplete. Why should the gay son report even more "distance" than the heterosexual son in the same family? Does the father really treat his gay son differently, or does the son provide us with an exaggerated report of this dimension? And if alcoholism is really more prevalent among fathers of gay sons, what is its significance? Clearly, the issue of distant paternal relationships cannot simply be dismissed as a homophobic stereotype but deserves serious and unbiased examination.

Do these data point to a genetic basis for sexual orientation? We cannot say for sure; they are consistent with a genetic factor, an environmental factor, or some combination of both. My own bias is that a combination of variables will eventually be identified as determinants of sexuality and that a genetic influence will be recognized as one component.

This chapter has indicated how a family study can contribute to the descriptive classification of homosexual and heterosexual orientations. The Kinsey scale proved to be a useful measure of orientation; our raters were able to apply it with a satisfactory degree of reliability, and it was validated by the results of the family study. Because the Kinsey scale measures one bipolar dimension, however, its usefulness may ultimately be limited. We and other investigators have come to feel that sexual orientation is better described on two dimensions, masculinization and defeminization, which provide a closer analogy to what is known about the development of sexual behavior in animals. At present, we do not have enough knowledge to make bidimensional ratings on an individual basis. Our effort is, I would like to think, congenial to Kinsey's attempts to classify and describe human sexual behavior, and I very much hope that it will be an enlightening and liberating effort.

Acknowledgment

Support for the research presented in this chapter was obtained in part from NIMH grant 32,170. I thank James D. Weinrich, Ph.D., Jeanette Poumadere, Ph.D., Ruth Carretta, and Joanne Greenfield.

References

Bayer, R. (1981). *Homosexuality and American psychiatry*. New York: Basic Books.

Bell, A. P., Weinberg, M. S., & Hammersmith, S. K. (1981). *Sexual preference: Its development in men and women*. Bloomington: Indiana University Press.

Endicott, J., Andreasen, N., & Spitzer, R. L. (1978). Family history—Research diagnostic criteria (3rd ed.). New York: Biometrics Research, New York State Psychiatric Institute.

Pillard, R. C. (1982). Psychotherapeutic treatment for the invisible minority. In W. Paul, J. D. Weinrich, J. C. Gonsiorek, & M. E. Hotvedt (Eds.), *Homosexuality: Social, psychological, and biological issues*. Beverly Hills: Sage.

Pillard, R. C., Poumadere, J., & Carretta, R. A. (1982). A family study of sexual orientation. *Archives of Sexual Behavior, 11*, 511.

Pillard, R. C., & Weinrich, J. D. (1986). Evidence of familial nature of male homosexuality. *Archives of General Psychiatry, 43*, 808.

Pillard, R. C., & Weinrich, J. D. (1987). The periodic table model of the gender transpositions: A theory based on masculinization and defeminization of the brain. *Journal of Sex Research, 23*, 425.

Weissman, M. M., Merikangas, K. R., John, K., Wickramaratne, P., Prusoff, B. A., & Kidd, K. A. (1986). Family-genetic studies of psychiatric disorders: Developing technologies. *Archives of General Psychiatry, 43*, 1104.

Zucker, K. J. (1983). Cross-gender identified children. In Steiner (Ed.), *Gender dysphoria: Development, research, treatment*. New York: Plenum.

8

Commentary: Biological Contributions to Sexual Orientation

John Bancroft

In this volume the implications of the Kinsey scale are examined from a variety of viewpoints. In this section we are concentrating on biology. To what extent does the Kinsey scale help us to understand or investigate a possible biological basis for homosexuality and heterosexuality? In the light of more recent knowledge of biological factors, does the Kinsey scale need reappraisal?

Before considering these questions in relation to Chapters 5, 6, and 7, let me briefly state my own theoretical position so that the reader can more readily follow my line of argument.I believe that the "state of being homosexual" in our society can be arrived at in a variety of ways. In other words, it is a consequence (and not necessarily an end state) of a multifactorial developmental process. I know of no convincing evidence that sexual preference or orientation is established early in development in either primates or humans. If biological processes are influential in this human developmental process, I would expect that parallel examples of such influences could be demonstrated in nonhuman primates. When we look at the primate literature, we find persuasive evidence that biological factors do indeed play a part, not in any direct sense but by interacting with forms of social learning to shape the pattern of adult behavior. (I have discussed this evidence at greater length elsewhere; Bancroft, 1989). The theme that emerges is that prenatal or perinatal hormones influence childhood behaviors such as mounting, which, in primate terms, serve both dominance and sexual functions. Prepubertally, the dominance aspect is more evident than the sexual; after puberty, the sexual consequences of such behavior become more powerful reinforcers; opposite-sex mounts increase, and same-sex mounts decrease. It is useful and valid to draw a parallel between dominance behavior in primates and gender role behavior in humans. This primate data, with its rich evidence of the powerful effects of social learning, take us a fair way toward a model of human sexual development in which biological factors can be seen to play a part. What the primate model does not do is to explain the development of exclusive homosexual or heterosexual preference. With the occasional rare exception, this exclusiveness, the Kinsey 6 or Kinsey 1 would appear to be a uniquely human phenomenon and, furthermore, one that as we shall see later in this volume, varies in importance across cultures. My favored explanation for this state of affairs in the human is that superimposed on the "primate model" of development are the effects of cognitive learning, that human characteristic of assigning things and people to categories, and that the categories relevant to sexual orientation are culturally dependent (Bancroft 1983). In Western societies the categories are "either heterosexual or homosexual"; people are either one thing or the other. In many societies that dichotomy does not apply. Perhaps the closest we can get to a "universal" category is that of the male who behaves like a woman. This type of individual seems to occur in all cultures, but how a society reacts to such individuals, how it expects them to behave sexually, and how it categorizes other individuals who interact sexually with them, varies considerably across cultures (Carrier, 1980).

It is to me ironic that it has been the exclusive "Kinsey 6" homosexual who is most likely to be regarded as "biologically determined," whereas if you accept my line of reasoning, it is this form of homosexuality that most emphasizes the importance of social and cognitive factors.

Whalen, Geary, and Johnson, in their principal conclusion in Chapter 5, reject the Kinsey scale as inappropriate for understanding the complexities of human sexuality. Whereas I would agree that this scale has not helped us in understanding the role of biological factors, for which a much more detailed analysis of the components of the sexual experience is required, the uncompromising nature of Whalen et al.'s rejection provokes me to defend Kinsey and suggest that Whalen et al. have missed the point. If one reads the relevant section of the Kinsey volume (Kinsey, Pomeroy, & Martin, 1948), it is very apparent that Kinsey was not in any way attempting to explain the complexities of the human sexual condition but something much more limited. He was unequivocally reacting to the polarized social stereotyping of people into either "straight" or "gay." To quote him, "This world is not divided into sheep and goats . . . it is a fundamental of taxonomy that nature rarely deals with discrete categories. Only the human mind invents categories and has to force facts into separate pigeon-holes" (p. 639).

The Kinsey scale can be seen as a method of summarizing the Kinsey group's mass of collected evidence so as to challenge this polarizing dichotomy of cultural belief. In what is best understood as a political objective, Kinsey succeeded in part, because he confronted the world with the extent of homosexual behavior. But in his main purpose, I believe, he failed, perhaps because he seriously underestimated the power of "human pigeon-holes" to influence human behavior. Whether our behavior can be placed on a continuum or not, we have this strong tendency to regard ourselves as either heterosexual or homosexual, from which a great many consequences stem. This, therefore, is my main criticism of the Kinsey scale. If Kinsey had intended the scale to aid our investigation of biological factors, I have little doubt he would have approached the task very differently. Whether he would have produced a nine-dimensional scale, as proposed by Whalen et al., is another matter. If one takes Whalen et al.'s argument to its logical conclusion, we would "describe" human sexuality with a series of highly detailed individual case histories. In practice, because of the limitations and needs of the human mind that Kinsey was being rude about, we are bound to summarize and simplify such complexity in order to draw useful conclusions. I would need to see Whalen et al.'s scheme applied in practice before being convinced that it is a useful substitute for Kinsey's scale. (I make the same criticism in relation to Klein's Sexual Orientation Grid presented in this volume. This does appear to be a useful way of summarizing the details of an individual case for clinical purposes, but it is difficult to see its research value.) I agree with Whalen et al. when they point out that we need a scale measuring aspects of masculinity and femininity that is more behaviorally oriented than the Bem Sex-Role Inventory. The Sex-Role Behavior Scale published by Orlofsky, Ramsden, and Cohen (1982) shows promise in this respect.

If this volume were to restrict itself to the merits and demerits of the Kinsey scale or alternatives, it would be of limited interest. The chapters in this section raise a number of other extremely interesting issues that deserve discussion in their own right.

Whalen et al. have correctly emphasized the need to use a multidimensional *model* to investigate sexuality. Whalen's 1966 paper "Sexual Motivation" remains a classic in the field. Much of the progress in analyzing hormone-sexual behavior relationships has resulted from this approach. I nevertheless take issue with some of the extrapolations from rodent to human. Whalen et al. state that not only are heterosexuality and homosexuality orthogonal dimensions, so too are masculinity and femininity. In other words, the degree of masculinity tells you nothing about the degree of heterosexuality or homosexuality or vice versa. Although I accept their rejection of the simplistic equation that masculinity in a man or femininity in a woman equals heterosexuality, the human evidence does strongly suggest that these dimensions of the human experience interact. Thus, Kagan and Moss (1962) found that the occurrence of "masculine" behavior early in childhood is predictive of earlier "dating" involvement in erotic heterosexual activity during adolescence. And a series of retrospective studies of adults and prospective studies of "effeminate" boys have shown an association between childhood gender nonconformity and later homosexual orientation. Pillard, in Chapter 7 of this volume, gives us further evidence of this kind. Carrier (1986) has reminded us that this developmental sequence only applies to a minority of homosexual adults and therefore is clearly not a *necessary* determinant. Nevertheless, this is the only characteristic that has repeatedly distinguished between the childhoods of heterosexual and homosexual men; therefore, it deserves serious attention. Gender nonconformity during childhood may influence the developmental process and *increase the likelihood* of homosexual orientation. And of particular importance to this discussion, it may be through their effects on gender role behavior that biological factors can influence, indirectly, the development of sexual preferences.

Whalen et al. next emphasize the independence of the two hormonally organized aspects of sexual differentiation of the brain, "masculinization" and "defeminization." This distinction is of crucial importance in understanding sexual differentiation in rodents, but how relevant is it to primates or humans? The main uncertainty is with "defeminization." This is manifested in two principal ways: the reduction of the female "lordosis" response and prevention of the basic female pattern of positive feedback response of the hypothalamus to estrogen, which underlies the LH surge and the ovarian cycle. As we shall see later, Gooren (Chapter 6) has effectively marshaled the evidence that this function of the hypothalamus, while clearly dependent upon early organization (i.e., "defeminization") in the rodent, is in the primate and human a function of the prevailing hormonal milieu, in other words, "organization" of a dynamic and mutable rather than structural immutable kind. The lordosis response, a complex reflex pattern highly dependent on hormones, also appears to have no meaningful counterpart in primates or humans. "Defeminization," in this sense, is therefore of doubtful relevance to human sexual development.

"Masculinization" of the brain by androgens is another matter. Gooren reminds us of the substantial body of data indicating that early exposure to androgens increases masculine-type behavior during the childhood of both primate and human females. There may therefore be value in extrapolating from rodents to humans in this respect.

Whalen et al. (Chapter 5 in this volume) go on to distinguish between androgen effects on sexual motivation and sexual orientation. "Thus, hormone levels, which may relate to sexual urge and the intensity of sexual activity, are not logically or empirically relevant to the issue of heterosexuality/homosexuality" (p. 00). I have already suggested that hormones may *indirectly* influence sexual orientation via their effects on gender role behavior. Gooren briefly reviews the evidence for homosexual development associated with abnormal endocrine states. He points out that whereas there is no evidence of any such link in males, females exposed to abnormal endocrine states during early development (e.g., excess androgen or DES which may act similarly to testosterone during central nervous system development, Ehrhardt et al., 1985) show evidence of homosexual imagery or interest *in a proportion* of cases, though not in the majority. Turning to studies of the endocrine status of adult heterosexual and homosexual men and women, Gooren, citing Meyer-Bahlburg's reviews, concludes that there are no hormonal differences between the two types of sexual orientation. He has somewhat misrepresented Meyer-Bahlburg in this respect and overlooked what could turn out to be a crucial difference between male and female sexual development. Meyer-Bahlburg (1979) found in a number of studies that lesbians showed somewhat raised testosterone levels in approximately a third of cases. He cautiously pointed out that this evidence is insufficient to be conclusive on this point, but the picture nevertheless looks interestingly different from that in the male. There is a comparable male-female difference in the evidence from transexuals. In spite of Gooren's own negative findings, other workers have reported abnormal endocrine states *in a proportion* of female-to-male transexuals. The most impressive has been reported by Futterweit, Weiss, and Fagerstrom, (1986), who found that a third of female-to-male transexuals were endocrinologically abnormal, most often showing polycystic ovarian disease. This accords with my own clinical experience, in which at least a third of such patients have raised testosterone levels before starting on exogenous androgens.

We thus have suggestive if not conclusive evidence of a sex difference in the relationship between endocrine status and sexual orientation. Why might this be so?

There is a sex difference in general when one considers the relationship between hormones and sexual behavior. Evidence from men is predictable and consistent across studies. Men need androgens for normal levels of sexual appetite (whether they are heterosexual or homosexual). The evidence for women, although of much greater quantity, is by comparison inconsistent and often contradictory. I have postulated a number of reasons why this might be so, including a greater genetic variability in behavioral responsiveness to hormones in women than in men (Bancroft 1986, 1988). But there is a particular aspect of this issue that is of potential relevance to the present discussion. Men normally have more circulating testosterone than they appear to need. Although there is still insufficient evidence on this point, it does look as though there is a threshold (no doubt varying in level from individual to individual) above which further increases in testosterone have no further effect, at least on behavior. Because it is likely that normal circulating levels of testosterone are commonly above that threshold, we should not be surprised that there is an absence of correlation between circulating testosterone and measures of male sexuality (Bancroft, 1988). In women, on the other hand, the levels of circulating testosterone are low, and the variations in level that occur are likely to be within the range that is behaviorally relevant. (This is shown diagrammatically in Figure 8.1.) If so, we might expect to find

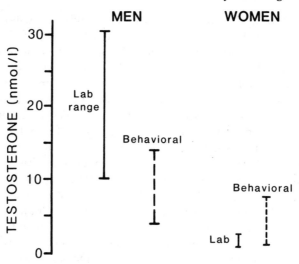

Figure 8.1. A comparison between men and women of the ranges of circulating testosterone levels (lab) and the ranges associated with behavioral effects.

significant correlations between circulating testosterone and sexual behavior. And indeed, this is what we find in a number of studies. But these correlations are not straightforward. Thus in our study of 55 women (Bancroft, Sanders, Davidson, & Warner, 1983) we found a high correlation between circulating testosterone and frequency of masturbation, whereas correlations with indices of heterosexual interaction were absent or in the opposite direction. Schreiner-Engel, Schiavi, Smith, & White, (1981),testing vaginal responsiveness to erotic stimuli in the laboratory, found that women with relatively high levels of testosterone produced stronger vaginal responses than those with low testosterone, whereas the associations with enjoyable and satisfactory heterosexual interaction were in the opposite direction. The "high testosterone" women had less satisfactory relationships. There is also limited evidence to suggest that women with high testosterone levels are more likely to be career oriented and less likely to be housewives (Bancroft et al., 1983; Purifoy & Koopmans, 1980). This led me to postulate that in women androgens might produce effects on both sexuality and personality that in certain social contexts (e.g., those in which a woman is expected to conform to the stereotype of the nonassertive, domesticated wife) might conflict with each other.In the male such conflict of effects is unlikely. The "stereotype" of the male would expect both the assertiveness and the sexuality associated with androgens. One can take this further and suggest that in some cases such conflicting hormonal effects in a woman might increase the likelihood of her adopting a lesbian life-style. The testosterone ensures a level of sexual drive that requires expression, whereas the lesbian life-style allows its expression without the conflict. This is a provocative and speculative hypothesis, but it is testable and it does provide an illustration of how hormonal and social effects may interact to influence the development of sexual preferences.

A unique study of hormone-behavior relationships in boys and girls around puberty has been reported (Udry, Billy, Morris, Groff, & Raj, 1985; Udry, Talbert, & Morris, 1986). In this study testosterone levels were the best predictors of all aspects of the boys' adolescent sexuality, including the likelihood of their having had sexual intercourse. The stage of pubertal development and various indices of social influence were by comparison less predictive. Whereas testosterone level in the girls predicted their level of sexual interest, it did not predict their involvement in sexual intercourse, which was more dependent on a variety of social variables. This points to a separation between "androgen induced" and "socially induced" sexuality in girls, a difference that is less evident in boys. This "separation" is consistent with the hypothesis about the conflicting effects of testosterone that I have already described and that may prove to be of considerable importance in understanding female sexual development.

So far I have been discussing the possible *activating* effects of androgens on sexuality and how they might indirectly influence the development of sexual preferences in girls if not in boys. A similar case can be made for the early *organizing* effects of androgens. Thus, males are relatively "overdetermined"—they are exposed to more androgen than is required to produce maximum masculinization—whereas females are exposed to low and variable amounts. As a consequence, females may develop with greater individual variability in their behavioral responsiveness to the later activating effects of androgens, contributing to the inconsistency in the hormone-behavior data from women that I referred to earlier. This raises a conundrum about male-female differences in androgen response that has been troubling me for some time. It is often implied that early exposure to testosterone sensitizes the target organ to later circulating hormone postpubertally. Whalen et al. refer to some evidence from Phoenix and his colleagues that explicitly states this. But if females are sexually activated by testosterone, and undoubtedly some are, they respond to levels of hormone that would be quite ineffective in normal males. Does this mean that the high levels of testosterone to which males are exposed during fetal development *desensitize* the male to later testosterone effects? This could be biologically necessary in order to permit the high levels of androgens that are necessary for somatic masculinization, muscle growth, and so on. But if that is the case, we will need to radically revise some of our concepts!

Although there is no consistent evidence to suggest that homosexual men are different from heterosexual men in their circulating hormone levels, the evidence published by Dorner (1979) that exclusively homosexual men come midway between heterosexual men and women in their hypothalamic response to estrogen provocation has remained a controversial finding, which on the face of it was replicated by Gladue, Green, and Hellman (1984). Dorner's interpretation of these data, that they indicate inadequate defeminization during the early development of homosexual men, and his other related ideas have provoked a strong reaction and understandably so. First, he takes the homotypical and heterotypical sexual behavior of the rat as a model of sexual preference in humans and then extrapolates from the rodent evidence of sexual differentiation of the brain to human sexual development. Whalen et al. point out the logical fallacies of his basic premise, a case that was also forcefully argued by Beach (1979). Dorner next concludes that the differences he has observed between homosexual and heterosexual men result from inadequate levels of testosterone during early development of the homosexuals. Finally and most provocatively of all, he suggests that appropriate hormonal treatment during pregnancy could prevent the development of homosexuality (Dorner, 1979). Whether Dorner's observations and his interpretation of them are scientifically correct or not, his suggestions for the "prophylaxis" of homosexuality takes the debate into the political and moral arenas. He was strongly attacked by Sigusch, Schorsch, Danneker, and Schmidt (1982) in an "official statement of the German Society for Sex Research," leading to a defensive response by Dorner (1983). It is not surprising that his work is not always appraised with complete scientific objectivity.

The most important part of Chapter 6 of this volume is Gooren's dismantling of Dorner's case. Gooren does this both conclusively and relatively objectively. First, as I have already commented, he destroys Dorner's basic premise—that the positive feedback response can be used as an indicator of early sexual differentiation of the brain in primates and humans. This leaves Dorner's data requiring some alternative explanation. This Gooren provides from his own research. A rise in LH following estrogen provocation was observed by him in a proportion of *both* heterosexual and homosexual subjects and was related to the degree of testicular suppression and the resulting reduction in negative feedback. In other words, the phenomenon being observed reflected testicular, not hypothalamic, function. What I find truly remarkable is that Gladue et al. (1984), by including measurement of testosterone in their study, something that Dorner had not done, also provided convincing evidence that the most likely explanation for their and Dorner's findings lay in the testis. Yet they dismissed this and persisted with the hypothalamic explanation. As Gooren points out, as soon as attention shifts from the hypothalamus to the testis, a whole range of factors, many related to life-style, could account for these effects. A comparable mistake was made in an earlier study of testosterone levels in homosexual men; these men were reported to have lower levels than heterosexual controls (Kolodny, Masters, Hendry, & Toro, 1971). Subsequent evidence indicated that the differences were probably due to greater marijuana use in the homosexual group (Kolodny, Masters, Kolodner, & Toro, 1974). Although such evidence may tell us something about the *consequences* of living as a homosexual, it is difficult to see how it has any relevance to the *origins* of sexual preference. It is time Dorner's hypothesis was laid to rest.

In Pillard's chapter we are dealing with a different type of evidence. The likelihood that genetic factors are relevant to homosexual development has already been demonstrated by studies showing greater concordance in monozygotic than dizygotic twins(Heston & Shields, 1968). Such evidence takes us only so far.It does not tell us what the relevant genotype is. If we accept a multifactorial development involving social and cognitive factors, this concordance may tell us little more than that genetically identical twins will tend to react in a similar way to environmental influences. It is thus of interest to pursue the possible sources of influence in family studies. Pillard's work is important in this respect. However, demonstrating an increased incidence of homosexuality among siblings of homosexual probands is only the first step. The crucial issue is whether there are characteristics that might help us to distinguish between genetic and social learning factors in such families. Obviously, the investigation of gender nonconformity is one possible route to follow, but as yet it is not possible to draw any relevant conclusions from Pillard's results.

Once again, a possible difference between male and female homosexuality is suggested: homosexual men are more likely to have homosexual brothers but not lesbian sisters, and vice versa. What can we conclude from this? Presumably, this finding makes it unlikely that there is an inherited nonspecific propensity for "same-sex preference." But that would seem inherently unlikely in any case. If inheritance of gender nonconformity were involved, would we expect it to be gender specific (e.g., a genetic tendency either to be inadequately androgenized, leading to male gender nonconformity, or to be over androgenized, which would only be relevant to female gender nonconformity)? Alternatively, are there specific types of family constellation or dynamics that from the learning point of view would be more likely to lead either to male or to female homosexual orientation? These are interesting questions, but they await answers.

In conclusion, nothing in the chapters in this section has caused me to revise my opinion that biological factors, insofar as they are relevant to development of sexual preference, need to be understood as interacting with the effects of social and cognitive learning rather than having direct effects of their own. To me, the single most interesting theme to emerge in this field is the possibility of a fundamental difference in the role of biological factors in the sexual development of the two sexes, an issue that may attract more attention in future research.

References

Bancroft, J. (1983). Problematic gender identity and sexual orientation. A psychiatrist's view. In M. F. Schwartz, A. S. Moraczewski, & J. A. Monteleone (Eds.), *Sex & gender: A theological and scientific inquiry* (pp. 102–104). St. Louis, MO: The Pope John Center.

Bancroft, J. (1986). The role of hormones in female sexuality. *Proceedings of the Eighth International Congress of Psychosomatic Obstetrics & Gynaecology.* Amsterdam: Elsevier.

Bancroft, J. (1988). Reproductive hormones and male sexuality. In J. Sitsen (Ed.), *Pharmacology of sexual function: Vol. 6. Handbook of sexology.* Amsterdam: Excerpta Medica.

Bancroft, J. (1989). *Human sexuality and its problems* (2nd ed.). Edinburgh: Churchill Livingstone.

Bancroft, J., Sanders, D., Davidson, D. W., & Warner, P. (1983). Mood, sexuality, hormones and the menstrual cycle. III. Sexuality and the role of androgens. *Psychosomatic Medicine 45,* 509–516.

Beach, F. A. (1979). Animal models for human sexuality. In R. Porter & J. Whelan (Eds.) *Sex, hormones and behavior*(pp. 113–132). Ciba Foundation Symposium 62 (new series). Amsterdam: Excerpta Medica.

Carrier, J. M. (1980). Homosexual behavior in cross-cultural perspective. In J. Marmor (Ed.), *Homosexual behavior: A modern reappraisal* (pp. 100–122). New York: Basic Books.

Carrier, J. M. (1986). Childhood cross-gender behavior and adult homosexuality. *Archives of Sexual Behavior, 15,* 89- 93.

Dorner, G. (1979). Hormones and sexual differentiation of the brain. In R. Porter & J. Whelen (Eds.), *Sex, hormones and behavior* (pp. 81–112). Ciba Foundation Symposium 62(new series). Amsterdam: Excerpta Medica.

Dorner, G. (1983). Letter to editor. *Archives of Sexual Behavior, 12,* 577–582.

Ehrhardt, A. A., Meyer-Bahlburg, H. F. C., Rosen, L. R., Feldman, J. F., Veridiano, N. P., Zimmerman I., & McEwen, B. S. (1985). Sexual orientation after prenatal exposure to exogenous estrogens. *Archives of Sexual Behavior, 14,* 57- 77.

Futterweit, W., Weiss, R. A., Fagerstrom, R. M. (1986). Endocrine evaluation of forty female-to-male transsexuals: Increased frequency of polycystic ovarian disease in female transsexualism. *Archives of Sexual Behavior, 15,* 69–78.

Gladue, B. A., Green, R., & Hellman, R. E. (1984). Neuroendocrine response to estrogen and sexual orientation. *Science, 115,* 1496–1499.

Heston, L. L., & Shields, J. (1968). Homosexuality in twins: A family study and a register study. *Archives of Sexual Behavior, 18,* 149–160.

Kagan, J., & Moss, H. A. (1962). *Birth to maturity: A study of psychological development.* New York: John Wiley & Sons.

Kinsey, A. C., Pomeroy, W. B., & Martin, C. F. (1948). *Sexual behavior in the human male* (p.639). Philadelphia: W. B. Saunders.

Kolodny, R, C., Masters, W. H., Hendry, V. J., & Toro, G. (1971). Plasma testosterone and semen analysis in male homosexuals. *New England Journal of Medicine, 285,* 1170–1174.

Kolodny, R. C., Masters, W. H., Kolodner, R. M., & Toro, G. (1974). Depression of plasma testosterone levels after chronic marihuana use. *New England Journal of Medicine, 290,* 872–874.

Meyer-Bahlburg, H. F. L. (1979). Sex hormones and female homosexuality: A critical examination. *Archives of Sexual Behavior, 8,* 101–119.

Orlofsky, J. L., Ramsden, M. W., & Cohen, R. S. (1982). Development of the revised sex-role behavior scale. *Journal of Personality Assessment, 46,* 632–638.

Purifoy, F. E., & Koopmans, L. H. (1980). Androstenedione, T and free T concentrations in women of various occupations. *Social Biology, 26,* 179–188.

Schreiner-Engel, P., Schiavi, R. C., Smith, H., & White, D. (1981). Plasma testosterone and female sexual behavior. In Z. Hoch & H. I. Lief (Eds.), *Proceedings of the Fifth World Congress on Sexology.* Amsterdam: Excerpta Medica.

Sigusch V., Schorsch, E., Dannecker, M., & Schmidt, G. (1982). Official statement by the German Society for Sex Research on the research of Prof. Dr. Gunter Dorner on the subject of homosexuality. *Archives of Sexual Behavior, 2,* 445–449.

Udry, J. R., Billy, J. O. G., Morris, N. M., Groff, T. R., & Raj, M. H. (1985). Serum androgenic hormones motivate sexual behavior in adolescent boys. *Fertility & Sterility, 43,* 90–94.

Udry, J. R., Talbert, L. M., & Morris, N. M. (1986). Biosocial foundations for adolescent female sexuality. *Demography, 23,* 217–229.

Whalen, R. E. (1966). Sexual motivation. *Psychological Review, 73,* 151–163.

III

EVOLUTIONARY
PERSPECTIVE

9

The Kinsey Scale in Biology, with a Note on Kinsey as a Biologist

James D. Weinrich

Can a man with poor heredity ever amount to much, even if his environment is good? Is a man of good heredity certain to find success, irrespective of the environment in which he lives? Which is more important, heredity or environment?

Let us see what the scientific facts of the matter are.

Kinsey (1926, p. 172)

When the Son of man shall come in his glory, and all the holy angels with him, then shall he sit upon the throne of his glory: And before him shall be gathered all nations: and he shall separate them one from another, as a shepherd divideth *his* sheep from the goats: And he shall set the sheep on his right hand, but the goats on the left.

Matthew 25:31–33

I have four goals in this chapter:

1. By way of background, to examine Kinsey's presexological writings in order to see how much (or how little) influence biology had on his thinking as a sexologist.
2. To clear up misconceptions about biological models, especially as they relate to biological determinism.
3. To explain the major sociobiological theories of human homosexuality.

4. To put these theories into the perspective provided by the two-dimensional model of sexual orientation/preference.

It turns out that points 2 and 4 are closely related, so after beginning with point 1, I will jump back and forth between them. Then I will cover point 3. Finally, I will go on to point 4 and again alternate with point 2 as necessary.

Kinsey as a Biologist

Kinsey received his doctorate (an Sc.D.) from the Bussey Institute, a quasi-independent entity affiliated with Harvard University and, for the purposes of academic geneology, considered by Harvard to grant a Harvard degree. (The Bussey Institute has been merged into the Harvard Herbaria.) Soon afterward, he joined the faculty of Indiana University and rose through the ranks to become a tenured professor in the Department of Zoology. At some point, the university decided to offer a course on marriage, and Kinsey was the one chosen to teach it. Kinsey later claimed that as a result of not being able to find answers to students' questions in this course, he decided to gather his own information about human sexuality.

His presexological writings are of interest to sexologists for several reasons. One of the most important ones is that he has sometimes been accused of being too much of a biologist. His use of the concept of "total outlet," for example, got him into trouble with reviewers such as Lionel Trilling (although frankly, why Trilling was regarded as an authority on human sexuality is a mystery to me). Total outlet was, roughly, the total number of orgasms a person had in a given time period, and for some analyses Kinsey divided it into "homosexual outlet," "marital outlet," and so on. In fact, this concept is arithmetic, not biological, and is unexceptionable as *one* of many measures that could be applied to a particular individual's sex history. It would only have been problematic if Kinsey had suggested that this was the *only* interesting measure, and this he did not do.

Another reason to be interested in Kinsey's presexological work is a simple scientific one: How good a scientist was the man? Was he a good biologist or a mediocre one? Did he move to sexology because his biology had reached a dead end or because sex was more interesting?

A third reason relates to the history of science: Was there anything in his biological work that prepared him positively—rather than negatively, as his critics would have it—for answering certain questions in sexology? Did he in fact bring insight and cleverness with him from biology, or was his change of field a complete break with the past?

I realized that I might have something special to contribute to this question when, on a hunch, I spent some time reading Kinsey's early biological papers—and discovered that they were not listed in the Kinsey Institute's card catalog! Not even the high school biology textbook he wrote was listed there. In a sense, Kinsey's own biological roots had, by inadvertence, been expunged from the official record of the very institute he had founded. But not, it turned out, his actual record; it took the library staff only about 15 minutes to turn up all I needed.

Kinsey was a more than competent evolutionary biologist. Official accounts tend to describe his work as taxonomy of gall wasps and leave it at that. But Kinsey's work was a lot more interesting than just deciding what species a wasp was in. One of the most important questions in evolutionary biology is, of course, the evolution of species: How does one species split and become two? This question was as important in Kinsey's time as it is today and has occupied every evolutionary biologist since Darwin. Kinsey was working at an exciting time, when this question was beginning to be answered in a better way than Darwin could possibly have answered it.

Another important question is this: What is a species? Interestingly, the modern answer to this question is explicitly sexological. Ernst Mayr, professor emeritus at Harvard and a grand old man of evolutionary biology, often explains how important it was (and is) that biology moved from a *typological* species concept to a *biological* one. A typological concept says: Species X of gall wasp has the following typological properties, by which you tell one species from another. Whether individuals x and y are members of the same or different species is sometimes a matter of opinion or ineffable professional judgment, a judgment about what the typological traits ought to be. In contrast, a biological species concept says: Members of species X can interbreed (and produce fertile offspring) with other members of their species and not with members of species Y. Whether individuals x and y are members of the same species or different species is an *empirical* matter, not a matter of opinion or judgment. Going from a typological concept to a biological concept was obviously a big step for biology; it moved the determination of a species boundary from an art to a science.

One contribution Kinsey made was to demonstrate the existence of a puzzle now well known in evolutionary biology: that the biological species concept could be slightly self-contradictory. Suppose that a and b are classed in the same species because they can interbreed, that b and c can do likewise, c and d the same, and so on, down to y and z. But now suppose it turns out that a and z can*not* interbreed. Are a and z of the same species? Such circularity puzzles exist in the real world—literally textbook examples. Kinsey discovered a puzzle of this sort in his gall wasps and described it in his textbook (Kinsey, 1926). It turns out, by the way, that modern evolutionary biologists *do* consider a and z to be in the same species in a case like this.

Another contribution Kinsey (1937) made was to clarify the mechanism of speciation (the formation of a new species). Evolutionary biologists have argued endlessly about this question and rightly so. Mayr's point of view is that speciation cannot come about unless two or more subpopulations of a species become *geographically isolated* from each other, preventing interbreeding for many generations. Thus, although x and y might be *able* to interbreed during this isolation period, in fact they never do because of the geographic barrier. Over those generations, each subpopulation becomes better adapted to its own habitat, and when the geographic isolating barrier is removed, one of two things has happened. Either the two subspecies can no longer interbreed (in which case they constitute separate species from then on), or for a while they can interbreed, but the adaptations to the respective environments are so important to reproductive success that a barrier quickly evolves to isolate the two reproductively (in which case they are considered separate species as soon as this genetic or behavioral barrier evolves).

Kinsey gathered gall wasps from everywhere. He recruited amateur naturalists to gather them for him, asking them to note exactly where the galls had been collected and to include some of the leaves of the plant on which they were found. All this was to test the theory that new species of gall wasps form *without* geographic isolation. There was a theory that one wasp species could become two by specializing on different plants in the same geographic locality—kind of an exception to prove the rule of geographic isolation. Kinsey could test this theory, and he did.

The relevance of this work for his later conceptualization of the homosexual/heterosexual continuum, what is now called the Kinsey scale, is obvious. Kinsey loved to say that telling "the homosexual" from "the heterosexual" (both words are used as adjectives, not nouns) was not like telling the sheep from the goats. That is, when it came to sexual orientation, Kinsey explicitly rejected what might naively have been expected to have been his response as a biologist. After all, he was a taxonomist. *It was his job to tell the sheep from the goats!* What would have been more natural than for him to rush into human sexuality and tell the homosexuals from the heterosexuals from the bisexuals? The normal from the abnormal? The average from the deviation?

But Kinsey did none of these things. I leave it to the historians of science (such as Robinson, 1976) to decide why not; but I do want to point out one thing. Kinsey was an empirical scientist. If someone proposed that heterosexual and homosexual were as different from each other as two species, Kinsey would have regarded this as an empirical question. Obviously, this hypothesis is not to be taken literally because it cannot be tested by seeing if homosexual and heterosexual interbreed. Instead, one would take it figuratively and gather data to see whether there is any reasonable dividing line that can be drawn between the two.

Kinsey seems to have been of the opinion that this is exactly what he did. He went out into the field, observed the answers people gave to questions about their sex life, and found no objective way to classify people into discrete categories of sexual orientation. Sexual orientation could be measured—as height can be—and the two poles of the measurement might even be contrasted—as tall people and short people can be. But there is no more of a dichotomous difference, he concluded *empirically*, between "the homosexual" and "the heterosexual" than there is between "the tall" and "the short."

Kinsey also wrote two editions of a high school biology textbook (Kinsey, 1926, was the first edition). The textbook was remarkable in two ways. First, it was explicitly evolutionary. It adopted the point of view that evolution by natural selection was a fact of scientific life, undeniable by anyone with the courage to look at the evidence. Politically, of course, this is still a controversial statement, although it is not scientifically controversial now any more than it was in Kinsey's time. But politics then as now was important in high school curriculum selection. Second, it was very empirical. The text is filled with suggestions to the teachers and students to take a field trip and *actually observe* what is going on in the world around them. Evolutionary biology is filled with fascinating stories of the niches species occupy in the great swarm of life. Kinsey knew this and knew how to turn other people on to this secret.

Sexology, of course, is filled with stories just as vivid, as any sex therapist knows. Society says we are not supposed to find out about the sexual niches various people fill, but that didn't stop Kinsey from figuring it out anyway, and it obviously doesn't stop most sexologists, either.

In sum, I find Kinsey was a very good biologist, whose work was among the best empirical work being done on important evolutionary questions. And I find the influence of his biological training on his sexology to be on the whole a good one rather than a bad one. His experience writing a high school biology textbook got him acquainted with telling the public truthful things some of its members did not want to hear. And the inevitable importance sex assumes in biology may, for all I know, have helped him get over the sex taboo.

Most biologists, by the way, overcome that taboo when it comes to their own organisms; botanists have no shame when discussing pistils and stamens, and entomologists have no trouble talking about damselfly penises. But they usually fall back into the taboo by refusing to talk (or think!) much about human sexuality. Kinsey broke that mold, too.

Misconceptions About Biology

With so many misconceptions about Kinsey as a biologist floating around, it should not be surprising that there are misconceptions about biology itself. There is nothing particularly sexological about this, of course. Good evolutionary biology is taught at very few universities in this country and in fewer high schools (good sexology at fewer still!). The misconceptions sexologists have about biology and the nature of biological models are shared, alas, by many scientists from many disciplines. When it comes to sociobiology—which, besides being biological and besides being evolutionary, has been subjected to a deliberate campaign of vilification and peripheralization—the misconceptions are even worse. I can't blame this campaign on Lionel Trilling, mind you, but I can blame it in part on the *New York Review of Books*, which published some of the earliest accusations.

The misconceptions I want to address are first, that sociobiology is biologically deterministic; second, that sociobiology is a theory that extrapolates from "lower" animals to "higher" humans; third, that sociobiology is only or mostly interested in the "How?" question of how behavior comes about in the proximate, mechanistic sense; and finally, that human learning and culture override any relevance biology may have for the explanation of human behavior.

Biological Determinism

Biological determinism is what people often think of first when they hear of a biological theory. That's a shame—because it's been years if not decades since "biological" has meant "biologically deterministic."

Here, for example, is the opinion of Peter Ellison (1984), a sociobiological anthropologist at Harvard, writing in *Ethology and Sociobiology*:

> [Boas and his students] helped to reject . . . an incorrect application of evolutionary theory to human behavior, an application that equates "inherited" with "fixed" and "unresponsive to environmental differences." The modern view suggests that what is inherited is more like a complex equation relating behavior to social and ecological conditions. Such an "equation" is probably the common heritage of all members of the species. In this view, it is indeed the external conditions that determine the result, by a process which is, however, fully biological and presumptively the result of natural selection. This is in a conceptual sense very close to Boas' notion of "universal human nature." (p. 69)

Notice that Ellison, a sociobiologist writing for other sociobiologists, *takes it for granted* that today's biological theories are not as deterministic as those in Boas's time were.

Ellison's view is exactly what I was taught as a graduate student and exactly what I read in the writings of every sociobiologist whom I respect. In fact, modern evolutionary theories are only as biologically deterministic as the data require them to be. Some human facial expressions, for example, seem cross-culturally universal, and some experiments (see Ekman, 1973, for example) suggest that the universal ones are genetically determined. Apparently, it is also universal to classify other humans on the basis of kinship, although which kin classification system will be used is variable. A predisposition to speak language is another apparently genetically determined, essentially human trait, although which language is spoken or signed of course is not.

But such biological determinism is not the reflexive choice some people take it to be. As I will describe later, there are many sociobiological theories that do *not* require that genetically influenced behaviors be fixed or rigidly determined.

The Ladder of Evolution?

The next misconception has to do with the nature of evolutionary logic. Some people think that evolution is hierarchical, that there is an evolutionary ladder, with slugs and worms and other slimy things at the bottom and *MAN* at the top (see Figure 9.1).

In this view, evolutionary biologists make generalizations based on phylogeny, or evolutionary descent. Consider, for example, the hypothesis that males tend to have more sexual partners than females do. To test this phylogenetically, you would observe copulations in various groups of animals, beginning at the bottom of the phylogenetic ladder and work your way toward the top, hoping that you could find some generalization that applied to all the rungs.

Assuming that you succeeded in showing that as a rule males had more sexual partners than females did, you would look for a mechanism. You might try to show that testosterone has some effect on the brain—prenatally, postnatally, or whenever—and thereby causes pleasure centers in the brain to be connected to and stimulated by the parts of the brain that detect novel sexual partners. If you found this true in the so-

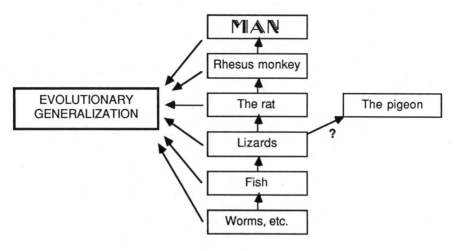

Figure 9.1.

called "lower" animals, you might cross your fingers and hope that it was true in humans, too.

This strategy is problematic because you can never be sure you've studied enough rungs of the ladder and because almost always the application to humans depends on an extrapolation—from the great body of observations to the last in a logical series. Extrapolations are always risky. Let me point out that although this view is presented in Figure 9.1 as a caricature, it really *is* valid in medicine, in physiology, and wherever you care about the underlying *mechanics* of behavior. Diseases, for example, often follow phylogenetic lines, and so do some hormonal mechanisms. In such contexts, an uncaricatured version of Figure 9.1 is appropriate.

But sociobiologists are not interested in the mechanics; they are instead interested in the *ultimate logic* of the behaviors under study, as I will explain in the next section. In sociobiology, the really exalted position is not held by any particular animal but by evolutionary theory (see Figure 9.2). There is no hierarchy and no necessity to depend only upon close relatives. Distantly related species can be similar in some *logical* way and thus test a single component of the theory. A theory is logically coherent and can be applied to many species across the animal kingdom because the logic should hold for every species on the face of the earth. Here the inference from animals to humans is not an extrapolation but an interpolation. The human case is, in some sense, *surrounded* by the cases of the other animal species. Interpolations are also risky, but not nearly as risky as extrapolations are.

Evolutionary Questions

At this point, let me pause to explain the questions evolutionary biologists ask. *Evolutionary biology* is the study of evolution by natural selection. Two

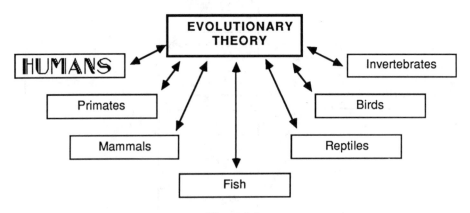

Figure 9.2.

branches of it are *ethology* and *sociobiology*, which ask slightly different questions about behavior.

First, there is the "What?" question, which simply asks what a behavior is. What happens? Under what circumstances? In what organisms or what societies? This is *natural history*, which interests both sociobiologists and ethologists.

Then there is the "Why?" question. Why did that organism do what it did? Why didn't it do something else? This is most interesting to sociobiologists, with ethologists following right behind.

Next, there is the "When?" question—when does this behavior start to occur in the organism's life, and when did it first occur in the course of evolution? This is more of interest to the ethologists.

And there is the "How?" question. How did it come about that a particular organism did a particular thing? How is the organism built to react to particular environments in particular ways? This question needs both sociobiology and ethology for a complete answer but is much more interesting to the ethologists.

Evolutionary theory is a connected body of hypothesis, experiment, and deduction—held together by simple logic—that explains why it makes sense for certain conditions of life to have particular evolutionary results. It is an attempt to answer the "Why?" question.

Think of the number-of-partners example. Sociobiologists don't care much about testosterone because it answers the "How?" question. Testosterone is part of a proximate physiological mechanism that itself is not really the cause of anything. God did not say, "Let there be testosterone, and let it be the cause of things." Instead, Darwin said, "Let me throw light on sexual selection," and testosterone was one of the results (generations later).

Sociobiologists think they know what one of the drivers of sexual selection is, and they call it *parental investment*, or *PI*—a term coined by sociobiologist Robert Trivers (1972). Trivers's parental investment theory says there is a relationship between the relative amounts of reproductive investment by each sex and several reproductive parameters, including the pattern of male and female partner seeking.

The theory *deduces* that the sex that invests more in offspring is the sex that will on average have fewer sexual partners. The sex that invests less in offspring will on average have more sexual partners. That is, the theory asks not How? but Why?

PI theory reasons that the sex that invests more in offspring will compete with other members of its sex for access to resources. If you are a member of the sex that invests more, then your reproductive success is limited by how much resource you can gather from the environment and turn into offspring, not by how many members of the other sex you can induce to mate with you (as long as one or two of them are available). But the sex that invests less in offspring will face a different picture; *their* reproductive success depends on finding members of the other sex willing to copulate with them. That is, they will compete with other members of their own sex for access to members of the sex that invests more.

This theory says nothing about phylogenetic descent and nothing about hormones or brain structures. It can be applied to any species on the face of the earth, so it is an extremely testable theory because it can be disproved by some weird little species of insect that only lives in the treetops near the Amazonian headwaters. And in fact the theory has spawned a minor industry as graduate students of particular weird little insects that live in Amazon-headwater treetops go out to the field to test it.

The theory is also gender neutral. Although usually it is females that invest more in offspring than males, this is not always the case. In species where females invest less than males, females should be the ones that have more sexual partners, and this seems to be so (see, for example, Petrie, 1983). In species where males and females invest about the same— humans, for example, and most birds—the difference in number of partners is expected to be fairly small and to be subtly influenced by a variety of environmental determinants. (For a more complete explanation, see Trivers, 1972, and Weinrich, 1987b, chap. 11.)

Now in order for this logic to go through, you *do* need some genetics, but you only need a little bit of genetics. In particular, you only need to believe that behavior can be influenced by genes that predispose those behaviors, at least in a probabilistic sense over evolutionary time. That is not an unreasonable hypothesis—even for human behavior. In fact, most reputable sociobiologists believe that the proportion of human behavior that is genetically predisposed is roughly the same as it is for any mammal (see Alcock, 1984; Konner, 1982; or Wilson, 1975, for chapter and verse on this point).

In sum, sociobiology is far more interested in the ultimate evolutionary logic of a particular trait than it is in the proximate mechanical question of how a particular behavior comes about.

Socialization and Culture

But what about socialization? What about culture? Don't they override genetic predispositions? Men *are* genetically predisposed to grow hair on their faces, but most American men override that predisposition every morning by performing an unnatural act in front of a mirror.

I don't have the space to give this point the attention it deserves. But there is a school in psychology that answers this question: the predisposition-in-learning work of people like John Garcia, Martin Seligman, James Kalat, and Paul Rozin. This school has shown that the laws of learning are *not* universal, that there are patterns in these laws, and that these patterns are exactly what one would expect from evolutionary theory (see Kalat, 1983; Lockard, 1971; and Seligman, 1970—for starters).

Animals, including humans, are *predisposed* to associate particular re-inforcers with particular kinds of stimuli—sometimes very strongly predis-posed.

It is easy to get pigeons to peck at a button that results in their getting food. But it is extremely difficult to get them to peck at a button in order to prevent themselves from getting an electric shock.

It is easy to teach cats to pull or push on something set up to open a door that is keeping them confined in a box. But it is extremely difficult to get them to lick themselves if that is what is set up to open the door.

It is easy to teach rats to avoid a stomach-upsetting X-ray dose by avoiding a certain flavor of food; it is nearly impossible to teach them to avoid the X ray by avoiding a certain size or shape of food. (For these three points, see Seligman, 1970.)

If you try to teach rats to choose, when presented with a set of similar items, the item different from the others, they don't do well when the items are pictures. But they do just fine if you give them the same kind of puzzle where the odd-man-out item differs in odor. Humans can easily choose the odd man out when the choices are pictures, but they don't do at all well with odors.

Horses and donkeys do a lot better than zebras do in most visual dis-criminations, but zebras do much better telling apart stripes of different widths. (For these two studies, see Kalat, 1983.)

When newly hatched chicks are shocked every time they approach their mother, they try harder and harder to reach her instead of staying away to avoid the shock (Kovach & Hess, 1963). This is because such chicks are preprogrammed to respond to such stress with attempts to seek help from their mother.

All these predispositions make perfect sense when you ask what the conditions were under which learning evolved. There is no reason, either theoretical or empirical, to believe that humans never evolved such predis-positions or that our tendencies toward them disappeared or became trivial the moment we acquired culture.

The Kinsey Scale and the Kinsey Plane [1]: Nature Versus Nurture?

By this point in this book, readers should be familiar with the one-dimensional *Kinsey scale* (see Figure 9.3), and its two-dimensional exten-sion, which I will call the *Kinsey plane* (see Figure 9.4).

You may also be familiar with the Bem scale of masculinity and feminin-ity, which inspired the Kinsey plane in the first place. The Bem scale can also inspire an idea in the philosophy of science. Let us make nature and nurture into two dimensions, also, and thus hasten the demise of the nature-versus-nurture debate by replacing it with a more flexible model (see Figure 9.5).

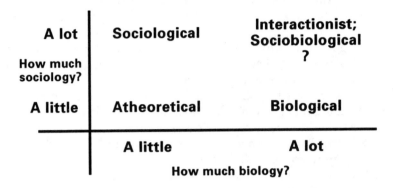

Figure 9.3.

Any given theory can be rated as to how biological it is and rated separately as to how sociological it is. In theory at least, these two ratings can be independent of each other; more biology in a theory does not necessarily mean less sociology, and vice versa. That means we can divide theories into four categories: biologically typed theories, sociologically typed theories, interdisciplinary theories, and atheoretical theories (the last category also known as "unpublishable").

Now one person or another may enjoy pushing theories in a particular direction. Biologists may want to push theories toward more biology, and sociologists toward more sociology. That's fine; the result may be a well-rounded interdisciplinary theory. But some people believe biology and sociology are opposites, as if a lot of biology in a theory means that there isn't any sociology in it, or as if a theory with no sociology in it can't get some without first throwing out any biology it might already have.

This is, of course, a fallacy. One place I see this fallacy working is in some of the early papers by Fred Whitam, a sociologist. He has taken the position that homosexuality is an orientation, not a preference (Whitam, 1977):

> While the term role usually implies prescriptions for behavior which have prior existence in the social structure, such prescriptions for homosexual behavior simply do not exist. While a role, as it is ordinarily understood, may be ascribed or achieved, children are neither socialized into the "homosexual role" nor do they ratio-

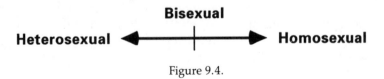

Figure 9.4.

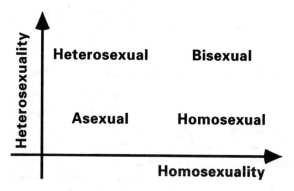

Figure 9.5.

nally choose it . . . Homosexuality is neither a [medical] "condition" nor a role but rather a sexual orientation and no useful theoretical purpose is served by regarding it as role behavior. (p. 1)

In this passage, Whitam falls for the either/or fallacy of nature versus nurture, biology versus culture; the phrase "neither . . . nor . . . but rather" gives him away.

Another place I see this fallacy is in the paper Whitam was attacking, sociologist Mary McIntosh's article on homosexuality as a social role. "The current conceptualization of homosexuality as a condition is a false one, resulting from ethnocentric bias. Homosexuality should be seen rather as a social role" (1968, p. 182).

Again, it is one little word—*rather*—that shows that McIntosh is seeing theories in one-dimensional terms, as roles *versus* conditions. So McIntosh and Whitam both have an inaccurate perception of what a biological theory is these days.

All right then, what *is* a biological theory? It's time to get specific.

Evolution's Questions

Sociobiology is interested in "Why?" questions that have an *adaptationist* answer. That is, sociobiologists begin by asking how the behavior might have been adaptive in the evolutionary past. Did individuals exhibiting the behavior have a higher reproductive success compared with individuals who did not? At first it seems paradoxical, but sociobiologists apply this approach to homosexuality just as they do to heterosexuality. Evolutionarily speaking, sociobiologists first look for what went right instead of what went wrong.

Sociobiological models of homosexuality have been advanced by Wilson, Spieth, and Trivers, by Kirsch and Rodman, by Lorenz, and by myself. Unorthodox sociobiological models have been proposed by Hutchinson, by Alexander, by Gallup and Suarez, and by Symons; these theories are "unorthodox" sociobiological because most do not hypothesize adaptation.

Trivers/Spieth/Wilson: Cross-Gender Homosexuality?

The Trivers/Spieth/Wilson model explains homosexuality in terms of a theory called *kin selection*. Without kin selection, evolution supposedly maximizes the number of offspring one has. With kin selection, natural selection reflects not only direct descendants but also indirect descendants. Genes permitting, predisposing, or causing a homosexual orientation in their carriers can increase under the action of natural selection if the homosexuals act reproductively "altruistically" enough to increase their *relatives'* reproductive success (RS), even at a cost to their own. That is, a reproductively altruistic act by definition increases someone else's RS (say, by an amount B, on average) at a cost to one's own RS (call it C). The theory of kin selection says that predispositions to perform such acts will spread under the action of natural selection if the predisposition is of a particular form. If the predisposition is to perform acts in which the benefit is large in relation to the cost, in particular, in which

$$B \times r > C,$$

then there will be a net benefit to the genes predisposing the individual to perform the act in the first place. (By definition, r is the *degree of relatedness* between the two individuals involved; think of it as the probability that a given individual shares the same gene as the person performing the act.)

Let me give an example. In Chapter 13 of this volume Herdt explains how there are three general patterns, cross-culturally, in homosexual behavior: the cross-gender pattern, the older/younger pattern, and the role-specialized pattern. The kin-selection theory of homosexuality fits the cross-gender pattern especially well.

It happens that there are animal species in which individuals of one sex perform acts usually or typically associated with the other sex. That's a paper in itself (Weinrich, 1980), but the point is there are species with a lot of cross-gender behavior, and there are also species with little or no cross-gender behavior. Sociobiologists ask, *why* are humans the kind of species in which cross-gender behavior is fairly common instead of the kind of species in which this is out of the question? And sociobiologists begin their answer by suggesting that it was probably reproductively advantageous for humans to be able to gender-nonconform under the appropriate circumstances.

Here is one model applying in a so-called primitive society in which a bride-price is paid. In bride-price societies marriage is very expensive for the groom; he and his extended family pay a carefully negotiated and very substantial sum to the bride's family, which distributes it along kin lines.

But what about those particular families that are unlikely to be able to raise a bride-price? Or those particular sons who, through injury or whatever reason, are especially unlikely to be able to raise a family? Such a family might benefit from a son who takes up the role of a girl because it would turn his marital liability into an asset. In the case of a poor family, the benefit to the extended family—the B, if you will—of having a son take the role of a daughter would be especially large. In the second case, the cost of the son's foregoing reproduction—the C—would be especially small. In either case, the probability that B would be greater than r times C for this particular son in this particular family would be especially high. *Anything*—genetic, cultural, or whatever—that favors sons wanting to act like daughters in such situations would become more likely by natural selection. Many societies allow this; among American Indians, anthropologists call this role the *berdache*.

Well, what about the family that pays the bride-price in such a marriage? What do they get out of it, evolutionarily speaking?

These societies are typically polygamous, and the berdache wives are typically the second or third wives of a man who already has some female wives. Theory predicts that the bride-price for a berdache would be lower than that for a reproductively capable genetic female, because the husband is only getting one of the two things that wives are valued for (these men say), work but not children.

Thus in some societies, accepting a man in the social role of a woman might be consistent with evolutionary theory for every person in the culture. That does not mean that it always *will* be, of course, but because of Wilson, Spieth, Trivers, and some elaborations by myself, it is no longer obvious that homosexuality runs counter to evolution.

These models, as they were originally presented, could be criticized from the point of view of the Kinsey plane, because they seem to imply that not taking up the role of a man means you have to take up the role of a woman instead. Well, in many societies it really is associated in that way, but this is not an essential hypothesis. The theory doesn't really require less masculinity in the berdache, just an increased amount of femininity—as defined by the culture. And in fact if you read these anthropological accounts carefully, you will find lots of cases where aspects of the male gender role are still subtly woven into the berdache's life. So it is easy to revise these kin-selection gender-nonconformity theories to take account of the Kinsey plane. However, I admit that the improvements gained by this would not be particularly spectacular.

Weinrich: Everyone Marries

There is another theory that meshes better with the Kinsey plane. It's one I've proposed (Weinrich, 1987a). It applies to societies that prescribe that everyone marry. What does "homosexuality" mean when parents arrange marriages and love is not presumed to be the basis of marriage? It would seem in this case that sexual orientation would range not from heterosexual to homosexual but from heterosexual to bisexual.

In a society like this, "homosexuality" means the homosexual axis of the Kinsey plane. Everyone is high on the heterosexuality axis, but people's behavior varies along the homosexuality axis. So homosexuality affects not so much whether you marry but whom you have sex with outside of marriage. If you are homosexual, you have affairs with people of the same sex as you. If you are heterosexual, you have affairs with the other sex.

In this kind of society, homosexuals and heterosexuals differ in two important ways of sociobiological interest. First, homosexuals would be involved in fewer extramarital pregnancies, all other things being equal. If universal-marriage societies are hard on illegitimacy, then extramarital pregnancies are especially troublesome, and this aspect is especially important.

Second, homosexuals would probably be less unwilling to marry the partner their parents have chosen for them. Heterosexuals, after all, might fall in love with someone other than the person their parents want them to marry, and this can cause a lot of conflict. But homosexuals would not expect to marry someone they are in love with, and so they ought to be more willing to go along with the choice their parents have arranged.

It turns out that both these suggestions have the same sociobiological consequence. They imply that homosexuals, in comparison with heterosexuals, are more reproductively altruistic. Trivers (1974) proposed, in a classic paper, that there is a fundamental sociobiological reason why parents and offspring are in conflict: the reproductive interests of parents would be better served if offspring would act more altruistically than the offspring themselves would find in their own best self-interests. He demonstrated this by a simple algebraic argument, for which there is not enough space here.

But in this paper, Trivers listed several traits involved in parent-offspring conflict—some of them subtle or surprising ones. One of those traits is refraining from extramarital reproduction when it is available, and another is being willing to marry the spouse your parents desire rather than the one who would maximize your own genetic interests. In short, in just the ways we deduced that homosexuals would differ from heterosexuals in a society in which everyone marries, Trivers said those ways constitute reproductive altruism.

So in this theory, homosexuality remains a reproductively altruistic trait; it is just that the magnitude of the altruism is smaller than in the cross-gender theory. That makes it easier to satisfy the $B \times r > C$ inequality. This theory also meshes very well with the Kinsey plane, calling attention to the fact that homosexual acts do not preclude heterosexual ones. This theory, by the way, fits the older/younger model better than the cross-gender model, for reasons I don't have space to explain.

KIRSCH AND RODMAN: HETEROZYGOTE ADVANTAGE

Now let's move on to Kirsch and Rodman's theory (Kirsch & Rodman, 1982). This one bridges the gap between the adaptationist models and the nonadaptationist ones. It hypothesizes the highest reproductive success for *bi*sexuals who are hetero*zygous* for a gene supposed to influence sexual orientation. Pure heterosexuals and pure homosexuals are inevitably produced by recombination.

The genetics in this model are analogous to those of sickle-cell anemia, which everyone learns about in high school. In its simplest form, Kirsch and Rodman's theory sets out some hypotheses: (1) there exists a gene or genes that tend to promote heterosexual reproduction, (2) there exists a gene or genes that tend to promote homosexual activity, and (3) people who get one copy of each kind of gene have higher reproductive success than those who get two genes of the same kind. Then the genetics of heterozygote advantage (or hybrid vigor) suggest that both kinds of genes will be maintained in the population, as the inevitable result of recombination taking place after selection for heterozygosity.

This theory is obviously the most genetically deterministic of those I have presented so far, but it fits the Kinsey plane like hand in glove. The Kinsey plane suggests that heterosexuality and homosexuality are empirically and theoretically independent of each other, and Kirsch and Rodman suggest that they are genetically independent, too.

Kirsch and Rodman developed their theory after reading an obscure paper by the evolutionary biologist G. E. Hutchinson (1959), who had the idea of applying heterozygote advantage to homosexuality but not the adaptationist idea explaining why heterozygotes would have a higher RS. Indeed, how might it happen that heterozygotes have a reproductive advantage? Well, in the everyone-gets-married theory, for example, people with the highest RS may be those with enough heterosexuality to get married and enough homosexuality to get some profitable extra-marital alliances going—but not so much as would produce illegitimate offspring. So Kirsch and Rodman's model fits the everyone-gets-married model pretty well. Hutchinson took care of the "How?" question, and Kirsch and Rodman answered the "Why?" question.

Social Consequences and Meta-Scientific Implications

Now I want to talk a bit about the meta-science in these theories. The fact that Kinsey assigned a positive number, 6, to the homosexual end of his scale, and a big fat 0 to the heterosexual end, was a signal, maybe an unconscious signal, that he did not want a theory that merely supported the status quo. Masculinity-femininity scales, for example, usually give high numbers to masculine scores and low numbers to feminine scores (as in the MMPI), and many feminists consider this a dead giveaway.

Sociobiologists and adaptation are like Kinsey and the Kinsey scale in this respect. It is a matter of historical record that sociobiologists first tried to explain homosexuality with exactly the same kinds of models they used to explain heterosexuality: adaptationist models. Neither Wilson, nor Trivers, nor Spieth, nor any other sociobiologist I knew from the early days ever flinched at such models. They did not hem and haw when they lectured about homosexuality, and they did not hesitate to choose words with "nice" associations such as "adaptive" or "kinship" in the same breath as they mentioned "homosexuality." They never got sheepish, never said anything like, "of course I don't mean to imply that homosexuals are *socially* altrustic," or anything like that.

Even worse, they described heterosexual reproduction as reproductively "selfish" because reproductive selfishness is defined as that which increases one's own RS—and having children usually does increase RS. No scientists with conservative politics dictating their terminology would let a nice word like "altruistic" be applied to homosexuals or let raising your own children be described as "selfish!"

It is fashionable, in this skeptical age, to claim that scientists always have a hidden agenda, usually the preservation of the status quo. But in the case of homosexuality and sociobiology, that claim is clearly false in the sense that the pioneers' behavior is far better explained by the old-fashioned pursuit of truth than it is by the hypothesis that they were merely promoting their personal prejudices.

Now although sociobiologists have a very good record, politically speaking, when it comes to homosexuality, it is not perfect by any means. In fact, maladaptationist models of homosexuality have appeared. I call them sociobiologically unorthodox models because they all conspicuously *fail* to hypothesize that homosexuality is in some way adaptive. Maladaptive theories of homosexuality have been proposed by Hutchinson (as I've already mentioned), by Alexander, by Gallup and Suarez, and by Symons.

MALADAPTIVE SOCIOBIOLOGICAL MODELS

Richard Alexander suggested that homosexuality might be a mistake, an accidental dead end resulting from selection for heterosexuality. That is, your own sex is what you settle for if you fail in the struggle to obtain a sufficiently good partner of the other sex. This idea has never been published outright. It was a suggestion Alexander made in a letter to a colleague, who was intrigued by it and brought it to the attention of a philosopher, who described it in a paper of his own (Ruse, 1981). To call this theory "obscure" is an understatement.

Gallup and Suarez (1983) made a similar suggestion, apparently unaware of Alexander's letter, but they were only able to publish it in an out-of-the-way journal. This paper is full of elementary logical errors and miscomprehensions of evolutionary theory that any decently trained graduate student could rebut.

Hutchinson (1959), as I mentioned, had a theory that theoretically compared homosexuality to heterozygote advantage. You can think of this as maladaptive in one sense, but it is easy to put this theory in an adaptive context, as Kirsch and Rodman (1982) did. Incidentally, Hutchinson got thinking about his theory as a result of reading the Kinsey *Male* volume, which showed homosexuality to be at a level far too high to be explained as a mutation or genetic mistake.

And Symons (1979) seems to have a theory of homosexuality, but it is a theory of omission. Symons views homosexuals as having the sexual traits that heterosexual men and women would have if they didn't have to put up with members of the other sex. That is, that homosexuals are more like members of their own sex than they are like members of the other sex, and that's all there is to it. Of course, there is much truth in this. But it is not the whole story because there are some well-established respects in which homosexuals on average are more like the other sex than they are like their own (childhood gender roles, for example). So I conclude that homosexuals are more like members of their own sex than they are like members of the other sex, *except when they're not*. As a generalization this is fine; as a falsifiable hypothesis it stinks.

The conclusion? When maladaptationist theories of homosexuality have been proposed within sociobiology, they haven't gotten very far, and rightfully so. Not everything is adaptive, but those things that are maladaptive are not very interesting, sociobiologically speaking.

Ethological Models

Now let me move on to ethology. Ethology asks the "When?" question and uses behavior to classify animal species by phylogenetic relatedness. The biology in the Kinsey *Male* and *Female* volumes is mostly ethology, for example. Kinsey was using an ethological approach when he argued that if a trait is widely distributed among our animal ancestors and animal relatives, then it is not fair to call similar human traits "unnatural." This argument is by phylogenetic descent; it is a "When?" question. It can be a good argument, but it is always tricky.

The most important ethological explanation of homosexuality was designed to answer the "How?" question. It is Konrad Lorenz's imprinting hypothesis that animals can imprint upon an atypical object (in infancy or a bit later) that turns out to be the sexually attractive object in adulthood. This raises the clear possibility that human homosexuals have imprinted upon a member of their own sex.

Lorenz found that it is not difficult to get male geese, at least, to imprint on other males in the juvenile period, so that when they grow up they seek males in courtship. This, along with the reports of female-female pair-bonds in the wild in some shorebirds (Hunt & Hunt, 1977), strongly suggests to me that birds are the best animal model of human homosexual pair-bonding—preferential homosexuality, if you will, because these animals bond with a member of their own sex over the space of more than one breeding season and do so even when members of the other sex are available. After all, if a species has no heterosexual pair-bonds, you're unlikely to find homosexual pair-bonds in it, either. Over 90% of bird species are, heterosexually speaking, at least as monogamous as humans are. So I suspect that more homosexual pair-bonds will be discovered in birds than in any other group of species.

As it happens, Lorenz had an explanation of how homosexual pair-bonds could be adaptive. He said in an interview (Evans, 1974) that a certain species of bird in Iceland formed male-male pair-bonds. Since males in this species are better fighters than females, a male-male pair could defend offspring from neighboring birds better than a male-female pair could. As it happens, cannibalism is common in many such shorebird species. So if the hatchling-to-fledgling success rate was more than double that of a heterosexual pair, natural selection could favor the formation of male-male pair-bonds, as long as there were unattached females around to insert themselves in between copulating males from time to time.

But alas, the naturalist who studied those birds in Iceland wrote to me that he had never sexed his birds, so he could not say whether the pair-bonds he saw were male-female, male-male, or female-female. (As predicted by PI theory for a monogamous species, the sexes are difficult to tell apart.) This sets Lorenz's theory back to square one, of course, but it underscores my point: adaptationism flows from the nature of evolutionary biology itself—even if it turns out to be wrong!—and does not depend upon the whim of any particular scholar. Ethologists and sociobiologists propose adaptive theories of homosexuality not because they're nice and not because they're trying to look like liberals; they propose adaptationist theories because that's what their disciplines are all about.

The Kinsey Scale and the Kinsey Plane [2]:
Social Consequences and Conclusions

Now it is time to return to point 4, social consequences. Sociobiology has social consequences, but they have not been those the cynics would predict. After all, a discipline focusing so strongly on reproduction might be expected to produce very unpleasant explanations of homosexuality. But biology has in fact produced just the opposite. How come?

Everyone knows that science is a social enterprise. It has social consequences, and it has hidden social assumptions. But what if scientific objectivity and social responsibility are not opposites but rather two separate dimensions? Then evidence that a hypothesis has social consequences is independent of our assessment of how scientifically unbiased it is.

Truly unbiased theories of sexual orientation should have certain properties. Unbiased theories should make predictions in which one sexual orientation gets the short end of the stick about as often as any other sexual orientation does. Now in a society that stigmatizes a particular sexual orientation, the actual distribution of such theories can be skewed by the sympathies of particular scientists, consciously or unconsciously. Many theories from the social sciences, for example, see homosexuality as an example of what can go wrong on the rocky road to heterosexuality, and in that respect leave a bad taste in your mouth. In contrast, sociobiological and ethological theories leave a good taste in your mouth.

So let's ask, are scientists as vigorous investigating and disseminating the controversial theories as they are the uncontroversial ones? At the very least, are they as willing to state controversial hypotheses as uncontroversial ones?

I hope it is clear that when it comes to sociobiology, the answer is yes. And for at least one pioneer invited to this symposium, the answer was also yes. Here is one example from her work published in the 1950s.

> It comes as no surprise that some homosexuals are severely disturbed, and, indeed, so much so that the hypothesis might be entertained that the homosexuality is a defense against open psychosis. But what is difficult to accept (for most clinicians) is that some homosexuals *may* be very ordinary individuals, indistinguishable, except in sexual pattern, from ordinary individuals who are heterosexual. Or—and I do not know whether this would be more or less difficult to accept—that some *may* be quite superior individuals, not only devoid of pathology but also functioning at a superior level.

This quotation is, of course, from Evelyn Hooker (1957, p. 29), and it is as true today—and as brave—as it was back in 1957.

It's brave because, alas, there are scientists today—even some openly gay scientists—who are scared of setting out all three of the logical possibilities: worse than, the same as, and better than. I know of one researcher, for example, who found in a survey that gay students reported a higher grade-point average than straight students did; this researcher *himself* took out the finding from his paper before it was published. I know of other researchers who were quick to describe the homosexual subculture as impoverished compared to ethnic subcultures, but they didn't look around very carefully to see if there are other respects in which it is richer.

Hooker was right. Homosexuals can do better, the same as, or worse than heterosexuals on any given task. Where homosexuals really do do worse than heterosexuals, in a biased society it is likely that these tasks have already been looked into. I don't know if it really is true that homosexuals have more pathological relationships with their parents than heterosexuals do, but the question has certainly been investigated, to the tune of millions of dollars. Where homosexuals might have done better, in contrast, scholars have not exactly rushed into print.

But some fraction of these gay-positive hypotheses *must* be true, presumably just as some of the gay-negative hypotheses must be true. If we assume that most of the gay-negative ones have already been looked into, we can deduce that gay-positive hypotheses right now promise a higher scholarly rate of return than gay-negative hypotheses do.

Sociobiologists have been in the lead in proposing such theories, for reasons that have less to do with social factors than with the scientific nature of sociobiology itself. Sociobiologists are not perfect, but in my humble (and obviously unbiased!) opinion they have been, so far, way above average. In that respect, their work on homosexuality resembles the pioneering work of Kinsey and Hooker—although sociobiology in general is not as obviously sexological, and thus probably not as risky to one's career. For all these reasons, I have been delighted to introduce you to it in this chapter.

References

Alcock, J. (1984). *Animal behavior: An evolutionary approach* (3rd ed.). Sunderland, MA: Sinauer Associates.

Ekman, P. (Ed.). (1973). *Darwin and facial expression: A century of research in review.* New York: Academic Press.

Ellison, P. T. (1984). Book review. [Review of *Margaret Mead and Samoa: The making and unmaking of an anthropological myth*]. *Ethology and Sociobiology, 5*, 69–70.

Evans, R. I. (1974). Lorenz warns: "Man must know that the horse he is riding may be wild and should be bridled." *Psychology Today, 8*(6), 82–93.

Gallup, G. G., Jr., & Suarez, S. D. (1983). Homosexuality as a by-product of selection for optimal heterosexual strategies. *Perspectives in Biology and Medicine, 26*, 315–322.

Hooker, E. A. (1957). The adjustment of the male overt homosexual. *Journal of Projective Techniques, 21*, 17–31.

Hunt, G. L., Jr., & Hunt, M. W. (1977). Female-female pairing in western gulls (*Larus occidentalis*) in southern California. *Science, 196*, 1466–1467.

Hutchinson, G. E. (1959). A speculative consideration of certain possible forms of sexual selection in man. *American Naturalist, 93*, 81–91.

Kalat, J. W. (1983). Evolutionary thinking in the history of the comparative psychology of learning. *Neuroscience and Biobehavioral Reviews, 7*, 309–314.

Kinsey, A. C. (1926). *An introduction to biology*. Philadelphia: J. B. Lippincott.

Kinsey, A. C. (1937). An evolutionary analysis of insular and continental species. *Proceedings of the National Academy of Sciences, 23*, 5–11.

Kirsch, J. A. W., & Rodman, J. E. (1982). Selection and sexuality: The Darwinian view of homosexuality. In W. Paul, J. D. Weinrich, J. C. Gonsiorek, & M. E. Hotvedt (Eds.), *Homosexuality: Social, psychological, and biological issues* (pp. 183–195). Beverly Hills, CA: Sage.

Konner, M. (1982). *The tangled wing: Biological constraints on the human spirit*. New York: Holt, Rinehart & Winston.

Kovach, J. K., & Hess, E. H. (1963). Imprinting: Effects of painful stimulation upon the following response. *Journal of Comparative and Physiological Psychology, 56*, 461–464.

Lockard, R. B. (1971). Reflections on the fall of comparative psychology: Is there a message for us all? *American Psychologist, 26,* 168–179.

McIntosh, M. (1968). The homosexual role. *Social Problems, 16,* 182–192.

Petrie, M. (1983). Female moorhens compete for small fat males. *Science, 220,* 413–415.

Robinson, P. (1976). *The modernization of sex.* New York: Harper & Row.

Ruse, M. (1981). Are there gay genes? Sociobiology and homosexuality. *Journal of Homosexuality, 6*(4), 5–34.

Seligman, M. E. P. (1970). On the generality of the laws of learning. *Psychological Review, 77,* 406–418.

Symons, D. (1979). *The evolution of human sexuality.* New York/Oxford: Oxford University Press.

Trivers, R. L. (1972). Parental investment and sexual selection. In B. Campbell (Ed.), *Sexual selection and the descent of man 1871–1971* (pp. 136–179). Chicago: Aldine.

Trivers, R. L. (1974). Parent-offspring conflict. *American Zoologist, 14,* 249–264.

Weinrich, J. D. (1980). Homosexual behavior in animals: A new review of observations from the wild, and their relationship to human homosexuality. In R. Forleo & W. Pasini (Eds.), *Medical sexology: The Third International Congress* (pp. 288–295). Littleton MA: PSG Publishing.

Weinrich, J. D. (1987a). A new sociobiological theory of homosexuality applicable to societies with universal marriage. *Ethology and Sociobiology, 8,* 37–47.

Weinrich, J. D. (1987b). *Sexual landscapes: Why we are what we are, why we love whom we love.* New York: Charles Scribner's Sons.

Whitam, F. L. (1977). The homosexual role: A reconsideration. *Journal of Sex Research, 13,* 1–11.

Wilson, E. O. (1975). *Sociobiology: The new synthesis.* Cambridge, MA: Harvard University Press.

10

Homosexual Behavior in Nonhuman Primates

Ronald D. Nadler.

The purpose of this chapter is to identify examples of homosexual behavior in nonhuman primates, determine the conditions under which they occur, and assess the usefulness of the data for insight into a possible biological basis for human homosexual behavior. It is important to emphasize that the domain of discourse is sexual behavior, not sexuality and not other forms of social behavior. Although this may represent a narrow perspective in the context of human homosexuality, to do otherwise in the case of nonhuman primates would raise considerable, if not insurmountable, problems of definition. This approach is supported, moreover, by the fact that it focuses on the behavior that distinquishes homosexual from heterosexual. That it is not entirely satisfactory is readily acknowledged.

There is a major difficulty inherent in defining homosexual behavior in nonhuman primates as a consequence of the somewhat less difficult but still present problem of defining what is (or what is not) heterosexual behavior in these species. These difficulties arise in part because behavioral patterns such as mounting and presenting, conspicuous elements of reproductive behavior in most nonhuman primates, also occur in situations deemed by most primatologists to have little or no direct sexual significance. As will be indicated, the early investigators of sexual behavior in nonhuman primates dealt with this problem more-or-less successfully. The approach taken in this chapter is to examine the reports that include or purport to include evidence of homosexual behavior and determine which ones meet the criteria proposed herein.

Homosexual behavior in nonhuman primates is defined as behavioral interactions between same-sex individuals that include (1) persistent genital stimulation (i.e., more than perfunctory), and (2) sexual arousal, in at least one of the individuals involved. Genital stimulation is usually observable, whereas sexual arousal is usually inferred from certain physiological and behavioral responses, especially, but not limited to, those responses that have been identified in the literature as components of the species-typical pattern of reproductive behavior. In the male, these components include penile erection, mounting with intromission, and pelvic thrusting and ejaculation. In the female, the most conspicuous component during heterosexual mating is presenting, either receptive, in response to a mount attempt, or proceptive, when observed spontaneously, in the absence of overt initiative by another individual. Homosexual behavior in nonhuman primates is therefore defined, in part, by the degree to which behavior between same-sex individuals resembles the typical heterosexual mating pattern of the species. The more closely the resemblance to the species-typical mating pattern and the more persistent the genital stimulation, the more confidence one has that the behavior includes sexual arousal. In general, confidence regarding the presence of sexual arousal in either sex is greater for the initiator of an interaction than for the recipient, for the mounter than for the mountee. The initiator, whether male or female, is usually the more active partner, and heightened sexual arousal is associated with heightened activity. An example of this relationship is seen in laboratory pair tests of heterosexual behavior in nonhuman primates, in which proceptive behavior is a more reliable indication of sexual arousal in the female than is receptive behavior (Nadler, Herndon, & Wallis, 1986). An ejaculatory pattern by a male (or its homologue in females of certain species), moreover, is a conspicuous indication of sexual arousal that occurs primarily in the mounter, whereas the responses of the mountee are generally more ambiguous.

In addition to using the components of reproductive behavior as indications of sexual arousal in nonhuman primates, there must be added other forms of genital stimulation between partners, such as ano-genital and oro-genital configurations and masturbation of another. Although these forms occur less frequently in natural than in captive conditions, they generally reflect sexual arousal and, as such, fall within the purview of the present review.

The foregoing criterion of resemblance to reproductive behavior is a more reliable indication for inferring sexual arousal of mature rather than immature nonhuman primates. Immature animals, although physiologically incapable of performing complete patterns of sexual activity, do perform some of the components of adult reproductive behavior. The same criterion is applied to immature individuals, with the understanding that the difference between sexual and nonsexual social behavior is smaller than in the adult, and hence the determination of sexual arousal is less certain.

Research on homosexual behavior in nonhuman primates is characterized by an early period of active interest from 1914 to 1942, followed by a
period of little or no investigation until the current era, beginning during
the late 1960s. The early period was stimulated by the initial introduction of
nonhuman primates into research on reproductive biology and by the controversy between some anthropologists and psychoanalysts of whether the
human being is unique in the animal world with respect to the regulation of
its sexual behavior. The anthropologist's position, as represented by
Malinowski (1927), maintained that the sexual behavior of all nonhuman
species is characterized by periods of "rut" or "heat," whereas, human
sexual behavior is not influenced by such physiological constraints but is
regulated instead by cultural factors. This assessment led the anthropologists to reject the proposal that research on nonhuman primates could
contribute to an understanding of human sexuality. On the other side,
there were those who, on the basis of some early reports, maintained that
there is continuity between human and nonhuman primate behavior and
that research on sexual behavior of the nonhuman primates reveals evidence on the origins of human sexual behavior, for example, "some zoological aspects of sex . . . are now given the place that they demand in specula-
tions bearing on these beginnings" (Miller, 1928, p. 273).

Early Research on Macaques, Baboons, and Chimpanzees

Foremost in Miller's (1928) thinking about the origins of human sexuality
were the results of a study carried out by Hamilton (1914), probably the
first "experimental" study on sexual behavior in nonhuman primates.
This and the other studies of the early period are described in some detail
because they established the conceptual basis for much of the research
that was to follow. They also illustrate the methodological problems encountered in such research, some of which are only now being resolved
by primatologists who are pursuing similar objectives (Beach, 1976; Bernstein, 1970; Goy, Wallen, & Goldfoot, 1974; Pomerantz and Goy, 1983;
Wallen, Winston, Gaventa, Davis-DaSilva, & Collins, 1984).

Hamilton's (1914) strong conviction regarding the value of the comparative approach for resolving human sexual problems is illustrated by his
assessment that "we still lack that knowledge of infrahuman sexual life
without which we may scarcely hope to arrive at adequately comprehensive conceptions of abnormal human sexual behavior" (p. 295). He sus-
pected that certain types of behavior that were then considered to be
abnormal "may be of normal manifestation and biologically appropriate
somewhere in the phyletic scale" (p. 295). He proposed that homosexual
behavior, in particular, was "a problem the solution of which awaits, first
of all, biological knowledge of homosexuality, which only the behaviorist
can supply" (p. 295).

Hamilton (1914) maintained a group of 20 monkeys—18 macaques, rhesus (*Macaca mulatta*), and cynomologus (*M. fascicularis*) and two baboons (*Papio sp.*) with which he conducted a series of "laboratory tests." Although most of the tests involved heterosexual pairs, several were conducted with animals of the same sex. Hamilton reported that several male castrates in his colony and a sexually immature male preferred "homosexual copulation" to copulation with females but that even the most dominant (intact) male exhibited such behavior on occasion, albeit less frequently than he engaged in heterosexual relations. Only a single case of homosexual relations between females was reported, that of a mother mounting a daughter following a year of separation. Hamilton concluded that homosexual behavior occurs frequently among male monkeys "even when opportunities for heterosexual intercourse are present" (p. 317).

Hamilton recognized two motives for homosexual behavior engaged in by the immature male monkeys: (1) a "sexual hunger" and (2) a means of defense or of recruiting the aid of an older, more dominant male. The lower frequency of male/male mounting behavior he observed in his adult males led him to conclude that male monkeys in their natural habitat probably abandon homosexual activity altogether when they reach sexual maturity. He proposed that females exhibit homosexual behavior primarily in response to threat and only rarely as a reflection of affection or of sexual arousal. As to the biological significance of his results, Hamilton proposed that homosexual behavior in immature males might serve several adaptive functions. In addition to the protection that such behavior might afford against attack, homosexual behavior might also serve as practice for adult heterosexual copulation.

It is apparent that Hamilton was able to distinguish several classes of mounting behavior in his monkeys despite the fact that he considered them all to be sexual. It is also apparent, from our present vantage point, that much of the mounting behavior he described as "homosexual copulation," that is, copulation associated with sexual arousal, probably was not so associated.

It is common practice among primatologists today to define as sexual only those mounts that contain clear indications of sexual arousal and to define other types of mounts as social mounts, the specific significance of which is defined on the basis of other contextual factors inherent in the interactions. In the early studies on nonhuman primates, however, the criteria for distinguishing among mounts were not clearly established because of inadequate knowledge of the species' behavioral repertoire and a limited perspective on the conceptual issues involved. As a result, some of the data purported to reflect "sexual hunger" undoubtedly relate to hierarchical interactions. Similarly, the "homosexual behavior" described by Hamilton as "prostitution" or the "offering of sexual favors" is readily recognized, from the accompanying descriptions provided, as submissive or appeasement behavior.

It is not clear from Hamilton's study, therefore, whether any of the "homosexual copulation" reported can be considered to be homosexual behavior in the sense of reflecting sexual arousal. As indicated in later sections of this paper, it was not until the research of Zuckerman (1932/ 1981) and Maslow (1936) that resolution of these issues was begun.

Kempf (1917), who, like Hamilton, was a psychotherapist, shared Hamilton's view regarding the value of comparative research on nonhuman primates for advancing our understanding of human sexual behavior, especially behavior considered to be aberrant. He proposed that in the monkey "we find man's phylogenetic determinants completely exposed" (p. 129).

Kempf studied a group of six rhesus monkeys, consisting of one immature female and five males, for a period of eight months. Like Hamilton, he observed mounting between males, but in this case, the mounting apparently included anal penetration and ejaculation. "Insertion of the penis into the anus was finally made, followed by rapid strokes and kissing of the lips until mild general convulsive movements resulted" (pp. 134–135). Kempf also recognized that all mounting was not sexually arousing. He considered presenting, in the absence of any clear stimulus, that is, spontaneous, to reflect a sexual motive. On the other hand, brief presenting in response to a fight and followed by the presenter's running away, he interpreted as defensive. If while running away, the animal exposed its teeth, Kempf thought this revealed anger as well as fear.

Kempf's limited experience in interpreting the behavior of his monkeys, however, is illustrated by his description of the subordinate animal in the group, which was frequently attacked by the others. "He would often *chuckle with delight* when he procured food, even though it fatally revealed his success to his companions" (p. 129, italics added). Most primatologists today would identify such behavior as an indication of fear and/or subordination. Kempf, moreover, did not specify which instances of mounting included anal penetration and ejaculation, making it impossible for the reader to judge its relative frequency in comparison to nonintromissive and probably social mounts. Also pertinent to the interpretation of his results, is the fact that the group of monkeys that he studied was essentially an all-male group. The "support" for his conclusion that a homosexual stage is the normal antecedent to a heterosexual stage in the development of individual males must therefore be viewed with more skepticism.

Kohler (1925) was another among the earliest investigators to report on homosexual behavior in nonhuman primates, in his case, common chimpanzees (*Pan troglodytes*). However, he recognized that his observations were inadequate for drawing any strong conclusions about such behavior in chimpanzees, generally, because there were no fully adult males in the group he observed. He reported that immature males and females mounted and thrusted on other immature animals of the same sex and that mature females, during maximal genital swelling, that is, during estrus, pressed themselves against one another so as to effect "mutual friction." Kohler proposed that this latter behavior by the mature females represented sexual substitution due to the absence of mature males. He maintained in addition, however, that what frequently appeared to be sexual behavior among the chimpanzees was a rather diffuse response "which can hardly be classed definitely under either the category of joyous and cordial welcome, or that of sexual intimacy" (p. 303). He proposed that such behavior also frequently reflected reassurance or consolation or occurred "just because life is so jolly" (p. 384). Later research on common chimpanzees in the wild (though provisioned) state (van Lawick-Goodall, 1968) suggests that some portions of Kohler's interpretations were quite accurate, for example, "Distinctly sexual approaches often actually appear as friendly greetings between these creatures" (p. 304). That Kohler's conservative assessment of the genital-stimulating behavior he observed was more astute than that of Kempf is suggested further by his interpretation of the chimpanzees' emotional expressions (which could well have been directed specifically at Kempf), for example, "the expression of a slight degree of fear is often mistaken for mirth, a great fear for rage" (p. 306).

Another study of common chimpanzees, this one a longitudinal study on the development of sexual behavior in four wild-born, captive immature animals, was conducted by the insightful psychologist Bingham. Bingham (1928) proposed that the various components of adult sexual behavior can be observed in very young chimpanzees but that they lack integration into a functional pattern as seen in adults. He observed pelvic thrusting in the ventro-ventral as well as the dorso-ventral position between the two young females he studied, with the more dominant female assuming the superior role in the dorso-ventral position. In another context, he had also observed dorso-ventral pelvic thrusting between two mature females, and in the same animals, a single example of genito-genital stimulation while the females stood quadrapedally, facing in opposite directions. This latter behavior occurred in the absence of any adult male chimpanzees, but the condition of the females' genital swellings during either of these activities, that is, their physiological status, was not specified. Although some covering (the great ape equivalent of mounting) of one of the immature males by the other was also observed, such behavior was much less frequent among the immature males than among the immature females.

Bingham thought that the reason one of the immature females engaged in "homosexual behavior" rather than heterosexual might be that this animal was dominant over the others, including the males. Presenting, he proposed, represented an incipient flight response (of a subordinate animal) and, as such, would not be exhibited by the dominant animal in the group.

Much of the genital-stimulating behavior Bingham observed between the immature females consisted of mutual clasping with thrusting, interpreted as comforting behavior by the dominant to the subordinate female. The dominant female was also observed to cover the subordinate (as in heterosexual copulation) and to make oral contact with the genitals of the subordinate, these as well as the preceding clasping behavior occurring in the context of play.

It is possible to conclude from these four early studies that mounting or otherwise effecting genital stimulation with another animal of the same sex is a relatively frequent occurrence among these immature nonhuman primates of both sexes. What functions such behavior might serve, its relative frequency in nonhuman primates of different species, and whether it is appropriately described as homosexual, in the sense of including sexual arousal, is not clearly deducible from these reports. It would also appear that such behavior is less common among adults of both sexes than it is among immatures, unless the adults are living in unisexual groups. In the latter situations, both males and females may engage in genital-stimulating episodes, but males perhaps, do so more frequently than females. Observation of ejaculatory patterns during anal intercourse among male rhesus monkeys (Kempf, 1917) clearly suggests that sexual arousal was a component of their interactions and that such interactions are appropriately labeled as homosexual behavior.

The significance of genital-stimulating behavior between the mature female nonhuman primates is less clear from these reports. That its occurrence among chimpanzees took place during maximal genital swelling (Kohler, 1925), the phase of the female cycle when female chimpanzees normally engage in heterosexual copulation, raises the possibility that this behavior included sexual arousal in the female. Left unanswered are the questions of preference for such behavior in comparison to heterosexual relations, the influence of such behavior during immaturity on adult behavior and preferences, and the persistence of such behavior in adults once it has occurred in adulthood under conditions of isolation with others of the same sex.

Zuckerman, the British anatomist who made extensive and substantive early contributions to our knowledge of reproduction in nonhuman primates, also discussed the role of homosexual behavior in these species. His perspective, however, was essentially the opposite of those of Hamilton and Kempf. In the postscript to the second edition of his 1932 book (Zuckerman, 1981) he states, "I totally fail to see how any analogical comparisons with the ways of monkeys and apes can help in the understanding of what some see as the major problems of human behaviour today" (p. 394). With respect to homosexual behavior, in particular, he states, "I fail to see any reason why . . . the fact that cows mount cows, dogs dogs, a baby monkey its mother, or a monkey mother its baby will help resolve the social problems or prejudices associated with human homosexuality" (p. 394).

This critical view of the value of extrapolating from nonhuman to human primates with respect to sexual behavior did not conflict, however, with his position that such knowledge of nonhuman primates was of considerable scientific interest in and of itself. Most of his observations of sexual behavior were conducted on hamadryas baboons (*Papio hamadryas*), newly introduced onto Monkey Hill in the London Zoological Gardens in the late 1920s, but he also had the opportunity to study wild baboons in South Africa. Zuckerman clearly recognized and described the predominant role played by dominance in the social organization of many nonhuman primates and discussed the relationships between dominance and heterosexual and homosexual behavior.

Zuckerman emphasized that dominance relationships of nonhuman primates differ from those of other animals in its pervasiveness throughout all forms of social interaction, including sexual. Along with his predecessors, he considered presenting to be both a sexual stimulus and an act of social submission. Thus, he proposed that the presenting of a subordinate animal to a dominant one distracts the dominant animal from its aggressive intentions because the sexual stimulus (presenting), in most cases, is more powerful than the stimulus for aggression. Homosexual behavior among males, he proposed, takes one form, that of one animal taking the feminine role of presenting while the other takes the masculine role of mounting. One of the two forms of homosexual behavior he described among females is essentially the same as that among males and is the predominant form in females. A second form of homosexual behavior he observed in females of some species consists of two animals rubbing their genitals together while facing in opposite directions, but this type of behavior had only been observed on two occasions. Bingham (1928), as cited earlier, had reported seeing it in mature female chimpanzees, and Zuckerman had observed a similar case in captive female bonnet monkeys (*M. radiata*). The observation by Kohler (1925) of two mature female chimpanzees effecting "mutual friction" may represent another observation of the same phenomenon, but Kohler did not specify the positions of the females during the activity. The positions used, however, are probably less significant than the fact of genital simulation.

With respect to the sexual significance of the behavior, Zuckerman (1932/1981) raised the question of "whether or not the terms homosexual and heterosexual behaviour have any basic significance with reference to the sexual activities of sub-human primates, apart from denoting the sexes of the animals engaged in sexual activity" (p. 286). In his analysis, he unfortunately focused on immature animals because homosexual behavior occurred more frequently among them than among the adults. With respect to immature animals, he proposed that mounting was clearly related to the dominance relationship and "it seems purely accidental whether a particular response is homosexual or heterosexual in its manifestations" (p. 289). Once maturity is reached, he suggested, heterosexual behavior predominates because of its relationship to reproduction.

This conclusion would appear to beg the question of the significance of homosexual behavior in adults. In other contexts, however, Zuckerman appears to accept certain aspects of the interpretation of others, for example, Hamilton (1914), Kempf (1917), and Miller (1928). This position states that homosexual behavior is resorted to primarily by subordinate animals in order to gain favors or protection from dominant animals or to divert their attacks, for example, "The sexual responses of sub-human primates may have no connection with sexual appetite" (Zuckerman, 1932/1981, p. 232).

It is worth noting that aggression was unusually high in Zuckerman's newly formed group of baboons, accounting for numerous injuries and at least 38 deaths (out of 137 animals introduced) in 6 years. He recognized that this level of aggression was related to the conditions of captivity and acknowledged also that "sexual behaviour may perhaps be intensified" (p. 217). He maintained, however, that the qualitative nature of "sociosexual adjustments are determined by the mutual responses of the animals, and not by environmental influences" (p. 217).

One of the most significant of the early contributions to the literature on dominance and sexual behavior of nonhuman primates was made by Maslow (1936), who studied captive rhesus monkeys at the Vilas Park Zoo in Madison, Wisconsin. Maslow distinguished two types of sexual behavior, functional and dominance, which he considered to represent a continuum rather than an absolute dichotomy. Functional sexual behavior was defined as that which "takes place typically in the adult pair when the female is in heat" and which, despite individual and species differences, typically consists of "mounting (with a few exceptions), intromission, pelvic movements of the mounting male, receptive posture in the female (presenting), and ejaculation" (p. 314). Dominance sexual behavior is similar to functional sexual behavior in that one animal (the dominant one) mounts another (the subordinate) but differs in that the other components "may be missing in the dominance mount, or they may be present in a merely nominal sense" (p. 322). The behavior of the subordinate animal also differs from that observed in the mounted animal engaged in functional sexual behavior and in a similar way; that is, it is perfunctory. Maslow proposed that sexual behavior that occurred between heterosexual pairs during the midcycle phase of the female cycle was *generally* of the functional type, whereas that which occurred at other times in the cycle was *generally* of the dominance type. Functional sexual behavior was therefore proposed to be regulated by gonadal hormone secretion, dominance sexual behavior by a dominance "drive." Maslow was careful to point out that his concept of drive referred only to some factor that served as the basis for "the high intercorrelation between the various parts of the dominance behavior syndrome" (p. 310), which he subsequently described in some detail. He also emphasized that any given mount might not be clearly distinguishable as functional or dominance and that a mount that appeared initially to reflect a dominance relationship could become functional as a result of the genital stimulation associated with the mount.

Maslow's hypothesis proposes that sexual behavior, including homosexual, that deviates from the cyclic functional pattern associated with elevated female hormone levels represents "the superimposing of socially motivated sexual behavior upon the hormonal cycle" (p. 330). According to Maslow, therefore, homosexual behavior in monkeys "is easily explained as dominance and subordination behavior" (p. 332). The significance of such behavior, he maintained, in agreement with Zuckerman (1932/1981), is of considerable importance to human beings but is essentially only an expression of dominance and subordination to the monkeys, irrespective of whether the pair is the same or of opposite sex. That this interpretation is accurate for much of the behavior described thus far is probable. Whether it is an adequate explanation for all forms is questionable.

The eminent psychologist R. M. Yerkes (1939) conducted a laboratory study of dominance and sexual behavior in common chimpanzees, related conceptually to that of Maslow's (1936). His specific interest was whether dominance and subordination between individuals varies with the phase of the female cycle. When pairs of mature females were tested, he found that both dominance and sexual behavior varied with cycle phase. A previously dominant female, at maximal genital swelling, might present and/or be covered by a previously subordinate female. Thrusting, similar to but slower than that of the male, was observed on some occasions. Also reported was the occurrence of genito-genital rubbing between females, as described earlier (Bingham, 1928; Zuckerman, 1932/1981). In the case described by Yerkes, it was a female during the menstrual phase of its cycle that backed against and rubbed its genitals against the swelling of a female at maximal tumescence.

Among pairings of mature with immature females, the mature females were dominant and generally were the ones that mounted (covered). The mountee was usually a female in estrus. Yerkes incorrectly stated that the female chimpanzee differed from other mammals in this respect because in the others, it was the estrous females that performed the mounting. Estrous females of different species may mount other estrous females at times, but the more consistent pattern is that of the mountee being the animal in estrus (Beach, 1948).

Carpenter (1942), another psychologist and one of the first investigators to study primates in their natural habitats, also conducted a study of sexual behavior on semi-free-ranging rhesus monkeys on Cayo Santiago, Puerto Rico. In addition to addressing the questions of length and discreteness of the estrous period in the rhesus monkey, he reported that homosexual behavior was engaged in by eight adult females living in mixed-sex groups and by young males living in two unisexual groups. For the females, "the behavior varied from single and sporadic mountings in some cases to persisting association and repeated mounting series" (p. 149). In one case, a female attacked and then mounted another female, which was apparently approaching estrus, approximately one month (cycle?) after the former female had passed through a normal estrous period. Under similar conditions, a female mounted another over a period of four days, until the latter female established a heterosexual consortship. In a third case, one estrous female, judged to be more highly motivated sexually than another, apparently estrous female presented and was mounted repeatedly by the second. Carpenter proposed that the presenting female was using its "homosexual relations" to gain access to a male that preferred the other female. In general, Carpenter found that the female being mounted was the one that was more highly motivated sexually, this in agreement with the data on the chimpanzee (Yerkes, 1939) and, as noted, a number of other mammals as well. Carpenter reported that "Homosexual behavior may occur along with, preceding, or following normal heterosexual behavior" (p. 150).

These observations are especially interesting because they were made on semi-free-ranging monkeys. They suggest that mounting behavior between the females of this species occurs more frequently than previously thought and in a more complete form. It should be noted, however, that Carpenter made his observations immediately after the monkeys had been released from a 6-week period of confinement for tuberculosis testing. That sexual behavior in general occurred more frequently under these circumstances than was normal is indicated by his statement that "more females became receptive than during any other comparable time in the history of the Colony" (p. 115). The frequency of mounting behavior between the females may therefore also have been unusually high.

The male/male mounting behavior that Carpenter observed was similar to that reported earlier for rhesus monkeys (Hamilton, 1914; Kempf, 1917). In the immature males living in unisexual groups, mounting of one by the other increased in frequency from infancy to the juvenile stage. Although the mounting closely resembled that of adult heterosexual pairs and included the possibility of anal penetration, no evidence of ejaculation was apparent. Mounting appeared to be stimulated in a variety of social activities, including play, aggressive encounters, dominance relationships, and so on, as reported earlier, with the dominant animal of the pair doing the mounting. Carpenter was uncertain as to whether this behavior in the immature males should be considered homosexual or nonspecific, or perhaps a displaced response related to fighting.

Carpenter reported that homosexual mounting also occurred between adult males in the heterosexual groups but most frequently among the more subordinate males. He interpreted these mounts as a means of gaining tolerance of others, an expression of friendliness, a response to insecurity, and a type of greeting. Since they were not performed in series and since they lacked ejaculation, Carpenter doubted that they were examples of "true sexual behavior."

Later Research on Chimpanzees and Rhesus Monkeys

Following a hiatus of 26 years in the reporting of homosexual behavior in nonhuman primates, there appeared two papers, one on sexual behavior of captive common chimpanzees (Kollar, Beckwith, & Edgerton, 1968) and the other, Jane Goodall's (van Lawick-Goodall, 1968) comprehensive monograph on wild common chimpanzees in Tanzania. Kollar et al., (1968) reported several examples of genital-stimulating behavior between captive chimpanzees of the same sex living as a large group (i.e., 25 to 45 animals) of both sexes and all age-classes. Most of the adult animals were wild-born and captured as infants, a factor that must be considered in evaluating their sexual behavior (Riesen, 1971; Rogers & Davenport, 1969).

In this study, one of three adult males that failed to show heterosexual behavior was observed to cover and execute pelvic thrusting with another male. Another of these three males manipulated the genitals of smaller males. Although the investigators also reported that "a number of these adolescent females were observed to rub their sexual skins together" (p. 453), they did not specify whether the females were facing in opposite directions, as in the earlier reports (Bingham, 1928; Yerkes, 1939).

The smaller females, of about 1 to 8 years of age, presented to others of both sexes. Also observed were presenting and mounting by same-sex animals involved in agonistic encounters, in situations suggesting an interpretation of "reassurance" for the presenting and during the excitement associated with feeding. Therefore, none of these examples suggest that sexual arousal was involved in the behavior.

A juvenile male was seen to intrude into the copulation of two other animals and present to the male, whereupon, the male covered the juvenile briefly and thrusted a few times. One older adolescent male and young juvenile "sat facing each other and rubbed their erect penises together" (p. 454). "Both males and females were observed to perform fellatio on Chuck, a large adolescent male," that solicited such performance "as he would for copulation" (p. 454). The same and another male solicited a juvenile male in a similar way, and the juvenile "responded by jerking their erect penises for several seconds" (p. 454)."Both males and females were observed to lick the vaginal area of females" (p. 454), in one case following copulation with ejaculation. Genital touching was also observed following initial meetings and reunions among animals; in the case of males, their penises were generally erect. This latter example is similar to the greeting behavior described by Kohler (1925). With respect to these various forms of genital contact between same-sex individuals, Kollar et al. (1968) proposed that "the fact that these perversions were most frequently observed in sex-segregated cage-raised adults suggests that this behavior was related to the abnormal living conditions during growth and development" (p. 458). The data suggest, at least, that chimpanzees possess the potential for a variety of genital-stimulating behavior and that early social and environmental conditions seem to account for the particular forms that these activities take.

Publication of Jane Goodall's monograph (van Lawick-Goodall, 1968) on wild (though provisioned) common chimpanzees in the same year as the preceding study provides a useful comparison with the data on captive chimpanzees. Sexual behavior, in general, occurred less frequently in the wild, and there were fewer examples of genital-stimulating behavior between same-sex animals. Two infant males were observed to thrust against infants of both sexes in the context of play, using both dorso-ventral and ventro-ventral positions while lying on the ground. Such behavior was rare among female infants. Adolescent and mature males frequently responded to a distressed infant of either sex by clasping and thrusting on the infant's back. This latter pattern was described as "reassurance mounting." Presenting and mounting during reunions of same- and opposite-sex individuals was also reported for wild chimpanzees, supporting Kohler's (1925) original interpretation.

The lower levels of genital-stimulating behavior among same-sex chimpanzees in the wild in comparison to captivity is probably related in part to the fact that heterosexual opportunities are already available in the wild at a very young age. Mature females in estrus, in addition to copulating with mature males, frequently encourage sexual interactions with infant and other young males, including the facilitation of intromission. Further observations on such behavior and additional examples of covering and thrusting on same-sex chimpanzees by infant and juvenile males was subsequently reported by others conducting field research in the same area (Plooij, 1984; Tutin & McGinnis, 1981). Apart from these early manifestations, however, there are few examples of interactions with a clearly sexual focus in same-sex wild common chimpanzees.

One of the more provocative of the recent studies of male/male mounting behavior with clear indications of sexual arousal in nonhuman primates was conducted on captive rhesus monkeys living as social groups in three relatively large (38.1 m^2) outdoor enclosures (Gordon & Bernstein, 1973). One of the enclosures contained a group of adult males and females, juveniles and infants, whereas the other two contained only males. The enclosures were spatially arranged so that one of the all-male groups had visual access to the breeding group and the other did not. Neither of the all-male groups could see the other.

Initial observations during the nonbreeding season indicated that only occasional mounts occurred in any of the groups (approximately one per 3 to 4 hours of observation). With the onset of the breeding season in October, the adult males and females in the breeding group underwent characteristic coloration changes, that is, reddening of the face and genital region (Vandenbergh, 1965), and engaged in frequent bouts of sexual activity (1.8 mounts per male per hour). The males of the all-male group that had visual access to the breeding group underwent the same physical and behavioral changes. These males were observed to sit at the fence closest to the breeding group and intently watch the animals in that group. The mount rate in this all-male group increased to about the same rate as that in the breeding group and included anal penetration (personal observation) and ejaculation. Following patterns, characteristic of consort relationships between males and females were also observed, such that, from a distance, the behavior of these males was frequently indistinguishable from that of heterosexual consorts. Some of the unisexual consortships persisted over days with maintenance of the mounter/mountee relationship. By contrast, the all-male group without visual access to the other groups showed none of the physical or behavioral changes normally associated with the breeding season.

Several factors suggest that the behavior observed in this study was associated with sexual arousal. (1) The behavior was confined primarily to the season when normal heterosexual behavior occurs, (2) the behavior was associated with physical changes that are induced by the same gonadal hormones that mediate heterosexual mating behavior, (3) the male/male relationships closely resembled typical heterosexual consortships and included the species-typical pattern of multiple mounts with intromission (anal) and ejaculation, and (4) the relationships between mounters and mountees was *not* related to the dominance relationships between the males. The homosexual behavior of these males, moreover, declined to minimal levels at the end of the breeding season, comparable to the heterosexual behavior of the breeding group. Of particular interest was the finding that when these males were later included in mixed-sex groups, they performed completely adequate heterosexual mating patterns and were never again observed in homosexual relationships (Gordon, personal communication). These data suggest, therefore, that the male/male mounting behavior of these adult male rhesus monkeys included sexual arousal, was stimulated in part by the observation of sexual activity in other monkeys, and occurred as a temporary substitute for heterosexual copulation, among males that were restricted from physical access to females. While not commonly observed under free-ranging conditions, a single example of male/male mounting with anal penetration and ejaculation was reported by another author for two rhesus macaques that were brothers (Sade, 1968). In this case, the homosexual behavior was attributed to heightened excitement at the time.

Several reports of homosexual behavior among female rhesus monkeys have also appeared. In one study (Akers & Conway, 1979), a group consisting of eight adult females and two adult males were observed for 6 months in an outdoor corral that measured 25 by 25 feet. Two forms of homosexual behavior between seven of the eight females were described: (1) mounts of several types that resembled heterosexual mounts, more or less, and (2) "ventral-hugging," seen in only one pair, in which face-to-face clasping occurred, sometimes accompanied by autosexual masturbatory behavior.

The homosexual behavior of the females included following, solicitations of various types, multiple mounts in series, and occasionally pauses resembling the ejaculatory pauses of males, all common to heterosexual mating. Examples of this behavior were observed throughout the study but varied in frequency among the different pairs and the months of observation. On average, the mounter was most likely in the follicular phase of the menstrual cycle, the mountee in the ovulatory phase, consistent with Carpenter's (1942) data. Cycle phase, however, was determined by counting backward from menstruation, thereby perhaps accounting for some of the variability observed among pairs. Among these females, dominance appeared to be implicated because the mounter was usually the dominant animal, but sexual arousal was clearly implicated because single, perfunctory mounts of the type that are typical in dominance interactions were excluded from the analyses. The homosexual behavior occurred despite the presence of two normal adult males and sometimes occurred on days when heterosexual copulation also took place.

Related data on serial mounting were reported for two 2-year-old rhesus females living in an all-juvenile group under semi-free-ranging conditions (Loy & Loy, 1974). As in the previous study, it appeared that the homosexual behavior occurred primarily during the ovulatory phase of the mountee's cycle and was also associated with heterosexual mating. Some of the mounts included genital rubbing by the mounter along the sacrum of the mountee, as also reported for female Japanese and stumptailed macaques (see below).

In another study (Ruiz de Elvira, Herndon, & Collins, 1983), two all-female groups consisting of five ovariectomized and eight intact female rhesus monkeys were observed in outdoor compounds (15.25 m × 15.25 m) through a nonbreeding and into a breeding season. In one of the groups (experimental), the ovariectomzied females (N = 2) were implanted with pellets of estradiol benzoate in an amount that produced serum levels of estradiol comparable to that of the late follicular/ovulatory phase of the cycle. The estrogen-treated, ovariectomized females "mounted repeatedly and displayed all the patterns usually associated with heterosexual mounting in this species except intromission and ejaculation" (p. 195). Despite continued treatment with the estrogen throughout the summer months (i.e., nonbreeding season), however, the homosexual behavior ceased after two weeks. Among the untreated females, one ovariectomized female and two intact females (one cycling, one noncycling) also showed homosexual behavior. In these animals, presenting and mounting occurred only infrequently until the beginning of the breeding season, when it increased in frequency and more closely resembled the heterosexual pattern. Dominance relationships in this study were not predictive of the mounter/mountee relationship nor were the levels of estradiol or progesterone correlated with sex skin coloration or the occurrence of homosexual behavior. The results of this study are interesting from several perspectives, including the indication that hormone levels under experimental conditions in this species cannot be inferred reliably from sex skin coloration or the frequencies of sexual activity. That hormone levels exerted some influence on the homosexual behavior observed is, however, apparent. That the behavior included sexual arousal seems likely.

The more frequent occurrence of female/female mounting in captive female rhesus monkeys in comparison to wild (Loy, 1971) or free-ranging groups (Kaufman, 1965) has been attributed to disturbances in "natural social bonds" (Fairbanks, McGuire, & Kerber, 1977). This interpretation was suggested, in part, from the results of group formation studies in which the highest levels of female/female mounting occurred immediately after group formation and declined therafter (Bernstein & Mason, 1963; Carpenter, 1942; Fairbanks et al., 1977). It was proposed that female/female mounting under these conditions facilitated the social bonding of the females, which then served as the basis for aggressive coalitions directed against other, unbonded females (Fairbanks et al., 1977; also see Chevalier-Skolnikoff, 1976). Although the female/female mounting in these studies of group formation was not described sufficiently to permit a judgment of whether or not the females were sexually aroused, the proposal that such behavior served to bond females together is worthy of further consideration.

Only one study was found in the literature in which two adult male nonhuman primates appeared to exhibit a homosexual preference for each other over a female (Erwin & Maple, 1976). The two males were rhesus monkeys, reared by mothers in individual cages until the age of 8 months and then reared together until 27 months of age. They then underwent a series of experimental separations and reunions with each other and with other conspecifics of both sexes, during which they exhibited apparently normal heterosexual copulation and with each other, male/male mounting with anal penetration, as well as mutual clasping and grooming at unusually high levels. When, as adults, they were simultaneously released into a room with an unfamiliar female they mounted each other as before and did not mount the female. The authors concluded that their bond was "based more on affection than sexual fulfillment" because "ejaculation was never documented during homosexual coitus" (p. 13).

In the absence of serial mounting and ejaculation between the males, it is difficult to assess completely the significance of their behavior and hence the basis of their relationship despite the occurrence of anal penetration. That their early rearing experience contributed to their relationship is clear. That they performed adequate heterosexual copulation with familiar and unfamiliar females is also clear. Unfortunately, however, evidence on their relationship with each other and with females beyond these test conditions is lacking.

Another study in which homosexual behavior related to early rearing experiences was reported for rhesus monkeys concerned two males, between 2 and 3 years of age, housed with two older female olive baboons (*P. anubis*) (Maple, Bernard, & McGlynn, 1977). "These interactions were characteristically reciprocal, were occasionally accompanied by lip smacking and reaching back (typical female sexual behaviors during copulation) and resulted in frequent anal intromission" (p. 25). Oro-genital interaction between the males was also described. This and the preceding study therefore suggest that early rearing experiences can facilitate the development of homosexual behavior in male rhesus monkeys. The long-term effects of such experiences, however, are not known.

More comprehensive experimental studies of the influences of early social experience on sexual behavior of rhesus monkeys have been conducted at the Wisconsin Regional Primate Research Center. Here rhesus monkeys were reared in isosexual or mixed-sex groups, with and without mothers present (Goldfoot, 1977). Mounting was increased in the isosexually reared females, especially the high-ranking ones, and presenting was increased in the isosexually reared males, especially the low-ranking ones. The data support the view "that social conditions can generate sex differences as a function of interactions between peers in a social group" (Goldfoot, Wallen, Neff, McBair, & Goy, 1984). The investigators emphasized the complexity of the problems in defining sexually dimorphic behavior, not only in terms of early rearing conditions but also in terms of the type of test conditions used to assess the behavior. They have not yet determined, however, the significance of the altered patterns of mounting and presenting at an early age for adult sexual behavior and adult sexual preferences.

Research on Other Simian Primates

Japanese Macaques (*M. fuscata*)

A number of investigators have reported mounting between same-sex partners in Japanese macaques of both sexes under semi-free-ranging conditions in captivity (Eaton, 1978; Fedigan & Gouzoules, 1978; Hanby, 1974; Hanby & Brown, 1974; Hanby, Robertson, & Phoenix, 1971; Wolfe, 1978, 1979) and in the wild (Enomoto, 1974; Takahata, 1980, 1982). Among infants and juveniles, males mounted same-sex partners more frequently than females did, but among adults, the opposite relationship was predominant.

Three forms of "mounting" by adult females were observed: (1) mounting similar to that of the male in heterosexual mating but usually not including the double foot-clasp, (2) sitting on, or (3) lying on the back of the mountee and rubbing the genitals back and forth along the sacrum of the mountee. In addition, ventro-ventral mountings were occasionally seen between young females (Wolfe, 1979). These female/female mountings were carried out in series by estrous females in the context of consortships that persisted for hours or days. The mounter/mountee role generally alternated and, in most cases, was independent of dominance status and age. Most instances occurred outside the kinship or matrilineal group, during the breeding season with adult males present. The proportion of females that engaged in these mountings varied among the groups and in different seasons for the same group. For the Oregon (Eaton, 1978) and Arashiyama West (Wolfe, 1979) troops, it was reported that the number of females that engaged in female/female mountings varied inversely with the number of adult males in the groups (but also see Fedigan & Gouzoules, 1978). An inadequate number of males, however, does not appear to account for differences in the frequency of female/female mounting within the wild groups (Takahata, 1980). It was reported for both captive (Fedigan & Gouzoules, 1978) and wild groups (Takahata, 1980) that most female/female mountings occurred postconception and in the captive group, that higher rates were observed in females that had not given birth in the previous birth season.

Same-sex mounting occurred much less frequently between male Japanese macaques than between females. The descriptions for the males are less complete than those for the females and do not suggest that the males were sexually aroused; for example, "Mounting between males rarely resembles that typical of heterosexual copulation" (Hanby, 1974, p. 843). At least one male, however, was observed to ejaculate twice in one day with the same male partner but without anal intromission. This seemed to be the proverbial exception to the rule.

Among Japanese macaques, therefore, there is a considerable amount of data to suggest that female/female mounting occurs to a significant degree and is associated with sexual arousal. Male/male mounting occurs less frequently, primarily as single mounts, suggesting a nonsexual, social basis.

Stump-Tailed Macaques (M. arctoides)

Perhaps the most extensive and varied examples of homosexual behavior in a simian species have been reported for the stump-tailed macaque. Both male/male and female/female interactions were reported with ample evidence of sexual arousal (Chevalier-Skolnikoff, 1974, 1976; Goldfoot, Westerborg-van Loon, Groeneveld & Slob, 1980). The interactions included same-sex mounting (in the female, resembling that described above for the Japanese macaque), as well as oro-genital and ano-genital contacts and manual masturbation of a partner. These observations were made on captive groups living in cages but were not observed in other groups living in large enclosures (Harvey, 1983; Murray, Bour, & Smith, 1985). Moreover, Harvey (1983), who did not observe such behavior in the stable mixed-sex group she studied, did see female/female mounting in a relatively large unisexual group and, initially, among a newly formed group of three females. Thus, while it seems clear that stump-tailed macaques have the potential for diverse forms of homosexual behavior, it does not appear that such behavior is typical of the species under natural conditions.

The potential for homosexual behavior in stump-tailed macaques was examined in another study in which three wild-born males were raised together for 9 years from the age of 3 years (Slob & Schenck, 1986). Unlike the rhesus monkeys described earlier (Erwin & Maple, 1976), the stump-tailed males preferred females to each other when tested as adults. As suggested by the authors, the most significant difference between the two studies is probably the earlier age at which the rhesus monkeys began living together. These data on the stump-tailed macaques are therefore not inconsistent with those on the rhesus monkey.

Squirrel Monkeys (*Saimiri sciureus*)

Same-sex mounting with thrusting by immature individuals has been reported for Roman arch (or Peruvian) and Gothic arch (or Colombian) squirrel monkeys of both sexes (Baldwin, 1969; DuMond, 1968; Latta, Hopf, & Ploog, 1967; Ploog, Hopf, & Winter, 1967). Such same-sex mounting is seen initially between 2 and 4 months of age and continues into the subadult stage of development. As in the other species considered, mounting at these early ages occurs in the context of play. By the juvenile stage, males are playing more vigorously and mounting others more frequently than females. It was proposed that males were more vigorous in their play than females, such that the females gradually withdrew from bouts of contact play (Baldwin, 1969). In general, older and larger animals assume the top position in dorso-ventral mounting, and the sex of the partner seems irrelevant to the monkeys. By the time the males reach the later stage of the subadult category, they begin pursuing heterosexual relations and no homosexual activity has been reported for fully adult male squirrel monkeys.

On the other hand, same-sex mounting has been reported for adult female squirrel monkeys of both the Peruvian and Colombian types living in laboratory cages (Travis & Holmes, 1974) and under semi-free-ranging conditions (DuMond, 1968). The behavior was reported to resemble typical heterosexual mating and occurred primarily during estrus, with the estrous female pursuing the other. The estrous females performed genital displays similar to males and vocalized in the male fashion (Travis & Holmes, 1974). Dominant females generally mounted subordinate ones, and subordinate females solicited and presented to dominant ones.

Female/female mounting occurred relatively frequently in a laboratory study of four females (Talmage-Riggs & Anschel, 1973) but was essentially eliminated after an adult male was added to the group (Anschel & Talmage-Riggs, 1977). The authors of the latter two studies concluded that this example of homosexual behavior "probably was an attempted substitution for heterosexual mating" (Talmage-Riggs & Anschel, 1973, p. 71).

The data on squirrel monkeys therefore resemble in certain aspects the data already reported for other primates. Animals of both sexes mount same-sex individuals as youngsters, but males at this stage of maturation eventually exceed the performance of females. Same-sex mounting of adult females is related to dominance status, occurs more frequently in unisexual groups, and is more common in females during the time of estrus. In contrast to the Old World monkeys, however, the estrous female squirrel monkey pursues and mounts the other female rather than assuming the present posture. The close resemblance of the female/female mounting to the typical heterosexual pattern and its association with estrus, suggests that sexual arousal is involved and that the behavior is appropriately termed homosexual. That such behavior by estrous females also stimulates mating by males in the vicinity suggests that the behavior may serve several functions (Travis & Holmes, 1974). Same-sex presenting and mounting has been briefly described in several other species of macaques, including *M. nemestrina* (Tokuda, Simons, & Jensen, 1968), *M. nigra* (Dixson, 1977), *M. silenus* (Skinner & Lockard, 1979), and *M. radiata* (Makwana, 1980; Simonds, 1965). In none of these reports, however, was there indication of persistent genital stimulation or sexual arousal. The same may be said for later studies on baboons (Anthoney, 1968; Bolwig, 1959), vervet (Gartlan, 1969), and talapoin monkeys (Dixson, Scruton, & Herbert, 1975; Wolfheim & Rowell, 1972), langurs (Jay, 1965), and tree shrews (Conaway & Sorenson, 1966) (also see Bernstein, 1970). One exception, in the case of langurs, was reported by Hrdy (1977, personal communication), who observed male/male mounting that was indistinguishable from heterosexual mating. This homosexual behavior occurred in all-male groups that had visual access to breeding groups, similar in this respect to the rhesus monkeys described earlier (Gordon & Bernstein, 1973).

Research on the Other Great Apes

Pygmy Chimpanzees (*Pan paniscus*)

A form of genital stimulation between adult females has been reported for pygmy chimpanzees, both in captivity (Savage & Bakeman, 1978; Savage-Rumbaugh & Wilkerson, 1978) and in the wild (Kano, 1980; Kuroda, 1979, 1980, 1984; Thompson-Handler, Malenky, & Badrian, 1984). "They embrace face-to-face and begin to rub each other's genitals together (probably clitoris) rhythmically and rapidly. Genital rubbing lasts from just a few seconds to 20 seconds. On rare occasions, it may last over one minute" (Kano, 1980, p. 253). This genito-genital rubbing (Kuroda, 1980) is observed most frequently during feeding, but it is observed at other times as well. Dominance relationships do not appear to be involved.

Genital stimulation occurs primarily among estrous females, but it is not restricted to this condition. Kuroda (1979, 1980, 1984) and Kano (1980) suggest that it serves to reduce tension, "to calm anxiety or excitement, to dissolve interindividual tension and thus to increase intimacy, and to express excited joy" (Kuroda, 1980, p. 190). Thompson-Handler et al. (1984), however, suspect that this interpretation may not be sufficiently comprehensive.

Male/male "mounting" has also been observed in the wild, but less frequently than the genito-genital rubbing of the females (Kano, 1980; Kuroda, 1980; Thompson-Handler, et al. 1984). This behavior between males occurs primarily in agonistic contexts, is related to dominance relationships, and gives little or no indication of sexual arousal. It is therefore questionable whether either of these behavior patterns in male and female pygmy chimpanzees should be considered to be homosexual, as defined in this review.

Gorillas *(Gorilla gorilla)*

Genital-stimulating behavior between same-sex individuals has been reported for both captive lowland gorillas (*G. g. gorilla*) and wild mountain gorillas (*G. g. beringei*). Hess (1973), who published an extensive report on the sexual behavior of lowland gorillas at the Basle Zoological Gardens, wrote, "All partner-related behavior can be observed between partners of the same or opposite sex" (p. 526). He described genital manipulation of relatively short and long periods of time and "copulation" developing out of the context of play. "Pseudocopulations can occur in the context of play; sometimes out of playing sexual motivation can develop. Generally, such activity with a partner is rarely observed in fully adult males and females, whereas young adult, subadult, and juvenile individuals indulge more often in activities of this type" (p. 577), especially during estrous periods of the females. That same-sex interactions of this type occur more frequently among females than males was suggested in another study of lowland gorillas (Coffin, 1978). Eleven of 29 "mounts" that were observed took place between young adult females, whereas none were observed between two young males. Thrusting in the dorso-ventral position was also observed by the author in pubertal and adult female lowland gorillas living as pairs or triads in cages. One of the females was generally in estrus. In the case of the pubertal female, it was seen to lie prone, rubbing its ventrum on the cage floor. A young adult female cage-mate covered and thrusted briefly on the younger female.

Similar observations of same-sex genital-stimulating episodes have been reported for immature (Harcourt, Stewart, & Fossey, 1981; Nadler,

1986) and adult wild mountain gorillas (Harcourt et al., 1981). Among the immature animals, thrusting against another was generally brief, although there were exceptions of longer duration. In one case, a black-backed (subadult) male that had been observed to copulate normally with a nulliparous female in estrus at another time thrusted against a 3-year-old male during a period of rough play (Nadler, 1986). In fact, as in other species, most genital-stimulating episodes in the immature gorillas occurred in the context of play. On several occasions, a juvenile female repetitively pressed female infants against its genitals while embracing and playing with the infants. That the genital stimulation involved same-sex individuals in these instances appeared to result in part from the composition of the group and from the fact that same-sex play was more common than opposite-sex play. The recipient of same-sex thrusting, moreover, was almost always younger and smaller than the actor.

Harcourt et al. (1981) proposed that same-sex "mounting" in adult females reflected sexual arousal because 7 of the 10 cases observed occurred in close temporal association with heterosexual copulation. In contrast to most of the other species described thus far (except the squirrel monkey), however, it was the estrous female that performed the thrusting. Similar same-sex behavior in males was observed on only three occasions and gave the impression that these interactions were agonistic.

Orang-utans (*Pongo pygmaeus*).

Surprisingly little evidence of homosexual behavior has been reported for orang-utans; surprising because both males and females of this species engage in sexual activity frequently in capitivity, heterosexual and autosexual (e.g., Nadler, 1977, 1982). Part of the explanation may relate to the fact that orang-utans live a semisolitary existence in nature and become increasingly intolerant of same-sex individuals as they mature. Moreover, in captivity adult orang-utans are generally maintained as heterosexual pairs.

MacKinnon (1974) reported a single instance of male/male mounting in immature orang-utans living in a zoo, but he saw no homosexual behavior during his field studies on Bornean (*P. p. pygmaeus*) or Sumatran (*P. p. abelii*) orang-utans. Rijksen (1978), on the other hand, reported a few interesting examples of homosexual behavior among rehabilitant (ex-captive) orang-utans in Sumatra. One female was seen to insert its finger into the vagina of other females while masturbating with its own hallux. Rijksen likened this behavior to the pattern of forcible copulation by subadult males because with respect to the females, the insertees struggled to free themselves from the inserter. It was also remarked that some of the female insertees later established affiliative relationships with the inserter.

Rijksen (1978) also reported a few examples of fellatio and anal intercourse with ejaculation among adolescent and subadult male rehabilitants. One adolescent that had been the recipient of fellatio by a subadult male "became very attached to the subadult male, and after a while followed him wherever he went" (p. 265). When the subadult male was moved to another area, the adolescent male established a similar relationship with another adolescent that had never before been seen to engage in homosexual behavior. In this case, the adolescent that had previously been the recipient of fellatio was seen being "forced" to perform fellatio by the other adolescent. "Later on this behaviour was seen several more times but with more cooperation on the part of the latter" (p. 265). A few cases of male/male mounting were also observed among juveniles.

With respect to captive orang-utans, Morris (1970) reported that two subadult males living together in a zoo regularly engaged in anal intercourse. When one of these males was later placed with a female, it copulated in a similar manner with the female. Apparently this male's early homosexual experience did not preclude later heterosexual copulation, albeit atypical and nonreproductive.

Another example of homosexual behavior among captive subadult male orang-utans was observed by the author at the Yerkes Regional Primate Research Center. The males, one a Bornean, the other a Sumatran, were wild-born but had been living together in a cage from about the age of 5 to 7 years. Fellatio was observed between them for several years until one began to develop the cheek flanges of a fully mature male. At about that time, serious fighting erupted between the two and they were permanently separated. It may be noteworthy that cheek flange development in these two males was delayed by several years in comparison with other wild-born males that had been obtained at the same time and whose ages were estimated to be about the same. Once separated, both males developed complete cheek flanges and subsequently copulated in an apparently normal manner with females. Maple (1980), who also observed fellatio in a juvenile male orang-utan, proposed that this behavior "may be nutritively rather than sexually motivated" (p. 118).

These observations on orang-utans, though scanty, include some provocative examples of extended periods of homosexual behavior in both males and females. Most of the examples, it should be noted, relate to captive or ex-captive individuals, and those males for which longitudinal observations were available later engaged in heterosexual copulation.

Conclusions

Rhesus Monkeys: Immature Individuals

The original observations of same-sex mounting by immature rhesus monkeys (Hamilton, 1914) were subsequently confirmed by other investigators studying animals under free-ranging conditions (Carpenter, 1942) and in experimental laboratory settings (Goldfoot et al., 1984). It appears that such mounting more likely reflects the availability of an animal that is susceptible to mounting, that is, one that is younger and/or smaller than the mounter, than it reflects the choice of an animal of a particular (the same) sex. That the choice of an animal is frequently one of the same sex may relate to sexually differentiated patterns of play in these primates (Goldfoot et al., 1984). Same-sex individuals play together more frequently than opposite-sex ones, and mounting occurs most frequently during play. The fact that the mounter is often the older and/or larger animal of the pair suggests that these interactions, in part, represent early manifestations of dominance relationships. Dominance in mounting, moreover, could serve either or both of two distinct functions: (1) the assertion of dominance per se or (2) the basis for restraining another animal so as to effect genital stimulation. Although it may not be possible to distinguish with confidence between these possibilities or between these and others, the focus of genital stimulation and especially its persistence in some cases suggest that sexual arousal is implicated to some degree in those cases. Therefore, according to the definition proposed earlier, those cases of same-sex mounting (with thrusting) of a persistent nature are appropriately labeled as homosexual behavior. On the other hand, because the sex of the mountee appears to be irrelevant and variable, the behavioral repertoire of animals so involved may be defined as ambisexual (Green, 1972).

Rhesus Monkeys: Mature Individuals

The data regarding homosexual behavior in mature rhesus monkeys are more easily interpretable than those on the immature ones. Certainly, a good deal of the behavior originally proposed to be homosexual in adults probably represents other nonsexual, social behavior. The study by Gordon and Bernstein (1973), however, suggests that Kempf's (1917) original observations of male/male mounting with anal penetration represent appropriate examples of male homosexual behavior. These two studies suggest that male homosexual behavior is readily elicited in response to the segregation of males apart from mature females. A stimulatory effect on homosexual behavior in the segregated males by observation of heterosexual mating is indicated. The analogy to prison populations and other sex-segregated conditions in humans (Kempf, 1917), seems relevant. Of particular interest in this regard was the finding that males that engaged in prolonged homosexual consortships that closely resembled the consortships of heterosexual pairs were never again observed in homosexual relationships after they were reintroduced into heterosexual groups (Gordon, personal communication; Gordon & Bernstein, 1973). Their behavioral repertoire, like that of the immature animals, is apparently ambisexual.

That same-sex mounting occurs among mature female rhesus monkeys in heterosexual (Akers & Conway, 1979; Carpenter, 1942) as well as unisexual groups (Ruiz de Elvira et al., 1983) was also reported. The observation of series mounting in these studies and indications of a response similar to the ejaculatory response of the male in one (Akers & Conway, 1979) provide strong evidence that the mounting included sexual arousal. The finding that heterosexual mating was observed in the same females on days they exhibited homosexual mounting is significant. It suggests that homosexual behavior in mature rhesus females (Fairbanks et al., 1977) may serve other functions in addition to that as a substitute for heterosexual mating. A qualification to this conclusion is necessary, however. Although it is true that mature males were present in one of the groups in which the female homosexual behavior was observed, there were far fewer than the number present in a natural group (Akers & Conway, 1979). The number of males available, therefore, and the number of choices available to the females were fewer than those under natural conditions and, as such, may have contributed to these results. Comparable observations in a natural setting are required before completely adequate evaluation of this phenomenon in mature female rhesus monkeys can be made.

A number of studies have shown that early conditions of rearing can have profound effects on the development of sexual behavior in rhesus monkeys. Most of these studies demonstrated that early social deprivation severely compromised the later performance of species-typical mating patterns (e.g., Mason, 1960). Several studies considered in this review, however, suggest that less severe modifications of rearing conditions, such as isosexual rearing, produce less severe behavioral disturbances (Goldfoot et al., 1984) and an increased probability that the animals will display homosexual behavior (Erwin & Maple, 1976; Maple et al., 1976). In fact, the only example of two nonhuman male primates with a possible homosexual preference was derived from an isosexual rearing experience (Erwin & Maple, 1976). This particular pair was one of three pairs reared under identical conditions but was the only one in which homosexual behavior was prominent (Erwin, personal communication).

The isosexually reared rhesus monkeys in the Wisconsin study (Goldfoot et al., 1984) were subsequently tested as young adults with animals of the same and opposite sex (Goldfoot, personal communication). Heterosexual mating was somewhat deficient but variably so, and no difference was found in same-sex mounting of isosexually reared and heterosexually reared individuals. In these tests, however, all the animals were paired with *unfamiliar* partners. This testing condition resulted in considerable aggression between same-sex individuals and, as such, was a relatively insensitive condition for the detection of homosexual behavior. Further observations on isosexually reared males in unisexual groups, on the other hand, revealed numerous occurrences of anal intercourse with ejaculation. Although the data from this study have not been completely analyzed as yet, they, together with those cited previously (Erwin & Maple,

1976), suggest that further study of developmental influences on homosexual behavior in rhesus monkeys is warranted.

Common Chimpanzees

The original observations of same-sex mounting by immature male and female common chimpanzees under captive conditions (Bingham, 1928; Kohler, 1925) were supported by comparable observations in the wild (Plooij, 1984; Tutin & McGinnis, 1981; van Lawick-Goodall, 1968). Kohler (1925) thought such behavior primarily reflected nonspecific, undifferentiated excitement, by which he meant a nonsexual basis. Bingham (1928) interpreted the same behavior as sexual play, implying some sexual arousal, and thought it served as practice for the perfection of adult copulatory behavior. That immature males in the wild exhibit such behavior even more frequently than immature females suggests that the opposite relationship reported by Bingham was related to the relatively few animals he studied (N = 4) and the fact that one of the females was dominant over both of the males. Thus, even at an early age, dominance appears to interact with sexual inclinations in the expression of sexual behavior in chimpanzees, as previously suggested for rhesus monkeys.

The distinction between homosexual and heterosexual behavior at this early stage of development seems to be irrelevant to the chimpanzees involved, as for rhesus monkeys. In the case of females, however, there are few if any indications of heterosexual mounting by immature individuals in contrast to the males, which mount both same-sex and opposite-sex partners. In young females of this species, therefore, same-sex mounting constitutes a greater proportion of their early sexual experience than it does in males. This could result from the fact that much of this early sexual behavior occurs during play, and males initiate play with the opposite sex more frequently than females do (Nadler, 1986).

The frequent and more varied examples of genital-stimulating behavior observed by Kollar et al., (1968) seem to be clearly related to the early rearing of the animals under conditions of social deprivation (Rogers & Davenport, 1969). Although a preoccupation with these more unusual forms of genital-stimulation is not characteristic of the species under more natural circumstances, its occurrence following social deficits in early experience could have implications for the interpretation of comparable behavior in other species, including our own.

Among adult chimpanzees, same-sex mounting of a sexual nature or genital-stimulating behavior in general between same-sex animals is rare or totally absent. The genito-genital rubbing between females reported by several investigators Bingham, 1928; Kohler, 1925; Yerkes, 1939) all took place under conditions in which there were no mature males present. The common interpretation was that some portion of these observations included a sexual component, but several other social functions were implicated, especially expressions of dominance and subordination. The only

male-male sexual activity reported for adult chimpanzees was that engaged in by the males that had had a socially deprived early rearing
experience (Kollar et al., 1968). It would appear, therefore, that homosexual interactions among adult chimpanzees of both sexes is rare under
normal circumstances.

Other Simian and Pongid Primates

The data on homosexual behavior of simian primates other than rhesus
monkeys indicate that there are differences in the extent to which such
behavior is reported for different species but that homosexual behavior is
included in the behavioral repertoires of many. The basis for the difference in reporting, moreover, is not necessarily related to a difference in
occurrence of homosexual behavior but rather a function of the extent to
which the species have been studied. In general, the data on these other
species appear to be fairly comparable to those on the rhesus monkey. The
repertoire of homosexual behavior in stump-tailed macaques, however, is
more extensive than those of the other species considered.

With respect to the great apes, there are more examples of homosexual
behavior among adult gorillas and orang-utans than there are among
chimpanzees. This does not appear to reflect unequal sampling but rather
a true species difference. Female pygmy chimpanzees engage in genito-
genital rubbing more frequently than common chimpanzees, but the full
significance of this behavioral pattern is not established.

Generalizations

It is apparent that much of the behavior of nonhuman primates that has
been described as homosexual lacks evidence of sexual arousal and is
more appropriately designated as some form of nonsexual, social behavior. It is also apparent that certain interactions are unquestionably homosexual in that they are indistinguishable from heterosexual mating, include an ejaculatory pattern, or in the case of females, an ejaculatory-like
pattern, and are carried out by individuals of the same sex. Of the 78
references reviewed, fewer than 20 fall into this latter category. It is necessary with the vast majority of cases, therefore, to assess the likelihood that
sexual arousal was involved from the descriptions provided. Completely
adequate assessments are generally not possible because relevant information is not provided. Most reports on homosexual behavior are derived
from studies with other objectives; the observations are frequently fortuitous and tangential to the major objectives of these studies. Despite these
caveats, it is possible to draw some generalizations about homosexual
behavior in nonhuman primates.

Table 10.1 contains a list of variables pertinent to such generalization.

1. Homosexual behavior has been observed in some species but
   not in others. This reflects, in part, the extent to which the

Table 10.1
Variables Pertinent to the Occurrence of Homosexual Behavior in Nonhuman Primates

1. Species
2. Sex
3. Developmental stage: immature versus mature individuals, including possible subdivisions within each developmental stage
4. Endocrine status
5. Dominance/subordination relationships
6. Experiential history
   a. Early rearing conditions
   b. Early and later specifically sexual as well as other experience with same-sex and opposite-sex conspecifics
7. Environmental conditions
   a. Physical conditions: captive versus wild, cage versus compound, or corral versus free- or semi-free-ranging conditions
   b. Group composition and social complexity: single sex versus mixed sex and absolute numbers of individuals, by sex and by age
   c. Tenure in a group or participation in tests: novel versus familiar individuals or conditions
   d. Test conditions: brief exposure versus group-living, contextual factors, e.g., feeding versus nonfeeding and restriction of contact (physical, visual, etc.)
   e. Season
8. Interactions among the foregoing

species have been studied, including age and sex distributions and environmental conditions. True species differences, however, are also apparent.

2. Homosexual behavior may occur between females but not males (wild mountain gorillas), or between individuals of both sexes (unisexual groups of captive rhesus monkeys), depending upon species and environmental conditions. Whether or not the reverse case of homosexual behavior between males but not females occurs among some species is not clear.

3. Homosexual behavior probably occurs in most immature nonhuman primates. Although technically termed homosexual behavior in that same-sex partners are involved, the sex of the partner seems to be irrelevant at this early stage of maturation.

4. Homosexual behavior occurs more frequently in females during the estrous phase of the cycle and perhaps more frequently among gonadectomized than intact males.

5. Homosexual behavior may or may not relate to dominance/subordination relationships. When such relationships are involved, the dominant animal may or may not take the superior position in mounting.

6. a. Homosexual behavior is facilitated by early isosexual rearing.

The full extent of the influence has not been determined. This is the area with the greatest potential for demonstrating a homosexual preference in a nonhuman primate.

b. Homosexual behavior is not maintained in individuals with early or later homosexual experience once those individuals have a heterosexual option (with one possible exception).

7. a. Homosexual behavior occurs more frequently in captive than in wild conditions, more frequently in cage, compound, or corral than in free- or semifree-ranging conditions.

b. Homosexual behavior occurs more frequently in unisexual than in heterosexual groups.

c. Homosexual behavior occurs more frequently in newly formed or otherwise socially unstable groups.

d. Homosexual behavior is stimulated by social excitement and visual access to copulating conspecifics.

e. Homosexual behavior in seasonally breeding species occurs during the breeding but not the nonbreeding season.

8. It should be clear that these generalizations apply to *some* sets of conditions but certainly not to all. Moreover, there is no intent to rank them according to the strength of their relative contributions to the performance of homosexual behavior.

Acknowledgments

Preparation of this review was supported by NIH Grant RR-00165 from the Division of Research Resources to the Yerkes Regional Primate Research Center and by NIH Grant HD-19060 and NSF Grant BNS87-08406 to the the the author.

References

Akers, J. S., & Conway, C. H. (1979). Female homosexual behavior in *Macaca mulatta*. *Archives of Sexual Behavior, 8*, 63–80.

Anschel, S., & Talmage-Riggs, G. (1977). Social organization of captive monandrous squirrel monkey groups *(Saimiri sciureus)*. *Folia Primatologica, 28*, 203–215.

Anthoney, T. R. (1968). The ontogeny of greeting, grooming, and sexual motor patterns in captive baboons (superspecies *Papio cynocephalus*). *Behaviour, 31*, 358–372.

Baldwin, J. D. (1969). The ontogeny of social behavior of squirrel monkeys (*Saimiri sciureus*) in a seminatural environment. *Folia Primatologica, 11*, 35–79.

Beach, F. A. (1948). *Hormones and behavior*. New York: Paul B. Hoeber.

Beach, F. A. (1976). Sexual attractivity, proceptivity, and receptivity in female mammals. *Hormones and Behavior, 7*, 105–138.

Bernstein, I. S. (1970). Primate status hierarchies. In L. A. Rosenblum (Ed)., *Primate behavior*, (Vol. 1, pp. 71–109). New York: Academic Press.

Bernstein, I. S., & Mason, W. A. (1963). Group formation by rhesus monkeys. *Animal Behavior, 11*, 28–31.

Bingham, H. C. (1928). Sex development in apes. *Comparative Psychology Monographs, 5*, 1–65.

Bolwig, N. (1959). A study of the behaviour of the Chacma baboon, *Papio ursinus. Behaviour, 14*, 136–163.

Carpenter, C. R. (1942). Sexual behavior of free ranging rhesus monkeys (*Macaca mulatta*). II. Periodicity of estrus, homosexual, autoerotic and nonconformist behavior. *Journal of Comparative Psychology, 33*, 143–162.

Chevalier-Skolnikoff, S. (1974). Male-female, female-female, and male-male sexual behavior in the stumptail monkey, with special attention to the female orgasm. *Archives of Sexual Behavior, 3*, 95–116.

Chevalier-Skolnikoff, S. (1976). Homosexual behavior in a laboratory group of stumptail monkeys (*Macaca arctoides*): forms, contexts, and possible social functions. *Archives of Sexual Behavior, 5*, 511–527.

Coffin, R. (1978). Sexual behavior in a group of captive young gorillas. *Boletin de Estudios Medicos y Biogolicos*, [Bulletin of Medical and Biologic Studies], Mexico City, *30*, 65–69.

Conaway, C. H., & Sorenson, M. W. (1966). Reproduction in tree shrews. *Symposium of the Zoological Society of London, 15*, 471–492.

Dixson, A. F. (1977). Observations on the displays, menstrual cycles and sexual behaviour of the "Black ape" of Celebes (*Macaca nigra*). *Journal of Zoology, London, 182*, 63–84.

Dixson, A. F., Scruton, D. M., & Herbert, J. (1975). Behavior of the Talapoin monkey (*Miopithecus talapoin*) studied in groups, in the laboratory. *Journal of Zoology, 176*, 177–210.

DuMond, F. V. (1968). The squirrel monkey in a seminatural environment. In L. A. Rosenblum & R. W. Cooper, (Eds.), *The squirrel monkey*, (pp. 87–145). New York: Academic Press.

Eaton, G. G. (1978). Longitudinal studies of sexual behavior in the Oregon troop of Japanese macaques. In T. E. McGill, D. A. Dewsbury, & B. D. Sachs (Eds.), *Sex and behavior* (pp. 35–59). New York: Plenum.

Enomoto, T. (1974). The sexual behavior of Japanese monkeys. *Journal of Human Evolution, 3*, 351–372.

Erwin, J., & Maple, T. (1976). Ambisexual behavior with male- male anal penetration in male rhesus monkeys. *Archives of Sexual Behavior, 5*, 9–14.

Fairbanks, L. A., McGuire, M. T., and Kerber, W. (1977). Sex and aggression during rhesus monkey group formation. *Aggressive Behavior, 3*, 241–249.

Fedigan, L. M., & Gouzoules, H. (1978). The consort relationship in a troop of Japanese monkeys. In D. J. Chivers & J. Herbert (Eds.), *Recent advances in primatology* (Vol. 1, pp. 493–495). New York: Academic Press.

Gartlan, J. S. (1969). Sexual and maternal behaviour of the vervet monkey, *Cercopithecus aethiops. Journal of Reproduction & Fertility, Supplement 6*, 137–150.

Goldfoot, D. A. (1977). Sociosexual behaviors of nonhuman primates during development and maturity: Social and hormonal relationships. In A. M. Schrier (Ed.), *Behavioral Primatology—Advances in research and theory* (Vol. 1, pp. 139–184). Hillsdale, NJ: Lawrence Erlbaum.

Goldfoot, D. A., Wallen, K., Neff, D. A., McBrair, M. C., & Goy, R. W. (1984). Social influences on the display of sexually dimorphic behavior in rhesus monkeys: Isosexual rearing. *Archives of Sexual Behavior, 13*, 395–412.

Goldfoot, D. A., Westerborg-van Loon, H., Groeneveld, W., & Slob, A. K. (1980). Behavioral and physiological evidence of sexual climax in the female stump-tailed macaque (*Macaca arctoides*). *Science, 208*, 1447–1479.

Gordon, T. P. & Bernstein, I. S. (1973). Seasonal variation in sexual behavior of all-male rhesus troops. *American Journal of Physical Anthropology, 38*, 221–226.

Goy, R. W., Wallen, K., & Goldfoot, D. A. (1974). Social factors affecting the development of mounting behavior in male rhesus monkeys. In W. Montagna & W. A. Sadler (Eds.), *Reproductive behavior* (pp. 1–12). New York: Plenum.

Green, R. (1972). Homosexuality as a mental illness. *International Journal of Psychiatry, 10,* 77–98.

Hamilton, G. V. (1914). A study of sexual tendencies in monkeys and baboons. *Journal of Animal Behavior, 4,* 295–318.

Hanby, J. P. (1974). Male-male mounting in Japanese monkeys (*Macaca fuscata*). *Animal Behavior, 22,* 836–849.

Hanby, J. P., & Brown, C. E. (1974). The development of sociosexual behaviours in Japanese macaques *Macaca fuscata. Behaviour, 49,* 152–196.

Hanby, J. P., Robertson, L. T., & Phoenix, C. H. (1971). The sexual behavior of a confined troop of Japanese macaques. *Folia Primatologica, 16,* 123–143.

Harcourt, A. H., Stewart, K. J., & Fossey, D. (1981). Gorilla reproduction in the wild. In C. E. Graham (Ed.), *Reproductive biology of the great apes* (pp. 265–279). New York: Academic Press.

Harvey, N. C. (1983). Social and sexual behavior during the menstrual cycle in a colony of stumptail macaques *(Macaca arctoides).* In H. D. Steklis & A. S. Kling (Eds.), *Hormones, drugs and social behavior in primates* (pp. 141–174). New York: Spectrum.

Hess, J. P. (1973). Some observations on the sexual behaviour of captive lowland gorillas, *Gorilla gorilla* (Savage and Wyman). In R. P. Michael & J. H. Crook (Eds.), *Comparative ecology and behaviour of primates* (pp.507–581). London: Academic Press.

Hrdy, S. B. (1977). *The langurs of Abu.* Cambridge, MA: Harvard University Press.

Jay, P. (1965). The common langur of north India. In I. Devore (Ed.), *Primate behavior* (pp. 197–249). New York: Holt, Rinehart & Winston.

Kano, T. (1980). Social behavior of wild pygmy chimpanzees (*Pan paniscus*) of Wamba: A preliminary report. *Journal of Human Evolution, 9,* 243–260.

Kaufmann, J. H. (1965). A three-year study of mating behavior in a free-ranging band of rhesus monkeys. *Ecology, 46,* 500–512.

Kempf, E. J. (1917). The social and sexual behavior of infra-human primates with some comparable facts in human behavior. *Psychoanalytic Review, 4,* 127–154.

Kohler, W. (1925). *The mentality of apes.* London: Routledge & Kegan Paul.

Kollar, E. J., Beckwith, W. C., & Edgerton, R. B. (1968). Sexual behavior of the ARL colony chimpanzees. *Journal of Nervous and Mental Disorders, 147,* 444–459.

Kuroda, S. (1979). Grouping of the pygmy chimpanzees. *Primates, 20,* 161–183.

Kuroda, S. (1980). Social behavior of the pygmy chimpanzees. *Primates, 21,* 181–197.

Kuroda, S. (1984). Interaction over food among pygmy chimpanzees. In R. L. Susman (Ed.), *The pygmy chimpanzee* (pp. 301–324). New York: Plenum.

Latta, J., Hopf, S., & Ploog, D. (1967). Observations on the mating behavior and sexual play in the squirrel monkey *(Saimiri sciureus). Primates, 8,* 229–246.

Lemmon, W. B. (1971). Experiential factors and sexual behavior in male chimpanzees. In Medical primatology 1970. *Proceedings of the Second Conference on Experimental Medicine and Surgery in Primates, New York 1969* (pp. 432–440). Basel: Karger.

Loy, J. (1971). Estrous behavior of free-ranging rhesus monkeys(*Macaca mulatta*). *Primates, 12,* 1–31.

Loy, J. & Loy, K. (1974). Behavior of an all-juvenile group of rhesus monkeys. *American Journal of Physical Anthropology, 40,* 83–96.

MacKinnon, J. K. (1974). The behavior and ecology of wild orang-utans (*Pongo pygmaeus*). *Animal Behavior, 22*, 3–74.

Makwana, S. C. (1980). Observations on population and behavior of the bonnet monkey, *Macaca radiata*. *Comparative Physiology and Ecology, 5*, 9–12.

Malinowski, B. (1927). *Sex and repression in savage society*. New York: Harcourt Brace Jovanovich.

Maple, T. L. (1980). *Orang-utan behavior*. New York: Van Nostrand Reinhold.

Maple, T., Bernard, D., & McGlynn, M. (1977). Dominance related ambisexuality in two male rhesus monkeys *(Macaca mulatta)*. *Journal of Biological Psychology, 19*, 25–28.

Maslow, A. H. (1936). The role of dominance in the social and sexual behavior of infra-human primates: III. A theory of sexual behavior of infra-human primates. *Journal of Genetic Psychology, 48*, 310–338.

Mason, W. A. (1960). The effects of social restriction on the behavior of rhesus monkeys. I. Free social behavior. *Journal of Comparative and Physiological Psychology, 53*, 582–589.

Miller, G. S., Jr. (1928). Some elements of sexual behavior in primates and their possible influence on the beginnings of human social development. *Journal of Mammalogy, 9*, 273–293.

Morris, D. (1970). The response of animals to a restricted environment. In D. Morris (Ed.), *Patterns of reproductive behavior* (pp. 490–511). New York: McGraw-Hill.

Murray, R. D., Bour, E. S., & Smith, E. 0. (1985). Female menstrual cyclicity and sexual behavior in stumptail macaques *(Macaca arctoides)*. *International Journal of Primatology, 6*, 101–113.

Nadler, R. D. (1977). Sexual behavior of captive orang-utans. *Archives of Sexual Behavior, 6*, 457–475.

Nadler, R. D. (1982). Reproductive behavior and endocrinology of orang-utans. In L. E. M. de Boer, (Ed.), *The orang-utan: Its biology and conservation* (pp. 231–248). The Hague: Dr. W. Junk Publications.

Nadler, R. D. (1986). Sex-related behavior of immature wild mountain gorillas. *Developmental Psychobiology, 19*, 125–137.

Nadler, R. D., Herndon, J. G., & Wallis, J. (1986). Adult sexual behavior: Hormones and reproduction. In G. Mitchell & J. Erwin (Eds.), *Comparative primate biology: Vol. 2A. Behavior, conservation, and ecology* (pp. 363–407). New York: Alan R. Liss.

Ploog, D., Hopf, S., & Winter, P. (1967). Ontogenese des Verhaltens von Totenhopfaffen *(Saimiri sciureus)*. *Psychologische Forschung, 31*, 1–41.

Plooij, F. X. (1984). *The behavioral development of free-living chimpanzee babies and infants*. Norwood, NJ: Ablex.

Pomerantz, S. M., & Goy, R. W. (1983). Proceptive behavior of female rhesus monkeys during tests with tethered males. *Hormones and Behavior, 17*, 237–248.

Riesen, A. H. (1971). Nissen's observations on the development of sexual behavior in captive-born, nursery-reared chimpanzees. In G. H. Bourne (Ed.), *The chimpanzee, 4*, (pp. 1–18). Basel: Karger.

Rijksen, H. D. (1978). *A field study of sumatran orang-utans (Pongo pygmaeus abelii Lesson 1827) Ecology, behavior and conservation, 78–2*. Wageningen, Netherlands: Meded. Landbouwhogeschool.

Rogers, C. M., & Davenport, R. K. (1969). Effects of restricted rearing on sexual behavior of chimpanzees. *Developmental Psychology, 1*, 200–204.

Ruiz de Elvira, M. C., Herndon, J. G., & Collins, D. C. (1983). Effect of estradiol-treated females on all-female groups of rhesus monkeys during the transition between the nonbreeding and breeding seasons. *Folia Primatologica., 41*, 191–203.

Sade, D. S. (1968). Inhibition of son-mother mating among free-ranging rhesus monkeys. In J. H. Masserman (Ed.), *Animal and human: Science and psychoanalysis* Vol. 12, (pp. 18–38). New York: Grune & Stratton.

Savage, S., & Bakeman, R. (1978). Sexual morphology and behavior in *Pan paniscus*. In D. J. Chivers & J. Herbert, (Eds.) *Recent advances in primatology*, Vol. 1 (pp. 613–616). New York: Academic Press.

Savage-Rumbaugh, E. S., & Wilkerson, B. J. (1978). Socio-sexual behavior in *Pan paniscus* and *Pan troglodytes*: A comparative study. *Journal of Human Evolution, 7*, 327–344.

Simonds, P. E. (1965). The bonnet macaque in south India. In I. DeVore (Ed.), *Primate behavior* (pp. 175–196). New York: Holt, Rinehart, & Winston.

Skinner, S. W., & Lochard, J. S. (1979). An ethogram of the liontail macaque (*Macaca silenus*) in capitivity. *Applied Animal Ethology, 5*, 241–253.

Slob, A. K. & Schenck, P. E. (1986). Heterosexual experience and isosexual behavior in laboratory-housed male stump-tailed macaques *(M. arctoides)*. *Archives of Sexual Behavior, 15*, 261–268.

Takahata, Y. (1980). The reproductive biology of a free-ranging troop of Japanese monkeys. *Primates, 21*, 303–329.

Takahata, Y. (1982). The socio-sexual behavior of Japanese monkeys. *Zeitschrift fur Tierpsycholgie, 59*, 89–108.

Talmage-Riggs, G., & Anschel, S. (1973). Homosexual behavior and dominance hierarchy in a group of captive female squirrel monkeys *(Saimiri sciureus)*. *Folia Primatologica, 19*, 61–72.

Thompson-Handler, N., Malenky, R. K., & Badrian, N. (1984). Sexual behavior of *Pan paniscus* under natural conditions in the Lomako Forest, Equateur, Zaire. In R. L. Susman (Ed.), *The pygmy chimpanzee* (pp. 347–368). New York: Plenum.

Tokuda, K., Simons, R. C., & Jensen, G. D. (1968). Sexual behavior in a captive group of pigtailed monkeys (*Macaca nemestrina*). *Primates, 9*, 283–294.

Travis, J. C., & Holmes, W. N. (1974). Some physiological and behavioural changes associated with oestrus and pregnancy in the squirrel monkey (*Saimiri sciureus*). *Journal of Zoology (London), 174*, 41–66.

Tutin, C. E. G., & McGinnis, P. R. (1981). Chimpanzee reproduction in the wild. In C. E. Graham (Ed.), *Reproductive biology of the great apes* (pp. 239–264). New York: Academic Press.

Vandenbergh, J. G. (1965). Hormonal basis of sex skin in male rhesus monkeys. *General and Comparative Endocrinology, 5*, 31–34.

van Lawick-Goodall, J. (1968). The behavior of free-living chimpanzees in the Gombe Stream Reserve. *Animal Behavior Monographs, 1*, 161–311.

Wallen, K., Winston, L. A., Gaventa, S., Davis-DaSilva, M., & Collins, D. C. (1984). Periovulatory changes in female sexual behavior and patterns of ovarian steroid secretion in group-living rhesus monkeys. *Hormones and Behavior, 18*, 431–450.

Wolfe, L. (1978). Age and sexual behavior of Japanese macaques (*Macaca fuscata*). *Archives of Sexual Behavior, 7*, 55–68.

Wolfe, L. (1979). Behavioral patterns of estrous females of the Arashiyama West troop of Japanese macaques (*Macaca fuscata*). *Primates, 20*, 525–534.

Wolfheim, J. H., & Rowell, T. E. (1972). Communication among captive talapoin monkeys (*Miopithecus talapoin*). *Folia Primatologica, 18*, 224–255.

Yerkes, R. M. (1939). Social dominance and sexual status in the chimpanzee. *Quarterly Review Biology, 14*, 115–136.

Zuckerman, S. (1981). *The social life of monkeys and apes* (2nd ed.). London: Routledge & Kegan Paul. (Original edition published 1932)

11

Primates, Homo Sapiens, and Homosexuality

Leonard A. Rosenblum

In decrying the problems of early efforts to establish the potential "biological basis" of human homosexuality through the study of nonhuman animal forms, Kinsey, Pomeroy, and Martin (1948) point to the confusions between object choice and the presumptive maleness or femaleness of the behaviors in which the subject engaged:

> In most of the literature on animal behavior it [the term *homosexuality*] is applied on the basis of the general conspectus of the behavior pattern of the animal, its aggressiveness in seeking sexual contact, its postures during coitus, its position relative to the other animal in the sex relation, and the conformance or disconformance of that behavior to the usual positions and activities of the animal during heterosexual coitus. (p. 613)

Modern observations of the sexual behaviors of human and nonhuman forms alike have underlined the diversity of behavior patterns observed in both males and females whether engaged with partners of their own or the other sex. Nowhere in the nonhuman portion of the animal kingdom has this variety been more in evidence than in the study of the nonhuman primates. In any number of species, males and females may spend the great majority of their time with either members of their own or the other sex, strong alliances and mutually supportive relationships may occur within or across sexual lines, and postures usually associated with male or female copulatory patterns may be observed in members of either sex while engaged with partners of either sex. Among the primates, under various conditions it is by no means unusual to observe either sex presenting the hindquarters to members of either sex, males mounting males, females mounting females, and even females mounting males in a manner that to the casual observer may be indistinguishable from reproductively successful male-female coitus.

In his comprehensive review of the nonhuman primate literature relevant to the question of whether any phylogenetic anlagen of human homosexuality can be discerned, Nadler (see Chapter 10) has chosen to follow more closely the admonition of Kinsey et al. (1948):

> It would encourage clearer thinking on these matters if persons were not characterized as heterosexual or homosexual, but as individuals who have had certain amounts of heterosexual experience and certain amounts of homosexual experience. Instead of using these terms as substantives which stand for persons, or even as adjectives to describe persons, they may better be used to describe the nature of the overt sexual relations, or of the stimuli to which an individual erotically responds. (p. 617)

Thus Nadler focuses his attention not on the interpretation of homosexual behavior as "male" or "female" behaviors that are considered incongruent with anatomical sex, but rather on the interactions between same-sex partners in which there appears to be reasonable evidence of sexual arousal. If one follows this guideline, answers to a number of significant questions regarding homosexual behaviors in nonhuman primates clearly emerge from the literature. The questions are these:

1. Do males and females of various primate species engage in sexually arousing interaction with members of their own sex?
2. Can primates show preferences for sexual interaction with same-sex partners even when heterosexual opportunities are present?
3. Are homosexual activities strictly determined by or always the mere expression of a dominance-subordinate relationship?
4. Are homosexual activities subject to neuroendocrine factors similar to those involved in heterosexual patterns?
5. Are there sex differences in the frequency with which primates engage in homosexual activities?
6. Can early experiences influence the frequency of homosexual activities?
7. Are any male and/or female primates exclusively homosexual?

It appears clear that the answer to the first six questions is yes, whereas at present the answer to the last question must be no; no evidence has as yet emerged to suggest that any nonhuman primate studied to date would rate a 6 on the Kinsey scale of heterosexuality/homosexuality. Similarly, in keeping with the general themes of the data presented in this volume, a variety of developmental, environmental, and circumstantial factors may influence the relative mix or preponderance of homosexual and heterosexual behavior in which any given individuals engage during any particular period of their lives. Thus, just as a variety of human data reflect, homosexual activity may be relatively common during the play of preadolescents. As Nadler correctly emphasizes, perhaps as a result of the more easily assessed sexual arousal in males, this behavior is more frequently recorded in males. Rearing in species-atypical groups, such as those including only one other animal or only members of the subject's own sex, may increase the likelihood of homosexual expression. Again, as has been repeatedly demonstrated in humans, conditions of confinement and physical or psychological restrictions of access to opposite-sex partners may also increase the frequency of homosexual behaviors. Hormonal factors relating to seasonality or to within-season cyclic fluctuations (or their experimental analogues) may influence the expression of homosexual as well as heterosexual interactions. Most significantly, virtually all subjects who at one time or another have been observed to engage in overtly sexual homosexual behavior, at other times, often both prior to and subsequent to the homosexual activities, have been observed to engage in active heterosexual patterns generally characteristic of their species.

In spite of the clarity of findings relating to these basic questions, Nadler's review also brings our attention to several essential theoretical issues that, because of their continued relevance to our concerns at the human level, require some additional comment. In maintaining a focus on the directly observable patterns of interaction and sexual arousal, our understanding of the literature still remains somewhat cloudier regarding the complex issues of motivation, that ubiquitous, unobservable bête noire of so much of psychology. As Nadler makes abundantly clear, sexual arousal may emerge as the by-product of playful interactions or dominance assertions. The subsequent continuance of the behavior at times appears to be sustained by the emergent sexual reinforcements but at other times appears ambiguously to be the product of the initial and subsequent motivations combined. Perhaps all behavior, human and nonhuman alike, is always multiply determined, that is, is always the product of the confluence of diverse motivational factors, some more and some less salient at any given time.

Notwithstanding the often unfathomable reaches of the unconscious motives of humans, at least with humans we have the ability to ask a subject "why?"—a luxury (or some behaviorists might say, a liability) that we lack when working with animal subjects. Since our concerns with human sexuality in general ultimately go far beyond issues of arousal and

orgasm and certainly require consideration of those aspects of relationships that prevail beyond periods of sexual arousal, our appreciation of
the relevance of nonhuman primate studies to an understanding of human homosexuality must confront the motivation issue. At present, it is
my judgment that we can only say that each action between same-sex
individuals (as with heterosexual encounters), whether overt sexual
arousal is present or not, reflects a number of motivational sources and
speaks to a number of dimensions of the relationship between those
individuals. In the absence of explicitly controlled, manipulative studies,
we can say no more than that.

This latter issue raises one additional point of interest, touched on
briefly in Nadler's amusing addendum to his chapter; that is, what can we
say about "homosexuality" rather than "homosexual behavior" in the
nonhuman primates? If, for example, as the Bell and Weinberg (1978) data
suggest, 16% of the white homosexual males and 29% of the white homosexual females in their sample (with somewhat lower but nonetheless
significant percentages in their smaller black sample) engaged in sexual
behavior once a month or less, how are we to think about the nonovertly
sexual relationships between same-sex members of primate groups?
Clearly, in some species both males and females spend considerably more
time and engage in a considerably greater number of close, affiliative
behaviors with members of their own as opposed to the other sex, accompanied by often relatively brief, seasonally delimited heterosexual copulatory patterns. It seems to me that future studies of nonhuman primates,
both within and across species and including those that are both naturalis-
tic and manipulative, should give consideration to the potentially separate genetic, experiential, and neuroendocrine factors that may underlie
the disparate dimensions of social interactions of same-sex partners, including those whose rewards fall within a more general sphere of affective and affiliative bonding. In the end, of course, we can draw no conclusions regarding the human condition from primate studies but only hope
to generate meaningful hypotheses worthy of testing at the human level.
Some matters may rest upon humans studying and understanding humans alone, and for those issues we can join Mark Twain in believing
"that our heavenly father invented man because he was disappointed in
the monkey."

References

Bell, A. P., & Weinberg, M. S. (1978). *Homosexualities: A study of diversity among men
and women*. New York: Simon & Schuster.
Kinsey, A. C., Pomeroy, W. B., & Martin, C. E. (1948). *Sexual behavior in the human
male*. Philadelphia: W. B. Saunders.

IV

CULTURAL
AND SOCIOLOGICAL
PERSPECTIVES

12

Gender Preference in Erotic Relations: The Kinsey Scale and Sexual Scripts

John H. Gagnon

The contemporary study of "homosexuality," "bisexuality," and "hetero-sexuality," or more generally "sexual orientation" or "sexual preference," is in a muddled state. It is tempting to call the current scientific situation of these topics "revolutionary," or more mildly, "interparadigmatic," but that suggests a more coherent program of research than has previously existed and presumes an equally coherent, though differently ordered, program may follow (Kuhn, 1970, 1977). In addition, the interdisciplinary character of sexual studies makes the vocabulary of paradigms seem less plausible than it appears to be when applied to marked changes within a delimited subfield of a larger discipline that has conventionally acceptable boundaries. The issue is both more diffuse and more complex and is perhaps better indicated by the quotation marks that have been placed around what are commonly taken to be scientifically unambigious terms.

The quotation marks are meant to suggest the coexistence of confidence and doubt. The routineness of use of terms such as *homosexuality* and *homosexual* in a variety of scientific and lay contexts expresses a widely held, perhaps near universal, belief that we know what these words instruct us to think and to study. At the same time there is a tendency within a number of fields concerned with sexuality to believe that these received classifications are in need of unpacking, so that we might ap-proach the conduct that they identify not as universals or singular es-sences but as complex assemblies of human conduct that may be funda-mentally unalike in different cultural spaces and historical times. This argument recognizes the importance, in some cases the priority, of the terminological, for it is the names that we are called that justify the sticks and stones that hurt us.

What is proposed in this chapter is to set forth an alternative conception of the relation between sexual studies, sexual conduct, and the cultural-historical context and to examine two examples of the ways in which this conception can lead to a different consideration of both sexual theory and sexual conduct. This will involve three tasks. The first is to discuss the relations between sexual science and its objects of inquiry as well as the culture of which both are constituents. This discussion will emphasize the multiplicity and interdependency of these relations rather than their singularity and independence. The second task is to apply the results of this discussion to Kinsey's treatment of homosexuality and heterosexuality, particularly as embodied in the heterosexuality/homosexuality scale. Kinsey's treatment of these matters is at the midpoint of the history of sexual studies and represents the first major break from the medical and psychoanalytic conceptions that dominated prior thought. The third task is to consider recent developments in sexual theory, particularly those associated with sexual scripting, and to discuss how these developments can be used to better understand the transformations in the conduct of gay men and lesbians since the middle of the 1960s.

Sexual Studies and Cultural Context

Sexual Studies and Sexual Reform

Until very recently sexual liberals commonly believed that the emergence of a scientific sexology at the end of the nineteenth century was an unalloyed triumph of "truth" over Victorian repressiveness (Weeks, 1981). Placing sex on the agenda of science meant that a new attitude of mind, as expressed in the scientific method, would provide an objective version of human sexual needs or capacities. This scientifically authorized version of the sexual would in turn serve as the basis for appropriate social reform. Freud did not entirely subscribe to this positivist vision of sexual redemption through science, although he was committed to those reforms that his theories and limited optimism could envisage. However, it was a matter of faith among the late nineteenth century sexologists such as Magnus Hirschfeld, Albert Moll, and Havelock Ellis that scientific knowledge would combat the antisexual values of the cultural majority (Robinson, 1976).

In the period between the turn of century and the present, this reformist spirit has continued to animate most sex researchers, including many psychoanalysts, in the United States, which has been the major center for research in sexuality. Whatever disputes might have existed among sex researchers about the particular explanations of different sexual practices, what all (here including Freud) would have agreed upon was the privileged character of the scientific enterprise. To them, science and its methods represented an independent and self-correcting system of knowledge production—though dominant groups in a culture could decide not to implement what scientists knew, they did so only out of error.

Despite the expressed views of many researchers that they only dealt with "what is" and not "what ought to be," from its beginnings this attempt to take a detached and "value-free" stance toward sexuality has always resulted in a constant struggle between the researchers and various religious and political groups. These groups correctly perceived that the existence of a relativistic attitude toward sexuality when embodied in independent scientific institutions would fundamentally erode the social dominance of the traditional cultural scenario in which gender and sexuality were exemplary moral functions. And indeed the practice of sex research has, in combination with other social forces, produced substantial changes in the moral and legal status of various sexual practices. Even the proliferation of new dichotomies with which we label conformity to or violations of rules governing sexual life attest to the role of sexual studies in changing the sexual landscape. What were once solely questions of vice/virtue or the unnatural/natural (e.g., the practice of oral sex or masturbation) have been transformed into issues of more variable moral intensity. Indeed oral sex is now treated by many of the sexually unadventurous (excluding the Supreme Court) in the United States as a matter of competent sexual technique rather than as sodomy (Gagnon & Simon, 1987). Practices that were once examples of the perverse, the infantile, the abnormal, the deviant are now, among many social groups, mostly matters of convention or taste.

That there now exists in most Western societies a spectrum of opinion on sexual matters ranging from vice to taste is in part the result of the success of liberal sexual ideologies and the legitimation of a variety of sexual practices (the prevalence of which often preexisted the legitimation). However, these continue to coexist with traditional sexual ideologies that have a less benign vision of even the limited set of sexual practices that they allow. While the weight of opinion has shifted in a more liberal direction, a shift supported by scientific sexology, most of the social orders in which such sex research programs have emerged remain deeply divided about many aspects of sexuality. In most large Western societies the erotic is simultaneously promoted and denied, homophobia remains the norm, the genders are segregated in many domains of social life, antiwoman practices and values are widespread, and there is usually no widely approved system for acquiring and practicing a sexual life at any stage in the life course. These conditions continue to shape not only the sexual lives that sex researchers study but the ways in which sex researchers think about those lives. As a consequence, research reports on pornography, scientific books on sadomasochism, studies of the internal secretions of homosexuals and heterosexuals, reports on the erotic experiences of women cannot be treated as merely the results of disinterested inquiry but represent moral and political acts in larger dramas of liberation and repression.

The Scientific Construction of Sexual Life

The recognition that sexual studies are ineluctably part of a larger arena of moral and political struggle and that debates about scientific knowledge (even those among scientists) are concerned with more than scientific knowledge is, however, only the first step in understanding the larger conceptual and intellectual difficulty within sexual studies. It is now better understood that the right to explain social phenomena is not neutral and that who explains a phenomenon and how it is explained are central to the control, or more strongly, the construction of that phenomenon (Foucault, 1978, 1979; Peckham, 1969, 1979). The analytic distinction between control in the weak sense of participating in the social management of a phenomenon and control in the strong sense that involves the social construction of a phenomenon is one of emphasis. Clearly, one merges into the other; medical doctors, when diagnosing and treating "homosexuals," participate both in the management of the behavior of the patient and in the maintenance of the cultural category "the homosexual."

In both of these senses of control—management and construction—scientists and their explanations are part and parcel of the phenomenon that they study. The research they conduct contributes to and is responsive to change in that phenomenon. While only some members of the community of scientists who deal with sexuality are directly involved with social control (e.g., psychiatrists who formulate diagnostic manuals, therapists who treat individuals and couples, those who castrate sex offenders), the majority indirectly influence the social order by providing the attitudinal and factual content of various forms of media (textbooks, television shows, science reports in the newspapers) and by affecting (again, indirectly) institutional practices and procedures in the public and private sectors (Scheff, 1968; Szasz, 1961). Even the promotion of a decline in traditional forms of social control over sexual practices based on scientific studies (e.g., repealing laws against obscenity) serves to change, at least in some modest ways, how sexual life is controlled (in the widest sense) in a society.

This understanding that sexual studies are an active ingredient in social control is not difficult to understand and is fairly widely understood. Indeed, in the weak form of social management it is not in opposition to a positivist view that the results of the scientific enterprise are privileged in terms of their truth value. Even a constructionist perspective might allow that explanations and facts based on a scientific method might be, in some sense, more "true" than those based on folklore, common sense, or religious praxis. However, what has been a less popular perspective (at least until the last decade) is that explanations of sexual conduct in the human sciences have a number of other, deeper connections with the surrounding cultural order. Probably the most important of these is the one that they share with all forms of human conduct, including those they claim to explain, which is that they bear the permanent mark of the time and place in which they are created. This historical grounding of explanatory statements, including scientific paradigms, places a fundamental limitation on understandings between different cultures and between the present and past in any culture (history being a variant of cross-cultural research) (Darnton, 1984). Members of the present are limited in their ability to understand the past in both its collective and individual dimensions because of fundamental cultural constraints on what can be known. These constraints mean that in any culture the not-knowable is a domain created by that which members now know and the conventional explanatory network that holds that knowledge together (Fleck, 1979). The not-knowable is composed of the past worlds we have lost, the future worlds we will never inhabit, and contemporary worlds that are so alien that they cannot be thought except by those who are natives (see Herdt, Chapter 13). Members of all cultures, including the culture of science, share with Veblen's engineers that trained incapacity is the mark of the native (Veblen, 1964).

This view that the theories, techniques, and observations of the separate scientific disciplines (indeed, even the existence of "separate disciplines") are historically and culturally situated and change in interaction with that historical and cultural situation has been most frequently discussed in the social studies component of sex research. It is most commonly held in sociology, anthropology, clinical psychology, and certain areas in historical studies, where the traditional boundaries between fields are weakening and where even the weak positivist assumptions about "science" are becoming more suspect (Geertz 1973, 1983). In these fields it is recognized that the human beings who are the objects of inquiry of these disciplines change both in interaction with and independently of changes in the disciplines themselves. Indeed, it is proper to observe that many of the conceptual difficulties that are treated as internal to the study of sexuality have actually resulted from changes in what have been treated as the field's "objects of inquiry." Thus, changes in the social, political, and economic status of women and their ideological correlate, feminism, have been the primary grounds for constituting a field called the study of gender. Similarly, the political and ideological efforts of gay male and lesbian liberation have transformed the study of gender preference in erotic relations.

The Cultural Specificity of Gender Preference

In the study of gender preferences in erotic relations (otherwise known as heterosexuality or homosexuality, gay sex, lesbianism, straight sex, or sexual orientation), the characteristics of the sexual actor and his or her conduct is increasingly recognized as a specifically cultural and historical artifact. Whatever the similarity in the arrangement of the sexes and their genitals, it is apparent that sex between men and women, men and men, and women and women is not the same in differing cultures and at differing moments in history. More specifically, neither the sexuality between married men and women nor the sexuality of older men with young men nor the sexuality praised by Sappho in classical Greece can be made comparable, without significant acts of translation, with married heterosexuality or male or female homosexuality in the modern United States (Gagnon & Simon, 1973). The conduct could not have been learned in the same contexts, it is not practiced for the same purposes, it is not maintained by the same social forces, and it does not cease to be practiced at the same moments in the life course for the same reasons. The social construction of sexuality (and even if sexuality exists as a separable domain in a culture) and its connnections to nonsexual conduct are specific to the cultural and historical circumstances of a particular social order.

What this means for the study of gender preference in erotic relations is that the facile application of modern "scientific" explanations of how persons in another time or place acquire, maintain, transform, and extinguish their "homosexuality" or "heterosexuality" and the relations of that sexuality to the larger social order usually involves unrecognized acts of translation and reconstruction. In most cases this makes the other historical moment or culture into a puppet through whose mouth the scientific ventriloquist speaks. Thus, the application of contemporary psychoanalytic, sociobiological, sociological, or biological theories of the origins of gender preference to sexual practices among the classical Greeks (Dover, 1978), the monks of the Middle Ages (Boswell, 1980), early nineteenth century romantics (Crompton, 1985), or the natives of Melanesia (Herdt, 1981, 1984) is an act of theoretical hubris. Even the decision to apply modern names to the conduct should require, though it usually does not, a certain delicacy since these usages bring with them the assumptions of the time and place in which they were invented.[1] Is it appropriate to call persons with same-gender erotic preferences in other times and places "gay" or "homosexual" or "lesbian?" In what sense do they possess a "sexual orientation" or a "gender preference?"

It is possible to argue that such terminological niceties are unreasonable or excessively strict and might result in our only using the natives' words for such conduct. And indeed there is some debate among contemporary natives about which of their words should be used for same-gender and other-gender erotic preferences: homosexuals, heterosexuals, gays, sodomites, fags, dykes, breeders, clones, woman-identified women, straights. It could be claimed that everyone knows what we mean when we label someone homosexual and at least it has the virtue of being widely used—more subtly it could be suggested that *homosexual* is the contemporary word and thus culturally applicable to the natives and the practices that it has served to name. Thus, homosexual and homosexuality could be construed to be merely provisional and weakly held labels for what everyone recognizes is a more complex reality. What is required, however, is more than a certain caution in naming, though that would be an advance. What is required is a constant recognition that acts of usage and explanation are acts of social control in the strong sense, that "homosexual" and "homosexuality" are names that have been imposed on some persons and their conduct by other persons—and that this imposition has carried the right of the latter to tell the former the origins, meaning, and virtue of their conduct.

This issue of names and explanations is thus linked to the conflict between the rights of members (in this case gay men and lesbians) and the rights of nonmembers (in this case psychoanalysts, sociologists, biologists, and other currently "authorized" scientific explainers) to explain the conduct of the membership. Within Western societies certain occupational groups have gained possession of explaining rights for same-gender erotic preferences, and the individuals and the conduct so marked are possessed as part of that group's turf. Such explanation rights bring, in addition to the pleasures of complex and dominating thought, such material benefits as career advancement, research grants and fellowships, professional deference, and opportunities for performing in the mass media. While these rights are always in contention there are constant within and between group struggles over what individuals or professions have such rights (e.g., biologists versus sociologists, feminists versus psychoanalysts, fundamentalists versus secular humanists, psychologist M versus psychologist E), there are often fairly long periods (though they have grown shorter in recent times) during which one voice or another drowns out the rest. In modern societies with the availability of message multipliers (the print media, radio, and television), such explainers can be widely heard and sometimes believed. The point is that authorized explainers, whoever they might be, are in the process of inventing social and psychological facts as often as they are discovering them, and such authorized facts are often "disproved" or at least "disbelieved" when a revisionist group of authorized speakers seize the means of communication.

Privileged and Everyday Beliefs

In modern societies authorized explanations often become the basis for everyday belief, replacing what would have been systems of folk belief in less media-dominated societies. In the area of sexuality this is most evident among the college educated, whose exposure to the cliches of authorized social science in various university courses provides them with scientifically acceptable "explanations" of conduct. Such explanations are often refinements of beliefs acquired earlier in life, but in some cases beliefs that are entirely novel are added to a student's repertoire of explanation. One consequence of this intimacy between explanation producers and explanation consumers is that future researchers are likely to hear answers to questions that are entirely congruent with prior explanations given in introductory textbooks. That a large body of scientific knowledge represents no better guide to action on the part of individuals (here think of volumes on the impact of child-rearing practices on personality development) than grandparents' tales or folklore has no bearing on the extent to which such knowledge is believed. Indeed, in many cases the formulation in the human science literature is folklore renamed and justified by "research data" (e.g., masturbation is not only a vice, it is a sign of mental disorder).

The historicity and culture boundedness of scientific ideas, the intimate relation and mutual influence of scientific ideas and everyday ideas, the power over the subjects and subject matter held by institutions and ideas of science, all belie claims to the cumulation of privileged knowledge, the detachment of the scientist, and the disinterestedness of both the enterprise and its practitioners. However, few in the human sciences wish to accept such "limitations" on their theoretical ambitions. Perhaps driven by what Ellul (1964) has observed as the drive for domination in Western science and technology, many human scientists strive for general and universal explanations of social and historical conduct. They have what the psychoanalyst Heinz Kohut (1977) described as "ambitions for their ideals," having perhaps idealized their ambitions, and they wish to impose their verbal constructions on the world itself. Having created a simulation of the world, they then wish to impose that simulation on the world itself (Baudrillard, 1983).

This desire for the universal and eternal on the part of the essentially transient is perhaps reason for the continued attractiveness of the great collective dramas of nineteenth-century romantic social thought, the tragic and hopeful visions subsumed under the names Marx, Darwin, and Freud. A more tempered vision can be found in the following social constructionist statement by the foremost member-theoretician of the radical sex lesbians:

> I no longer believe that there is some ahistorical entity called homosexuality. Sexuality is socially constructed, within the limits imposed by physiology, and it changes over time, with the surrounding culture. There was no thing such as a Castro clone, a lesbian feminist or a Kinsey 6 a century ago, and 100 years from now, these types will be as extinct as Urnings. (Califia, 1983, p. 27)

The correlative point is that the explanations of contemporary sexual studies that have helped to create these types will become fossils in the verbal record as well. The types, their conduct, and the explanations will become historical artifacts. In the same way that contemporary explanations of contemporary types fail to explain the extinct Urnings of the nineteenth century, theories of whatever "homosexuality" will be called a century from now will not explain the Castro clone, the lesbian feminist, or the Kinsey 6.

The Kinsey Scale
The Cultural Context of the Kinsey Research

The attempt to richly recollect past experiences in periods of even moderate collective and individual change—to locate the selves, the others, and the social contexts and to script them into plausible narratives—strains the limits of most people's skills at verstehen. It is thus very difficult for those who lived through the period from the World War I to the end of World War II, and perhaps impossible for those who did not, to accurately experience the pleasures and pains of sexual life in the United States during those decades. The changes in sexual life that have occurred since the 1950s have perhaps permanently estranged us from a world in which the underwear advertisements in the Sears Roebuck catalogs were the source of rural and small-town boys' erotic fantasies, when nudist magazines were sold in brown wrappers in certain bookstores in larger cities, and when a bare breast in a photograph was the grounds for an obscenity trial. It was a time when J. Edgar Hoover was an expert on sex crime and pornography, and the sex moron and the sex fiend graced the pages of urban tabloids. Pluralistic sexual ignorance was the norm, carrying with it the usual corollaries of sexual guilt and misadventure. The literary, visual, and interpersonal landscapes of the times were filled with good girls and boys (June Allyson and Andy Hardy) and bad girls and boys (the young Jane Russell and Studs Lonigan), who enacted quite traditional tales of sexual excess and constraint and experienced community exile and redemption. Even the voices of present-day religious fundamentalists carry only a faint echo of a period when the views they now espouse were those of a confident majority occupying the American Protestant center.

These decades were also a period in which new social forms for desire were being created, especially for the young. The independent girl with her bare legs and short hair, young people dancing first to jazz and then to swing, double-dating in cars while listening to the sounds of Glenn Miller and Guy Lombardo, the exquisite pleasures and anxieties of truly forbidden and dangerous unbuttonings and touchings were all inventions of this period. These spots in time and space for romance and eros were detached from immediate community and familial surveillance and the usual religious constraints. For the majority these delights were perhaps more often offered at the movies than in real life, but holding hands and (for that passionate minority) necking while watching the screen in the great dream palaces was thrilling in any case. A sexuality created out of glimpses, denials, fears, going only part of the way, and waiting for true love certainly had its appeal.

These sexual lives that now seem so far away, even to those who lived them, were conducted in a nation that was in the process of radical social and cultural transformation. The United States entered the 1920s a nation composed of cultural regions, of natives and immigrants divided by ethnicity and religion, and of urban dwellers segregated from those who lived in small cities and towns and on farms. The four decades of the 1910s through the late 1940s saw the country transformed, by economic and political upheaval, internal migration, and the mobilization of the society for purposes of two world wars, into a national economy and polity that, increasingly stratified by class and education, offered the potential for a national culture. The sexual recollections of this period, whether journals, autobiographies, or other fictions, usually entirely or in their early passages, record the sound of these regional, even local, accents. It was only toward the end of the period, when the tide of immigrants had been stemmed and their children provisionally Americanized and when radio and the cinema had begun to create a national character for the new middle classes, that a national culture actually began to emerge.

The Impact of the Kinsey Studies

The work of Alfred Kinsey and his colleagues exactly spans the concluding years of this first period and the first years of what was to be the next cultural epoch in the history of the United States. Kinsey conducted his first interviews in 1938 and continued to interview throughout the end of the depression and during World War II. It is remarkable that no one has commented on the fact that during what was thought to be a total mobilization, it was possible to conduct a major sex research project (involving travel, research grants, and face-to-face interviewing) that was irrelevant to the war effort. There has been no discussion of the impacts on Kinsey's findings of the large numbers of men who were in the military service (for example, such impacts as delaying marriage, separating spouses, increasing sexual permissiveness because of the wartime climate). Indeed, about 34% of the males and 48% of the females were interviewed during the war years. Equally remarkable are the facts that such research could have been conducted at a site universally considered to be politically and religiously conservative and that the research did not receive serious public notice until the publication of *Sexual Behavior in the Human Male* in 1948 (Kinsey, Pomeroy, & Martin).[2,3]

Kinsey and his work—the volume *Sexual Behavior in the Human Female* (Kinsey, Pomeroy, Martin, & Gebhard) was published in 1953; Kinsey died in 1956—represent an important marker in the historical transformation of United States society from a regional to a national culture. Sexuality in the largest sense was out of the closet; words previously unspoken outside of professional groups and those privy to the culture of psychoanalysis and never written in the popular press became part of national discourse. Penis, vagina, oral genital contact, orgasm, homosexual, extramarital coitus dropped from people's lips and appeared on the printed page.[4] Conduct heretofore unmentioned, or mentioned only in the most negative terms, was reported to be exceedingly common: nearly all men masturbated and so did a majority of women, oral sex was practiced by lots of married folks, about a third of men had had a homosexual experience, perhaps 5% exclusively desired such experience, half of women were not virgins when they married, and a quarter of those married had sex with men other than their husbands (the number of men in the last category was much higher). Kinsey was violently assailed by religionists, conservative congressmen, and some methodologists; he and his work were caricatured in the press; and the sex researcher and sex research were freely lampooned. This backlash may well have shortened Kinsey's life; what it did not do was to discredit the work itself (Pomeroy, 1972). The Kinsey studies, whatever their weaknesses, came to be treated as a national report on the state of sexuality in the United States.

It is in the larger framework of social change that Kinsey's general treatment of sexuality needs to be understood. Kinsey reported upon the conduct primarily of what was then an emergent national middle class that was being detached from region and ethnicity. It should be pointed that nearly all studies of sexuality from Freud to Masters and Johnson have been conducted on this changing social formation, and the social formations that it has supplanted are worlds we have lost. Kinsey's subjects were predominantly young, native born, socially liberal, and college attending or college educated (Gagnon & Simon, 1987). And the audience for his work were members of that same growing class, many of whom were already alienated from or resistant to traditional sexual values. What Kinsey supplied, under the banner of science, was a legitimation of the sexual lives that many middle-class persons were already living. His findings suggested that the dominant cultural scenarios for sexual conduct of the period from 1920 to 1940 only weakly applied to the actual sexual lives of the new middle class. If Kinsey offered a mirror to the society, it was restricted to this expanding social formation and it reflected far more of the society's future than its past.

Kinsey and the Relation of Heterosexuality and Homosexuality

Kinsey's treatment of the relation between heterosexuality and homosexuality was more than a simple mirror in which conventional persons could recognize themselves. Unlike his view of premarital sex, heterosexual erotic techniques, even extramarital experience, Kinsey's view of heterosexuality and homosexuality dealt primarily with the experience of an alien minority. Even though many men reported having a few homosexual experiences in their early and late adolescences, homosexuality remained a matter of the abnormal and the normal. It was exactly this dichotomy that Kinsey attacked on the level of sexual theory and individual experience. Theoretically, he argued specifically against prior conceptions of the homosexual and homosexuality, and by creating the 0 to 6 scale (or as it was called at the Institute for Sex Research at that time the H-H scale), he proposed that people's heterosexuality and homosexuality could be best understood as the proportion of other-gender and same-gender sexual acts (here including fantasies) in which they had engaged. The relation between heterosexuality and homosexuality was to be treated as continuous rather than discrete, and individuals could move from one place to another on the continuum by adding new acts of the two different types.

What Kinsey opposed was the theoretical belief, well-established among psychiatrists and psychoanalysts, that persons with substantial amounts of same-gender erotic experience represented a unitary category of persons with similar psychological or biological biographies whose lives were entirely governed or at least strongly influenced by the the gender of the persons they sexually desired. Assimilated into this conception was a prior folk belief shared by both "heterosexuals" and "homosexuals" (and enacted by some of the latter) that "homosexuality" was grounded in a gender defect (either constitutional or learned). This defect meant that homosexual men were somehow insufficiently masculine (and therefore effeminate) and that homosexual women were insufficiently feminine (and therefore masculine). More complex readings of these relations between psychosexual normality, gender, and sexual desire were formulated (e.g., the obligatory, the situational, the masochistic, the situational homosexual), but at the center of the theory was the assumption of a common class of persons whose pathological conduct depended on common pathological origins (Socarides, 1978).

Kinsey's theoretical counter to this view that each homosexual was possessed of a defect in biology or very early education was to take a strong biological line, but one that emphasized the evolutionary history of the species rather than the defective status of the individual (see Weinrich, Chapter 9). This is essentially the theoretical position he took about *all* sexual conduct, approved and disapproved. He argued that homosexuality, masturbation, and oral sex (to take the triad he most often discussed when dealing with these issues) were common activities in "the mammalian heritage" as well as among human groups where cultural repression of the sexual was not the norm. Hence such activities represented the diversity of nature rather than perversities and deviations from a biological or cultural standard for the sexually correct individual (Kinsey et al., 1948). This is an argument of extraordinary originality, one that allowed Kinsey to bring what was thought to be unnatural under the umbrella of a larger and more copious nature. It shares with the Freudians a view that there is a severe tension between the offerings of nature and the strictures of culture; however, Kinsey's vision of what nature offers is closer to Rousseau's than it is to Hobbes'.

The moral and political legitimacy of homosexuality could thus be created by treating it as part of a natural world that should not be limited by the artifices of culture. Kinsey's opposition between nature and culture thus rests on a distinction between the bounty and variety of the natural world (read here the diversity of species in an unmanaged nature) as opposed to a civilized world of agriculture in which nature is pruned and limited. In much the same way as agriculture gives the fields over to monocrops, sexually repressive cultures cultivate procreative heterosexuality as their sole flower, treating all else as weeds. Kinsey remained true to his prior evolutionary and ecological concerns; it is in the biology of abundance and adaptation that he found the template for the normal, not in the individual organismic views that characterize the defect-finding traditions in psychiatry, psychology, and biology.

The H-H Scale: Acts Against Essences

The H-H or 0 to 6 continuum rests at least in part on Kinsey's understanding of nature. As he wrote:

> Males do not represent two discrete populations, heterosexual and homosexual. The world is not to be divided into sheep and goats. Not all things are black nor all things white. It is a fundamental of taxonomy that nature rarely deals with discrete categories. Only the human mind invents categories and tries to force facts into separated pigeon-holes. The living world is a continuum in each and every one of its aspects. The sooner we learn this concerning human sexual behavior the sooner we shall reach a sound understanding of the realities of sex. (Kinsey et al., 1948, p. 639)

That continua are as much human inventions as dichotomies and that there is, for certain purposes, a utility to distinguishing between sheep and goats are reasonable intellectual responses to Kinsey's positivist view that the continua in the mind mirror the sexual facts in the world. However, the important issue is Kinsey's decision to make heterosexuality and homosexuality a question of acts rather than a question of common origins, common personalities, or common behavioral performances (in the case of males: effeminacy, artistic temperament, a broader pelvis, occupational preference, scores on Terman-Miles MF scale) (Kinsey et al., 1948, p. 637). It is the mixture of heterosexual and homosexual performances that impressed Kinsey; the record of "experience and psychic reactions" (p. 639) that fluctuates across the life course, even within a single sexual occasion.

It is this record of experiences and psychic reactions that were collected during the sex history that became the basis for placing an interviewee on the 0–6 scale. Interviewers returned from the field and counted up, necessarily in somewhat crude ways, the frequency of sociosexual experiences, with and without orgasm, with the same or different partners (independent of marital status and other factors) that occurred with people of the same or opposite gender. In addition, the frequency of sexual dreams with and without orgasm that could be classified as having same-gender and other-gender content and the proportion of masturbation accompanied by same-gender or other-gender *fantasy*, were estimated. These calculations were somewhat less precise than those from sociosexual experience for a variety of reasons, most significantly the result of weaker attention given to fantasy in the interviews. Such counts were made for each year of life and cumulated for the life span as well as for other periods in the life course.

Perhaps the best analogy for this method would be to think of each year of a person's life as a jar into which a white ball is dropped for each heterosexual experience and a blue ball for each homosexual experience. The total number of balls is then divided into the number of white balls and a place on the continuum is assigned for that year. What this does not account for is the total volume of sexual experience, so that someone who had 10 other-gender sexual experiences with the same person and ten same-gender sexual experiences with 10 persons in a single year would be a 3 as would someone who masturbated 150 times with only homosexual fantasy but who had marital coitus 100 times and coitus with female prostitutes 50 times in a single year. This actually suggests a greater accuracy of counting events than could be attained from the sex histories and a rather more mechanical practice in the assignments than was practiced.[5] A good deal of judgment was involved in the assignments, and researchers often estimated the "importance" of different kinds of sexual activity when assessing their contribution to the final number assigned.

The scale is an empirical attempt to undermine all of the usual sharp distinctions that were made between individuals who had sexual contacts with the same and the other gender. By focusing on flexibility and change in conduct across the life course, it counters arguments that same-gender erotic preferences start early in life, are fixed across the life course, and are influential in all spheres of life. By focusing on acts rather than persons, Kinsey tried to protect those who are persecuted as "homosexual" because of a few homosexual acts as well as to counter the argument that there is an essential homosexual personality. Thus a single act or a small number of same-gender erotic acts does not a homosexual make (Kinsey did not make the corollary argument that a single or small number of heterosexual acts did not a heterosexual make). More trenchantly, there is no such thing as a homosexual person, only persons with various mixtures of acts. Kinsey remained quite consistent in arguing that the intermediate numbers on the scale are not to be treated as a social type called "bisexuals," but are rather persons with a mixture of homosexual and heterosexual acts.

The Subversion of the Kinsey Scale

Kinsey actually did not propose a specific theory of the acquisition, maintenance, or transformation of either heterosexuality or homosexuality in his 1948 volume. The closest he came was to argue,

> If all persons with any trace of homosexual history, or those who were predominantly homosexual, were eliminated from the population today, there is no reason for believing that the incidence of the homosexual in next generation would be materially reduced. The homosexual has been a significant part of human sexual activity ever since the dawn of history, primarily because *it is an expression of capacities that are basic in the human animal.* (Kinsey et al., 1948, p. 666, italics added)

As in nearly all discussions of heterosexuality and homosexuality the central focus was on the latter, with the former treated as a residual category. In the volume on the female, largely in response to critics of this argument, he wrote:

> The data indicate that the factors leading to homosexual behavior are (1) the basic physiological capacity of every mammal to respond to any sufficient stimulus; (2) the accident that leads an individual into his or her first sexual experience with a person of the same sex; (3) the conditioning effects of such an experience; and (4) the indirect but powerful conditioning which the opinions of other persons and the social codes may have on an individual's decision to accept or reject this type of sexual contact. (Kinsey et al., 1953, p. 447)

The grudging readmission of what was at least a stripped down version of the roles of psychology and culture in sexual life was an important shift, one that was characteristic of a change in Kinsey's views as he wrote about female as opposed to male sexuality (Gagnon, 1978). Culture remains, however, only responsive to the mammalian heritage and the accidents of experience and conditioning.

What is problematic for Kinsey's view that persons are mixtures of acts is that most individuals with same-gender erotic experiences actually lived in terms of the social types that Kinsey fought so hard to dissolve. Persons with same-gender erotic experiences viewed themselves and were viewed as enacting or resisting the social roles provided in the contemporaneous existent homosexual culture. Sissies, queers, dykes, fems, butches, trade, faggots were experienced as real states. No one has ever experienced himself or herself as a jar filled with 50% heterosexual and 50% homosexual acts. Contra Kinsey, persons with what they thought to be equal desires for or experiences with women and men have labeled themselves "bisexuals." It is one of the ironies of research history that some of these persons have now substituted Kinsey "numbers" for such labels as exclusive homosexuality or bisexuality. Thus "bisexuals" might refer to themselves (in front of a sophisticated audience) as a 3 or as a Kinsey 3. Most commonly these labels will be used by persons with predominantly same-gender partners as a summary measure, "I'm a Kinsey 6." A recognition of the extent of this knowledgeability is evident in recent studies that use various forms of the Kinsey scale as the basis for self-ratings of respondents (Bell & Weinberg, 1978). What was once an "objective" count of experience has become part of the culture of gay life and part of self-labeling by members of that community.

It would raise our confidence in the scientific enterprise if it could be argued that Kinsey's ideas, as embodied either in his theories or in his scale, had some deep impact on the main strands of work that followed his publications. However, neither his notions of the importance of the "mammalian heritage" nor his treatment of heterosexuality/homosexuality as a mixture of acts independent of the existence of role packages has been deeply influential. What have been consequential are Kinsey's arguments against the negative essentialism of psychoanalytic and psychiatric formulations and the belief, based on his interviews, that same-gender erotic conduct was fairly common as an exclusive desire and very common as incidental conduct.

During the 1950s and 1960s, the way was opened for a large series of studies that emphasized the importance of social oppression and local cultural circumstances as critical to the life-ways of persons with same-gender erotic preferences. In addition to scientific interest, there was an increase in political activism with what was to become the community of gay men and lesbians (Humphreys, 1972). This activism was interactive with the activities of liberal social scientists, and in many cases the activists took over an important role both in performing research and in transforming the subjects of research. In its early phases this work focused on four themes: (1) that same-gender erotic preferences were not acquired through special or pathological pathways and that there was no evidence of special or frequent pathology among persons with such preferences that could not be explained by social oppression; (2) that the importance of origins was, in any case, both overemphasized and probably insoluble given the weakness of recollection and the enculturation of gay men and lesbians by dominant psychoanalytic theories; (3) that the observed similarity among persons with same-gender erotic desires did not result from common individual origins but was a function of group membership (learning how to be gay in a specific culture) and enhanced when performing for others in contexts specific in the culture (clones are more masculine in clone bars and health clubs); (4) that the nonsexual aspects of such persons' life-ways were often more important in shaping their sexual lives than vice versa (Gagnon & Simon, 1973, chaps. 5 and 6).

This work during the 1950s and 1960s and the social activism associated with "homosexual activists" were directly consequent on the existence of Kinsey and the publication of his data rather than being responsive to either his theory or his scale. It was Kinsey and his research as a societal rather than as a scientific event that provided an opportunity to quite different programs of research and social activism than he foresaw. This confluence of research and activism became the basis for the creation of the new cultures and communities of gay men and lesbians that emerged in the 1970s.

Changing Scripts for Same-Gender Desire
Social Scripts for Sexual Conduct

The social-scripting perspective on sexual conduct was first articulated in the late 1960s. Its specific conceptions were framed by the larger intellectual traditions of sociological symbolic interactionism, the dramatistic analysis of literature and culture, and a view of human action and the human life course as understandable only in specific historical and cultural contexts (Burke, 1936, 1966, 1984; Mead, 1934; van den Berg, 1975).[6] The examples of the scripting of conduct were primarily drawn from the sexual realm and were thus heir to all of the advantages and limitations of responding to the particular scientific and intellectual conditions of that field at that time. Scripts were most often treated as heuristic devices to be used by observers to better interpret sexual conduct at three levels: cultural scenarios (such as pornography and the cinema), interpersonal interactions (as in specific sexual acts), and intrapsychic processes (e.g., sexual fantasies, plans, remembrances). When interpreting concrete role enactments, for instance, persons were thought of as engaging in sequences of interaction that are scripted in terms of *who* persons are, *what* is to be done, *when* and *where* it is to be done, and perhaps most importantly, *why* it is to be done. This first wave of work dealt in most detail with the heterosexuality of young people and young adults, the sexual conduct of gay men, lesbians, imprisoned persons and female prostitutes and with pornography (Gagnon, 1973; Gagnon & Simon, 1973; Simon, 1973).[7]

More recent formulations of these conceptions have more explicitly recognized that using a scripting perspective to interpret conduct is not solely the activity or property of privileged observers. Many everyday actors, particularly those aware of popular approaches to understanding conduct, self-consciously "script" or near script their own interactions as they negotiate their lives (Berne, 1966; Gagnon, Rosen, & Leiblum, 1982).[8] Thus, in making plans, people often script the interactions that are to take place and practice conversations for the purpose of self-control and to manage the conduct of the other persons involved. The ubiquity of this *internal rehearsal*, even among those shielded from *pop-soc* and *pop-psych* interpretations of conduct, suggests the closeness of the practices of the scientific observer and the everyday actor in scripting conduct (Steiner, 1984). What one would hope distinguishes the majority of scientists from the majority of laypersons is that the former are more systematic and self-conscious in treating the script as a molar unit that can be used to package roles, contexts, expectations, and motives into plausible narratives.

Scripting Same-Gender Desire

The social-scripting perspective converges with Kinsey's work on homosexuality by accepting his empirical findings that in this culture and at this moment in its history there is a great variety in the types of persons who have homosexual experience, that such experience is not the expression of a specific pattern of early learning, and that it is quite common for persons to change their gender preferences in erotic relations across the life course. At the same time, this perspective diverges from Kinsey in rejecting his conception of homosexuality as an inheritance from humanity's mammalian ancestors, a legacy that is expressed either in cooperation or in conflict with the surrounding culture. From the perspective of scripting theory, same-gender erotic preferences are elicited and shaped by the systems of meaning offered for conduct in a culture. What is usually construed as culture against "man" or culture against nature is thus actually conflict among differently enculturated individuals or groups. Another major divergence is from Kinsey's belief in the continuous character of the relation between heterosexuality and homosexuality as represented in the heterosexuality/homosexuality scale. This conception fails to account for the felt experience of most persons in Western cultures that having sex with a person of the same gender is qualitatively different from having sex with persons of the other gender. Persons usually experience themselves and others through relatively discontinuous social types (and stereotypes), even when confronted with a "continuous" variable such as age.

The scripting perspective treats the causal history of homosexuality and heterosexuality (*Why* are you homosexual or heterosexual?) and the motivations offered for proximate performances (*Why* did you have sex with that particular man or woman?) as culturally plausible accounts, whether they are offered by scientists or everyday actors (Peckham, 1969, 1979; Rorty, 1979). In general, such motivational accounts are offered only for same-gender conduct (being heterosexual is not a "marked" form of conduct, though some types of heterosexual conduct, e.g., extramarital sex, may well be), and as such they are usually restricted to causes or motives that are drawn from the conventionalized domains of sexuality or gender. It is also not uncommon that historical accounts are conflated with motives for current conduct. Thus, the proximate motive for a man having sex with another man is treated as being verbally equivalent to being "caused by" (where cause means "motivated by" as well as "explained by") having had a seductive mother and a detached hostile father at critical moments in childhood. Such ways of explaining conduct should be understood as cultural conventions rather than scientific truths. The instability of such causal or motivational statements (e.g., whether fire starting is seen to express a sexual or an economic motive may depend on whether the analysis is conducted by a psychoanalyst or the arson squad) should suggest that they serve more than purely scientific interests.

Struggles over explanation are central to cultural change. They are engaged in to reconstruct the past, to justify the present, and to propagandize for alternative futures. The idealized and gendered explanations for women's sexuality offered by some lesbian feminist intellectuals have been countered by the lesbian sex radicals who have proposed an ungendered and erotic set of motives for same-gender erotic conduct among women.[9]

> It is odd that sexual orientation is defined solely in terms of the sex of one's partners. I don't think I can assume anything about another person because I have been told they are bisexual, heterosexual or homosexual. . . . For many people, if a partner or a sexual situation has other desirable qualities it is possible to overlook the partner's sex. Some examples are: a preference for group sex, for a particular socioeconomic background, for paid sex, for S/M, for a specific age group, for a physical type or race, for anal or oral sex. (Califia, 1983, p. 2)

It is increasingly plausible to provide histories and motives for same-gender and other-gender erotic preferences that are entirely independent of either sexual desire or gender. Thus, the promotion of social mobility, the opportunity to earn money, the desire for personal security, assuaging terror in the midst of battle, the chance to participate in religious communions, and the desire to bear children are all nonsexual motives for sexual conduct. Such motives can be read as explaining or motivating either the acquisition or the maintenance of same- or other- gender preferences.

This perspective, with its emphasis on the socially constructed and culturally and historically variable character of sexual conduct, indeed all conduct, seems more appropriate to the understanding of the lives of sodomites, pederasts, homosexuals, as well as gay men and lesbians, than do perspectives that emphasize essentialist continuities in the biography and conduct of "the homosexual." In part this appropriateness is a consequence of the rapidity of ideological and, to some extent, behavioral change within the communities of gay men and lesbians since the early 1970s (Levine, 1986; Plummer, 1981; Warren, 1974; Wolf, 1979). The decision of gay male and lesbian/feminist activists and intellectuals to rename themselves and to play an active role in reconstituting their selves and their culture has been critical in recasting the conduct of nonelites in the gay male and lesbian communities. The actions have also resulted in the decline of scientific privilege in naming and explaining same-gender erotic conduct and in a change in the mass media representation of the "homosexual." Debates over the importance of early fixing of "sexual orientation," the stability of gender preference in erotic relations over the life course, the gender bases for differences between the life-styles of gay men and lesbians are no longer quarrels among scientists but part of intense political-ideological debates within the gay male and lesbian communities. It is part of the ideological ferment of the contemporary situation that it is even possible to find strong support within the gay male and lesbian communities for a "neo-essentialist" gayness or lesbianism.

Scripts Before and After Stonewall

In the post-Stonewall era, the changes in what was to become the gay male and lesbian communities (as opposed to the homosexual community) changed not only "who" gay men and lesbians thought they were (in the sense of gay identity and gay pride) but also changed the scripts for sexual and nonsexual encounters among gay people as well as relations with straights.[10] The pre-Stonewall "homosexual community" was for many persons, who for one reason or another were unpersuaded by or uncomfortable with heterosexuality, their first point of access to a collectivity that they might join. In most locales this quasi-underground community was an anonymous collection of public meeting places (usually bars and taverns serving alcohol and therefore restricted to those "of an age to drink") predominantly utilized by a somewhat fragmented collection of individuals primarily for sexual contacts and transient sociability. Many homosexual men and some women found their friends and lovers in the community as well. When coupled affectionate and sexual relationships were going well, individuals often withdrew from the community. If such coupled relations broke up or became sexually unsatisfying, individuals often returned to the public life of the homosexual community. This cycle of withdrawal and reentry gave untutored observers the idea that a constant search for new sexual partners was characteristic of all homosexual men. However, this penumbra of more stable affectional relationships could be found around a more constant population of regulars and workers for whom the institutions of the homosexual community were primary sources of identity and provided social and economic well-being.

Except in the very largest of cities, the homosexual community was male dominated with few all-women institutions. It was also a community with few of the resources of other communities, one that emphasized, particularly among men, the virtues of youth, sexuality, and attractiveness. Many of its members were "in the closet" to most of the significant others in their lives; they were properly fearful of the police, their own families, and their coworkers. Such fears often extended to the people with whom they were having sex, since blackmail and violence were both endemic and not reportable to the police. At the same time, the homosexual community was one of the sole ports of entry to friendship and affectional relations and sometimes to jobs and social mobility. It also provided a place in which persons could be what they thought was "themselves." For those who were lucky—the affluent, the talented, and the beautiful—there also existed zones of tolerance, often in the arts and other culture-producing institutions, in which a more open homosexual life-style could be enacted. The scripts for male same-gender erotic relations were learned and reinforced, indeed given content, in this secretive and persecuted community. The identity and experience of the lesbian was far less dependent on this community, in part because it was far less visible to most women and because it was dominated by male cultures. As a result, lesbianism remained far more tied to traditional women's gender values, was often come upon by accident, and was enacted within isolated pairs and small friendship circles (Gagnon & Simon, 1967).

The contemporary gay male and lesbian communities in the major metropolitan centers are far more than just a "sexual marketplace," though prior to the AIDS crisis, the gay male community was that as well.[11] There are now specialized institutions for both gay men and lesbians: newspapers, magazines, political groups, restaurants, counseling organizations, bookstores, travel agencies, physicians, housing cooperatives, and neighborhoods as well as intellectual/political elites. Surrounding this open community is a radically changed climate of public discussion in the nongay media of the existence of gay men and lesbians. Well in advance of the AIDS crisis, homosexuality and homosexuals, gay men and lesbians had become part of public discourse. The publicity afforded same-gender erotic desire, both in the majority media and in the existence of a gay and lesbian cultural apparatus, has not only changed the very character of the process of "coming out" (acquiring a gay or lesbian self-definition), but it has also offered the possibility of "being out" to a wide variety of audiences. Being gay or lesbian is now a more reasonable possibility, often a positive alternative to what heterosexuality offers, and there is now the opportunity for both anticipatory socialization in and practical experimentation with gay and lesbian role enactments that require relatively modest levels of erotic commitment.

Since this environment offers new attractions to wider audiences, there have been changes in the who, when, and why individuals are attracted to it (White, 1980). This is particularly true among the young, who now know about gay and lesbian possibilities at an earlier age and who are better informed about the content of these life-styles. The existence of a richer and more complex gay and lesbian culture also sustains the interest of those who would have been put off by what they saw as the oversexualized or culturally impoverished character of the homosexual community. Older women and men, including those formerly married and with children, more easily find a gay or lesbian commitment plausible. These enlistees from a wider base of persons with more various biographies and life experiences may well reduce the power of the community to shape and homogenize gay and lesbian identities. Moreover, their presence will further falsify in cultural practice the belief that gay men and lesbians have similar biographies and common personalities.

The Flexibility of Gender Preference

A more varied set of new members and a more diffuse pattern of conceiving of oneself as having the capacity for same-gender desire and erotic relations have also influenced the stability and fixity of same-gender erotic relations. In the very recent past many persons reported that they had had the experience of first knowing "who they really were" or being "at one with themselves" when they first publically identified themselves as homosexual. This dramatic revelation could be produced by what now appears to be the very simple act of going to a gay bar and being in the company of others "like me." These experiences of rapid identity crystallization were often treated by those who experienced them (and by observers) as evidence that an individual had found his or her "true identity." This felt sense of "belonging" needs to be understood not as evidence of a prior hidden identity now properly expressed but as a result of the oppressive sexual climate of the period that produced intense personal sexual isolation among nearly all adolescents and young people regardless of the usual gender of their erotic preferences (White, 1983). Anxieties about sexual matters were endemic among young people; these included anxieties about most aspects of sexual performance as well as preference. Even a marginally competent sexual experience was more often a relief from anxiety and doubt than it was an expression of intense desire. It is only a cultural and scholarly prejudice that the acquisition and early enactments of other-gender eroticism are not treated as a form of "coming out."

This is not to argue that the acquisition and enactments of same-gender desire were not more sharply felt than their other-gender correlates. That the culture was generally antisexual should not blind us to the fact that it was violently antihomosexual. For the majority, a same-gender preference in erotic relations was usually constructed in a context of extraordinary ignorance, doubt, avoidance, and fear.[12] As the content of the desire became better understood, its fatefulness in terms of traditional relationships became apparent, as did its consequences, for an individual's life chances in general. As a result of what were often long periods of isolated intrapsychic scripting of the self (Who am I?), it was common for many individuals to treat their desire as permanent even if no one else knew of it. The pain of the process of taking the ego-alien into the self (to mix two discourses) was sufficient evidence of the condition. The disclosure of the private label to other audiences, both the rejecting conventional and the accepting nonconforming, was important in confirming but not initiating the preference. Thus, prosecuting and stigmatizing an individual may help to limit his or her return to the larger community, but negative labels are not the sole agent in this adhesion (contra the work of labeling theorists following the work of Howard Becker, 1963). Once the public disclosure is made, however, the individual, the new membership group, and the conventional community cooperate in constructing a mutually plausible biography for the marked condition.

Other aspects of the sexual conduct of "homosexuals" could be understood in terms of this climate of persecution. Thus, the vigorous pursuit of sexual partners by male "homosexuals" during this early period of commitment (given the argot name "honeymoon") must also be understood as a response to specific historical conditions of becoming a male homosexual in the homosexual community. The scholarly emphasis on the sexual aspects of the coming out period conceals the difficulties of the acquisition of the major elements of being an accomplished "member" of the homosexual community—sexual skills, argot, jokes, differentiation among partners, falling in love, coupling, falling out of love—none of which are acquired "naturally."

Under contemporary circumstances a conception of same-gender desire as an irreversible orientation is less plausible to many gay and lesbian individuals as well as to scholarly opinion. It is now possible to recognize that changes in gender preference in erotic relations, both in fantasy and conduct, may occur throughout the life course. This instability seems particularly prevalent in adolescence, when gender-appropriate sexual scripts are in the process of acquisition. While it is possible "after the fact" to know how a large number of persons have become distributed in terms of gender preference, it is quite clear that during the ages of 12 to 17 the gender aspects of the "who" in the sexual scripts that are being formed are not fixed (Kinsey et al., 1948). A deeper complication is that it is not obvious whether it is the gender aspects of the "who" that have provoked the nascent desire or even if the desire is linked to a "who" at all. The desire may be focused on someone who is successful, someone whom we or others admire for his or her purity, or someone we can dominate or by whom we can be dominated. The "who" in these circumstances may be genderless, or gender may be important only insofar as success, purity, and domination are linked to gender itself.[13]

Changes in Gender Preference During Adulthood

In addition to gender preference instability among the young, there is evidence that in recent years a substantial number of previously married men and women have been publicly entering the gay and lesbian communities. [It is estimated that one gay man in five has had children; this estimate increases to two in five among lesbians (Bell & Weinberg, 1978).] This represents an important addition to the pathways into same-gender erotic relations, particularly for men. It is likely that some of these men under earlier historical conditions would have been "tearoom trade," that is men who would have sought secretive and transient sexual contacts in public toilets and parks (Humphreys, 1970). With changing attitudes toward divorce and same-gender erotic relations, such men have been able to make a less concealed choice of their objects of desire. Many of these men also appear to have been have been disproportionately selected from the more affluent and from those who were able to sustain relations with their children after divorce and becoming openly gay.

Similar changes in gender preference have historically more often come later in the life course for women, largely as a result of women's ignorance about lesbianism and the salience of love, marriage, and children in women's lives. The disappointments of other-gender relations (e.g., male violence, emotional indifference, and erotic incompetence) as well as the attractions of women's emotional and interpersonal company have always been the grounds for women to change their gender commitments. There is, however, an increase in the number of women moving into lesbian roles from those women who would have formerly remained celibate or who would have remained in an undemanding other-gender marriage. The increasing cultural complexity of the lesbian community now provides reasons to adopt a lesbian commitment other than the emotional support offered by sororal communities or even same-gender erotic desire.

These new patterns of enlistment, in terms of who enlist and when in the life course they enlist, undermine the general essentialist positions, whether they are held by traditional scientific theorists or by gay male or lesbian neo-essentialists. There is little evidence that these persons share a common biography, that they are recognizing their true identities, or that they have common psychological profiles as measured through standard psychological inventories. In actual fact, there was little evidence that such commonalities characterized those in the homosexual communities of an earlier era. Such homogeneities that did exist were the consequence of community membership and not historical or contemporaneous psychological commonalities. It was often the similarities produced by cultural conformity to homosexual roles that scholars treated as the result of similar personal histories.

There is also evidence that more persons with previously exclusive or near exclusive same-gender erotic preferences are experimenting with other-gender erotic conduct. In some cases these are transient erotic encounters, but equally often these sexual relationships are conducted for reasons based on gender differentiation, social conformity, desire for marriage, physical beauty, mental health, romantic love, even reproduction. Many lesbians who wish to have children are now engaging in coitus solely for this purpose. There is also evidence that numbers of persons with predominantly same-gender sexual histories are experimenting with other-gender erotic relations for ideological reasons. Hence:

I have no way of knowing how many lesbians and gay men are less than exclusively homosexual. But I know that I am not the only one. Our actual behavior (as opposed to the ideology that says homosexuality means being sexual only with members of the same sex) leads me to ask questions about the nature of sexual orientation, how people (especially gay people) define it, how they choose to let those definitions control and limit their lives. (Califia, 1983, p. 2)

It is difficult to estimate how often such shifts from exclusive same-gender erotic commitments (the Kinsey 6) take place, but the amount of interpersonal and ideological policing of this kind of conduct suggests that many gay men and lesbians feel an acute sense of personal and political vulnerability when confronted with such conduct. The strong negative reaction to "bisexuality" and "political lesbians" and the construction of identity tests for culturally "correct" gayness or lesbianism represents a recognition by some members of the gay male and lesbian community that the community is itself relatively permeable and that the preferences that have organized it are potentially very unstable. Conducting research on this movement from same- to other-gender erotic preferences is very difficult in that the persons involved are often treated as socially dead by the gay and lesbian communities. Such persons are also declared to have been false group members, never to have been truly homosexual, since the mark of the true native is his or her total commitment.[14]

It is among those who have been traditionally called "bisexuals" that these mixed patterns of gendered eroticism have been best documented. The evidence is that these shifts in desire and practice are mediated by both nonerotic and erotic factors. Thus, the changing weight given to nonsexual exigencies such as love, children, or occupational aspirations may shape which gender preference is salient. In more specifically sexual contexts, individuals may exhibit different erotic "preferences" when enacting sexual scripts that specify different "whos." A young man who is a straight hustler to men and who uses the money he is paid to take out his woman friend, the woman who is a lesbian for feminist reasons and who has a male lover, the wolf or jocker in prison who views being fellated as "heterosexual" since the man who does it is "like a woman" are all enacting gender-appropriate, but gender-segregated erotic scripts (Gagnon, 1977). These patterns may mean that bisexuality as a gender-*indifferent* erotic preference may be relatively rare or is being constructed as a general cultural possibility at the present moment (Duberman, 1974).

Conclusion

In the period from 1950 to the present there has been a remarkable shift in thinking about same-gender erotic relations and in the conduct of those relations. The complexity of the relation between changes in thinking and changes in conduct needs to be constantly kept in mind since the relation has been constantly dialectical. The pre-1950s essentialist theories influenced the thinking of "homosexuals" about who they were and indirectly sustained the repressive machinery and attitudes of the larger society toward the "homosexual." Such essentialist theories underrepresented the actual variety of homosexual life-styles that existed even within the narrow cultural repertoire of the homosexual community and homogenized the biographical origins of those who were identified as homosexual. Kinsey and his colleagues offered a new empirical view of the homosexual that emphasized their biological normality and their personal diversity. Following Kinsey, a number of primarily sociological researchers focused empirically on the conditions of the homosexual community, the processes of "coming out," the psychological normality of members of the gay community, and theoretically set out to deconstruct psychoanalytic and other essentialist theories.

By the late 1960s these views were widely held among homosexual intellectuals and became part of the ideological apparatus of resistance to heterosexism. With the transformations of the homosexual community into the gay male and lesbian communities these social constructionist views of gender preference in erotic relations were widespread. In addition, a large number of gay scholars, including persons with and without professional licenses, began actively to participate in the construction of the history, psychology, and sociology of gay male and lesbian life. During the late 1970s and early 1980s the intellectual weight in scholarly research began to shift from the "objective and disinterested" heterosexuals to publicly identified gay and lesbian scholars.[15] The intimacy between theory construction and culture construction is now far more complete, as self-conscious intellectuals attempt not only to discover but to construct culturally that which was once thought to be only an expression of nature.

The instability of gender preference in erotic relations, both in its recognition and in fact, must be seen as part of a general decline in the constancy and rigidity of appropriate role packages in the society. Thus, trustworthy bank tellers and bank presidents no longer have to be white, church-attending, Christian men over a certain age with wives and children. As the traditional gender, race, age, religious, and ethnic prejudices have weakened, so too have prejudices against variations in sexual conduct weakened. Changes within the sexual domain have thus been driven not only by theories about sex and sexual factors but also by changes in the larger culture, particularly in the area of gender theory and practice. The recognition of the extraordinary complexity of the relation between gender and eros is in part the result of the collapse of both folk and traditional scientific views that were built upon them. The result of moving the primary sources of explanation of gender and sexual conduct into the domain of science, which is the least stable source of explanation in the culture, may be that theory will now change far more rapidly than practice.

This chapter, which started out as a discussion of same-gender and other-gender erotic relations, has focused, as do all such works, on the minority preference. Given this bias, one might ask if there is nothing interesting to be said about the origins, acquisition, maintenance, transformation, and disappearance of heterosexuality in person's lives. This turns out to be quite difficult when the discussion begins in a constrastive or polarized mode. In the traditional folk and scientific views of the mid-nineteenth century to the mid-twentieth century, heterosexuality was treated as the normal pole of a gendered opposition; it existed as a moral and biological monolith requiring no explanation. Kinsey kept the two poles, but turned the dichotomy into a continuum and made its entire length normal. From a scripting perspective it seems best to treat the interpretation of other-gender erotic relations and same-gender erotic relations as independent puzzles. It may well be that our understanding of why men and women desire each other is obscured by thinking that it is analogous to why men and men or women and women desire each other. It may be our belief that they are related in some deep way that has made the preference so critical in moral, political, and scientific debates. To return to the deconstructive mode:

> I live with my woman lover of five years. I have lots of casual sex with women. Once in while I have casual sex with gay men. I have a three year relationship with a homosexual male who doesn't use the term gay. And I call myself a lesbian. . . . I call myself a fag hag because sex with men outside the context of the gay community doesn't interest me at all. In a funny way, when two gay people of opposite sexes make it, it's still gay sex. (Califia, 1983, 25)

Acknowledgment

My thanks to Professor Cathy Stein Greenblat for her comments on this chapter.

Notes

1. The name homosexuality was given to same-gender erotic relations in the mid-nineteenth century as part of the general medicalization of sexual nonconformity. Heterosexuality as a label appeared somewhat later (Katz, 1983).

2. Indiana University is located in Bloomington, Indiana, 40 miles south of U.S. Route 40. The entire state was historically characterized by old-time religion and Republicanism, and its southern portion was long characterized by an intense racism. Until 1935 the university administration fired all faculty who divorced, and until 1960 the barber shop located in the Indiana Memorial Student Union did not cut the hair of what were then Negro students.

3. The success of the research enterprise may have been aided by the turmoil

of the times during which it was conducted. The decade of research activity contained the end of the depression (1938–1940), the preparation for and conclusion of World War II (from 1940–1946), and the period of massive family formation and occupational resettlement between 1946 and 1948. It was a period in which persons were far too seriously engaged in making critical life choices to be concerned with such minor issues as sex research. This intense involvement of people in their own lives also prevented them from being swept away by the moral panics of anticommunism, antidrugs, and antisexuality that marked the early to middle 1950s. The physical isolation of the Bloomington campus also meant an insulation from the still heavily regionalized press and radio news systems. It was not until the mid-1960s that the privacy of cultural life disappeared in the face of a fully developed and voracious national television and print system that began to treat behavioral science topics of various sorts as newsworthy.

4. This process was of course not completed in that period. The word *penis* did not appear in the *New York Times* until the mid-1960s, and discussions of anal sex in print and on television have had to await the advent of AIDS. Thus the televised statements of the surgeon general and the National Academy of Science in October of 1986 have contained reasonably explicit references to same- and other-gender anal practices.

5. It is rarely noted that the 0–6 scale contained an additional category of "X," which meant no sexual activity at all. Kinsey reported that at age 15 one male in 5 had no overt sexual activity and no psychosexual reactions (about one in 20 for the entire period from age 16 to age 20). There is no separate definition of the X category in the 1948 volume (Kinsey et al., 1948, p. 641); however it is defined in the 1953 volume (Kinsey et al., 1953, p. 472) because of the large number of women in this category throughout the life course (Ibid., p. 499). Xs account for 15–20% of the never married respondents, 1–3% among the married, and 6–8% among the previously married. The gender preferences of these large numbers of sexually inactive persons should be treated with some caution.

6. As the careful reader has noted there is no necessary relation between the idea of scripting and these larger traditions except perhaps for dramatism. These traditions shape the way that scripts are thought of, what they contain, and how variable they are rather than the choice of the script metaphor itself.

7. A quite different concept of scripting has been used in artifical intelligence research, and distinguishing that usage from social scripts may serve to further clarify the latter (Schank, 1982; Schank & Abelson, 1977). In research on computerized story interpreters, which involves programming computers to read narrative and make choices based on their interpretations, the word *scripts* refers solely to fixed sequences of action. For example, in a restaurant script when the meal is finished the computer is expected to "understand" that the next move is to ask for the check. Scripts in this context are the lowest-level units in a hierarchy of modular units. *Scripts* are the basic elements that are assembled into *plans*, which in turn become the elements in *schemas*, and so forth. The higher the modules are in the hierarchy, the more general and flexible they are thought to be. In social scripting, a script is the sole molar unit that is descriptive of all actions; as such, scripts can be used to interpret mental processes (e.g., plans for the future, remembrances of the past), the guidance of public interactions, and the semiotic structure of environments. They are nonhierarchical in the sense that they are not a "level" in a larger information-processor/decision-maker or personality system. They are also variable in terms of flexibility, ranging from the ritualistic to the improvisational, depending on cultural and historical context.

8. The tradition of transactional psychotherapy explicitly used the metaphors of script and game as heuristics for patients to analyze their "self-defeating" conduct (Berne, 1966).

9. The complexities of this debate among feminists, whatever their gender preferences, about the role of sexuality in women's lives and what sexuality is "correct" in hewing to various political lines are exceptionally passionate and often intellectually dense. It would be too easy to dismiss all of these debates as merely sectarian (which they often are) since they are full of very serious argument about the problems of cultural reconstruction.

10. The Stonewall riot in which gay men defended themselves against the police is the mythic historical marker that divides the homosexual from the gay epoch. The Stonewall was a gay male bar in Greenwich Village.

11. The impact of the AIDS crisis on the gay male community will not be well understood for another decade. It is clear, however, that there was a rapid adoption of "safe sex" practices among most gay men. This change in sexual practices was strongly supported by the media institutions of the gay community, and the community itself has become the primary source of support for those afflicted with the syndrome. The ability of gay men to change their sexual practices supports a view of same-gender erotic preferences as relatively loosely structured both as intrapsychic and interpersonal phenomena.

12. This is a generalization that is probably true for a majority of those with same-gender erotic desires, particularly during their early adolescent and young adult years. There are persons, however, who report wonderfully cheerful and satisfying same-gender erotic lives even during adolescence and many more who report lives of great personal and sexual fulfillment during their adulthood. Considering the level of sexual oppression, it is remarkable how many happy "homosexuals" there turned out to be.

13. Paralleling the relative diffuseness of the gendering of erotic desire during this period, it is also likely that romantic love is less gender specific in this period for both boys and girls. Passionate friendships with persons of the same or the other gender are actually quite common for both boys and girls; the ways in which such patterns of love and admiration facilitate erotic preferences are not well understood.

14. The increased politicalization of the gay male and lesbian communities has made boundary maintenance between these communities and the straight world a critical ideological and practical issue. As a result these communities look more and more like those Lewis Coser (1974) describes in his work on greedy institutions.

15. Journals such as the *Journal of Homosexuality*, *Speculum*, *Signs*, and *Chrysalis* all carry works by persons who identify themselves as gay or lesbian. The works of gay and lesbian historians, sociologists, psychologists, and literary figures represent most of the useful work now being conducted on the relation between culture and the self.

References

Baudrillard, J. (1983). *Simulations*. New York: Semiotext(e).

Becker, H. (1963). *The outsiders*. New York: The Free Press.

Bell, A., & Weinberg, M. (1978). *Homosexualities: A study of diversity among men and women*. New York: Simon & Schuster.

Berne, E. (1966). *Games people play*. New York: Grove Press.

Boswell, J. (1980). *Christianity, social tolerance, and homosexuality: Gay people in Western Europe from the beginning of the Christian era to the fourteenth century*. Chicago: University of Chicago Press.

Burke, K. (1936). *Permanence and change: An anatomy of purpose*. New York: New Republic.

Burke, K. (1966). *Language as symbolic action: Essays on life, literature, and method.* Berkeley: University of California Press.

Burke, K. (1984). *Attitudes toward history.* Berkeley: University of California Press. (original work published 1937)

Califia, P. (1983, July). Gay men, lesbians and sex: Doing it together. *The Advocate,* pp. 24–27.

Coser, L. (1974). *Greedy institutions: Patterns of undivided commitment.* New York: Free Press.

Cromptom, L. (1985). *Byrons and Greek love: Homophobia in 19th-century England.* Berkeley: University of California Press.

Darnton, R. (1984). *The great cat massacre and other episodes in French cultural history.* New York: Free Press.

Dover, K. J. (1978). *Greek homosexuality.* Cambridge, MA: Harvard University Press.

Duberman, M. (1974, June 28). The bisexual debate. *New Times Magazine,* pp. 34–41.

Ellul, J. (1964). *The technological society.* New York: Knopf.

Fleck, L. (1979). *The genesis of a scientific fact.* Chicago: University of Chicago Press. (Original work published 1935)

Foucault, M. (1978). *The history of sexuality: Vol. 1. An introduction.* New York: Pantheon.

Foucault, M. (1979). *Discipline and punish: The birth of the prison.* New York: Pantheon.

Gagnon, J. H. (1973). Scripts and the coordination of sexual conduct. In J. K. Cole & R. Dienstbier (Eds.), *Proceedings of the Nebraska Symposium on Motivation* (pp. 27–59). Lincoln: University of Nebraska Press.

Gagnon, J. H. (1977). *Human sexualities.* Glenview, IL: Scott, Foresman.

Gagnon, J. H. (1978). Reconsiderations: A. C. Kinsey et al., *Sexual behavior in the human male* and *Sexual behavior in the Human Female. Human Nature, 1*(10), 92–95.

Gagnon, J. H., Rosen, R., & Leiblum, S. (1982). Cognitive and social aspects of sexual dysfunction. *Journal of Sex and Marital Therapy, 8*(1), 44–56.

Gagnon, J. H., & Simon, W. (1967). Femininity in the lesbian community. *Social Problems, 15*(2), 212–221.

Gagnon, J. H., & Simon, W. (1973). *Sexual conduct.* Chicago: Aldine.

Gagnon, J. H., & Simon, W. (1987). The scripting of oral genital conduct. *Archives of Sexual Behavior, 16*(1), 1–25.

Geertz, C. (1973). *The interpretation of cultures.* New York: Basic Books.

Geertz, C. (1983). *Local knowledge.* New York: Basic Books.

Herdt, G. (1981). *Guardians of the flute.* New York: McGraw-Hill.

Herdt, G. (1984). *Ritualized homosexuality in Melanesia.* Berkeley: University of Calfornia Press.

Humphreys, L. (1970). *Tearoom trade: Impersonal sex in public places.* Chicago: Aldine.

Humphreys, L. (1972). *Out of the closets: The sociology of homosexual liberation.* Englewood Cliffs, NJ: Prentice-Hall.

Katz, J. (1983). *Gay/lesbian alamanac: A new documentary.* New York: Harper & Row.

Kinsey, A. C., Pomeroy, W. P., & Martin, C. (1948). *Sexual behavior in the human male.* Philadelphia: W. B. Saunders.

Kinsey, A. C., Pomeroy, W. P., Martin, C. & Gebhard, P. H. (1953). *Sexual behavior in the human female.* Philadelphia: W. B. Saunders.

Kohut, H. (1977). *The restoration of the self.* New York: International University Press.

Kuhn, T. S. (1970). *The structure of scientific revolutions* (2nd ed.). Chicago: University of Chicago Press.

Kuhn, T. S. (1977). *The essential tension*. Chicago: University of Chicago Press.

Levine, M. (1986). *Gay macho: Ethnography of the homosexual clone*. Unpublished doctoral dissertation, Department of Sociology, New York University.

Mead, G. H. (1934). *Mind, self, and society*. Chicago: University of Chicago Press.

Peckham, M. (1969). *Art and pornography: An experiment in explanation*. New York: Basic Books.

Peckham, M. (1979). *Explanation and power: The control of human behavior*. New York: Seabury.

Plummer, K. (Ed.). (1981). *The making of the modern homosexual*. Totowa, NJ: Barnes & Noble.

Pomeroy, W. B. (1972). *Alfred C. Kinsey and the Institute for Sex Research*. New York: Harper & Row.

Robinson, P. (1976). *The modernization of sex*. New York: Harper & Row.

Rorty, R. (1979). *Philosophy and the mirror of nature*. Princeton, NJ: Princeton University Press.

Schank, R. C. (1982). *Dynamic memory: A theory of reminding and learning in computers and people*. Cambridge, England: Cambridge University Press.

Schank, R. C., & Abelson, R. P. (1977). *Scripts, plans, goals and understanding: An inquiry into human knowledge structures*. Hillsdale, NJ: Lawrence Erlbaum.

Scheff, T. (1968). *Being mentally ill: A sociological theory*. Chicago: Aldine.

Simon, W. (1973). The social, the erotic, the sensual: The complexities of sexual scripts. In J. K. Cole & R. Dienstbier (Eds.), *Proceedings of the Nebraska Symposium on Motivation* (pp. 27–59). Lincoln: University of Nebraska Press.

Socarides, C. W. (1978). *Homosexuality*. New York: Aronson.

Steiner, G. (1984). The distribution of discourse. In G. Steiner, *A Reader*. London: Pelican.

Szasz, T. (1961). *The myth of mental illness*. New York: Dell.

van den Berg, J. H. (1975). *The changing historical nature of man: Introduction to a historical psychology*. New York: Delta. (Original work published 1961)

Veblen, T. (1964). *The instinct of workmanship and the industrial arts*. New York: W. W. Norton. (Original work published 1914)

Warren, C. A. B. (1974). *Identity and community in the gay world*. New York: John Wiley & Sons.

Weeks, J. (1981). *Sex, politics, and society: The regulation of sexuality since 1800*. London: Longmans.

White, E. (1980). *States of desire*. New York: E. P. Dutton.

White, E. (1983). *A boy's own story*. New York: E. P. Dutton.

Wolf, D. G. (1979). *The lesbian community*. Berkeley: University of California Press.

13

Developmental Discontinuities and Sexual Orientation Across Cultures

Gilbert Herdt

Anthropology has pioneered the understanding of variations in sexual practices across the spectrum of human groups on the basis of intensive ethnographic study. The speculative hierarchical taxonomies of Victorian evolutionists in the nineteenth century, for instance, gave way to the encyclopedic surveys of Havelock Ellis (1936) and Westermarck (1917), among others, in the early twentieth (reviewed in Bullough, 1980; Foucault, 1980; Herdt, 1984a; Money & Ehrhardt, 1972); this in turn was succeeded by Freud (1905/1962). By 1925, Freud (1925/1961), in a classical paper on sex differences, could speak confidently of "universals" in psychosexual development as if cross-cultural variations were irrelevant. The influence of the Freudians was great, and it shifted interest to the psychic level of gender meanings. Malinowski (1927) complained of this universalism, but he could not provide a counterpoint to the view that "anatomy is destiny." Margaret Mead's (1935) classic work on New Guinea, *Sex and Temperament in Three Primitive Societies*, attempted such a response, however. From the available evidence it would seem that Mead and her followers succeeded to a remarkable extent.[1] Since the 1930s many other ethnographers have provided insights on the extent to which, as Carrier (1980) has put it, "Intercultural variations in patterns of human sexual behavior are mainly related to social and cultural differences occurring between societies around the world" (p. 100). (See also Ford & Beach, 1951; LeVine, 1979; Mead, 1949; Minturn, Gross, & Haider, 1969; Ortner & Whitehead, 1981). Yet while anthropology has examined cross-cultural differences in sexual patterns across societies, it has had little to say regarding cross-cultural similarities on another dimension of sexual social-ization: developmental discontinuity across the life span.

How do sexual behavior and experience change across the developmen-tal cycle of a person, and how do cultural practices and related psy-chosexual mechanisms structure such variance? This general problem area—which surely is one of the more perplexing and controversial in the study of our own society—has been largely ignored in the study of other cultures. In this chapter, I explore similarities and differences in develop-mental change in sexuality from an anthropological perspective. I suggest that when we sort the considerable cross-cultural archives, we discover that change in sexual behavior and experience after childhood is a clear part of the human condition. This point regarding the potential for change is supported by accumulating evidence from life-span development studies of a wide-ranging nature in our own society (Brim & Kagan, 1980; Honzik, 1984). In a recent review that includes sexual development, Kolberg and his colleagues (Kolberg, Ricks, & Savarey, 1984) suggest "that there is more change than constancy between childhood and adolescence or adulthood" (p. 156). Because of its exploratory nature, I will not undertake a systematic survey of all the literature here.[2] Moreover, in keeping with the focus of this volume, I will study issues related to understanding the structure and meaning of homosexuality and bisexuality, especially in non-Western cul-tures. Because homosexuality cannot in my view be disengaged from the study of heterosexuality—since both forms of sexual action occur in the same ongoing social field of institutions, roles, and symbols, which take as their objects male and female experience (De Cecco & Shively, 1984)—we must also ground our analysis in broader social contexts.

The relationship between discontinuity and homosexuality across cul-tures is not, I think, fortuitous or trivial, and indeed, their co-occurrence helps explain both the absence of studies on discontinuity by anthropolo-gists and how I have arrived at the present problem in my own work. With a few exceptions, such as Ruth Benedict's classic paper (1938) discussed below, anthropologists have not taken continuities and discontinuities in sexual development as problematic in cross-cultural work. Benedict used institutionalized homosexuality in Australian and New Guinea tribes as a key example of how in developmental time children in some cultures must "unlearn" cultural things to learn other adult cultural practices. By con-trast, Benedict's student, Mead (1935), saw homosexuality as a form of "deviance" and as an unanticipated outcome of unusual temperaments who could not accommodate themselves to the norm. Later work did not change this ambiguous treatment; for as various writers have said (Carrier, 1980), the data on homosexual behavior in anthropology were until very recent skimpy and poor. New studies have improved the situation (re-viewed in Blackwood, 1986; Herdt, 1981, 1984a; Read, 1980). These studies are only now beginning to alter our understanding of developmental change in sexual socialization in other cultures.

The historical treatment of sexuality by anthropologists must be seen in the broader context of functional studies of culture and personality associated with the work of Benedict, Devereux, Mead, Whiting, and others from the 1920s onward. These psychoanalytically oriented studies were holistic and largely ahistorical; they focused on adults and normative outcome variables. Homogeneity of experience and behavior were often stressed, so that in understanding particular cultural "ways," even sexuality, ethnographies stressed the equation of culture with the "basic personality" of a tribal people. Furthermore, descriptive relativism—the view that all cultural elements are meaningful in their native context—led to normative relativism: the idea that moral judgments about cultures cannot be made, because they are all of equal worth (Spiro, 1986). Functionalism and relativism thus operated together in the epistemology of anthropology. Since cultures were "adaptations" and "functioned," they must be consistent, integrated, and relatively useful accommodations—nonpathologic (cf. Spiro, 1984; Wallace, 1969, pp. 24–25). Culture was nearly self-contained in providing the necessities of adult rational adaptations to environments (Benedict, 1934). So strong was the view that cultural adjustment requires normative homogeneity in beliefs and practices shared by *all members* of a group, that Margaret Mead, for example, once suggested that cultural heterogeneity is *"ipso facto* pathogenic" (quoted in Wallace, 1969).[3] Added to this situation was the general trend that anthropologists avoided the study of sex (LeVine, 1979) per se; kinship, family, marriage, and the like were a priori concerns (see Herdt & Stoller, in press).

Thus, when it came to dealing with it, homosexuality was a strange intruder in the garden of functionalist anthropology. Let us take, as a case in point, Marvin Opler, an anthropologist who worked with the Ute Indians and who also authored an early review on homosexuality (1965). First, Opler thought of homosexuality solely in the context of Freud's (1910/1955a) Schreber case, as a defensive manifestation of the Oedipal complex. However, he argued that Freud's model was historically culturebound to middle-class Viennese society. He suggested contra the Freud of *Totem and Taboo* (1913/1955b) that initiation and penis mutilation have nothing to do with "castration anxieties" or erotic matters among Australian aborigines, although no evidence was adduced to support his contention (Opler, 1965). Apparently Opler was unaware of institutionalized homosexual practices among certain aboriginal societies (Herdt 1984c).[4] Following this, almost as a non sequitur, Opler then stated: "The point about these societies and other nonliterate hunting and gathering societies is that homosexuality is generally rare and, in some instances, virtually nonexistent" (p. 111). Opler proceeded to dismiss the resilient findings of Ford and Beach (1951) on the frequency of homosexual practices across cultures,[5] arguing that their survey data were decontextualized and unreliable. (Rado, 1956, however, who felt that homosexuality was situation-specific to prisons and associated with "impulse-ridden schizophrenics," was more reliable, according to Opler.[6]) After suggesting further that this "deviant homosexuality"—astonishingly, the term is never defined—occurs also in "aberrant" Siberian shamans and Norwegian rats, Opler concluded: "One thing is clear: In the absence of an organic or hormonal basis, homosexuality in practically all cultures is regarded as a deviation from the majority values and norms of conduct" (p. 114). The prosecution rested, its case against homosexuality in other cultures firmly made.[7]

Is there any wonder that virtually a generation has passed and now a new breed of younger anthropologists has come along to disagree and reopen the case to critical inquiry (Blackwood, 1986; Carrier, 1980; Davenport, 1977; Herdt, 1981; Murray, 1984; Nanda, 1986; Stoller & Herdt, 1985)? And is it to be further wondered that the range and types of homosexual and bisexual behavior, their role and meanings in the developmental cycle of people, should today be so poorly understood?[8] Only now may we return to issues of continuity and discontinuity in sexual socialization across cultures.

What Did Kinsey Measure?

It was during the heyday of functional anthropology, the 1930s and 1940s, that Kinsey began his ambitious project on American sexual practices. Kinsey did draw upon anthropology in contextualizing some of his findings, as we can see in *Sexual Behavior in the Human Male* (Kinsey, Pomeroy, & Martin, 1948), wherein he cited ethnographers with regard to variations in sexual norms. He used Margaret Mead's work, for instance, in comparing American practices of premarital intercourse and extramarital intercourse to those of other cultures. Kinsey's use of cross-cultural references was generally citational, not expository, however, and the references are positioned textually at the beginnings of chapters, usually to raise the question of the universality of sexual practices.

Kinsey's great and lasting contribution, from a comparative perspective, was to disengage monolithic cultural categories—homosexuality, heterosexuality—from the disparaging discourse of the 1940s and 1950s by demonstrating *variation* in sexual behavior among normative males and females. His empirical findings challenged moral and political images of the normative in psychosexual development. Everyone was at one point "deviant" with regard to heterosexuality. However flawed the data, either by sample, procedures, or analysis, Kinsey's insistence upon behavioral variation opened the way for far-reaching and critical cultural transformation in Americans' understanding of sexual orientation. Process replaced prototype. Kinsey challenged, that is, the biological essentialist and morally flawed deficit views of human nature—in man and woman—as social and psychological prototypes in Western thought. We need not belabor the point that his critics, among them the infamous Joseph Mc-

Carthy, exacted from Kinsey and his associates a heavy price for this scientific and societal progress. Nor must we forget its scientific benefits for the emergence of the remarkable research of the 1950s and 1960s, such as the seminal contributions on sexuality of John Money (1956) and his colleagues or the later survey studies (see Bell, Weinberg, & Hammersmith, 1981). Subsequent dissatisfaction with the Kinsey scale, the notion of sexual orientation, the analysis of bisexuality as a residual category, and the polarization of homosexuality and heterosexuality as psychosexual prototypes distilled in a different form than that in which Kinsey found them must not overshadow the historical and cultural domains into which Kinsey and his colleagues brought genuine enlightenment.

Kinsey has been criticized on various grounds, not the least of which concerns the implied universality of his American study. Responses by anthropologists at the time ranged from the very critical (Gorer, 1955) to the more positive Kluckhohn (1955). Geoffrey Gorer, a British anthropologist, felt that Kinsey exaggerated sex as behavior as a mere "device for physical relaxation. . . . Not only is sex, in Dr. Kinsey's presentation, as meaningless as a sneeze, it is also equally unproductive; after the equivalent of blowing the nose, that is the end of the matter" (1955, pp. 51–52). This point, while perhaps overinflated, raises a cultural critique agreed upon by many in gender research, including John Gagnon (Chapter 12) and John De Cecco (Chapter 21) in this volume: that Kinsey studied disembodied acts, discrete behaviors, rather than meaning-filled patterns of action. As De Cecco sees it, Kinsey had four conceptions of sex: that it was a physical activity, that it developed in a mechanistic way, that robust sexual performance was to be admired, and that its chief outcome was not reproduction but erotic pleasure. These attributes all are related to the question of sex as meaning-filled symbolic expression of normative development and sexual socialization in culture. By emphasizing acts instead of symbolic action, Kinsey managed to create a field of sexual study amid a moral climate that had hindered it (Kluckhohn, 1955), yet he did so at the cost of divorcing sex from the lives and meanings of whole persons (see also Stoller, 1985).

Why this is important to me is that Kinsey's work fostered a view that sexual acts can be seen apart from the developmental life-span stages in which they are studied. This implied a "steady state" view that sexual development is always based on *continuities* in cultural conditioning, if not in fact in actual *experienced* successive continuities, in people's lives. Such a preconception is based on a cultural conception of human nature that characterizes Western countries such as the United States.

But to return to my own question. What Kinsey *thought* he measured were overt sexual experiences that indicated the individual's developmental continuity in sexual behaviors. He looked for a linear trend. Kinsey et al. (1948) specifically believed that attitudes, fantasies, and other "subjective" materials were too introspective to be reliable measures of experience.[9] This eliminated inconsistencies between acts in the head and those in the real world. Furthermore, because Kinsey scores for the same person were not aggregated, the sexual preference and behavior of the individual was studied at one point in time, not as successive sequelae but as outcome variable. Cross-sectional studies of different age-groups were held up as a composite picture of the "meaning" of psychosexual development in American society. But this was problematic in view of retrospective bias (Ross, 1980). This approach had the effects of eliminating sexual change within the same person's life, of making the act more important than its inner experience, and therefore of concentrating on the mechanics of how, not the meanings of why, people engage in erotic intercourse.

Ruth Benedict on Discontinuity

During the start-up period of Kinsey's research, Ruth Benedict (1938) contributed an insightful paper for the first issue of *Psychiatry*, a paper entitled "Continuities and Discontinuities in Cultural Conditioning." Her text outlined a powerful critique of Kinsey's treatment of sexuality in cultural and developmental perspective. "All cultures must deal in one way or another with the cycle of growth from infancy to adulthood," Benedict began.

> Nature has posed the situation dramatically: on the one hand, the new born baby, physiologically vulnerable, unable to fend for itself, or to participate of its own initiative in the life of the group, and, on the other, the adult man or woman. Every man who rounds out his potentialities must have been a son first and a father later and the two roles are physiologically great in contrast; he must first have been dependent upon others for his very existence and later he must provide security for others. This discontinuity in the life cycle is a fact of nature and is inescapable. Facts of nature, however, in any discussion of human problems, are ordinarily read off not at their bare minimal but surrounded by all the local accretions of behavior to which the student of human affairs has become accustomed in his own society. (p. 160)

The "facts of nature" are not "natural" for humans, Benedict argued: between this nature and human behavior, culture is a great "middle term," a mediator. Transitions in the life course involve "cultural bridges" (Ibid.). Such bridges—social practices, roles, expressive ceremonies such as initiation rites, and so on—embody underlying conceptions of human nature; what it is, how it is made, and how it changes over time (Geertz, 1973).

In Benedict's view, then, cultures differ in the degree of continuity of experience, task-assignment, rules, norms, beliefs, expectation, goals, and roles structured across the developmental cycle from infancy to adulthood. Continuity means, Benedict (1938) wrote, "that the child is taught nothing it must unlearn later" (p. 165). As a mundane example of continuity in cultural conditioning, Benedict cited the practice in America of eating three meals a day. By age 2 or 3, infants achieve the adult schedule. No change in this occurs or is expected. Modesty is another illustration she used: "We waste no time in clothing the baby, and in contrast to many societies where the child runs naked till it is ceremonially given its skirt or pubic sheath at adolescence, the child's training fits it precisely for adult conventions" (pp. 161–162). For examples of discontinuity, Benedict selected three domains: "responsible-nonresponsible status role," "dominance-submission," and "contrasted sex role." On responsibility, she argued that Americans and other Westerners treat the child as wanting to play, whereas the adult has to work. Child labor laws in England and the West changed a historical pattern in which, during the Middle Ages, children were regarded as small adults who had heavy work responsibilities (Aries, 1962). Agrarian children in the United States and other Western countries also differ in this way. Benedict (1938) cited the Papago Indians as a people who draw less distinction than do we in expecting children to be socially and productively responsible like adults. Mead (1930), in her *Growing Up in New Guinea*, stressed discontinuity in the responsibility of Manus Island children, who shunned the concerns of adults. "The contrast with our society is very great," said Benedict (1938, p. 163). And thus it was with dominance/submission distinctions: in American society, children are expected to obey adults, their superiors. Benedict felt that our society loaded every situation with the seeds of a power relationship. By contrast, many simple societies make use of kinship terminology systems that emphasize continuity and reciprocity, rather than power and hierarchy, across the life span. In support of this view, a classic study by Barry, Child, and Bacon (1959) has demonstrated training for independence and autonomy among hunters and gatherers and training for obedience and submission among horticultural peoples around the world.

Discontinuity in sex role training, Benedict's third domain, is most relevant to my analysis. The discrepancy between facts of physiological maturation and cultural concepts of sexual differentiation between children and adults poses a great challenge to the adult outcome of sexual development. Is the child regarded as neuter or sexless? Are children permitted to experiment sexually? Are homosexual acts considered morally neutral or repugnant? And how is sexual variation handled in adulthood? The answers to such questions vary enormously across cultures (Herdt, 1987b; Mead, 1961). Discontinuity is not linked in any simple way to whether a people are prudish or sexually tolerant. Benedict (1938) noted that among the Dakota Indians, for instance, "Adults observe great privacy in sex acts and in no way stimulate children's sexual activity," so there is no developmental discontinuity because the child "is taught nothing it does not have to unlearn later" (p. 165). In such societies, sexual experimentation is viewed as harmless because it poses no serious consequences for adult behavior. Yet in our society, in which preadolescent sexual activity is generally disapproved and sexual variations are punished, the potential for unlearning values and attitudes is very great and may be associated with a kind of emotional and cognitive amnesia of childhood (Cohler, 1982; Gagnon, 1971; Neisser, 1962).

With regard to homosexuality, Carrier's (1980) review categorizes societies around the world into three types of response: accommodating societies, which are approving; disapproving societies; and societies that do not formally sanction same-sex activity but utilize social regulations to inhibit its free expression. An important form of accommodation to homosexual practices is that of tribal initiation and secret male cults. Ruth Benedict (1938) cited two well-known examples from New Guinea, the Keraki of the Trans-Fly River (Williams, 1936) and the Marind-anim of Southeast New Guinea. Both groups have what she referred to as "Making of Men" initiations, which are widespread in Melanesia and Australia (Herdt, 1982). Here is Benedict's summary:

> Among the Keraki it is thought that no boys can grow to full stature without playing the [passive homosexual] role for some years. Men slightly older take the active role, and the older man is a jealous partner. The life cycle of the Keraki Indians includes, therefore, in succession, passive homosexuality, active homosexuality and heterosexuality.
>
> There is no technique for ending active homosexuality, but this is not explicitly tabu for older men; heterosexuality and children, however, are highly valued. (p. 166)

In fact, the Marind-anim do not sanction but rather expect even old men to take part in ritual homosexual activity (Van Baal, 1984). This example of cultural discontinuity shows, Benedict (1938) believed, the way in which cultural institutions can "furnish adequate support to the individual as he progresses from role to role or interdicts the previous behavior in a summary fashion" (p. 167). She concluded by arguing how strikingly different is our culture in the existence of "maladjusted persons" who become "fixated" at a pre-adult level. Obviously she was referring to homosexual or gay people when she said that they were blamed for not manifesting "behavior which up to that time has been under a ban"—namely, heterosexuality—even though this exacts from them a "great psychic cost." This problem in developmental discontinuity should be seen not as an individual issue, Benedict chided, but rather one of contradictory cultural "institutions" and "dogmas." Instead of creating more dogmas about sexual neurosis we ought to develop new social institutions that would remove these pressures.

   Benedict seems to have been responding to the medicalization of homosexuality. Her plea for a new social fabric—one heard before and since—
was in keeping with the cultural determinism, humanism, and relativism
already outlined. Although she hinted at ideological conceptions of human nature and elsewhere indicated that these were always to be seen as
ethnocentric folk models all peoples exhibit (Benedict, 1934), she did not
say how these were related systematically to problems of sexual discontinuity. Take note that she never defined homosexuality, though her reference to "jealous" Keraki partners implied that this was more than a ceremonial performance. It involved the whole feeling person. Note, too, her
assumption that the imposed discontinuities of ritualized homosexuality
do not create psychosocial problems for either the individual or society.
Benedict responded to the medical model with a relativist account of
homosexuality, and like Kinsey, she thereby expanded our discourse on
human sexuality by using examples from other cultures. Her relativism
suggested that our society was "worse" than others in how it accommo-
dated individuals to "natural" developmental changes. In spite of the
differing conceptual approaches, however, Kinsey and Benedict shared in
common the notion that homosexuality is not *necessarily* abnormal and
may, indeed, be but one of many potentials humans have for fluidity and
change in their essential "nature."

Developmental Changes in Sexuality

Suppose that we agree with the view that the "facts of nature" impose
inevitable psychophysiological changes upon the life course of sexuality
in humans; where do we go from there? Sexual differentiation from infancy to adulthood certainly involves numerous changes in primary and
secondary sex traits (Luria, 1979), not all of which are developmentally or
socially problematic, or even of conscious interest, to human groups
(Maccoby, 1979; Ortner & Whitehead, 1981; Shapiro, 1979). This potential
for flexibility in sexual accommodations to culture is a "two-edged
sword," Margaret Mead (1935, p. 310) once wrote, because it allows for
both positive and negative imposition[10] of external structure and goals
upon the person in development.
   The difficulty with Kinsey's scale of measurement in this regard was
that it placed too much emphasis upon discrete acts of sex and not enough
stress upon the cultural context and total developmental outcomes to
which these acts are related. This is the same failure that today manifests
itself in enormous quantitative sociological surveys of homosexuality that
decontextualize the culture and lives at issue (Bell et al., 1981). Benedict's
corrective was the point that conceptions of developmental changes must
be seen in the context of social structure and "dogmas" of human nature
that make them seem "normal and natural." What she failed to do, however, was to explicate these systematic cultural patterns and folk concepts

of human nature underlying the direction of psychosexual changes. Yet this latter perspective must not be seen as an analogy to the onion peel: a physical nature with culture wrapped around it. Kinsey et al. (1948) seemed to have this image in mind. Humans are neither innate capacities nor discrete bundles of actual behaviors, however. "When seen as a set of symbolic devices for controlling behavior," Geertz (1973) has said, "extrasomatic sources of information, cultures provide the link between what men are intrinsically capable of becoming and what they actually, one by one, become" (p. 52).

The nonbiological changes that co-occur with sexual differentiation—social and psychological differentiation—are complex; while the biological transformations can be modeled as universals, the psychosocial correlates vary greatly, and must be modeled as local contingencies (Ehrhardt, 1985). Such changes, to which the person must adapt, include ideas about the human nature folk model thought to cause and result from the changes, ideas about gender roles, ideologies, rules for sexual conduct, and normative images of appropriate gender behavior that guide action in nonsexual domains, some of which function as cultural ideology for work and love, and others of which become internalized as subjective scripts. Although this is quite a bit, it does not exhaust the content of personal and cultural experiences, which are contingent upon, among other things, early attachment, learning experiences, and their related fantasies (Obeyesekere, 1981; Stoller, 1979, 1985). In this area I maintain, with Freud (1905/1962), a "presumption of bisexuality" in human potential.[11] Although many, but by no means all (Ford & Beach, 1951), human groups associate appropriate gender and erotic behavior with moral institutions (the family, inheritance, religion), other cultures do not make such assumptions or social connections. Departures from norms may thus be "disapproved" (Carrier, 1980), but only if they are idiosyncratic, not cohort-normative. Discontinuities of the type discussed by Benedict may therefore be problematic for the individual but not so for the society in which cultural guidelines anticipate developments of "human nature." This is particularly evident in cultural systems that institutionalize dramatic change in sex role development (Cohen, 1964; Stephens, 1962). Gagnon's (1971) seminal review made this point in our society, and my work in Melanesia has also illustrated this general pattern.

One means of sorting out this variance is to establish a normative typology of societies relative to how prescribed or preferred sexual conduct is structured across the life cycle. From this we can infer how underlying conceptions of human nature are felt to contribute to normative developmental changes in sexual being and action. Following this typology, I will examine how major structural forms of homosexuality found around the world can be classified.

For the sake of brevity, I will use a three-category typology of sexual development regimes cross-culturally. These types are idealized models and could be further subdivided into component subtypes, which I will not consider here. All three structural types attempt to capture the degree[12] and range of continuity experienced by people in regard to sexual practices and associated attitudes across the life span.

1. *Linear development* is an unbroken developmental line (Kohlberg et al., 1984) of sexual behavior that is constructed on the basis of fully anticipated outcomes by parents and other caretakers. No dramatic change—unlearning—in sexual conduct or orientation and little discontinuity from early childhood onward are experienced by the person. As ethnographic examples of linear sexual development, I would cite the !Kung bushmen (Shostack, 1980), the Trobriand Islanders (Malinowski, 1927), and the Tahitians (Levy, 1973), though others could be identified as well (Mead, 1961).

2. *Sequential development* is a broken developmental line of sexual behavior with marked and sometimes dramatic changes in anticipated outcomes between childhood and adulthood (see also Money & Ehrhardt, 1972). Variable and even discrepant norms and rules here radically transform sexual being and action from one life cycle stage to another. One or both parents may avoid or be unaware of adult anticipated sexual practices, so that no *direct* preparatory socialization enters into childhood teaching. For examples of avoidant regimes, I would cite Victorian England (Foucault, 1980) and, somewhat less so, contemporary America (Fine, 1988), in which many caretakers still regard children as erotically naive and sexless, as Benedict argued. For illustration of unawareness of parents, I would cite, for instance, those cultures in Melanesia that institutionalize secret homosexual contact (hidden from women and children) as a paradigmatic case (Herdt, 1984b). The question of nonconscious or unconscious awareness of eventual sequential change is problematic and will be discussed shortly. However, my operational rule is that for inclusion in this category, at least one and possibly both parents must share in the cultural image of the eventual career of the child, even though the anticipated changes are hidden or not spoken of by both the socializers (Herdt, 1987a). Thus, sequential development can still be analyzed as a system of serial stages or consequences that logically succeed one another.

By its very nature, a sequential sexual socialization regime is phasic or episodic. John Money (1987) has reviewed various instances of this. Two patterns of such phasic development stand out. First, the dramatic changes in sexual behavior are not handled by the primary socialization group (e.g., the nuclear family) but rather by secondary socializing groups or institutions (e.g., ritual cults, peer groups, etc.). Herdt (1987b) illustrates this for the Sambia of New Guinea. Second, some elements of the sexual code will be continuous even in the face of radical change in other components of sexual orientation. To take the example of age-structured homosexual activity in Melanesia, ancient Japan, Greece, and elsewhere, all caretakers and children seemingly share in the norm that boys and girls will marry and reproduce; this norm does not alter across the lifespan, in spite of the introduction and experience of homosexual activity as a radically different change in sexual status between childhood and adulthood (Herdt 1987a). We can thus refer to phasic and nonphasic patterns of sexual and nonsexual behavior in systems of sequential development. By contrast with "linear" systems, more elements of both sexual *and* nonsexual behavior change in societies that institutionalize discontinuous sequential change in development.

3. *Emergent development* refers to a more "open-ended" culture or subculture in which new sexual values and practices are based upon uncertainty and ambiguity in future outcomes of development as socialized by caretakers. New values, for instance, replace or transform older ones. For total social systems in which dramatic change occurred, but which did not fundamentally affect the sexual code, I would cite the instances of Manus Island (Mead, 1956) and postrevolutionary Mexico (Wolf, 1969). Societies that have undergone far-reaching change in social *and* sexual being and behavior would include the Israeli kibbutz and the People's Republic of China, (Tavris & Offir, 1977), particularly insofar as gender equality has been touted as a public ideology. The so-called "sexual revolution" in the United States of the 1960s brought new values in the areas of sexual contact, the decision to marry or have children, and the like, although the long-term consequences and retrenchment of this period of change have yet to be seen (Gagnon, 1971; Weeks, 1985). In the classificatory scheme used below, the cultural concept "gay" and the notion of a gay subculture or community (Adam, 1987), seem to belong to emergent developmental regimes. Structurally, emergent regimes have a core; not everything changes (Herdt, 1988). Some deep-seated premises of sexuality endure, while other surface features (such as beliefs and roles) may change. Androgyny in dress and cosmetic styles, for example, may become acceptable and eventually normative, as in the case of "punk culture" (Plummer, 1989). Emergent, as a label, implies that socializers are less sure of the absolute outcomes of sexual behavior codes in the future. Emergent sexual regimes are found in rapidly changing, technologically advanced societies, although emergent values and their attendant social changes are certainly occurring in developing countries of the third world (reviewed in Herdt, 1989).

The sketch of these three types of sexual developmental regimes implies somewhat different conceptions of human nature that can only be hinted here.[13] Such "dogmas," to use Benedict's term, are translatable into ideologies and sexual practices, at the collective level, and internalized experience or scripts, for the individual. Suffice it to say in the present context that variability in the normative sexual "careers" of societies involves factors of sexual practice, emotion, cognition, and relationships—key variables of the Kinsey scale (Klein, Sepekoff, & Wolf, 1985). But this variability has not been transferred into our theory of

Kinsey scale findings. The conception of human nature implied by linear developmental regimes is one in which the fundamentals of the expected adult normative outcome are believed to be present at birth or in early childhood and do not require additional "biological" or "social" treatment. There may be flexibility in relation to sexual experimentation, yet the consequences of this are perceived to be insignificant for the outcome. Why is this so? Because the "normal and natural" adult repertoire of sociosexual roles is limited; the requirements of adult personhood are met by marriage and parenthood; and no internal contradictions within the society challenge this or allow for major exceptions to the outcome (see Adam, 1987).

In contrast, the conception of human nature in sequential systems is one of unfinished requirements or prerequisites that necessitate unlearning. Additional biological essentials, psychosocial training, or sexual experiences are necessary after childhood to attain normative adult outcomes. The boundaries of gender roles are subject to careful scrutiny and sanctioning. Fluidity of human potential is thus perceived as a preconception of developmental changes across the life span. Sexual fertility may be seen as a kind of dynamic, electrical force that flows into and out of people, with children and the aged perceived to be sexually infertile (Herdt, 1984a; Strathern, 1988). This fluidity must be seen in the context of important internal contradictions in societies of this type (Herdt, 1981; Herdt & Poole, 1982; Lindenbaum, 1984; Shapiro, 1979).

The emergent regime is the most complex type in its conception of human nature, apparently implicating assumptions of both linear and sequential regimes, but going beyond them. This has, no doubt, to do with the parallel existence of *traditional* notions of, say, Anglo-Saxon societies, such as America and England, alongside of post-Enlightenment *scientific* views coincident with industrialization and the market-economy image of the "individual" in the development of persons (see Foucault, 1980; Mead, 1961, pp. 1456–1457).[14] My sense of this cross-cultural variability is that Kinsey assumed the American conception of human nature, in the image of emergent sexual development, to be universal, an assumption that now seems false. In the conclusion, I will return to a discussion of Kinsey's work in the light of this critique of forms of developmental regime.

Four Forms of Homosexuality

The further examination of developmental changes in sexuality across the life span and across cultures will be facilitated by understanding the structural forms of homosexual organization. The model of the forms I use has been presented in greater detail elsewhere (Herdt 1987a, 1988), and this departs from previous models in several ways. Westermarck (1917), for example, thought that homosexuality, cross-culturally, showed two trends: either homosexual behavior was kept confined or peripheral enough that it did not challenge the biological and social reproduction of a society across generations, or it was institutionalized in such a way (by social role or by age-grading) that homosexual bonding was restricted and did not "get out of hand" in its effects upon later developmental goals for a person. Other authors, including Ford and Beach (1951) and Margaret Mead (1961), have assumed institutionalized cross-dressing or transvestism to be the most frequent form of homosexuality (see also Carrier, 1980). The work of Adam (1986), Murray (1984), and Trumbach (1977) has, however, produced new insights into the structural variants of homosexual activity around the world. We can build upon these synthetically in a new model of homosexual variation as it relates to the regimes of developmental discontinuity already outlined.

1. *Age-structured homosexuality*. This type refers to same-sex contact between people of different ages. Typically, age-structured homosexuality involves older and younger males between the period of late childhood and adolescence or early adulthood, although exceptions occur among some groups. Many societies prescribe this homosexual activity as a regular and normal part of development. Often, but not always, it is associated with militarized societies and the inculcation of courage, prowess, aggressiveness, and masculine valor (e.g., the ancient Greeks, ancient Japan, the Azande of Africa, New Guinea societies, and others). Age-structured homosexuality is also strongly correlated with ritual mechanisms, such as initiation ceremonies (Herdt, 1984c). Age-structured homosexuality occurs in many places and times in history; although it is not universal, it could be argued that it is the most frequent form of *institutionalized* same-sex erotic contact around the world (Herdt, 1987a), contrary to the suggestion of previous surveys (Ford & Beach, 1951). Age-structured examples of female homosexuality are rare (Blackwood, 1986; Herdt, 1984a), a fact no doubt related to social status and prestige systems (Rosaldo & Lamphere, 1974).

Age-structured homosexuality nearly always involves the notion that the person will later marry and have children. In this way, the nature of same-sex erotic contact is sequential, not linear; in time it evolves into a different mode of sexual experience for the person. Age-graded societies of this type do not regard homosexuality as an end in itself, in other words; it is a transitional or phasic state. There is no concept here of "homosexuality" in the modern Western sense of a person who is habitually and exclusively sexually bonded to a same sex-partner across the life span (Stoller, 1985). Homosexuality is not treated as a noun, as an object; it can only be applied as an adjective to specific acts or relationships. Nonetheless, it would be incorrect to refer to such persons as "bisexual" (Davenport, 1977) in the temporal sense because they are usually prohibited from simultaneous heterosexual contact. Moreover, they are usually enjoined to only homosexual contact (Carrier, 1980). What this suggests for their measurement on the Kinsey scale will be discussed shortly.

Age-structured "homosexuality" (which here implies both identity and role components) is commonly associated with developmental discontinuity across the life span. This means, to use Benedict's idea, that sexual models learned in childhood must be unlearned later to accommodate the person to this normative homosexual activity (cf. Stoller & Herdt, 1985). The reasons for this change are related to the secrecy, ritual, and social structure of the homosexual experience in such societies (see Herdt, ed. 1984). I know of no absolute exceptions to such hypothetical discontinuity; the instances of the ancient Greeks and Japanese, however, and perhaps the ancient Arabians and Azande of Africa, are potential test cases (Adam, 1986; Herdt, 1987a). Virtually all age-asymmetric societies indicate strong developmental change in this way.

2. *Gender-reversed homosexuality.* This form of same-sex activity involves reversal of normative sex-role comportment: males dress and act as females, and females dress and behave as males. Institutionalized examples of gender-reversed homosexuality are well known and include the North American Indian *berdache* (Blackwood, 1986; Devereux, 1937; Mead, 1961; Whitehead, 1981) and the Tahitian *mahu* (Levy, 1973). Although it was assumed that berdache were always male, Blackwood (1986) has shown the frequency of female berdache among American Indian tribes, some even excelling to become noted warriors and hunters who took "brides." The Indians were not confused as to the anatomical sex of these individuals; indeed, Mead (1961, p. 1452) argued that it was not *until* they were sure of the correct sex that they would pronounce the person to be a "true" gender-reversed berdache (see also Callendar & Kochems, 1983).

The question of developmental continuity in gender-reversed homosexuality is necessarily speculative. Many authors have wondered about the mechanism of selection of the child who would reverse and cross-dress (Levy, 1973; Whitehead, 1981). Mead (1961) believed that ultimately the selection was based on a kind of genetic predisposition to the role, a suggestion that remains controversial. What is known is that these societies institutionalized heterosexual marriage and parenthood as normative. Gender reversal of this norm therefore again implies discontinuity in childhood to adult development. What remains further problematic is the possibility, in core gender identity (Stoller, 1968), of the person's feeling that he or she was always of the opposite sex (i.e., primary transsexualism). Whether this is true remains to be seen; yet the possibility of an anlagen of bisexuality tending to social and erotic identification with the anatomically opposite sex cannot be ruled out.

3. *Role-specialized homosexuality.* This form of homosexual practice occurs in societies for which same-sex activity is recognized only for people who occupy a certain status role. The Chukchee shaman, for instance, may have a vision-quest experience that leads to the feeling that he should cross-dress and engage in homosexual activity (Eliade, 1964). In this case,

homosexuality may be forbidden to the society at large but required for the person by virtue of divine revelation by gods or spirits (cf. Hoffman, 1984). Some analysts, most recently Blackwood (1986), have also further divided role-specialized groups into class-stratified and nonclass societies. For class societies, she cites Chinese women who were silk workers in nineteenth-century Kwangtung Province, China; and for classless groups she cites women among the Azande of Africa (Evans-Prichard, 1970), who lived in polygamous households and underwent a ritual that "created a permanent bond" between them (Blackwood, 1986, pp. 10–13). Such examples seem to indicate that our modern notion of "lesbian" is strongly related to the advent of role specialization in a generalized way, which has been persuasively argued for the historical gay male role in a parallel manner (see Adam, 1987). Moreover, Blackwood (1986) suggests that factors of male dominance and economic dependence make it "impossible for women to assume a cross-gender role because such behavior poses a threat to the gender system" (p. 14) of most cultures.

Once again these illustrations suggest that in role-specialized homosexuality we see discontinuity in sexual development. The role is provided for and may only be performed by specialists. For the societies in general, heterosexual development is otherwise normative and leads to marriage and parenthood as adult outcomes. Something special must be added and adapted to this generalized goal to engage in homosexual practices and relationships. Here, as in gender-reversed homosexuality, the possibility of enduring homoerotic bonds arises. This is generally not true of age-structured homosexuality (Adam, 1986). Moreover, the existence of clearly organized female forms of role-specialized homosexuality raises the general issue of the distribution of sex-specific homosexuality across these types, with lesbianism on an institutionalized basis becoming more recognizable in transitional societies with class, industrialization, and modernity as social features.

4. *The modern gay movement.* In my typology, "gay" is a social movement, a political cause, a new form of gender identity, and a life-style (Herdt, 1989). Many social theorists and historians have written of the origins of the category "gay" (Boswell, 1980; Bullough, 1976; Herdt, 1988; Murray, 1984; Weeks, 1985). There is controversy over how early and fully developed the concept is; how it relates to the social role of "the homosexual" or "the lesbian" (McIntosh, 1968); and how to think about the meaning and existence of the gay community in modern society (Adam, 1987; Murray, 1984). Because this form of homosexuality involves the diverse elements mentioned and because the concept is now virtually pervasive in the major urban centers of most Western countries, gay has become more than a specialized role, as in type three homosexuality. It may indeed have evolved out of role specialization of the form previously sketched with regard to, say, the role of "molly houses" and "artists" as

cultural images (Adam, 1987; Plummer, 1975; Trumbach, 1977), but it has now transcended this. In the same sense, it is false, in my view, to argue, as does Boswell (1980), that gay is a monolithic and invariant identity label culturally valid for ancient and medieval societies (Murray, 1984). Certainly the gay movement is specialized somewhat to class and urban social formations, and it must be seen from the perspective of the decontextualization of sex. Only by disengaging sexuality from the traditions of family, reproduction, and parenthood was the evolution of the gay movement a social and historical likelihood (Herdt, 1987b).

Being and acting gay and lesbian is a developmental discontinuity in our society. The norms, values, and roles familiar to children are those of their parents and peers, who are heterosexual or perceived to be. This is in line with the generalized dichotomization of human nature in Anglo-Saxon traditions, mentioned previously, to which Kinsey first implicitly directed his work. Dank's (1971) classic study showed clearly that self-identification as "homosexual" involves change in conventional cognitions and affects. People must "unlearn" certain normative attributes and socialization orientations and learn new ones appropriate to the gay or lesbian role and life-style (reviewed in Herdt, 1989). The well-known stage models of homosexual development all assume that significant sequential changes are antecedents of homosexual "identity consolidation" as an adult outcome (Cass, 1983–1984; Troiden & Goode, 1978). It could be remarked that "bisexuals" pose a challenge to these developmental models (Paul, 1984). Thus, where Kinsey's work tended to dichotomize people into the more or mostly "heterosexual" or "homosexual," with bisexuality a residual category, some work on contemporary gays has tended to the same direction. This seems mistaken for several reasons, not the least of which is that many chapters in this volume suggest that 1s and 6s on the Kinsey scale are rare; most people fall somewhere in between these extremes, when viewed across the life span and on multiple dimensions of gender and erotic measurement. Moreover, it is unlikely, for the reasons already stated, that we shall find many gays for whom being and living gay is a developmental continuity from childhood to adulthood.[15] Even though living a gay life-style is an understandable outcome of modern, technologically advanced, urban life, it does not stem from a linear sexual regime.

We would do well, on the other hand, to study the "bisexuals" more, for they, in their sense of themselves and their sexual practice, may more closely approximate developmental continuity through the life cycle. If this is true—and if it is experienced consciously as such in the face of differential social pressures and stigma that should have forced them to "make a choice" on either side—we are presented with a great opportunity to understand the biopsychological and cultural factors that constrain developmental continuity and discontinuity in human sexuality.

The Measurement of Age-Structured Homosexuality:
A Comparative Note

To round out my discussion of sexual development in cross-cultural perspective, I will conclude with a comment on the measurement of continuity and discontinuity in certain Melanesian societies. By and large the
Kinsey scale has not been used to measure sexual orientation in traditional societies. There are several reasons for this, but the facts that sex is
a sensitive topic and is seldom directly observed are critical (Mead, 1961).
Though I did not use the Kinsey scale, longitudinal study of many Sambia
males, from children to the aged, makes it possible to assess them norma-
tively and constitute sexual histories using the dimensions of a modified
Kinsey scale (Klein et al., 1985).[16]

Elsewhere I have described discontinuities in Sambia male development in normative terms (Herdt, 1981, 1987b). When the Klein scale is
used in normative assessments, the pervasive nature of such changes
becomes evident. These changes are shown in Table 13.1. No dimension
of scale assessment remains constant across development. Emotional and

Table 13-1
Normative Developmental Changes in Sambia Males

Variable	Childhood	Early Adolescence	Late Adolescence	Adulthoot
Sexual attraction	Unknown	6	5	2
Sexual behavior	Not applicable	7	7	1
Sexual fantasies	Unknown	6	6	2
Emotional preference	2	6	6	6
Social preference	2	7	7	7
Self-identification	3	6	6	7
Erotic style	Heteroerotic	Homoerotic	Bierotic	Heteroerotic

1	2	3	4	5	6	7
Other sex only	Other sex mostly	Other sex somewhat more	Both sexes equally	Same sex somewhat more	Same sex mostly	Same sex only

Note: Modified from Klein, Sepekoff, & Wolf, 1985, pp. 39–41.

social preferences for the same sex come closest in approaching developmental continuity, but these changes are so profound, following the separation of boys from mothers and boys' initiations in middle childhood (ages 7–10), that I have referred to the transformation as one of "radical resocialization" (see Herdt, 1981). Sambia male sexual behavior is apparently extremely malleable. Other ethnographers who have worked in "age-structured homosexual" societies of Melanesia have generally interpreted erotic expression in the same way (see Herdt, 1984a). Little is known in general of erotic fantasy, although Stoller and Herdt (1985) describe homosexual *and* heterosexual fantasies in the same Sambia teenage male. Take note that the dimensions of self-identification and gay lifestyle are either inappropriate or simply wrong for the Sambia male; they are too culture-bound. The degree of discontinuity in sexual development for Sambia contrasts with that of other Melanesian cultures in certain respects. The sheer presence of age-structured homosexuality as a cultural form does not mean that sexual development is identical in these societies. For example, because the Sambia sanction childhood sex play, the possibility of more continuity in sexual behavior is limited compared to, say, the Kaluli people (Schieffelin, 1976), to whom this seems more acceptable. Likewise, because the Sambia forbid adult homosexual practice after fatherhood, continuity in overt sex practice is here blocked as compared to the Marind-anim (Van Baal, 1984) mentioned before, who not only permit but require older men to engage in homosexual activity even though they are married and have children. Such variants must make us cautious in generalizing about continuity even in tradition-bound and seemingly similar societies.

What general patterns can be adduced from the Melanesian material? I have reviewed these elsewhere (Herdt, 1984a) and wish here to mention only five findings. First, age-structured homosexuality occurs in approximately 10% to 20% of all Melanesian societies. Second, with the exception of Malekula Island (Deacon, 1934) and possibly the Casuarina Coast (Boelaars, 1981), all of these societies practice male but not female institutionalized homosexuality. The rarity of ritualized lesbianism, as previously noted (cf. Blackwood, 1986), suggests that same-sex practice is more complex and more socially controlled for females. What role does developmental continuity play in this? There is no simple answer, yet females in Melanesia nearly everywhere seem to experience more generalized developmental and sexual continuity than males. This suggests the possibility of alternative sexual regimes in the same society: linear for Sambia females, sequential for Sambia males (Herdt, 1987b). Third, ritual is a uniform mechanism of sexual discontinuity across the life span in these groups. Not surprisingly, male initiation is almost universal, whereas female initiation is uncommon in Melanesia (see Brown, 1963, and Shapiro, 1979, on this correlation more widely). Fourth, change in sexual development occurs in a normative trajectory that leads to marriage and parenthood, in spite of the previous and profound homosexual experience. This does not mean that marriage always excludes subsequent homoerotic activity, as we have seen in the instance of the Marind-anim and a few other Melanesian groups or, for that matter, the ancient Greeks (Hoffman, 1984). The point is that heterosexual marriage and simultaneous homosexual or bisexual relationships are not incompatible to these peoples (Herdt, 1984a). Therefore, they do not make an exclusive sex-object "choice" in the way defined as normative in Western culture. Fifth and last, the profound changes on these normative dimensions of sexuality defy an easy "scoring" of the kind that Kinsey made famous for Americans. This idea deserves a final comment.

How should we "rate" the Sambia in normative terms? As a 6? No. Certainly not a 1. Perhaps we could score them somewhere in between. But to do so would require that we stipulate the exact variable at the exact developmental stage being measured: childhood, early or late adolescence, or adulthood. To do otherwise would be a serious disservice to them; it would inaccurately take account of the changes that come before or after; and it would tell us little about their sexual histories. Nor can we, in any simple way, describe the Sambia as exclusively homosexual, bisexual, or heterosexual in their overt behavior, because to do so would imply a sexual continuity that simply is not there. This is what I believe the Kinsey scale implies: that people's prior behavior and experience are irrelevant to understanding who they are—their whole sense of themselves and their world—today. Such an explanatory approach goes completely against the grain of the conception of human nature built into the Sambia developmental cycle and probably that of other traditions as well. In this regard, Kinsey's model of nature and culture was limited; moreover, the one he used is now dated. We need something better.

Conclusion

The cross-cultural archives of anthropology have often been used to demonstrate variation in sexuality across human groups. Today, this is still as valuable a general perspective in a volume of this kind as it was in 1961, when Margaret Mead (1961) could state: "Sex role assignment may be far more complex in other cultures than in our own" (p. 1453). All of us know that there is diversity in standards across cultures; yet it is easy to ignore this multiplicity in constituting representative models of *human* sexuality. The variables we include must be more extensive than the Gallup poll images drawn upon by Kinsey et al. (1948). The main contribution of this chapter has been to add another primary variable to such models— developmental continuity across cultures. Kinsey fleshed out his study from a skeleton based upon Western preconceptions about human nature and sexuality. Too much emphasis was placed upon assumed continuity in sexual behavior and experience. While this assumption of continuity is plausible in the biological realm, it tends to evade the psychological and symbolic reality of humans in society. Kinsey's work had the enormous benefit of opening up the study of sexuality and its potential for change in our societal discourse. He got us to think of sexual development as more of a wardrobe of possibility and less a straitjacket of inevitability. Yet his conception of humans was too bound to a folk model arising from zoology: too much weight was placed on sex drive, sexual performance, sexual acts, and a single sex-object "choice." When is a sexual act a preference and when not? Only a developmental perspective that focuses upon the lives of whole persons in context can answer this question (cf. Cohler, 1982; Gagnon, 1971). Can we have more than one sexual preference? Is it possible to have multiple "sexual identities?" For Kinsey et al. (1948), heterosexuality was a monolithic single and simple entity, unlike homosexuality, which was heterogeneous and complex. Nowadays we might more properly say that there are multiple heterosexualities and homosexualities, which are neither simple nor "natural" but rather complicated developmental pathways to varied outcomes (Bell et al., 1981; Stoller, 1985). These assumptions about human sexuality were built into the Kinsey scale and its interpretation, and we are only now beginning to unpack them. Adding a developmental framework to our studies will go a long way in clarifying these preconceptions. There are at least three major and distinct types of sexual development regime across cultures: linear, sequential, and emergent. Each takes the assumptions about human nature of the socialization agents as "givens" or "constants" in the formation of a young person's sexual behavior and related attributes of personhood. The development of gender identity is but one of these, though an important one (Stoller & Herdt, 1982). In studying the forms of homosexual organization around the world, it becomes apparent that these are not random; they cluster around types. These cultural forms of homosexual (and bisexual) behavior are in turn correlated with many other psychosocial characteristics and institutions. Yet all of them, in varying degrees of occurrence, intensity, exclusion of other acts, and in meaning, are associated with developmental discontinuity across the life cycle. That such peoples as the Sambia may not experience these changes as discontinuous is a significant and an as yet little-understood aspect of the argument; the degree to which they interpret the process as constant must be tested empirically, however. Whatever the final answer, the observer's point of view here—the behavioral/experiential discontinuity related to homosexual relationships—has far-reaching implications that beg for study at home and abroad.

One is reminded here of Benedict's (1938) insight that in systems of discontinuity people must "unlearn" things in order to "learn" the necessary elements of expected adult outcomes. Learning is, however, probably too rational and cognitive to refer to the process. For discontinuity involves many complexities of mind, sometimes by reaction to previous developmental sequences. The timing is important, perhaps critical, to the subsequent changes, as Freud[17] and others have said, as is the severity of the early socialization regime, which led Freud (1905/1962) to joke, "Harsh rulers have short reigns" (p. 107). Meaning, in short, is what is needed in pushing further the interpretation of such dimensions. When the whole person in cultural and developmental context is restored to the study of sexuality, we will have come a long way in the study of such sexual meaning systems.

Notes

1. Social scientists (including anthropologists) have been critical of Mead's findings, as she herself noted in her 1963 preface to *Sex and Temperament* (1935); the controversy on her Samoan case study has continued and renewed such criticism (Freeman, 1983). But in other fields and in sex research and popular culture (Rappaport, 1986), Mead's influence on gender ideas was powerful. I would point out that most textbooks still utilize Mead's 1935 study as a crucial cross-cultural example, the Katchadourian and Lundt 1980 text—the widest-selling college text-book of its kind—being a case in point.

2. I will not here deal with exceptions, but I have no doubt that some could be found. These do not obviate a *general* theory, for in cross-cultural studies it is difficult to find any generalization other than the most vacuous for which exceptions cannot be found.

3. A. F. C. Wallace quotes Mead:

In a heterogeneous culture, individual life experiences differ so markedly from one another that almost every individual may find the existing cultural forms of expression inadequate to express his peculiar bent, and so be driven into more and more special forms of psychosomatic expression. (p. 72)

4. Probably so, in my own survey of Australian and Melanesian societies (Herdt, 1984c), I found areal experts who either did not know of or ignored the evidence on forms of structural homosexuality.

5. Ford and Beach (1951) found, for example, that "in 49 (64%) of the 76 societies other than our own for which information is available, homosexual activities of one sort or another are considered normal and socially acceptable for certain members of the community" (p. 130).

6. Had Opler and Rado forgotten that Freud himself, in the *Three Essays on the Theory of Sexuality*, (1905/1962), believed that homosexuality was "remarkably widespread among many savage and primitive races" (p. 5)?

7. Stoller (1985) has recently said of psychoanalytic research on homosexuality: "We have transformed diagnosis into accusation, covering our behavior with jargon. But though it hides hatred, it promotes cruelty; jargon is judgment. It serves hidden agendas" (p. 183).

8. Clyde Kluckhohn (1955), one of the great anthropologists of Mead's cohort, remarked in the context of reviewing Kinsey's work from an anthropological perspective:

One may perhaps infer that even anthropologists are insufficiently emancipated from their own culture to investigate sexual behavior with the same detachment and scrupulous attention to detail that they have devoted to basketry, primitive music, and kinship systems. Of course, it must in all fairness be added that, even if the individual anthropologist were emotionally free to be truly scientific, he might be realistic enough to realize that published researches upon sex were unlikely to lead to secure teaching positions or even to scientific recognition (p. 333)

9. Manus children stayed free of adult concerns until age 10 or 12. "Where the adults were a driven, angry, rivalrous, acquisitive lot of people . . . the children were the gayest, most lively and curious" (Mead, 1956, p. 110). Neisser (1962) states:

In these circumstances, coming of age involved drastic reorientation of the child's entire way of life. It would seem, then, that infantile amnesia among the Manus of that period should have been both deeper and longer than among ourselves. (p. 68)

10. Mead used examples such as the Nazis in Europe to show how social engineering could retard and regress sexual enlightenment in societies.

11. According to Freud (1905/1962):

Psychoanalytic research is most decidedly opposed to any attempt at separating off homosexuals from the rest of mankind as a group of special character . . . It has found that all human beings are capable of making a homosexual object-choice and have in fact made one in their unconscious . . . .

Psychoanalysis considers that a choice of an object independently of its sex—freedom to range equally over male and female objects—as it is found in childhood, in primitive states of society and early periods of history, is the original basis from which as a result of restriction in one direction or the other, both the normal and inverted types develop (pp. 11–12).

12. Degree of discontinuity is here meant to index such variables as (1) the age at which change is introduced to the person; (2) the number of domains that change affects; (3) the radical transformations in beliefs, values, and norms involved across these domains; (4) their obligatory nature for the person; (5) the public or secretive and thus unexpected quality of the imposed change; (6) the extent to which antecedents of the change are consciously or preconsciously known to the person and his caretakers; and, (7) among other things, the impact of such revisions of the perceived symbolic environment upon the self-concept of the person and his synergistic responses to socially constructed reality in the society.

13. Mead (1935, 1949, 1961) was among the few anthropologists who consistently studied sex, and she was probably the only one of the previous generation of major standing to discuss developmental aspects of sex and gender. In a major piece on cultural determinants of sexual behavior, she outlined all possible "sexual careers" in human groups (1961, pp. 1451–1452), a piece that deserves fuller scrutiny elsewhere. For more recent reviews, see LeVine (1979), Ross and Rapp (1981), and Shapiro (1979).

14. Shweder and Bourne (1984) review concepts of personhood across cultures and argue that "all cultures are confronted by the same small set of existential questions," which includes "the problem of the relationship of the individual to the group" (pp. 189–190).

The group" (pp. 189–190).
There seem to be relatively few "solutions" to this last problem; the "sociocentric" solution subordinates individual interests to the good of the collectivity while in the "egocentric" solution society becomes the servant of the individual, i.e., society is imagined to have been created to serve the interests of some idealized autonomous, abstract individual existing free of society yet living in society. (Ibid., p. 190)

Here we have a fundamental existential contrast that could be used to differentiate linear regimes (sociocentric) from sequential (egocentric and sociocentric, in a mixture of elements) and emergent regimes (fully egocentric). This contrast, in other words, is not reducible to "traditional" versus "modern" societies, as

Shweder and Bourne (1984) hint, but involves attributes of folk models of human nature only roughly correlated with technological/scientific structures in society.

15. I do not mean here merely the sense that a person has always felt "different" or has always been attracted (at some level of awareness) to the same sex (Troiden, 1989). To fully meet the requirements of continuity in development, people would always have had to feel they were gay, have engaged in same-sex contact, and lived in a gay life-style as children, adolescents, and adults. I am not certain what this would entail for children or preadolescents. Although I can imagine that a few people have experienced this full inside-and-outside expression of developmentally being gay their whole lives, I know of no such examples described in the literature. There are many issues related to this problem, such as presumed biological precursors of homosexuality (Whitam, 1983) and how stigma structures parental and peer influences on adult sexual orientation (Bell et al., 1981; Harry, 1982). We need to rethink the antecedents and consequences of bisexuality and homosexuality in the light of the kind of developmental social regimes outlined in this chapter.

16. See Herdt and Stoller (in press) for a description of the total subject pool and age ranges of these Sambia males.

17. "Divergence in the temporal sequence in which the components come together invariably produces a difference in the outcome" (Freud, 1905/1962, p. 107).

References

Adam, B. (1986). Age, structure, and sexuality: Reflections on the anthropological evidence on homosexual relations. In E. Blackwood (Ed.), *Anthropology and Homosexual Behavior*, pp. 19–34. New York: Haworth Press.

Adam, B. (1987). *The rise of a gay and lesbian movement*. Boston: Twayne Publishers.

Aries, P. (1962). *Centuries of childhood* (R. Baldrick, Trans.). New York: Vintage Books.

Barry, H. A., Child, I. L., & Bacon, M. K. (1959). Relation of child training to subsistence economy. *American Anthropologist, 61,* 51–63.

Bell, A. P., Weinberg, M. S., & Hammersmith, S. (1981). *Sexual preference.* Bloomington: Indiana University Press.

Benedict, R. (1934). *Patterns of culture*. Boston: Houghton Mifflin.

Benedict, R. (1938). Continuities and discontinuities in cultural conditioning. *Psychiatry, 1,* 161–167.

Benedict, R. (1946). *The chysanthemum and the sword*. Boston: Houghton Mifflin.

Blackwood, E. (Ed.). (1986). *Anthropology and homosexual behavior*. New York: Haworth Press.

Blackwood, E. (1986). Breaking the mirror: The construction of lesbianism and the anthropological discourse on homosexuality. In G. Blackwood (Ed), *Anthropology and homosexual behavior*, pp. 1–17.

Boelaars, J. H. M. C. (1981). *Head-hunters about themselves*. The Hague, The Netherlands: Martinus Nijhoff.

Boswell, J. (1980). *Christianity, social tolerance, and homosexuality*. Chicago: University of Chicago Press.

Brim, O. G., & Kagan, J. (Eds.), (1980). *Constancy and change in human development*. Cambridge, MA: Harvard University Press.

Brown, J. K. (1963). A cross-cultural study of female initiation rites. *American Anthropologist, 65,* 837–853.

Bullough, V. L. (1980). *Sexual variance in society and history*. Chicago, IL: University of Chicago Press.

Callendar, C., & Kochems, L. (1983). The North American Indian Berdache. *Current Anththropology, 24,* 443–470.

Carrier, J. (1980). Homosexual behavior in cross-cultural perspective. In J. Marmor (Ed.), *Homosexual behavior: A modern reappraisal* (pp. 100–122). New York: Basic Books.

Cass, V. (1983–1984). Homosexual identity: A concept in need of a definition. *Journal of homosexuality, 9,* 105–126.

Cohen Y. A. (1964). *The transition from childhood to adolescence.* Chicago: Aldine.

Cohler, B. (1982). Personal narrative and life course. In B. Baltes & O. G. Brian, Jr. (Eds.), *Life span development and behavior* (Vol. 4, pp. 205–241). New York: Academic Press.

Dank, B. (1971). Coming out in the gay world. *Psychiatry, 34,* 100–197.

Davenport, W. H. (1977). Sex in cross-cultural perspective. In F. A. Beach (Ed.), *Human sexuality: Four perspectives* (pp. 115–163). Baltimore, MD: The Johns Hopkins University Press.

Deacon, A. B. (1934). *Malekula: A vanishing people in the New Hebrides.* London: George Routledge.

De Cecco, J. P., & Shively, M. G. (1984). From sexual identity to sexual relationships: A contextual shift. *Journal of Homosexuality, 9*(2/3), 1–26.

Devereux, G. (1937). Institutionalized homosexuality of the Mohave Indians. *Human Biology, 9,* 498–527.

Ehrhardt, A. (1985). The psychobiology of gender. In A. Rossi (Ed.), *Gender and the life course* (pp. 81–96). Chicago: Aldine.

Eliade, M. (1964). *Shamanism* (W. R. Trask, Trans.). New York: Pantheon.

Ellis, H. (1936). *Studies in the psychology of sex* (Vol. 2). New York: Random House.

Evans-Prichard, E. E. (1956). *Nuer religion.* Oxford, England: Clarendon Press.

Evans-Prichard, E. E. (1970). Sexual inversion among the Azande. *American Anthropologist, 72,* 1428–1434.

Fine, M. (1988). Sexuality, schooling, and adolescent females: The missing discourse of desire. *Harvard Educational Review, 58,* 29–53.

Ford, C. S., & Beach, F. (1951). *Patterns of sexual behavior.* New York: Harper & Row.

Foucault, M. (1980). *The history of sexuality* (R. Hurley, Trans.). New York: Pantheon.

Freeman, J. D. (1983). *Margaret Mead and Samoa.* Cambridge, MA: Harvard University Press.

Freud, S. (1955a). Leonardo da Vinci, and a memory of his childhood. In J. Strachey, (Ed. and Trans.), *The Standard Edition of the Complete Psychological Works of Sigmund Freud,* (Vol. 11, pp. 59–137). London: Hogarth. (Original 1910).

Freud, S. (1955b). Totem and taboo. In J. Strachey, (Ed. and Trans.), *The Standard Edition of the Complete Psychological Works of Sigmund Freud,* (Vols. 4–5). London: Hogarth. (Original 1913).

Freud, S. (1961). Some physical consequences of the anatomical distinction between the sexes. In J. Strachey (Ed. and Trans.), *The Standard edition of the complete phsychological works of Sigmund Freud,* (Vol. 19, pp. 243–258). London: Hogarth Press. (Original 1925).

Freud, S. (1962). Three essays on the theory of sexuality (J. Strachey, Trans.). New York: Basic Books. (Original 1905).

Freud, S. (1963). On the mechanism of paranoia. In J. Strackey, (Trans.), *General Psychological Theory,* (pp. 29–48). New York: Collier Books.

Gagnon, J. H. (1971). The creation of the sexual in early adolescence. In J. Kagan and R. Coles (Eds.), *Twelve to sixteen: Early adolescence* (pp. 231–257). New York: W. W. Norton.

Geertz, C. (1973). Thick description: Toward an interpretive theory of culture. In *The Interpretation of Cultures*, (pp. 3–30). New York: Basic Books.

Gorer, G. (1955). Nature, science, and Dr. Kinsey. In J. Himelhoch & S. J. Fava (Eds.), *Sexual behavior in American society*, (pp. 50–58). New York: W. W. Norton.

Harry, J. (1982). *Gay children grow up*. New York: Praeger.

Herdt, G. (1981). *Guardians of the flutes: Idioms of masculinity*. New York: McGraw-Hill.

Herdt, G. (Ed.). (1982). *Rituals of manhood: Male initiation in New Guinea*. Berkeley: University of California Press.

Herdt, G. (Ed.). (1984a). *Ritualized homosexuality in Melanesia*. Berkeley: University of California Press.

Herdt, G. (1984b). Preface to G. Herdt (Ed.), *Ritualized homosexuality in Melanesia* (pp. vii-xvii). Berkeley, CA: University of California Press.

Herdt, G. (1984c). Ritualized homosexuality in the male cults of Melanesia, 1862–1982: An introduction. In G. Herdt (Ed.), *Ritualized homosexuality in Melanesia* (pp. 1- 81). Berkeley, CA: University of California Press.

Herdt, G. (1987a). Homosexuality. *The Encyclopedia of Religion* (15 volumes), Vol. 6, pp. 445–452. New York: MacMillan and Co.

Herdt, G. (1987b). *Sambia: Ritual and gender in New Guinea*. New York: Holt, Rinehart and Winston.

Herdt, G. (1988). Cross-cultural forms of homosexuality and the concept "gay." *Psychiatric Annals, 18*, 37–39.

Herdt, G. (1989). Introduction: Gay and lesbian youth, emergent identities, and cultural scenes at home and abroad. In G. Herdt (Ed.), *Adolescence and homosexuality* (pp. 1–42). New York: Haworth Press.

Herdt, G., & Poole, F. J. (1982). Sexual antagonism: The intellectual history of a concept in the anthropology of New Guinea. In F. J. P. Poole, and G. H. Herdt (Eds.), *Sexual antagonism, gender, and social change in Papua New Guinea, Social Analysis* (Special Issue) No. 12: 3–28.

Herdt, G., & Stoller, R. J. (in press). *Intimate communications: Erotics and the study of culture*. New York: Columbia University Press.

Hoffman, R. (1984). Vices, gods, and virtues: Cosmology as a mediating factor in attitudes toward male homosexuality. *Journal of Homosexuality, 9*, 27–44.

Honzik, M. P. (1984). Life-span development. *Annual Review of Psychology, 35*, 309–331.

Katchadourian, H. A. (1979). The terminology of sex and gender. In H. A. Katchadourian (Ed.), *Human sexuality: A comparative and developmental perspective* (pp. 8–34). Berkeley: University of California Press.

Katchadourian, H. A., & Lundt, D. (1980). *Fundamentals of human sexuality*. 3rd ed. New York: Holt, Rinehart and Winston.

Kinsey, A. C., Pomeroy, W. B., & Martin, C. E. (1948). *Sexual behavior in the human male*. Philadelphia: W. B. Saunders.

Klein, F., Sepekoff, B., & Wolf, T. J. (1985). Sexual orientation: A multi-variable process. *Journal of Homosexuality, 11*, 35–50.

Kluckhohn, C. (1955). Sexual behavior in cross-cultural perspective. In Jerome Himelhoch & S. F. Fava (Eds.), *Sexual behavior in American society* (pp. 332–345). New York: W. W. Norton.

Kohlberg, L., Ricks, D., & Savarey, J. (1984). Childhood development as a predictor of adaptation in adulthood. *Genetic Psychol. Mono., 110*, 91–172.

LeVine, R. A. (1979). Anthropology and sex: Developmental aspects. In H. A. Katchadourian (Ed.), *Human sexuality: A comparative and developmental perspective* (pp. 309–319). Berkeley: University of California Press.

Levy, R. (1973). *The Tahitians*. Chicago: University of Chicago Press.

Lindenbaum, S. (1984). Social and sexual transformations. In G. H. Herdt (Ed.), *Ritualized homosexuality in Melanesia* (pp. 337–361). Berkeley: University of California Press.

Luria, F. (1979). Psychosocial determinants of gender identity, role orientation. In H. A. Katchadourian (Ed.), *Human sexuality: A comparative developmental perspective* (pp. 163–193). Berkeley: University of California Press.

Maccoby, E. E. (1979). Gender identity and sex-role adaption. In H. A. Katchadourian (Ed.), *Human sexuality: A comparative and developmental perspective* (pp. 194–203). Berkeley: University of California Press.

Malinowski, B. (1927). *Sex and repression in savage society*. Cleveland, OH: Meridian Books.

McIntosh, M. (1968). The homosexual role. *Social Problems, 16*, 182–192.

Mead, M. (1930). *Growing up in New Guinea*. New York: Dell.

Mead, M. (1935). *Sex and temperament in three primitive societies*. New York: Dell.

Mead, M. (1949). *Male and female: A study of the sexes in a changing world*. New York: William Morrow.

Mead, M. (1956). *New lives for old. Cultural transformation: Manus 1928–1953*. New York: William Morrow.

Mead, M. (1961). Cultural determinants of sexual behavior. In W. C. Young (Ed.), *Sex and internal secretions* (pp. 1433- 1479). Baltimore, MD: Williams & Wilkins.

Minturn, L., Grosse, M., & Haider, S. (1969). Cultural patterning of social beliefs and behavior. *Ethnology, 8*, 301–317.

Money, J. (1987). Sin, sickness, or status. *American Psychologist, 42*, 384–399.

Money, J., & Ehrhardt, A. (1972). *Man and woman, boy and girl*. Baltimore, MD: Johns Hopkins University Press.

Money, J., Hampson, J. G., & Hampson, J. L. (1956). Sexual incongruities and psychopathology: The evidence of human hermaphrodism. *Bulletin of John Hopkins Hospital, 98*, 43–57.

Murray, S. (1984). *Social theory, homosexual realities*. New York: Gai Sabre Monographs.

Nanda, S. (1986). The Hijras of India: Cultural and individual dimensions of an institutionalized third gender role. In E. Blackwood (Ed.), *Anthropology and homosexual behavior* (pp. 35–54). New York: Haworth Press.

Neisser, U. (1962). Cognitive and cultural discontinuity. In *Anthropology and human behavior*. Washington, DC: Anthropological Society of Washington, DC.

Obeyesekere, G. (1981). *Medusa's hair*. Chicago: University of Chicago Press.

Opler, M. K. (1965). Anthropological and cross-cultural aspects of homosexuality. In J. Marmor (Ed.), *Sexual inversion* (pp. 108–123). New York: Basic Books.

Ortner, S., & Whitehead, H. (Eds.). (1981). *Sexual meanings*. New York: Cambridge University Press.

Paul, J. (1984). The bisexual identity: An idea without social recognition. *Journal of Homosexuality, 9(2/3)*, 45–63.

Plummer, K. (1975). *Sexual stigma*. Boston: Routledge and Kegan Paul.

Plummer, K. (1989). Coming out in England. In G. Herdt (Ed.), *Adolescence and homosexuality*. New York: Haworth Press.

Rado, S. (1956). A critical examination of the concept of bisexuality. In J. Marmor (Ed.), *Sexual inversion* (pp. 175- 189). New York: Basic Books.

Rappaport, R. (1986, summer). Desecrating the holy woman. *American scholar*, pp. 313–347.

Read, K. E. (1980). *Other voices*. Novato, CA: Chandler & Sharp.

Rosaldo, M. Z., & Lamphere, L. (1974). Introduction in M. Z. Rosaldo and L. Lamphere (Eds.), *Woman, culture, and society* (pp. 1–15). Stanford, CA: Stanford University Press.

Ross, E., & Rapp, R. (1981). Sex and society: A research note from social history and anthropology. *Comparative Studies in Sociology and History, 23,* 51–72.

Ross, M. (1980). Retrospective distortion in homosexual research. *Archives of Sexual Behavior, 9,* 523–531.

Schieffelin, E. (1976). The sorrow of the lonely and the burning of the dancers. New York: St. Martin's.

Shapiro, J. (1979). Cross-cultural perspectives on sexual differentiation. In H. A. Katchadourian (Ed.), *Human sexuality: A comparative and developmental perspective* (pp. 269–308). Berkeley, CA: University of California Press.

Shostack, M. (1980). *Nisa: The life and words of a !Kung woman.* New York: Vintage Books.

Shweder, R. A., & Bourne, E. J. (1984). Does the concept of the person vary cross-culturally? In R. A. Schweder & R. A. Levine (Eds.), *Culture Theory,* pp. 158–199. New York: Cambridge University Press.

Spiro, M. (1986). Cultural relativism and the future of anthropology. *Cultural Anthropology, 1,* 259–286.

Stephens, W. N. (1962). *The Oedipus complex: Cross-cultural evidence.* New York: The Free Press.

Stoller, R. J. (1968). *Sex and gender: Vol. 1. On the development of masculinity and femininity.* New York: Science House.

Stoller, R. J. (1979). *Sexual excitement.* New York: Pantheon.

Stoller, R. J. (1985). *Observing the erotic imagination.* New Haven, CT: Yale University Press.

Stoller, R. J., & Herdt, G. (1982). The development of gender identity: A cross-cultural contribution. *Journal of the American Psychoanalytic Association, 30,* 29–59.

Stoller, R. J., & Herdt, G. (1985). Theories of origins of male homosexuality: A cross-cultural look. *Archives of General Psychiatry, 42*(4), 399–404.

Strathern, M. (1988). *The gender of the gift.* Berkeley, CA: University of California Press.

Tavris, C., & Offir, C. (1977). *The longest war: Sex differences in perspective.* New York: Harcourt Brace Jovanovich.

Troiden, R. R. (1989). The formation of homosexual Identities and roles. In G. Herdt (Ed.), *Adolescence and homosexuality* (pp. 43–74). New York: Haworth Press.

Troiden, R. R., & Goode, E. (1980). Variable related to the acquisition of a gay identity. *Journal of Homosexuality, 5,* 383–392.

Trumbach, R. (1977). London's sodomites: Homosexual behavior and Western culture in the 18th century. *Journal of Social History, 11*(1), 1–33.

Van Baal, J. (1984). The dialectics of sex in Marind-Anim culture. In G. Herdt (Ed.), *Ritualized homosexuality in Melanesia* (pp. 128–166). Berkeley: University of California Press.

Wallace, A. (1969). *Culture and personality* (2nd ed.). New York: Random House.

Weeks, J. (1985). *Sexuality and its discontents.* London: Routledge & Kegan Paul.

Westermarck, E. (1917). *The origin and development of the moral ideas,* (Vol. 2, 2nd ed.). London: Macmillan and Co.

Whitam, F. L. (1983). Culturally invariable properties of male homosexuality. *Archives of Sex Behavior, 12,* 207–222.

Whitehead, H. (1981). The bow and the burden strap: A new look at institutionalized homosexuality in native North America. In S. B. Ortner & H. White-head (Eds.), *Sexual meanings* (pp. 80–115). Cambridge, England: Cambridge University Press.

Williams, F. E. (1936). *Papuans of the trans-fly*. Oxford, England: Clarendon Press.

Wolf, E. (1969). *Peasant wars of the twentieth century*.New York: Harper Torchbooks.

V

IDENTITY DEVELOPMENT PERSPECTIVE

14

The Implications of Homosexual Identity Formation for The Kinsey Model and Scale of Sexual Preference

Vivienne C. Cass

The study of homosexual identity formation, the process whereby someone comes to adopt a lesbian/gay/homosexual identity, is a relatively new field. Since the early 1970s, when homosexual identity first began to be discussed in the literature, numerous articles have been written outlining theories and research results.

This interest is indicative of a significant change in community thinking about homosexuals, a change as evident in gay/lesbian people themselves as in heterosexuals. In simple terms, there has been a shift away from viewing the gay person as a psychiatric aberration and toward seeing him or her as a member of a minority group. In scientific circles this shift is reflected in the increasing emphasis being placed on asking questions such as "How did she/he come to adopt a gay/lesbian identity?" and "What is it like to live as a gay person?" rather than "What factors caused this person to become homosexual?"

This change can best be understood as an outcome of the development and increasing refinement of the social category or social type of the "homosexual" in Western societies.

Social categories or types are a way in which society summarizes and makes sense of the immense array of information available about its members. On the basis of some social attribute such as race, education level, age, individuals are given a label (e.g., black, professional, youth) that is commonly understood by all. The people fitting such a label may then apply this to themselves as well as have others apply it to them. In time, those labeled may come actually to develop an inner sense of themselves as *being* members of the groups to which they have been assigned. This "inner sense" or *identity* (see Cass, 1985, for a full definition of *typological identity*) will hold psychological importance in a person's overall sense of "who I am."

"Homosexual/gay/lesbian," "bisexual," and "heterosexual" have been designated as labels of sexual preference or sexual orientation. The historical process by which this took place began in the late eighteenth and early nineteenth centuries (Boswell, 1980; Foucault, 1978; Greenberg & Bystryn, 1982; Katz, 1983; Weeks, 1977, 1981) and continues in various forms into our present time. Within the scientific literature the changes are apparent in the lessening interest in specific sexual *behaviors* and greater concern for describing characteristics of a *person* having a particular sexual preference (Cass, 1985).

It was not until the late 1960s and early 1970s that the notion of homosexual identity began to be documented in the homosexual literature. Until that time, the label "homosexual" had been used primarily by members of those professions (e.g., medical, legal) concerned with the social control and medical documentation of individuals practicing "unacceptable" sexual behaviors. By the mid-1970s, homosexuals themselves had taken the label and transformed it into an expression of identification with the gay minority group.

Thus the changes to Western conceptions of sexual preference from the beginning of the last century until the present time have been quite remarkable. In a short space of time (historically speaking) acts of "sodomy" have become reclassified as "perversion," "perversity," and "homosexual," and the influence of the church replaced by that of the medical and legal professions as the groups within which society vests the powers of social control.

In this century we have seen the proposals of Freud and his followers draw interest away from the *activities* and onto the *personality* of the homosexual, bisexual, and heterosexual. We have seen the influence of the medical and psychiatric professions decline, while the 1960s ideologies of individual rights, tolerance of differences, and the importance of self-fulfillment gain acceptance. Groups such as homosexuals could now claim to be minorities having the same right to self-expression as other minorities. There was concern to present the homosexual's *own* view of the world and self. The label "homosexual/lesbian" and later "gay/dyke" came to be used by homosexuals themselves as a means of identifying membership in a group rather than as an indication of pathology. In essence, the homosexual became viewed as a *person* rather than as a clinical condition.

The homosexual's own self-perceptions were seen to be an important component of the expression of sexual preference and their documentation a significant way of recording the inner lives of this particular minority group. The homosexual *identity* became the means for referring to all those personal aspects of identification with the societal group known as "homosexuals." Everything that related to *belonging* to the gay group was seen to be relevant to holding a gay identity.

As these changes have become incorporated into the scientific literature of recent years, we are now beginning to see a further development— greater focus on the bisexual person and the bisexual identity. Interest in the heterosexual person and heterosexual identity, however, remains peripheral since by virtue of their majority and "normal" status heterosexuals have been largely ignored.

Having briefly sketched one of the significant themes of change in attitudes toward sexual preference during the last century and a half, I am now in a position to examine Kinsey's part in those changes.

Quite clearly, Kinsey and his colleagues (Kinsey, Pomeroy, & Martin, 1948; Kinsey, Pomeroy, Martin, & Gebhard, 1953) began their work on the documentation of sexual behaviors in the United States at a time when these attitudinal changes were well under way. Nonheterosexual sexuality was still viewed as an abnormal condition by clinicians and as immoral by church groups, the heavy weight of the law menaced anyone not conforming to the heterosexual example, and present-day conceptions of the homosexual were not in sight. Against this setting, Kinsey presented ideas radical for their rejection of the moralistic foundation upon which sexual behavior had been based so long.

There can be no question of the impact of the Kinsey volumes upon the scientific and general communities. The mammoth task undertaken by Kinsey and his associates resulted in findings and theoretical proposals that, decades later, still retain the attention of sexuality researchers.

This is as evident in the area of sexual preference as in other areas. The Kinsey publications provided a new perspective on homosexuality and bisexuality, one that differed significantly from the prevailing medical and moralistic view. Following soon after Kinsey were other researchers such as Hooker (1957) and Ford and Beach (1951), who through their research were also instrumental in undermining the established psychiatric view of homosexuality, as well as in promoting the notion of the sociological and psychological "normality" of homosexuals.

So significant and impactful were the Kinsey publications on sexual preference that it was not until the middle of the 1970s that the theoretical assumptions upon which they were based began to be examined seriously or questioned. Even then, however, there was little evidence that the attention given to the Kinsey scale or model of sexual preference was diminished to any significant degree.

Nevertheless, the changes mentioned earlier, whereby the focus has moved to seeing the homosexual as a *person*, someone who belongs to a stigmatized minority group, have taken place, as documented in both the popular and the scientific literature. The impact such developments have had on our view of the homosexual cannot fail to have implications for Kinsey's ideas.

These implications need to be addressed if we are to assess Kinsey's work on sexual preference in the light of its relevance for today. Specifically, this chapter examines the area of gay/lesbian identity and its development and the way that it points to modifications to the model of sexual preference proposed by Kinsey. It will be argued that the theoretical assumptions and perspectives underlying the identity literature raise many questions about the nature and characterization of sexual preference as portrayed during the first half of this century.

Interestingly, few researchers and theorists of homosexual identity have explicitly examined this issue. Indeed, when developing my own theory of gay identity formation, I believed that this process could be conceptualized as separate from that of sexual preference development, which I defined in the traditional way to mean the development of a relatively permanent sexual and emotional attraction for someone of the same and/ or opposite sex. I saw the identity formation process as one that occurred *after* sexual preference had evolved.

It was only over time that I came to believe that the two processes are intricately interwoven in the development of the modern-day homosexual, that the formation of identity can be influential in the development of sexual and emotional preference, and vice versa. Some theorists have hinted at the relationship between the two processes (e.g., Coleman, 1981–1982; Minton & McDonald, 1983–1984) but appear to have little awareness of the implications that these ideas have for their conceptualizations of either gay identity or sexual preference.

Curiously, these implications have been implicitly present from the moment I first became interested in the issue of homosexual identity. As a clinician, I was originally drawn to the area because of difficulties in helping those who were extremely distressed about becoming homosexual. At the same time I was fascinated by those who openly acted in a homosexual way without labeling themselves or their behavior as homosexual/lesbian. I concluded that understanding sexual behavior or attraction alone gave a very limited picture of what was happening in these people's lives. In finding existing ideas on sexual preference to be so unhelpful, I then chose to develop a model that incorporates the element of homosexual functioning that I consider to be crucial—the individuals' own perceptions of themselves and their social world. As other theorists began to publish similar ideas, I became convinced of the need to attend to the person's self-perceptions in order to understand the experience of the modern homosexual. It has taken nearly a decade for me to realize that I was also questioning existing beliefs about the nature of sexual preference (epitomized by Kinsey in his sections on *homosexual outlet* in Kinsey et al., 1948, and Kinsey et al., 1953).

So although the area of homosexual identity and identity formation remains a legitimate one for study in its own right, it also raises important questions about the nature, development, and expression of sexual preference, questions that need to be addressed if we are fully to understand the usefulness of Kinsey's model of sexual preference for the present time.

Kinsey's Model of Sexual Preference

Although Kinsey did not explicitly outline a theoretical framework for sexual preference, his chapters on homosexual outlet in both Kinsey et al., 1948, and Kinsey et al., 1953 provide enough information for us to draw conclusions about his beliefs. Frequently, this information is in the form of what he did *not* agree with, leaving the reader to infer what ideas Kinsey did hold.

Kinsey et al. distinguished between the *expression* of sexual preference and the *development* of sexual preference.

Expression of Sexual Preference

Kinsey proposed that sexual preference could be assessed by monitoring the two ways in which it was expressed: (1) "psychic reactions," reactions to being erotically stimulated by a particular type of person (such as someone of the same or opposite sex), and (2) sociosexual contacts.

Kinsey stated clearly that his scale was based on both these factors but gave little information as to how "psychic reactions" were measured. Sociosexual contacts, on the other hand, were precisely defined as engagement in sexual activity to the point of orgasm with someone of the same or opposite sex.

Frequency or intensity of behavior resulting from psychic reactions and sociosexual contacts was not the important factor. Rather, it was the *balance* between the homosexual and the heterosexual that decided preference.

Kinsey's scale clearly indicates that a person may express his or her sexual preference via one of three preference patterns: exclusive homosexuality, exclusive heterosexuality, or bisexuality (responsivity to both the same and opposite sexes *in some degree*, either concurrently or serially). It is a mutual exclusivity model. That is, someone can show *high preference* for choosing a partner of the same *or* opposite sex but not both at the same time. The term *bisexuality* is used when this choice is neither exclusive nor nearly exclusive, to either the same sex or the opposite sex.

Kinsey deplored the use of the terms *homosexual* and *heterosexual* as nouns representative of discrete and independent groups. His data did not fit this conception. Rather than focus on types of people, Kinsey maintained that it was more correct to examine degrees of homosexual and heterosexual behaviors.

While Kinsey proposed that both psychic reactions and sexual contacts must be taken into account in the measurement of the expression of sexual preference, he suggested that the former is more truly indicative of preference than the latter since social opportunity can influence the level of activity engaged in. Some people, he noted, may engage in sexual contacts simply because circumstances make them available and not from any strong preference. Similarly, those with a strong homosexual preference may choose not to express themselves overtly because of fears about behaving in such a manner. Thus, psychic responses and sociosexual activity represent independent but related dimensions of behavior. The more specific the psychic reactions, the more they direct the person toward one of the sexes for sexual contact.

Further, an individual can be erotically aroused by others of the same sex without engaging in homosexual sexual activity and, likewise, can engage in sexual activity with others of the same sex without experiencing any sexual arousal.

Significantly, Kinsey was aware that the meaning a person gives this behavior may not coincide with the definition accorded it by virtue of the gender of the sexual partner. "The homosexuality of certain relationships between individuals of the same sex may be denied by some persons, because the situation does not fulfill other criteria that they think should be attached to the definition" (Kinsey et al., 1948, p.616). Kinsey did not, however, consider it necessary to incorporate the individual's interpretation of his or her own behavior, or the difference between this meaning and his or her behavior into his ideas on the expression of sexual preference. It is sexual response, not the individual's perceptions of that response, that is important.

Kinsey had other things to say about sexual preference. Frequently, his views were illustrated by reference to what it is *not*.

1. He argued for the differentiation of sexual preference from *inversion*, a state in which individuals express characteristics of the opposite sex. While inversion and homosexuality *may* coincide, they are essentially two different types of behavior.
2. He also pointed out that sexual preference is not designated by a personality or body type or by certain mental attributes.
3. Sexual preference is not made up of discrete categories and therefore should not be used to classify people into separate groups of homosexuals, heterosexuals, and bisexuals. Rather, there are people who show a preference *in some degree* for partners of the same and/or opposite sex.
4. The balance between homosexual and heterosexual behavior, he emphasized, is not fixed and may vary during a person's lifetime.

Although not referred to specifically, it may be inferred that the dimensions on which sexual preference is expressed were believed to be similar for women and men.

The Development of Sexual Preference

Kinsey strongly advocated the idea that *all* forms of preference in sexual response are learned. Although people are considered to be born with the capacity to respond sexually, the direction in which this capacity comes to be expressed is learned. He rejected, therefore, the notion that people are innately heterosexual, homosexual, or bisexual.

He proposed that sexual response is learned through the processes of conditioning and suggested three ways in which this can occur:

1. through *vicarious learning*, whereby a person becomes sexually stimulated by sharing another's sexual experience and, via conditioning, becomes in turn stimulated by elements of those shared experiences without the presence of the other person; thus preference can be acquired without a person's engaging in any actual sexual activity;
2. through *associated learning*, in which sexual activities and response become linked, through learning processes, with other factors (such as body type, sounds, etc.); and
3. through *sympathetic responses*, whereby people react to sexual responses or to material depicting sexual activity and response with a sexual response of their own and through conditioning processes acquire certain preferences in accordance with the stimulating experiences or material.

The development of sexual response, and therefore of sexual preference, is, according to Kinsey, the result of both childhood *and* adult experiences, not just childhood experiences as some early theorists had stated.

The first sexual experience, as well as the most intense sexual experience with the same sex exerts a significant conditioning effect on the individual's sexual preference. The opinions of others and social codes can, indirectly, also have a significant effect on conditioning by influencing the decision to reject or accept sexual contacts.

Women, Kinsey noted, are less susceptible to conditioning in this way, but he did not offer alternative routes of development.

As noted earlier, the work of Kinsey and his colleagues had an enormous impact on the way others thought about sexual preference. His model was used as an example for the next two decades. However, his scale of heterosexuality/homosexuality was soon adapted to define someone as *a* homosexual/heterosexual/bisexual. It would seem that the idea of sexual preference *types* was too heavily built into psychiatric and sociological theory to overturn prevailing thought. In addition, encouragement for this viewpoint came from the modern development that differentiated the homosexual *group* from the heterosexual group and characterized members of such groups as being distinguishable on the basis of separate homosexual and heterosexual *identities.*

It was not until the late 1970s that researchers began to question the theoretical assumptions upon which Kinsey's model and scale were based (e.g., De Cecco, 1977; Shively & De Cecco, 1977; Storms, 1979, 1980), in particular examining the proposal that homosexuality and heterosexuality represent opposite ends of a unipolar continuum. Later, other researchers (e.g., Klein, Sepekoff, & Wolf, 1985; Suppe, 1984) added voice to De Cecco's claim that components other than sexual behavior are also significant to the expression of sexual preference. The factors of emotional response, relationships, life-style, self-identification (with regard to sexual preference), and self-concept were all mentioned as relevant. For those theorists interested in the *components* of sexual preference, the focus has been on identifying which variables may be important to understanding the expression of that preference. Little attempt has been made to hypothesize the way these variables interrelate with each other.

It is important to note the emphasis on the psychological components of self-concept and self-identification, areas of human functioning that Kinsey did not include in his documentation of sexual preference expression.

Most researchers have skirted the difficult task of examining Kinsey's proposals on the development of sexual preference. Storms (1979, 1980), however, expanded Kinsey's theories to formulate a theory of erotic development. Significantly, no attempt has been made to examine comprehensively the influence of variables such as self-identification and self-concept on the development of preference. With increasing weight being given to the concept of gay/lesbian identity, it would now seem time to examine the implications of homosexual identity formation for our understanding of both the expression and development of sexual preference.

Defining Homosexual Identity and Homosexual Identity Formation

Homosexual Identity

Gay or lesbian identity is the sense that a person has of *being* a homosexual/ gay man/lesbian. It is a very personal sensation, experienced as a recognition of "who I am." The experience of identity is frequently described by the individual as "I know who I am," "I feel like a homosexual/gay man/ lesbian," "I am a homosexual," "This is me." Two aspects of identity are of interest to the psychologist: an objective aspect and a subjective aspect.

The objective side to identity is the image or cognitive picture that someone has of himself or herself as "a homosexual." As human beings, we have the capacity to look objectively at ourselves and identify our own characteristics, using labels prescribed by society. Based on societal and personal definitions of what constitutes a homosexual, individuals can come to label their own behavior as "homosexual." This label, in reality, is simply a term used to cover a multitude of different characteristics that when grouped together are defined by the individual as related to homosexuality. Individuals will vary in which characteristics make up their particular definition of "homosexual." They will also differ on other factors, such as the importance given to each characteristic, the clarity in which each is seen, and the degree to which each is positively evaluated.

The subjective side of identity is less easily described. It is the feeling or sensation a person has of *being* a homosexual. It is a *knowing* and experiencing of the self at any moment as opposed to the objective aspect of identity, which refers to *thinking about* the self. People may differ in the strength with which they feel themselves to be a homosexual/gay man/ lesbian.

Homosexual Identity Formation

Both the objective and subjective aspects of identity are developed through a complex process called homosexual identity formation (Cass, 1979, 1983/1984, 1985). I have described this process as comprising six stages of development. Within each stage different paths may be taken toward the formation of a gay/lesbian identity.

The process of homosexual identity formation begins when people are able to acknowledge that there is something about their behavior that they define as "homosexual." This awareness can act as a trigger for a complex process of change that sees a person develop an increasingly unambiguous and accepted image of self as "a homosexual." This image is gradually disclosed to others, and acceptance (validation) by them encourages the individual to develop a deepening sense of self as a homosexual. The process of identity formation ends with the development of a gay/lesbian identity that is accepted as a significant and positive part of the self.

Individual differences are apparent in the rate of progression through the stages, the final stage of development reached, the paths of development taken within each stage, and strategies adopted to cope with the tasks of each stage. At each stage the individual can foreclose development, in which case he or she will remain at the point of identity formation achieved prior to foreclosure. Thus, it is possible for someone to move through the process until any particular stage and then carry out strategies aimed at preventing further development.

During the identity formation process, changes are evident within the individual in the areas of cognition (thoughts, fantasies, hopes), emotions, and actions. Development in one of these can bring about changes in the other two areas. Similarly, changes within the individual can promote new ways of interacting outwardly with the social environment, which in turn may influence internal factors. For example, individuals who come to perceive that they "probably are homosexual" (Stage 3) are likely to become aware of social, sexual, and emotional needs that remain unsatisfied. This awareness may lead to first moves to make contact with gay people. If acceptable and fulfilling, these actions may then lead to a greater sense of positiveness about being "a homosexual."

Two motivational systems are considered to provide the impetus for movement from one stage to the next: the self-consistency motive and the self-esteem motive. The former, applicable to cognitive changes in identity formation, works on the principle that people strive to maintain a consistent image of self that is related to sexual preference. The latter, applicable to the emotional changes of identity formation, states that people have a need to develop positive feelings about the self relevant to sexual preference while avoiding negative ones.

Stage 1: Identity Confusion

Stage 1 begins when the individual recognizes "there is something about my behavior [this can include actions, feelings, and/or thoughts] that could be called homosexual/gay/lesbian," and ends when he or she proclaims, "I may be a homosexual."

With the realization that the behavior can be defined as "homosexual," emotional tension is experienced in the form of confusion, bewilderment, anxiety, and so forth. Previous sexual preference identities (e.g., heterosexual) are questioned. This results from being forced to consider the question "If my behavior may be called homosexual, does that mean that *I* am a homosexual?" Three paths of resolution of this crisis are described, the first where the homosexual meaning is rejected, the second where it is accepted as correct but seen as undesirable, and the third where it is accepted as correct and also evaluated as desirable.

Stage 2: Identity Comparison

Stage 2 begins with the tentative acceptance of a potential homosexual identity ("I may be a homosexual") and finishes with the acknowledgment that such an identity is likely to be applicable to self ("I probably am a homosexual"). This stage marks the first step toward a commitment to a homosexual self-image. Now the wider implications of that tentative commitment can be contemplated (e.g., loss of family support, feeling different from others, loss of future plans, etc.) and this provokes feelings of social alienation.

In order to deal with these feelings four paths of development are proposed. Selection of path will depend on whether the individual perceives the image of himself or herself as a homosexual to be a desirable one or not and to what extent the adoption of such an identity is considered to entail greater costs or rewards. Strategies such as inhibiting sexual behavior and rejecting stereotypes of homosexuals may be used. Final outcomes at this stage will include either identity foreclosure, a self-image of self as "probably homosexual/not heterosexual" viewed positively or negatively, or a self-image of "bisexual," "temporarily homosexual," or "a special case."

STAGE 3: IDENTITY TOLERANCE

In Stage 3 the changes range from "I probably am a homosexual," the end point of Stage 2, through to the acknowledgment of a homosexual identity ("I am a homosexual"), although as the name suggests, this identity is not fully accepted. The individual begins to experience the minority status of a gay person while giving validity to the majority (heterosexual) perspective. This leads to a toleration of the homosexual identity rather than an acceptance of it.

With the greater commitment to a homosexual identity and the greater clarity with which it is perceived, the individual begins to focus on those social, emotional, and sexual needs that remain. In order to fulfill these needs, attempts are made to seek out other gay people. Where such contacts are seen as rewarding, this generates further identification with homosexuals, raises self-esteem, and encourages further contact with gay people. A negative experience may encourage the devaluation of homosexuals, the minimization or cessation of contacts with homosexuals, and lowered self-esteem. Socialization with homosexuals, at whatever level, allows for the rehearsal of the homosexual role, which then encourages others to identify the individual as a homosexual.

As consistency between one's own views and others' views of self increases, the individual experiences a deepening commitment to a homosexual identity.

STAGE 4: IDENTITY ACCEPTANCE

Stage 4 is characterized by a clearer and more positive image of self as a homosexual and greater security in carrying out the homosexual role. There is increasing contact with the gay subculture and the development of a network of homosexual friends. The world is clearly divided into homosexuals (likely to be supportive) and nonhomosexuals (likely to be hostile), although selective disclosure about one's identity to the latter group may blur the division a little. Attempts are made to fit in with the surrounding environment and to avoid confrontation with regard to homosexuality, and to this end passing as heterosexual is commonly played out.

Where this is acceptable, the developmental path will lead to foreclosure at a stage that is relatively peaceful and fulfilling. For those unable to accept the secrecy and negative status of homosexuals tolerated at this stage, the developmental path will be different. The inconsistency between one's own positive feelings about being gay and the negative feelings attributed to nonhomosexuals leads the individual out of Stage 4 and into the next stage of development.

STAGE 5: IDENTITY PRIDE

Those entering Stage 5 do so with a strong sense of the incongruency between their own positive attitudes toward their homosexuality and society's disapproval of such an identity.

In response to the alienation arising from this situation, feelings of pride and anger are generated. Pride is felt toward oneself and other homosexuals. Gay people are valued positively and heterosexuals negatively. Anger is felt about the negative status assigned to homosexuals. This leads to confrontation and disclosure. The world is clearly divided into gays and nongays, with a preference for mixing with the former. When confrontation and disclosure evoke negative responses, this reinforces beliefs about the nongay world and foreclosure takes place. When positive reactions occur this creates an inconsistency, the resolution of which leads the individual into Stage 6.

STAGE 6: IDENTITY SYNTHESIS

In Stage 6, the individual develops a full sense of self as a homosexual and integrates this with all other aspects of the self—the homosexual identity is seen as an important part of self but is not the only identity. The rigid "them and us" attitude adopted in Stage 5 is dropped, and the feelings of anger and pride are less overwhelming. Attacks on homosexuals are perceived not as personal vendettas but rather as reactions to a minority group.

Disclosure becomes almost automatic in Stage 6 as greater security is felt in the identity, and interaction in the heterosexual world is experienced as generally rewarding. Nonhomosexuals come to be considered a significant reference group. There is less need to adhere to the gay community as a defense maneuver. As the public and private aspects of self become synthesized into one, the person gains a sense of well-being and peace. Greater self-actualization is possible now than previously.

As is apparent from the foregoing description, homosexual identity is seen to develop by degrees, arising out of the interplay between individual (interpersonal *and* intrapersonal) and social factors within the immediate and broader social contexts. In order to measure the degree of identity formation attained, it is necessary to examine a range of variables that make up each of these factors. No one variable will describe either the overt expression of identity or the developmental process that is being undergone.

It is worth noting that whether the concept of homosexual identity has been constructed by social scientists, by the times in which we live, or both, as was discussed earlier, is irrelevant at this point. The fact remains that individuals develop a sense of themselves as "a homosexual" and that this sense and process can be documented as a phenomenon of our present time.

Implications of the Study of Homosexual Identity Formation for Kinsey's Views of Sexual Preference

We are now in a position to examine the relevance of gay identity to the study of sexual preference. Can we use some of the principles of homosexual identity formation to extend our understanding of sexual preference as we know it today? Does identity formation suggest *new* directions, questions, or issues for our consideration?

Simply contemplating the possibility of a connection between identity formation and sexual preference prompts us to ask new questions. What type of relationship might exist between these two concepts? Can, for example, different stages of homosexual identity formation (i.e., the degree of identity development) influence the direction or strength of sexual preference and vice versa? If these two are mutually influential, then we are faced with additional questions.

What might be lost in our understanding of sexual preference if we ignore individuals' own perceptions of themselves as well as the complex interactions that take place between people and their environments?

What effects might there be on the expression and/or the development of sexual preference if the self-images comprising someone's gay identity emphasize emotional, social, role, political factors, or physical characteristics? For example, if someone believes that a gay person is someone who is involved in fighting for gay rights, where such a picture is unacceptable to him or her, will this influence the taking on, strength, or direction of a homosexual preference?

What effects might there be on the expression and/or development of sexual preference if a person holds a negatively valued homosexual identity as opposed to a positively valued identity? Where a person encounters positive sexual/emotional contacts with someone of the same sex at a time when his or her homosexual identity is evaluated negatively, will this encourage, for example, a stronger attraction to the same sex or a lesser attraction, or will it have no impact at all? Can it influence the direction of sexual preference?

To what extent can self-identity as homosexual be influential in the development of sexual preference when such an identity differs from the presented identity (image of self presented to the world) or perceived identity (image of self that other people hold)? Is it easier to develop preference when all of these identities are in accord with each other?

What are the ways in which individuals might *actively* attempt to alter sexual preference through the manipulation of their self-identity?

Can the attribution of permanency by individuals to their self-identity influence the development/expression of sexual preference?

Can having to cope with different societal reactions in the process of developing a gay identity influence the strength or direction of sexual preference?

The remainder of this chapter will be devoted to the presentation of some of the more pertinent issues that arise from the identity literature and can be seen as relevant to our understanding of modern-day sexual preference. In outlining these issues two fundamental questions present themselves for consideration. (1) Does the area of gay identity and its development illustrate a fundamental change in the notion of sexual preference? (2) If so, is Kinsey's rating scale based on factors broad enough to cover all those aspects of human behavior relevant to the measurement of modern-day Western sexual preference?

Interrelationship of Identity Development and Sexual Preference

In order for homosexual identity formation to begin, it is essential that the individual experience some type of behavior that indicates, to him or her, attraction to someone of the same sex. This behavior may be an infrequent occurrence, a regular and fixed aspect of the individual's sexual preference, or something in between these two. Essentially, some form of behavior occurs *first* (whether as activity, cognitions, or feelings), and identity formation may follow.

In the gay identity literature, little, if any, attention has been paid to the *quality* of the behavior that prompts identity formation. Specifically, the distinction between behavior that reflects a regular, stable, or fixed characteristic of the person (which in Western societies would be referred to as a sexual preference) and behavior that does not has not been addressed.

What might be the effect of the identity formation process on each of these modes of behavior? We could hypothesize that both the *direction* and the *strength/intensity* of the behaviors could be influenced by the identity formation process. It would seem logical to suggest that the less "set" the behavior leading to identity formation, the more likely it is to be influenced by any process of change and development. In particular, the direction of preference is less likely to be affected where the initiating behaviors are given psychological significance (that is, where they are already a "set" part of a person's functioning). There is no reason to assume, however, that in such circumstances the strength or intensity of the preference cannot be further increased by identity formation processes. Where initiating behaviors are not fixed characteristics, we would expect that identity formation could influence both direction and strength of preference development. Some of the ways in which identity formation could influence sexual preference development are narrowing opportunities for sexual/social/emotional expression, building attitudes that attach a fixed quality to identity and preference, reinforcing behaviors that are consistent with identity, and providing a system of rewards that encourages commitment to a particular mode of behavior.

As described earlier, homosexual identity formation brings about, and is brought about by, changes in self-attitudes, actions, and feelings. With increasing development, there is a greater acceptance of homosexuality and a homosexual life-style. Stereotypes of gay men and lesbians are discarded, and the opportunities for expressing sexual, emotional, and social needs with others of the same sex are increased. These and the other changes mentioned earlier may provide circumstances in which sexual and emotional responsiveness to someone of the same sex is more readily acceptable.

These points can be illustrated by using the example of the woman who perceives herself as bisexual and demonstrates a sexual history of attraction to both sexes, emotionally and sexually. What might happen if such a person were to become very attracted to another woman, fall in love, and eventually come to share living arrangements with that other woman? First, we might expect her to close off options for expressing attraction for the opposite sex (assuming the relationship is a positive experience). Second, we might see the integration of the two women within a social group from the larger gay subculture that encouraged a lesbian identity as consistent with the (perceived) lesbian life-style. Third, we could also hypothesize that with time and the continuation of a rewarding relationship, sexual and emotional responsiveness toward her partner would become enhanced, leading to a more generalized conditioning to females rather than males.

Before continuing our discussion, it must be noted that the argument presented here rests on several assumptions. First, it is accepted that sexual preference is not something so rigidly developed that it cannot be modified. Second, it is assumed that change and development of sexual preference can occur in the adult years and are not necessarily simply a childhood development. Third, any changes that occur do not necessarily reflect the concept of latency, that is, the idea that later development is really an uncovering of development that has taken place at an earlier time. Fourth, learning processes are perceived to play a part in the development of preference. Fifth, something called "sexual preference" can be identified and distinguished from experiences of sexual attraction. And sixth, it is assumed that individuals can consciously alter their behavior.

Although sexual preference is frequently depicted as something that happens without direct control from the individual concerned, there are in fact many examples seen in a clinical setting of people who for various reasons *do* alter, withhold, diminish, or replace one form of response with another. For example, the refusal by some people to entertain the idea of being a homosexual can bring about a cessation of activities considered indicative of such an identity and increased involvement in heterosexual activities. For some, this may encourage greater interest in and eventually greater responsiveness to heterosexual experiences.

Gay identity formation may also provide the circumstances whereby different components of sexual preference may be redirected and/or strengthened. Recalling the proposals of De Cecco (1977), Klein et al. (1985), and Suppe (1984), who have advocated several components of sexual preference, it is important to keep in mind that at the time identity formation begins, different components may be directed toward different genders and experienced with different strengths. For example, the erotic component of De Cecco's model may be strongly felt toward those of the same gender while the emotional component may be weakly felt toward same-sex individuals but intensely felt toward someone of the opposite sex.

It is hypothesized that during homosexual identity formation any component of sexual preference may be affected either in direction or strength. Again, we can suggest that components that have a fixed quality will be less likely to be altered than those that do not.

Let us take the example of a man who after several chance sexual encounters with other men decides that on the basis of these experiences he may be a homosexual, at least at the present time. His emotional attachments for men are limited, and he believes that eventually he will fall in love with a woman. If such a person is to move through the identity formation process to Stage 3, he may find himself beginning to mix in social situations where emotional involvements in the form of relationships with men may be expected of him. His contacts with aspects of the gay subculture may also encourage him to drop any interest he has for women since this may be seen as a cop-out from accepting a gay identity.

Each of these factors may then provide the stimulus and conditions for such an individual to become interested in forming emotional ties and increased sexual contacts with men. This interest could lead, in turn, through learning factors, to a strengthening of his sexual preference for the same sex.

Another example can be cited using the woman who, through involvement in the women's movement, in which close emotional ties with other women are accepted, becomes involved in a sexual/emotional relationship with another woman. She has had no such previous contact and does not recall being sexually attracted to women at an earlier time in her life. Her emotional attraction is considerably stronger than her sexual attraction largely because of the circumstances in which she entered into the relationship. If she were to sever the emotional ties with the other woman, she would be unlikely to experience strong sexual urges toward other women at this time.

What effect might identity formation have on this woman? It could be hypothesized that with an acceptance of the label of "lesbian" as applicable to herself and where such a label includes the characteristic of "being sexual with another woman," this may lead to a greater focus and interest in the sexual aspects of relating with her partner. If seen positively, this could then pave the way for a strengthening of both the intensity and frequency of her sexuality to the extent that she considers this a preference.

The preceding discussion does not mean that *all* those who move through the process of gay/lesbian identity formation will be influenced to alter either the direction or strength of their sexual preference. Rather, it is suggested that this may be *one* way in which sexual preference is developed. If this proposal is true, then it would seem more accurate, in the formulation of a model of sexual preference, to acknowledge the influence of identity formation processes.

HOMOSEXUAL IDENTITY IS DEVELOPED SEPARATELY FROM OTHER SEXUAL PREFERENCE IDENTITIES

People may develop identities that relate to any of the three broad sexual preference types promoted by Western society: homosexual, heterosexual, bisexual. Preference identities need not be limited to these types, however. If "asexual" or "celibate" or any other concept is seen by members of society to constitute a social type related to sexual preference, it too can feature as an identity to be developed.

The development of a homosexual identity is a separate process from that engaged in by those who develop other sexual preference identities (although the nature of that process may contain similar elements). Thus, the identities "bisexual," "heterosexual," and "homosexual" are perceived as separate entities, having separate developmental processes, the components of which may be similar or different.

Given present conceptions of sexual preference in Western society (in which preference focuses on gender of partner), it is probably difficult if not impossible for someone to entertain the idea of developing more than one sexual preference identity. People invariably develop one identity only, although this identity may be replaced with another in serial fashion. For example, a person may move through the homosexual identity formation process with the result that a gay/lesbian identity is formed. If, however, this same person engages in particular behaviors that are seen as indicative of a *different* preference (e.g., strong sexual interest in someone of the opposite sex), this may lead to a questioning of self that initiates movement through a *bisexual* identity formation process.

In other words, it is theoretically possible for someone to begin to develop an alternative identity that (because of present ideas about sexual preference) replaces an existing one. Whenever new meaning is attributed to behavior seen as relevant to sexual preference, this may initiate the identity formation process leading to the development of the alternative identity.

If we make the assumption that identity formation can influence sexual preference development, then it may be hypothesized that as a particular identity is being formed, this will heavily influence the development and maintenance of sexual preference in a direction congruent with that identity. For someone who dislikes inconsistency, to give one example, any behavior that does not fit current sexual preference identity may be discounted, denied, or invalidated in some way. Attempts may even be made to avoid situations in which such behavior might arise again.

Homosexual Identity Is Not Fixed but May Be Long-Lasting

Kinsey and his associates found that sexual preference is not necessarily a fixed aspect of a person's life, although there are some people for whom little variation is seen in sexual preference during their adult years. From the preceding discussion it may be stated that *one* of the factors leading to the variability/rigidity of preference may well be identity formation.

However, while sexual preference identity may not necessarily be a fixed entity, it can be characterized by long-lasting and intense qualities. Sexual preference identities may be treated as permanent, fixed, and irreversible structures by those holding them, as well as by their friends, acquaintances, and so on. These attitudes are generally perpetuated by a number of sources.

1. Present societal beliefs stress that identity is fixed and each person must eventually choose one identity only.
2. This philosophy is also held by most segments of the gay community, which promote the ideas of "once a gay, always a gay" and "the truly gay person."
3. The social structures of people's environments promote consistency in the way people behave and present themselves. Inconsistency is punished in social ways.
4. Individuals, themselves, have a preference for congruency and wish to avoid conflicting and ambiguous behaviors that give rise to unpleasant psychological states.
5. With increased commitment to a homosexual identity, more social and psychological structures are included in the maintenance of that identity. To give up such an identity means giving up something that the person experiences as an integrated aspect of self. There may be anticipation of a sense of loss.
6. There is a human propensity for changing the focus from the act to the actor, that is, from the behavior to the identity, when that behavior is considered to be an indication of something about self as opposed to a consequence of the situation (Matza, 1969). Identities are usually given a fixed status.

It is therefore important to recognize both the potentially flexible nature of homosexual identity and other sexual preference identities as well as the inflexible characteristics attributed to such identities. As noted previously, the attribution of a fixed state may work to solidify and narrow sexual preference into one direction only.

ALL DIMENSIONS OF HOMOSEXUAL EXPERIENCE ARE RELEVANT

Although Kinsey noted that individuals' interpretations of their own behavior may differ from the meaning given to it by someone else (i.e., a researcher), he chose to include only overt behavior as the dimension relevant to sexual preference expression and development.

The study of gay/lesbian identity suggests, however, that many other dimensions of behavior are involved in the experience of being a homosexual. These include both overt and covert components of behavior, of which cognitions, affect (emotional), and/or activity components may be involved. Under the heading of cognitions we may find reference to fantasies, ideal images of self, knowledge about the homosexual stereotype, and thoughts about being a homosexual. Affect may include hopes and fears, evaluation of self or behavior, a feeling of love for someone, and anxiety about mixing with gay people. Activity may cover participating in gay-pride marches, avoiding gay meeting places, reading about homosexuality, acting sexually, and acting "in love."

The relationship between these areas of functioning is interactive, with each being able to influence the others during identity formation. In the description of the stages of identity formation, the example was offered of those who upon admitting that they could possibly be "a homosexual," then feel alienated from other people. This in turn may motivate them to seek out gay people on a social basis in order to deal with that alienation. This contact may prove a rewarding experience and encourage participation in sexual/emotional activities.

Equal significance is attributed to internal and external aspects of functioning. Overt behavior is considered no more significant overall than cognitive or emotional factors. However, for different people, different combinations of factors may be important to identity. For example, someone who puts great emphasis on thinking problems out may ignore many of the emotional components of identity. Moreover, at various stages of identity development, different factors may play a central role in development as noted earlier.

Thus, two points stand out for us here. First, it is apparent that a variety of factors may be involved in varying degrees in both the development and expression of homosexual identity and therefore of sexual preference. Sexual responsiveness, traditionally seen to be *the* most significant factor in preference, is given a less central place. Second, significant individual differences may be documented among those at similar stages of gay/lesbian development. Even sexual response is not the simple variable that it has frequently been portrayed as but can be broken down into a number of different factors that may be experienced in varying ways by different people.

In understanding homosexual identity and sexual preference, it is considered necessary to examine all such variables and to note the relative influence of each. It is simply too narrow to attempt to cover the entire complexity of sexual preference by reference to one or two variables. It is also irresponsible to suggest that it is more effective to focus only on those aspects that are easily measured or classified.

THE MEANING OF BEHAVIOR IS IMPORTANT

Homosexual identity cannot be understood without recognizing the particular importance of the *meaning* that a person places on his or her actual behavior. Identity theorists recognize that the individuals' own interpretation of his or her behavior can influence the direction of development.

As Kinsey found, human beings have the capacity for interpreting their actions in any way that feels comfortable to them, and because of this, homosexual behavior may not necessarily be classified as homosexual. From a modern viewpoint, there are people for whom homosexual expression may be perceived as, for example, "making a political statement," "an outlet," "a spiritual expression," or "something I had no control over."

Can we fully understand sexual preference without recognizing and documenting such meanings? I believe not. It seems no longer to be acceptable or realistic to use only the researcher's interpretation of what is happening. It is necessary to include people's *own* accounts of their sexual preference in order to develop an understanding of preference that is relevant to the present.

Some writers claim, however, that such meanings should not be taken seriously in our attempts to understand sexual preference. They would argue that since the social type of "homosexual" has been socially constructed and therefore is relevant only to the present-day homosexual, we give validity to a picture of the homosexual that is neither universal nor a concrete entity.

Indeed, the homosexual type as we characterize it today *has* evolved out of social developments, as described earlier in this chapter. Some of these developments may have involved the promotion of a particular image of the homosexual by social scientists, as some critics claim. However, the experience of holding a homosexual identity is a very real and significant one *to the individual concerned* and is an important part of his or her sexual preference. (See Cass, 1983/1984, for an outline of this debate.) Should we ignore this experience on the grounds that the homosexual of the twenty-first century may be entirely different, or may not exist at all, or because identity is an illusive concept?

If we assume a model of sexual preference that cuts across all time and cultural barriers and considers preference to be some common and invariable human experience, it might be argued that meaning of behavior is irrelevant. The study of gay/lesbian identity does not claim to fit this model. To a large extent it is reactive. Researchers and theorists aim to document what they see happening around them *at the present time.* The sense of being a homosexual is seen to be a complex human experience accounted for by reference to a number of different dimensions of human functioning. Identity formation and the interrelationship between identity and sexual preference development and expression are recognized as pertinent self-experiences for the individual and as such must be given due respect by theorists and researchers.

THE PERSON PLAYS AN ACTIVE ROLE IN THE ACQUISITION OF HOMOSEXUAL IDENTITY

Within the gay/lesbian identity formation process, the individual is seen to play an active role. This proposal contrasts markedly with the traditional view of sexual preference that sees the development and expression of preference as largely unconscious or at least out of awareness. According to this view, the individual is simply a passive vehicle upon which change processes take place and through which behaviors are expressed.

For those theorists, researchers, and clinicians working with personal development, this concept of passivity does not fit what is known about change and development in human beings. Although much human development can occur out of awareness, people also have the capacity to carry out change at a conscious level, making decisions and taking actions designed to bring about change.

These dynamic qualities of personal development also include the capacity to choose from a range of alternatives, the capacity to motivate oneself, the ability to recognize consequences and implications, the ability to select from a range of strategies aimed at self-enhancement and self-fulfillment, and the capacity to engage in decision-making processes, to name a few.

In the homosexual identity formation process it is recognized that the individual has the capacity to promote or prevent further change. To give an example, a man having an awareness that he likes fantasizing about other males may consciously decide to let this continue, or he may choose to switch his fantasies to females. Of course, choosing to engage in these strategies does not necessarily mean that he will be successful in achieving his intention since this will depend on any number of personal and social factors. To the extent that he is successful, however, it could be suggested that this may contribute to the reinforcement of sexual responsivity in the direction nominated.

Because of this possible link between the dynamic qualities of homosexual identity formation and sexual preference development and expression, it would seem important to reconsider existing models of sexual preference based on a passive view of personal development.

The study of gay/lesbian identity formation suggests that the traditional view of sexual preference as being largely unconscious with the individual simply a passive recipient does not fit what is known about change and development in human beings.

IDENTITY FORMATION CAN OCCUR AT ANY AGE

To a large extent Kinsey was radical for his time in stating that although childhood factors are important in the acquisition of sexual preference, adult learning factors can also contribute significantly. He inferred that adult experiences, which can provide important learning conditions, may account for variations in adult sexual preference behavior. Not all subsequent theorists have taken up his ideas about adult experiences.

Interestingly, the study of homosexual identity also promotes the idea of development that can take place during later childhood and/or adulthood. The development of gay/lesbian identity may begin and end at any age provided that two prerequisites are met. First, the ability to place meaning onto one's own behavior must be present. Thus, a young child or someone who is severely intellectually handicapped will not have the ability to objectively classify his or her own actions, feelings, or thoughts. Second, there must exist a cognitive schema or template about homosexuality and homosexuals. A cognitive schema is like a blueprint of what "a homosexual" or "homosexuality" *is*. Individuals can apply this blueprint to their own behavior or the behavior of others in order to decide whether their actions, thoughts, or feelings can be assigned the meaning "homosexual." The majority of people in Western societies develop such a template through childhood and into adulthood. Some social groups (e.g., young children, members of religious groups that repress information about sexuality) may not have had the opportunity to formulate a cognitive schema of "homosexual."

Of interest to identity theorists is the fact that there may be a significant time gap between the first expression of sexual response to someone of the same sex and the attribution of homosexual meaning. This may result from several factors. Some individuals, for example, deny the homosexual meaning of their behavior because of the negative attitudes attached to it in Western societies. This will cause them to foreclose on a homosexual identity. Others may be unable to assign homosexual meaning because the behavior being expressed is not included in their cognitive schema of "homosexual." Women, for example, frequently classify feelings of love for another woman as a "special friendship," while men may perceive sex with other men as "fooling around—nothing serious."

It is not uncommon for someone to have childhood experiences with another person of the same sex without attributing homosexual meaning (which results in the formation of a homosexual identity) until well into adulthood. What is of interest to us here is to what extent the delay in the attribution of meaning may influence the development of sexual preference. In other words, what is the effect of early or late identity formation in relation to the expression of sexual preference behavior?

This issue adds weight to the argument put forward earlier that homosexual identity formation should be seen as part of the overall process in which sexual preference is developed in Western societies at this point in time. At the very least, consideration of the identity factor can provide one explanation as to why people move from one preference to another at different times in their lives.

Interestingly, the study of homosexual identity formation essentially reinforces Kinsey's notion of sexual preference as not being specific to any particular age-group.

WOMEN'S EXPERIENCE DIFFERS FROM MEN'S

Although Kinsey suggested that different learning factors may enter into the sexual preference development of men and women, he seemed clearer as to the factors responsible for male development than he was for the factors responsible for female development. With regard to the *expression* of preference, he applied the heterosexuality/homosexuality scale to both sexes.

In the acquisition of gay/lesbian identity it is recognized that different factors operate as a result of different socialization patterns for men and women and different societal expectations for gay men and lesbians. These different variables may result in different paths of development being taken within each stage of identity formation, in different images forming the content of homosexual identity, and in different ways of expressing identity and sexual preference.

For example, because of the emphasis on the relationship of emotional factors to sexual expression evident in the socialization of women, lesbians are less likely to have used sexual stimulation as a stimulus to identity formation than to have used emotional or social events. In other words, falling in love with another person of the same gender is more likely to initiate the identity formation process for woman than for men.

It is not uncommon to see a woman who in mid-life "falls in love" with another woman for the first time in her life. This experience may not necessarily include sexual responses, although the quality of the emotional experience is similar to other love relationships she may have had with men. Where a sexual component does become present, this may occur after a period of time or after the emotional responses have been reciprocated. Some women choose not to share their feelings with the other woman. Many repeat the "in love" experience several times at various points in life, while others simply have the single experience.

Women are also more likely to reject the female sex role of women as passive and nurturing of others as an early step in their acceptance of a lesbian identity. This is probably because the image of a lesbian, or the societal expectation for lesbians, is of someone who is focused on her own needs without reference to a male standard.

In addition, women are more likely to perceive the rejection of the female sex role, as well as the need for female support, as also being an indicator of homosexual meaning, and they can give greater weight to these factors in the assignment of meaning to their behavior than to sexual response.

Males are more likely to enter the identity formation process on the basis of sexual stimulation and to *adjust* to the male stereotype by dressing or acting in appropriate ways. Given the status and power differential between the male and female sex roles, there is probably less incentive for the gay male to reject the male sex role with its focus on independence, power, and intellect than there is for the lesbian to reject the female sex role.

Another major difference between women and men lies in the tendency of the former to develop a homosexual identity later than men. It is not uncommon for women to begin the identity formation process as adults, with few if any prior sexual preference experiences of a sexual or emotional nature other than the immediate behavior that has triggered the developmental process.

An example of this, which does not have a replica in the male situation, is that of women coming to adopt a lesbian identity as a result of their association with femininist groups and philosophies. This association helps to develop attitudes that give emotional and sexual associations with other women high and positive status. This acceptance of women-women relationships, as well as the readier access of information about lesbianism within the women's community than can be seen in the general community, provides an environment in which previous views can be reexamined. Out of this, some women choose to become involved in an emotional and/or sexual encounter with someone of the same sex. Some even identify as a lesbian prior to having any such experiences. Where lesbian contacts prove to be rewarding (for a number of reasons such as emotional fulfillment, sexual excitement, political satisfaction, reduction of philosophical conflict that may arise in an encounter with a male), this in turn may contribute to the development of a lesbian sexual preference.

It is clear that the experiences of the modern lesbian simply do not fit the Kinsey model with its emphasis on the measurement of *sexual* response. Since it is hard to believe that lesbians in Kinsey's day were radically more sexual and less emotional than they are now, we can only conclude that first, the Kinsey scale has been modeled solely on the male example and, second, his model of sexual preference, again based on male experiences, did not recognize emotional responses as components of sexual preference.

It is important that acknowledgment be made of the way in which women's experience of sexual preference can differ from men's. The example from the homosexual identity literature suggests that a more accurate account of sexual preference is one that covers patterns of emotional responsiveness, as well as interaction between the sexual and emotional, with recognition given to the complex social and political factors linked with gender role.

PRESENTING HOMOSEXUAL IDENTITY TO OTHERS

Another example of the impact of identity formation on sexual preference may be cited by drawing upon the capacity, recognized in identity formation, of people to present a picture of themselves (presented identity) that is quite different from the one they actually apply to themselves (self-identity)—and in addition, to recognize that these two pictures may differ from the identity attributed to them by others (perceived identity). For example, an individual may believe that he or she is a homosexual but present an image to others of being asexual. Other people, on the other hand, may assume this person to be heterosexual.

What might be the effect of these different images on the individual's sexual preference? It could be hypothesized that where they are related to different sexual preference types, there may be less inducement for the individual to become further involved in the preference related to the self-identity. For example, when someone leads others to believe that she or he is heterosexual, while personally identifying as homosexual, the result may well be restricted opportunities for the expression of a homosexual sexual preference, which in turn may effect the development of such a preference. This effect would be strongest when the homosexual identity was evaluated negatively.

INITIATION OF IDENTITY DEVELOPMENT DOES NOT REQUIRE OVERT BEHAVIORAL EXPRESSION

Identity formation theory proposes that the initial step toward developing a gay identity does not require the actual presence of others or engagement in any overt sexual or emotional contact with others of the same sex. The development of a homosexual identity may be initiated and continued on the basis of *symbolic* representation (that is, mental images) of interactions with others such as occurs in fantasies, daydreams, and so on.

In other words, a person can label fantasies, daydreams, and inner feelings as "homosexual" in the same way they identify actual sexual encounters as homosexual. Thus, celibate people having had no overt emotional or sexual contacts with others may come to see themselves as homosexual (e.g., some lesbian nuns).

It should be noted that in my theory of gay/lesbian identity formation, such a self-image could not be classified as a fully developed homosexual identity. The stages of development represent *degrees* of identity formation. A fully developed identity is one in which self-identity, presented identity, and perceived identity are congruent in describing a positive homosexual image. That is, the individual's picture of self is confirmed by others with a resulting positive sense of self being achieved. In order to obtain this situation, the person concerned is required to overtly express his or her homosexual self-image. Therefore, it is the *early* stages of identity formation that can be achieved through symbolic functioning rather than later ones.

It is significant to note that a person who begins identity development in a symbolic manner cannot be classified on Kinsey's scale. Once again, this points to the limited ability of this instrument to encapsulate sexual preference as we know it today.

It is interesting, too, if we accept the premise put forward in this chapter that identity formation can influence the development of sexual preference, to speculate about what effect the process of forming a homosexual self-image without overt expression of sexual preference may have on the development of preference. It might be, for example, that this image will act to direct the individual's attention to a homosexual sexual preference. This, in turn, might lead to attempts to express the homosexual self-image overtly, resulting perhaps in a conditioning to these patterns of behavior.

Conclusions

Kinsey's scale of heterosexuality/homosexuality is intended to measure current sexual preference. No allowance is made for variations in the strength of preference between individuals at a particular point on the scale or in the factors leading a person to a particular point in sexual preference development. Someone who registers as a 4 on the scale is not necessarily similar to another 4 in anything other than the balance between heterosexual and homosexual sexual behaviors.

We now have to ask ourselves whether having the information that someone measures 4 is useful and whether it is adequate as a description of the individual's sexual preference. Indeed, is there any difference between classifying someone as a Stage 5 or a Kinsey 4? From the stage descriptions presented earlier in the chapter, it should be apparent that there *is* a difference. Knowing which stage of development has been achieved can be useful to clinicians in their work with people having identity problems. The stages themselves represent a composite picture summarizing the involvement of a large number of variables responsible for identity development to that particular point. To describe people as being at a certain stage of development is to say many things about them on the basis of whichever factors are involved at that point of identity formation.

To designate someone as a 4 on Kinsey's scale, however, is to describe only the most overt of characteristics, the balance between sexual responses to men and to women. Because of this, the usefulness of the scale in describing a person's sexual preference is quite limited. Even the suggested amendments of Shively & De Cecco (1977), Storms (1979, 1980), and De Cecco (1977) to make the heterosexual and homosexual scales orthogonal still paint a two-dimensional picture of sexual preference. What is needed is a three-dimensional representation that includes reference to the complexity of factors involved in the expression of sexual preference.

The reader who takes the time to examine Kinsey's work cannot be filled with anything but admiration for the innovative way in which he tackled areas long entrenched in the rigid sexual perspectives and morals of the nineteenth century.

Yet admiration not withstanding, it must be concluded from the review of homosexual identity formation presented in this chapter that the approach taken by Kinsey in his model and scale of sexual preference is now too narrow to be applicable to the experiences of the present-day lesbian or gay man.

Indeed, the issues we have pursued suggest much more than a simple revision of Kinsey's scale. For in claiming that the Kinsey view of sexual preference is obsolete, we are also stating that an *alternative* perspective can be described. In other words, any reassessment of Kinsey's rating scale along the lines suggested by the literature on homosexual identity formation leads us to examine the very dimensions upon which sexual preference is both expressed and developed.

We are left, therefore, with a task far greater than might have been predicted—that of examining the very nature of sexual preference. The question before us now is "What *is* the nature of sexual preference as we know it today?" It has been suggested in this chapter that this question can be partially answered by examining the concept of homosexual identity and the way in which it develops.

References

Boswell, J. (1980). *Christianity, social tolerance and homosexuality*. Chicago: University of Chicago Press.

Cass, V. C. (1979). Homosexual identity formation: A theoretical model. *Journal of Homosexuality, 4*, 219–235.

Cass, V. C. (1983/1984). Homosexual identity: A concept in need of definition. *Journal of Homosexuality, 9*, 105–126.

Cass, V. C. (1985). *Homosexual identity formation: The presentation and testing of a socio-cognitive model*. Unpublished doctoral dissertation, Murdoch University, Western Australia.

Coleman, E. (1981/1982). Developmental stages of the coming out process. *Journal of Homosexuality, 7*, 31–43.

De Cecco, J. P. (1977). *Research on social sex-roles and sexual orientation*. Unpublished manuscript, San Francisco State University.

Ford, C. S., & Beach, F. (1951). *Patterns of Sexual Behavior*. New York: Harper & Bros.

Foucault, M. (1978). *The history of sexuality* (Vol. 1). New York: Pantheon.

Greenberg, D. F., & Bystryn, M. H. (1982). Christian tolerance of homosexuality. *American Journal of Sociology, 88*, 515- 548.

Hooker, E. A. (1957). The adjustment of the male overt homosexual. *Journal of Projective Techniques*, *21*, 18–30.

Katz, J. (1983). *Gay/lesbian almanac: A new documentary*. New York: Harper & Row.

Kinsey, A. C., Pomeroy, W. B., & Martin, C. E. (1948). *Sexual behavior in the human male*. Philadelphia: W. B. Saunders.

Kinsey, A. C., Pomeroy, W. B., Martin, C. E., & Gebhard, P. H. (1953). *Sexual behavior in the human female*. Philadelphia: W. B. Saunders.

Klein, F., Sepekoff, B., & Wolf, T. J. (1985). Sexual orientation: A multi-variable dynamic process. *Journal of Homosexuality*, *11*, 35–49.

Matza, D. (1969). *Becoming deviant*. Englewood Cliffs, NJ: Prentice-Hall.

Minton, H. L., & McDonald, G. J. (1983/1984). Homosexual identity formation as a developmental process. *Journal of Homosexuality*, *9*, 91–104.

Shively, M. G., & De Cecco, J. P. (1977). Components of sexual identity. *Journal of Homosexuality*, *3*, 41–48.

Storms, M. D. (1979). Sexual orientation and self-perception In P. Pliner, K. Blankstein, & I. Spigel (Eds.), *Perception of emotion in self and others*. New York: Plenum.

Storms, M. D. (1980). Theories of sexual orientation. *Journal of Personality and Social Psychology*, *38*, 783–792.

Suppe, F. (1984). In defense of a multidimensional approach to sexual identity. *Journal of Homosexuality*, *10*(3/4), 7–14.

Weeks, J. (1977). *Coming out: Homosexual politics in Britain from the nineteenth century to the present*. New York: Quartet Books.

Weeks, J. (1981). Discourse, desire and sexual deviance: Some problems in a history of homosexuality. In K. Plummer (Ed.), *The making of the modern homosexual*. London: Hutchinson.

15

Toward a Synthetic Understanding of Sexual Orientation

Eli Coleman

NARCISSUS: Yes, You've hit the nail on the head. That's it: to you, differences are quite unimportant; to me, they are what matters most. I am a scholar by nature; science is my vocation. And science is to quote your words, nothing but the "determination to establish differences." Its essence couldn't be defined more accurately. For us, the men of science, nothing is as important as the establishment of differences; science is the art of differentiation. Discovering in every man that which distinguishes him from others is to know him.

GOLDMUND: If you like. One man wears wooden shoes and is a peasant; another wears a crown and is a king. Those are differences, I grant you. But children can see them, too, without any ·science.

NARCISSUS: But when peasant and king are dressed alike, the child can no longer tell one from the other.

GOLDMUND: Neither can science.

NARCISSUS: Perhaps it can. Not that science is more intelligent than the child, but it has more patience; it remembers more than the most obvious characteristics.

GOLDMUND: So does any intelligent child. He will recognize the king by the look in his eyes, or by his bearing. To put it plainly: you learned men are arrogant, you always think everybody else is stupid. One can be extremely intelligent without learning.

NARCISSUS: I am glad that you're beginning to realize that. You'll

soon realize, too, that I don't mean intelligence when I speak of
the difference between us. I do not say, you are more intelligent;
better or worse. I merely say, you are different.

Herman Hesse, "Narcissus and Goldmund"

There have been several notable paradigm shifts in thinking about sexual
orientation over the past 100 years. First, the construct of the homosexual
identity developed by Karl Heinrich Ulrichs and Magnus Hirshfield represented a shift to understanding variations in sexual identity to essentialist
scientific anomalies rather than sins of moral turpitude. Sexual beings
could be divided into male, female, and third sex (the last describing
homosexuality). It was assumed that individuals developed these identities from biological regulations. Anomalies of these biological regulations
could then be regulated to disease states. These developments coincided
with the development of a science of sex, formally christened sexology in
1906 (Haberle, 1983).

Freud (1905/1962) believed that social environment, expecially parent-
child relationships, determined the destiny of the child's sexual orientation. As a biologist, he believed that men and women were not born with
destinies to become heterosexual or homosexual (or third sex) but as
males and females, both with a bisexual orientation. While Freud appeared to take a relatively neutral view of what constituted a psychological anomaly in sexual orientation, his followers certainly labeled homosexuality as an illness state caused by a failure in normal psychosexual
development. They believed that through psychosexual development a
more permanent and polarized sexual orientation is established (Bieber et
al., 1962).

The American scientists (Hall, Watson, and Terman) continued to free
sexuality from moral and religious restrictions (Minton, 1988). Yet their
observations still mirrored societal standards regarding sexual anomalies
and gender roles.

The pioneering efforts of Alfred C. Kinsey (Kinsey, Pomeroy, & Martin,
1948; Kinsey, Pomeroy, Martin, & Gebhard, 1953) achieved the second
paradigm shift. Like others before him, Kinsey was interested in taking a
scientific approach to human sexuality (Pomeroy, 1972). However, he
sought to investigate sexual behavior in a purely empirical and scientific
manner—dissociated from current societal morals or mores. He attempted to study sexuality within the context of the individual's own
experiences and interpretations—recognizing the complexity of the human organism as dynamically interacting with its environment (see
Minton, 1988).

Kinsey rejected the traditional essentialist assumption that human sexuality was inherently heterosexual. However, he believed the sexual instinct could be expressed in a varity of ways, ranging from exclusive
homosexuality to exclusive heterosexuality. Therefore Kinsey's studies

viewed homosexuality and heterosexuality as opposite poles of a continuum of human sexual expression. These orientations were divorced from previously held conceptions of gender role determinations.

There has now been a third paradigm shift away from previous views that sexual orientation can be reduced to the physical and the behavioral (and more specifically the orgasmic) experience to the view that sexual orientation must reflect more psychological and sociological aspects of human sexuality. The Kinsey scale, while representing an important historical, sociological, and political paradigm shift, has been criticized by several authors in this volume for its assumptions regarding sexual orientation for its orgasmocentric and androcentric bias and for the reductionistic and deterministic assumption that sexual orientation is determined by one's own gender and the genitalia of the individual to whom one is attracted. However, humans (and many other animal species) have shown that attraction can be based upon many other dimensions.

Recent scientific work builds upon Kinsey's studies. In a new paradigm, a broader view of sexual orientation is offered—one that incorporates a number of dimensions that various researchers up to now have found to be salient.

First and foremost is the recognition by Shively and De Cecco (1977) that sexual orientation identity is only one of four components of sexual identity. One's biological or physical identity, gender identity, and social sex role identity need also to be included in a description of sexual identity. These four components are clearly distinct from one another.

In clinical practice, I see these various components operating and illustrating the complexity of sexual orientation identity and the dilemmas it presents. For example, one may see a biological male with a female gender and social sex role identity who is attracted exclusively to males with male gender and social sex role identities. Is this man (woman?) a heterosexual or homosexual individual? Does it matter whether this person is a preoperative or a postoperative transsexual? In many transsexuals, the gender role is a much more important variable in understanding their sexual orientation. Changing their physical identity through sex reassignment surgery does not, in many cases, alter their sexual orientation. This has been disturbing to some biologically male transsexuals (presurgery) who are attracted to females and remain attracted to females after their sex reassignment surgery. They have hoped (or expected) that by becoming a woman, they would become attracted to males and would be able to live the culturally expected life of a heterosexual individual. In fact, these individuals not only face the transition from a male to female physical gender and sex role identity, but they also must face the difficulties of developing a "lesbian" identity after surgery.

For others, social sex role is as important to their sexual orientation identity as other sexual identity components. Is the biological female with a male gender identity and a social sex role identity who is attracted to biological males with male gender and social sex role identities a homosexual or a heterosexual individual? One of my colleagues said to me, "I am a (biological) female with a predominately male gender and social sex role identity, and I am attracted to males with male gender social sex role identities. Therefore, I consider myself, basically, a gay man."

From this viewpoint, it is clear that the labels homosexual, bisexual, heterosexual, gay, straight, and so on can be understood only within the context of other components of sexual identity (Suppe, 1984). (Please note that I have not begun to describe the many combinations of individuals with various sexual identities. The possibilities are endless).

There are a few other important and salient variables to better understand or illustrate sexual orientation.

The unidimensional seven-point scale developed by Kinsey and his associates attempted to include both overt experiences and erotic arousal and responses, and yet the number of annual sexual performances apparently outweighed the psychological material in importance (De Cecco, Chapter 21 of this volume). In an effort to improve on this measurement of sexual orientation, Bell and Weinberg (1978) used two seven-point rating scales—one for sexual behavior and one for erotic fantasies. Although this view of sexual orientation clearly represented an improvement in measurement, Shively and De Cecco (1977) suggested that the conceptualization of sexual orientation should include physical factors (sexual behavior), intraspsychic factors (erotic fantasy), and interpersonal factors (affection).

Klein (1980) and Klein, Sepekoff, and Wolf (1985) further illustrated the complexity of sexual orientation and include seven dimensions of orientation that can be rated on a seven-point scale (sexual behavior, fantasies, emotional attraction, sexual attraction, social preference, self-identification, and heterosexual/homosexual life-style preference).

Klein has also argued for the concept of fluidity of sexual orientation over time, and so for purposes of assessment, the Klein Sexual Orientation Grid (KSOG) includes ratings for the respondents' past, present, and ideal choices on all seven dimensions.

Suppe (1984) and others have argued that qualitative descriptors are needed as well as quantitative descriptors. The typologies of homosexual life-style and adaptation that were found by Bell and Weinberg (1978)—closed (monogamous) coupleds, open (nonmonogamous) coupleds, functionals (single life-style), dysfunctionals (single life-style), and asexuals—are also useful constructs in assessing sexual orientation. Besides these qualitative descriptors, Bell and Weinberg found through cluster statistical analysis that psychological adjustment was correlated with life-style. These researchers found that closed coupleds, open coupleds, and functionals were healthier psychologically and had more of an integrated sexual orientation identity than the dysfunctionals and asexuals. So a person's self-acceptance about his or her identity is also an important qualitative descriptor.

Identity integration and synthesis is another valuable construct. The process of developing a mature self-identity has been described by Cass (1979), Coleman (1981/1982), and others. Cass and I discuss identity integration and matured self-concept as a stage that recognizes fluidity and the nature of change in one's integrated identity (Coleman, 1981/1982). While some express concern about the reductionistic assumptions of identity development theories, the constructs of identity synthesis and integration are admittedly reductionistic, yet the concepts keep the important elements of dynamism, fluidity, and diversity. However, although Cass (1979) and I both agree that our theoretical formulations of homosexual identity development are just social constructs, we do think these concepts provide a pragmatic and, in some sense, a "truthful" picture of reality given the current sociocultural-political *milieu*. As Cass has noted, homosexual identity is a descriptor of genuine human response as well as a theoretical construct devised to organize homosexual experiences, and she recognizes that both perspectives are embedded within the values and attitudes of Western society.

A Proposed Model of Clinical Assessment of Sexual Orientation

The proposed synthetic model of assessment is built upon the components model of sexual identity offered by Shively and De Cecco (1977), the KSOG (Klein, 1980), the Bell and Weinberg (1978) typologies, and a clinical methodology developed by the author (1987).

The proposed model measures nine dimensions of sexual orientation (see Figure 15.1). The first dimension is a descriptor of life-style or current relationship status.

Self-identification is the second dimension, followed by idealized self-identification. Fourth, a global measure of comfort of self-acceptance of the individual's current sexual orientation is used. Four more dimensions measure the four components of sexual identity (physical, gender, social sex role, and sexual orientation identity) (Shively & De Cecco, 1977).

In terms of assessing sexual orientation identity, the three dimensions suggested by Shively and De Cecco (1977) are utilized (sexual behavior, fantasies, and emotional attachments). The remaining dimensions of sexual orientation identity suggested by Klein (1980) and included in this volume are not used because of a pragmatic effort to simplify matters in the clinical setting. This decision not to use the remaining dimensions is generally supported by the research conducted on the KSOG (see Klein, Sepekoff, & Wolf, 1985) and Wayson (1983).

The final dimension comes from Klein's argument for fluidity of sexual orientation (Klein, 1978, 1980, and Chapter 16 in this volume). In Klein's

ASSESSMENT OF SEXUAL ORIENTATION

© Eli Coleman, Ph.D.

1986

Name or Code Number:_____ Age:_____ Date:_____

What is your current relationship status:

○ Single, no sexual partners

○ Single, one committed partner Duration_____

○ Single, multiple partners

○ Coupled, living together (Committed to an exclusive sexual relationship)

○ Coupled, living together (Relationship permits other partners under certain circumstances)

○ Coupled, living apart (Committed to an exclusive sexual relationship)

○ Coupled, living apart, (Relationship permits other sexual partners under certain circumstances)

○ Other_____

In terms of my sexual orientation, I identify myself as . . .

○ Exclusively homosexual

○ Predominantly homosexual

○ Bisexual

○ Predominantly heterosexual

○ Exclusively heterosexual

○ Unsure

In the future, I would like to identify myself as . . .

○ Exclusively homosexual

○ Predominantly homosexual

○ Bisexual

○ Predominantly heterosexual

○ Exclusively heterosexual

○ Unsure

In terms of comfort with my current sexual orientation, I would say that I am . . .

○ Very comfortable

○ Mostly comfortable

○ Comfortable

○ Not very comfortable

○ Very uncomfortable

Figure 15.1A

INSTRUCTIONS:

Fill in the following circles by drawing lines to indicate which portion describes male or female elements. Indicate which portion of the circle is male by indicating (M) or female by indicating (F).

Example:

If the entire circle is male or female, simply indicate the appropriate symbol in the circle (M or F).

Example:

Fill out the circles indicating how it has been up to the present time as well as how you would like to see yourself in the future (ideal).

UP TO PRESENT TIME

Physical Identity
I was born as a biological . . .

Gender Identity
I think of myself as a physical . . .

In my sexual fantasies, I imagine myself as a physical . . .

Sex-Role Identity
My interests, attitudes, appearance and behaviors would be considered to be female or male (as traditionally defined) . . .

Sexual Orientation Identity
My sexual behavior has been with . . .

My sexual fantasies have been with . . .

My emotional attachments (not necessarily sexual) have been with . . .

FUTURE (IDEAL)

Physical Identity
Ideally, I wish I had been born as a biological . . .

Gender Identity
Ideally, I would like to think of myself as a physical . . .

In my sexual fantasies, I wish I could imagine myself as a physical . . .

Sex-Role Identity
I wish my interests, attitudes, appearance, and behaviors would be considered to be female or male (as traditionally defined) . . .

Sexual Orientation Identity
I wish my sexual behavior would be with . . .

I wish my sexual fantasies would be with . . .

I wish my emotional attachments (not necessarily sexual) would be with . . .

Figure 15.1B.

methodology, he asks individuals to rate their past, present (including the past year), and idealized future sexual orientation on his seven defined dimensions. In this methodology, past and present orientations are collapsed, while the idealized future orientation is retained. It is this comparison of the present to the future that yields the most valuable clinical information.

Therefore, the nine dimensions measured by this instrument include the following:

1. Life-style or current relationship status
2. Self-identification of sexual orientation identity
3. Idealized self-identification of sexual orientation identity
4. Global measure of comfort or self-acceptance of one's current sexual orientation identity
5. Physical sexual identity
6. Gender identity
7. Sex role identity
8. Sexual orientation identity including measures of sexual behavior, fantasies, and emotional attachments
9. A measure of past and idealized future sexual identity (physical, gender, sex role, and sexual orientation identity)

The other deviation from other assessment methodologies is the use of circle graphs rather than Kinsey-type (0–6) ratings. Instead of individuals being placed or placing themselves on a horizontal line, circles are used so that the individuals can divide the circles into percentages or slices of a pie. This method yields more of a graphic illustration of sexual orientation, and the ends of the Kinsey continuum (heterosexuality and homosexuality) are not viewed as so distant or different from one another. This concept of the circle also implies integration of male and female aspects of sexual identity into a conceptual whole. Once this assessment tool is filled out, the clinician can discuss the implications, meanings, possible sources of distress, developmental deficits, and goals of therapy with the client.

This clinical tool has been useful to many clients in understanding their concerns about their sexual orientation/identity. It gives them a more complete understanding of sexual orientation than the dichotomous or trichotomous labels (homosexual, heterosexual, or bisexual) a Kinsey scale can give them. This assessment method helps clients define themselves, recognize and value the complexity of their sexual orientation, and further their overall sexual identity development and satisfaction.

Suggestions for Further Research Regarding Sexual Orientation

The clinical tool described here can easily be modified for research purposes by using the discrete categories of life-style, self-identification, idealized self-identification, and self-comfort and by measuring the degrees of the circles to derive numerical values for the measures of sexual identity. Otherwise, Kinsey-type (0–6) ratings could be substituted for the circle graphs. Or for the measurement of sexual orientation, the entire KSOG could be used. For broader studies of large groups of self-identified homosexuals, the entire form of the KSOG would not need to be utilized; a portion of this scale could be used or a formula could be devised to collapse categories. This might be needed for some methodological studies (see Wayson, 1983). Other more sophisticated measures of gender identity, sex role identity, self-concept, self-esteem, and psychological adjustment could also be utilized.

However, the results of such investigations need to be reported more specifically as to how sexual orientation is measured and groups are defined. Using more dimensions or measures of sexual orientation allows investigators to conduct interesting post hoc analyses, which might yield greater understanding of the results and the formulation of future hypotheses.

Conclusion

In further research on sexual orientation, multiple dimensions of assessment of sexual orientation must be used. Sexual orientation identity should be viewed in its complexity, using various dimensions (minimally, measures of sexual behavior, fantasies, and emotional attachments). Sexual orientation should also be viewed in its relationship to other components of sexual identity (physical, gender, and social sex role). Moreover, some qualitative descriptors should be utilized to measure life-style, self-identification, and comfort with sexual orientation identity. Finally, all these measurements need to be understood as social constructs born out of the cultural, sociological, and political climate of our time.

References

Bell, A. P., & Weinberg, M. S. (1978). *Homosexualities: A study of diversity among men and women*. Bloomington: Indiana University Press.

Bieber, I., Dain, J. J., Dince, P. R., Grundlach, R. H., Drellich, M. G., Grand, H. E., Kremer, M. W., Rifkin, A. H., Wilbur, C. B., & Bieber, T. B. (1962). *Homosexuality: A psychoanalytic study*. New York: Basic Books.

Cass, V. C. (1979). Homosexual identity formation: A theoretical model. *Journal of Homosexuality, 4*, 219–235.

Coleman, E. (1981–1982). Developmental stages of the coming out process. *Journal of Homosexuality, 7*(2/3), 31–43.

Coleman, E. (1987). Assessment of sexual orientation. *Journal of Homosexuality, 14*(1/2).

Freud, S. (1962). *Three contributions to the theory of sex*. New York: E. P. Dutton. (Original work published 1905)

Haeberle, E. J. (1983). Sexology: Conception, birth and growth of a science. In R.

T. Seagraves & E. J. Haeberle (Eds.), *Emerging dimensions of sexology* (pp. 9–28). New York: Praeger.

Hesse, H. (1981). *Narcissus and Goldmund*. New York: Bantam. (Original work published 1930)

Kinsey, A. C., Pomeroy, W. B., & Martin, C. E. (1948). *Sexual behavior in the human male*. Philadelphia: W. B. Saunders.

Kinsey, A. C., Pomeroy, W. B., Martin, C. E., & Gebhard, P. H. (1953). *Sexual behavior in the human female*. Philadelphia: W.B. Saunders.

Klein, F. (1978). *The bisexual option*. New York: Arbor House.

Klein, F. (1980, December). Are you sure you're heterosexual? or homosexual? or even bisexual? *Forum Magazine*, pp. 41–45.

Klein, F., Sepekoff, B., & Wolf, T. (1985). Sexual orientation: A multi-variate dynamic process. *Journal of Homosexuality, 11*(1/2), 35–49.

Minton, H. L. (1988). American psychology and the study of human sexuality. *Journal of Psychology and Human Sexuality, 1*(1), (pp. 17–34).

Pomeroy, W. B. (1972). *Dr. Kinsey and the Institute for Sex Research*. New York: Harper & Row.

Shively, M. G., & De Cecco, J. P. (1977). Components of sexual identity. *Journal of Homosexuality, 3*, 41–48.

Suppe, F. (1984). In defense of a multidimensional approach to sexual identity. *Journal of Homosexuality, 10*(3/4), 7–14.

Wayson, P. (1983). *A study of personality variables in males as they relate to differences in sexual orientation*. Unpublished doctoral dissertation, California School of Professional Psychology, San Diego, California.

16

The Need to View Sexual Orientation as a Multivariable Dynamic Process: A Theoretical Perspective

Fritz Klein

Being identified by one's sexual orientation is relatively new in the history of humankind. As Boswell (Chapter 2 of this volume) has pointed out, it goes back only to the nineteenth century. Now however, people act as if this classification of human sexuality is a fixed axiom in relationships between people. Because there is confusion about the notion of sexual orientation among investigators as well as laypeople, it may be helpful to consider some of the underlying assumptions that support the concept and how it is used in research. My own introduction to the field of sexual orientation began with my studies of bisexuality. In order to obtain a large enough population, I established a social organization in New York City called the Bisexual Forum. Over many years, we held weekly meetings in which the issues of bisexuality in particular and sexual orientation in general were discussed. The people who attended had answered an advertisement in the *Village Voice*, a weekly newspaper, giving a telephone number of a support group for bisexual men and women.

It became clear before very long that most of the people who showed up were confused as to their sexual orientation. Their confusion lay not in what they thought or felt themselves but rather in the definition they could use for themselves and others. Many thought that they only had the option of two categories to describe their sexual orientation, namely, homosexuality and heterosexuality. Only a small percentage perceived the possibility of the third category of bisexuality.

Invariably the meetings with newcomers to the forum would settle down to a discussion of the definitions of the three categories. It became quite evident that limiting sexual orientation to only three possibilities would not do justice to what these people knew about themselves and others. So we began to educate the newcomers to the Kinsey notion of a seven-point heterosexual/homosexual scale. A seven-point scale helped somewhat in that a continuum made more sense than having only the choice of two or three labels.

However, even Kinsey's scale did not meet the needs of the group because too many questions were still left unanswered as to the meaning of who a person was. If, for instance, we said a person was a 2 or 3 on the Kinsey scale, what did that mean exactly? The seven-point continuum did not answer at all the complexity of the concept of sexual orientation, the definition of which must take into account a number of variables.

As we know, the Kinsey numbers are as follows:

0 Exclusively heterosexual
1 Predominantly heterosexual, only incidentally homosexual
2 Predominantly heterosexual, but more than incidentally homosexual
3 Equally heterosexual and homosexual
4 Predominantly homosexual, but more than incidentally heterosexual
5 Predominantly homosexual, only incidentally heterosexual
6 Exclusively homosexual

Let me illustrate with the following example the difficulty of using the Kinsey scale in trying to decide where a particular man would fit on the scale. A married man who dearly loves his wife has sex with her on the average of once a week. However, he also goes to the baths for sex with men on the average of once a month.

Using only the man's sexual behavior, we already run into trouble with the scale in that if we look at the number of his partners, the man should be classified as a 5 since he had sex with 12 men but only one woman. If on the other hand, we look at the frequency of sexual outlets, he is clearly a 2 in that he had 52 experiences with a female but only 12 with males.

Sexual orientation is, however, more complex than just counting sexual experiences. If one thinks seriously about the concept, it seems that we must include other variables. We have identified seven variables that are important when looking at the concept of sexual orientation. Let us look at them one at a time and see where this man fits on the scale.

The first variable is sexual behavior, and we just saw that by looking at number of outlets, this man is a 2; number of partners places him in the category of 5, while if we ask him (and we did) what he thinks he is in terms of sexual behavior, he answers that he is a 3.

What about the man's emotional life? He only loves his wife while on this level; he has never had any loving feelings toward men. Using the variable of emotional preference in sexual orientation, we must classify the man as a 0.

Sexual fantasies is another important variable. This past year, the man told us that his sexual fantasies were exclusively limited to men. This gives him a Kinsey number of 6 on this variable.

With respect to sexual attraction, the man rates himself a 5, namely, predominately homosexual and only incidentally heterosexual.

How about social preference? Does a person like to socialize with members of his or her own sex or the other sex? This man enjoys the social company of men and women equally. This places him in the category of 3.

A sixth variable is that of heterosexual, bisexual, or homosexual life-style. Does a person live in the heterosexual social world, does he or she have bisexual or homosexual friends, go to homosexual bars or clubs, and so on? This particular man lives almost exclusively among heterosexuals, and outside of the baths that he visits, he does not have any knowledge-able association with homosexual or bisexual organizations or people. In this, he is a 1 on the scale.

The last variable is self-identification. What a person thinks he or she is makes a large difference in what that person does or feels. This man labels himself a 4 on this variable.

This example, using the diversity of a man's numbers to show the complexity of the concept of sexual orientation, gives the man the follow-ing profile: 3, 0, 6, 5, 3, 1, and 4. Now where does that place him if we only use one number as most of us have been doing when classifying people according to the Kinsey scale? If we would use the labels of hetero-sexual, bisexual, or homosexual, this man evidently does not fit easily into any of the three categories. In my experience, however, I have heard arguments to support all three labels as the "true" label for any particular person.

Yet looking at sexual orientation as having these seven variables does not completely cover its complexity. What we have left out of the defini-tion so far is that people change with respect to their sexual orientation over time. Where a person is today (in terms of behavior, feeling, and identification) is not necessarily where he or she was in the past or for that matter where he or she will be, or would like to be, in the future. The concept of a dynamic process must be included if we are to understand a person's orientation.

Rather than use one number to describe someone's sexual orientation, it becomes necessary to use a grid. This grid lets us see and understand at one glace who a particular person is with respect to his or her orientation. Following is the Klein Sexual Orientation Grid (KSOG), which was devel-oped to take these considerations into account.

We have tested this grid on hundreds of people and have found it to be both a reliable and a valid instrument. For a more detailed analysis of the instrument, see Klein (1985).

Variable	Past	Present	Ideal
A. Sexual attraction			
B. Sexual behavior			
C. Sexual fantasies			
D. Emotional preference			
E. Social preference			
F. Self- identification			
G. Hetero/homo life-style			

Note: For categories F and G, use Kinsey's definition for 0 to 6. For categories A through E, change Kinsey's definition for 0 to 6 from heterosexual/homosexual to other/same sex.

Figure 16.1. Klein Sexual Orientation Grid (KSOG).

That we are on the right track in thinking about sexual orientation can be seen from the other chapters in this volume that address the issue that one number does not adequately describe a person. Among those who have come up with other variables for measuring sexual orientation are Whalen, Geary, and Johnson (Chapter 5), who include the variables of arousability, sexual behavior, sexual fantasy, and masculinity/femininity of the person and of the partner; Pillard (Chapter 7), who differentiates between fantasy and behavior; Coleman (Chapter 15), who using pie charts instead of numbers includes gender identity, social sexual roles, comfort level, and patterns of relationship, as well as the already mentioned variables of sexual behavior, fantasy, affection, and self-identification; and Nichols (Chapter 20), who has not created a scale herself, but does mention the need for taking the variables of sexual fantasy, masculinity/femininity, and monogamy into consideration.

We see that other researchers in the field of sexual orientation have different ideas as to what variables are the important ones to measure when we try to differentiate the various populations from each other. At this stage, our knowledge is limited and we may disagree as to what variables to use, but more than one variable seems to be necessary. Where I disagree with my colleagues is in maintaining that the dimension of time is a very important one and must be taken in consideration. Herdt (Chapter 13) and Blumstein and Schwartz (Chapter 18) have pointed out the necessity of viewing the discontinuities with respect to a person's sexual orientation.

In reviewing the literature, I found that many studies of "homosexual" populations have lumped together many people most of us would classify as bisexual. These research endeavors had to be flawed in that various populations were grouped into one category, namely, that of homosexuality.

Another major difficulty in using the Kinsey scale and one number to describe a person's orientation is that the definition is fuzzy and we might be talking about different populations even if we use only one Kinsey number. Using the KSOG, we notice that a person might be labeled a 4 even if in one case the 4 is made up of 4, 4, 4, 4, 4, 4, 4, and in another case the numbers are 3, 5, 2, 6, 1, 6, 5.

The histories of many people who would be clearly labeled as either bisexual or homosexual show that over time their numbers in the various categories have changed, some to a very large extent. When asked about their ideal, their values sometimes change remarkably. Therefore, in addition to looking at the seven variables, it becomes necessary to see a person's orientation as one that changes over time; for some there is little change, for others change is gradual, for still others change occurs from one day to the next. This is why it is important to use a grid that includes the dynamic factor of time.

The obvious advantages in using the KSOG is that no matter how a researcher defines his or her population, that definition can be spelled out and the study may be replicated with a similar group. The grid also eliminates the confusion of defining the three categories that people are put into: heterosexual, bisexual, and homosexual. Whatever definition we may wish can be explicity spelled out. In fact, several authors who have used the KSOG have clearly demarcated their populations. Thus, even though they have used different definitions as to who their populations were, the people under investigation could easily be identified and the studies easily replicated. For example, if to be included in a bisexual group for a particular study a person had to have a 2 to 4 average in both the sexual and nonsexual variables, a reader knows precisely who was considered bisexual and included in the study.

The KSOG is not written in stone. As long as the researcher or expert uses a clear scale or grid that includes the different variables that are deemed important, we will be able to follow and define sexual orientation. I still use the KSOG even though it does have limits and does not cover additional aspects that some experts have observed might be important in certain populations or certain studies. Following are some of the points not covered by the KSOG:

1. The age of the partner is not looked at.
2. There is no category for nonapplicable behaviors. This is easily

remedied with the inclusion of an X in addition to the values of 0 to 6.

3. Love and friendship have not been differentiated with respect to emotional preference.
4. Sexual attraction does not separate out lust and limerance.
5. The grid does not make clear what is meant by sexual behavior with respect to frequency. Are we measuring the number of partners or the number of sexual occurrences?
6. Sex roles as well as masculine/feminine roles are not included.
7. Questions of monogamy, both with respect to behavior as well as attitude are not measured; i.e., does a person have many sexual relationships such as one-night stands, or does the person have only one life partner?
8. Having only one category called "Past" does not give us details about changes in a person's history or about the continuous or discontinuous variables throughout the past. One solution might be to break the past into 5-year periods. The advantage is obvious; the disadvantage is that the grid becomes more complicated and cumbersome to fill out.

Some have felt that the KSOG is too complicated for research purposes. As it is now comprised, I have found that to the contrary, the grid is quite simple to administer and rate. It takes only 10 minutes to fill out, and it is much shorter than most questionnaires. In addition, the KSOG values are easily analyzed by a computer.

In conclusion, the seven variables and three time frames eliminate the shortcoming of the Kinsey heterosexual/homosexual scale while taking into account the complexity of the sexual orientation concept. Many a person who has filled out the KSOG has had the "Aha" reaction about his or her own sexual orientation.

Reference

Klein, F. (1985). *Bisexualities: Theory and research*, New York: Haworth Press.

17

Psychoanalytic Theory and the Therapy of Gay Men

Richard A. Isay[1]

Psychoanalysts have postulated that homosexuality necessarily reflects an unfavorable unconscious solution to developmental conflict and that the entire personality of the homosexual shows the effects of early fixation. The basis of these conceptualizations lies in Freud's early theory that homosexual men have a "compulsive longing for men" because of their "ceaseless flight from women" (1905, p. 145). Freud's model implicated a number of "accidental" factors, most prominently, the child's fixation to his mother, which motivates him to find love objects "whom he might then love as his mother loved him" (1922, p. 230). Attachment to the mother, narcissism, fear of castration, and at times, jealousy against older brothers, along with "the influence of the organic factor which favors the passive role in love" (1922, p. 231) were all mentioned by Freud as determinants of the homosexual object choice.

In spite of this pathological model, Freud's theory of innate bisexuality, his openness to new clinical data, and an emphasis on constitutional as well as "accidental" factors led him to equivocate about both the nature and origin of homosexuality (1930). He grew to believe that it was as difficult to convert a "fully developed homosexual into a heterosexual" as to do the reverse (1920, p. 151). His libertarian instincts, even as early as October 1903, caused him to write, "I am even of the firm conviction that homosexuals must not be treated as sick people . . . . Homosexual persons are not sick, they also do not belong in a court of law" (1903). In 1930, along with several other leading Austrian intellectuals, he signed a petition urging the repeal of a law that had criminalized homosexual behavior

(1930). His humane letter to an American mother (1935) is well known. Less well known was Freud's support for the admission of homosexuals to psychoanalytic institutes unless the applicant had "other qualities" that might militate against such a decision (see Isay, 1985, p. 252).

After Freud's death, psychoanalysts seemed intent upon removing any ambiguity in his theory of sexual-object choice and decisively settled on the pathological model. Rado (1940) criticized the concept of bisexuality as biologically unsound and of little clinical or heuristic value. Later (1949) he wrote that homosexuality was a reparative attempt on the part of men who were "incapacitated by their fear of women." Other workers, for example, Bergler (1956), Bieber et al. (1961), Ovesey (1965), and Socarides (1968, 1978), later elaborated and consolidated the theory that the same sex object choice was motivated by anxiety evoked by the opposite sex. Emphasis has been placed upon pre-Oedipal disturbances, especially binding, engulfing mothers who interfere with the separation-individuation process, resulting in the failure to separate from the mother of infancy and early childhood, with a consequent disturbance in gender identity. Those men most accepting of their homosexuality, the "obligatory" homosexuals, are those believed to have had the most disturbed early mother-child relationship, and conseqently, the most severe ego defects and the most severely impaired character structures because of early developmental failure (Socarides, 1978). They are also said to "inevitably have disturbances in self identity, gender identity and gender role" (Ovesey & Woods, 1980, p. 332). Homosexual men who regress from conflicts around Oedipal stage competitive issues are felt to be less disturbed and to have greater flexibility in their object choice (Socarides, 1978). There is a current emphasis on the importance of the father in assisting in the stage of disidentification from the mother (Stoller, 1979, Tyson, 1982). Whether implicating an engulfing mother or a distant, absent father (Bieber et al., 1962) or both, most psychoanalysts make no distinction between the development of sexual-object choice in the gay man and the development of male gender identity. (For a review and critique of psychoanalytic theories of homosexuality, see Friedman, 1986).

The view of the severity of psychopathology of gay men has been maintained in spite of evidence accumulated from nonanalytic studies. The statistics cited by Kinsey (1948) would throw this view into question by virtue of the large numbers of homosexuals in the population. Evelyn Hooker's (1957) study utilizing projective psychological tests failed to discern any demonstrable psychopathology in large numbers of her homosexual sample. A number of other investigators, using both projective and objective standardized tests, have been unable to differentiate homosexual from heterosexual subjects and suggest that there is no greater pathology among homosexuals than heterosexuals (see the review by Riess, 1980).

Attempts to Change Sexual Orientation

I am defining as homosexual a man who has a predominant erotic attraction for others of the same sex; that is, those whose sexual fantasies are either almost entirely or are exclusively directed toward others of the same sex. Most homosexuals do engage in sexual activity. However, one need not do so to be homosexual because of the inhibition of sexual behavior caused by censorious social pressures or intrapsychic conflict. There are also those who may be homosexual but are unaware of their sexual fantasies because of the repression, suppression, or denial of these fantasies. In adults, the homoerotic attraction can usually be recollected as being present from the latency years, preadolescence, or from early adolescence (ages 8 to 13) and sometimes even earlier. There are, of course, heterosexuals who for developmental reasons (some adolescents), for opportunistic motives (some delinquents), for situational reasons (some prison inmates) or to defend against anxiety may engage in homosexual behavior for varying periods of time and not be homosexual. I will discuss this last issue later in this chapter (see also Isay, 1986a, 1989).[2]

One clinical consequence of the theory that homosexuality is a symptom based upon developmental conflict and early fixation has been the view of most analysts that it is both possible and in the best interest of their homosexual patients to become heterosexual. The psychoanalytic literature is replete with recommendations in support of a "flexible" analytic technique that might be of assistance in changing the sexual orientation of the gay patient. Kolb and Johnson (1955) suggest that the therapist should terminate treatment if homosexual behavior persists rather than encourage the patient's "self-destruction" (p. 513). Bieber et al. (1962) stated, "We are firmly convinced that psychoanalysts may well orient themselves to a heterosexual objective in treating homosexual patients rather than adjust even the most recalcitrant patient to a homosexual destiny" (p. 319). Wiedeman (1974) noted that a "purely analytic approach consisting only of interpretations, without any other elements of support, clarification, and confrontation with reality, hardly exists in discussions of the psychoanalytic therapy of homosexual men (p. 676).

In my practice I have seen many gay men who have sought additional help after interrupting or completing a previous analysis or therapy, where the analyst's goal (either explicitly stated or implicitly guiding the treatment) had been to assist the patient in changing his sexual orientation. My clinical material suggests that such efforts may cause symptomatic disturbances such as severe anxiety, depression, and dysphoria, resulting from the disruption of a lifelong process of sexual identity formation and from injuring self-esteem. In some cases it may result in severe social difficulties in later life. My conclusion in working with these patients is that the analyst's internalized social values interfere with the proper conduct of an analysis by causing the analyst to be unable to convey appropriate, positive regard for his or her patient or to maintain therapeutic neutrality. I have presented extensive illustrative clinical material in a previous publication (Isay, 1985) and will relate only two examples here.

Alan, age 20, was referred for further treatment after he had left his previous psychotherapist, who was an experienced analyst with a fine reputation. Alan initiated therapy again because of dissatisfaction with his life, complaining of an inability to form satisfying relationships, an unsatisfactory college performance, and having no goals in his life. He also complained about being gay because his parents wished he were straight. He wanted to be able to please his mother, who badly wanted grandchildren. Although he had friendships with girls and on one occasion had had intercourse, his sexual fantasies from the age of 9 or 10 had been almost exclusively about other boys, and he felt little sexual interest in girls. He wanted to be able to fall in love and to have a boyfriend because he felt so lonely, but when a man liked him, he found the man unattractive and lost interest. His sexual activity, therefore, had been largely confined to the bathroom of the college library or to the stalls of the pornographic bookstore, performing or being the recipient of oral sex.

Alan's previous three times weekly analytically oriented therapy came to a halt because of his continued feeling that his therapist disapproved of him. He was never told explicitly not to be homosexual, but whenever he cruised a bookstore or had sex, the therapist discouraged this behavior. Going out with another boy would cause his therapist to wonder aloud why he did not devote similar energy to some girl. The therapist's interventions appeared to increase Alan's need for random sexual encounters as he grew to feel that such comments and interpretations were motivated by the therapist's disapproval of his homosexuality and the manner in which he was expressing it. Alan's belief that his therapist disapproved of his homosexual behavior would be interpreted as projection. He felt increasingly depressed, anxious, defeated, and self-critical.

It is, of course, always difficult to evaluate a patient's description of a previous therapeutic experience. However, his description appeared to be more than distortions due to past or current transference phenomena. His initial expression of dissatisfaction with his sexuality, which invited disapproval, was a reflection of poor self-esteem from his early narcissistic injuries and his introjection of hostile social values. It also became increasingly clear that his need to be a "good boy" to please his mother was reflected in the wish to change his sexuality, to which his previous therapist had responded not by attempting to understand the conflicts underlying the wish but by complying with it.

I did not view Alan's homosexuality as his problem. Because he had had an exclusive, or nearly exclusive, homosexual fantasy life since childhood and long-standing homosexual activity with little or no real heterosexual interests, I considered him to be gay. It became clear, therefore, that there was no clinical justification for attempting to change his basic homosexual orientation. This attitude enabled us to analyze those aspects of his wish to be heterosexual that were related to the acquiescence to internalized critical social values and made it possible for us to understand projections of these as well as other feelings and values in the transference. It also became possible to have a clearer view of the early injuries and conflicts that made intimacy so painful for him.

I will now turn to Benjamin, whose first analyst, unlike Alan's, gave the appearance of being nonjudgmental and unmanipulative. No modifications in analytic technique had been necessary to discourage homosexual behavior because this patient had not engaged in homosexual sex during his previous treatment.

Benjamin began his first analysis when in his early 20s because of conflict about homosexual fantasies and lack of interest in women. Although homosexual masturbation fantasies and daydreams had persisted since childhood, he had never engaged in homosexual activity, except for occasional adolescent sexual play. Throughout the first analysis the analyst had interpreted homosexual fantasies as a defense against assuming aggressive male roles, which included having heterosexual sex. Benjamin, ambivalent about his sexuality, readily acquiesced to his analyst's view that his homosexuality could be analyzed and would disappear. He continued to have exclusive homosexual fantasies, but because of his powerful transference needs, he did occasionally engage in sex with women, although he was frequently impotent. Shortly after the termination of this analysis he married. Sexual interest in his wife rapidly waned, and after several years of marriage he began to have homosexual sex for the first time. I first saw Benjamin when he was in his late 30s. He was depressed, agitated, despairing, and confused.

The previous analyst's heterosexual bias was largely expressed in the interpretation of homosexual fantasy as a defense against fears of heterosexuality and of competition. Benjamin's perception of his prior analyst's unconscious intolerance of homosexual behavior and fantasy did appear to be accurate, even though it was clear that this man had a need to feel enraged and to see his analyst, like his parents, as being negligent and uncaring. The analyst's inability to help Benjamin discover his sexual identity contributed to his later symptoms and to the painful social situation he found himself in at the beginning of his subsequent treatment.

Both these cases demonstrate how the transference may be exploited for hoped for therapeutic gain. In the first case the therapist admonished the patient for homosexual behavior and overtly encouraged heterosexual behavior to overcome what he believed to be his patient's avoidance of sex with women. In the second illustration the analyst used interpretation implicitly to encourage heterosexual behavior. I believe that both cases illustrate an analyst's exploitation of transference wishes, particularly the patient's wish to please and be loved, to express his own value system and countertransference. Such an analytic attitude adds a measure of insidious conviction to any patient's long-standing belief in his being intolerable or evil.

I want to make it clear that I am not underestimating the value of questioning, uncovering, and interpretative work with gay men. Nor do I advocate the unquestioning acceptance of a patient's views and values. Rather, I am attempting to emphasize the therapeutic dangers inherent in a position that is not neutral by virtue of the analyst's being oriented to changing the patient's sexuality, for by doing so he or she encourages the analysand "to persevere in sadomasochistic fantasizing and acting out, or to engage in wholesale repression of disturbing factors" (Schafer, 1983, p. 5). It appears to me that the judgment that it is both possible for gay men to become heterosexual and that it is in their best interest to do so is not truly a "health value" that is in the service of our patients. Such efforts seem to derive from the confusion of "health ethics" with moral values, so that "empirically subjected values are posited as if they were objective and accessible to empirical validation" (Hartmann, 1960, p. 67).

At this point I wish briefly to mention work with bisexuals, who can gain varying degrees of satisfaction and pleasure with either same-sex or opposite-sex persons. Analysts, in general, believe that bisexuals are either sick heterosexuals, who use their homosexuality to avoid anxiety-provoking heterosexual impulses, or that they are in fact homosexuals, who with proper treatment will become functioning heterosexuals. My experience suggests that while there are indeed some who appear to be bisexual who are defending against one or another aspect of their sexuality, there are truly bisexual men, whose sexual arousal patterns are established at a very early age.

An important distinction between such men and gay men is that if they wish to do so, they may be enabled to live a heterosexual life, relatively unencumbered by their homosexuality, through a neutral, traditional psychoanalytic or psychotherapeutic process. The comfort of their lives as functioning heterosexuals will depend upon the degree to which they are made conscious of and accepting of their homosexual fantasies and impulses, which can then be used in the service of their heterosexuality and productivity. My impression is that bisexual men have enough emotional gratification and satisfying sexual discharge with women that their homosexual longings may be suppressed for varying lengths of time without placing excessive stress on a heterosexual relationship. Although treatment will not lead to the disappearance of homosexual fantasies, the increasing tolerance of the homosexual component of their sexuality leads often to an increasing enjoyment of heterosexuality and to a relative increase in heterosexual fantasies.[3]

Defensive Homosexuality in Heterosexuals

The case of Benjamin illustrates how the pathological model may lead to a blurring of clinical goals and to the obfuscation of distinctions between heterosexuals who use homosexual fantasies and behavior as a defense against heterosexuality and homosexual men, who do not do so. I now turn to an example of defensive homosexuality as seen in a predominantly heterosexual man to illustrate some of these distinctions.

Charles was 23 when he began his analysis. He had graduated from college two years before with only fair grades after excelling in high school in both academic studies and extracurricular activities. He went to law school after college but dropped out after the first year because of loss of motivation. Subsequently, he got a job on a newspaper but quit after 6 months because of his loss of interest. When I started to work with him, he was a waiter in a natural food store. He wanted treatment because of concerns about his work history, his lack of motivation, and his sexual inadequacy. He had a history of premature ejaculation and impotence with a girlfriend of two years, whom he had subsequently stopped seeing one year before beginning his analysis. He was not dating at all when he began treatment. His masturbation fantasies were predominantly of erect penises, sometimes of performing fellatio, and less frequently, of having heterosexual sex in which he would force a woman to submit to him.

His father was a highly successful businessman, competitive, powerful, and emotionally detached. Charles was cognizant of his closeness to his beautiful mother, who was sometimes subservient to her husband but at other times contemptuous of him. Charles became increasingly aware during the course of his analysis of sadistic and spiteful rage toward her and toward other women because of frustrated sexual longings and the feeling of being demeaned by her.

By the third year of his analysis Charles had successfully completed graduate school and was working for a corporation. This period of renewed success was accompanied by feelings of competitiveness and increasing homosexual fantasies, both in and outside of the analysis, motivated by the fear that, like his father, I would injure him if he did not please me by being submissive. He had the following dream the night after being complimented by his boss for an innovative solution to a complicated business problem:

> I was underneath some blankets with my shorts on. All of a sudden this guy was rubbing his leg against me. I wanted to get out from underneath the blankets but couldn't because my shorts were off and he'd see I had a hard on. He wanted to kiss me and I wanted to kiss him too. I had this sexual feeling even though I was resisting it.

His associations were of sexual feeling toward me, feeling small, power-less, and helpless. A further elaboration of the manifest dream was that his legs were spread like a woman's. He felt that his penis was small like a clitoris and that he was helpless and unable to do anything by himself—"just like a woman." He wondered what it would feel like to be anally penetrated by me.

As his analysis progressed, Charles was able to permit himself greater success in different areas of his life, including increased sexual pleasure with women; but his anxiety correspondingly increased, and he had fre-quent conscious homosexual fantasies of fondling my penis or some other man's, of being anally penetrated or of performing fellatio. Although these fantasies were sexually arousing, he had no homosexual activity or any significant interest in doing so. Rather, he continued to have a pervasive heterosexual drive and increasingly satisfying sexual activity. Analysis of his anxiety around competitive strivings and his fear of injury as a result of his competitiveness both reduced the frequency and intensity of his homoerotic fantasies and increased his success in competitive endeavors.

This case is illustrative of the most frequent form of homosexual-like behavior and fantasy seen in adult heterosexual males: they serve as a defense against conflicts about assertiveness by the expression of the unconscious wish to be a woman. In such patients, feminine is per-ceived unconsciously as being passive and noncompetitive and opposes what are perceived as the dangers inherent in being masculine, competi-tive, and assertive. It is, of course, of interest that the symptomatic expression of the wish to be a woman takes the form of homosexual fantasies, for such fantasies express the perception that all homosexual men are passive and submissive, that heterosexual men are necessarily assertive and competitive.

The following characteristics may be helpful in distinguishing clinically between such heterosexual men who use homosexuality defensively from the true homosexual as defined earlier in this chapter.

1. In the heterosexual, the homosexual fantasy usually has the uncon-scious meaning of being womanlike and nonmasculine. The sexual fan-tasy may have that same unconscious significance at times in some homo-sexuals, but it is not of exclusive or predominant significance. The mean-ing of the homosexual fantasy of homosexuals, like the heterosexual fan-tasy of heterosexuals, is dependent on many aspects of character and determined by conflict and compromise formation.

2. Homosexual behavior and fantasy in the heterosexual ward off and defend against heterosexual attachment. The homosexual behavior and fantasy of the homosexual have attachment to another man as their aim. As with any heterosexual, however, such attachment is not the only aim of the sexual behavior or fantasy nor is it necessarily the conscious aim. Both homosexuals and heterosexuals may use sexualization and hypersexuality as a way of avoiding such attachment.

3. Most, although not all, heterosexual men enjoy in their childhood stereotypical male, aggressive "rough and tumble" activities. Most, although certainly not all, homosexual men have a history of aversion to and avoidance of these activities in childhood (Friedman & Stern, 1980; Green, 1985). Gay men also have a feeling of being different from their same-sex peers, which in some measure is based upon their preconscious perception of their sexual orientation (see Isay, 1986b).

4. In the heterosexual, the onset of the homosexual fantasy is usually recollected as starting in late adolescence or early adulthood. The fantasies of the homosexual have their onset in childhood. They are usually consciously recollected as starting in the latency years or early adolescence and often earlier.

5. In heterosexuals, the homosexual fantasy is distressing and feels unnatural (ego dystonic). To most gay men, the homosexual fantasies and behavior feel natural, although at times, because of social intolerance, they may be unwanted.

6. In the heterosexual, homosexual fantasies either disappear or are greatly mitigated in an uncoercive neutral therapy or analysis. In the homosexual, in a properly conducted treatment, fantasy and sexual activity become less conflicted.

7. In the heterosexual man, homosexual fantasies are most likely to appear at times of heightened transference around conflicted aggression and competitiveness. In the homosexual, while the nature of the same-sex fantasy and behavior may change during analysis as they become less distorted by neurotic conflict, such fantasy and behavior remain comparatively constant during treatment. (For elaboration and illustration of these issues, see Isay, 1986a.)

I view those gay men who come for analysis or therapy because they are dissatisfied with themselves as homosexuals and with their sexuality to be responding to real and immense social pressures and prejudices that face them and to conflicts engendered by these, or to internal conflicts that are interfering with and inhibiting the acceptance and expression of their sexuality and homosexual identity, and/or to conflicts unrelated to their sexuality but displaced onto it. Like the majority of gay men who enter treatment for other than conscious conflict about their sexual orientation, the analysis of such conflict should enable them to have less encumbered, more conflict free, less inhibited, more gratifying lives as homosexuals. I will illustrate in my work with Alan, the young man described earlier, some aspects of the neutral and accepting attitude that I believe to be essential in working with such patients, as well as some of the clinical issues that arise in treatment.

Alan was attracted to men who were either attached to someone else, had previously rejected him, were conflicted about their homosexuality, or were heterosexual and disinterested. Anyone who was available was perceived as being like him and became repugnant after the first sexual encounter. After he left college, he had expanded social opportunities and began to date. It became clear in his analysis that when he developed affection for another man, he became impotent.

Throughout much of our work Alan articulated that he was not attracted to "older men," men in their 40s, feeling that they were "lecherous" and they would take advantage of his youth. He also had intense anxiety about being the recipient of anal sex and was usually too tight to permit anal penetration, especially if he felt affection for his sexual partner. He was attracted to passive, feminine-appearing boys but had masturbation fantasies of powerful black men with large penises. These symptoms, along with the manner in which they were manifested in and intensified by the transference, suggest a discomfort around his passive longings and his wish to be dominated.

One manifestation of his anxiety around these wishes in the transference was his need to appear to be oblivious of me, in spite of his occasional seductiveness and exhibitionist behavior on the couch. He would ignore my interpretations or clarifications or focus on an insignificant aspect of what I had said to defend against feeling taken over by me. As the analysis progressed, he became increasingly aware of the fear and the wish that I dominate him. At times this appeared to repeat a perceived domination and fear of his mother; but at other times these conflicted wishes expressed his wish for a powerful father. He returned often, especially when he was anxious, to a memory of his father having spanked him, one of the few signs in his mind of his father's dominance, an incident he turned to in fantasy as a reminder of masculine strength and power.

As the transference was analyzed and he became more tolerant of his wishes to get close to a man he perceived as powerful, the affectional-sexual split very gradually began to heal. This coincided with the less disguised, more clearly expressed transference wishes and fears of getting close to me. In his third year of analysis he reported this dream: "I am in a room. It looks like a cell. Some guy comes after me. I hear his heavy breathing. I dig my heels into the floor, going backward, trying to get away."

His associations were to his lying on the couch, sometimes being distracted by noises I made behind him. He became angry about my silence and how long the analysis takes. "I don't know what I want from you anymore," he stated, with considerable longing in his voice. He felt that he could not get what he needed from me. He wondered whether I was good enough or smart enough to help him, or whether I was weak and ineffective like his father. Although he felt affection for his father, he was frightened of getting close to him both out of a fear of disloyalty to his mother and because of anxiety engendered by his erotic attachment to his father.

As these issues became clearer to Alan, he had the following dream in his fourth year of analysis:

I meet this guy. He is selling something. I am in a cave or some dark environment. I really want to sleep with him. I don't know if he's gay. He's tall and skinny. He has long, nonstyled hair, almost like Tarzan. His pants are open. I reach out and grab his leg. He has a bathing suit underneath. We start making out. I say something like "Let's take off our clothes; let me suck your dick." There is something on the underside of his dick like a swelling or herpes. It looks like it's been cut and has scar tissue around it. I suck his cock and then I sit on it. I don't remember his coming; just the wonderful feeling. I woke up very hard and jerked off.

He associated to seeing his physician at a gay resort and having spoken with him there. He wondered what he would do if he saw me there. He remembered recently reading about an article I had written 20 years ago when I was in the navy and commented that I must have looked good in a uniform. He then acknowledged for the first time some attraction to me.

This dream expressed the least disguised sexual transference wish that he had had up to that time, and it was followed by affectionate feelings for me and positive feelings about our work together and the progress he was making. It appeared to usher in an even less ambivalent, but still tentative, appreciation of a young man whom he had been going out with for several months and whom he was now thinking of living with.

Normal Developmental Pathway

Because psychoanalysts contend that genital heterosexuality is the baseline for all human sexuality, our understanding of the development of such homosexual men as Alan or Benjamin has been directed solely to understanding how they deviate from the heterosexual developmental path. In the following brief outline of a normal developmental pathway for homosexual men, I hope to contribute to our further knowledge of gay men and to provide a conceptual framework for understanding some of the developmental impediments that may interfere both with the formation of a positive self-image and with the full and gratifying expression of their sexuality.[4] (See Isay 1986b for an elaboration of this developmental perspective.)

Every gay man I have seen reports that beginning at age 3 or 4 he experienced that he was "different" from his peers. This feeling is described as having been more sensitive, crying more easily, having his feelings hurt more readily, having more aesthetic interests, and being less aggressive than others of his age. Such differences make children feel like outsiders in relation to peers and often to family as well.[5]

Part of the experience described by gay men as being "different" appears to have been a perception of same-sex fantasies and early homoerotic arousal patterns. I have found that the feeling of being different, consistently acknowledged by gay men, may be unconsciously used as a screen for these earlier repressed childhood memories of sexual arousal by others of the same sex. The childhood fantasy may be recalled by the adult, but like the heterosexual's childhood sexual fantasies, most often they are reconstructed from the transference or from derivative memories manifested in other current relationships. I will briefly describe one man who illustrates how a child's actual experience of being different at age 6 or 7 acted as a screen for early sexual feelings.

David is a 32-year-old, masculine-appearing, well-muscled, tight and rigid but handsome man with a small mustache. He entered psychotherapy because of feelings of loneliness, dysphoria, anxiety, and dissatisfaction with the quality of his relationships. He had no apparent conflict over his homosexuality, easily speaking in the initial session of his attraction to other men, but also of his difficulty in feeling close to them. Early in therapy he recollected having felt different from his peers during his childhood. He described this in part as "not liking to hit people or rough stuff. I was more sensitive. I never liked being demanding. I liked playing the piano."

David's father was described as having been somewhat distant. His mother was described as clinging, depressed, and the dominant force in this family in which David was favored by both parents over a brother two years older. In his artistic and musical interests, he perceived himself as being more like his mother, and in his acquiescence, passivity, and emotional distance, as being like his father.

The transference initially took the form of indifference toward the therapist, suggesting a need to deny my importance to him. As our work progressed, he met and moved in with a new lover, who was comfortably open in his expression of affection and tenderness toward the patient. David gradually became less frightened of his feelings within the transference and much more open and giving in this new relationship. It was during this period of gradually increasing comfort with the showing of sexual feelings that he recalled sexual fantasies from when he was 3 or 4 that were centered on muscular comic book heroes. Eventually, he recalled that it was his father who read Superman and Captain Marvel comic books to him while he was sitting on his lap. He began to remember his father as warm, tender, and affectionate rather than distant. It seemed likely from our continuing work, especially from the nature of the transference, that an early interest in and excitement over boys in his class from about age 8 were displacements from and expressions of his repressed sexual feelings toward his father.

It has become clear from my analytic and therapeutic work with men such as David, as well as many other gay men, that homoerotic fantasy is present from the age of 3 or 4 years. I conceptualize this period as being analogous to the Oedipal stage of heterosexual boys except that the primary sexual-object in gay men appears to be their fathers. There is no evidence in the transference or in the nature of their sexual-object choice of a defensive shift in erotic interest from their mothers to their fathers. The experience of being different from peers is focused on in analysis or therapy as a way of defensively excluding other, more deeply repressed memories of "difference," namely, the early homoerotic attraction to peers and the even earlier erotic attachment to the father. This period of childhood homoerotic sexual attachment is the first stage in the acquisition of a homosexual identity. The guilt around such early homoerotic fantasies and the actual experience of being different from peers both contribute to the low self-esteem and negative perception many gay men have of themselves. I turn now to the stage of consolidation of the homosexual identity in adolescence and then to some of the developmental impediments that may hinder a healthy consolidation and continuing integration in adulthood of a homosexual orientation as part of a positive identity.

Consolidation of Sexual Orientation

David's sexual fantasies and attraction to his classmates continued throughout grade school and high school without abating, but he also never had any sexual experience. He was popular with his peers in high school because of a combination of masculine appearance, intelligence, sensitivity, and good looks, and like most adolescents, he cultivated and appreciated peer group recognition. In order to be accepted he dated girls steadily throughout high school, but he was so apprehensive that sex would be required that he became physically ill before going out. Throughout this period he continued to deny that he was gay.

In college his closest friend was gay. Although this friend had wanted to have sex with David and the attraction was mutual, David still could not associate this attraction with a sexuality that was not acceptable to him. In his first year of graduate school, when he was about 23, he fell in love and then suddenly and with a great sense of relief recognized and acknowledged to himself that he was homosexual. He then had sex for the first time and has subsequently been appropriately open about his sexuality.

David's experience was similar to that described by others who acknowledge their sexual orientation after a sudden and dramatic breakthrough of barriers of denial, repression, and suppression. What is often described by a gay man as his "Aha" experience is caused by the coming together of the long-established sexual arousal pattern with a sexual object and feels like the pieces of an old puzzle falling into place. The sense of relief and well-being that usually follows signifies the conscious recognition of his sexuality and the beginning of its acceptance as part of his identity. As one man put it: "The feeling is one of a clearing, a freeing, of being in and of others and the world rather than at odds with the world." Because of internalized social prohibitions and the fear of loss of parental and peer approval, this initial stage of consolidation of sexuality does not often occur as early in the homosexual boy's adolescence as it does in the heterosexual boy's. David's development in this regard may therefore be regarded as normal. However, not all homosexual men "come out" to themselves with the suddenness and unexpected great relief David experienced. In those who have less need for peer recognition than David or less hunger for parental love, recognition and integration may occur more gradually, with less suppression and denial of their sexuality during adolescence (see Isay, 1986b).

Edward, for example, had his first sexual experience at the age of 8, when he was fondled by an older man. He was uncertain how this had occurred, but he felt that he had been a reluctant accomplice in the event remembered with considerable anxiety and guilt. At age 12 Edward became aware of his attraction to some of his teachers whom he had identified as being gay. He recognized a strong wish to be close to them, although not specifically to be sexual with them. His adolescent masturbation fantasies were of a man lying on top of him, making him feel submissive and cared for. He traveled abroad when he was 15 or 16 and had his first mutual sexual contact with a man working in a hotel. It was in his second year of college that he acknowledged in a conversation with a friend that he was homosexual. There was no rush of relief following this recognition, as was true of David, since the acknowledgment of his sexuality had been at a preconscious level, with the process of integration occurring more gradually over the preceding years of early and middle adolescence.

Edward appeared to have had a more nourishing maternal environment than David, which enabled him to rely less on peer and social conformity for self-esteem enhancement, making it less necessary for him to please in order to feel lovable and therefore possible for him to acknowledge his sexual orientation more gradually and with less discomfort. This integration of one's homosexuality into a cohesive and positive self-image is part of the normal development of a healthy gay man. My clinical experience suggests that conflicts related to impaired relationships with the mother or father in early development is one of the impediments that may interfere with this normal process.

Frederick, who entered analysis because of extremely low self-esteem, illustrates the effects of such an impaired relationship on the formation of his gay identity. He had a severe masochistic character disorder, having suffered narcissistic injuries that affected the manner in which he expressed his sexuality. His sexual experiences were almost exclusively with hustlers who could dominate him. He made nightly forays into dangerous areas of the city, where he would pick up partners indiscriminately, at times jeopardizing his property, physical well-being, and of course his health as well.

His conflicts also affected the difficulty he had in accepting himself as a homosexual man. For example, in his initial interview he spoke of his sexuality as though it were a foreign appendage that he would like to have excised. He was very fearful that his homosexuality would be discovered at work, and he would go out of his way not to associate with other gay men.

During the course of his long analysis it became clear that he perceived his mother as having treated him as a narcissistic extension of herself and that she did not convey to him a sense of his separateness from her. He had an unconscious perception of and strongly identified with her hatred of him, and he had little capacity to feel lovable or to accept any aspects of himself without either compensatory inflation or intense hatred. His sexuality became a focus for aspects of himself that made him feel hated and hateful, and he had no capacity to sustain a sense of himself as a good person in a society that was inimical to and censorious of his sexuality.

Alan, mentioned earlier in this chapter, also had a tendency to enjoy random sexual encounters to the exclusion of a relationship. He also had impaired self-esteem that appeared to be associated with his early relationship with his mother. She, too, had conveyed that her unrealized goals and gratifications were to be accomplished through his achievements and that his failures and unhappiness would result in her disappointment and despair. Having little sense of himself as a separate person or of his own goals, Alan was very dependent on peer and social approval for self-esteem regulation, and censorious social attitudes toward his sexuality weighed heavily on him. A binding relationship with an impaired and hostile mother made him rageful and full of self-hatred, eventuating in his profound difficulty in permitting himself pleasurable sexual activity within the context of a gratifying, loving relationship. Like Edward, Alan's sex was tinged with masochism, contributing to the feeling that his sexual orientation was bad and dirty and to his failure to integrate it as part of a positive identity. During their analyses the self-image of both men gradually improved as they began to recognize their early feelings of humiliation and rejection. Consequently, the quality of their object relations also improved, and they became better able to have sustained relationships for varying periods of time with people who cared about them. These more nourishing relations in turn enhanced their self-esteem and their image of themselves as gay men.

The process of the development of sexual identity as a homosexual man is, of course, lifelong. As we have seen, the acquisition of the sexual orientation occurs in childhood, as does the beginning of sexual identity formation, with the feeling of being different and the preconscious recognition of same-sex fantasies. Consolidation occurs during late adolescence and early adulthood with the expression of sexuality motivated by the surge of sexual needs. Continuing integration of the sexual identity occurs throughout adulthood by both sexual and social relations with other homosexual men and with varying degrees of involvement in gay social networks.

The process of "coming out" to other gay men usually leads to "homosocialization," by which I refer to the nonsexual contacts with other gay men either within or outside of an established gay community. There are homosexual men with a relatively healthy, comfortable acceptance of their homosexual orientation who do not have extensive social gay contacts, for the degree and nature of involvement in the gay community is usually determined by social and vocational needs, by marital status, and by the availability of other gay men (Weinberg & Williams, 1974, p. ll). Furthermore, the support provided by a network of gay friends or by living in a gay community, when this is available, may be unnecessary for those who receive adequate gratification from social and vocational activities within the heterosexual community. It is, however, generally easier for a homosexual man in our society to be integrated into a heterosexual community when he is not coupled and when he has not "come out," and most men find it more comfortable to be in a long-term relationship within the supportive and relatively unprejudiced structure offered by a gay community and gay friends.

The freedom to be homosocial may also be related to one's having less need for support from heterosexually oriented peer and social organizations; therefore, it is often indicative of the healthy acceptance of one's sexual orientation and of the self-assurance that precludes the necessity for continued traditional sources of support. For Alan and Edward, there was a connection between their poor self-esteem, the consequent inability to have a positive image of their sexuality, and a need to avoid contact with other gay men. As their self-esteem improved through the analysis of early conflict, especially around the problematic relations with their mothers, homosocial contacts increased measurably, as did their capacity for having homosexual relations. For others, whose self-esteem was not significantly disturbed by early conflict, there is a capacity for an interest in nonsexual relationships with other gay men. Insofar as availability and other obligations permit, homosocial relations are necessary for the continuing consolidation and integration of identity. The capacity for such relationships is a sign of relatively positive self-regard. Conversely, the inability or unwillingness to have such relationships suggests impaired self-esteem.

Conclusion

It would not be accurate to conclude from what I have written that all homosexual men who engage in random sexual encounters are beset by neurotic difficulties or that only those who have sustained relationships are necessarily "healthy." The selection of multiple partners is best understood as being determined by a number of interactive issues that include social as well as dynamic factors. Furtive, anonymous sexual activity in public restrooms may be carried out by gay men who cannot afford to risk discovery and disclosure and who are well integrated into a heterosexual community (Humphreys, 1972). The expression of defiance at antihomosexual attitudes, the lack of legal and social sanctions of homosexual relationships, the absence of children to bind these relationships, the availability of partners, and the interdictions of our society probably all foster random sexual encounters. There is also evidence that biological factors related to male sexuality play a role in the nature of the homosexual man's sexual activity, for the human male in general is less object directed then the human female, who appears to be less interested in the variation of partners (Kinsey, 1948, p. 589).

By pointing out these social and biological issues I am not minimizing the importance of the intrapsychic factors that motivate the different types of sexual behavior in all human beings. Nor am I underestimating the difficulties some gay men may have in maintaining and sustaining long-term relationships, which may be caused by those same social and biological factors, as well as by unconscious conflict. I do believe, however, that to view the sexual behavior of homosexual men in the consultation room as being unconnected to an external social reality leads to simplistic unifactorial dynamic explanations of such behavior. In the homosexual man, social factors interact with, help to shape, and even modify intrapsychic forces formed in early development.

One can view retrospectively any clinical history, such as Alan's or Frederick's, and say that the determinants of his selection of another man instead of a woman as a love object appear clear. The homosexual object choice could appear to have been determined by his need to establish and experience closeness to a longed for, distant, and demeaned father or because of a frightening closeness to his mother during infancy and early childhood. However, such psychodynamic explanations of possible determinants of homosexual object choice are not satisfactory. First, there is nothing specific or particular to such families that one does not find in many heterosexuals. Second, the basis of all dynamic explanatory efforts is to understand why these men avoid women, while the natural flow of a properly conducted analysis with a gay man who is not encumbered by neurotic anxiety about his sexuality is toward the unfolding of and understanding of conflicts interfering with gratifying relations with other men.

While I have seen gay men such as these with family constellations as described in the psychoanalytic literature, namely, a strong, binding mother and/or a father who is perceived as being weak, I have also seen heterosexual patients with similar family constellations and many gay men who appear to have had "average" expectable parenting, for example, Edward, described before. In my practice I have seen as many different types of homosexual men as heterosexual men, and these include gay men capable of forming lasting, loving relationships, as well as those whose relationships are conflicted. As is true of heterosexuals, there are homosexuals who are sadistic, masochistic, narcissistic, depressed, borderline, or psychotic, that is, who run the spectrum of psychological disturbances. Those men who are gay and have such psychological disturbances dynamically resemble their heterosexual counterparts more closely than they do each other. The manner in which they express their sexuality, sometimes adaptively but sometimes, like heterosexuals, with inhibitions or self-destructive conflict, appears to be determined by the nature of the parenting and other early environmental factors. Questions about the origin of a gay man's sexuality and the nature and origin of his psychopathology, when it exists, must be separated if we are going to understand our gay patients and be of adequate therapeutic assistance to them.

With regard to the origin of the homosexual object choice itself, some have claimed that the genetic model best explains the development of sexual orientation. At present the evidence is not entirely convincing because of methodologic and sampling errors. However, Kallman's studies (1952), in spite of such difficulties, are suggestive of a genetic factor. So are studies by Hoult (1984), and Eckert, Bouchard, Bohlen, and Heston (1986), and Pillard's family studies (Chapter 7 of this volume). It also seems to me that we can say with certainty that human beings have an inherent capacity for flexibility in sexual response. The capacity for flexible sexual response, the major contribution of constitutional factors, a possible variety of early environmental conditions, and whatever social and biological advantages may accrue from being homosexual (see Weinrich, Chapter 9 of this volume) may all be necessary for the establishment of sexual orientation. The understanding of conflict incurred by early familial environment can neither change sexual orientation nor explicate it. Furthermore, our capacity to understand that some early environmental issues contribute to the manner in which a homosexual orientation is expressed should not suggest that such behavior is necessarily maladaptive, since what once originated in conflict may later become adaptive, growth-enhancing behavior.

Finally, the viewpoint presented in this chapter should not be taken as a nihilistic view of analytic or psychotherapeutic work with gay men. The clinician may be helpful in the same manner and for the same spectrum of problems as with heterosexuals. Analysis carried out with appropriate neutrality and with regard and respect for the patient may help to ease the burden that society has imposed on every gay man and may help him resolve conflicts that interfere with the full and gratifying expression of his sexuality.

Notes

1. A more extensive and comprehensive discussion of the ideas presented in this chapter may be found in my book, *Being Homosexual: Gay Men and their Development*, New York: Farrar, Straus and Giroux, 1989.

2. The men I am calling homosexual would in general be rated as 5s and 6s on Kinsey's scale. He emphasized in his determinations sexual "reactions," that is, overt, observable behavior (1948, p. 641). Kinsey's aim was to accumulate as large and objective a body of data on sexual behavior as possible through questionnaires and interviews. My intent is therapeutic, my sample of approximately 40 men is comparatively minuscule, and my method, of course, is to observe the unraveling unconscious and preconscious as well as conscious reported material.

3. My experience has been only with bisexual men who wanted to get married or remain married and who entered treatment because they feared that their homosexuality would be harmful to their marriage. In such men the homosexual component of their bisexuality usually causes a great deal of anxiety.

4. In this chapter I am using "healthy" and "normal" interchangeably. By these terms I am referring to the homosexual man's potential to have a well-integrated personality (Klein, 1960), that is, a personality in which there is reasonable intrapsychic harmony so that he may feel positively about his personal identity as a homosexual and may work and live without significant hindrance from intrapsychic conflict.

5. Extensive longitudinal studies by Green (1979, 1985) and by Zuger (1978, 1984) corroborate earlier studies by Saghir and Robbins (1973), which demonstrate a high incidence of adult homosexuality among children who display effeminate behavior in childhood. These studies suggest that gender identity disorders in childhood are good indicators of the later development of homosexuality, but it is unclear from these studies what proportion of adult homosexuals have gender disorders in adulthood. In my much smaller clinical sample I have found that many of the same characteristics described in these studies of effeminate boys, except for the cross-dressing, are recollected in gay men whom I do not consider to have gender identity disorders, that is, they experience and perceive themselves as men and not women. Nor have I observed any qualitative distinction in the early experiences described by those men who as adults are more conventionally masculine in appearance and those whose behavior and appearance are more androgynous or feminine.

References

Bayer, R. (1981). *Homosexuality and American psychiatry*. New York: Basic Books.

Bergler, E. (1956). *Homosexuality: Disease or way of life?* New York: Hill & Wang.

Bieber, I., Dain, H. J., Dince, P. R., Drellich, M. G., Grand, H. G., Gundlach, R. H., Kremer, M. W., Rifkin, A. H., Wilbur, C. B., & Bieber, T. B. (1962). *Homosexuality: A psychoanalytic study*. New York: Basic Books.

Eckert, E. D., Bouchard, T. J., Bohlen, J., & Heston, L. L. (1986). Homosexuality in monozygotic twins reared apart. *British Journal of Psychiatry*, 148, 421–425.

Freud, S. (1903, October 27). Interview. *Die Zeit* (Vienna), p. 5.

Freud, S. (1905). Three essays on the theory of sexuality. In J. Strachey (Ed. and Trans.) *The Standard Edition of the Complete Psychological Works of Sigmund Freud*, (Hereafter S.E.) (Vol. 7, pp. 125–245). London: Hogarth Press, 1953-1974.

Freud, S. (1922). Some neurotic mechanisms in jealousy, paranoia and homosexuality. In S.E., vol. 18, pp. 223–232.

Freud, S. (1930). Civilization and its discontents. In S.E., Vol. 21, pp. 59–145.

Freud. S. (1920). The psychogenesis of a case of homosexuality in a woman. In S.E., Vol. 18, pp. 145–172.

Freud, S. (1935, 1981). Letter to an American mother. In R. Bayer, *Homosexuality and American psychiatry*, p. 27. New York: Basic Books. (Original letter published 1935)

Friedman, R. C., & Stern, L. O. (1980). Juvenile aggressivity and sissiness in homosexual and heterosexual males. *Journal of the American Academy of Psychoanalysis, 8*, 427–440.

Friedman, R. M. (1986). The psychoanalytic model of male homosexuality: An historical and theoretical critique. *Psychoanalytic Review, 73*, 4.

Green, R. (1979). Childhood cross-gender behavior and subsequent sexual preference. *American Journal of Psychiatry, 36*, 106–108.

Green, R. (1985). Gender identity in childhood and later sexual orientation. *American Journal of Psychiatry, 143*(3), 339- 341.

Hartmann, H. (1960). *Psychoanalysis and Moral Values.* New York: International Universities Press.

Hooker, E. (1957). The adjustment of the male overt homosexual. *Journal of Projective Techniques, 21*, 18–31.

Hoult, T. J. (1984). Human sexuality in biological perspective: Theoretical and methodological considerations. *Journal of Homosexuality, 9*, 137–155.

Humphreys, L. (1972). *Out of the closets: The sociology of homosexual liberation.* Englewood Cliffs, NJ: Prentice-Hall.

Isay, R. A. (1985). On the analytic therapy of homosexual men. *Psychoanalytic Study of the Child, 40*, 235–254.

Isay, R. A. (1986a). Homosexuality in homosexual and heterosexual men: Some distinctions and implications for treatment. In G. Fogel, F. Lane, & R. Liebert (Eds.), *The psychology of men: New psychoanalytic perspectives,* New York: Basic Books.

Isay, R. A. (1986b). The development of sexual identity in homosexual men. *Pyschoanaltyic Study of the Child, 41.*

Isay, R. A. (1989). *Being homosexual: Gay men and their development.* New York: Farrar, Straus, & Giroux.

Kallmann, F. J. (1952). A comparative twin study on the genetic aspects of male homosexuality. *Journal of Nervous and Mental Disease, 115*, 283–298.

Kinsey, A. C., Pomeroy, W. B., & Martin, C. E. (1948). *Sexual behavior in the human male.* Philadelphia: W. B. Saunders.

Kolb, L. E., & Johnson, A. M. (1955). Etiology and therapy of overt homosexuality. *Psychoanalytic Quarterly, 24*, 506–515.

Klein, M. (1960). On mental health. *British Journal Medical Psychology, 33*, 237–247.

Marmor, J. (Ed.) (1965). *Sexual inversion.* New York: Basic Books.

Marmor, J. (Ed.) (1980). *Homosexual behavior: A modern reappraisal.* New York: Basic Books.

Ovesey, L. (1965). Pseudohomosexuality and homosexuality in men. In J. Marmor (Ed.), *Sexual inversion,* (pp. 211–233). New York: Basic Books.

Ovesey, L., & Woods, S. M. (1980). Pseudomosexuality and homosexuality in men: Psychodynamics as a guide to treatment. In J. Marmor (Ed.), *Homosexual behavior: A modern reappraisal,* (pp. 325–341). New York: Basic Books.

Rado, S. (1940). A critical reexamination of the concept of bisexuality. In *Psychoanalysis of behavior: Collected papers,* New York: Grune & Stratton, 1956.

Rado, S. (1949). An adaptational view of sexual behavior. In P. Hoch & J. Zubin (Eds.), *Psychosexual development in health and disease,* (pp. 159–189). New York: Grune & Stratton.

Riess, P. F. (1980) Psychological tests in homosexuality. In J. Marmor (Ed.), *Homosexual behavior: A modern reappraisal,* pp. 296–311, New York: Basic Books.

Saghir, M. & Robbins, E. (1973). *Male and female homosexuality: A comprehensive investigation.* Baltimore, MD: Williams & Wilkins.

Schafer, R. (1983). *The analytic attitude.* New York: Basic Books.

Socarides, C. W. (1968). *The overt homosexual.* New York: Grune & Stratton.

Socarides, C. W. (1978). *Homosexuality.* New York: Aronson.

Stoller, R. (1979). Fathers of transexual children. *Journal of the American Psychoanalytic Association, 27,* 837–866.

Tyson, P. (1982). A developmental line of gender identity, genderrole and choice of love object. *Journal of the American Psychoanalytic Association, 30,* 61–86.

Weinberg, M. S., & Willians, C. J. (1974). *Male homosexuals.* New York: Oxford University Press.

Wiedeman, G. H. (1974). Homosexuality. *Journal of the American Psychoanalytic Association, 22,* 651–696.

Zuger, B. (1978). Effeminate behavior in boys from childhood. *Comprehensive Psychiatry, 19,* 363–369.

Zuger, B. (1984). Early effeminate behavior in boys. *Journal of Nervous and Mental Disease, 172,* 90–96.

VI

RELATIONAL
PERSPECTIVE

18

Intimate Relationships and the Creation of Sexuality

Philip Blumstein and Pepper Schwartz

The study of human sexuality has been dominated by the presumption that male and female behavior is biologically programmed, and much research has concerned itself with understanding what these programs are and to what extent biological predispositions are modified by social forces. Another prominent assumption posits that each individual has a *true* sexual core self that does not change. Some researchers emphasize that this self emerges over time, through a process of socialization, while others stress that desires are genetic and/or hormonal in origin, but both perspectives share a belief in the immutable core disposition.

The combined force of these two research traditions in the study of human sexuality has almost dismissed from serious scholarly discussion what we believe to be the true nature of human sexuality: that sexuality is situational and changeable, modified by day-to-day circumstances throughout the life course. In our perspective there are few absolute differences between male and female sexuality. What differences are observed are primarily the result of the different social organization of women's and men's lives in various cultural contexts. "Essentialist" theories, that is theories that assume immutable selves, ignore data that would disturb the assumption. One startling example of the field's willingness to be misled is the unfortunate interpretation of the ground-breaking Kinsey studies and the misuse of the Kinsey heterosexuality/homosexuality scale (Kinsey, Pomeroy, & Martin, 1948; Kinsey, Pomeroy, Martin, & Gebhard, 1953). We would like to reexamine the scale, using it to direct research away from essentialist reifications and more in the direction we believe

Kinsey himself would have preferred: toward a kinetic model of sexual desire and away from a static and categorical model.

Unfortunately, when the Kinsey group constructed the scale of 0 to 6, they unintentionally endorsed and extended essentialist ways of thinking by establishing a typology allowing for seven kinds of sexual beings instead of only two. After Kinsey, there were such people as "Kinsey 4s" instead of simply heterosexuals and homosexuals. While the seven-point scale does enormously more justice to the range and subtlety of human sexuality, in its common usage it does not do justice to Kinsey's own belief in the changeability and plasticity of sexual behavior. As researchers have inevitably used Kinsey's scale as a shorthand system of sexual identification, they have reified the person as a sexual type. His or her "real" sexuality is discovered and seen as an essence that has been uncovered. It is the final summation of the person's sexual behavior and "psychic reactions."

Such essentialist thinking allows one to ignore concrete behaviors in assigning people to sexual categories. Even the verbal descriptions made by respondents and patients of their *own* behavior and feeling states may be swept aside in an essentialist judgment. As Katz (1975) has written on this general subject, "Persons conceive of essences as inherent qualities which may be manifested, reflected, indicated, or represented by, but do not exist in, conduct . . . Essences exist independent of observable behavior" (p. 1371). Essentialism also allows one to capture the actor with one great biographical sweep, for example: "She is a homosexual" or "He is a bisexual." The Kinsey scale, as it is frequently used to aggregate behavior over a finite length of time or even over a lifetime, encourages the categorization of an actor's biography, for example: "She is a Kinsey 3."

The application of the Kinsey scale is hardly unique in this respect. Essentialism has dominated both lay and professional thinking about sexuality. Sexuality has been perceived as emanating from a core or innate *desire* that directs an individual's sex life. Before Kinsey, this desire had to be either homosexual or heterosexual; after Kinsey, this desire could be ambisexual. But in either case, it originated in constitutional factors or in the person's early experience and was a fixed part of the person. This desire has been seen as so powerful that even though behavior might vary over a lifetime, many psychotherapists and sex researchers have continued to believe in the existence of a basic predisposition reflecting the true nature of each individual's sexuality.

We do not deny that there are men and women who come to a therapist with unacted-upon homosexual desires that they believe reflect their true sexual selves. Nor do we deny that most Americans who call themselves heterosexual or homosexual feel strongly that their sexuality is highly channeled. They feel that they have only *categorical desire*, that is, desire for people of only one specific gender.[1] But the commonly held belief in the generality of this pattern has not been challenged to see if it reflects a truly universal experience. And indeed there is evidence to call that belief into question (e.g., Blumstein & Schwartz, 1976a, 1976b).

It is our position that it is not primarily categorical desire that determines whether people's sex partners are male or female. Fundamental categorical desire may not even exist. Rather, it is culture that creates understandings about how people are sexual and thus determines whether people will be able to have only one sexual focus, to eroticize both sexes, or to experience categorical desire for one sex at one point in their lives and categorical desire for the other sex at another point in their lives (e.g., Herdt, 1981). In our society, because virtually everyone partakes of the dominant essentialist theory of sexuality, large numbers of people experience categorical sexual desire and see it as determining their sexual lives. But it is critical not to confuse this particular cultural pattern with scientific confirmation that there is a core sexual orientation within every human being. In our society there are also people whose fundamental sexual desire seems to be produced within the context of a relationship rather than by an abstract preference for women or men, or whose sense of sexual self never becomes consistently organized. The essentialist understanding of sexuality skirts questions of what experiences and understandings lead to the behaviors that create a sense of self. Essentialism ignores the *process* of the creation of a sense of self.[2]

But it is not only the essentialist nature of the Kinsey scale to which we object. The Kinsey scale, particularly as it is presently used in lax scientific discourse, is limited because it was based on a single cultural model of sexuality. The Kinsey group inadvertently took the dominant model of middle-class male sexuality as a guide for understanding human sexual behavior when other models, also cultural but perhaps ultimately more productive, could have been utilized. In the male model, behavior provides the critical data used to categorize core sexual selves. This is because in the modern Western world, men and their observers have used behavior as the indicator of internal psychic processes. This has been particularly true in the analysis of homosexuality because a homosexual behavior so violates cultural proscriptions that it has been assumed that such behavior must surely demonstrate an irrepressible core sexual self. Thus, once homosexual acts were discussed scientifically, the use of behavior as an indicator of an individual's true sexuality became more important.[3] Oddly enough, however, homosexual acts tend to be given greater weight than any heterosexual acts that the individual might also perform. In most cases, it is assumed that "psychic reaction" is the crucial factor to resolve any empirical oddities. If psychic arousal is more dramatic in homosexual relations, then a homosexual core self is adduced. How cross-situationally consistent such psychic arousal might be, however, is seldom contemplated.

The cross-cultural record amply suggests that the essentialist model of human sexuality has far from universal fit. Indeed one does not need a cross-cultural perspective; if one looks at the relatively ignored facts of modern Western female sexuality, the essentialist model's inadequacies become clear. As we have observed elsewhere (Blumstein & Schwartz, 1976a, 1977), female sexuality in our culture does not justify an essentialist position. Women are less likely than men to view their sexual acts as a revelation of their "true sexual self," and female sexual choice seems to be based as much on situational constraints as on categorical desire. Desire seems to be aroused frequently by emotional intimacy rather than by abstract erotic taste.

Our sociological vision of sexuality is far different from the essentialist approach of many other sex researchers. Our thesis is simply that desire is created by its cultural context. Sexuality emerges from the circumstances and meanings available to individuals; it is a product of socialization, opportunity, and interpretation. For example, male sexuality in our cultural view is shaped by the scripts boys are offered almost from birth, by the cultural lessons they learn throughout the life course, among them, the belief in a sometimes overpowering male sex drive and the belief that men have immutable sexual needs that are manifested over and above individual attempts at repression.

Our approach leads to a different question than the one posed by essentialists. As sociologists, we do not wish to proliferate sexual categories but rather ask, "What circumstances create the possibility for sexual behavior—either homosexual or heterosexual?" This question cannot be approached fruitfully when one is relying on the seven-point Kinsey scale since concrete behaviors are lost in the data aggregation process used in applying the scale to people's lives.

Within a specific cultural setting there are many factors that facilitate or deter sexual behavior, both homosexual and heterosexual. The two key factors, which we will concentrate on in this chapter, are (1) the *gender roles* culturally available and (2) the *societal organization of opportunities*.

Biological sex is constrained and directed by the roles each society offers men and women. Expectations of role performance organize male and female sexuality. Thus, in order to understand human sexual behavior and the meaning of that behavior to people, it is crucial to know what members of each sex have learned is appropriate to feel and to do and what sanctions exist for inadequate or noncompliant role performance.

While there is still much to be understood about the subtle relationship between sexuality and gender, we are substantially more ignorant about the second factor, the social organization of opportunity. By this we mean how society does or does not offer circumstances that permit certain behaviors to occur. These circumstances may be as concrete as a woman's being unable to have heterosexual experience within an institution of chaperonage or as subtle as her being unable to have sexual relations outside of her marriage because she is a suburban housewife who, in the course of her typical day, never finds herself in the company of men. Even a wife who is propositioned may not have a real opportunity if the cost of giving in to temptation is ostracism from her community, expulsion from her marriage, and a future of being unacceptable to any other loving partner. Similarly, a boy who goes to all-male schools will have different sexual opportunities than one who is never in an all-male adolescent peer group, and a salesman who travels constantly is more likely to have extramarital temptations than a man who never leaves his small home-town.

Opportunity is also shaped in a less objective fashion by the meanings the culture makes available. A wife may not be able to be sexually respon-sive even if she is alone with a man other than her husband if she has learned that a healthy woman has little sexual appetite and that what appetite she has can only be aroused in the context of her role as wife and companion to her husband. A man may have difficulty experiencing ho-mosexual desire in himself if he has been taught that such attractions do not exist in typical heterosexually active men.

From these examples it should be clear that we are not describing forces that affect individuals idiosyncratically, but rather we are focusing on the way society organizes social life. This does not mean that everyone acts according to a single cultural mandate. Sometimes social directives are in flux or they are actually in conflict with one another and leave room for individual choice. For example, when women in large numbers were first allowed college education, there was no deliberate social plan to make them men's equals or for them to have sexual appetites resembling men's. The same can be said of the development of safe and effective contracep-tive technologies. The latent consequence of men and women having more similar lives, however, has been that attitudes and norms that had functioned well to maintain very different sex lives for women and men were no longer able to sustain their potency and legitimacy.

We would argue that understanding the dynamics of gender roles and social opportunities is a more fruitful approach to the question of why sexual behavior occurs and under what circumstances sexual identities are adopted than is the essentialist paradigm. We do not in this chapter perform the larger sociological task of developing a theory of how social opportunities arise in sexual life. Rather, we proceed from the idea that social opportunities exist and examine one type of opportunity structure in depth in order to show the utility of the concept. The source of opportu-nities we focus on here is intimate relationships, which we see as pro-foundly important in determining what behaviors will take place.

As an immediate caveat we must say that in our culture, this is truer for women than for men. If Kinsey had used female sexuality as a model, his scale might have been conceptualized not so much in terms of accumu-lated acts and psychic preoccupations but rather in terms of intensity and frequency of love relationships, some of which might have only incidental overt erotic components.

Women have been so effectively socialized to link love and attachment, love and sex, that eroticization is more often a consequence of emotional attraction than the trigger for the involvement. In cases where eroticization comes first, it is unlikely to continue without a relationship context; if the attraction is powerful, a relationship may have to be invented in order to sustain and justify continuing the liaison. Whether this attraction process is the result of women's relatively low position in the social structure (de Beauvoir, 1953), or whether it is a response to cultural themes governing female sexuality (Laws & Schwartz, 1977), or whether women's erotic cues are biologically different from men's (Symons, 1979; van den Berghe, 1979) is a large question, and we are unable to put it to rest in this chapter. We can, however, show that in our culture women's sexuality is organized by other than physical cues. For modern Western women, the recognition of love or admiration or the pleasure in companionship or deep friendship most often leads to erotic attraction and response. While women are not incapable of seeking sex for its own sake, this pattern of sexual behavior is relatively rare among them (Blumstein & Schwartz, 1983). Our research indicates that it is overwhelmingly more common for the relationship (or the desire for such a relationship) to establish itself first.

This pattern is less common among men in our culture. While homosexual and heterosexual erotic feelings can develop in an intimate relationship, it is much more common for a man to have sexual attractions (as early as adolescence) to a number of specific persons (some or all of whom may be total strangers), or to a generalized other, or to fantasized persons. If an opportunity exists and any personal or cultural interdictions can be overcome, he may seek to realize his erotic preferences in one or many concrete sexual contacts. An intimate or committed relationship is not necessary for excitation and in some cases may even be counterproductive to sexual arousal. Nonetheless, most men do form intimate relationships, and this leads us to ask, "What is the relevance of such relationships for their subsequent sexual behavior and self-identification?"

This is a complex question since in some cases the relationship, for example, marriage to a woman, seems to organize the man's sexual behavior and identity, while in other cases, such as the self-defined homosexual man who is married to a woman, it is less central. The husband who has sexual experiences with other men may feel torn, dishonest and fearful of exposure, but frequently he also feels a need to have a family and an approved social identity (Ross, 1971; Ross, 1983). He also finds the attraction of conventionality more compelling than the opportunity to have a less compromised homosexual sex life. A different but related example is a man with a previously exclusively homosexual life who decides that heterosexual marriage is important to him and that his homosexuality is too costly. We interviewed such a man, who decided to learn how, in his words, to "be heterosexual" in order to facilitate having children and, as he saw it, stability and respectability. While we cannot say that 20 years after this decision he would experience no residual homosexual desire, we can certainly claim that his attachment to a heterosexual relationship changed his behavior and, we believe, his self-identification.

How it is possible for men such as these to organize their lives in these ways is a question that needs and deserves further research. There is, however, some relevant information in the anthropological and historical records on the interaction of appetites, intimate relationships, and sexual self-identity. It is far from culturally universal to expect intimate relationships to be the major or sole outlet for the expression of sexual feelings or appetites. The modern Western desire for sexual, emotional, and life-style coherence is probably a rare accommodation. In the ancient world, for example, a gentleman was expected to marry and father children regardless of his attraction to males, and even in modern times, there are numerous examples of homosexual behavior occurring in the private lives of married men (e.g., Humphreys, 1970; Ross, 1971; Ross, 1983). This homosexual behavior has not exempted men from performing the male role of their time.

An interesting question is whether the separation of family and sexuality has been possible because of innate sexual flexibility or because of male socialization to be able to separate sexual, loving, and obligation impulses so that sex can be accomplished within whatever format is necessary. Or has this ability led to the existence of dual lives so that the appetite could be fulfilled without threatening home and family? Thus homosexual behavior could occur without homosexual self-identification, thereby inhibiting the development of an exclusively homosexual life-style.

An important question is why is there now such great emphasis on shaping one's life on the basis of one's intimate relationships. Perhaps the same social forces that helped create a bond between love and family and sex for women are starting to apply to men as well. Moreover, recent cultural themes of individual fulfillment and personal growth encourage and shape sexuality by giving people the impression that any disjunction between parts of the self is unhealthy and ultimately an inappropriate way to live. In addition, the ability to identify oneself as a homosexual man or lesbian and be viewed as gay by friends and acquaintances probably diminishes ability to identify with or practice heterosexual desire. The predominance of the essentialist paradigm leads men and women to create a coherent package of behavior, identity, and community, and they are thus more motivated to form same-sex relationships.

While sex role differences are a critical factor in understanding the impact of intimate relationships on sexuality, it is also important to consider the type of relationship. Sexuality is different in marriage as compared to heterosexual cohabitation, and opposite-sex relationships have a different sexual dynamic from same-sex relationships (Blumstein & Schwartz, 1983). An individual's sense of self is in part created by the relationship she or he is in, and most individuals find a transition that might occur—that is, from cohabitation to marriage or from an opposite-sex to a same-sex partner—has an enormous impact on their identity. For example, a man whom we interviewed had married his childhood sweetheart and had what he considered a happy, fulfilling, and monogamous marital sex life until unexpectedly his wife died. This man subsequently, in his words, "became in touch with" early homoerotic feelings and entered into a relationship with a man. He describes himself as having been "obsessed" with his new partner but also feels that he had been equally taken with his wife. While this man could be labeled as a Kinsey 3, or for that matter as a Kinsey 0 who changed to a Kinsey 6, we argue that it would be more fruitful to look at the circumstances that shaped his sexuality, courtship, marriage, and homosexual relationship. One might also want to know why this man, unlike most men in his society, was sexually galvanized by a tender relationship rather than by independent erotic desire.

Another example is the case of a woman, unhappily married for 23 years but feeling a profound absence of a real "soul mate." She met a woman at her son's college graduation ceremony, and over a long period of time, the two women gradually fell in love and left their husbands. Not only did the respondent's sense of self change but so did her sexual habits and desires. Again, instead of trying to determine who the "real person" is, we think it more productive to discover how changing relationships produced some new forms of behavior.

All of this would be theoretically trivial if we were only talking about individual histories. What makes these stories more compelling to a social scientist is that they are reflections of twentieth-century Western opportunities. The manner in which the intimate relationships are conducted is a cultural and historical phenomenon, which when studied in the aggregate can show us how sexuality is created.

The organization of opportunity in modern life is formed by the instability of marriage, a high remarriage rate, the ability to survive as an independent unmarried person, and the possibility of meeting eligible sex partners of either sex in institutions that have developed expressly for the purpose of bringing people together. The scenarios described in this chapter are uniquely twentieth-century stories and would not have been possible, for example, in nineteenth-century America. There would have been few opportunities for divorce, little ability to live a single or private life, and no conceptualization of the importance of sexual fulfillment or entry into a gay life-style. In fact "life-style" is a uniquely modern concept. Life-style incorporates the notion of sexual choice, and choice has simply not existed for most people in most historical periods. Furthermore, how people behaved within marriage or with a same-sex partner would have been entirely different from the way they would act today. A same-sex relationship in the nineteenth century would probably not be perceived as an appropriate public lifetime commitment.[4]

We are not historians and cannot do justice to the meanings and constructions of everyday sexuality in periods other than our own. We have, however, gathered data in the 1970s and 1980s that show how sexuality is shaped by the relationship scripts available. Our observations are based on two pieces of research: (1) the study of the antecedents of sexual identity and bisexuality, based on a sample of 150 interviews (Blumstein & Schwartz, 1976a, 1976b, 1977), and (2) the study of same-sex and opposite-sex couples, involving questionnaire, interview, and observational data, the overall sample representing approximately 1,000 male homosexual couples, 800 lesbian couples, 3,600 heterosexual marriages, and 650 heterosexual cohabitation relationships (Blumstein & Schwartz, 1983).

Two areas of couples' sexual lives—frequency of sexual activity and monogamy—are presented to illustrate the contention that intimate relationships shape sexuality.

Sexual Frequency

In all four groups of couples in our research, sexual frequency declines with the duration of the relationship (see Table 18.1). From this we infer that there is some habituation effect in all kinds of couples that serves to reduce sexual appetite.[5] Within heterosexual couples, this pattern varies by the simple fact of whether or not the pair is legally married. People who live together without marriage are surely different from those who marry, and such differences may in some measure account for the differences in sexual frequency. But they probably do not account entirely for the differences. Rather, we suggest, it is the differences between marital and nonmarital heterosexual relationships themselves that create different opportunities and different motivations for sexual expression.

When we look at the three groups in our study that include women, we notice that those in relationships with men (both married and unmarried) have a greater sexual frequency than those in relationships with other women. We also note that the sexual frequencies in male homosexual relationships come closer to the heterosexual frequencies. The probable

Table 18.1
Percentage of Couples Reporting Sex Three Times a Week or More

Years Living Together	Married Couples	Cohabiting Couples	Male Couples	Female Couples
2 or less	45% (344)	61% (349)	67% (309)	33% (357)
2–10	27% (1505)	38% (288)	32% (472)	7% (350)
10 or more	18% (1754)		11% (169)	1% (61)

Note: Numbers in parentheses are the numbers of couples on which the percentages are based. Very few of the cohabitors were together more than 10 years.

reason for these differences in sexual profiles is that men in our culture are allowed and encouraged to desire and demand more sex. They have fewer costs for experiencing or acting on sexual desires (i.e., no reduced marketability, no fear of becoming pregnant), and therefore they establish a fairly high sexual frequency in both heterosexual and homosexual relationships. We do not think women in heterosexual relationships have essentially different sexual appetites from women in lesbian relationships, since both groups of women have had similar sexual socialization and have learned similar inhibitions. If the heterosexual women in our study were suddenly put into a same-sex relationship, their sexual frequency would probably resemble lesbians' sexual frequency. The reduction in sexual frequency would occur because the norms of lesbian relationships are different from heterosexual relationships and because two women bring different cultural scripts to a sexual relationship than a man and a woman.[6]

In our study, men more often than women initiated opposite-sex relationships.[7] Men are assigned this role, and women in our society are taught to be receptive rather than aggressive in sexual matters.[8] It makes sense, then, that in lesbian couples, where both partners have experienced female sexual socialization, there would be a mutual reluctance to take the sexual lead. Such inheritance of social conditioning might contribute to lesbians having an overall lower initiation rate than other couples and hence a lower rate of sexual activity.

This reluctance to initiate, however, does not simply stem from the internalization of sexual prohibitions directed at women. Additionally, themes in some lesbian subcultures stigmatize sexual aggressiveness as "power plays" and male-type sexuality and place a lower premium on genital sexuality, with a corresponding emphasis on other forms of physical intimacy. Moreover, higher standards of relationship satisfaction are demanded in order to legitimate sexual intimacy. Relationship dynamics rather than essential core sexuality orient the individual's sexual frequency and sexual pattern.

The internal dynamics of the relationship can affect sexual experience in subtle ways. For example, among all four groups of couples in our study, the greater power one partner has, the more likely he or she is to refuse a sexual overture (Blumstein & Schwartz, 1983, pp. 219–221). And among the women in heterosexual couples, the more power they have, the less likely the couple's intercourse is to be restricted to the male-prone/female-supine position (Blumstein & Schwartz, 1983, pp. 229–230).

On the basis of these findings and with every indication that there will be greater equality between the sexes in the future, one might hypothesize that the sexual patterns of heterosexual couples will change in response to a more liberated female sexuality. In some couples frequency may increase and in others it may decrease, but in either event these changes will be responses to the structure of the relationship between the partners, not to some inherent capacity of women.

Monogamy

The rules of monogamous conduct provide insight into how male sexuality is affected by intimate relationships. With the exception of the male homosexual couples in our study, the majority of each group of couples feels that the rules of monogamous conduct are a cornerstone of the relationship and should not be broken.[9] Homosexual men, while presently intimidated by the risk of contracting AIDS, nonetheless have a long history of separating sexual desire from intimacy and love, and have evolved a norm of having relationships that allow either occasional or a great deal of sex with persons other than one's partner.

Heterosexual men, both married and cohabiting, have frequently mentioned in our interviews that they would like greater permission for "recreational" sex in their relationship, but the data show that they tend not to pursue it (see Table 18.2). If these men were in a same-sex relationship, they would have a higher rate of nonmonogamy because the rules of acceptability would be altered.[10] Thus an element of their sexuality is constructed by their female partner's wishes and by the norms that are shaped by the institution of marriage. Compliance to the norm is, of course, not perfect: many husbands do have extramarital sex, and sex outside their relationship is even more common among male cohabitors. The latter face less stringent guidelines within their relationship and are merely asked to comply with their partner's wishes rather than with the directives of marital vows. Looking at the difference between married men's and cohabiting men's extrarelationship sex tells us how much the norms of marriage organize sexuality.

This cursory look at sexual expression in intimate relationships is not intended as more than an illustration of the analytic mileage to be gained by conceptualizing sex within the context of social circumstances. Even by

Table 18.2
Percentage of Respondents Reporting at Least One Instance of Nonmonogamy in the Previous Year (couples living together between two and ten years)

Husbands	11%	(1510)
Wives	9%	(1510)
Male cohabitors	25%	(288)
Female cohabitors	22%	(288)
Homosexual males	79%	(943)
Lesbians	19%	(706)

Note: Numbers in parentheses are the numbers of respondents on which the percentages are based.

looking at relatively crude survey data we can see that sexual behavior is created by relationship expectations and traditions rather than by sexual essences. If we were to look more microscopically within relationships, we could see the subtle ways in which intimate interaction affects participants. We could see how friends, neighborhoods, community, law, and other constraints, affect sexual conduct. If research on sexuality were to proceed in this direction, if more attention were paid to opportunity structures—of which intimate relationships are but one—we would uncover the social construction of sexuality.

In sum, we look forward to research in which situational variables and cultural meanings are seen as the foundation of sexuality. But new research needs to avoid androcentrism so that opportunity structures are not chosen because of their relevance only to men's lives. A useful approach will take into account individual biography without producing a static and individualistic explanation of sexuality. Sexuality is best comprehended by noting and understanding the *processes* that encourage the occurrence of acts and the reason for their discontinuance. We should focus on the act, behaving not as accountants tabulating frequencies but as behavioral scientists looking at the meaning of the act for the actors. If we continue as we have in the past, focusing on the individual rather than on the social context that creates his or her behavior, we may end up with interesting biography but relatively little ability for further prediction or theory construction. We then run the risk of thinking we understand something merely because we have given it a number on a scale.

Acknowledgment

The authors would like to thank Mary Rogers Gillmore, Judith A. Howard, and Barbara Risman for their helpful comments on an earlier draft of this chapter.

NOTES

1. We would also argue that for most members of contemporary Western society, because of the hegemony of sexual essentialism, once an individual develops a sexual identity, it funnels much of his or her social experience into erotic and nonerotic circumstances that continually reinforce a subjective sense of categorical desire.

2. On the social construction of sexuality, see, among others, Gagnon and Simon (1973), McIntosh (1968), Plummer (1975), and Weinberg (1978, 1983).

3. The Kinsey scale was originally aimed at both behavior and "psychic reactions." The inclusion of the latter construct implicitly acknowledged ways in which purely behavioral tabulations could mislead. However, the conceptual and measurement problems associated with "psychic reactions" have remained largely unresolved.

4. It is important to note that homosexual behavior leads to the existence of gay male and lesbian couple relationships only under extremely rare historical and cultural circumstances. This means that most homosexuality occurs in very different contexts than much (we do not know how much) heterosexuality. This fact, as

obvious as it is, has important implications. Most sensible researchers would be wary of equating heterosexual intercourse between two strangers (e.g, a man with a female prostitute) with that in a 25-year marriage. Neither situation reflects an "essence of heterosexuality." Researchers have been less sensitive in the case of homosexual behavior, as though the slogan were "Sodomy is sodomy is sodomy . . . " It is critical to see human sexual behavior as context embedded rather than as a simple expression of the underlying sexuality of the individual.

5. Two other interpretations of these data come immediately to mind. First is the argument that physical aging, which is correlated with relationship duration, is the real causal factor. Multivariate statistical analyses allowed an evaluation of the aging effects net of duration and the duration effects net of aging. On the basis of these analyses, we concluded that both physical aging and habituation independently reduce sexual frequency. The other interpretation to consider is that couples with relatively low sexual frequency have greater likelihood of longevity. While we have no direct empirical test of this causal hypothesis, it seems implausible in light of substantial positive correlations between sexual frequency and sexual happiness and substantial negative correlations between sexual happiness and relationship durability.

6. Another way of looking at these data is to imagine a woman living in a heterosexual relationship for 10 years followed by a homosexual relationship of the same duration. In the typical case, the total number of sexual acts in the heterosexual relationship would be much greater than the total number of acts within the lesbian relationship. Ought we to label such a woman a Kinsey 3 because she was in two 10-year relationships? Or would she be a Kinsey 1 because her sexual activity was more frequent in the heterosexual union? Or would we label her a Kinsey 5 or 6 because of her most recent sexual life, especially if asserted that this relationship was permanent? These data suggest caution in the use of a scale that does not take into account the context and changing meaning of people's emotional and sexual lives.

7. Fifty-one percent of husbands say they initiate sex more than their wives as compared to 16% who say the reverse pattern holds true and the remainder who say initiation is equal ($N = 3,612$). While the wives are not in perfect agreement with their husbands, they are very close (48 percent and 12 percent, $N = 3,616$). Thirty-nine percent of male cohabitors say they initiate more, and 19% say their female partner initiates more ($N = 646$). The female percentages are 39% and 15% ($N = 648$).

8. Sociobiologists have argued that this difference is a reflection of the different reproductive strategies of men and women. Indeed Symons (1979) has applied this argument to the sexual behavior of lesbians. His discussion, however, does not adequately deal with the influence of cultural learning.

9. We asked respondents how important they felt it is that they themselves be monogamous. The percentages saying it is important are husbands, 75% ($N = 3,635$); wives, 84% ($N = 3,640$); male cohabitors, 62% ($N = 650$); female cohabitors, 70% ($N = 650$); lesbians, 71% ($N = 1,559$); and male homosexuals, 36% ($N = 1,924$).

10. It should be noted that the percentages in Table 18.2 are based on data gathered just before the AIDS crisis began to receive widespread attention in the gay community.

References

Blumstein, P., & Schwartz, P. (1976a). Bisexuality in women. *Archives of Sexual Behavior*, 5, 171–181.

Blumstein, P., & Schwartz, P. (1976b). Bisexuality in men. *Urban Life, 5*, 339–358.

Blumstein, P., & Schwartz, P. (1977). Bisexuality: Some social psychological issues. *Journal of Social Issues, 33*(2), 30–45.

Blumstein, P., & Schwartz, P. (1983). *American couples: Money, work, and sex.* New York: William Morrow.

de Beauvoir, S. (1953). *The second sex.* New York: Knopf.

Gagnon, J. H., & Simon, W. (1973). *Sexual conduct: The social sources of human sexuality.* Chicago: Aldine.

Herdt, G. H. (1981). *Guardians of the flutes: Idioms of masculinity.* New York: McGraw-Hill.

Humphreys, L. (1970). *Tearoom trade: Impersonal sex in public places.* Chicago: Aldine.

Katz, J. (1975). Essences as moral identities: Verifiability and responsibility in imputations of deviance and charisma. *American Journal of Sociology, 80,* 1369–1390.

Kinsey, A. C., Pomeroy, W. B., & Martin, C. E. (1948). *Sexual behavior in the human male.* Philadelphia: W. B. Saunders.

Kinsey, A. C., Pomeroy, W. B., Martin, C. E., & Gebhard, P. H. (1953). *Sexual behavior in the human female.* Philadelphia: W. B. Saunders.

Laws, J. L., & Schwartz, P. (1977). *Sexual scripts: The social construction of female sexuality.* Hinsdale, IL: Dryden Press.

McIntosh, M. (1968). The homosexual role. *Social Problems, 16,* 182–192.

Plummer, K. (1975). *Sexual stigma: An interactionist account.* London: Routledge & Kegan Paul.

Ross, H. L. (1971). Modes and adjustments of married homosexuals. *Social Problems, 18,* 385–393.

Ross, M. W. (1983). *The married homosexual man.* London: Routledge & Kegan Paul.

Symons, D. (1979). *The evolution of human sexuality.* New York: Oxford University Press.

van den Berghe, P. L. (1979). *Human family systems: An evolutionary view.* New York: Elsevier.

Weinberg, T. S. (1978). On "doing" and "being" gay: Sexual behavior and homosexual male self-identity. *Journal of Homosexuality, 4,* 143–156.

Weinberg, T. S. (1983). *Gay men, gay selves: The social construction of homosexual identities.* New York: Irvington.

19

A Relationship Perspective
on Homosexuality

Letitia Anne Peplau and Susan D. Cochran

Research on the interpersonal relationships of lesbians and gay men represents a relatively new direction in the study of homosexuality. Only during the past decade have studies of close homosexual relationships emerged as a recognizable scientific perspective on homosexuality (see reviews by Blumstein & Schwartz, 1983; Harry, 1983; Larson, 1982; McWhirter & Mattison, 1984; Peplau, 1982; Peplau & Amaro, 1982; Peplau & Gordon, 1983). In this chapter, we examine the close relationships of gay men and lesbians. We begin by outlining important issues raised by a relationship perspective on homosexual experiences. We then discuss the goals of relationship research. We conclude with a review of recent empirical findings about homosexual couples in the United States.

Three Perspectives on Homosexuality

Human experience can be studied from many perspectives. To understand a relationship approach, it is useful to contrast it with two more established perspectives on homosexuality—approaches that focus on the individual and on the society or culture.

Most research on homosexuality has taken the *individual* as the focus of analysis. Kinsey's pioneering work investigated the sexual behaviors of the individual and used biographical information to locate the person on a continuum from exclusive homosexuality to exclusive heterosexuality. Other individualistic approaches include studies of the personality characteristics, psychological well-being, and life histories of gay men and lesbians (e.g., Morin, 1976). More recent work exploring individual homosexual "identity" (see Cass, Chapter 14 of this volume; De Cecco & Shively, 1984; Shively, Jones, & De Cecco, 1984) also represents a person-centered analysis. These lines of inquiry have in common their focus on describing and/or explaining the behavior and subjective experiences of individuals. What individual approaches often neglect, however, is the extent to which homosexuality also involves interpersonal experiences and behaviors occurring between two people of the same sex.

Sociocultural analyses, typically undertaken by anthropologists, historians, and sociologists, focus on the societal patterning of homosexuality. Sociocultural researchers seek to describe and explain societal reactions to homosexuality, cultural and subcultural variations in homosexuality, social rules and institutions that regulate homosexuality, and so on. For example, Boswell's (1980) historical analysis, tracing social attitudes toward homosexuality from the beginning of the Christian era to the fourteenth century, showed that there have been periods of relative tolerance toward homosexuals, and questioned the role of Christianity in shaping intolerance toward homosexuality. Herdt's (1981, 1987) ethnography of the Sambia provided a detailed description of the nature and social meaning of ritualized male homosexuality among a tribe in New Guinea. Closer to home, Warren's (1974) early sociological account of the "gay world" described such features of the gay community as gay bars, styles of socializing, gay vocabularies and ideology, and strategies for maintaining secrecy. Wolf's (1980) work described the development of a lesbian feminist community in San Francisco in the mid-1970s. What these investigations have in common is their concern with describing and explaining social institutions and public attitudes concerning homosexuality.

In contrast, a *relationship* perspective takes as the central phenomenon of interest the sexual and romantic relationships that occur between same-sex partners. As De Cecco and Shively (1984) noted, a relationship perspective shifts the focus of inquiry "from isolated individuals to their mutual associations" (p. 1). A relationship perspective seeks to describe the characteristics of homosexual pairings, addressing such issues as the extent of commitment in gay relationships, the balance of power between partners, and the nature of sexual expression in long-term couples. A relationship perspective also explores the goals and values that individuals have about relationships and their subjective experiences in relationships. A further goal of relationship research is to analyze the causes of variations among homosexual couples and to understand the factors that lead relationships to change over time.

Conceptual Issues in Studying Homosexual Relationships

A first question for those interested in gay and lesbian relationships is seemingly obvious: "What is a homosexual relationship?" One answer to the question is provided by the specific criteria or operational definitions that empirical researchers use when enlisting the participation of members of homosexual couples. In practice, researchers have usually studied romantic/sexual relationships of some duration between partners who describe themselves as gay, lesbian, or homosexual. For example, in their study of gay male couples, McWhirter and Mattison (1984) included as participants only male couples who had lived together in the same house for at least a year and who considered themselves to be a "couple." In a study of lesbian relationships, Mays (1986) identified eligible participants by asking women to indicate if they were currently in a "serious, committed romantic/sexual relationship with a woman." In a comparative study of lesbian, gay male, and heterosexual relationships, Duffy and Rusbult (1986) used a broader criterion that permitted participants to describe any relationship, past or present, of any duration and any level of seriousness. These examples make it clear that current research encompasses a range of relationships, with some researchers using considerably more restrictive operational definitions of homosexual relationships than others.

Little attention has been given to the more difficult *conceptual issues* involved in defining a homosexual relationship. In an insightful article titled "The Fallacy of Misplaced Precision," Koertge (1984) used examples from the history of science to argue that current research on homosexuality can benefit from the use of "cluster concepts" and "fuzzy sets." Koertge argued convincingly that efforts to impose single, rigidly precise definitions in work on homosexuality are premature. We agree, and think it useful to consider some of the difficult issues involved in conceptualizing the meaning of a "homosexual relationship"—namely, what we mean by "relationship" and when we will consider a relationship to be "homosexual."

What Is a Relationship?

We believe that it is essential to conceptualize homosexual relationships without using heterosexuality as a model or standard. Assumptions about relationships based on the values and experiences of heterosexuals may not necessarily apply to gay and lesbian couples. The extent to which actual gay and lesbian relationships resemble heterosexual marriages is an open question—and should not be an implicit assumption guiding research hypotheses and practices. Instead, we argue for a broader concept of relationships. For these purposes, a useful starting point is provided in the book *Close Relationships* by Kelley et al. (1983).

Kelley et al. presented a framework for understanding the range of close human relationships and defined close relationships in terms that can be applied to relations with lovers, friends, family, coworkers, and others. The key feature of any relationship is that two people are interdependent, that each partner influences the other. Relationships can range from fleeting encounters between strangers to enduring relationships between partners whose lives are deeply intertwined. Of central interest are *close relationships*, those that are both relatively enduring and important to the participants. In technical terms, Kelley et al. defined close relationships as involving four core ingredients.

1. The partners interact or otherwise affect each other *frequently*. In most cases, people in close relationships see each other often. But when partners are separated, their mutual influence may continue because they think about each other, take actions on behalf of the other, make plans for future joint activities, and so on.

2. The influence that partners have on each other is *strong* and intense. This could mean that partners are able to create strong positive or negative feelings in each other, that they are highly dependent on the relationship to satisfy important psychological or material needs, that they are able to change each other's thoughts and behaviors in important ways, and so on.

3. The influence that partners have on each other spans a range of *diverse* activities, domains, or topics. In a close romantic relationship, for example, partners may talk about many issues, spend time in various leisure pursuits, exchange advice and presents, communicate both verbally and physically, share stories about the past and make plans for the future, create a circle of mutual friends, or begin a joint household.

4. Close relationships are characterized by relatively long *duration*.

In sum, close relationships are influential associations in which partners have a great deal of impact on each other.

This definition identifies the core features common to all close relationships. The definition is deliberately phrased in very general terms that can encompass a broad range of different types of pairings. Many other possible features of relationships—whether the partners are male or female, whether the partners love each other or feel committed, whether the relationship involves sexual behavior, whether the partners share power equally, whether the influence that partners have on each other is "good" or "bad," whether the relationship is formally recognized and approved by society, and so forth—are seen as dimensions along which close relationships can meaningfully vary. Indeed, the description of variation and diversity among close relationships is an important research goal.

When Is a Relationship Homosexual?

More difficult than defining a relationship is specifying when a relationship is "homosexual." Of all close same-sex relationships between friends, relatives, coworkers, acquaintances, or others, which shall be considered homosexual relationships? Social scientists would probably agree on the *prototype* or most typical description of a close homosexual relationship in our society, namely, a couple in which same-sex partners build a life together that includes both love and sex. But what of other cases—two women who live together as loving partners but do not have sex with each other? College roommates who have a lengthy sexual affair but insist that they are "not gay" and just love this one special partner? A long-term couple who continue to live together, even after sexual interest and passionate love have disappeared? Examples such as these raise dilemmas about conceptualizing homosexual relationships. Several rather different approaches have been taken to defining the core features of a close *homosexual* relationship.

Sex and Love

One approach to defining homosexual relationships focuses on specific characteristics of same-sex relationships, most commonly sexuality and love. In this view, a close same-sex relationship is homosexual if, or only if, the partners have sex and/or experience love.

One view has been that *sexuality* is crucial to defining homosexual relationships. For example, De Cecco and Shively (1984) argued for the value of shifting discourse on homosexuality from "sexual identity" to "sexual relationships" (p. 14). Bullough (1984) echoed this point, encouraging "the attempt to shift from equating homosexuality with sexual identity" to "emphasizing sexual behavior" (pp. 3, 5). Certainly in the public mind, it is the fact of sex occurring between same-sex partners that most readily distinguishes homosexuality from heterosexuality. Participants in same-sex relationships may themselves use sexual interest or behavior as evidence of whether their relationship is a homosexual one rather than a platonic friendship. For example, when we (Peplau, Cochran, & Mays, 1986) asked a large sample of black lesbians whether or not they were in a "serious, committed" lesbian relationship, all those who responded yes indicated that they had had sex with their partner. This is not necessarily true for heterosexuals, who may consider themselves to be dating or engaged without having sex. Lacking the social institutions that define and structure heterosexual courtship and marriage in America, homosexuals may emphasize the occurrence of sexual behavior as a key to labeling their own same-sex relationships.

A focus on sexuality as the distinguishing feature of homosexual relationships entails several difficulties, however. One is the problem of defining sexuality and specifying whether sexuality must involve explicitly genital acts—or can be construed more broadly to include other forms of physical affection and/or "latent" sexuality. De Cecco and Shively (1984) acknowledged this difficulty when they wrote that "still unanswered is the question of what distinguishes a relationship that is *sexual* from one that is not sexual" (p. 2).

Further, the use of sex as a definitional criterion appears, by omission, to ignore other facets of a relationship such as love, communication, commitment, and shared activities that may be of equal or greater importance, either to the partners or to researchers. The sexual interaction criterion also seems to exclude from consideration partners whose love and commitment are not expressed in sexual ways, and leaves uncertain the status of couples whose relationship may once have been sexual but subsequently continues without sexual activity. In a discussion of contemporary lesbians, Miller and Fowlkes (1980) flatly discounted the usefulness of sex as a defining criterion:

> For Masters and Johnson, as for Kinsey, the sex act is the problem. It is a problem for the remainder of contemporary research on lesbianism as well, but here it is a problem because it is not a problem. In recent scholarly work [on lesbians], there is widespread agreement that the sex act itself is not a fruitful area for study. (p. 797)

A similar point was made by Faderman (1984) in her discussion of contemporary lesbian feminists:

> Women who have come to lesbianism through radical feminism reject the notion that *lesbian* is a *sexual* identity . . . . [S]exual activity is for them, generally, only one aspect, and perhaps a relatively unimportant aspect, of their commitment to a lesbian life-style. . . . Lesbian-feminists define lesbianism in much more inclusive terms: A lesbian's entire sense of self centers on women. While sexual energies are not discounted, alone they do not create the lesbian-feminist. (pp. 86–87)

It makes good sense to include sexuality as a key feature in the "fuzzy set" that defines the prototype of a homosexual relationship in contemporary America, but it seems unwise to require sexual interaction as a criterion in all cases.

Another key element in defining homosexual relationships concerns the *emotional quality* of a relationship and the experience of love between the partners. For example, in a discussion of women's relationships in the nineteenth century, Faderman (1981) argued that the term *lesbian*

> describes a relationship in which two women's strongest emotions and affections are directed toward each other. Sexual contact may be a part of the relationship to a greater or lesser degree, or it may be entirely absent. By preference the two women spend most of their time together and share most aspects of their lives with each other. . . . [I think that most] female love relationships before the 20th century were probably not genital. (pp. 17-18)

Faderman also provided the interesting observation that many of the "lesbian" cases discussed by Havelock Ellis, Sigmund Freud, and other early sexologists were Victorian women whose same-sex love relationships were nongenital.

The dilemma of whether love or sex or both are requisites for a homosexual relationship has not been resolved. It seems to us that gender sometimes plays a part in how people think about the matter. It appears that observers are more likely to emphasize sexuality in discussing men's relationships and to focus on love in discussing lesbian relationships. This may, in some measure, mirror the way that lesbians and gay men themselves conceptualize and talk about their own relationships. We can also speculate that male and female researchers may differ in the relative importance that they attach to love and sex in their scholarly research on homosexual relationships. We are not sure of the accuracy of these impressions or certain about their possible origins in gender role socialization and stereotypes, but we think the topic warrants further examination.

As relationship researchers, we propose that *neither* sex nor love be taken as a necessary or an exclusive definitional criterion for homosexual relationships. To insist on either would unnecessarily narrow the scope of research on homosexual relationships. Any particular researcher will, of course, need to use specific operational definitions of gay or lesbian relationships. Some may decide, as we ourselves have done (Peplau & Cochran, 1981; Peplau, Cochran, Rook, & Padesky, 1978), to study relationships that participants define as "romantic/sexual." But other criteria, such as living together or being in a "serious/committed" relationship, may be equally reasonable. We think that scientists should view sex and love as common and potentially important elements in cultural prototypes of homosexual relationships but not necessarily as the best or only criteria for researchers to use in defining homosexual relationships scientifically.

In practical terms, we suggest that researchers use general indices of close relationships to identify homosexual couples, such as objective measures of relationship duration or living together, and subjective measures of the partners' perceptions of themselves as being a "couple," or having a serious or important relationship. Measures such as these do not prejudge the motivations of the partners or the character and quality of their relationship. Rather, the proposed measures permit and encourage researchers to investigate naturally occurring variations in love and sexual behavior in homosexual relationships. Further, researchers may be well advised to use multiple indicators of a homosexual relationship rather than relying on a single criterion such as living together.

Homosexual Identity

Another issue in conceptualizing homosexual relationships centers on the *personal and/or social identities* of the partners. Most researchers have included in their conception of a homosexual relationship that the partners must define themselves as gay, lesbian, or homosexual. Thus, for example, Mays (1986) excluded from her study of lesbian relationships those women who were currently in a "serious/committed relationship" with another woman but who described themselves as bisexual. McWhirter and Mattison (1984) required that the participants in their couples study identify themselves as "gay men." The criterion that a relationship be considered "homosexual" only if the participants define themselves as homosexual has clear merits. It permits researchers to describe their research participants with greater precision and provides a more homogeneous sample of homosexual relationships. In doing so, it probably enables researchers to study couples who more closely approximate contemporary prototypes of homosexual relationships.

This approach also has disadvantages, however. For those who argue that homosexuality research should move away from a focus on sexual identity and who see relationship research as an alternative to the identity approach (e.g., De Cecco & Shively, 1984), the use of homosexual self-identification to define homosexual relationships is problematic. A further criticism is that the use of an identity criterion may be heavily biased by contemporary American cultural beliefs and values. In our society, individuals may feel considerable pressure to define themselves in such categories as gay, lesbian, heterosexual, or bisexual. As Bullough (1984) noted, both personal needs for self-identification and the impact of the political gay movement encourage individuals to adopt specific self-labels such as gay or bisexual. In other times and places, however, homosexual relationships have not invariably been associated with a personal or social identity as homosexual. According to Bullough (1984), "homosexuality has always existed, but if it is defined to meet present-day requirements, then it becomes difficult to identify those in the past who were homosexuals" (p. 4).

As relationship researchers, we believe that important questions should be raised about the varied links between personal identity and experiences in close same-sex relationships. In a critique of traditional work on sexual identity, De Cecco and Shively (1984) noted that sexual identity has frequently been "conceived as an essence, interiorly lodged within the individual, one which determines whether the individual has only female or only male sexual partners or both" (p. 2). From such a perspective, same-sex relationships are an expression and consequence of sexual identity. But other patterns are also possible. For some, the first experience of having a close same-sex relationship may be a major factor causing a person to question his or her personal identity and to adopt a new identity as gay or lesbian. In still other cases, same-sex relationships may be seen as irrelevant to sexual identity. For instance, Vicinus (1984) provided a fascinating description of the intense friendships or "crushes" that developed among boarding-school girls in the late nineteenth century and noted that although these relationships were often passionate, they were not labeled as homosexual. Both Tripp (1975) and Hencken (1984) have discussed the processes by which individuals can engage in homosexual behavior but avoid the self-definition of being gay. For example, casual same-sex liaisons may be defined as simply "experimentation" or "just physical," or can be excused because the person was intoxicated at the time. For more involved relationships, "special friendship" and love may be emphasized so that the relationship is seen as an expression of unique feelings for the partner that have no implications for sexual identity. These brief examples indicate that the links between same-sex relationships and personal identity may be more complex than is frequently assumed and merit further investigation.

RESEARCH IMPLICATIONS

Most studies of homosexual relationships have not discussed these conceptual issues in depth. Operationally, researchers have commonly defined homosexual relationships on the basis of characteristics of the relationship (e.g., living together, defining the relationship as "romantic/ sexual") and self-definition by participants as gay or lesbian. Individual researchers must, of necessity, make such choices in operationally defining homosexual relationships. We encourage researchers to think carefully about these choices, to consider the use of general indices derived from research on close relationships, and to use multiple indicators to identify homosexual relationships.

We believe that a comprehensive understanding of homosexual relationships will require broadening the scope of empirical investigations in several directions. Current studies have provided much useful information about what might be considered "prototypical" homosexual relationships in America today. Research has focused on couples who define themselves as homosexual and whose relationship involves both love and sex. Future research will benefit from studying relationships that depart from the cultural prototype, such as relationships between same-sex partners who experience passion or commitment without overt sexuality, same-sex partners who define themselves as something other than homosexual, or people who relate simultaneously or sequentially to both same-sex and other-sex partners. For example, both Ross (1984) and Kaplan and Rogers (1984) have suggested that the physical sex of a partner may not be the central basis for attraction in homosexual relationships, that researchers should investigate social and psychological factors that may be more important than physical sex, and that to explore these issues, relationship studies should include bisexuals. In general, we need to know more about the diversity among homosexual relationships.

We also think it will be essential to broaden the comparisons used to understand homosexual relationships. It has been fairly common for researchers to compare same-sex relationships to other-sex relationships, asking for instance, about sexuality or love in homosexual versus heterosexual couples. It may be equally illuminating to consider homosexual relationships in the context of other same-sex relationships, looking for similarities and differences in relationships with one's closest same-sex partner and with other same-sex friends. Adrienne Rich's provocative essay "Compulsory Heterosexuality and Lesbian Existence" (1980) used the term lesbian continuum to

> include a range—through each woman's life and throughout history—of woman-identified experience; not simply the fact that a woman has had or consciously desired genital sexual experience with another woman. If we expand it to embrace many more forms of primary intensity between and among women, including the sharing of a rich inner life, the bonding against male tyranny, the giving and receiving of practical and political support . . . we begin to grasp the breadth of female history and psychology which have lain out of reach as a consequence of limited, mostly clinical, definitions of "lesbianism." (pp. 648–649)

A parallel continuum might also be proposed to explore the range of men's relations with other men. The implication of Rich's comments is that we should consider a full range of same-sex relationships and not limit our investigations to those that meet prevailing social "tests" for homosexuality.

The Goals of Relationship Research

In recent years, there has emerged an interdisciplinary field of inquiry into close relationships (see Gilmour & Duck, 1986; Hinde, 1979; Kelley et al., 1983). This field recognizes the central importance of relationships to human life, from the first attachments between newborn and parent to peer relations, adult love relations, and ties with friends, neighbors, and coworkers. This approach focuses on questions about the nature of relationships themselves, recognizing the importance of individual and sociocultural factors that shape relationships. Our own relationship perspective on homosexuality draws heavily from this new social science work on close relationships. Broadly speaking, relationship research has three interrelated goals.

Description. As in all science, adequate description is essential—in this case, efforts to describe the nature and diversity of close homosexual relationships. In so doing, we seek to identify the key dimensions that characterize these relationships and to describe the range of variation that occurs on these dimensions. The description of homosexual relationships includes both studies of patterns of interaction in couples and studies of partners' perceptions and attitudes about the relationship—their "experiences" in the relationship. Thus, we might ask: What is the emotional quality of homosexual relationships? What is the range and meaning of sexuality in gay and lesbian couples? How common is it for partners to share equally in decision making? What types of problems arise in homosexual couples? Are there typical changes in homosexual relationships as they develop over time?

Causal analysis. A second goal is to explain variations and changes in homosexual relationships by analyzing such factors as gender, personal values, and social norms that influence homosexual couples. Causal analyses most often ask how individual and social factors affect relationships. Causal questions might include the following: Why are some lesbian relationships happy and satisfying, while others are miserable and conflict-ridden? Why are some partnerships characterized by equal power and shared decision making, while others have one clearly dominant partner? What effects do differences in age or income have on the nature of gay male couples? What impact has the gay rights movement had on the nature of homosexual relationships? Also of interest are questions about the effects that homosexual relationships have on individuals and society. For instance, how does the experience of being in a long-term homosexual relationship affect an individual's sense of personal identity and psychological well-being? What effects have women's romantic friendships had on the feminist movement or on the development of predominantly female professions?

Theory building. A third goal of relationship research is to construct and evaluate theories about relationships. One approach has been to test the applicability of general theories to homosexual relationships. For instance, can the principles of social exchange theory predict the balance of power in homosexual relationships? Are existing models of commitment to relationships helpful in understanding the longevity of gay and lesbian couples? Another theoretical approach has been to develop new models based on gay or lesbian relationships. The stage model of gay men's relationship development proposed by McWhirter and Mattison (1984) is illustrative.

Studies of Lesbian and Gay Male Relationships in the United States

In this section we review research conducted in the United States about homosexual relationships. Our goal is to highlight major areas of research and to identify new research directions. Space limitations preclude a completely comprehensive review. Most of the available studies are based on younger, urban, primarily Anglo individuals. Although a few studies have involved fairly large samples, none has been completely representative of either lesbians or gay men.

Most lesbians and gay men want to have enduring close relationships. Bell and Weinberg (1978) asked homosexuals how important it was to them to have "a permanent living arrangement with a homosexual partner" (p. 322). In their sample, 24% of the lesbians and 14% of the gay men indicated that this was "the most important thing in life;" 35% of lesbians and 28% of gay men said it was "very important." Less than 13% of lesbians and 19% of gay men indicated that a permanent, living-together relationship was "not important at all," and some of these individuals may have preferred a close relationship in which partners lived apart.

Several studies have investigated the extent to which lesbians and gay men are actually involved in close relationships. In surveys of gay men, between 40% and 60% of the men questioned were currently involved in a steady relationship (e.g., Bell & Weinberg, 1978; Harry, 1983; Jay & Young, 1977; Peplau & Cochran, 1981). Harry (1983) argued that these figures may underrepresent the actual frequency of enduring relationships because men in long-term relationships tend to be somewhat older and less likely to go to bars—both factors that would make these men less likely to be included in current studies. In studies of lesbians, between 45% and 80% of women surveyed were currently in a steady relationship (Bell & Weinberg, 1978; Jay & Young, 1977; Peplau et al., 1978; Raphael & Robinson, 1980). In most studies, the proportion of lesbians in an ongoing relationship was close to 75%.

Harry (1983, p. 225) estimated that approximately half of all gay male couples live together, compared to about three quarters of lesbian couples. We presently know little about the factors that lead some homosexual couples to live together and others to live apart. Possible causes might include efforts to maintain secrecy about being gay, a rejection of a "marriage" model in which lovers must live together, a reluctance to pool finances, the requirements of partners' jobs, and the like. From a methodological standpoint, researchers who use living together as a criterion for the selection of homosexual couples will have a significantly more restricted sample than those who use other criteria of couplehood, although we do not know the specific differences such a choice creates.

These estimates may not be completely representative of all lesbians and gay men in the United States. They do suggest, however, that a large proportion of homosexuals have stable close relationships and that a higher proportion of lesbians than gay men may be in steady relationships. We do not yet have good information on how such factors as age, ethnicity, or social class influence the likelihood that gay men and lesbians form close relationships. It should also be stressed that those lesbians and gay men who are not currently in a close relationship are a diverse group. They include people who have recently ended a close relationship through breakup or death, people who are eager to begin new relationships, and others who do not currently want committed relationships.

The Quality of Gay and Lesbian Relationships: Satisfaction and Love

Several studies have examined satisfaction in lesbian and gay male relationships (e.g., Duffy & Rusbult, 1986; Jones & Bates, 1978; Kurdek &

Schmitt, 1986a, 1986b; Peplau, Padesky, & Hamilton, 1982; Peplau et al., 1986). In general, research has found that most gay men and lesbians perceive their close relationships as satisfying and that levels of love and satisfaction are similar for homosexual and heterosexual couples who are matched on age and other relevant characteristics.

Comparative studies. In an early study, Ramsey, Latham, and Lindquist (1978) compared samples of 26 lesbian, 27 gay male, and 25 heterosexual couples from Southern California on the Locke-Wallace Scale measure of "marital" adjustment. All couples scored in the "well-adjusted" range, and the homosexuals were indistinguishable from the heterosexuals. Dailey (1979) used several standardized measures to compare 26 heterosexual couples, 5 lesbian couples, and 5 gay male couples living in Kansas. In general, all couples appeared to be "successful," and no significant group differences were found for satisfaction, expression of affection, or cohesion. A small but statistically significant difference was found on a measure of couple "consensus," with homosexual couples scoring lower than heterosexuals. Cardell, Finn, and Marecek (1981) compared partners in 10 heterosexual, 10 lesbian, and 5 gay male couples in Pennsylvania on a standardized measure of couple adjustment and found no group differences. More recently, Kurdek and Schmitt (1986a) compared somewhat larger samples of lesbian, gay male, and heterosexual cohabiting and married couples. They found no significant differences among groups on measures of love or relationship satisfaction, with the exception that heterosexual cohabitors scored lower than the other three groups.

In research at UCLA (Peplau & Cochran, 1980), we selected matched samples of 50 lesbians, 50 gay men, 50 heterosexual women, and 50 heterosexual men—all involved in "romantic/sexual relationships." Participants were matched on age, education, ethnicity, and length of relationship. Among this sample of young adults, about 60% said they were "in love" with their partner; most of the rest indicated they were "uncertain." On a standardized love scale, lesbians and gay men generally reported high love for their partners, indicating strong feelings of attachment, caring, and intimacy. They also scored high on a liking scale, reflecting feelings of respect and affection toward their partners. On other measures, lesbians and gay men rated their current relationships as highly satisfying and very close. We found no significant differences among lesbians, gay men, and heterosexuals on any of these measures.

In the UCLA research, we also asked lesbians, gay men, and heterosexuals to describe in their own words the "best things" and "worst things" about their relationships. Responses included such comments as these: "The best thing is having someone to be with when you wake up" or "We like each other. We both seem to be getting what we want and need. We have wonderful sex together." Worst things included, "My partner is too dependent emotionally" or "Her aunt lives with us!" Systematic content analyses (Cochran, 1978) found no significant differences in the responses of lesbians, gay men, and heterosexuals—all of whom reported a similar range of joys and problems. To search for more subtle differences among groups that may not have been captured by the coding scheme, the "best things" and "worst things" statements were typed on cards in a standard format, with information about gender and sexual orientation removed. Panels of student judges were asked to sort the cards, separating men and women or separating heterosexuals and homosexuals. The judges were not able to identify correctly the responses of lesbians, gay men, or heterosexual women and men. (Indeed, judges may have been misled by their own preconceptions; they tended, for instance, to assume incorrectly that statements involving jealousy were more likely to be made by homosexuals than heterosexuals.)

Correlates of satisfaction. Which couples are happiest? Social exchange theory predicts that satisfaction is high when a person perceives that a relationship provides many rewards and entails relatively few costs. Duffy and Rusbult (1986) tested these predictions among heterosexuals, lesbians, and gay men. They found that in all groups, greater satisfaction was significantly associated with the experience of relatively more personal rewards and fewer personal costs. Kurdek and Schmitt (1986a) provided similar results. In a study of lesbian relationships, Peplau et al. (1982) found support for another exchange theory prediction, that satisfaction is higher when partners' are equally involved in (committed to) the relationship.

Many contemporary lesbians and gay men strive for power equality and shared decision making in their relationships. Three studies have found that satisfaction is higher when lesbians and gay men perceive their current relationship as egalitarian (Harry, 1984; Kurdek & Schmitt, 1986a; Peplau et al., 1982).

Some plausible factors have *not* been shown to predict relationship satisfaction. Individual characteristics of partners such as their age, education, or income have not been associated with satisfaction (Kurdek & Schmitt, 1986a; Peplau et al., 1982). For instance, a study of 295 black lesbians (Peplau et al., 1986) found that relationship satisfaction was unrelated to living together versus apart, to age, education, income, religion, or to whether the respondent's partner was black versus nonblack. Harry (1984) also found that for gay men, living together was unrelated to satisfaction.

Finally, a few studies have examined the impact of similarity or matching between the partners on satisfaction. Harry (1984) found that satisfaction was lower when gay men's incomes were different, but satisfaction was unrelated to age differences. Kurdek and Schmitt (1987) found that differences in partners' age, income, or education had no effect on satisfaction in lesbian or gay male couples. Peplau et al. (1982) discovered that the degree of similarity between partners on age, religion, or work status was not linked to satisfaction. In interpreting these findings, however, it is important to note a methodological issue: in most research to date, there has usually been relatively little variation in satisfaction scores (most people surveyed tend to be happy); neither has there been much variation in levels of matching (most couples tend to be at least somewhat matched). This makes it difficult to test the matching hypothesis. It is also likely that having similar attitudes and values is more important to relationship happiness than matching on demographic characteristics (see Kurdek & Schmitt, 1987; Peplau et al., 1982).

Commitment and the Duration of Relationships

Love is no guarantee that a relationship will endure. For homosexuals, as for heterosexuals, relationships begun hopefully and lovingly can and do fall apart. Love and commitment do not necessarily go hand-in-hand (see Kelley, 1983). Little empirical work is currently available on commitment and permanence in homosexual relationships (see Blumstein & Schwartz, 1983; Duffy & Rusbult, 1986; Lewis, Kozac, Milardo, & Grosnick, 1980).

Commitment refers to those forces that cause a relationship to endure over time. Commitment is affected by two separate factors (Levinger, 1979). The first concerns the strength of the *positive attractions*, including love, that make a particular partner and relationship appealing. Current data suggest that homosexuals do not differ from heterosexuals in the love and satisfaction they experience in steady relationships. But the possibility always exists that attractions may wane and that people may "fall out of love." Such a decrease in attraction could encourage the ending of a relationship.

A second set of factors affecting the permanence of relationships consists of *barriers* that make the ending of a relationship costly, in either psychological or material terms. The lack of alternative partners, the perception of having invested a great deal in a relationship, an awareness of the personal costs of leaving a relationship—these and other nonpositive factors cause relationships to endure. For heterosexuals, marriage usually creates many barriers to dissolution, including the costs of divorce, a spouse's financial dependence on the partner, joint investments in property, the presence of children, and so on. Such factors may encourage married couples to "work" on improving a declining relationship rather than end it. In extreme cases, these barriers can also keep partners trapped in an "empty-shell" relationship. Researchers have speculated that gay men and lesbians may experience fewer barriers to the termination of relationships than heterosexuals (e.g., Duffy & Rusbult, 1986; Peplau & Gordon, 1983). If this is true, lesbians and gay men will be less likely to become trapped in hopelessly unhappy relationships. But they may also be less motivated to rescue deteriorating relationships that may warrant saving.

In an empirical comparison of lesbian, gay male, and heterosexual relationships, Duffy and Rusbult (1986) found that for all types of relationships, higher levels of perceived commitment were significantly linked to feeling greater personal satisfaction, having made greater investments in the relationship, and feeling less confident of finding an alternative partner. They also found that regardless of sexual orientation, women reported having made greater investments and feeling greater commitment than did men. Kurdek and Schmitt (1986a) compared attractions, barriers to leaving, and available alternatives for partners in gay, lesbian, and heterosexual married relationships. They found no differences in attractions. But married partners perceived more barriers than did either gay men or lesbians; and both lesbians and married individuals perceived fewer available alternative partners than did gay men.

Data on the longevity of relationships are provided by Blumstein and Schwartz (1983), who followed a large sample of lesbian, gay male, and cohabiting heterosexual couples over an 18-month period. At the time of original testing, lesbians, gay men, and heterosexuals were about equal in their personal expectations of staying together, although both lesbians and gay men speculated that gay men usually have less stable relationships than lesbians. During the 18-month period, fewer than one couple in five broke up. Breakups were rare among couples who had already been together for more than 10 years (6% for lesbians and 4% for gay men). Among shorter-term couples, lesbians had the highest breakup rate (about 20%), with roughly 16% of gay male couples and 14% of cohabitors breaking up. Although these differences among groups are quite small, they do run counter to the suggestion that lesbians are more likely to have enduring partnerships. These three studies provide interesting information about commitment and permanence in homosexual relationships, but definitive conclusions will have to await additional research.

Sexuality

Relationship researchers view sexuality as one facet of experience in couples. In the domain of sexuality, differences between men and women may be at least as important as differences between homosexuals and heterosexuals.

SEXUAL FREQUENCY AND SATISFACTION

Research has investigated both the frequency of sexual activity in homosexual couples, and partners' evaluations of sexual satisfaction. In their large-scale study *American Couples*, Blumstein and Schwartz (1983) have provided the only detailed comparative investigation of sex in lesbian, gay male, heterosexual cohabiting, and married couples. They reached several conclusions that seem generally consistent with other studies of sexuality in homosexual relationships (e.g., Jay & Young, 1977; Lewis et al., 1980; McWhirter & Mattison, 1984; Peplau & Cochran, 1981; Peplau et al., 1986; Peplau et al., 1978).

First, across all couples, the median frequency of sex is about one to three times a week. But there is enormous variation among couples in the average frequency of genital sex—ranging from couples who have sex less than once a month to couples who have sex daily. We know little about factors that create these differing patterns. It appears that the frequency of sex declines the longer a couple stay together and, to some extent, with age (Blumstein & Schwartz, 1983; McWhirter & Mattison, 1984).

Gender is an important factor in sexual frequency. There is some evidence that at all stages of a relationship, average sexual frequency is lower among lesbian couples than among gay male couples, heterosexual cohabitors, or married heterosexuals. For instance, Blumstein and Schwartz (1983, p. 196) reported that among couples who have been together less than two years, only 33% of lesbians had sex three or more times a week, compared to 45% of married couples, 61% of cohabitors, and 67% of gay men. In other words, the proportion of couples who had sex often varied with the gender composition of the couples. The reasons for this pattern are unclear. Blumstein and Schwartz speculated about the possible importance of traditional socialization that represses women's sexual expression but encourages men to be sexually active, the possibility that women may put more emphasis on nongenital activities such as hugging and cuddling, or possible problems that lesbians may have with initiating sex. Blumstein and Schwartz also reported an interesting pattern of sexual frequency for gay men. For the first several years of a relationship, gay men had sex with their primary partner more often than heterosexuals did, but later on gay male couples showed a reversed pattern of lower sexual frequency than heterosexuals. In many gay couples, sex with men outside the relationship compensated for the declining frequency of sex with the primary partner, at least for relationships studied prior to the AIDS crisis.

In general, lesbians and gay men report high levels of sexual satisfaction with their partner (e.g., Peplau & Cochran 1981; Peplau et al., 1986; Peplau et al., 1978). For example, Blumstein and Schwartz found that roughly 70% of lesbians, gay men, and heterosexuals were satisfied with the quality of their sex life. For all groups, satisfaction was higher among couples who had sex more frequently and who reported that the initiation of sex was equal in their relationship. In McWhirter and Mattison's (1984, pp. 278–279) study of gay male couples, 83% reported having a satisfactory sex life, 7% said it was very satisfactory, and only 10% reported dissatisfaction. Most men (91%) said that the level of sexual satisfaction with their partner had improved since the beginning of their relationship. At the same time, there is also a growing awareness that gay and lesbian couples are not immune to sexual difficulties (e.g., McWhirter & Mattison, 1980; Toder, 1978).

SEXUAL EXCLUSIVITY

Few relationship issues are as controversial for Americans as whether a couple should be sexually exclusive or sexually open. In this century, we have seen a steady shift toward more permissive attitudes about sex out-side a primary relationship. Very recently, however, the growing aware-ness of the dangers of AIDS and other sexually transmitted diseases may once again be changing attitudes about sexual conduct. At present, most published studies of sexual exclusivity in gay and lesbian relationships predate the AIDS crisis and so do not yet reflect possible recent changes in attitudes and/or behavior.

A number of studies have investigated sexual exclusivity in homosexual relationships, particularly among gay men (e.g., Bell & Weinberg, 1978; Blasband & Peplau, 1985; Blumstein & Schwartz, 1983; Harry, 1984; Harry & DeVall, 1978; Harry & Lovely, 1979; Kurdek & Schmitt, 1986; Peplau & Cochran, 1982; Peplau et al., 1978; McWhirter & Mattison, 1984). In gen-eral, homosexuals—especially gay men—appear to have more permissive attitudes about sexual fidelity than do heterosexuals (Peplau & Cochran, 1980). Blumstein and Schwartz (1983, p. 272) reported that *for men* in couples, 75% of husbands and 62% of heterosexual cohabitors believe monogamy is important, compared to only 35% of gay men. *For women,* 84% of wives, 70% of heterosexual cohabitors, and 71% of lesbians believe monogamy is important. For all groups except gay men, a majority en-dorse the virtues of sexual fidelity; among gay men, sexual exclusivity is the minority view.

Blumstein and Schwartz (1983, p. 274) provided comparative data on the extent of actual "nonmonogamy" in couples. The likelihood that a partner has ever been nonmonogamous increased over time. For lesbians, nonmonogamy was uncommon in the first 2 years of a relationship (15%), as it was for heterosexual wives (13%) and husbands (15%). For gay men, however, 66% of those surveyed reported nonmonogamy during the first 2 years of their relationship. Among couples together for more than 10 years, 22% of wives, 30% of husbands, 43% of lesbians, and 94% of gay men reported at least one instance of nonmonogamy. McWhirter and Mattison (1984) found a similar pattern for the gay male couples in their study; all men in relationships lasting more than 5 years reported at least one instance of nonmonogamy. There has been much discussion of the possible reasons for the high incidence of sexual openness in gay men's relationships (e.g., Blumstein & Schwartz, 1983; McWhirter & Mattison, 1984; Silverstein, 1981). Suggested factors include sex role socialization that may teach men to value sexual variety, a tendency for men to sepa-rate sexuality from emotional commitment, norms of the gay male commu-nity that encourage sexual openness, and the availability of many opportu-nities for casual sex.

Some studies have taken a closer look at sexual exclusivity in gay male relationships (Blasband & Peplau, 1985; Blumstein & Schwartz, 1983; Harry, 1984; Kurdek & Schmitt, 1986b; McWhirter & Mattison, 1984). Research has investigated the ways couples negotiate sexual exclusivity, studying for instance the extent to which partners keep their behavior secret and the extent to which couples develop agreements about circumstances in which sexual openness is mutually acceptable. Other research has examined the links between sexual openness and satisfaction within the relationship, finding that nonmonogamy is not necessarily a sign of problems or dissatisfaction in the primary relationship. What seems most important is that partners in a relationship reach some degree of agreement about this issue.

We do not yet know what impact the AIDS crisis will have on sexuality in gay male couples. A study by McKusick et al. (1985) followed a group of gay men from 1982 to 1984 and reported a general decrease in the number of encounters gay men had with new partners and a decrease in the frequency of high-risk sex behaviors. Men who had a primary relationship were more likely than single men to reduce encounters with new partners. McKusick et al. also found a statistically significant decrease in the frequency of sex with the primary partner (from 10.8 times per month in 1982 to 8.5 times per month in 1984), which they speculated may reflect a general inhibition of sexual activity. A clearer understanding of the impact of AIDS on gay male couples must await further research.

Power

Power refers to one person's ability to achieve his or her own ends by influencing another person (Huston, 1983, p. 170). Powerful people can use interpersonal influence to "get their own way." Research on homosexual relationships has investigated both the balance of power (dominance structure) in relationships and the specific influence tactics that partners use with each other.

THE BALANCE OF POWER

In general, it appears that most lesbians and gay men value power equality as a goal for relationships. For example, in a study comparing the relationship values of matched samples of younger lesbians, gay men, and heterosexuals, Peplau and Cochran (1980) found that all groups rated "having an egalitarian (equal power) relationship" as quite important, although women, both lesbians and heterosexuals, gave equal power even more importance than did men. On another question asking what the ideal balance of power should be in their current relationship, 92% of gay men and 97% of lesbians said it should be "exactly equal." But although most participants wanted equal-power partnerships, not all of those currently in a relationship said that it met this standard. Only 59% of lesbians, 38% of gay men, 48% of heterosexual women, and 40% of heterosexual men reported that their relationship was "exactly equal." What factors tip the balance of power in favor of one partner?

Social exchange theory predicts that a partner who has relatively greater personal resources (e.g., more money, education, or status) will have a power advantage in the relationship. Several studies have tested this hypothesis for gay male couples. Harry and DeVall (1978) studied 243 gay men from Detroit. About 60% said that decision making in their relationship was shared "half and half," 24% said they personally made more decisions, and 16% said the other partner made more decisions. Harry and DeVall tested the impact of money as a resource and found that the partner whose income was relatively greater had a power advantage. In a more recent study, Harry (1984) replicated this finding. More than 65% of men currently in a relationship said decision making was joint. Unequal power was significantly linked to differences in income and also to differences in age, with the power advantage going to men who were wealthier and older. This theme is echoed by Blumstein and Schwartz (1983), who concluded from their data that "in gay male couples, income is an extremely important force in determining which partner will be dominant" (p. 59).

For lesbians, the impact of personal resources on power is not well understood. Caldwell and Peplau (1984) found that differences in income and education were significantly related to power in a sample of 77 younger lesbians from Los Angeles. In contrast, Reilly and Lynch (1986) found that differences in age, education, income, and assets were not related to the balance of power in 70 lesbian couples from the Northeast. Blumstein and Schwartz (1983) studied the effects of income on power, concluding that "Lesbians do not use income to establish dominance in their relationship. They use it to avoid having one woman dependent on the other" (p. 60). The reasons for these inconsistent findings are unknown. It could be that the concept of "resources" is somehow less relevant to lesbian couples than to gay men and heterosexuals or that the material resources typically studied (e.g., money, education) are less significant in this group than are other perhaps less tangible resources (e.g., status in the lesbian community, social skills).

The "principle of least interest" is another prediction from social exchange theory (Blau, 1964). This states that when one person is more dependent, involved, or "interested" in a relationship than the partner, the more dependent person will have less power. In studies of heterosexuals (e.g., Peplau, 1984), such lopsided dependencies have been strongly associated with an imbalance of power. Only one study has tested this hypothesis among homosexuals. Caldwell and Peplau (1984) found support for the principle of least interest among lesbians. Among the women who said the partners were equally involved, 72% also reported equal power. Among women who reported unequal involvement, 82% reported that the less involved partner had relatively more power. Caldwell and Peplau also found that women in equal-power relationships were more satisfied and anticipated fewer problems than did women in unequal relationships. Similarly, Blumstein and Schwartz (1983) reported that power imbalances were a factor in the breakup of lesbian and gay male relationships (although not for married couples.)

Virtually nothing is known about how the balance of power affects face-to-face interaction in homosexual couples. One fascinating exception comes from a study by Kollock, Blumstein, and Schwartz (1985). They compared the conversational patterns of lesbian, gay male, and heterosexual couples. Of interest was the extent to which partners showed conversational dominance by using a disproportionate amount of the "air" time available, by using interruptions to gain the floor, or by asking questions. Their complicated results are not easily summarized, but a few examples will illustrate. In both lesbian and gay male couples, the amount of talking and the number of interruptions were significantly linked to power—the more powerful person was more loquacious and interrupted more. Results for asking questions were different for lesbians and gay men. In male couples, more powerful partners asked substantially more questions than did less powerful partners, perhaps using questions as a way of structuring or controlling the conversation. For lesbians, power had no impact on asking questions. Studies such as this, which investigate the dynamics of power in interpersonal interaction, provide an important direction for future research.

INFLUENCE STRATEGIES

A few studies have begun to examine the specific strategies or behaviors used by lesbians and gay men to influence their partners. In a study comparing self-reports of power strategies by lesbians, gay men, and heterosexuals, Falbo and Peplau (1980) found no overall differences between the strategies used by homosexuals and heterosexuals. Gender affected influence tactics only among heterosexuals: whereas heterosexual women were more likely to withdraw or express negative emotions, heterosexual men were more likely to use bargaining or reasoning. Among homosexuals, women and men did not differ significantly in the strategies used. Regardless of sexual orientation, people who perceived themselves as relatively more powerful in a relationship tended to use direct and mutual strategies, such as persuasion and bargaining (i.e., the strategies characteristic of heterosexual men.) Low-power partners tended to use more unilateral approaches, such as doing what they wanted without the partner.

In another study, Howard, Blumstein and Schwartz (1986) also compared influence tactics in the intimate relationships of homosexuals and heterosexuals. They found that in power-unequal couples, regardless of sexual orientation, the partner with less power tended to rely more on "supplication" and manipulation, both "weak" strategies. Those in positions of strength were more likely to use bullying and autocratic tactics, both "strong" strategies. They also found that individuals with male partners (i.e., heterosexual women and homosexual men) were more likely to use manipulation and supplication. These two studies provide beginning insights into the impact of gender and sexual orientation on influence tactics, but more research is clearly warranted.

Roles

In any close relationship, partners develop consistent patterns of interaction—characteristic ways of being together, specialization in terms of who does what in their relationship, shared hobbies and interests, special rituals and terms of endearment, agreements about goals for the relationship, and so on. The concept of social roles is typically used to describe and/or explain these relationship patterns (Peplau, 1983).

ROLE TAKING AND ROLE MAKING

Relationship roles emerge or develop in two ways (e.g., Turner, 1962). Role taking refers to the processes by which partners adopt or conform to preexisting cultural or social guidelines for their relationship. For many types of relationships, such as heterosexual marriage or relations between teacher and student, there exist fairly explicit, conventional guidelines and social models. In contrast, role making refers to the processes by which partners create their own idiosyncratic rules, expectations, and goals for a relationship. Partners may actively discuss and think about their relationship, hammering out agreements, and discussing points of difference. They may "fall into" habit patterns or discover what seems to "work best" for them on the basis of their individual values, interests, and skills. Close relationships usually involve a mix of both role taking and role making. Presumably, when preexisting guidelines for relationships are explicit and detailed, partners are more constrained in their interactions and less likely to innovate.

The nature and extent of cultural guidelines for homosexual relationships vary both cross-culturally and historically. Some societies define institutionalized patterns of homosexuality. Among the Sambia of New Guinea, for example, all boys are expected to spend part of their teenage years in all-male groups that practice specific forms of homosexuality (Herdt, 1981, 1987). Elaborate ceremonies are conducted to teach young boys about these culturally prescribed practices. Social rules control the selection of partners, the nature of the sex acts, and the circumstances under which sex can occur. The patterning of these homosexual relationships is well defined as part of male Sambian culture, although individuals undoubtedly vary in the specfics of how they play out the prescribed roles. It is further expected that after this period of adolescent homosexuality, adult men will marry women and father children.

In contrast, in contemporary American society, gay relationships are "largely lacking in institutional supports and cultural guidelines" (Harry, 1977, p. 330). As a consequence, homosexual partners must rely more on innovative processes of role making than on enacting culturally defined scripts for homosexual relations. Nonetheless, it seems likely that aspects of other cultural roles such as marriage or friendship do influence patterns of interaction in homosexual partnerships.

POSSIBLE MODELS FOR HOMOSEXUAL RELATIONSHIPS

At least three different patterns for male homosexual relationships have been described (e.g., Harry, 1982). Some gay male relationships are structured at least in part by *gender roles*, with one partner playing a more "masculine" role and the other a "feminine" role. Here, heterosexual roles for dating and marriage are used as a model for gay relationships. A second pattern is based on *age differences*, such as a relationship between an adult male and an adolescent boy or between an older man and a younger man. This pattern bears some similarity to other age-structured roles as between teacher and student or mentor and apprentice. A third pattern is based on *peer relations*, with partners being similar in age and emphasizing sharing and equality in the relationship. This pattern seems more similar to cultural roles for friendship. In each case, homosexual patterns incorporate elements of other, conventional social roles in the society.

The three patterns identified for men may also have parallels in lesbian relationships. Descriptions of lesbian experiences in the 1950s (Martin & Lyon, 1972; Wolf, 1980) suggest that the influence of heterosexual role models was strong:

> The old gay world divided up into "butch" and "femme." . . . Butches were tough, presented themselves as being as masculine as possible . . . and they assumed the traditional male role of taking care of their partners, even fighting over them if necessary, providing for them financially, and doing the "men's" jobs around the house. Femmes, by contrast, were protected, ladylike . . . . They cooked, cleaned house, and took care of their "butch." (Wolf, 1980, p. 40)

Age-differences as a basis for women's romantic relationships are reported by Vicinus (1984) in her description of the adolescent "crushes" experienced by young girls living at boarding schools around the turn of the century. In this instance, the girls developed passionate attachments toward an older woman, usually a teacher. Finally, relationships modeled after friendship or peer relations are found in Faderman's (1981) description of late nineteenth century "Boston marriages." These were long-term monogamous relationships between two unmarried women. The women were typically financially independent of men, were involved in social causes, and were identified as feminists.

These three forms for homosexual relationships—modeled loosely after husband-wife roles, mentor-student roles, and friendship roles—may not exhaust the range of diversity among gay and lesbian relationships. In complex industrial societies such as ours, it seems likely that these and perhaps other relationship patterns may all exist.

RESEARCH ON AMERICAN COUPLES

Empirical research on role patterns in contemporary homosexual relationships has focused primarily on the question of how closely homosexual relationships resemble heterosexual pairings. Stereotypes would suggest that "butch-femme" roles are widespread. Tripp (1975) notes that "when people who are not familiar with homosexual relationships try to picture one, they almost invariably resort to a heterosexual frame of reference, raising questions about which partner is 'the man' and which 'the woman' " (p. 152). A good deal of research on this issue has been generated (see reviews by Harry, 1983; Peplau & Gordon, 1983).

In general, research suggests that most lesbians and gay men today actively reject traditional husband-wife or masculine-feminine roles as a model for enduring relationships. Most lesbians and gay men are in "dual-worker" relationships, so that neither partner is the exclusive "breadwinner" and each partner has some measure of economic independence. Further, examinations of the division of household tasks, sexual behavior, and decision making in homosexual couples find that clear-cut and consistent husband-wife roles are uncommon. In many relationships, there is some specialization of activities, with one partner doing more of some jobs and less of others. But it is rare for one partner to perform most of the "feminine" activities and the other to perform most of the "masculine" tasks. That is, a partner who usually does the cooking does not necessarily also perform other feminine tasks such as shopping or cleaning. Specialization seems to be based on more individualistic factors, such as skills or interests.

Nonetheless, it has been found that a small minority of lesbians and gay men do incorporate elements of husband-wife roles into their relationships. This may affect the division of labor, the dominance structure, sexual interactions, the way partners dress, and other aspects of their relationship. In some cases, these role patterns seemed to be linked to temporary situations, such as one partner's unemployment or illness. For other couples, however, masculine-feminine roles may provide a model of choice. Evidence suggests that this pattern has declined in recent years, at least in part as a response to the gay liberation and feminist movements.

Only a few analyses have explicitly looked at age-differentiated relationships, notably among gay men. Harry (1982, 1984) suggests that the age-difference pattern characterizes only a minority of gay male couples. When it does occur, the actual differences in age tend to be relatively small, perhaps 5–10 years. Harry has found that in these couples, the older partner often has more power in decision making.

Those who have reviewed the research on today's homosexual couples have concluded that the majority of relationships develop roles similar to friendship—with expectations that partners should be similar in age and equal in power and should share responsbilities fairly equally.

An important direction for research on relationship roles is to investigate the impact of gay and lesbian subcultures and, more recently, of gay rights and lesbian feminist movements on relationships. An illustration is found in Barnhart's (1975) description of "friends and lovers in a lesbian counterculture community." In the early 1970s, counterculture lesbians living in Oregon formed small "communities" of about 30 women that served as a psychological "kin group" for members. The community developed fairly explicit expectations and norms about love relationships and encouraged members to conform to these group standards. For example, loyalty to a partner was to be secondary to loyalty to the community. Sexual openness and equality were considered important values for relationships. If a couple broke up, they were expected to remain friends. Studies examining how other elements of homosexual culture affect relationships would be useful.

In summary, contemporary homosexual relationships follow a variety of patterns or models. Relationships patterned after friendship appear to be most common. Among both lesbians and gay men, a decreasing minority of couples may incorporate elements of traditional masculine-feminine roles into their relationships. For others, age differences may be central to role patterns. More efforts are needed to describe relationship roles in lesbian and gay male couples. Further, we currently know little about the causal factors responsible for these patterns. Why, for instance, are some men attracted to older partners and others to peers? Why do some partners prefer to share tasks and responsibilities and others prefer to develop patterns of specialization? These and other questions remain for future investigations.

Final Thoughts

In the 40 years since Kinsey and his colleagues published their pioneering work on homosexual behavior, research on relationships has emerged as an important perspective in the study of homosexuality. Our knowledge about gay and lesbian couples has increased markedly in the last decade.

Research Questions

Existing research on homosexual relationships leaves many important topics unexamined. For instance, we know little about conflict in couples and the ways that partners strive to avoid and resolve their differences. The process of "breaking up" and the aftermath of separation are also worthy of study. McWhirter and Mattison (1984) took an important first step in their analysis of developmental trends in gay male couples. But more work needs to be done to understand the developmental course of relationships among gay men and among lesbians. Close relationships are often affected by ties to third parties—to children, aging parents, siblings, and others. How, for instance, does the decision to have a child affect a lesbian relationship? There is growing awareness that close relationships can provide important kinds of social support that help us to meet major crises and to deal with the hassles of daily life. What types of social support are available to lesbians and gay men, and which types of relationships are most important? (See Aura, 1985; Collins, D'Augelli, & Hart, 1985.) Finally, how are close homosexual relationships affected by social and historical changes? In particular, how is the current AIDS crisis affecting homosexual couples?

Research Methods

Those who study homosexual relationships face a major methodological challenge. We know that accurate description is a keystone of good science, and yet we also know that we are not able to obtain truly representative samples of gay and lesbian couples. At the very least, this dilemma should make us cautious in generalizing from results of single studies to "all" homosexual couples. It should also make us critically aware of the importance of replication across many studies and should encourage us to describe the couples we study with care and precision. In addition, however, we need to increase the diversity of our information base by broadening the samples we investigate. Studies of homosexual relationships among people from varied ethnic and racial groups, from working-class backgrounds, from closeted professional elites, and from rural areas will be especially valuable. Our knowledge about young adults should be supplemented with studies of relationships among teenagers and older adults. Detailed "ethnographic" studies that attempt to provide comprehensive descriptions of relationships in defined communities or specific groups may be extremely useful.

References

Aura, J. (1985). *Women's social support: A comparison of lesbians and heterosexuals.* Unpublished doctoral dissertation, University of California, Los Angeles.

Barnhart, E. (1975). Friends and lovers in a lesbian counterculture community. In N. Glazer-Malbin (Ed.), *Old family/new family* (pp. 3–23). New York: D. Van Nostrand.

Bell, A. P., & Weinberg, M. S. (1978). *Homosexualities: A study of diversity among men and women.* New York: Simon & Schuster.

Blasband, D., & Peplau, L. A. (1985). Sexual exclusivity versus openness in gay male couples. *Archives of Sexual Behavior, 14*(5), 395–412.

Blau, P. M. (1964). *Exchange and power in social life.* New York: John Wiley & Sons.

Blumstein, P., & Schwartz, P. (1983). *American couples: Money, work, sex.* New York: William Morrow.

Boswell, J. (1980). *Christianity, social tolerance, and homosexuality.* Chicago: University of Chicago Press.

Bullough, V. L. (1984). Weighing the shift from sexual identity to sexual relationships. *Journal of Homosexuality, 10*(3/4), 3-14.

Caldwell, M. A., & Peplau, L. A. (1984). The balance of power in lesbian relationships. *Sex Roles, 10,* 587–600.

Cardell, M., Finn, S., & Marecek, J. (1981). Sex-role identity, sex-role behavior, and satisfaction in heterosexual, lesbian, and gay male couples. *Psychology of Women Quarterly, 5*(3), 488–494.

Cochran, S. D. (1978, April). *Romantic relationships: For better or for worse.* Paper presented at the Western Psychological Association meeting, San Francisco.

Collins, C., D'Augelli, A. R., & Hart, M. M. (1985, August). *Social support patterns in a rural network of lesbians.* Paper presented at the annual meeting of the American Psychological Association, Los Angeles.

Dailey, D. M. (1979). Adjustment of heterosexual and homosexual couples in pairing relationships: An exploratory study. *Journal of Sex Research, 15*(2), 143-157.

De Cecco, J. P., & Shively, M. G. (1984). From sexual identity to sexual relationships: A contextual shift. *Journal of Homosexuality, 9*(2/3), 1–26.

Duffy, S. M., & Rusbult, C. E. (1986). Satisfaction and commitment in homosexual and heterosexual relationships. *Journal of Homosexuality, 12*(2), 1-24.

Faderman, L. (1981). *Surpassing the love of men.* New York: William Morrow.

Faderman, L. (1984). The "new gay" lesbians. *Journal of Homosexuality, a0*(3/4), 85–95.

Falbo, T., & Peplau, L. A. (1980). Power strategies in intimate relationships. *Journal of Personality and Social Psychology, 38*(4), 618–628.

Gilmour, R., & Duck, S. (Eds.). (1986). *The emerging field of personal relationships.* Hillsdale, NJ: Lawrence Erlbaum.

Hansen, C. E., & Evans, A. (1985). Bisexuality reconsidered: An idea in pursuit of a definition. *Journal of Homosexuality, 11*, 1-6.

Harry, J. (1977). Marriage among gay males: The separation of sex and intimacy. In S. G. McNall (Ed.), *The sociological perspective: Introductory readings* (4th ed., pp. 330–340). Boston: Little, Brown.

Harry, J. (1982). Decision making and age differences among gay male couples. *Journal of Homosexuality, 8*(2), 9–22.

Harry, J. (1983). Gay male and lesbian relationships. In E. Macklin & R. Rubin (Eds.), *Contemporary families and alternative lifestyles: Handbook on research and theory* (pp. 216–234). Beverly Hills: Sage.

Harry, J. (1984). *Gay couples.* New York: Praeger.

Harry, J., & DeVall, W. B. (1978). *The social organization of gay males.* New York: Praeger.

Harry, J., & Lovely, R. (1979). Gay marriages and communities of sexual orientation. *Alternative Lifestyles, 2*(2), 177–200.

Hencken, J. D. (1984). Conceptualizations of homosexual behavior which preclude homosexual self-labeling. *Journal of Homosexuality, 9*(4), 53–63.

Herdt, G. H. (1981). *Guardians of the flutes: Idioms of masculinity.* New York: McGraw-Hill.

Herdt, G. H. (1987). *The Sambia: Ritual and gender in New Guinea.* New York: Holt, Rinehart & Winston.

Hinde, R. A. (1979). *Towards understanding relationships.* London: Academic Press.

Howard, J. A., Blumstein, P., & Schwartz, P. (1986). Sex, power, and influence tactics in intimate relationships. *Journal of Personality and Social Psychology, 51*(1), 102- 109.

Huston, T. L. (1983). Power. In H. H. Kelley et al., *Close relationships* (pp. 169–219). New York: W. H. Freeman.

Jay, K., & Young, A. (1977). *The gay report: Lesbians and gay men speak out about sexual experiences and life styles.* New York: Summit Books.

Jones, R. W., & Bates, J. E. (1978). Satisfaction in male homosexual couples. *Journal of Homosexuality, 3*(3), 217- 224.

Kaplan, G. T., & Rogers, L. J. (1984). Breaking out of the dominant paradigm: A new look at sexual attraction. *Journal of Homosexuality, 10*(3/4), 71-75.

Kelley, H. H. (1983). Love and commitment. In H. H. Kelley et al., *Close relationships* (pp. 265–314). New York: W. H. Freeman.

Kelley, H. H., Berscheid, E., Christensen, A., Harvey, J. H., Huston, T. L., Levinger, G., McClintock, E., Peplau, L. A., & Peterson, D. R. (1983). *Close relationships*. New York: W. H. Freeman.

Koertge, N. (1984). The fallacy of misplaced precision. *Journal of Homosexuality, 10*(3/4), 15–21.

Kollock, P., Blumstein, P., & Schwartz, P. (1985). Sex and power in interaction: Conversational privileges and duties. *American Sociological Review, 50,* 34–46.

Kurdek, L. A., & Schmitt, J. P. (1986a). Relationship quality of partners in heterosexual married, heterosexual cohabiting, gay, and lesbian relationships. *Journal of Personality and Social Psychology, 51,* 711–720.

Kurdek, L. A., & Schmitt, J. P. (1986b). Relationship quality of gay men in closed or open relationships. *Journal of Homosexuality, 12*(2), 85–99.

Kurdek, L. A., & Schmitt, J. P. (1987). Partner homogamy in married, heterosexual cohabiting, gay, and lesbian couples. *Journal of Sex Research, 23,* 212–232.

Larson, P. C. (1982). Gay male relationships. In W. Paul, J. D. Weinrich, J. C. Gonsiorek, & M. E. Hotvedt (Eds.), *Homosexuality: Social, psychological, and biological issues* (pp. 219–232). Beverly Hills: Sage.

Levinger, G. (1979). A social psychological perspective on marital dissolution. In G. Levinger & O. C. Moles (Eds.), *Divorce and separation* (pp. 37–63). New York: Basic Books.

Lewis, R. A., Kozac, E. B., Milardo, R. M., & Grosnick, W. A. (1980, August). *Commitment in lesbian and gay male living-together relationships.* Paper presented at the annual meeting of the American Sociological Association, New York.

Lynch, J. M., & Reilly, M. E. (1986). Role relationships: Lesbian perspectives. *Journal of Homosexuality, 12*(2), 53- 69.

Marecek, J., Finn, S. E., & Cardell, M. (1982). Gender roles in the relationships of lesbians and gay men. *Journal of Homosexuality, 8*(2), 45–50.

Martin, D., & Lyon, P. (1972). *Lesbian/woman.* San Francisco: Glide Publications.

Mays, V. M. (1986, August). *The black women's relationships project: A national survey of black lesbians.* Paper presented at the annual meeting of the American Psychological Association, Washington, D.C.

McKusick, L., Wiley, J. A., Coates, T. J., Stall, R., Saika, G., Morin, S., Charles, K., Horstman, W. R., Conant, M. A. (1985). Reported changes in the sexual behavior of men at risk for AIDS, San Francisco, 1982–84: The AIDS Behavioral Research Project. *Public Health Reports, 100*(6), 622–629.

McWhirter, D. P., & Mattison, A. M. (1980). Treatment of sexual dysfunction in homosexual male couples. In S. R. Leiblum & L. A. Pervin (Eds.), *Principles and practice of sex therapy.* New York: Guilford Press.

McWhirter, D. P., & Mattison, A. M. (1984). *The male couple.* Englewood Cliffs, NJ: Prentice-Hall.

Miller, P. Y., & Fowlkes, M. R. (1980). Social and behavioral constructions of female sexuality. *Signs: Journal of Women in Culture and Society, 5*(4), 783–800.

Morin, S. F. (1976). Annotated bibliography of research on lesbianism and male homosexuality (1967-1974). *JSAS Catalog of Selected Documents in Psychology, 6*(1), 15 (58 pages).

Peplau, L. A. (1982). Research on homosexual couples: An overview. *Journal of Homosexuality*, *8*(2), 3–7.

Peplau, L. A. (1983). Roles and gender. In H. H. Kelley et al., *Close relationships* (pp. 220–264). New York: W. H. Freeman.

Peplau, L. A. (1984). Power in dating relationships. In J. Freeman (Ed.), *Women: A feminist perspective* (3rd ed., pp. 106–121). Palo Alto, CA: Mayfield.

Peplau, L. A., & Amaro, H. (1982). Understanding lesbian relationships. In W. Paul, J. D. Weinrich, J. C. Gonsiorek, & M. E. Hotvedt (Eds.), *Homosexuality: Social, psychological, and biological issues* (pp. 233–248). Beverly Hills: Sage.

Peplau, L. A., & Cochran, S. D. (1980, September). *Sex differences in values concerning love relationships*. Paper presented at the annual meeting of the American Psychological Association, Montreal, Canada.

Peplau, L. A., & Cochran, S. D. (1981). Value orientations in the intimate relationships of gay men. *Journal of Homosexuality*, *6*(3), 1–19.

Peplau, L. A., Cochran, S. D., & Mays, V. M. (1986, August). *Satisfaction in the intimate relationships of black lesbians*. Paper presented at the annual meeting of the American Psychological Association, Washington, D.C.

Peplau, L. A., Cochran, S., Rook, K., & Padesky, C. (1978). Women in love: Attachment and autonomy in lesbian relationships. *Journal of Social Issues*, *34*(3), 7–27.

Peplau, L. A., & Gordon, S. L. (1983). The intimate relationships of lesbians and gay men. In E. R. Allgeier & N. B. McCormick (Eds.), *The changing boundaries: Gender roles and sexual behavior* (pp. 226–244). Palo Alto, CA: Mayfield.

Peplau, L. A., Padesky, C., & Hamilton, M. (1982). Satisfaction in lesbian relationships. *Journal of Homosexuality*, *8*, 23- 35.

Ramsey, J., Latham, J. D., & Lindquist, C. U. (1978, August). *Long term same-sex relationships: Correlates of adjustment*. Paper presented at the annual meeting of the American Psychological Association, Toronto, Canada.

Raphael, S. M., & Robinson, M. K. (1980). The older lesbian: Love relationships and friendship patterns. *Alternative Lifestyles*, *3*(2), 207–230.

Reilly, M. E., & Lynch, J. M. (1986). *Power sharing in lesbian partnerships*. Unpublished manuscript, University of Rhode Island, Kingston.

Rich, A. (1980). Compulsory heterosexuality and lesbian experience. *Signs: Journal of Women in Culture and Society*, *5*(4), 631-660.

Ross, M. W. (1984). Beyond the biological model: New directions in bisexual and homosexual research. *Journal of Homosexuality*, *10*(3/4), 63–75.

Shively, M. G., Jones, C., & De Cecco, J. P. (1984). Research on sexual orientation: Definitions and methods. *Journal of Homosexuality*, *9*(2/3), 127-136.

Silverstein, C. (1981). *Man to man: Gay couples in America*. New York: William Morrow.

Toder, N. (1978). Sexual problems of lesbians. In G. Vida (Ed.), *Our right to love: A lesbian resource book* (pp. 105–113). Englewood Cliffs, NJ: Prentice-Hall.

Tripp, C. A. (1975). *The homosexual matrix*. New York: Signet.

Turner, R. H. (1962). Role-taking: Process versus conformity. In A. Rose (Ed.), *Human behavior and social processes* (pp. 20–40). Boston: Houghton Mifflin.

Vicinus, M. (1984). Distance and desire: English boarding-school friendships. *Signs: Journal of Women in Culture and Society*, *9*(4), 600–622.

Warren, C. A. B. (1974). *Identity and community in the gay world*. New York: John Wiley & Sons.

Wolf, D. G. (1980). *The lesbian community*. Berkeley: University of California Press.

20

Lesbian Relationships: Implications for the Study of Sexuality and Gender

Margaret Nichols

In large part because of the legacy left by Kinsey and his colleagues at the Kinsey Institute for Research in Sex, Gender, and Reproduction (formally the Institute for Sex Research), research on homosexuality in the last two decades has evolved beyond the "pathology" model that, aside from its moral judgmentalism, inappropriately restricted the study of sexual orientation to an overly narrow domain of interest. We have a growing body of work that, instead of asking "what pathology has produced this aberrant behavior," asks the far more relevant question "how and why does human sexuality diversify in such interesting ways, particularly regarding the *gender* of the sexual or romantic partner?"

The new researchers in sexual orientation recognize the foresight of Kinsey's conceptualization of a continuum of attractions based on the gender of object choice, and they recognize the limitations of this 40-year old model. They understand not only that attractions to same and opposite sex can exist side by side in the same person; they are beginning to catalog the many ways in which both heterosexual and homosexual attractions have been manifested in different time periods and cultures and by different individuals within a culture. Because issues of sexual orientation are so complex, they are also linked to topics of gender and gender role socialization and questions about human love and sexual relationships. Thus the study of any subsegment of homosexual or bisexual expression has the potential to enlighten us about human sexuality in many ways.

Lesbianism has always been less understood than male homosexuality. In part because of simple sexism, in part because most research has found the incidence of lesbianism to be lower than rates of male homosexuality, women who love other women are less frequently studied. And yet ample evidence exists to suggest that lesbians are not simply female reproductions of gay men. In fact, because lesbians seem so different from gay men at times, contrasting gay male relationships with lesbian relationships with heterosexual relationships, as Blumstein and Schwartz (1983) did in their highly creative work, gives us exciting opportunities to observe the interaction of gender, sex, and relationships. Such study yields important knowledge about the social construction of our sex roles, our sexuality, and our loves.

To emphasize what we can learn about socialization does not exclude the possible contribution that biology, including genetic and prenatal influence, plays in the development of sexuality. Yet certain social forces seem undeniable. To anyone studying lesbianism in any depth, the role of sex role socialization and cultural attitudes toward women seems unmistakable. One of the thrusts of this chapter will be to highlight what lesbian relationships have to tell us about all women.

Indeed, even the lower incidence of homosexuality in women may be in part a reflection of the socialization of women. For example, it has been amply documented that lesbian women, when compared to gay men, tend to recognize and act upon their same-sex attractions at a later age. Higher percentages of lesbians have had heterosexual sex and a higher percentage marry heterosexually (Bell & Weinberg, 1978; Jay & Young, 1979). However, married gay men stay married longer and report being happier in their marriages, prompting Bell and Weinberg to say:

> Women were less likely to behave sexually in accordance with their true interests . . . It is possible that lesbians' greater heterosexuality simply reflects a history of accommodation to males in a sexual context or of conformity to social expectations. (p. 60)

In other words, the relative ratio of gay men to lesbians may reflect men's relatively higher rates of *all* kinds of sexual activity coupled with women's relative lack of personal freedom to live their lives as they choose. Women in this culture have generally fewer life options than men, including the option to openly live out one's homosexuality.

In order to elucidate some of the ways in which lesbian relationships can cast light upon our knowledge of women, this chapter will consider four aspects of female homosexuality: a historical overview of the various forms lesbian relationships have taken in this century, a discussion of research findings of bisexual women, the dynamics of lesbian couples, and breakthroughs of the emerging lesbian sex radical movement.

A Brief Historical Overview of Lesbian Relationships

When one takes even a cursory look at historical and anthropological evidence, it becomes clear that the "essentialist" view of sexual orientation, which regards orientation as an almost immutable trait like skin color or height, cannot encompass all the variations of same-sex behavior that we know to exist and to have existed in the past. Three illustrations of the forms that lesbian relationships have taken in this country in the last century and a half will clarify this point. For example, Lillian Faderman's fascinating book *Surpassing the Love of Men* (1981) describes the "romantic friendships" common among upper-middle-class women of the previous two centuries. During these years, a number of single, childless women lived in lifelong companionships with other women that often enabled them to live more career-oriented or at least intellectually oriented lives than would have been possible in traditional wife/mother roles. From accounts that some of these women have left behind (diaries, letters, and so on), Faderman concludes that many "Boston marriages," as they were often called, were emotionally passionate, intimate relationships comparable to heterosexual marriage but often probably without a genital sexual component. The women involved in these companionships did not consider themselves "lesbians;" indeed, for much of this time period neither the word nor the concept for lesbianism existed. Nevertheless, Faderman, who has since drawn parallels between these women and today's radical lesbian feminists (1984), argues that they be considered "gay" relationships on the basis of their romantic/emotional component and their structural similarities to heterosexual marriage. Faderman's analysis raises interesting questions about how one defines sexual orientation (Is a relationship lesbian if genital sexual contact is absent?), but also highlights the interaction of sexual orientation/sexual identity with the sociopolitical functions served by the homosexual role. It is extremely important to recognize that women in romantic friendships were, by virtue of their "lesbianism," able to be free of many of the social constraints experienced by heterosexually married women. Thus, seen in this context, sexual orientation means far more than the seemingly neutral choice of gender of the romantic or sexual partner. When cultures use gender as a primary organizing principle for the structuring of nearly every aspect of an individual's life, then the choice of gender of partner must of necessity be laden with social meaning and implication. As we will see in the next section, there is increasing evidence that at least for some people, sexual attraction is not immutably determined from birth. Given this, it is almost irresistible to conclude that the social meanings, roles, and functions attached to gender must in some way influence the development and expression of sexual orientation.

Looking at history shows us that the theme enunciated by "romantic friendships"—that of escaping the traditional roles culturally assigned to women—repeats itself over and over again in lesbian relationships. Jonathan Katz (1976) documents the phenomenon of "passing women" in America around the turn of the century. During this era, a number of women dressed as men and used male names, taking on male identities and roles and often "marrying" women. They disguised themselves in this way and often assumed a male persona for their entire adult lives, unknown as women to their closest associates, and sometimes even to their "wives." Some achieved great prominence in business and politics, holding elected office as men, and they were not discovered to be female until after death, upon autopsy or preparation of the body for burial. What we know of these individuals comes largely from newspaper accounts after death revealed their true identities, less frequently from personal diaries. The few accounts they left behind in their own words strongly suggest that "passing women" were motivated at least as much by their desire to escape the limited social roles available to women as they were to actualize their same-sex erotic attractions. Again, the social meanings attached to gender appear to interact with sexual orientation.

The third piece of historical data we can consider is the growth of lesbian-feminist culture in the 1970s (Faderman, 1984). During this decade, many women seemed to come to a recognition of their same-sex attractions through the vehicle of the women's movement. Typically, the lesbian who "came out" in this way was largely unaware of her same-sex impulses until adulthood. Often she had married heterosexually and was dissatisfied with her relationships with men for a variety of reasons that found articulation through the political philosophy of feminism. Many such women began actively pursuing a lesbian life-style only after a personal political transformation and after seeing lesbianism validated by women's groups and organizations. They often consider their lesbianism a "choice" and rationalize their new life-style with the rhetoric of feminism:

> Women who came to lesbianism reject the notion that lesbianism is a sexual identity. This is not to say that sexual expression is usually absent in the new gay women's lives; rather, sexual activity is for them generally only one aspect and perhaps a relatively unimportant aspect of their committment to a lesbian lifestyle. Lesbianism in this context, or, more precisely, lesbian-feminism, is defined as a political choice more than a sexual preference . . . less a personal choice about who to sleep with than a uniting of women against patriarchal power. Lesbian femininsts deny that the choice to be lesbian arises from sexual interest or sexual proclivity . . . Instead, lesbian feminists define lesbianism in much more inclusive terms: a lesbian's entire sense of self centers on women. (Faderman, 1984, pp. 86–87)

In some ways, lesbian feminists have articulated in defiantly political terms what "passing women" articulated in an individualistic framework and what remained without voice for women in romantic friendships (Nichols & Leiblum, 1986).

It is not suggested here that sexism is the sole determinant of lesbian relationships. In addition to personal, interpersonal, and family dynamics, biologic or innate predisposition is quite likely to play a role in the unfolding of sexual orientation. For some individuals, the cultural loading of gender may have little or nothing to do with their expression of sexual identity. Moreover, it is just as likely that for many people the social functions assigned to gender may shape the manifestation of sexual orientation but not the initial formation of erotic attractions. For example, lesbians in the 1950s often assumed rigid "butch-femme" roles in their couple relationships, and the butch-femme phenomenon seems more related to an imitation of existing heterosexual models of relationships than to the formation of erotic attraction (Nichols & Leiblum, 1986). As we shall see in the section on lesbian couples, sex role socialization may influence the dynamics of female-female pairings in a way independent of the origins of same-sex erotic pull. Nevertheless, the study of the differentiation of sexual orientation can be greatly enhanced by considering the various functions, roles, and meanings that directly or indirectly accrue to a homosexual versus heterosexual life-style. Same-sex erotic attraction is probably a necessary but not sufficient condition for homosexual behavior or identity. For some lesbians, the cultural roles assigned to women seem to influence the expression of attraction.

Bisexuality in Women and Its Relationship to Lesbianism

Additional insight about sexual orientation in women can be achieved by reviewing some of the newer research on bisexuality in women. The study of bisexuality is made more difficult by lack of a precise definition. Do we use as our criterion fantasy, attraction, or behavior, and do we attend to quantity or quality of contact, sexual versus relationship aspects, history over a life span or recent behavior? Masters and Johnson (1979), for example, found what they termed "cross-preference encounter" sexual fantasies to be quite common for all their subjects. Lesbian sexual fantasies were the fifth most common fantasy among women who identify as heterosexual, and heterosexual fantasies ranked third for self-identified lesbians. Bell and Weinberg (1978) reported that only half of lesbian women rate their feelings and attractions as exclusively gay. Hyde (1982), in interpreting data from both the Kinsey surveys and the Hune survey of the 1970s, estimated that on the basis of same- and opposite-sex behavior in adulthood, approximately 15% of women are bisexual and less than 1% exclusively homosexual. Bell and Weinberg additionally estimated that more than one third of their lesbian sample exhibited what they called a "partial bisexual style," that is, some current pleasurable heterosexual activity and attractions despite a predominantly gay life-style and lesbian identity. Moreover, even among their "heterosexual control group," 10% of women were behaviorally bisexual. These statistics suggest that (1) far more women *behave* bisexually and/or experience bisexual fantasies and attractions than are self-labeled as bisexual; (2) lesbianism is something of a residual category in this culture, that is, large percentages of women who self-label as gay are in fact both erotically and behaviorally bisexual, not just in terms of life history but also with regard to their current behavior and feelings. Lesbian means "not exclusively heterosexual" as much as it means "exclusively homosexual." In a sense, these data make lesbianism an even more interesting phenomenon. Clearly, lesbianism is not merely a matter of an overwhelming, single-focus sexual attraction. These facts about bisexuality make the nonbiologic factors operative in lesbianism even more relevant and give insight into the claim of some gay women that they "chose" their sexual orientation.

Three more pieces of research on bisexuality shed additional light on the complexity of sexual attraction and orientation in women. Nichols (1985) asked gay, lesbian, bisexual, and heterosexual subjects to rate themselves on a series of Kinsey-style scales with regard to various dimensions of behavior, fantasy, and emotional attractions for both past and current time periods and related these dimensions to self-identified sexual orientation. Gays and lesbians, but particularly lesbians, showed little internal consistency in their ratings. Among lesbians, it was not at all uncommon to find "heterosexual" ratings of fantasy and behavior; only *behavior in the last year* was highly related to self-label. Again, this work suggests that women often identify as lesbians and live a lesbian life-style for reasons more complex than merely strength of erotic attraction. Two other studies of bisexual women in marriages suggest that erotic attraction itself may be more fluid and variable in women than has previously been believed. Both Coleman (1985) and Dixon (1985) found fewer than half of these married women to have been aware of homosexual feelings prior to marriage. Many appeared to make dramatic swings in Kinsey ratings of both behavior and fantasy over the course of the marriage. These findings cast doubt upon the widely held belief in the inflexibility of sexual orientation and attraction over a lifetime, as well as the assumption that homosexual attractions are developed and "fixed" in early childhood or adolescence. For some women, at least, sexuality is fluid and changeable over time. Dixon, who studied women in "swinging" marriages, found that few of her subjects reported homoerotic fantasies or attractions before engaging in lesbian activities during "swinging" scenes, but most reported such fantasies and attraction *after* pleasurable lesbian sex. It seems, then, that for some women, fantasy can follow pleasurable behavior rather than be an antecedent to it. From a cursory examination of bisexuality in women, we see that female sexual orientation, at least for some, can be fluid and dynamic and that by implication lesbianism is a multifactored life-style, not merely the expression of a biological imperative or of some intransient orientation fixed early in childhood.

Lesbian Couples: Implications for the Study of Relationships

If we examine the loving relationships that lesbians form with each other, we discover that although in many ways lesbian couples are like any other kind of couple, there are several interesting differences that illuminate not only the dynamics of woman-to-woman pairings but also other kinds of relationships as well. Lesbian relationships represent, above all, the inter-actions of women with each other in the absence of a male influence, or at least in a setting that is as free of male influence as one can get given the early sex role socialization that affects us all.

What do we know of contemporary lesbian relationships? First, because lesbians as a group have been underresearched, we know less about lesbian couples than about any other kind of pairing. For example, there is no work on lesbians to compare with the pioneering research on gay male couples conducted by McWhirter and Mattison (1984) or Silverstein (1981). But we do know that like heterosexual women, lesbians value relationships very highly. For example, Bell and Weinberg (1978) found that 82% of the lesbians they interviewed were currently living with part-ners. In addition, they found that a majority of lesbians rated being in a committed relationship as the most important value in their lives. Like other women, most lesbians have been socialized to value relationships more highly than careers or other life goals. Furthermore, lesbians ideal-ize their relationships in a way that is somewhat different from others in the culture. Peplau, Cochran, Rook, and Padesky (1978) found that lesbi-ans value egalitarianism in their relationships more than do others, al-though they may not always achieve the egalitarianism. Blumstein and Schwartz (1983) noted that lesbians are less concerned with physical beauty and age of a partner. Thus, it appears that many lesbians cherish committed relatiohships as the most important aspect of life and attempt to incorporate feminist values of equality into their partnerships, al-though not always with more success than heterosexual women or gay or heterosexual men.

The most striking differences between lesbian couples and other kinds of couples have to do with sexuality and sexual frequency. *Single* lesbians have less frequent sex and fewer different partners than do gay men (Bell & Weinberg, 1978; Jay & Young, 1979). This is not surprising because at least until the advent of AIDS, gay men were probably more sexually active than anyone else in the culture. And some research suggests that, overall, lesbians may be more sexually responsive and more satisfied with the sex they do have than are heterosexual women (Coleman, Hoon, & Hoon, 1983; Masters & Johnson, 1979). Masters and Johnson speculate that the sexual techniques of lesbians, which tend to be sensuous, less genitally and orgasm focused, and less oriented to vaginal penetration, are generally more suited to the sexual needs of women than is heterosexual sexual activity.

Lesbians do not seem to have pervasive sexual problems. Clinical reports do not suggest, for example, that gay women have significant rates of orgasmic dysfunction, and dyspareunia and vaginismus are almost unheard of among gay women for reasons probably related to sexual technique. But lesbians do seem to have strikingly low rates of sex *within long-term committed relationships*.

Most clinicians and sex therapists working with lesbian couples have noted the high prevalence of sexual desire disorders among such couples (Burch, 1982; Decker, 1984; Kaufman, Harrison, & Hyde, 1984; Nichols, 1982, 1987, 1988; Roth, 1985). Sociologists Blumstein and Schwartz (1983), comparing heterosexual married and unmarried couples, gay male, and lesbian couples, have given us the most comprehensive data we have on this topic. They found that lesbian couples in long-term relationships have sex far less frequently than any other type of couple studied. Only about one third of lesbians in relationships of 2 years or more had sex once a week or more. Forty-seven percent of lesbians in relationships of over 5 years had sex once a month or less. This is in striking contrast, for example, to heterosexual married couples: two thirds of these couples together more than 5 years had sex once a week or more, and only 15% had sex once a month or less.

That this dynamic is related to lesbians' status as women rather than to their homosexual nature of the coupling is evident from the Blumstein and Schwartz (1983) data on gay male couples. Gay men have slightly less sex in their primary relationships than do heterosexual couples; on the other hand, gay males have the highest rates of extramarital sex. This means that lesbians in couple relationships are less sexual both within and outside the relationship than any other group, just as uncoupled lesbians have less frequent sex and fewer partners than do gay men.

Moreover, Blumstein and Schwartz's findings indicate other differences as well. Their lesbian subjects preferred hugging, cuddling, and other nongenital physical contact to genital sex, reminiscent of reports from heterosexual women in such surveys as the *Hite Report* (1976). Similarly, both Blumstein and Schwartz (1983) and Jay and Young (1979) found lesbians to be more constricted in their range of sexual techniques than other couples. For example, 61% of lesbian couples have oral sex "infrequently or not at all," leaving the repertoire of the majority of couples limited to manual stimulation and tribadism. Lesbians have about the same rates of nonmonogamy as do heterosexuals (28% report at least one extramarital episode), although they have far less "outside" sex than gay men, for whom nonmonogomy is the norm rather than the exception. Moreover, both lesbians and gay men tend to have sex in the context of an "open" relationship in contrast to the secretive "infidelities" common among heterosexuals. But lesbians, like heterosexual women and unlike both gay and straight men, are likely to have "affairs" rather than just sexual encounters. Finally, Blumstein and Schwartz (1983) reported that one half of lesbians in couples with a low frequency of genital contact said that they were dissatisfied with their sexuality. And in an 18-month follow-up of all couples, lesbian couples had the highest rates of dissolution of any couple type. The pattern of breakup was significant: one partner had an outside affair and subsequently left the primary relationship for the new lover.

How are we to explain these findings? They fly in the face of not only the belief that women culturally form the "glue" that holds relationships together but also findings showing the high value lesbians place on relationships, the high percentages of lesbians that are members of committed couples at any given time, and the general level of satisfaction lesbians report about the sexual encounters they do have. It seems clear, given the dissimilarities between gay male and lesbian couples, that we must interpret these findings as dynamics of woman-to-woman pairings, the effects of female socialization multiplied rather than concomitants of homosexuality. Given that, what sense can be made of the data on lesbian couples to shed light upon femininity as expressed in this culture?

It appears, first, that the recognizably feminine values of relationship orientation and egalitarianism may influence the tendency to *be* coupled but not necessarily the ability to make a relationship last. On this point, it is important to stress that we have only one study—the Blumstein and Schwartz (1983) research— that gives us hard data on longevity of lesbian couples. Moreover, Blumstein and Schwartz themselves are quick to remind us that the variable of *social sanction* seems to be the predominant factor correlated with relationship longevity. That is, heterosexual married couples stay together longer than any type of unmarried couple, be it heterosexual, gay male, or lesbian, and the differences between longevity of married versus unmarried couples are far greater than differences among any type of unmarried couple. Nevertheless, it is safe to assume at this juncture that lesbian couples do *not* experience more longevity than other types of couples, which is what one would assume from the stereotype that women provide the "glue" of relationships. Further, although lesbian sex may be more pleasurable and intrinsically/biologically "right" for women than more genitally/orgasmically focused sex, this does not seem to contribute to frequency of sexual encounters within a long-term relationship.

To an extent, the data on frequency of sex within lesbian relationships forces us to examine our beliefs about the significance of sexual interaction within any committed relationship. Just as Faderman (1981) argued, in her work of "romantic friendships," for a definition of lesbianism that did not necessarily include genital sex, so it is probably true that some lesbians are not disturbed by the infrequency or even total absence of genital sex in their relationships. Tripp (1975) and others have observed numerous long-term lesbian relationships devoid of genital sexual contact without apparent disturbance, and Blumstein and Schwartz (1983) revealed that many of their lesbian subjects expressed a preference for hugging and cuddling over genital physical contact. Some lesbians simply do not place a high priority on sex, and in this regard they resemble some heterosexual women. Schreiner-Engel (1986), for example, reported that even among heterosexual subjects who define themselves as suffering from problems of low sexual desire, men and women differ markedly, with men reporting situational or secondary desire disorders and women reporting primary problems: half of these women report *never* experiencing sexual desire. And all surveys of sexual behavior show women, overall, to be less sexually active than men. To an extent lesbian couples may simply enact the sexual desires of women in general. While it may not be true that women provide the "glue" in relationships, it is possible that men tend to provide the major push for frequent sex in long-term relationships.

Thus, one interpretation of the data on sexuality in lesbian relationships is that the low frequency of genital sex coupled with a relatively constricted sexual repertoire and high frequency on nongenital physical expressions of affection represents a "true" expression of female sexuality. For some lesbians this is undoubtedly the case. However, just as some women have high sexual needs and desires for a broad range of sexual/genital activities, some lesbians clearly are dissatisfied with the sexual patterns that predominate in their long-term relationships. Some evidence for this is direct: many lesbians *report* dissatisfaction, and low sexual frequency is often noted as a complaint of lesbians seeking couple counseling. Other evidence is indirect: we can infer that the relatively higher dissolution rate for lesbian relationships found by Blumstein and Schwartz (1983) may be related to low rates of sexual contact. In fact, the pattern found in the Blumstein and Schwartz (1983) study is one frequently noted by clinicians working with lesbian couples. That pattern consists of a sharp decrease or even absence of sex in the couple after a few years, followed by one member's seeking an outside lover and eventually leaving her partner for that lover.

This evidence suggests that we need to consider the low rates of sexual expression found in long-term lesbian relationships as a problem for at least some gay women rather than simply an expression of female sexuality in its "natural" form (i.e., not influenced by a male presence). What might be the source of this sexual dysfunction?

The sources of low sexual frequency among lesbian couples have been discussed elsewhere in depth (Nichols, 1982, 1987,1988), but a brief discussion of three of these causes will illustrate points about female sexuality as well as lesbian relationships.

To an extent, the behavior of lesbians in couples may reflect an extreme example of the general approach women take to sexuality and relationships. While it is true that women tend to value committed relationships highly, it may be that at times they choose to be in relationships at the expense of individual differentiation and the development of personal autonomy and emotional self-sufficiency. Moreover, women, somewhat more than men, tend to fuse sex and love, expressing their sexuality primarily in the context of an emotional pair-bond. Thus, it is not surprising that lesbians, manifesting these female tendencies, tend to be coupled in such high numbers. Many gay women spend little of their adult lives as single women, moving directly from one love relationship into another. Moreover, lesbians often tend to interpret sexual attraction as love and move very rapidly from the initial limerent stage of a relationship to a live-in commitment within weeks or even days. This quick progression from attraction to commitment allows little opportunity for partners to explore the practical feasibility of the relationship, that is, to ascertain differences that might lead to conflict. Thus, the high dissolution rate of gay women's partnerships probably reflects to an extent the initial inappropriateness of partner choice, an inappropriateness that might have been discovered before a commitment was made had the women been a little more comfortable with their status as single adults and a bit more at ease with the idea of sex without commitment. These twin tendencies—to value relationships at an extreme over being single and to express sex only within the context of a relationship—partially account for lesbians' patterns of nonmonogamy and movement from one relationship to the next. When lesbians are dissatisfied with a primary relationship (often because of low sexual frequency), they seek outside outlets but seem able to do this only by "falling in love" with a new woman, breaking the old commitment, and rapidly recommitting to the new lover.

Two other factors that influence the low sexual frequency in lesbian relationships are worthy of mention. The first is that the low sexual frequency and constricted sexual repertoires of lesbian couples probably reflect the general socialization women receive in this culture to fear sex and thus to devalue it and repress their own sexual desires. As Carol Vance (1984) has written:

> Women—socialized by mothers to keep their dresses down, their pants up, and their bodies away from strangers—come to experience their own sexual impulses as dangerous. Self-control and watchfulness become necessary female virtues. As a result, female desire is suspect from its first tingle, questionable until proven safe, and frequently too expensive when evaluated within the larger cultural framework which poses the question, Is it really worth it? When unwanted pregnancies, street harrassment, stigma, unemployment, queer bashing, rape, and arrest are weighed on the side of caution and inaction, passion often doesn't stand a chance. (p. 4)

We see no reason to believe that lesbians have escaped the conditioning Vance describes, which seems ironic in light of the fact that some lesbian feminists maintain they have "chosen" their lesbianism in part precisely in the hope of escaping these dynamics.

Finally, low sexual frequency in lesbian relationships is often a correlate of what has been noted by clinicians as the phenomenon of *fusing* (Kaufman et al, 1984; Nichols, 1982; Roth, 1984, 1985). Kaufman et al. (1984) described fusion, which appears to be very common in lesbian relationships, in the following way:

> [This] relationship distress is characterized by excessive closeness between women, extreme and intense ambivalence, and a failure to establish emotional, territorial, temporal, and cognitive space for each individual . . . These lesbian couples . . . appeared to be too closely merged and symbiotic . . . For these couples the initial merging that occurred with the early stage of falling and being in love would not yield to increasing pressures from the environment. The oneness, a kind of narcissistic failure to allow for separateness or a defense against difference, had become the norm or the expected state they would strive to achieve and maintain through more and more closeness . . . Each ignored her own needs for space as well as those of her partner. (p. 530)

Kaufman et al. proceeded to describe a cluster of behaviors typical of fused lesbian couples. These behaviors include attempts to share all social, recreational, and sometimes professional activities; the absence of individual friendships; little or no separate physical space or belongings, including clothing; regular telephone intrusions into the workday so that partners rarely spend even a few hours without being in contact with each other; and communication patterns that indicate assumptions of shared thoughts, values, and ideas (e.g., sentences started by one woman may be completed by another).

These couples represent an extreme version of the kind of closeness and intimacy in which all women are trained so well. In one sense, lesbians achieve what many other women idealize. Or, as Kaufman et al. (1984) suggest:

> [T]hese behaviors are strongly reinforced by cultural descriptions of the idealized romantic relationship of lovers riding off into the sunset, escaping worldly pressures and reality in their isolation, making promises of lifelong fidelity, and believing that they belong to one another. (p. 531)

To an extent, lesbian couples achieve what is represented in women's pulp romantic novels, and in doing so they show us the "down side" of intimacy, what the need and desire for intimacy can do when is it unmitigated by the more typically male attitude that emphasizes distance and autonomy. Individual differences are suppressed in favor of the dyad, and closeness comes to be defined as sameness. This need to supress individuality, although it can be comforting and can enhance a certain kind of egalitarianism, often produces tension and ambivalence, which are expressed by avoiding intimate genital sexual contact. Avoidance of genital sexuality can be seen as a way to achieve distance in relationships severely in need of space. Additionally, if one sees sexual contact as a method couples use to achieve oneness, it is clear that this mechanism is simply unnecessary in fused relationships. And finally, to the extent that sexual desire is sparked by difference between partners and the desire to overcome the boundaries established by difference, this means of fueling desire is absent in fused lesbian couples. Thus, the examination of these dynamics in lesbian relationships can potentially teach us a great deal, not only about female socialization regarding love and sexual behavior but also about the negative and positive contributions this type of socialization makes to sexual and relationship dynamics.

The Lesbian Sex Radicals

To conclude this review of lesbian relationships, let us mention one of the most recent movements to develop out of the lesbian community, one that stands in contrast to much of our discussion of lesbian couple dynamics. In the late 1970s some lesbians, borrowing from the gay male sexual liberation activities that proliferated during that decade, began to organize groups and organizations to radicalize sexuality for women. Activities of the lesbian sex radicals have included the production of written, auditory, and visual erotica; the dissemination of information regarding a broad range of sexual techniques; the exposition of theoretical tracts about female sexual liberation; and the development of support groups for women wishing to experiment with casual sex, multiple sexual partners, bisexuality, and unusual sexual practices such as domination/submission, bondage, and so on. If traditional female sexual conditioning emphasizes the fusion of sex and love, the lesbian sex radicals quite consciously emphasize the separation of the two, but in an atmosphere that stresses female-oriented values such as equality of power, consensuality, safety, and emotional nurturance. While it is beyond the scope of this chapter to detail or describe this movement, it is worth noting that some lesbians themselves seem conscious of the pitfalls of feminine cultural socialization regarding sex and love and are deliberately attempting to change traditionally held values and behaviors. This movement is without parallel in the heterosexual female culture at large. It will be interesting to see whether it can survive and what role it will play in shaping the character of lesbian relationships in the future.

References

Bell, A. P., & Weinberg, M. S. (1978). *Homosexualities: A study of diversity among men and women*. New York: Simon & Schuster.

Blumstein, P., & Schwartz, P. (1983). *American couples*. New York: William Morrow.

Burch, B. (1982). Psychological merger in lesbian couples: A joint ego psychological and systems approach. *Family Therapy, 9*(3), 201–208.

Coleman, E. (1985). Bisexual women in marriages. *Journal of Homosexuality, 11*(1/2), 87–99.

Coleman, E., Hoon, P., & Hoon, E. (1983). Arousability and sexual satisfaction in lesbian and heterosexual women. *Journal of Sex Research, 19*(1), 58–73.

Decker, B. (1984). Counseling gay and lesbian couples. *Journal of Social Work and Human Sexuality, 2*(2/3), 39–52.

Dixon, J. K. (1985). Sexuality and relationship changes in married females following the commencement of bisexual activity. *Journal of Homosexuality, 11*(1/2), 115–133.

Faderman, L. (1981). *Surpassing the love of men: Romantic friendship and love between women from the renaissance to the present.*New York: William Morrow.

Faderman, L. (1984). The "new" gay lesbian. *Journal of Homosexuality, 10*(3/4), 85–96.

Hite, S. (1976). *The Hite Report*. New York: Macmillan.

Hyde, J. S. (1982). *Understanding human sexuality*. New York: McGraw-Hill.

Jay, K., & Young, A. (1979). *The gay report*. New York: Summit Books. Katz, J. (1976). *Gay American history*. New York: Thomas Crowell.

Kaufman, P., Harrison, E., & Hyde, M. (1984). Distancing for intimacy in lesbian relationships. *American Journal of Psychiatry, 14*, 530–533.

Masters, W., & Johnson, V. (1979). *Homosexuality in perspective*. Boston: Little, Brown.

McWhirter, D., & Mattison, A. (1984). *The male couple*. Englewood Cliffs, NJ: Prentice-Hall.

Nichols, M. (1982). The treatment of inhibited sexual desire in lesbian couples. *Women and Therapy, l*(4), 49–66.

Nichols, M. (1985, September). *Relationships between sexual behavior, erotic arousal, romantic attraction, and self-labeled sexual orientation*. Paper presented at the SSSS Conference, San Diego.

Nichols, M. (1987). Doing sex therapy with lesbians: bending a heterosexual paradigm to fit a gay lifestyle. In Boston Lesbian Psychologies Collective, *Lesbian psychologies*. Urbana, IL: University of Illinois Press.

Nichols, M. (1988). Low sexual desire in lesbian couples. In S. Leiblum and R. Rosen (Eds.), *Treatment of sexual desire disorders*. New York: Guilford Press.

Nichols, M., & Leiblum, S. (1986, Spring). Lesbianism as personal identity and social role: A model. *Affilia: Journal of Women and Social Work*, pp. 48–59.

Peplau, L., Cochran, S., Rook, K., & Padesky, C. (1978). Loving women: Attachment and autonomy in lesbian relationships. *Journal of Social Issues, 34*(3), 7–28.

Roth, S. (1984). Psychotherapy with lesbian couples: The interrelationships of individual issues, female socialization, and social context. In E. Hetrick & T. Stein (Eds.), *Psychotherapy with Lesbians and Gay Men*. Washington DC: American Psychiatric Press.

Roth, S., (1985). Psychotherapy with lesbian couples: Individual issues, female socialization, and the social context. *Journal of Marital and Family Therapy, 11*(3), 273–286. Schreiner-Engle, P. (1986, September 20). *Clinical aspects of female sexuality*. Paper presented at the meeting of the International Academy of Sex Research, Amsterdam, the Netherlands.

Silverstein, C. (1981). *Man to man: Gay couples in America*. New York: William Morrow.

Tripp, C. (1975). *The homosexual Matrix*. New York: McGraw-Hill.

Vance, C. (1984). *Pleasure and danger: Exploring female sexuality*. London: Routledge & Kegan Paul.

VII

CONCEPTUAL AND THEORETICAL PERSPECTIVES

21

Sex and More Sex:
A Critique of the Kinsey
Conception of Human Sexuality

John P. De Cecco

I say that old traditions should be retained not because they are *old*, but because they are *different* from the status quo, because they permit us to see it in perspective and because many people are still interested in them and want to live accordingly. I also favor imagination and emotion but I don't want them to *replace* reason, I want them to *limit it*, and to *supplement* it.

Feyerabend (1978, p. 189)

From Christian Lust to Unfettered Sex: The Kinsey Transmutation

Through the rituals of science, the Kinsey reports (Kinsey, Pomeroy, & Martin, 1948; Kinsey, Pomeroy, Martin, & Gebhard, 1953) redeemed the evil "flesh" of Christian lust by transforming it into the "mammalian capacity" for boundless sexual experience and thereby made a memorable contribution to Western civilization. Christianity, for its contribution to our happiness, should be given the credit for bequeathing us *lust*.

Lust was not an issue for the classical Greeks. In *The Use of Pleasure*, Michel Foucault (1985) concluded that the ancient Greeks were more likely to be preoccupied with food than sex. For them, sexuality did not exist as a unified concept. Its importance was inherent in its relationships to physical health, which was not to be compromised by sexual behavior; to marriage, as the means of begetting legitimate children; and to love, which was tied more to honor and self-esteem than sexual gratification

(Lloyd, 1986). What worried the Greeks was not erotic desire itself, in either its heterosexual or homosexual form, but the threat of becoming a slave either to one's own desires or an instrument of somebody else's pleasure, sexual or otherwise. Their single fear about sexuality was the ancient, ecological one, that the loss of semen in ejaculation might become a serious drain upon the life force (Elia, 1987).[1]

It was the fulminations of such Christian Fathers as St. Paul and St. Augustine against the evils of the *flesh* and *carnal desire* that fostered the idea of *lust*, an "inordinate appetite for venereal pleasure" (Attwater, 1941, p. 317), as my Catholic dictionary defines it, and in church doctrine, one of the seven deadly sins and an "unnatural" form of sexual expression. There was, however, a contradiction in the application of the idea of "natural" to human sexuality, and it is evident in the work of the reigning medieval theologian, St. Thomas Aquinas. John Boswell (1980) observes that "Despite his [St. Thomas's] absolute conviction in every other [i.e., nonsexual] context that humans were morally and intellectually superior to animals and therefore not only permitted but obliged to engage in many types of activity unknown or impossible to lower beings, St. Thomas resorted again and again to animal behavior as the final arbiter of human sexuality" (p. 319). This inherent contradiction led him to condemn as "promiscuity" in humans the kind of random sexual behavior that can be commonly observed in domestic pets and farm animals. It was the untenable position that what was sexually "natural" for animals was "unnatural" for humans, as if there were two "natures," which the Kinsey group unwittingly capitalized on when they implied that as humans we should have at least as much sexual freedom as our pets.

Our sexual legacy, therefore, includes both the Christian horror of "lust" and the Kinsey appreciation of the possibility of less restrictive experience. Based on the assumption that sexual expression was natural and even biologically commendable, the Kinsey reports wove a different conception of human sexuality that was (1) essentially physical in content, (2) mechanical in mode of acquisition, (3) robust in performance, and (4) hedonistic, in that pleasure was its chief aim.

The Physical Nature of Sexuality

In the first place in the Kinsey work, it appears to me that all sexuality was conceived as a physical phenomenon—anatomical structure and physiological function. Its functional unit was the *orgasm*, defined as the "moment of sudden release" (Kinsey, et al., 1948, p. 158). This functional end point follows "erotic arousal" (p. 157), which, in turn, was defined as a "*material* phenomenon which involves an extended series of physical, physiological, and psychologic changes" that quicken the pulse; raise the blood pressure; swell the eyes, lips, ear lobes, and nipples as well as penis, labia, vaginal walls, and clitoris; and stiffen the muscles. The "sudden release" consisted of local spasms and "all-consuming" convulsions.

Total outlet was the observable sexual performance that accompanied the physical changes, "the sum of the orgasms" derived from six various sources, including masturbation, nocturnal emissions, petting, and intercourse. The orgasm was clearly anchored in the physical as the source of both arousal and subjective experience. *Sexual Behavior in the Human Male* (p. 158), for example, noted that when individuals refer to this physiologic state as being "emotionally aroused," they are usually unaware of the *"material* sources of the emotional disturbance."

Even the presumptive "psychologic" side of human sexuality consisted of physical images of performers and performances that sparked physical arousal, those composed by the individuals for themselves or those portrayed for them, for example, in magazines, films, or strip shows. When asked about sexual fantasies, respondents were directed to answer questions about whether they fancied females or males, who were blonde or brunette, tall or short, thin or stocky, masculine or feminine in dress and demeanor, and so on (Pomeroy, Flax, & Wheeler, 1982).

The Mechanistic Acquisition of Sexuality

The second fundamental assumption of the Kinsey conception of human sexuality was, as I see it, the mechanistic process through which it was acquired. "It is a picture," the 1948 report states, "of an animal who, however civilized or cultured, continues to respond to the constantly present sexual stimuli, albeit with some social and physical restraints" (p. 204). If the response were sexually reinforced, that is, gratified, then it would become conditioned and thereby repeated in the future in the presence of identical or similar stimuli. All forms of sexuality, the Kinsey group held, could be explained as products of learning and conditioning, from the preference to blondes and brunettes as sexual partners to "behavior which may appear bizarre, perverse, or unthinkably unacceptable to some persons . . . [but] may have significance for other individuals because of the way in which they have been conditioned" (Kinsey et al., 1953, p. 645).

The Performance Level in Sexuality

The third aspect of the Kinsey conception of human sexuality that strikes me as critical was its emphasis on robust performance. The individual's position in the hierarchy of sexual performance was determined by her or his record of outlets. In the *Male* volume (p. 216) the Academy Awards for record numbers of sexual outlets were bestowed upon six individuals who were able to attain between 25 and 38 outlets per week and as many as five ejaculations with each sexual encounter. [The Oscar for best male performance went to a black prostitute (p. 217) who, in addition to his regular heterosexual outlets, averaged 3 homosexual outlets a day and, at the age of 39, was still capable of six to eight ejaculations per encounter.] On the contrary, the 179 males with "low outlet" (p. 208), were unflatteringly described as being in poor health, physically incapacitated, sexually apathetic, slow starters, deprived (as in the case of prisoners), or sexually timid and inhibited.

The Moral Perspective of Sexuality

Finally, the moral tone of the Kinsey view was implicitly hedonistic. The Christian position was that the primary purpose of human sexuality was procreation. Pleasure was thrown in as a serendipitous gain in lives otherwise dedicated to the service and love of God.[2] The authors of the reports did a teleological somersault, replacing one primary sexual purpose with another: sex for reproduction was replaced by sex for pleasure—for its own intrinsic gratification. For them, human sexual expression was learned through the mechanism of reinforcement, which referred to the pleasurable physical consequences that followed sexual performance. Since the pursuit of sexual pleasure was portrayed as an evolutionary, biological capacity fortuitously shaped by responses to the physical environment, the Kinsey view equated the natural with the moral.

The Biological Morality of the Kinsey Reports

What makes the Kinsey reports remarkable documents is how this view of human sexuality was so punctiliously documented along several demographic dimensions and how it was argued with such unwavering moral zeal.[3] For the authors, human sexual experience did not require the usual extrinsic justifications found in religion and the law, such as the propagation of the human race, rearing of offspring, passionate love, and enduring relationships. Their proclamation to the world was that human sexuality is an intrinsic good, a pleasure that should be enjoyed for its own sake.

If the Kinsey group had stopped here, in my opinion, they would have stood on defensible scientific and moral ground. However, the general tone of the reports is that their material, quantitative, mechanistic, and hedonistic view described the nitty-gritty of human sexuality. In referring to the depiction of human sexuality in psychoanalysis, literature, and art, the first report asserts: "Such thinking easily becomes mystical, and quickly identifies any consideration of anatomic form and physiologic function as scientific materialism which misses the 'basic,' the 'human,' and the 'real' problems in behavior" (Kinsey et al., 1948, p. 642). Again, in the historical introduction to the first volume, the following assessment of previous studies of human sexuality appears:

> There is not one aspect of human behavior about which there has been more thought, more talk, and more books written . . . . It is, at once, an interesting reflection of man's absorbing interest in sex, and his astounding ignorance of it; his desire to know and his unwillingness to face the facts; his respect for an objective, scien-

tific approach to the problems involved, and his overwhelming urge to be poetic, pornographic, literary, philosophic, traditional, and moral. (pp. 21–22)

This quotation typifies the scientific hubris that pervades the reports—that at last the *truth* about human sexuality was to be starkly revealed. The reports would lift the veil of social values and moral injunction so that we could now look the truth in the face and see that sexuality is an essentially physical, mammalian capacity that humans share with the primitive anthropoid. Moreover, our wild, primate ancestors were less "hampered in the pursuit of sexual contacts" than the human male, who was restricted by "two thousand years of social monitoring" (Kinsey et al., 1948, p. 268).

The Humanist Counterresponse

The humanists did not take this lying down. Lionel Trilling (1950), the famous literary critic, rose to the occasion in a rhetorical essay, published after the first Kinsey report, which concluded with this statement:

The preponderant weight of its argument is that a fact is a physical fact, to be considered only in its physical aspect and apart from any idea or ideal that might make it a social fact, as having no ascertainable personal or cultural meaning and no possible consequences— as being, indeed, not available to social interpretation at all. (p. 229)

Trilling held that the reports committed both the reductive and psychologist's fallacies, the former referring to the reduction of the personal, cultural, and moral aspects of human sexuality to the physical and behavioral, the latter to the authors' erroneous assumption that their view of human sexuality was the phenomenon itself.[4]

The theologian Reinhold Niebuhr (1954) believed that the Kinsey reports ignored a cardinal assumption of the humanities, that is, the "radical freedom of the human person:"

This freedom makes for the uniqueness of the individual. It also creates a field of complex causation about which it is hazardous to draw any causal sequences, because every fact is so complexly related to previous events that a purely scientific judgment is impossible. It is impossible in the sense that events do not follow each other "in a necessary manner" in such a way that a scientific judgment would be possible . . . . Kinsey makes no room for responsible criticism of extant moral codes and attitudes, due to the consistency of his hedonism and his blindness to all the complexities of the relation of the sexual impulse to the institutions of civilization. (pp. 69–70)

I suspect that the Kinsey authors, as well as the rest of us in our calmer moments, feel that the "truth" about our sexuality is indeed complex and confusing and extraordinarily difficult to come by. Those of us who are deeply invested in our homosexuality, as individuals and scholars, perceive very keenly the dimensions of our sexuality that lie beyond the physical and behavioral. Unlike heterosexuality, which is socially *pre*scribed, homosexuality is *pro*scribed. As Vivienne Cass (1979) and Eli Coleman (1981/1982) have pointed out in their theories on the homosexual identity, it is bequeathed to us as the cracked mirror of heterosexuality. Indeed, because gay people cannot derive their sexuality from that imperfect reflection of what is judged to be a basically biological phenomenon, we must depend heavily on our own experience. In general, this experience is at first egregiously physical for the men and engulfingly emotional for the women, until we grasp the fact that we must develop our own vision of sexuality as the means of absorbing its social, political, and moral impact on our lives.

All That Glitters Is Not Gold: The Sexual and the Erotic

The Kinsey reports made no clear distinction between objective *sexual* performance and subjective *erotic* experience. Rather than narrowly targeting the orgasm as the sole source of gratification, the *erotic* dimension of our sexual experience is its perceptual and emotional qualities, which I will conceptualize as *sensuosity* and *desire*. It is my contention that erotic desire is fulfilled by the increments of sensuous gratification that occur along the way to orgasmic release.

Sensuosity, as one component of the erotic, embraces islands of satisfaction derived from the various senses, for example, the delight in hearing the soothing sound of your partner's voice, the sight of shadows moving over your bodies, the smell of freshly bathed and faintly scented skin, and the soft touch of hair brushing against your face. As erotic gratification, physical release should represent the culmination of a sensuous experience rather than its obsessive preoccupation.

Physical sexual contact is erotically renewing not because of its slavish obedience to the laws of learning but because it depends upon the changing contours of erotic desire, the spontaneous, fluid, sensuous qualities of the actual experience that elude habit. As the Kinsey level of *sensual* appetite and conditioned learning, the primary, perhaps the only, prospect of future gratification was more of the same performance one had experienced in the past, a genital drudgery that had to meet the stringent demands of what Herbert Marcuse (1955/1962), in another regard, called the "performance principle."[5]

The Kinsey reports therefore are explicitly about objective performance and only inferentially about subjective pleasure. The first report, for example, drew a distinction between *orgasm*, the "moment of sudden release" (Kinsey et al., 1948, p. 158), and the corresponding term once preferred by psychoanalysts, *orgastic pleasure* (e.g., Rado, 1949). The Kinsey group believed that orgastic pleasure referred to *degrees* of physiological change or sexual satisfaction occurring in sexual experience. The authors unequivocally asserted that their study did not delve into the *quality* of sexual experience: ." . . . we have no statistics on the frequencies of physiological differences, or the various degrees of satisfaction, and, in the present study, all cases of ejaculation have been taken as evidence of orgasm, without regard to the different levels at which the orgasms have occurred." (pp. 159–160).

Note that *quality* is defined as *degrees*, as if one were rating meat, so that you presumably can have "utility," "choice," or "prime" performance. This is like equating the appearance of the meat with the experience of preparing and tasting it. From the perspective of the erotic, the Kinsey recipe was the fast-food version of sex, brimming over, I'm afraid, with emotionally empty calories.[6]

The emphasis on the physical and behavioral also characterized their conception and assessment of homosexuality, "homosexual outlet," as they called it. Regarding the use of the heterosexual/homosexual rating scale, we are told that the ratings were based on two dimensions, *overt experience* and *psychologic reactions* (Kinsey et al., 1948, Figure 161, p. 638). *Overt experience* referred to physical contacts, specifically touching, that led to physical arousal but not necessarily to orgasm (Pomeroy, 1986). *Erotic arousal* has been operationally defined by Pomeroy and his associates (Pomeroy, Flax, & Wheeler, 1982) as "awareness of deep breathing, warm skin, rapid pulse, and lubrication (female) or erection (male") (p. 203). *Psychic responses*, you will recall, referred to reactions to fantasies or portrayals of sexual activity involving either female or male performers or both.

These definitions provided the operational guidelines for assigning ratings to respondents. They clearly subsumed the erotic aspects of sexual experience under the physical and behavioral. We should therefore not be surprised when informed by the Kinsey authors that although subjects were rated on the two criteria, overt experience and psychic responses, that the ratings were usually quite similar (Kinsey et al., 1948, p. 647). In effect only one aspect of their sexuality was being rated—physical performers and performance—real or fantasized.

Erotic Desire: A Freudian View

Finally, *desire*, the second component of the erotic, refers to the emotional aspects of sexuality, more specifically, to individuals to whom we are emotionally drawn and with whom we desire to form affectionate and romantic ties. Although it is hardly fashionable in sexology to do so, I think we can turn to Sigmund Freud to gain a different view of the nature of erotic desire as we turn to the Kinsey reports for the demographic intricacies of physical performance. Because an important focus of the current volume is homosexuality, for illustrative purposes I shall use Freud's depiction of how it develops (Freud, 1910/1955a, 1920, 1924, 1925/ 1961). Freud believed the child's homosexuality largely emerged in the struggle to acquire the femininity or masculinity that was exemplary of her or his biological sex. In the Freudian conception of ideal sexual maturity, the normal male turned out to be male in physical appearance, masculine in his attitudes, and attracted to females as sexual partners. Ideally, the mature female would be female in appearance, feminine in her mentality, and erotically drawn to her mature male counterpart. Together these constituted Freud's delineation of the heterosexual identity. Although the Kinsey group identified homosexuals by their sexual behavior, Freud believed homosexuals were essentially distinguished by their cross-sex feminine and masculine attitudes. For Freud, heterosexuality and homosexuality were more mental than physical phenomena.

The acquisition of the heterosexual or homosexual identity, in Freudian theory, rested upon the resolution of the Oedipal conflict in which the child's sex role identification as a boy or girl came to rest more, but almost always imperfectly, with one parent or the other, incorporating the child's interpretation of the parental portrayals of femininity and masculinity. In Freud's conception the individual's personality or character finally congealed at some point along a continuum for which femininity and masculinity served as polar opposites. In this feminine-masculine balance, heterosexual men and homosexual women were on one side of the psychological fulcrum, heterosexual women and homosexual men on the other.

The Oedipal conflict was also the child's first love affair, passionate because it involved the child's untamed emotions and tragic because, regardless of its resolution, the child was fated to lose the beloved parent since the child could not replace the rival parent as an adult lover. The Oedipal resolution was fateful and tragic in a second sense: because it was ignited by the child's erotic desires, the child's psychologcal identification as feminine or masculine would determine once and for all whether the direction of those desires would be heterosexual or homosexual. The Oedipal theory, therefore, was the means whereby Freud linked femininity and masculinity to heterosexual and homosexual desire.

Whatever the merits of Oedipal theory, and remember not all psychoanalysts accept it, it at least illustrates how erotic desire can be shaped by seemingly unrelated factors and understood in nonphysical terms.[7] What Freud was attempting to show was that the origin of erotic desire is often unconscious and that desire itself is often disguised in expression and intricately interwoven with other desires and with our actions. Not every physical sexual act was performed for erotic purposes and apparently nonsexual acts could be erotically motivated.[8]

The Kinsey interviewers were not blind to the relationship between feminine and masculine attraction and the sexual performance of respondents whom they elliptically identified as having "extensive homosexual experience."[9] However, they lacked Freud's insight into how, in our sharply sex-dimorphic Western culture, the dynamic tension between our femininity and masculinity profoundly shapes erotic desires.[10] This life-long conflict between femininity and masculinity, in my experience, is felt very keenly by individuals whose desires draw them to others of their own sex since these desires fall outside the psychological and social domains culturally assigned to men and women. Moreover, this same conflict profoundly affects the emotional qualities of the relationships of gay people with both men and women so that they are not mere simulacra of heterosexual relationships.

Anything You Can Do I Can Do Better: The Gay Identity

The Kinsey authors' conception of Western society and culture, especially its political and moral traditions, was as ingenuous and impoverished as their insight into the erotic content of our sexual acts. In their reports the cultural dimension of human sexuality consisted of the institutional constraints imposed upon an animal appetite innocently adrift in a sea of sexual stimuli. Society was the detour in the route that stretched between the natural sexual capacity of us noble savages and free sexual expression.

This conception of civilization amounted to a sweeping rejection of Western tradition by the Kinsey authors. It was difficult for them to understand that tradition is all that each generation starts out with. The past has existed for its own reasons, which may no longer be ours, but which we must respect as long as there are those who wish to continue to live by it. The past we inherit is the product of the needs and aspirations of our predecessors as we hope the future will reflect ours.

The historical and cultural naivete of the Kinsey group eventually resulted in their engulfment by traditions and changes that they misunderstood. It was difficult for them to understand that the nineteenth-century creation of the idea of the homosexual identity by such leaders as Karl Heinrich Ulrichs (Kennedy, 1980/1981) and Magnus Hirschfeld (1914) spontaneously evolved from their hopes of removing the institutional constraints that criminalized their sexual conduct and pathologized their erotic desire. The Kinsey authors believed this identity concept was false because it did not jibe with the physical facts of homosexuality as they conceived and recorded them.

The Gay Identity and the Kinsey Scale

A further examination of our experiences in the realm of sexual identity make clear the limitations and distortions thata physicalist/performance perspective imposes on us. Without the idea of the "gay identity" and a "gay community" to foster it, most of us who have done so would lack the words, the occasions, the courage to make public disclosures of our homosexuality and, for many of us, to make it the core of our professional and scholarly endeavor. Although we are not entirely certain of our motives or how the announcement will be received, many of us who have "come out" feel that somehow our lives will never be the same again. As Cass (1979) has shown, at the very least we know that a large deception has been shed and we hope that the truth will make us free. Coming out is a very personal act, but it is also ideological; it is a moment in our lives when the behavioral, emotional, political, and moral aspects of our sexuality powerfully converge. It is this convergence of meanings that makes the gay identity and the political movement that has sponsored it unique historical phenomena of the nineteenth and twentieth centuries.[11]

In performing this ritual I believe most of us realize that the "gay" label only hints at the complexity of our sexual experience and its shifting meanings in our lives. On the other hand, our research has hardly begun to uncover the meaning of "coming out" regarding the ways in which heterosexual or homosexual orgasms and outlets, patterns of sensuosity, erotic desire, social scripts, and ideological and moral commitments are woven together to form the fabric of the individual's sexuality. Although the failure to come out is often attributed to cowardice, ["foreclosure," in Cass's (1979) dispassionate terminology], in some cases I think it is because the individual feels he or she may be personally and socially misrepresented by taking on the gay or lesbian label. Moreover, some may believe that affixing the label to themselves and subscribing to membership in the gay community can become as prescriptive of their lives as the heterosexual label—that they will have sacrificed more personal autonomy than they would stand to gain (De Cecco, 1981).

The Use, Disuse, and Misuse of the Kinsey Scale

The Kinsey notion of the *heterosexual-homosexual balance* was as an explicit repudiation of the idea of a gay identity. This is made clear in *Sexual Behavior in the Human Male*, which rejects Hirschfeld's concept of a homosexual identity, the belief "that a person is really homosexual only when his psychic or overt contacts are more or less exclusively so" (Kinsey et al., 1948, p. 620). The idea of the *heterosexual-homosexual balance* was designed to emphasize the continuity of gradations between exclusively heterosexual and exclusively homosexual performances and reactions and the relative amounts of heterosexual experience or response in each sex history.[12]

There was little the Kinsey group could do to prevent the engulfment of their notion of "balance" by an idea whose time in history had arrived, that is, the gay identity. As Paul Robinson (1976) has pointed out, the ratings never succeeded in completely counteracting the idea that individuals were either heterosexuals or homosexuals. Ironically enough, wherever their use survives, the ratings themselves have become identities so that one can now be, for example, a "Kinsey 3" or a "Kinsey 5." There was at least a little confusion even in the minds of the Kinsey investigators as to whether they were rating individuals or their sex histories. The explanation of the ratings in the reports (e.g., Kinsey et al., 1948, p. 639) indicates that "individuals" are to be rated, but we know that in practice it was their annual inventories of sexual performances.[13]

We also know that in those relatively few studies (e.g., Bell & Weinberg, 1978; Masters & Johnson, 1979) in which the scale has been used, the ratings usually have been collapsed to form two groups of subjects, heterosexuals and homosexuals. The classification of individuals as homosexuals whose rating are as low as '2' or '4' now has had the investigators of bisexuality up in arms (e.g., Klein & Wolf, 1985; MacDonald, 1981; Paul, 1983/1984).

In a survey undertaken at CERES (Center for Research and Education in Sexuality, San Francisco State University) of the ways in which sexual orientation has been conceived in recent research on homosexuality (Shively, Jones, & De Cecco, 1983/1984), we found that only 2 out of 228 studies published since 1974 used the Kinsey scale to make the initial identification of subjects, although sexual orientation was assessed by some modified version of the scale in 30 others. On the basis of the examination of studies in which the scale had been employed, it is fair to conclude that its use has been infrequent and that it has *never* been applied in the way it was intended—as a series of ratings applied by interviewers to annual installments of a respondent's sex history.

Indeed, over the past decade or so, I would conjecture that we have produced a vast research literature on homosexuality that is based on subjects whose sexual performances were a total mystery to their authors and remain so for their readers. But I don't believe the blame lies entirely with the authors. The ignoring of the Kinsey scale in the subsequent research on homosexuality can be attributed to the fact that the research was politically inspired by the desire to detoxify the homosexual identity within the framework of sociological rather than behavioral theory. Its misuse, as in the case of Masters and Johnson (1979) and Bell and Weinberg (1978), was inevitable because the idea of the gay identity was so popularly entrenched that in classifying subjects, it outweighed in importance the proper interpretation of the ratings.

Not only has the Kinsey scale itself been engulfed by the idea of the gay identity, but so has the entire Kinsey conception of human sexuality as a physical phenomenon. I refer to the current effort to discover the biological basis of the gay identity. This effort constitutes a most improbable marriage among the psychobiologists of homosexuality, (e.g. Richard Green, 1974, 1985, 1987; Heino Meyer-Bahlburg, 1984), the sociobiologists of homosexuality, (e.g., Pillard and Weinrich, this volume), and a group mostly composed of sociologists, (e.g., Bell, Weinberg, & Hammersmith, 1981; Harry, 1984; Whitam, 1981; Whitam & Mathy, 1986).

With misguided compassion, they are attempting to prove that homosexuals are born, however imperfectly, not made—a fact not appreciated by either their families or fellow humans, who ignorantly mistreat them for failing to measure up to normative expectations.[14] Although the Kinsey authors explicitly rejected hormonal explanations of homosexuality as premature in a climate of prejudice, I contend that their strictly physical conception of human sexuality has unwittingly contributed to these recent efforts to biologize the gay identity. (See Gooren's refutation of the hormonal research in Chapter 6 of this volume.)

All Is Fair in Love and War: Sexuality Beyond Moral Reproach

I have already pointed out that the Kinsey group equated the natural and the moral. What I see as their conception of human sexuality as animal capacity, mechanistically reactive to fortuitous stimuli though a conditioning-like process, places our sexual conduct apart from moral rules, such as keeping promises, telling the truth, showing gratitude, making reparation, and not interfering with another's liberty, although Kinsey would certainly not have countenanced the last of these. These *prima facie* rules embody moral tradition, a nasty phrase in the Kinsey vocabulary, and represent the accumulated wisdom of the ages about the consequences of particular forms of conduct (Hyack, 1973). Of course, like anything else we humans create, moral rules congeal over time and need to be replaced with others. However, throughout Western civilization at least, it is generally believed that our sexual conduct is not exempt from moral restrictions and, indeed, that all is *not* fair in love, war, and sex.

Ethical theory addresses the question of right and wrong conduct, of moral obligation and responsibility.[15] Although it asserts that right conduct promotes good over evil, it does not tell us what the good is, what is worthwhile in life, or most crucially, what the standards are upon which we can base such judgments (Frankena, 1963). In the case of human sexuality, good can be considered on at least three bases: (1) it is *extrinsically* good, for example, in its usefulness for producing offspring and as a means for establishing intimacy; (2) it is *intrinsically* good as a rewarding experience—try it, you might like it; and (3) it is a *contributory* good—it makes life happier. Unfortunately, these standards do not always work together harmoniously. For example, the sexual pleasure of a new partner (intrinsic good) may conflict with sustained intimacy with a previous partner (contributory good) or with the extrinsic good of keeping free of sexually transmitted diseases.

The Kinsey reports leave one with the impression that any restrictions placed on sexual appetite served society rather than the individual. Ruddick (1984) cautions, however, that "we must distinguish between giving up some occasions for sexual pleasure and giving up sexual pleasure itself" (p. 290). Perhaps the classical Greeks struck an ideal balance between sexuality and other aspects of life. In the same sense that morality is made for humankind and not humankind for morality, I believe that sexual pleasure exists for us and not we for sexual pleasure.

Sexuality Without Mind or Will: Reductionism and Determinism

In research on human sexuality and, in particular, homosexuality, the Kinsey studies are not alone in committing the reductive and psychological fallacies that Lionel Trilling mentioned. The Kinsey authors fallaciously assumed that the mental, cultural, political, and moral dimensions of human sexuality were mere appendages of a unitary, physical phenomenon. The Freudians and gay identity theorists have fallen victim to these same fallacies. In the Freudian attempt to disentangle erotic desire from other motives and to chart its many roles in our mental life, sexuality as physical performance evaporates into the recesses of the mind and one is left with the impression that orgastic pleasure no longer requires a body. Freudians tend to subordinate the physical to the mental. The gay identity theorists, in their commendable efforts to detoxify homosexuality, have developed a new brand of performance anxiety. The puritanical strain in recent gay research makes it sometimes appear as if gay people now have emotional and political commitments but no longer do they have orgasms. The physical is now erased by the social.

In the various chapters appearing in this volume, we see the dangers of both reductionism and determinism in almost every direction. In particular, the mental life of individuals, that which comprises thought, imagination, emotion, and will—their uniqueness as celebrated in philosophy, literature, and art—is squeezed into oblivion as biological forces press in from one side and social forces from the other. Veering wildly between anthropomorphizing the animal kingdom and brutalizing the human being, we have seen the labored attempts of the primatologists and sociobiologists to depict human sexuality as a biological given and to weave it into an evolutionary theory that assumes that reproduction is its essential ingredient. (e.g., Money, Chapter 4; Nadler, Chapter 10; Pillard, Chapter 7; Rosenblum, Chapter 11; Weinrich, Chapter 9). Reproduction may be the essential *biological* ingredient in human sexuality, but it is no more or no less important or subject to interpretation than erotic desire and esthetics, social and cultural prescriptions, or political and moral commitment.

The sociologists and social psychologists, in their grim resolve to escape the clutches of biological and psychoanalytic determinism, have apparently abandoned the individual, whom they therefore describe only in terms of social demography, group membership, social structures, or normative expectations (Blumstein & Schwartz, Chapter 18; Gagnon, Chapter 12; and Peplau & Cochran, Chapter 19). All such factors are essential *social* ingredients, but they are no more "givens" than the biological. They constitute elements of sexuality that are variously interpreted, modified, incorporated, and resisted by the individual. Although efforts by psychiatrists and psychologists such as Isay (Chapter 17) to construct a mental theory for the development of a nonpathological homosexuality may escape the perils of biological and sociological reductionism, they fall into the trap of scientific determinism by assuming that there is (a) an ineffable sexual "passion" that dictates whether the object choice is heterosexual or homosexual and (b) a single "normal" pathway for the development of a "healthy" homosexuality, which mirrors that for healthy heterosexuality and ideally (although not invariably) leads to gay monogamy.

Some social historians have their own brand of reductionism. Boswell (1980, 1982, 1982/1983) has committed the historical fallacies of anachronism and *post hoc, ergo propter hoc* in reducing the modern notions of the gay identity and movement to male love and friendship circles in the early Middle Ages (e.g., De Cecco & Shively, 1983/1984; Hoffman, 1984). Hoffman (1984) asserts: "[For] *pace* scholars like Boswell, gay people did not and do not exist in other centuries or cultures. Like beatnik and hippie, gay is symbolic of a cultural phenomenon linked to the present generation and in other countries in the same way we study *la vie boheèmienne* of 19th-century Paris" (p. 48). Boswell's historical fallacies are probably attributable to his presupposition that homosexuality is essentially an inherited biological condition and that nature, in its wisdom and bounty, provides every century with its quota of "gay people" (cf. Boswell, 1980, p. 9n).

It is my opinion that primarily the cultural anthropologist and the clinicians have consciously and more or less successfully struggled against reductionist and determinist views of human sexuality. Herdt (Chapter 13) has explained how factors that the Kinsey authors viewed as "continuities" of sexual development (e.g., the constancy of heterosexuality *or* homosexuality throughout an individual's sex history) constitute *discontinuities* in non-American cultures. Nichols (Chapter 20) raises the question about how the fluidity of the individual's sexual desires and behavior succumbs to social pressures. Similarly, in arguing that sexuality is not a fixed state, Klein (Chapter 16) has shown how sexual and nonsexual dimensions of the individual's life form complex and changing configurations. Cass (Chapter 14) has sketched the subjective dimensions of "sexual preference" and their possible relationships to a homosexual social identity. Proceeding one step further, Coleman (Chapter 15), using clinical insight and a model of sexual development developed by Shively and De Cecco (1977), has shown how the individual's mental organization of her or his sexuality may dramatically differ from that person's self-ascribed stereotype, so that the "gay male," for example, might be more aptly designated a "lesbian" if one knew enough about the mental organization of his sexuality.

Quite clearly, it is the reductionists and determinists, whatever their disciplinary loyalties may be, who view homosexuality as a permanent or distinguishing biological, psychological, or social characteristic, a "marker" of the individual, whether biologically given or socially constructed, and who either ignore or deal awkwardly with change. It is generally the cultural anthropologist and clinicians who view homosexuality as an aspect of personal development that includes stability and change. This should not be surprising, particularly in the case of the clinicians, who deal with those who seek change or are confronted with the need to change.

Horizons Beyond the Orgasm: Future Research Gratifications

As biological and social scientists we have been so thoroughly schooled in analysis, reducing the whole to its parts and then focusing only on particular parts, that we neglect synthesis, the examination of our presuppositions about the whole. If each facet of sexuality is studied from one approach in isolation from the others, as in the case of the Kinsey studies, the case for that particular facet may be overstated.

The Kinsey studies, including the heterosexual/homosexual rating scale, are unsurpassed as sociological surveys of sexual behavior. In the annals of sexology, no similar research has yet approached them in grandness of conception, in number and diversity of respondents, in diligence and thoroughness of interviewing, in the careful analysis and reanalysis of data, and in cogency and clarity of presentation. Moreover, they are unexcelled in their fortitude in publishing conclusions, especially those showing the high incidence of homosexuality in the American population, a finding that stirred widespread controversy in academic and professional ranks. What the Kinsey authors have bequeathed to those of us who would carry on their work *is* the knowledge of the social demography of sexual performance in American in the mid-twentieth century and the methodology for obtaining histories of sexual performance.

By stating clearly and forthrightly their particular beliefs about human sexuality, the Kinsey reports have also given us a very special opportunity, that is, the chance to formulate our own beliefs in the process of weighing theirs—not just to ask new questions or make new group comparisons, but to make explicit the assumptions upon which they are based. They have provided a rich foundation for those scholars who have been invested personally and academically in homosexuality, for those whose family lives and professional interests have been dedicated to reproductive heterosexuality, and for those whose lives are committed to both, each with our own particular sensibilities. They have enabled us to construct an edifice of human sexuality that, of course, includes the biological and behavioral, but only in reference to the mental, the cultural, the political, and the moral elements—all this, while avoiding judgments about which is basic or essential. Obviously, if it is *human* sexuality that we seek to understand, what is important is the knowledge of their varied configurations rather than their preferential ranking or the conquest by one view or approach of all others.[16] It is this historic opportunity and challenge for studying and understanding human sexuality in its rich, individual, and cultural complexity that the Kinsey authors have bequeathed to those who would follow in their footsteps.

Acknowledgment

I wish to thank Dr. Wardell Pomeroy for his cordial assistance in clarifying the conceptual basis for the heterosexual/homosexual rating scale and its use in assessing sex histories. Dr. Jay Paul has my deep appreciation for his critical appraisal of this chapter and, in particular, for helping me distinguish between the erotic and sexual. Finally, I thank my colleagues in Human Sexuality Studies at San Francisco State University for our sometimes vociferous theoretical confrontations, which certainly influenced and speeded up my reflections on human sexuality.

Notes

1. Foucault's and Lloyd's view of sexual attitudes in ancient Greece differs somewhat from that presented by Boswell (this volume), who suggests that sexuality was perceived as generally dangerous.

2. An astonishing aspect of the Kinsey reports is that so little was devoted to sexuality as reproduction despite Kinsey's biological background, the portrayal of human sexuality as an expression of mammalian capacity, and the fact that three of the six surveyed outlets were related to marriage. This omission may have been due to Kinsey's plan (according to Pomeroy) to publish their third volume on pregnancy and birth control.

3. Professor Gagnon correctly pointed out that the Kinsey reports are essentially sociological studies. They included the following demographic variables: sex, race, age, age at onset of adolescence, marital status, educational level, the subject's occupational class, the parental occupational class, rural-urban background, and religious affiliation.

4. Trilling credits the definition of the psychologist's fallacy to William James (1890), who defined it as "the confusion of his own standpoint with that of the mental fact about which he is making the report" (pp. 196–197). Dr. Rosenblum, astonishingly enough, defended the use of this fallacy as a useful way of operationally defining the "sexual" in his analogy of the umpire who declares "they [i.e., the baseball plays] ain't anything until I call them."

5. The Kinsey authors paint a bleak picture of sexuality and aging. They reported that the types of sexual outlets changed insignificantly for most individuals over a lifetime but that physiological and psychological "fatigue" overtakes their sexuality as they grow older (cf. Kinsey et al., 1948, p. 227).

6. Dorothy Bromley (1954) believed that it would have been easy enough for the Kinsey authors to phrase interview questions that would have shed light on the emotional content of sexual acts and that the absence of such questions suggests that the authors were not interested in it.

7. In what, by now, is the orthodox, empirical study of homosexuality by psychoanalysts (Bieber et al., 1962, p. 34), some of the participating analysts were described as "culturalists," who believed that the Oedipal complex occurred only in highly pathological families.

8. The Kinsey authors seem to delight in assailing the Freudian belief that sexuality lurked in every corner of human experience. For example, in Kinsey et al., 1948, regarding the elementary tactile experiences of infants, the authors declare: "We are not now concerned with recording every occasion on which a babe brings two parts of its body into juxtaposition, every time it scratches its ear or its genitalia, nor every occasion on which it sucks its thumb" (p. 63).

9. For example, in *Sexual Behavior in the Human Male*, the list of items for the sex histories includes "preference for masculine or feminine types" and the "subject's self-analysis" regarding such factors as "physical stigmata," "carriage and movements," "hip movements," and "voice" (pp. 69–70).

10. The agrarian sensibility of the Kinsey authors apparently leaned toward the lusty, masculine homosexuality of males in western, rural areas, who are described as "virile" and physically active (1948, p. 457), as opposed to that of the "city group" with its "affectations."

11. The issue of the historical origins of the idea of the "gay identity" and "gay movement" arose early in the symposium. Boswell presented evidence of friendship circles, love affairs, and marriages in the early Middle Ages, several involving male members of the regular clergy. To call such people "gay" or their relationships a "movement" is, however, anachronistic. For one thing, if Boswell is correct in asserting that there was considerable tolerance of homosexuality in the early Middle Ages, no "movement" would have been necessary in the modern sense of that word, which signifies a concerted political effort to win tolerance that is withheld or lacking. As a vogue word *gay* is used to mean almost anything you want it to mean. However, as a historical phenomenon of our generation, it symbolizes a unique combination of the sexual, personal, and political for the individuals and groups to whom it uniquely applies.

12. Vern Bullough stated that the rating scale was developed by Kinsey after collecting only a few sex histories. This statement squares with one made by John Gagnon, that the scale represented an ideological commitment of the Kinsey authors to win popular acceptance of homosexuality by showing that it was a form of sexual behavior (*not* the psychic identity of a few) widely dispersed throughout the American population.

13. In Pomeroy's (Pomeroy et al., 1982) monograph on the sex history methodology, the respondents are asked to rate themselves, but only for the last year of their history. Although respondents are not assigned a single, comprehensive rating by the interviewer, given the categorical nature of our thinking, particularly with regard to sexuality, the temptation to do so, even with such distinguished historical figures as Michelangelo, is practically irresistible.

14. I have identified some of the presuppositions upon which the psychohormonal and related sociological research is based (De Cecco, 1987a & b). For a most astute (and devastating) review of sociobiological theory on homosexuality, see Futuyma & Risch (1983/1984), a paper to which Weinrich alludes in his chapter.

15. For this brief excursion into moral philosophy I have relied on my colleague, Dr. Robin Assali, and the treatise he supplied me, by William Frankena (1963). As further recommended, I have also perused two edited volumes dealing with philosophy and sexuality, Baker & Elliston (1984) and Soble (1980).

16. John Gagnon, following the philosopher of science, T. S. Kuhn (1970), argued that we had reached a crisis in the study of human sexuality that could only be resolved with a shift in paradigms, presumably away from biological, behavioral, and clinical assumptions and toward the historical, ideological, and social. Following the lead of Dr. Assali, I believe this would merely substitute one form of reductionism and determinism for another, with little gained for a general understanding of human sexuality. It would also preclude such promising, interdisciplinary cooperation as that exemplified in this volume in which the issue of disciplinary versus sexological is addressed. It seems to me, however, if the effort to understand, for example, homosexuality, ends at the border of the single discipline in which the investigator has had formal training, that the methodological and theoretical presuppositions about human sexuality inherent in that discipline will not be recognized and examined.

References

Attwater, D. (Ed.). (1941). *A Catholic dictionary*. New York: Macmillan.

Baker, R., & Elliston, F. (Eds.). (1984). *Philosophy and sex* (rev. ed.). Buffalo, NY: Prometheus.

Bell, A. P., & Weinberg, M. S. (1978). *Homosexualities: A study of diversity among men and women*. New York: Simon & Shuster

Bell, A. P., Weinberg, M. S., & Hammersmith, S. K. (1981). *Sexual preference: Its development in men and women*. Bloomington: Indiana University Press.

Bieber, I., Dain, H. J., Dince, P. R., Drellich, M. G., Grand, H. G., Gundlach, R. H., Kremer, M. W., Rifkin, A. H., Wilbur, C. B., & Bieber, T. B. (1962). *Homosexuality: A psychoanalytic study*. New York: Basic Books.

Boswell, J. (1980). *Christianity, social tolerance, and homosexuality: Gay people from the beginning of the Christian era to the fourteenth century*. Chicago: University of Chicago Press.

Boswell, J. (1982). *Rediscovering gay history: Archetypes of gay love in Christian history*. The fifth Michael Harding memorial address. London: Gay Christian Movement (in Xerox).

Boswell, J. (1982/1983). Revolutions, universals, and sexual categories. *Salmagundi, 58/59*, 89–113.

Bromley, D. D. (1954). Doctor Kinsey's summum bonum. In D. P. Geddes (Ed.), *An analysis of the Kinsey reports on sexual behavior in the human male and female* (pp. 143–153). New York: New American Library.

Cass, V. C. (1979). Homosexual identity formation: A theoretical model. *Journal of Homosexuality, 4*, 219–235.

Coleman, E. (1981/1982). Developmental stages in the coming out process. *Journal of Homosexuality, 7*(2/3), 31–43.

De Cecco, J. (1981). Definition and meaning of sexual orientation. *Journal of Homosexuality, 6*(4), 51–68.

De Cecco, J. (1987a). Homosexuality's brief recovery: From sickness to health and back again. *Journal of Sex Research, 23*(1), 106–114.

De Cecco, J. (1987b). The two views of Meyer-Bahlburg. *Journal of Sex Research, 23*(1), 120–123.

De Cecco, J. P., & Shively, M. G. (1983/1984). From sexual identity to sexual relationships: A contextual shift. *Journal of Homosexuality, 9*(2/3), 1–26.

Doerner, G. (1976). *Hormones and brain differentiation*. Amsterdam: Elvesier.

Elia, J. P. (1987). History, etymology, and fallacy: Attitudes toward masturbation in the ancient Western world. *Journal of Homosexuality, 14*(3/4), 1–19.

Feyerabend, P. (1978). *Science in a free society*. London: NLB Enterprises, Ltd.

Foucault, M. (1985). *History of sexuality: The use of pleasure. Vol. 2*. New York: Pantheon.

Frankena, W. (1963). *Ethics*. Englewood Cliffs, NJ: Prentice-Hall.

Freud, S. (1955a). Leonardo da Vinci and a memory of his childhood. In J. Strachey (Ed.), *Standard edition of the complete psychological works of Sigmund Freud, 11* (Vol. 11, pp. 59–137). London: Hogarth Press. (Original work published 1910).

Freud, S. (1955b). Some psychical consequences of the anatomical distinction between the sexes. In J. Strachey (Ed.), *Standard edition of the complete psychological works of Sigmund Freud*, (Vol. 19, pp.243–258). London: Hogarth Press. (Original work published 1925).

Freud, S. (1953). Psychogenesis of a case of homosexuality in a woman. In J. Strachey (Ed.), *Standard edition of the complete psychological works of Sigmund*

Freud, (Vol. 18, pp. 146–172). London: Hogarth Press. (Original work published 1920).

Freud, S. (1953). The dissolution of the Oedipus complex. In J. Strachey (Ed.), *Standard edition of the complete psychological works of Sigmund Freud,* (Vol. 19, pp. 172–129). London: Hogarth Press. (Original work published 1924).

Futuyma, D. J., & Risch, S. J. (1983/1984). Sexual orientation, sociolobiology, and evolution. *Journal of Homosexuality, 9*(2/3), 157–168.

Green, R. (1974). *Sexual identity conflict in children and adults.* New York: Basic Books

Green, R. (1985). Potholes on the research road to sexual identity development. *Journal of Sex Research, 21*(1), 96–101.

Green, R. (1987). *The "sissy boy syndrome" and the development of homosexuality.* New Haven, CT: Yale University Press.

Harry, J. (1984). Sexual orientation as destiny. *Journal of Homosexuality, 10* (3/4), 111–124.

Hirschfeld, M. (1914). *Die homosexualitat des mannes und des weibes.* Berlin: Louis Marcus.

Hoffman, R.J. (1984). Clio, fallacies, and homosexuality. *Journal of Homosexuality, 10* (3/4), 45–52.

Hyack, F. A. (1973). *Rules and order: Law, legislation, and liberty* (Volume 1). Chicago, IL: The University of Chicago Press.

James, W. (1890). *Principles of psychology* (Vols. 1 and 2). New York: Holt.

Kennedy, H. C. (1980/1981). The "third sex" theory of Karl Heinrich Ulrichs. *Journal of Homosexuality, 6*(1/2), 103–112.

Kinsey A. C., Pomeroy, W. B., & Martin, C. E. (1948). *Sexual behavior in the human male.* Philadelphia: W. B. Saunders.

Kinsey A. C., Pomeroy, W. B., Martin, C. E., & Gebhard, P. H. (1953). *Sexual behavior in the human female.* Philadelphia: W. B. Saunders.

Klein, F., & Wolf, T. J. (Eds.). (1985). *Bisexualities: Theory and research.* New York: Haworth Press.

Kuhn, T. S. (1970). The structure of scientific revolution. Chicago: University of Chicago Press.

Lloyd, G. E. R. (1986, March 13). The mind on sex. *New York Review,* pp. 24–28.

MacDonald, A. P. (1981). Bisexuality: Some comments on research and theory. *Journal of Homosexuality, 6*(3), 21–37.

Marcuse, H. (1962). *Eros and civilization: A philosophical inquiry into Freud.* New York: Vintage. (Original work published 1955).

Masters, W. H., & Johnson, V. E. (1979). *Homosexuality in perspective.* Boston: Little, Brown.

Meyer-Bahlburg, H. F. L. (1984). Psychoendocrine research on sexual orientation: Current status and future options. In J. DeVries (Ed.), *Progress in brain research* (pp. 375–398). Amsterdam: Elsevier.

Niebuhr, R. (1954). Kinsey and the moral problem of man's sexual life. In D. P. Geddes (Ed.), *An analysis of the Kinsey reports on sexual behavior in the human male and female* (pp. 62–70). New York: New American Library.

Paul, J. (1983/1984). The bisexual identity: An idea without social recognition. *Journal of Homosexuality, 9*(2/3), 45–64.

Pomeroy, W. B., Flax, C. C., & Wheeler, C. C. (1982). *Taking a sex history: Interviewing and recording.* New York: Free Press.

Pomeroy, W. B. (1986). Personal communication.

Rado, S. (1949). An adaptational view of sexual behavior. In P. Hoch & J. Zubin (Eds.), *Psychosexual development in health and disease* (pp. 9–23). New York: Grune & Stratton.

Robinson, P. (1976). *The modernization of sex: Havelock Ellis, Alfred Kinsey, William Masters, and Virginia Johnson*. New York: Harper & Row.

Ruddick, S. (1984). Better sex. In R. Baker & F. Elliston (Eds.), *Philosophy and sex* (pp. 280–299). Buffalo, NY: Prometheus.

Shively, M. G., & De Cecco, J. P. (1977). Components of sexual identity. *Journal of Homosexuality, 3*, 41–48.

Shively, M. G., Jones, C., & De Cecco, J. P. (1983/1984). Research on sexual orientation: definitions and methods. *Journal of Homosexuality, 9*(2/3), 127–136.

Soble, A. (Ed.). (1980). *Philosophy of sex: Contemporary readings*. Totowa, NJ: Littlefield, Adams.

Trilling, L. (1950). The Kinsey report. In L. Trillings, *The liberal imagination*. New York: Viking.

Whitam, F. L. (1981). A reply to Goode on the homosexual role. *Journal of Sex Research, 17*(1), 66–72.

Whitam, F. L., & Mathy, R. M. (1986). *Male homosexuality in four societies: Brazil, Guatemala, the Phillipines, and the United States*. New York: Praeger.

22

Constructing Concepts of Sexuality: A Philosophical Commentary

Noretta Koertge

Humans find their way around the world by using language to divide and describe. Like children watching "Sesame Street," we sort people, objects, and experiences into little conceptual baskets, like with like, carefully separating sheep from goats and the cooked from the raw. We then generalize about these categories, noting which bundles of items are pleasant or permanent or friendly or good to eat. Humans occasionally are forced to revise or refine their divisions and descriptions; children seem to do this rather easily. I like to think that scientists are also able to do so, although understandably with more agony—the larger and more closely knit our conceptual scheme, the more energy it takes to change our filing system.

The purpose of this volume is to look critically at our concepts of homosexuality, bisexuality, and (serving mainly as a residual category) heterosexuality. How can we best sort out sexual phenomena so as to produce scientifically useful descriptions, generalizations, and explanations?

To remind us of the clutter in our conceptual closet, let me pull out a few assorted files from one cupboard.

1. Here is the story of Prudence—as far as we can tell, she never had, or wished to have, sexual contact with her lover Patience. Theirs was a romantic friendship, one that surpassed the love of men.[1]

2. Next I present Boise Suburb. He has four beautiful children and loves his wife. Every Friday evening he has hot sex with young hustlers. He pays well and never asks their names. He always picks ones with nice hair and straight teeth. Boise claims to be heterosexual although he

admits to having an unusually strong sex drive—one too strong for women to handle.[2]

3. Ms. Artemis Moonglow chose to become a lesbian after working for three years in a battered women's shelter. She experiences varying depths of erotic intimacy with different women at different times, sometimes leading to orgasm. She denies that she ever "has sex," because that is a phallic concept. For men, the principal organ of pleasure also happens to be the organ of reproduction and the organ of penetration. But women's genitals (i.e., the parts principally involved in biological reproduction) have nothing to do with the bodily sources of their sensuality. And for Artemis, erotic fulfillment is inhibited by penetration, or feelings of being "had" or possessed.[3]

4. Robin Queensland has always enjoyed dressing up. When he was 3, he had a Carmen Miranda costume and danced for his hunky uncles at family reunions. Robin's friends are all straight women who are into clothes and makeup. Robin constantly complains to them about what brutes men are and cries whenever his current boyfriend leaves him (which is frequently). Robin doesn't really feel like a woman although he likes pretty things, but he believes he's too sensitive and fragile to be a real man. "I guess God threw away the cookie cutter after making me— I'm one of a kind."[4]

And so on. Having sampled this diversity, one is reluctant to file all these cases back in one bin under the label homosexuality. Even arranging them on a Kinsey scale of 0 to 6 doesn't help that much. What do we do with Prudence? And although Artemis and Robin are both now 6s they seem to be *very* different types of people. Small wonder that new dimensions or components of sexual orientation have sprung up in the literature like mushrooms.[5] To Kinsey's scales of homosexual fantasy and sexual behavior have been added measures of homophilia, homolimerence, and homosocial patterns of affection, attraction, and friendship. Some stress various aspects of the individuals' self-definitions or social roles. What is their gender identity? What sort of relationships are they looking for? Are they moderately successful in achieving their desires? How do they label themselves? How do they present themselves to others? Are they integrated into a gay subculture? How do they deal with stigma? And so on.

As a result of this proliferation of dimensions we can now generate almost as many combinations as Kinsey found species of gall wasps. And it is humanistically satisfying to describe the little idiosyncratic whorls and spirals of each of our sexual fingerprints. But the scientist is always balancing descriptive richness against a desire for systematicity and economy. Which concepts are best for theory construction? And some of us may still be closet essentialists. "Come on now," we say. "There's got to be *something(s)* that all homosexuals have in common. We/they sure as hell aren't the same as heterosexuals."

Concept formation in science is always a gradual evolutionary process in which many variations are proliferated and a few eventually prove to be fruitful.[6] It is rarely wise to legislate definitions, and that is certainly not the job of the philosopher of science. What I will do instead is give a partial framework for the *evaluation* of concepts by describing some of the different kinds of concepts that operate in science, the different roles they play, and some of the ways in which they can be evaluated.[7] I will illustrate these general principles with some examples of concepts used in the study of homosexuality.

The Search for Natural Kinds

Most sciences begin with a search for natural kinds, that is, classes of objects or processes that share many important properties. Early physicists investigated the behavior of levers, planets, magnets, and lenses. Chemists studied the properties of metals, acids, and the products of combustion. Biologists described and classified the species of plants and animals.

When they exist, natural kinds (which are then labeled by natural kind terms) are useful to the scientist in many ways. First of all, they provide the matrix for simple inductive inferences.[8] Is there lead in this mug's glaze? If so, without experimenting on this piece of pottery, I can infer that it would be unwise to drink from it because other materials that contain lead are poisonous. Is your pet fish, Cuddles, a piranha? Then despite its name I am not about to invade his bowl with my little finger. Have astronomers discovered an additional moon close to Jupiter? Then we predict that it will obey Kepler's Laws (at least approximately).

Second, natural kinds can often be related to each other in a systematic way, either through a classification system (cf. the Periodic Table or the Phylogenetic Trees of Evolutionary Biology) or through a more abstract theoretical structure (cf. Newton's Laws or Atomic Theory). Natural kinds, when they can be discovered, truly seem to "carve nature at the joints." But the search is never easy. Typically, scientists start with commonsense categories and look for shared features that lie outside the range of our ordinary language concepts. A child knows that drinking water is colorless and wet. Science reveals that it boils at 100° C at sea level and consists of H_2O molecules that form a tetrahedral lattice when ice is formed.

Often the scientific concept corrects the commonsense notion—whales are not fish to the taxonomist, window glass is not a solid but a super cooled liquid, and to the physicist the moon is constantly falling toward the earth. And sometimes the most deeply entrenched commonsense categories do not correspond to natural kinds at all. Color terms do not pick out natural kinds. Red apples are good to eat, but some red berries are poisonous. Red objects seem to share no properties beyond their redness. Likewise, for geometrical shapes—spherical vegetables do not taste better than elongated ones. And textures—furry animals are not as a rule friendlier than sleek ones.

So we see that concepts vary enormously in their inferential import. Some concepts (the ones that have traditionally been called natural kind terms) support a variety of inferences. If my cat is diagnosed via a blood test as having feline leukemia, I (or my veterinarian) can infer a good deal about the future symptoms it is likely to develop, what its chances for survival are, the vectors by which the disease was transmitted to it, and so on. Disease concepts are particularly rich because they often permit inferences both to specific preceding causes and to the effects that generally follow. From the fact that my cat is anemic, I cannot infer a specific cause (there are a variety of precipitating conditions), but I may be able to make fairly precise predictions about the outcome of untreated anemia. However, from the fact that my cat is gray, I may be able to make some probabilistic inferences about the color of its ancestors or offspring, but that is about all. From the weight of my cat, I can infer how it will affect a seesaw or whether it will break the chandelier if it climbs up on it, but very little about its life *qua* cat (although its weight may be relevant to its success in cat fights). And the fact that my cat has a tattoo, though very useful for identification purposes, permits no further inferences whatsoever.

There are two important morals to draw. Some concepts (such as color terms) can be made quite clear and precise, they may be very useful in *describing* features of the world, and yet they may have very little *inferential* import. And concepts (such as weight) that figure importantly in one domain of inquiry (mechanics) may have very limited predictive value in another field (e.g., cat psychology).

All of this might make us wonder about the concept of *homosexuality*. It could be that no matter how hard we work at making the notion clear and precise, we will never arrive at a concept that is inference-rich. For example, it might turn out that knowing that certain people were homosexuals (in some precisely specified sense, maybe using a refined Kinsey scale) would permit us to infer *nothing* about their psychological adjustment, hormone balance, rating on a masculinity/femininity scale, prenatal environment, childhood popularity, present income, or future chances of going to heaven.

Since most (though not all) research concludes that homosexuals are remarkably similar to other folks, should we now conclude that there can be no science of homosexology because no amount of ingenuity can produce a natural kind where there isn't one? Or to put it another way, does present research indicate that both homosexuality and heterosexuality are *un*natural kinds? There can be no definitive negative answer to such concerns. First, it is always possible that we have not yet discovered the appropriate network of properties. Perhaps all (or most) homosexuals slept diagonally in their cribs as children or drank cranberry juice while hanging upside down from a tree limb.

Another possibility is that we have not made our divisions fine-grained enough. Maybe homosexuality is a broad generic category like the class of minerals or the set of warm-blooded animals, and impressive generalizations will only appear when we further subdivide. Bell and Weinberg's (1978) typology of homosexualities is a step in this direction.[9] Maybe to get to the level of basic natural kinds, we will need to focus on categories such as promiscuous former-sissy-boy homosexual weight lifters with lots of attitude, average testosterone levels, and weak fathers! But if we use too many properties in defining our clusters, what will be left to infer?

Social Constructions

At this point some readers may be quite impatient with all of this talk about "natural" kinds, illustrated with examples from the "natural" sciences. "Of course, homosexuals don't comprise a natural kind," such a reader might argue. "But they have been marked off as a stigmatized group in our society. And the implications of this socially constructed categorization are enormous. It is only people blinded by the positivisitic approach characteristic of much of natural science who could fail to see the inferential power of such concepts. To a biologist, race may be a rather impoverished concept that correlates only weakly with distributions of blood types and the odd disease such as sickle-cell anemia. But to someone living in South Africa, the socially constructed categories of race are rich with consequences. It is only when we begin to view homosexuality as a social construct that we will make any theoretical progress."

"Of course, societies such as ours are not monolithic and change over time so we should not expect the sexual constructs of New England in the nineteenth century to necessarily be the same as those operating in late twentieth century California. But we can hope to find meaningful patterns emerging from the flux of history."

This outburst from an imagined critic[10] combines two claims that often come together in a package but that I wish to separate because I largely agree with one, but not the other: (1) Homosexuality is best viewed as a social construct (here I have some sympathy). (2) Social constructs can best be studied using methods that differ from those of natural science, for example, methods of *verstehen*, hermeneutics, or critical political analysis (here I largely disagree).

Let us look at some simple examples of how socially constructed concepts work. Astrology provides an extreme case. Using the physical property consisting of the position of certain celestial objects on her birth date, a person is classified, say, as a Libra. For many people in our society, this description is rich with inferential import about the individual's personality, her suitability as a friend, how she will react in stressful situations, and so on. Even if the Libra herself doesn't take astrology seriously, the chances are very good that she will at least read her own horoscope in the newspaper.

The example of astrological signs is typical of social constructions in many respects. First of all, on the basis of a few easily detectable properties (viz. birth date), individuals are placed in a social category. Having once been labeled, stereotypical inferences are drawn about important aspects of their personality and behavior. There is no attempt to correct these inferences in any systematic way, although people are willing to make exceptions—"Jones is not your typical Libra." The cluster of properties associated with the socially constructed concept is remarkably resistant to change even when there is absolutely no scientific basis for the purported correlations. Already at the time of Plato it was believed that Libras were judicious in their judgments; that Capricorns were stubborn, and so on.

However, this example is also atypical in two important respects. First, although there is a widespread *casual* belief in astrology within contemporary Western society, astrological expectations are not strong enough to influence significantly the actual personalities and behaviors of individuals today. Thus, when Gauquelin's statistics are corrected, there is no correlation between being born under Mars and being a military officer. Second, in the astrological case there are powerful theoretical reasons for arguing that the planetary influences on which the construct is based could not be physically relevant. (So even if it turned out that people born under Mars tended to become generals, one would *know* that the causes were social in nature.)

In the more typical case, it is very difficult to factor out the respective roles of nature and culture. In the case of premenstrual syndrome, for example, how much of the distress stems from hormones and how much from internalized social expectations? Or is there a complicated feedback or synergistic relationship between the two?[11]

The zodiac example also lacks a wrinkle that will probably turn out to be very important in the case of homosexuality. Since Libras are not stigmatized in our society, there are no important differences between how Libras see themselves and how the "others" see them—there is no queer/gay dichotomy. The question of the reality base of social constructions becomes crucial when they are used to harm people. Although many intellectuals worry about the popularity of astrology (so much so that Nobel-prize-winning scientists publish manifestos against it), this system of beliefs seems far less dangerous than institutionalized concepts of racism, sexism, and homophobia.

Clearly, there are a variety of socially constructed conceptions of homosexuality, and these can have very direct consequences on our behavior and well-being, as when internalized homophobia contributes to a lesbian's alcoholism, or AIDS hysteria causes a gay man to lose his job. Yet many researchers, for a variety of reasons, seem reluctant to give these aspects a central role.

First, it might be argued that as my astrology example illustrates, socially constructed labels must have at least some minimal basis in material conditions for them to be very effective. (Or, to use Marxist terminology, superstructure is of secondary importance to infrastructure).[12] In this view, systems of belief should be deconstructed, not incorporated into the fundamental concepts of our theories.

Second, if one deals only with purely social aspects, one could be reduced to the absurd cultural relativism of Carlos Castañeda's account of Don Juan.[13] Surely, it is important to know what was really happening when the Yaquis *thought* he was flying around like a bird. Likewise, the fact that our friend Boise Suburb *labels* himself heterosexual should not distract us from his behavior.

There is another extreme position that has been adopted by some sociologists of knowledge, according to which madness, homosexuality, and pregnancy must be social constructs because *all* scientific concepts are. According to this view, concepts such as gene, oxygen, and electron cannot be said to represent reality; rather, they are the results of social agreements negotiated in the laboratory.[14] To critique this position thoroughly would take us too far afield. Suffice it to say here that even if the doctrine of universal sociologism (like the doctrine of theory-ladenness of all observations) has some merit, it would still be worthwhile to talk about degrees and there would remain an important difference between the amount and kind of "negotiation" needed to declare someone a witch and the social procedures involved in describing her as having a wart on her nose!

But let us try to set possible excesses and ideological prejudices aside. What new methodological or theoretical issues arise if we introduce cultural components into our basic conception of sexuality?

First, would it make our conjectures less testable? Probably somewhat. It is easier to get reliable data on hormone levels, pupil dilations, and penile extensions than on the degree of one's assimilation into a subculture. Yet many purely behavioral concepts, such as Kinsey's scale based on the relative proportions of same-sex/different-sex sex acts, could only be measured in practice through self-reporting. And I would expect that memories of sexual fantasies would be very unreliable in cases where a person feels conflict over his or her sexual identity. However, in every science one may sometimes have to work with variables whose values are difficult to determine in order to tackle interesting questions.

A second problem: Since social constructions are strongly influenced by context, won't introducing them vitiate any attempt to find universal theories that hold across all cultures? Some social constructionists are content to find local patterns and would feel no regret if we decide that Sappho has very little in common with her post-Stonewall admirers. However, it might turn out that local culture strongly conditions sexuality and yet that there are also invariant principles that govern these formations. A conjectural example would be the following: Gender roles seem to be important in every culture studied so far (universal), although there is much local variation in what counts as appropriate behavior. Perhaps *every* society also prescribes some pattern of linkage between genders of participants and appropriate genital activity, although the specific patterns vary. Then in every society the possibility for deviations from the local gender/genital norm exists. One would expect that serious deviations would always be stigmatized, although the form of disapproval would be local.

My conjectural example is trivial and obvious, but one hopes there are more interesting universal patterns that could be discovered. Once again, however, there may be a trade-off—this time between universal applicability and descriptive detail.

Another concern: Since animals have little or no culture or sense of self, isn't too much emphasis on self-identity and societal labeling tantamount to saying *a priori* that comparative studies are irrelevant? (Even Dorner deserves better than that!) I think it must be admitted that the social constructionist is betting that human sexuality is about as loosely connected to animal sexual behavior as our liking for gourmet banquets is related to protein requirements. Nevertheless, strong biological determinants might be uncovered. In that case the meaningfulness of human sexual activity would be like the complicated dreams we generate after the fact in order to "explain" the loud noise that disturbed our sleep. Time will tell!

A fourth query: If sexuality is largely constituted by *belief* systems, why aren't sexual orientations more labile? Shouldn't I just be able to *think* myself into a new sexual category? Yet psychoanalysts, experts in the talking "cure," are remarkably unsuccessful in changing the preferences even of clients who really want to change.

Several points in reply: First, as the case of Artemis Moonglow, a so-called political lesbian, reminds us, some people *do* appear to think their way into a new form of sexual life, and relatively few longitudinal studies have been conducted, so this may be common. Second, the social constructionist might argue that since our society expects sexual orientation to be stable (at least in adults), most people believe that they cannot vary it—and so they don't. Third, this query overlooks the fact that most people's individual belief systems are very conservative—children tend to vote like their parents, attend the same churches, belong to the same social class, and so on. Small wonder that sexual affiliations are stable. (This is *not* to say they will match those of one's parents. It is simply to point out that if one has always been told that one is a heartbreaker, or a ballbreaker, Mommy's right-hand girl, or a man's man, or too independent to stay tied down for long, eventually one is inclined to believe it.)

I conclude that the introduction of social constructs into our conception of sexuality does not predetermine what the structure of a mature theory of sexuality will look like. In particular, it does not rule out a search for universal laws and invariant patterns. Sensible social constructionists do not deny that "sticks and stones may break my bones;" they do, however, emphatically point out that words can also be causally efficacious, both in hurting us and in healing us.

From Typologies to Multidimensional Variables

I began this chapter with a discussion of the search for natural kinds, that is, classes of items that are relatively homogeneous with respect to a variety of properties. We saw that the search for uniform categories of sexual orientation led to finer and finer subdivisions characterized by properties ranging from the chromosomal sex of the individual to his or her state of existential authenticity. However, not all successful scientific theories rest on the sort of simple typologies we have been looking for. For example, I said that acids constitute a natural kind for chemists. But equally important to the similarities among acids are their variable properties, such as their degrees of concentration, oxidizing power, volatility, and so on. How might we construct theories of sexuality that exploit variations in human beings instead of looking only for similarities? The original Kinsey measures provide a good preliminary example. Although most researchers divide the Kinsey scale into three classes—homosexual, heterosexual, and in between—what Kinsey actually provided was a continuous spectrum. Furthermore, the values of the sexual behavior scale could in principle have been measured by computing the actual proportions of sexual encounters. (Thus it was conceptually more precise than a scale that merely records values from "strongly disagree" to "strongly agree" in seven arbitrary steps.)

Since Kinsey had two scales, one for behavior and one for fantasy, scientists could immediately ask whether the components are strongly correlated (they are) and how they are causally related (does fantasy precede behavior or vice versa?). Equally interesting are the cases in which the values differ dramatically. Do incongruities between fantasy and behavior cause dissonance, or do they enrich the individual's overall sex life? Do they presage a dramatic change in sexual orientation? And so on. Notice that in the course of such inquiries we are *not* arriving at interesting generalizations about homosexuals *per se*. Rather, what we are finding is how these two components of sexuality fit together and what happens when they do not.

As we add new dimensions, the questions that we can study proliferate rapidly as we search for internal connections among the components as well as their relationships with external factors such as mental health, intelligence, childhood experiences, hormone levels, or what have you.

Does this mean that the more dimensions of sexuality we postulate, the better our theory? Not at all. As a hypothetical example let me pick on the homosocial dimension simply because I have a hunch it isn't very important. Suppose it turned out that whether one's best friends were largely of the same sex or not correlated with none of the other dimensions. Furthermore, whether one's lovers and friends were of the same sex made no difference in one's sexual satisfaction, ability to find lovers, ability to hold down a job, and so on. Then this dimension would not contribute systematically to a study of sexuality, no matter how broadly construed, and should be dropped. (Of course, the homosocial dimension might be valuable elsewhere—perhaps in the study of people's choice of professions or preferences in hobbies.) An intermediate result is also possible—perhaps the homosocial dimension is connected with sexuality in some groups (distinguished perhaps by age, gender, or culture) but not in others. Only empirical inquiry can decide.

The current proliferation of dimensions of sexuality complicates the field, and some of the components will eventually be dropped if it is found that they do not contribute to our ability to give systematic descriptions and explanations of human sexuality. But what about the examples I started with? Are those romantic friends Patience and Prudence really lesbians or not? Is Boise Suburb a homosexual, or isn't he? At the present state of inquiry, there is simply no nonarbitrary answer to such questions. Many definitions can be stipulated, but as yet none are embedded in a successful system that is rich in inferential import. This is no cause for disappointment or embarrassment, however. It was two millenia after Democritus before scientists sorted out what atoms were, and then they turned out to be divisible! The Kinsey scales have been around only half a century—our understanding of sexuality is just beginning.

Notes

1. See Lillian Faderman, *Surpassing the Love of Men: Romantic Friendship and Love Between Women from the Renaissance to the Present* (New York: Morrow, 1981) and also her historical reconstruction of a famous nineteenth-century trial, *Scotch Verdict: Miss Pirie and Miss Woods v. Dame Cumming Gordon* (New York: Quill, 1983).

2. Frederick Suppe alluded to such cases in his "In Defense of a Multidimensional Approach to Sexual Identity," *Journal of Homosexuality* Vol. 10, Nos. 3/4 (1984), pp. 7–14.

3. This analysis of "having sex" was presented in a paper by Claudia Card, "Intimacy and Responsibility: What Lesbians Do," at a meeting of the Midwest Division of the Society for Women in Philosophy, Madison, WI, October, 1986.

4. Friendship patterns are discussed in Letty Cottin Pogrebin's book, *Among Friends* (New York: McGraw Hill, 1987).

5. In addition to the chapters in this volume, see two issues of the *Journal of Homosexuality* Vol. 9, Nos. 2/3 (1984) is entitled "Bisexual and Homosexual Identities: Critical Theoretical Issues" followed by *Vol. 10*, Nos. 3/4 (1984), called "Controversy Over the Bisexual and Homosexual Identities: Commentaries and Reactions."

6. A variety of examples are presented in my article "The Fallacy of Misplaced Precision," *Journal of Homosexuality*, Vol. 10, Nos. 3/4 (1984), pp. 15–21.

7. In discussing concept evaluation, both social scientists and philosohers of science tend to emphasize desiderata such as reproducibility or operational definitions. See, for example, Carl G. Hempel's classic monograph, *Fundamentals of Concept Formation in Empirical Science* (Chicago: University of Chicago Press, 1952). My main concern, however, is in evaluating the theoretical and systematic fruitfulness of concepts.

8. An early recognition of the importance of natural kinds for induction is found in John Stuart Mill, *A System of Logic*, which first appeared in 1843.

9. See Alan Bell and Martin Weinberg, *Homosexualities: A Study of Diversity Among Men and Women* (New York: Simon and Schuster, 1978).

10. The idea that the category of homosexuality is a fairly recent invention is best argued by Michel Foucault in *The History of Sexuality* (New York: Random House, 1978).

11. A telling criticism of our continual backsliding into nature-culture dualisms is found in Lynda Birke, *Women, Feminism and Biology: The Feminist Challenge* (New York: Methuen, 1986).

12. See Marvin Harris, *Cultural Materialism: The Struggle for a Science of Culture* (New York: Random House, 1979).

13. See my "Beyond Cultural Relativism" in G. Currie and A. Musgrave, eds., *Popper and the Human Sciences* (Dordrecht: Nijhoff, 1985), pp. 121–31.

14. For a good summary of Latour and Woolgar's *Laboratory Life* and Knorr-Cetina's *The Manufacture of Knowledge*, see Paul Tibbitts, "The Sociology of Scientific Knowledge: The Constructivist Thesis and Relativism," *Philosophy of Social Science*, 16, (1986), pp. 39–57.

Epilogue

Evelyn Hooker and Mary Ziemba-Davis

In the Prologue to this volume, David McWhirter graciously acknowledges the contributions of Alfred C. Kinsey and myself (EH) to the study of sexual orientation—the ever expanding and important area of scientific knowledge and human concern addressed by this second volume in The Kinsey Institute Series. I, too, owe a great debt of gratitude to Alfred Kinsey without whom I would have had neither the courage to pose my questions nor the knowledge to frame them in the manner in which I did. Because most people recognize the immense importance of Kinsey's legacy insofar as his work legitimized the scientific study of sex, thus providing both credibility and courage to its students, in this Epilogue we would like to focus on Kinsey's contributions to the questions we ask and the ways in which we ask them.

The genius of Kinsey, as reflected in his seven-point rating scale, was to think of the "purity" versus the "impurity" of sexual orientation. As Gilbert Herdt (Chapter 13) and others have made clear, heterosexual, homosexual, and bisexual men and women do not represent homogeneous groups, either across or within cultures. Rather, as Kinsey's scale first suggested, they are quite heterogeneous. Thus, although the Kinsey scale may have practical limitations, it highlights some important theoretical issues in the study of sexual orientation.

In Chapter 19, Anne Peplau and Susan Cochran note that the Kinsey scale might fruitfully be used in studies of individual differences in personality and relationships. Along these lines, although popular lore suggests that all men who score a 6 on the Kinsey scale reject women, we know of few, if any, empirical data which fully support this idea. While it is reasonable to assume that a majority of these men have a positive reaction to the male, their reaction to the female, possibly neutral, negative, or positive is poorly understood. My own work (EH's) suggested to me that men who qualify as Kinsey 6s differ in many or all of the ways that men typically differ. Thus, for example, these men, like other men, may vary with respect to the valence that sex with women is given, both at puberty and throughout their lives. Other possibly relevant differences, as noted by Richard Isay (Chapter 17) and Vivienne Cass (Chapter 14), are reflected in the fact that, whereas some homosexuals are totally comfortable with their gay identity, others suffer considerable distress. In light of these observations, it may be important to examine individual differences among both male and female 6s more closely with an eye to discovering which, if any, of such differences are germane to the fact that they are gay. Similarly, it also would be valuable to investigate potential variation within groups other than the 6s, such as the 3s, 4s, and 5s.

Kinsey's continuum further prompts us to ask "What differentiates a 'pure' 6 from a 4 or a 5" or, for that matter, the 1s and the 2s from the 0s. Between-group comparisons of personality, life satisfaction, and social or generational factors may assist us in understanding the variety of ways individuals come to identify themselves as heterosexual, homosexual, or bisexual (see Cass, Chapter 14). How and why do people choose a nominal sexual self-label—that is, heterosexual, homosexual, or bisexual? How do people using similar self-labels vary on the Kinsey scale with respect to partner selection and erotic fantasy? How or why, for example, do some men and women who commence their lives as completely content and well-adjusted 0s later, often after years of marriage and children, become transformed into equally content and well-adjusted 6s? What makes heterosexuality and homosexuality differentially compelling during different phases of the life cycle? Although answers to such questions may require additional knowledge about the circumstances under which erotic desire transforms itself into sexual behavior, it may be useful to begin by assessing the similarities and differences among individuals who fall along different points on the Kinsey scale.

Kinsey's conceptions of heterosexuality and homosexuality, like all products of science, are subject to continual scrutiny and revision as new information and insights become available. Most notably, the notion of a unidimensional continuum of sexual orientation may need to be revised (see Whalen, Geary, & Johnson, Chapter 5). As a number of the contributions to this volume (Cass, Chapter 14; Coleman, Chapter 15; De Cecco, Chapter 21; Klein, Chapter 16; Koertge, Chapter 22) have discussed, in and of itself, the Kinsey scale fails to capture the multileveled psychological, social, and behavioral complexity of particular sexual orientations; nonetheless, Kinsey's scale has and will continue to provide a framework for empirical investigations and to provoke many questions which have yet to be fully explored in investigations of sexual orientation. More specifically, the foundation laid by Kinsey directs us to ask: "What differentiates the 'closer neighbors' on this scale," both within and across nominal sexual orientation groups.

In conclusion, we would like to note one other contribution of Dr. Kinsey: his validation of the many different variants of sexual orientation. Kinsey was very explicit in stating that, for example, homosexuality was as valid and as "normal" as heterosexuality for the individuals involved. This concept was initially very hard to accept, even among social scientists. For example, when I (EH) chaired the Task Force on Homosexuality of the National Institute of Mental Health (1967–1969), a number of distinguished members of the task force refused to accept Kinsey's position (which I espoused and validated with empirical data). Yet, only four years later, the American Psychiatric Association deleted homosexuality from its diagnostic handbook. Prejudice, even among scientists, dies hard. As this volume demonstrates, however, Dr. Kinsey has at last come into a full measure of acceptance.

A major theme to emerge from this second Kinsey volume, as well as virtually all of contemporary behavioral science, is a cry to elaborate the qualitative characteristics of people in a given category. In advocating and implementing such an approach, the editors and contributors to this book have taken a great step toward providing reliable answers for future generations who undoubtedly will continue to confront many of these same issues both inside and outside of the research context.

Author Index

Subject Index